Javits

_____

Javits

THE AUTOBIOGRAPHY
OF A PUBLIC MAN

Senator Jacob K. Javits

with Rafael Steinberg

BOSTON
HOUGHTON MIFFLIN COMPANY
1981

Library of Congress Cataloging in Publication Data

Javits, Jacob K. (Jacob Koppel), date
Javits : the autobiography of a public man.

Includes index.
1. Javits, Jacob K. (Jacob Koppel), date.
2. Legislators — United States — Biography. 3. United
States. Congress. Senate — Biography. I. Steinberg,
Rafael, 1927–   .
E748.J28A34   328.73′092′4 [B]   81–1139
ISBN 0–395–29912–8   AACR2

Printed in the United States of America

V 10 9 8 7 6 5 4 3 2 1

A portion of this book has appeared in the *Washington Monthly*.

I dedicate this account of my life to those who have had the greatest influence in shaping it: to Marian, my wife, and to Joy, Joshua, and Carla, our children; to the memory of my mother, Ida, of my father, Morris, and of my brother, Ben, and to Ben's family, Lily, Joan, and Eric, and their children; to teachers and friends who have guided me; and to the voters of the state of New York who placed their hopes for the future in my hands and entrusted me with the power to lead them in the paths of peace, justice, and freedom.

Contents

Illustrations xi

1 · The Urban Log Cabin 1

2 · The Education of a Kid Brother 16

3 · Letters from Europe: Laying
the Foundations 27

4 · Trial Lawyer 39

5 · World War: A Turning Point 55

6 · Searching for a Role 77

7 · On the Stump 91

8 · Marian and Me 114

9 · The Congressman in Domestic Affairs 132

10 · The Congressman in Foreign Affairs 154

11 · Adventures in New York Politics 189

12 · The Lie That Failed 213

13 · Victory and Vindication 239

14 · The Most Exclusive Club in the World 252

15 · The United States and Israel 271

16 · The Nation's Health versus the Nation's
Politics 291

17 · Endowing the Arts 305

18 · The Struggle for Civil Rights 320

19 · Republicans Divided 347

20 · The Governor and the Senator　362

21 · Winning and Losing for Labor　378

22 · Vietnam and the Power to Make War　393

23 · Watergate and After: The 1974
　　　 Elections　415

24 · Crisis in New York City　434

25 · Our Troubled World　448

26 · The Explosive Middle East　465

27 · The Last Campaign　490

　　　 Index　509

Acknowledgments

This book springs from my memory, but it contains much more than I could possibly hold in my mind. A great deal of it is based on the contents of two thousand file drawers of documents, the record of a public life. For bringing order to the material, I owe a special debt to my archivist, Ilana Stern, who spent several years arranging my files and culling from them the most important and interesting material. She was most ably assisted by Caroline Ehlers and Tom King.

Richard M. Clurman is in a real sense the godfather of this book. He guided me, facilitated the process, and performed the indispensable task of bringing me together with my collaborator — and keeping us together throughout the work.

Members of my family to whom I have dedicated this book also played a working role. To my wife, Marian, for her constant recollection of elements of our lives that appear in the book and for her extraordinarily generous and enlightened approach to the chapter on our married life, I express my gratitude. Our children, Joy, Josh, and Carla, contributed their own recollections as they bore upon the substance of the book; my sister-in-law, Lily, supplied me with many details about my relations and Marian's with her and my brother; and Joan and Eric Javits, like my own children, filled in those relationships and supplied views and facts about their own relationships with me. I thank them all.

Many friends and associates generously gave me time and thought in order to add the fruits of their memories to mine. I acknowledge especially the cooperation of Herbert Brownell, Richard M. Clurman, Peter Cusick, Charles Goodell, Leonard Hall, Isaiah Kenen, William Macomber, Tex McCrary, Sam Roman, Arthur Schwartz, Morris Shapiro, and John Trubin.

I also frequently turned for assistance to those men and women who made my staff one of the best on Capitol Hill; some of them were still with me when I called on them and some had gone on to other work, but all of them cooperated when asked to help tell my story with precision and accuracy. Of my staff members in Washington and New York, I owe a particular debt of gratitude to Richard Aurelio, Frank Cummings, Jay Cutler, Mike Gordon, Sheldon Kaplan, Robert Kaufman, Don Kellermann, Sheila Kelley, Peter Lakeland, Allen Lesser, Robert Locke, C. Burton Marshall, Roy Millenson, Gene Mittelman, Patricia Perlman, John Rother, Peter Turza, and Win Wheeler.

There are several other people whose aid was indispensable. Max Fisher, Albert F. Gordon, Sr., the late Andre Meyer, Arthur Ross, and John Hay Whitney encouraged me in the course of writing the book. R. Burdell Bixby and Hugh Morrow helped me assemble some of the bits and pieces. Arthur Moscowitz's study of my early campaigns was extremely useful. Sarah Lewis tirelessly assisted my collaborator in searching for facts and tying together the threads of my life.

The patience, understanding, and dedication of my editor, Daphne Abeel, was an important factor in the completion of this work. She gave an unusual amount of time to the task, and her wise comments and textual suggestions improved and sharpened the book. She was in every way a model editor and a good friend.

Renata Adler and Sidney Hyman read the manuscript and offered most helpful comments, for which I am very grateful.

Esther Newberg, my agent, also helped in putting the book on the right path and sketching its general design.

And finally, of course, my collaborator, Rafael Steinberg, as historian, reporter, writer, and patient investigator, played a great role in what was to him and to me a historic process. I am deeply grateful.

It would be impossible to identify by name the thousands of people who, without knowing it, may have contributed indirectly to this work by supplying me with information and insights over the years. I thank them now, and I hope that if they see a shadow of themselves in these pages they will recognize it and be pleased.

J.K.J.
January 1981

Illustrations

following page 242

Morris Javits, JKJ's father

JKJ at three and a half

Ida Javits, JKJ's mother, with JKJ and his brother, Ben

JKJ as a young bachelor

JKJ, just promoted from major to lieutenant colonel

JKJ bringing petitions to the Board of Elections, 1946

JKJ and the former Marian Ann Borris on their wedding day

Two young congressmen, JKJ and John F. Kennedy

JKJ gets a hit in the annual baseball game

A Javits campaign tool, comics for constituents

JKJ announces candidacy for mayoralty of New York City

JKJ with Adlai Stevenson

JKJ with Pope Pius XII

Senator Javits with his wife, Marian, and their children

JKJ with David Ben-Gurion in Israel

JKJ with Congressman Adam Clayton Powell

JKJ with his fellow senator from New York, Kenneth B. Keating

Marian and JKJ

Playing tennis in Florida

Nelson Rockefeller and JKJ in a television studio after the election of 1958

JKJ with "Der Alte," Konrad Adenauer, chancellor of West Germany

JKJ with Bernard Baruch

JKJ with President Dwight D. Eisenhower

JKJ with Helen Hayes

JKJ's staff gathers for his birthday, circa 1960

JKJ and Rockefeller campaigning together in a store in Flushing, Long Island

JKJ being hugged by an enthusiastic constituent

JKJ and Rockefeller, campaign photo

Dressed for winter and the first trip to the USSR

Vice President Lyndon B. Johnson swears JKJ in to the Senate

JKJ at the 1963 civil rights March on Washington

Senators celebrating the passage of the Civil Rights Act, 1964

Herblock cartoon from the *Washington Post*

Cartoon by Hy Rosen

JKJ with marines in Vietnam

JKJ with Rabbi Sherer, examining an ancient scroll

JKJ proposing a toast

Former Vice President Richard Nixon, Governor Rockefeller, and JKJ

JKJ and George Romney

Senators Edmund Muskie, JKJ, and Hubert H. Humphrey

Reelection to the Senate in 1974

President Richard Nixon, JKJ, and Secretary of State Henry Kissinger

Senator Edward Kennedy and JKJ

JKJ with Golda Meir, prime minister of Israel

JKJ with Egyptian President Anwar Sadat

Senator Henry "Scoop" Jackson, JKJ, and Senator Abraham Ribicoff with President Gerald Ford

JKJ and Senator Ribicoff with President Jimmy Carter

JKJ and Senator Frank Church with Deng Xiaoping in China, 1979

JKJ leaving the Capitol after a long day

Javits

ONE

The Urban Log Cabin

For a New York politician of my generation, I was born and brought up in the right place. Manhattan's Lower East Side — the twentieth-century equivalent of a log cabin — was the first home in America for masses of hopeful immigrants from Europe, and for them and generations of their children it was the cradle of a great adventure. The crowded tenement houses of the Lower East Side in the early years of this century provided much of the muscle and many of the brains that transformed America into an industrialized society. The immigrants and their children labored in sweatshops and factories, built cities, shaped the country's arts and sciences and professions, energized our business and commercial establishments, and developed new principles of government, politics, and economics. Their adventure is my adventure; their problems have been mine — and our country's — and I feel a part of their hopes and their triumphs and their disappointments. As a legislator it was always natural for me to represent their interests and concerns, and as a politician I won their support, for we share an inheritance of struggle, privation, hard work, a passion for justice — and a tenement-bred conviction that the world can be changed.

At the time, of course, hardly any of us on the Lower East Side would have discussed our lives in such lofty terms. We were all poor. We were cut off from the mainstream by religion, language, social customs, and a boundary called East Fourteenth Street. Immigrants in the early 1900s worked long hours, at strenuous, wearying, and often demeaning jobs, to earn the pittance that would ensure survival — while unwittingly building a modern United States. They lived on the Lower East Side because they had to, and most of them left it as soon as they could.

My particular corner of the Lower East Side was the intersection of Stanton and Orchard streets, in a bustling Jewish market area of small shops, clothing stalls, pushcarts, and crowded tenements. My father was the janitor for three tenement houses on that corner, and I was born in one of them, 85 Stanton Street, on May 18, 1904.

For the first thirteen years of my life, my world centered on that house, those streets, that neighborhood — and a busy, varied, stimulating world it was. Local policemen, shopkeepers, and assorted characters wandered in and out of our kitchen to drink tea or beer, to visit, gossip, and argue. I played one o'cat with the other kids on Stanton Street, which was a thoroughfare for horsecars; in the middle of one game, while I was looking the other way, I suddenly found myself entangled with a horse and was laid up with a very bruised thigh for two weeks. Around the corner, on Orchard Street, I helped my mother sell secondhand housewares from a pushcart and dry goods from a stall. Three blocks away from our corner were the University Settlement, Public School 20, and a public library.

Although most of the people I knew were Jews like ourselves, I grew up very much aware of ethnic, cultural, and religious diversity: There were Italians three blocks to the west and Irish and Germans nearby; there were Jews from Russia, Austria-Hungary, Poland, and the Baltic countries, each with their own traditions, all desiring to become Americans. Thanks to my brother, Benjamin, who was ten years my senior, I became aware also, at an early age, of the possibilities that awaited me in the broader America outside the Lower East Side ghetto.

My parents had immigrated to the United States by 1890, so they were both somewhat accustomed to American ways by the time I was born. My father, Morris Jawetz (as the immigration officers spelled it on his papers when he arrived), was born in Mielnieza, in Galicia, which was then part of the Austro-Hungarian Empire and now belongs to the Soviet Ukraine. It was a small town in a backward, economically stagnant area, and the Jewish community faithfully followed the ancient orthodoxy, by and large suffering less religious persecution than their brethren in czarist Russia. My father's father was a relatively prosperous flour merchant, and he sent Morris to study under the local rabbi — the Mielniezer *reb*. Morris did well in his studies of the Talmud and the Scriptures; he became a *yeshiva bucher* and a favorite of the rabbi, and he might have been on the way to becoming a rabbi himself.

But when Morris was nineteen his father and the rabbi arranged a marriage for him; his bride came from another village and he saw her for the first time on their wedding day. He tried it for a year, but he did not like her at all. So about 1882, at approximately the age of twenty, leaving his family, abandoning his bride, and breaking with his tradition, Morris picked himself up, escaped from a disagreeable marital situation, and joined the growing stream of migration to the United States. It was an amazingly brave and adventurous thing to do, and I have never been able fully to understand the reasons for the sudden burst of courage that made it possible for him. He must have been a spirited youth.

Morris arrived penniless at Castle Garden, in lower Manhattan, where immigrants were processed; this was before the reception point on Ellis Island was established. To be admitted, each person had to be healthy and have at least one U.S. dollar. My father was healthy enough, but the dollar was a problem. He often told us later how the immigrants, with the unofficial complicity of the inspectors, passed a silver dollar back to those behind them as they went through final clearance; each immigrant held a dollar at that moment, but when he left Castle Garden and found himself in the strange streets of New York he had nothing at all.

Probably guided by others who spoke Yiddish, Morris made his way to the Lower East Side and slept that night in a butcher's wagon. A series of odd jobs soon led him into New York's rapidly expanding garment industry, the ideal field of work for a Jewish immigrant. In the 1880s clothing was manufactured either in tiny apartments, where families or groups of people from the same European villages worked and ate and lived together, or in sweatshops operated by individual bosses. Since the contractor who farmed out the piecework paid a set price for the completed garments and not an hourly or weekly wage, the immigrant work teams could arrange their own schedules. That allowed them to keep their Sabbath and their holidays and eat kosher food and observe their orthodox rituals, which would have been nearly impossible while working in a factory on a Christian calendar and timetable. Even the sweatshops with hired labor were run by Orthodox Jews, so the holidays and rituals were observed there as well.

This was very important for my father. Although he had immigrated alone, without a family, he cherished his religion, and in the garment industry he could preserve both body and soul.

So Morris Jawetz became an "operator" on men's pants, which meant that he operated one of the new sewing machines. At some point he managed to purchase a sewing machine of his own, and carrying it on his back, he walked from workshop to workshop hiring out his machine and his new skills to whatever family work team or shop operator needed an extra hand. The Lower East Side was becoming the leading U.S. producer of ready-made clothing, so there was plenty to do during the "season," but the work was arduous, the hours required to earn enough to survive were long, and the season was short — only about four months of furious activity a year.

About seven years after his arrival in New York, my father met Ida Littman, a more recent immigrant; they married in 1893 and I was their second son and their youngest child. Only in the turmoil and adversity of an immigrant community in America could two people of such different backgrounds have met to fall in love and produce a family. Both of them were poor, both were Jewish, and both worked in the garment industry; other than that, Morris and Ida Javits would seem to have had little in common. Morris, a Talmudic scholar with a quick, warm smile — and a fierce temper that came and went just as quickly — was always uncomfortable, and sometimes almost helpless, in the practical world of moneymaking. Ida was illiterate when they married; but having worked since she was a child, she readily appreciated the dynamics of business, and it was she who tried to make the extra dollar to ease our lives. My father was impatient, possibly because he had been brought up to expect a better life. My mother had never been promised anything but hard times, so she accepted and endured, refusing to get angry and taking disasters in stride. These two very different people, while enduring poverty and hard work, remained deeply in love with each other until the ends of their lives.

My mother was born in Safed, Palestine, which was then part of the Turkish Empire. I have an early memory of her in shirtwaist and dark skirt, dancing with her friends in our living room, all of them linked together with long colored ribbons in the Turkish manner. When my mother was an infant her father abandoned his family. Her mother turned the baby over to *her* mother and went off to Odessa, in Russia. So Ida was brought up by her grandmother, who ran a small grocery store in Safed. She was given no schooling and had to work hard from the age of six or seven. In later years, usually when we complained about something, she would tell us how she had had to wash clothes in lye, which caused painful skin burns on her hands.

When Ida was sixteen her mother sent for her. The young girl walked the sixty-five miles from Safed to Beirut and then took a sailing ship to Odessa — where her life of toil continued. Her mother, with a new husband, was running a small tearoom, and Ida worked there as a waitress for three years, until her stepfather died. Then, in about 1889, she and her mother, stepsister, and half-brother emigrated to New York. The garment industry claimed them too, and my mother became an operator on men's ties, working literally day and night during the season.

Soon after my parents married, the arrival of my brother, Benjamin, compelled them to think of some more reliable and settled method of earning a living than the uncertainties and drudgery of the garment seasons. It was my mother, always alert to economic opportunities, who realized that the family could live more comfortably in a permanent home, and with a better income, if my father could find a job as a janitor. On her own initiative, she went looking for such an opening and found one on Allen Street. The Second Avenue Elevated Railway thundered overhead, and the street was one of the dirtiest and most crowded in the ghetto, but they moved into the janitor's basement apartment. For the rest of his life Morris Javits, Talmudic scholar, earned his living taking care of tenement houses.

After Benjamin was born, my mother gave birth to two girls; both of them died in infancy because of unsanitary conditions or the accidents of tenement life. The move to Stanton Street, a few years before I came along, probably represented a small step up in the world, but even there we lived in abysmally bad conditions. For cleaning and taking care of three tenements, my father received a free apartment plus heating coal in the winter and a salary never exceeding $45 a month. There was just one toilet on each of the five floors of each building; four families lived on each floor and shared the single toilet in the hall. Despite the efforts of my father, who was generally assisted by an old black man named Charlie who slept in the cellar and loved a drink, the hallways reeked eternally of every human odor, and the alleys between the buildings were always packed with the garbage that the tenants persisted in throwing out the windows. I can well remember — but will not repeat — the Yiddish curses my father directed at these miscreants. Morris the scholar was clearly miscast as a janitor, but his eloquence when he castigated those who added to his burdens was really impressive.

My mother tried to supplement the family income by operating a number of small businesses, which generally ended up unsuccessfully. She started a home-furnishings store in one of the houses my father tended, but that went bankrupt. For a while she sold dry goods from an Orchard Street stall; that enterprise was too small to go bankrupt, but it did not last very long.

I remember going along with my mother in a hired horse and wagon to a warehouse on Worth Street where we purchased a large stock of defective crockery and pots and pans. We hauled the load home, soldered the holes and straightened the dents and painted the stuff, and then piled it all on a pushcart. My job was to hawk it: In as loud a voice as I could muster — and it was necessary to shout to be heard in the cacophony of Orchard Street — I extolled the virtues of our patched-up wares and emphasized the bargain prices. I was about ten years old at the time, and I did that about once every two or three weeks and regarded those episodes as exciting adventures.

Looking back at that ten-year-old street peddler, I believe I learned something important on Orchard Street. I have never felt the least embarrassment or shyness about getting up in front of a crowd — even a hostile political one — to speak or argue or to explain and persuade. Within a year or two of my pushcart days, my public-school teachers were giving me prizes for declamation, and I was always the first in my class to be called upon to recite. And I never hung back. It is not a matter of self-confidence; often in my life I have been less than confident. But I learned on that pushcart how to attract attention and make a point, and public speaking has never frightened me since. In high-school and law-school debates, during several years as a salesman, then as a trial lawyer, and later, of course, in political speeches, congressional debates, and before television cameras, speaking out in public came naturally. Beyond that, public speaking is enjoyable for me, often exhilarating — something like the thrill a poet or a painter or a composer gets when his work is well done. I am not a musician, I do not paint; my art is in my audience. There are many reasons why I made my career in politics and statecraft, but the public-speaking talent that enabled me to succeed at it began to develop when I hawked chinaware from a pushcart on Orchard Street.

We lived in four small rooms. Facing the street was the living room, usually occupied by the three or four boarders we had to take in to make ends meet; then came the kitchen, then a bedroom for Benjamin and me, and then my parents' bedroom in back. Each bedroom had one window facing the alley and a blank wall, the bleak outlook enlivened only by those occasional bags of garbage hurtling earthward.

There was plenty of life within the apartment, because our kitchen was also our dining room and a neighborhood hangout. With its big stove, the kitchen was the only warm room during winter (we had no central heat), and the winter habit carried on through the year, making the kitchen a gathering place in all seasons. We were supposed to bathe there, too — in a big washtub — but it was difficult to do so in such a populous kitchen. Tenants, boarders, neighbors, shopkeepers, and friends drifted in and out, and the cops on the beat used our kitchen as an unofficial rest stop.

One Irish cop, named Jim Melody, showed up regularly for a cup of tea — or, if fortune had smiled on us, a nip of something stronger.

He must have had a special affection for me when I was small, for he would carry me around the block in his arms, to the delight of the neighbors.

Another local character who made himself at home in our kitchen was a man named Spitnick. Spitnick earned a marginal living, I think, peddling cheap diamonds to the ghetto residents, but in my mind he was our local intellectual. I ascribed this status to him for three reasons. First, he never put his arms through his coat, but always wore it draped over his shoulders in the manner affected on Second Avenue and East Broadway, where, we all knew, the Jewish intelligentsia gathered. Second, his pockets were stuffed with the newspapers he was always reading. And third, he made his own Russian-style cigarettes and smoked continually.

For Spitnick, making cigarettes was an exacting and complicated procedure, which I watched in fascination. He had a little tube into which the tobacco was packed, an elegant mouthpiece, and several other tools, all carried in an ornate box. He would sit down at our kitchen table, open his box, and with great flair manufacture one or two or more cigarettes — depending on how much time he could spare from his more sophisticated pursuits. His tea, which he would take only in a glass, he would pour into a saucer to cool, and drink from that. The sugar never went into the glass; he would hold a cube of it between his teeth and drink the tea through it. And that was our house intellectual.

Most of my memories of that apartment are centered on the Sabbath and the Jewish holidays; it was then that my mother managed to create a mood of tranquility and stability that contrasted with the hardships of our daily existence. On the Sabbath the house was quiet and clean, the food was specially prepared, and everyone dressed as appropriately as they could, considering our limited means. A relative quiet and dignity pervaded the streets as well as our home, for the area then was almost completely a Jewish ghetto and the throngs of people going to and from synagogue were the major part of the Saturday traffic.

In my memory of those days the holiday that stands out most clearly is Passover, with its special foods and utensils and its reminders of our deliverance from bondage in Egypt, of our heritage of the Holy Land, our belief in one God, and the thirst for justice. I am somewhat sentimental about all holidays and birthdays and special observances, but to this day Passover remains for me the most beautiful holiday of all.

My mother welcomed and appreciated the Sabbath and the Holy

Days as a respite from her daily grind. They provided a chance to spend a few extra hours with her family. To my father, however, religion meant much more. The rituals of orthodox Judaism were the core of his life; despite all of his life's vicissitudes, he never forgot his rabbinical training and never lost his passionate faith in the law of the Torah. Upon arising in the morning, he strapped to his forehead and to his left arm the little leather-bound *tefilin*, phylacteries, containing prayers and passages from the Torah. Then, with these symbols of the Hebrew faith near his mind and his heart, he would pray. Except on the Sabbath and on Jewish holidays — which required of him longer, more intricate rituals and prayers — my father prayed with his phylacteries every morning of his life.

By the time I became aware of these things, perhaps at the age of six or seven, the question of religion had already caused a deep split within my family. Benjamin, like many Jews born in the New World, had abandoned the practice of orthodoxy as soon as he had begun to earn a living. My father could not forgive him for this, and the struggle between them went on continuously in the background of my early life.

Benjamin had been sickly as a child. At a very early age he was operated on for pleurisy. The operation took place on the kitchen table in the Allen Street apartment; a piece of his rib was cut out and he was left with a deep scar in his back. Until he was about ten, he did not walk and play like other kids, and my mother had to wheel him around in a baby carriage. During those years he obeyed my father, and when he became a man under Jewish law — at his bar mitzvah at age thirteen — he began praying with the phylacteries as the Torah dictates. But by that time Ben was beginning to overcome his physical frailty. Soon thereafter, with an explosion of will echoing my father's courage in leaving Mielnieza, young Ben summoned up a powerful inner drive to make himself strong, intellectual, successful — and aggressive. This determination to triumph over weakness and adversity shaped his whole life — and influenced mine as well — and in its first manifestation it brought him into conflict with my father. Four or five years after his bar mitzvah, Benjamin rebelled. He refused to lay the phylacteries in the morning, he stopped going to synagogue, and he even denounced the rituals as superstition. In his teens he had become what was then called a free thinker, and there was no place for established religion in his life.

This rebellion led to furious arguments between my father and brother — Ben having inherited Morris's quick and violent temper. Ben's renunciation of established religion was a grievous affront to my father, who felt particularly hurt by his oldest son's refusal to lay the phylacteries. One of the four bits of Scripture contained in the *tefilin* says, "Sanctify unto me your first-born male child." And Morris Javits's first-born son was refusing to have anything to do with Morris's orthodoxy. Again and again my father berated Ben as an unworthy son to have abandoned the rituals in which he was raised, as an ungrateful man to have abandoned the God who had restored his health.

Ben was just as passionate and stiff-necked. With all the doctrinaire fervor of a young man discovering "Truth," he railed against the narrow orthodoxy of our father, and he was not too nice about it. I can almost still hear him exclaiming: "With all the problems and misery in the world, how can you worry about a superstition like the *tefilin* in the mornings?" A more tolerant young man might have gone through the motions of ritual just to please his father, but Ben's was too forceful and positive a personality for that. I think he expected that the force of his ideas, or the strength of his arguments, would eventually persuade my father to give up. But he protested in vain.

The struggle was very hard on my mother. She was not as attached to the orthodox rituals as was my father, so the argument itself did not move her; but she was torn — between her love for him and her love for and pride in Ben. It was in the context of this tension that I think I first became aware of my mother's capacity to accept whatever fate provided. Nothing fazed her. She could endure hardship and abuse for as long as necessary. Without appearing to be stubborn, she was unbelievably persistent. She went her own way, avoiding confrontations by simply ignoring whatever she disagreed with. Her habit was to continue on what she thought was the right course as if she had not heard the contrary, and in the end she almost invariably prevailed. Sometimes, when my father and brother had been arguing for a long time, my mother would suggest mildly that "it's time to stop already." At which point *she* would be yelled at by my father. But that did not bother her in the least, for she had been yelled at since her childhood and had survived. Afterward she would find a rational excuse to forgive them, to forgive anyone who had behaved badly. "He was getting too excited," she might say, or "This is a difficult time for him."

These impassioned arguments and frequent displays of temper had something to do with my lifelong reluctance to let loose my own emotions or to get involved in angry disputes. Emotionally, one could say, I am a very private person. Certainly I have inherited much of my mother's "thick skin," her capacity to take criticism, and her dislike of violent argument.

Although I never dared to say anything during those arguments,

I tended to agree with my brother's contention that he was free to do as he liked.

It was impossible to grow up on the Lower East Side without becoming sensitive to change and diversity. The older generation, holding to customs and beliefs that seemed alien, was always among us. My grandmother, my mother's mother, was an old-fashioned Russian Jewish woman who dragged herself up five flights of stairs to her tiny apartment on East Seventh Street until well into her seventies. She died when I was only seven or eight and I have only one clear memory of her: She believed in a simple remedy for every illness, whether it was chilblains, arthritis, a sore throat, or weak eyes. Her remedy was Colgate toothpaste. She did not know what it was, but she was convinced it could cure anything.

Another ancient lady who provided a kind of health care was a midwife named Rifka. She was eighty-five when she delivered me, I was told, and it is said she lived to be a hundred, having brought hundreds of Lower East Side babies into the world. Rifka was a medicine woman as well as a midwife. Until my tonsils were removed by a charity doctor when I was about twelve, I often had to miss school because of tonsillitis. Whenever my tonsils flared up, my mother would send me to Rifka to exorcise this devil. Rifka would concoct a brew in a frying pan and chant some incantations over it while I looked on, mesmerized. From this ritual I was supposed to get well. Of course, I did not.

Ethnic diversity was never very far away, either. Three blocks west of our home was Chrystie Street, the border of the Italian neighborhood. We regarded the Italians as strange and different: They had large, very close-knit families; seemed to us to be very excitable; and, as we saw it, were all in the business of selling ice cream or ice. Their view of us must have been similarly distorted; I imagine they saw the Jews as sharp businessmen lacking in spirit. There was no hostility or even unfriendliness between the Jewish and Italian communities, but we got into a lot of street scraps with the Italian kids. In the winter our weapons were snowballs into which a small piece of coal was embedded. For defense we turned to the large elliptical tops of the tin kettles in which our mothers boiled clothes; the kettle tops had handles and they made great shields. Once, though, I was not quick enough with my shield, and I still bear a small scar over my eye where I was hit by a piece of coal packed in a snowball.

Of course, we also went to school with the Italian kids, and sometimes we made friends with them. I remember being very proud that I had a friend from the other side of Chrystie Street. My best childhood friend, however, was Herman Feinstein, who lived on my block. We were classmates, we played together from the age of about six, and we kept in touch with each other for decades thereafter. His father's clothing store on Stanton Street later expanded into a clothing manufacturing enterprise, Admiration Clothes, which Herman and his brothers operated very successfully, and it pleased Herman — and me — that I bought my suits there.

Diversity within the Jewish ghetto itself offered us plenty of details for forming childish stereotypes. The Hungarians were dreamers, the Lithuanians were herring and potato eaters, and the Rumanians, whom we regarded with suspicion, were known for the consumption of large quantities of a corn pudding called *mamaliga*.

We were also aware of the American Irish Catholics, although we did not have an ethnic caricature for them because they lived farther away. They were the police, like Jim Melody, and they controlled Tammany Hall and provided our link to politics and government. My father was involved with the Tammany organization, so at a very early age I was exposed to the realities of the New York political system.

My father supplemented his janitorial income by performing small political chores for the Tammany machine. At election time he disbursed to the tenants in his buildings the two or three dollars that Tammany paid for each vote. The cash for this vote-buying enterprise came from an Irish politician who, according to my best recollection, was called Porges, and who kept a saloon on the corner of Allen and Rivington streets. Occasionally I tagged along when my father went to Porges's saloon to pick up the money. Porges wore a black derby, tilted back on his head, and a vest, like a faro dealer; he was slender and beetle-browed and he always seemed to have a mug of beer in front of him as he counted out the bills that my father would then carry to the tenants. The Tammany connection entailed other duties: Pushcart peddlers would run to my father if they got a summons for a minor violation, and he would take it to Porges to get it quashed. Whether it *was* ever quashed I do not know, but that was the mission.

I do not think it ever occurred to my father that there was anything wrong with what he was doing; it was to him simply part of settling in New York City's ghetto. I did not grasp its meaning as a child, but later, as I learned about politics, I felt a revulsion against this corruption, and it was one of the main reasons I joined the Republican Party rather than the Democrats when I grew up.

Despite my mother's hard life — or perhaps because of it — she wanted her sons to be gentlemen. I was always dressed in clean clothes,

I was encouraged to read and study, and I was taught to be polite. I do not think this made me a "mama's boy," for I did get into street fights and I hung around with the neighborhood boys, but I was certainly not a tough East Side kid. One summer day, when I was about nine years old, I tagged along when the kids on the block trooped down to swim in the East River, which was not so polluted in those days. A barge had been moored to a pier and filled with river water to make a free swimming pool for the Lower East Side. I was standing around watching, for I could not swim, when suddenly one of the boys tossed me into the pool, clothes and all. I scrambled out — how, I will never know — frightened, humiliated, and determined to learn to swim.

I clung to that determination for a year, and the following summer I got my chance. Somehow — probably because Ben was working by then — our family managed to spend several weeks on the beach at Coney Island. We shared a tiny rented apartment on Surf Avenue with two young women, and they taught me to swim. I was avid to learn, and I worked hard at it and became quite a good swimmer. So the unpleasant incident at the East River pool provided me with a lifetime pleasure.

Occasionally during those years my family took trips out of the city. My mother's half-brother ran a small ice-cream parlor in Rockville Centre, Long Island. We would go out there on warm weekends, and I helped sell ice cream to the fans at the local baseball game. It was with a sense of becoming a responsible grownup that I took in the money and turned it over to my uncle. Another place we went to was Jersey City, where my mother had a friend whose husband manufactured pipes. It was like going to the country; to get to their house we walked from the "tube" station down a broad tree-lined street. "Aunt" Mary always fed us very well, and we worked in the afternoon, the work children could do, cementing the stems into the bowls of the pipes. In those days no one from the busy ghetto just went to visit friends and relatives: Each person always had a purpose and a task; no one could afford to waste any time. Those experiences marked me. Pure relaxation, the simple wasting of time, still makes me uncomfortable; I am happiest when I am working, and I cannot remember when I have taken a vacation without bringing work along — to the despair of my wife and the concern of my staff.

Of all the influences on my early life, that of my brother was the most profound and lasting. Philosophically, professionally, and to a degree economically, he made me. When I was a kid growing up in the poverty and turmoil of the Lower East Side, reading avidly and exploring ideas, Ben provided the inspiration that neither my wise but uneducated mother nor my displaced orthodox father could give me — much as they would have wanted to. It was through Ben's efforts that we escaped from the Lower East Side; he found me my first jobs, encouraged me to attend law school, took me into partnership with him. (He also changed the spelling of our family name, to Javits, to make it phonetic.) In later years Ben and I disagreed about many things, and to become "my own man" I had to struggle to free myself from his domination, but our love for each other endured. I have never forgotten, nor do I want to forget, that Benjamin Javits did more than anyone to shape my mind and character in those formative years and thus made it possible for me to accomplish everything I have achieved since.

When I was twelve and thirteen, Ben used to take me on long walks from Stanton Street up Second Avenue as far as Fourteenth Street, the limit of our turf. Second Avenue in those days was an exciting, thriving thoroughfare, the Times Square or Champs-Elysées of the Jewish ghetto. On Second Avenue there were Yiddish theaters, where my mother had taken me on rare and special occasions, and the cafés where Jewish writers, actors, artists, and scholars gathered to discuss politics and literature. We seldom could afford to go anywhere that cost money; but we often stopped and looked in the window of the famous Café Royale. Occasionally Ben took me to the social and discussion club to which he belonged. It was on East Seventh or East Eighth Street, just off Second Avenue, and I think it was called the Emmanuel Club. That is where I first heard serious discussions of the great social and political controversies of the day, and where I first heard the names of the Lower East Side heroes: Meyer London, the Socialist congressman, and Morris Hillquit, the Socialist candidate for mayor. There, sitting quietly and just listening to Ben and his pals, I first became politically aware.

But mostly we just walked while Ben talked endlessly and I listened in love and admiration. He gave me his side of the conflict with our father, explaining his impatience with the limitations of the orthodox religion as our father practiced it. He told me of his dreams and his plans. And he inspired me with his social and political ideas.

Ben was in law school then, going to Fordham at night and working during the day to help support the family. He had been earning money for some years; he had even attended high school at night. Having been brought up as one of the working poor, Ben had developed a passion for financial security and an acquisitiveness for money — as well as influence. But the poverty and injustice he had seen, and his own struggle against illness, also instilled in him a social conscience; and the political ferment and the labor movement on the Lower East Side offered him a platform for it.

In those years Ben was a Socialist, passionately devoted to the study of social and political issues, but also dedicated to the practice of democracy. On those long walks I learned much about his beliefs. Soon he was taking me to Socialist meetings, where I heard Eugene Debs and actually met Algernon Black, Hillquit, and other Socialist leaders of the time. We even attended a sendoff rally at Carnegie Hall for the anarchist leaders Emma Goldman and Alexander Berkman, who were on their way to Washington to protest the draft in the First World War. I can remember them marching out of the hall to great cheers and applause.

It was natural for ghetto youth to be Socialists in those years. We all saw firsthand the sweatshop conditions of the garment industry and the inequities of the economic system. The bitter fight to organize labor was then under way, and almost every worker recognized that only by forming unions could working men and women better their lot. Many of our boarders were involved in union organizing activities and sometimes they would come home with bandaged heads, the result of having been clubbed by a policeman — or a goon — on a picket line or at a labor rally. My mother used to keep a little pot on the stove with each boarder's dinner, so that they could eat even if they came home late. I remember watching one of them who had been roughed up trying to eat despite what must have been a splitting headache. The belief that the trade union movement embodied the cause of social and economic justice thus became a very important part of my early upbringing and has remained with me all my life. Even without Ben's influence, I might have emerged from the Lower East Side as a firm believer in the principle of trade unionism.

What those walks and talks with Ben gave me, in my very impressionable years, was a fascination with political and social action and a conviction that injustices can be eliminated, that bad laws can be changed, that it is possible to make the world a better place. I have spent most of my life trying to live up to that conviction, and Ben devoted much of *his* later life to the belief that *capitalism* could produce everything that socialism promised, to wit, social and economic justice and equal and full opportunity for economic security.

Were it not for Ben, however, I might never have emerged from the Lower East Side at all. His primary ambition at the time of those walks was to get the family out of the ghetto, and in 1917 he managed it. He was only twenty-three, still in law school, but somehow he scraped together enough money for us to move to Brooklyn. We took an apartment at 1187 Eastern Parkway in Brownsville, which was another Jewish area but much cleaner and more comfortable than Stanton and Orchard streets.

One reason Ben wanted us to make that move was to remove my father from the dirt and drudgery of a janitor's life, but it did not work out that way. My father refused to leave his job. My mother tried to persuade him to join us in Brooklyn; he was in bad health and we were sure he would live longer on Eastern Parkway. But he was a proud man, and I think he simply could not bring himself to become the dependent of a son who had forsaken his God.

So he remained on the Lower East Side, tending to his tenements, while my mother and Ben and I lived in Brooklyn. Every day my mother traveled back and forth between Eastern Parkway and Stanton Street — a trip of forty-five minutes or an hour by trolley over the Williamsburg Bridge — bringing my father his meals and then hurrying back to take care of us. She loved him dearly; she was probably the only person who remembered or cared that Morris Javits had once been a Talmudic scholar. But the struggle between father and eldest son was too much even for her. In her stoic way she carried on, equally tolerant of my father's stubbornness and my brother's drive. So my brother prevailed, and my father abdicated his role as the main provider for the family.

Six months or a year later, my father fell ill, and after an operation for gallstones he could no longer work. Only then did he join us in Brooklyn. But he never recovered. In the summer of 1919 he came with us to Arverne, in the Rockaways, where Ben had managed to rent a summer bungalow. There, in the Far Rockaway Hospital, and literally in the arms of his family, Morris Javits died from a post-operative infection. He was an economic failure, my father, but a dear man with a beautiful smile, who was sustained by the profound comfort of his faith.

TWO

The Education
of a Kid Brother

I was a good student. Very early I found that books could provide not only knowledge but pleasure and excitement as well. My mother's passion to see her children learned and well educated nurtured my love of books, as did the example of Ben, who had graduated from public elementary school by the time I entered it and who was already at home in the world of ideas. The thirst for knowledge was great in the ghetto, for we all realized knowledge could lead to social position and financial achievement and a better life.

My first experience with the institutions that made books available to us and encouraged their use was at the University Settlement — where Eleanor Roosevelt had been a social worker — three blocks from our house. The University Settlement and a dozen or so settlement houses like it led my generation, the children of immigrant parents, into the mainstream of our country's life; they made us eager for the American experience. Uptowners — Eleanor Roosevelt was only one of many — gave unstintingly of their time, some of them coming to live in the area for weeks or months, others making generous financial donations at a time when there was no income tax against which to claim charitable deductions. The settlements improved the immigrants' health, diet, sanitation, and education; they lobbied successfully for parks, playgrounds, public baths, nursing homes, and recreation facilities. (The East River swimming pool into which I was dumped was probably provided by one of the settlements.) The University Settlement may also have had something to do with my prolabor feeling: A number of unions covering workers in the garment trades met regularly at the settlement, where the injustices to workers were recognized and discussed.

I attended kindergarten at the University Settlement, and the first thing I learned, I think, was how to take a shower, for we had no such amenity at home. Later I joined the Cornell Club at University Settlement and played a lot of basketball and baseball on club teams. My parliamentary experience began with the club meetings. We discussed club and settlement-house activities in accordance with parliamentary rules and under the guidance of the adult adviser — usually a lawyer or a teacher — who was assigned to each club.

To me, the most memorable settlement-house occasions were our picnic expeditions to the Palisades in New Jersey. Girls' clubs came along, too — my first exposure to girls. We took the subway to Dyckman Street in upper Manhattan and walked to the ferry for the ride across the Hudson River. At the Palisades we played baseball, climbed the rocks, and ate hot dogs and sandwiches. After a full day in this outdoor paradise, a world away from the teeming streets in which we lived, we would troop home again, dead tired but joyous on the subway ride back to Lafayette and Spring streets and the long walk home.

At Public School 20, across the street from the University Settlement, I made the honor roll and enjoyed my English and history classes. Spencerian penmanship was still taught in those days and I worked my way through that as best I could: My handwriting is still hard to read. The most exciting school moments came when I was chosen to recite to the assembly of the entire student body, the teachers having discovered this aptitude in me. I remember doing Felicia Hemans's "Casabianca" ("The boy stood on the burning deck") and Walt Whitman's "O Captain! My Captain!"

One of my teachers at P.S. 20 was a wise and distinguished gentleman named Mittleman. Teaching arithmetic was his specialty, but he did more than that. He instilled in us qualities I was already learning from my mother: gentility, dignity, scholarliness, good manners. My mother had a natural grace in personal conduct; Mittleman encouraged that in me and taught us the American forms of courtesy. From an early age I was impressed with the lasting value of good manners — standing for a lady or an older person, tipping my hat, opening a door for someone, or giving up my seat in the subway.

Half a block from the University Settlement on Rivington Street was a branch of the New York Public Library. I spent an enormous amount of time there, and I came home loaded with volumes on history and biography and novels by James Fenimore Cooper, Victor Hugo, and Alexandre Dumas. These works wove a rich tapestry of adventure, provided glimpses of other societies that inspired my youthful imagination, and revealed to me the joy and power of good writing. I owe a great debt to public libraries, and I have tried to repay it by working for Congress's support for the U.S. public-library system.

I graduated from P.S. 20 in February 1917, near the top of my class, and enrolled in De Witt Clinton High School. De Witt Clinton was regarded at the time as one of the best academic high schools in the city, and it was something of an honor to be admitted to it. But for some reason the half semester I spent there was disastrous for me. I flunked algebra — the only course I ever failed — and had to repeat it later; and I was very unhappy. I was younger than most of the other students and I could not adapt to what I remember as a highly competitive atmosphere. It may have been the teachers, whom I found too busy to listen; or it may have been that only a few of the boys I knew from P.S. 20 were with me or that the best students from all over the city gave me tough intellectual competition. Or I may have been jolted at finding myself, for the first time, outside a familiar environment. Or it may have been merely geographical: De Witt Clinton was at Fifty-ninth Street and Tenth Avenue, and to get there I had two long walks and a rush-hour subway ride. Most likely, the combination of these factors contributed to my unhappiness at De Witt Clinton.

Fortunately, I was rescued from this situation before much damage was done; I had been at De Witt Clinton only half a semester when Ben moved us to Brooklyn. There I entered Boys' High School and everything started going well for me again. With great determination I repeated the algebra course I had failed at De Witt Clinton, and I passed with a mark of 100 percent. I studied hard and enjoyed it, and I remained in the upper quarter of my class for most of the two years I attended Boys' High, even though those years were marked by the tragedy of my father's illness and death.

At Boys' High I tried out for the swimming team; the jostling bothered me, and though I became a good swimmer there, I did not make the team. I played a lot of sand-lot baseball in Brownsville (first base was my favorite position) and also joined some of the unofficial "sports" of my schoolmates. One of these offered the challenge of riding the trolley car to school without paying the nickel fare. The cars were open, with a running board along the outside, so you could get off from any part of the car. The trick was to keep moving ahead of or behind the conductor and then hop off just before he got to you. If you were lucky, you would have reached the school by then; if not, there would be only a block or two to walk.

My political activities began in Brooklyn, too. Ben noticed that public speaking came naturally to me, and when I was fourteen or fifteen he enlisted me to help the Socialists at street-corner meetings. I never joined the Socialist Party, but often I stood on a soapbox at some corner in Brownsville and spoke to a crowd about the need for social and economic justice, about trade unionism, about unemployment and welfare and civil liberties and other planks of the Socialist platform. I talked about the Espionage Act of 1917, which had endangered our civil liberties, and immediately after the Armistice I spoke about the hysterical fear of "labor agitators" that was sweeping through many communities in the United States. For someone who had grown up with labor sympathies, there were obviously many battles to fight.

Ben and I talked fervently about these issues on long walks that we continued to take in Brooklyn as we had on the Lower East Side. At night we used to stroll down Eastern Parkway to Pitkin Avenue, the brightly lit commercial center of Brownsville that always excited me.

On one of these walks, my brother, as concerned as a father, asked me what I wanted to do when I graduated from high school. Up to that time my ambition had been to become a doctor. Health — or rather often the absence of it — had ruled the lives of all the people I knew on the Lower East Side, and I had always looked with awe on the miracles a doctor could perform. There had been a Dr. Michael Katz down the street from us on Stanton Street. He came to our house often (at fifty cents a visit) because of my tonsillitis. He seemed to have been particularly attached to our family and especially respectful of my mother, probably because she was known in the neighborhood as someone who was always ready to lend a hand to anyone who needed it. He was a warm and good-hearted man and made me feel — as he did everyone else — that he was giving me his personal and devoted attention. At any rate, I admired and loved him — and that may have had something to do with my early desire to become a doctor.

So I told Ben I was still interested in medicine. Ben, struggling through law school, was certain that the legal profession was much more interesting and important. As a lawyer, he said, I would have many more opportunities to be socially useful, many more paths to follow later. Lawyers with our commitment to social justice were needed in the world, he said — and I had to agree there. Ben and I had discussed my ambitions before that evening, and our conversation on that walk was the culmination of these talks. He impressed me with the intensity of his conviction that I should become a lawyer. In those days, certainly — when I was fifteen and he was twenty-five — and even for many years thereafter, Ben's influence on me was great, and besides, I liked the idea of being associated with him. So then and there I decided to study law.

There were times, later, when I had some doubts about this course.

But at that moment, influenced not only by Ben but by all the hopes and fears in post-Armistice America, I made the decision that was eventually to propel me into public life.

During that period Ben was supporting the family as a collector of bad debts. Traveling from our home in Brooklyn to his law courses at Fordham, which was then in lower Manhattan, and to his collection business in midtown became a burden. So in the summer of 1919, soon after our father died, he moved us again, this time to Washington Heights, in upper Manhattan. We took an apartment at 600 West 192nd Street, and that fall I transferred to George Washington High School.

It was a golden year for me. I plunged into student affairs, took on a great deal of responsibility for the student body's postwar relief activities, won a prize for scholarship — and had a very good time. The school was brand-new and was located in what felt to me like a rural area, in Inwood, just beyond Washington Heights, with playing fields and open space. George Washington High School seemed to me almost like a country club, and most of the students were ladies and gentlemen — relaxed, genteel, civilized people who did not feel they had to scramble to outdo each other every moment. Many of them were from well-to-do families and most of them were Christians; I was in the minority, but I was elected president of my official class — that is, my homeroom — and I enjoyed the role of leader. My classmates introduced me to a new world that seemed to suit me. There was one tennis player who never stepped on the court unless he was wearing his proper white flannels; the game intrigued me and I started to play tennis, too — a lifetime avocation. The school was coeducational, and the girls added a new and fascinating element to my life.

I graduated in June 1920, having completed my high-school education in three and a half years. My classmates elected me chairman of the Senior Class Day Committee, and the "Futuristic Fish Bowl" page of the class yearbook predicted that I would become a "political boss." Under my picture appears the legend "You can't tell from first appearances." Twenty-six years later, my classmates still living in the area had a second look and a chance to vote for me again: Washington Heights helped elect me to Congress four times.

My graduation from high school was followed almost immediately by the depression of 1920–22. The initial shock of it was almost as severe as the Great Depression of the 1930s, and American farmers did not recover from it for twenty years, but it is barely remembered now except by economic historians — and by me. The 1920–22 depression forced me to go to work early, for it hit my brother's debt-collection business hard. With unemployment rising and businesses failing, not even a keen and aggressive debt collector like Benjamin could function effectively: The money just was not there. So I had to postpone any thought of college or law school and start earning a living and helping to support the family.

Ben found a job for me. One of his clients was a wholesaler of lithographic stones and inks, and Ben asked the firm to take me on. So, soon after my high-school graduation, I became a traveling salesman of lithographic supplies.

My sales territory stretched from New York to Norfolk, Virginia. For nearly two years I traveled over this area, taking long solitary train rides to Philadelphia, Washington, Richmond, and Wilmington, and then bus and trolley trips to lithographers in industrial areas. There I would show my samples, give my sales pitch and take orders, and after a round of such visits make my way back to my employer's warehouse in what is now known as the SoHo district of Manhattan. My commissions and salary came to $85 or $90 a week.

That was very good money in those days, and I earned every penny of it — with loneliness. It was a bleak routine for a young man — a boy, really — who was not given to the traditional pleasures of a traveling salesman's life, or who perhaps was simply not old enough to find or enjoy them. I was a student, quite shy, and I did not make friends quickly. Furthermore, I had never before spent so much time away from my family. The long, empty evenings in cities where I knew no one stick in my memory; only the busy workdays made the trips tolerable. I would return to New York and the warmth of family with great eagerness and relief. My sales rounds took me frequently to Washington, where I would sometimes find a concert to go to; I had no idea, of course, that it was the city where I would spend the better part of my life.

My only friends on those journeys were the books I carried with me. I was still something of a socialist, and I was reading Marx's *Das Kapital*, Charles and Mary Beard's history of the United States, Carlyle on the French Revolution, Gibbon's *Decline and Fall of the Roman Empire*, and other books on history and political theory. Then I came upon a work that was to have an even greater influence on my thinking. It is a book that is largely ignored today, although its ideas have become an accepted element in our sociopolitical beliefs.

The book is the *History of Civilization in England*, by Henry Thomas Buckle, a brilliant and erudite English historian and philosopher who lived in the nineteenth century. Buckle, who is said to have taught himself eighteen languages, intended to write a history of all civilization, then scaled it down to a sixteen-volume opus on intellectual development in Britain, and eventually published only two volumes before he died.

Buckle was one of the first exponents of the concept that history may be a science. Impatient with the traditional historians' emphasis on wars, politics, and the careers of individual leaders, Buckle insisted that history depends on the influences of soil, food, and climate, that these geographical and environmental factors affect national character, and that the mass behavior of societies and nations is much more important than the roles of individuals. Although some of Buckle's "laws" and theories merely reflected the prejudices of his time and his country — for instance, his view that only the European climate could support a high level of civilization — he was the first to try to apply the methods of natural science to the study of human political behavior, and his ideas profoundly affected all the social scientists, including Marx. Certainly they had a profound effect on me. I recall learning about Buckle in Arthur Brisbane's "Today" column in the *New York Evening Journal*; I borrowed the books from the library and read them avidly. They confirmed my instinct that society's problems can be solved rationally because they depend on factors that are often predictable. Buckle made me optimistic, for if man's social problems are correctable, then we can hope for the ultimate triumph of the rule of law over the rule of force.

Despite the need to work, I had not, of course, abandoned my intention to study law. Rather than follow in Ben's footsteps precisely, by going to Fordham, I applied to the dean of New York University Law School, Frank Henry Sommer. At that time it was not necessary to graduate from college in order to enter law school, but some college credits or their equivalents were needed. Dean Sommer, a very kind and considerate gentleman, outlined a program for me; while working as a salesman, I took some college courses at Columbia, cramming my study into whatever odd hours I could find. Since I was not able to attend regularly, it took me nearly three years to amass the necessary credits, which probably amounted to no more than one year of a normal college program.

In addition to the academic courses, Columbia required its students to take some kind of physical education, so I enrolled in a boxing class. On the first day, the instructor lined up a group of us and told us to put up our hands. We did so, and the next thing I knew I was sitting on the floor wondering what had happened. "You put your hands up," the instructor said. "The first thing you've got to learn in boxing is hit 'em from where you are. Wherever you are, hit 'em. Don't make a ceremony out of putting up your arms or putting down your arms. Just hit 'em." The lesson of that punch has stayed with me: No matter where you are you can do things; there is nothing to be gained by wishing you were someplace else or waiting for a better situation. You see where you are and do what you can with that.

In the fall of 1923 I entered NYU Law School, where I was fortunate to find some remarkable teachers. The most gifted, in my opinion, was Professor Daniel F. Burnett, who taught courses in equity and real property. His explanations of legal principles and the rationales of cases were always crystal clear, always perfectly paced. He did not try to slow down for the dullards or speed up for the gifted students. From Burnett's teaching style I learned never to take anything for granted when giving an explanation, never to assume knowledge or the lack of it on the part of your listeners. You always explain your terms; you do not assume the other fellow knows. Maybe he does and maybe he does not, but if you are too arrogant to explain something you may lose him; so you must carry him with you all the way. But Burnett was always careful not to insult us by assuming we knew nothing; he made his explanations and gave his definitions as pieces of a logical puzzle that we deserved to have put before us whether we had heard them before or not. That, too, I absorbed and remembered — and used.

Another lesson Burnett taught me about a legal argument is to grasp and enunciate the central point first: You say, "The point of this case is such and such," and then go on to deal with its complexities. But first you must give your listener something to hang on to while he is listening to you, something to which he can anchor every fact and detail.

With Burnett and other good teachers to guide me, I took quickly to the intricacies of the law, to the research, the thinking, and the issues. The process seemed to come naturally to me. I made good grades and won the position of anchor man on the NYU Law School debating team.

In those days legal studies required eighteen hours of classes a week, which enabled me to work my way through law school. Ben by then had finally been admitted to the bar and had opened up a small law office. He gave up his debt-collection business and helped me get started in one of my own. So I ended my lithographic sales career and, while carrying my full schedule of law courses, began chasing down debtors as my brother had been doing for six years.

For about a year I ran the little business myself from an office at 500 Fifth Avenue. From 8:00 A.M. to 3:30 P.M. I went out soliciting business and making collections. Then I hurried to my classes on Washington Square and came back to the office a little after 8:00 P.M. to telephone debtors and to study law. From about 10:00 P.M., when it got too late to phone people, my law books took over exclusively. I had a radio in the office — quite a primitive apparatus by modern standards. It had an enormous loop antenna and earphones. Night after night I would sit there, listening to classical music and poring over cases on contracts, torts, crimes, equity, and real property.

As a debt collector I may not have been as tough and aggressive as Ben had been — and when you are running after reluctant debtors aggressiveness is certainly a useful trait — but I was persistent. You cannot collect bills without clients who give you their bills to collect. I was shy, and to walk off the street and ask for business was hard for me, but I made myself do it and was quite successful at it.

I did that at a big men's-underwear manufacturer on West Twenty-third Street, Lax and Burgheimer. It was one of those magnificent cast-iron loft buildings with a huge street-level store. I walked in, inquired for the credit manager, introduced myself to him, and asked him to give me a chance to prove myself by letting me go after some of his toughest deadbeats. I had nothing: no references, very little experience. But for some reason the credit manager was impressed enough to try me out, and the firm became one of my best clients. My experience as a salesman, as well as my public-speaking skill, helped me that day, but it was not easy: This time the product I was selling was myself.

After I had been collecting bills for about two years, Ben and I tried to expand my business. Ben found me a partner, a Southerner named Leonard Crone, who was a systems-management expert very fond of color-coded filing methods. He was also fond of a loaded pistol that he carried around in his pocket. One day Leonard and I, the working partners, and Ben, who had put some money into the enterprise, sat down in our new office on Forty-fourth Street to discuss how much salary we should draw and how the profits should be split. Leonard took his gun out and put it on the table. He did not threaten us and we were not defying him. But it was like a scene out of a George Raft movie: "Now let's talk, fellas," with a gun on the table.

That joint enterprise did not last long. I never saw Leonard Crone use his gun, but he turned out to be a better money spender than money maker, and neither Ben nor I felt secure about the partnership. So we parted company. I think we just turned the business over to Leonard and felt happy to get out.

By that time Ben's law practice was looking up and he needed help. So I supported myself through the latter part of law school by clerking for my brother. Right from the start, even though I was still a student, Ben and I established the division of labor that was to characterize the firm of Javits & Javits for many years. Ben was my mentor, my preceptor; I benefited from his determination, his vigorous and animated spirit, his fertile mind always teeming with new ideas and plans. But I profited from his weaknesses as well. He was not too good with the law books, not very adept in handling the technical aspects of the law. So, even when I was Ben's clerk, I had the opportunity to handle much of the basic legal drafting for the office, while he brought in the business, set the fees, and negotiated with clients and adversaries. When I was admitted to the bar, Ben's dynamic, innovative thinking and boldness and my legal skill soon made us an effective team. He took great pride in that and liked to point out that he was one lawyer in New York who was never reluctant to say "We'll see you in court."

Even before this teamwork began, however, Ben and I had our first serious disagreement. It was more significant than I may have realized at the time, because it sprang from our contrasting temperaments and foreshadowed the differences that would eventually lead us to go our separate ways professionally.

Toward the end of 1920, my mother and Ben and I had moved from Washington Heights to an apartment in a brownstone building on Eighty-seventh Street near West End Avenue. For some reason, although both Ben and I were working, we fell behind in our rent payments and were threatened with eviction.

In response to the landlord's legal action against us, Ben filed a counterclaim against the landlord for failure to maintain the building properly, asserting that we were withholding the rent until our demands were met. The fact was that we just could not manage to pay that month, as I pointed out to Ben, but he refused to admit it. I was still not much more than a kid and my arguments did not change my brother's mind, so my mother and I were forced to appear in court and testify to the poor condition of the apartment and the building.

That was a very uncomfortable and distasteful experience for me. It was not that we testified falsely, for indeed there was fault on the landlord's side, but I felt, objectively, that we did not have adequate legal grounds for the counterclaim. If we could not pay the rent, I thought, we should have either moved or tried to persuade the landlord to give us a period of grace. But Ben had his way.

That case, right at the outset of his legal career, characterized Ben's aggressive style as a lawyer. On occasion he became combative over some client or issue that I did not think was worth it. I have always said that as a lawyer I would never offer another lawyer a settlement I would not take myself; Ben was always much more determined to get the last possible dollar out of a situation. There were to be many cases in which I might have settled for less than Ben got — and I might have been wrong. My inclination was to follow my mother's peaceful path of avoiding unnecessary confrontations. Ben, who had inherited the more volatile temperament of my father, would never let anybody "get away with it," as he saw it.

Shortly after our legal battle with the landlord (the precise outcome of which I have forgotten), our family living patterns changed. My mother remarried and went to live in Brooklyn with her new husband. Ben and I and Ben's fiancée, Lily, took a small apartment in Forest Hills at about the time I started law school.

Ben and I had met Lily a year or two earlier at a dance in a Catskill Mountains resort. She was a gorgeous young woman: small, very feminine, with a perfect complexion and a lovely figure; Ben was smitten immediately. Lily was a milliner, working first for her aunt and later for the Shubert theater organization, but she eventually gave up her very promising career for Ben. She came to live with us in Forest Hills, where Ben and I shared one bedroom and Lily occupied another. The three of us were very close. Lily became as dear to me as a sister, and Ben's courtship of her was one of the most beautiful things in my life. My brother was an unusual man: Who else could have tolerated that kind of triangle? One Lincoln's Birthday, Ben and Lily disappeared, and when they came back they announced they had been married.

After graduating from law school in 1926 and taking the bar examination, I had to complete a year of full-time legal clerkship before I could be admitted to the bar, so I continued clerking for Ben and living with him and his bride. Finally, in June 1927, I was admitted to the bar. I was a lawyer at last, and only five years behind my brother. The financial difficulties that Ben had faced as a youngster had delayed his education, and his aid to me had speeded mine up, so that professionally the age difference between us had been cut in half. But, at twenty-three, I still walked in my brother's shadow; I was not yet my own man.

THREE

Letters from Europe: Laying the Foundations

Only once in my life have I taken a three-month vacation: From July to October 1927 I toured Europe; the trip was a gift from Ben in celebration of my admission to the bar. I traveled alone, and nearly every other day I wrote to Ben or Lily. There are about fifty letters and Ben saved all of them, envelopes included.

I read these letters now with a mixture of emotions: astonishment that I have forgotten places and problems that were once so critically important to me; awe at the sensitivity of the perceptions of this twenty-three-year-old who bore my name; embarrassment at his errors, his naiveté, his easy youthful certainties; envy of his freedom; sympathy for his anguish and indecision — mixed with a little wonder at the seriousness of it all — and a sweet nostalgia for his romanticism.

The letters refer often to unexplained crises and conflicts. Ben knew the background, whatever it was, so there was apparently no need to spell it out; I am unable to shed much light on these matters fifty years later. Underlying all of them, I know, was the search for my own identity and independence. I had completed my legal education and been admitted to the bar — as Ben had wished. I was planning to join his firm — as he had wished. I was touring Europe — on his generosity. Yet I was now a lawyer in my own right, and I wondered whether I was merely a creature of Ben's and whether the role he had written for me really matched my own wishes. As the letters show, I was even then considering other career choices: writing, for example. Ben was unhappy at this incipient rebellion (although he always insisted that I make up my own mind), and to please him I took every opportunity to reiterate what was true, my love and devotion to him.

My grand tour lasted longer than any previous absence from New York. It thus gave me a chance to think things over and come to some

decisions on my own, away from Ben's direct influence. The introduction to Europe that the trip provided was the most broadening
experience of my life up until then. I was not only an indefatigable
tourist tasting the joys of the art, culture, and monuments of the Old
World — which I felt keenly was the world from which I came — but
I was fascinated also by the politics, history, economics, and national
characteristics of the Europeans, and as a good student of Buckle I
sought constantly to relate these phenomena to one another. (If some
of my generalizations sound too pat, I plead only that I was twenty-
three and on my first trip abroad.) Visiting a foreign country or city
naturally makes it more real and less foreign; my tour of Europe in
1927 made me an internationalist and kindled my lifelong interest in
foreign affairs.

I sailed on July 23, 1927, on the Cunard liner *Carmania,* and I
started writing letters the first day out. Characteristically, I had brought
several books with me.

> I have been reading Papini's *Life of Christ....* The real Christ
> does shine through despite Papini's apparent attempts to deify
> him.... Jesus, according to Papini, recommended absolute pov-
> erty and an avoidance of wealth. The "glorification in poverty"
> today would make us slothful, narrow and weak. It is the urge
> for acquisition that has made for many scientific conquests. Strug-
> gle has sharpened and strengthened our faculties.... We have
> found that most men are too weak to be spiritually free when
> they are economically chained, and that the material comforts add
> great joys to life and give more time and more space for spiritual
> expression.... But to minimize the necessity for material things,
> and the joy they give, to encourage in this age poverty and sub-
> mission, not only seeks to deprive us of great joys but dries up
> the very wells of energy and the inspiration, bred of struggle,
> which created a Christ.

In thus almost sanctifying materialism, I was reflecting the optimistic spirit of the boom years and echoing Ben's emerging theories
of radical capitalism. We were both putting socialism behind us.

As the next letter shows, I was also afflicted with a severe case of
Weltschmerz:

> My being is dissolving into vagrant urgings, soarings of the soul
> annexed to no particular thing, leading nowhere, concerning no
> one, nebulous, incomprehensible, joyous with a choking pain.
> Something may yet come of this poor clay. This is, too, a sense of
> utter present futility. Not the futility of despair, but the futility
> of being lost....

Possibly tomorrow I shall write a letter for Lily about a little girl of Spanish-English parentage whose eyes are filled with the guile and experience of ages of woman, who has suffered much and is bitterly in love with life.

Apparently that girl was not so little. A day later I wrote Ben to "tell Lily that the Spanish girl fizzled — she is quite all right — but my taste is rather vagrant."

From the Imperial Hotel on London's Russell Square I described the "harmonious" English countryside, which looked to me "as if one eye had envisaged the whole of it and then spent centuries of patient application molding and shaping." I was intrigued with the ceremonial attitudes of even the railway porters, and by the old-fashioned oakwood railway cars. And then I wrote of London, "the first of the magic cities":

> I have seen a good deal for one day. Westminster Abbey for morning prayer, the government buildings, Horse Guards, National Gallery, Parliament, St. James's and Hyde Parks, the palaces, and an English girl, *tout fini.* . . . The interesting thing here is . . . the people. They are almost all alike. Few without interesting faces, all pragmatic, all rather selfish, all involved with how difficult it is to live. A people unconcerned with higher values or with common weal, a vast mass physically. It is good soil for politicians and artists. . . . I saw men who I am sure belong to the political class, I am certain it is almost a hierarchy here, men whom centuries of inbreeding have taught that honesty and public service are the best policy for staying in office longest, gaining most . . . and keeping the mass dull — and safe. We will do things first long before these people awake.
>
> I, my loves, as you can see, am keenly awake and more observant than I ever knew I could be. . . . If Lily inquires about the English girl, she was gravely a pathological subject, lower middle class, pretty and unexciting.

I seem to have made a point of telling Lily about every woman I met on the trip, to assure her that I was not getting romantically involved.

On August 8 I flew from London to Paris, quite an adventure in those days. Paris, I wrote,

> is broad and sweeping and people who pass are dynamic and alive. The far famed dames du Paris look like very hardened sinners, and not very attractive. I shall love Paris, though sans dames. . . .
>
> The people here are very puzzling. They are joyous, apparently carefree, lovers of beauty, strongly nationalistic, avid of

fame, reputation and glory. They love liberty but liberty militant. None of your lovely Anglo-Saxon utopias.

At the Fontainebleau Palace the Sèvres pottery, the carvings, the gold, the tapestries and paintings overwhelmed me and prompted some musings on the fate of kings:

These French monarchs spared themselves nothing. . . . Each of these kings decorated a room of his own . . . and each tried to outdo the other. . . . I can see why the French kings fell so suddenly. They spent too much money, and they were individualists. In England the king built almost self-effacingly, he built for kingship, for the nation. . . . But in France each king built for his own glory, he put his initial on everything that someone else's initials were not already on. Napoleon . . . put his on the same thing three times. That struck me as a very important social factor and as a mirror of France. . . .

While I was in Paris the Sacco-Vanzetti case was approaching its climax in Boston. The last legal appeals for the two men had failed, they were about to be executed, and a great wave of agitation and protest swept Europe. Frenchmen blamed me and every American for what they regarded as a horrible miscarriage of justice. I had my own doubts about the guilt of Sacco and Vanzetti, but I was even more concerned by the wholesale condemnation of the United States that I heard all about me. So, as a conscientious and patriotic new lawyer, I took it upon myself to educate France about the American legal system. On August 10 I sent a long letter to the editor of the Paris edition of the *New York Herald*.

My letter anticipates a legal and legislative strategy that later was to characterize an aspect of my public life. I took no position on the guilt or innocence of Sacco and Vanzetti and I said that having no knowledge of the facts of the case I wished to emphasize the legal issues and how they were dealt with in the United States. I was attempting to blunt the anti-Americanism that the case had stimulated. I was trying to salvage something from an awkward situation.

I pointed out that Frenchmen seemed to be charging the entire American people with "judicial murder." I explained that under the U.S. federal system jurisdiction in the case rested entirely in Massachusetts, "a state which contains less than 5 percent of the total population of the United States, which is the most conservative of the forty-eight states and whose constitution and laws still seriously restrict the franchise." Respect for the administration of the law is "the surest bulwark of democracy," I said, and added that Americans expect their officials to "stand by the law, despite ... public clamor." And I went on:

> The world must understand that we cannot discard a philosophy of government which is firmly rooted in every American mind. To override the administration of the law means to most Americans opening the door to tyranny and injustice. If Sacco and Vanzetti are innocent, the American people will inflict political oblivion and public obloquy on those who have been consciously unjust. But to accuse the American people ... would only harden their hearts, and erect a barrier in their minds.
>
> If this case can teach men to correct each other kindly, to live like men and not to hate like beasts, then Sacco and Vanzetti, guilty or not, can become great public benefactors.... If they had lived for a hundred years, agitating in their own small way, they could not have worked so great a good. I believe that they are brave enough to be glad to die, if they must, in such a cause.

An awkward view of what so many then condemned as "judicial murder," but that was youth and inexperience talking. A few days later I was writing to Ben on quite a different subject:

> My last days in Paris were spent in walking on the streets and mixing with the people.... I did not look at the women too closely before, but I have now. It is they who are the great thing of France. They have a fiery eye and keen quick insight that I have not seen in any man here.... I walked on the boulevards and, struck with a sudden inspiration, stopped to talk with one of those ladies whose office it is. She spoke only French but I understood her and I am quite sure she understood me. She was accustomed to uplifters but she gasped when I told her that I respected her more than a great many of her disdainful suitors because of her honesty. The one thing that moved me was only a short sentence, "Oui, c'est triste, Paris." For the rest her philosophy consisted of inviting me to "couchez avec moi." She was amazed at my kind behavior and departure "seulement," although it was a very philosophical amazement. As my taxi drove by her I noted that she was looking up at the moon, a glorious full one, with her chin in her hand, wondering. I had asked her how she could make believe on a night of such great beauty.

Pre-Hitler Germany awed and disturbed me. I wrote from Berlin:

> Germany is tremendously busy, everything is being either built or repaired, the railroads, the buildings, the houses, farms, everywhere activity.... Those wiry bespectacled, studiously purposeful engineers abound. Everywhere along the countryside are factories,

going full blast. The trains are filled with businessmen. Everyone seems intent on going somewhere or doing something, everyone has a purpose, and peculiarly enough I cannot say why the purpose appears to be the same. Business with us is a form of play. Here it is a study and a science. This land clicks. . . .

There is a fixed purpose in every glance, and the appearance of a terrific universal will. This people is strictly pragmatic. There is far more sexual neuroticism here than in Paris. There they played at it, but here they live it. . . . I have a continual feeling that they are still the old Goths and Visigoths, the martial terror of civilization in Roman days. Only this people could honestly believe in might. They have a vast brain, a deep soul, but little heart.

On the train from Berlin to Munich I was intrigued by the peasant villages I saw through my window, the barefoot women in the fields, the farmyards filled with cackling geese. "Exactly the sort of place we always imagined Dad hailed from," I wrote Ben.

Vienna had undergone a period of violent riots shortly before my arrival there. It is, I wrote,

a beaten city, the people laugh, but mechanically to sustain a reputation. There is no spark in any of them. . . . They have no guts, no stomach for the fight. . . . These people are too timid for rebellion, they must have been crazed with hunger or fear when they rose up.

From Lucerne, Switzerland:

Returning to myself again I found that I . . . had no power to create within me. I felt deeply but I could not articulate, emotion died in my throat. . . . I diagnosed it as fear, of what kind I find it hard to tell, but it is probably the greatest fear of all, the fear of being afraid. It is that which raises such a tempest within me that every fair bark which ventures forth from some little beauty within me is immediately torn and sunk. I must learn to walk like a little child or like a convalescing paralytic.

I perceive so much that is beautiful or ugly or instructive that I wish in turn to be an artist or a sculptor or a musician so that I may give men my conception.

At Interlaken I received "one great gulp" of mail from home. The letters indicated Lily was depressed about something, perhaps an illness, so I wrote directly to her to cheer her up. Actually, in urging her to feel free I was talking to myself; she, like me, was in danger of being completely absorbed by her husband.

Dear Little One [I wrote]. I do not believe that you quite see the import of Ben's counsel yet. To breathe, to exercise, to play, to work, are not any of them the exact point. They are not manifestations of the inner light, which is nurtured by freedom and beauty. . . .

Please, therefore, sweet girl, do not breathe because Ben asks you to, do not write because he asks you to, or read or work, but only because you are being free, because you are living more and giving more, because it is a great joy to feel the life stream flow in open sunlight unhampered, basking in its beauty, playing in its strength. Unflagging devotion to your ideal of perfect womanhood . . . will lift you over your barrier, yourself, and then your greater barrier . . . which when mounted will let you kiss high heaven.

Was that "greater barrier" the towering personality of Ben?

All through my trip I had felt the special pull of Italy. I finally reached Venice on September 5.

Italy — at last! And so beautiful. But let me not forget a few things. . . . They are animated and ambitious these Italians, they have been awakened to their own might. . . . The whole country is an armed camp, black shirts as militia, and soldiers in training. The esprit de corps is apparently high, the officers freely fraternize with the civilians. . . . This is a people which is preparing for its new day, but it will be a race of benevolent despots or conquerors because it is too romantic to be consistently oppressive. . . .

It is apparent that only the intelligentsia, the theorists, currently oppose Mussolini. To the other Italians he is a mastermind, Italy's savior, and as honest as Christ. As long as he remains that in their imagination they will protect him against the world. This people is the same exactly as those Romans who tore Caesar's murderers to shreds. . . .

Ben's letters had chided me for not meeting some lawyers he wanted me to see and for not writing often enough. From Florence I wrote, "I thought I had been doing quite well, writing a complete letter every two days." Ben's reproaches must have hurt me, for later that night I wrote:

I am terribly ill at ease tonight. My soul cries out for something more than it can find within itself. It's probably the search for perfection turned without when it cannot find a man within. The pain and the struggle now so keen would be a divine expression if I could rest upon a loving arm and feel a reigning peace within.

And the next day was only a little better:

> I have been continually assailed with doubts, doubts as to my
> own capacity, doubts as to my spirit, doubts as to my honesty. . . .
> I have had moments of terrible fear, of deep grief, of transcen-
> dental joy. But the moments of question have predominated. . . .
> Perhaps I shall never express a thing of beauty. But God, how I
> have felt it, how it has pounded within me.

Seeking to get back into Ben's good graces, I found an opportunity to express my loyalty to his emerging new theories of radical
capitalism. I had attended a dinner party, I wrote, and had "talked
myself out" on politics, economics, and international relations.

> The text was the usual one, better organization, larger units,
> prosperity through spending, a higher standard of living. . . . The
> ideas you know because they are quite your own. I am becoming
> a staunch upholder of the virtues and the possibilities of Amer-
> ican intellect. . . . I have not yet determined exactly what I wish
> to do. I know that I wish to write, and I know that I wish to
> extoll and inculcate those virtues which man must have or acquire
> before he will do justice to your magnificent plans of organization.

The crisis passed. Still from Florence, on September 15:

> These people do not realize how closely activity, strife, and public
> unrest are bound up with the great artistic expression, which they
> apparently revere. They are totally surrounded with thrilling
> triumphs of mind and imagination, yet they are very common-
> place and manifest little or none of this great well of beauty in
> their lives. . . . They are nationally worshippers of Mussolini, so
> happy are they to have found someone who will save them the
> trouble of . . . doing for themselves.

And then Rome. I knew history and I was overwhelmed by the
place where so much of it had been made.

> The great Colosseum with its yearning arches and powerful bal-
> conies like a broken old man whose muscles still stand out clear
> and hard, drawn and plundered to mold palaces for robbers and
> cardinals. . . . The Forum is tremendously impressive. It is only
> a vast rubble heap but people it with . . . Caesar . . . Anthony . . .
> Constantine . . . hear the clash of arms and blare of trumpets and
> shrieks of the delirious populace. . . .
> All of man's ambitions, urgings, desires . . . lie buried in these
> stones. Great ecstasy, great faith, great treachery, great public
> spirit, great love, all here, inspiring every stone. . . . "That too
> shall pass away" is apparent in every bit of earth, yet I feel that

it did not, that something remained, that I have something of what did remain. Call it vast sum total of human spirit, call it soul or God or conscience, I have it, I feel these men and I knew them.

In Michelangelo's figure of Moses I found a special significance, and it became there and then an irreplaceable part of my life. I have never gone to Rome since without a pilgrimage to San Pietro in Vincoli, where the Moses stands.

Moses is the essence of law. He is social justice, ethical right, he is supremely sure, more than confident. Obey but the law, deviate not. Moses does not threaten, he is eternal, he knows that the law ... eventually will be obeyed.... The figure is marble but the eyes blaze, the muscles are tense. Moses rises even as he sits, he is force, he is assurance, he knows.

And I could not ignore the modern Rome:

Fascism is so typically a Latin manifestation that I am finding it hard to comprehend. The day I arrived here a great parade moved by me on the Caso. The enthusiasm of these men, young and old, their cheers, their songs, bespoke a new faith. The set of their jaw was determined, the look in their eye fanatical. These are neither reasoning men nor thinkers. They are worshippers of heroes and phrases.

I spoke with a Fascist editor last night. He was full of the new simplicity of Italy. The going back to the land. The return to a naturalism reminiscent of Rousseau. He told me that Fascism meant placing the accent and the national unity on family, not on economic classes.... You see how utterly ingenious these men are, how utterly unaware of the new world. The same shining spirit is author of the pronounced opinion, shared I fear by most Italians, that women should be neither accomplished intellectually nor free.

That letter ended with the remark that I would return about October 8. Ben and Lily were anxious for me to hurry back; I was expressing a little newfound independence by taking my time. There was still much to explore, as this letter indicates:

I went through some intense mental anguish today but I am all right now.... Curiosity so got the better of me yesterday that I applied for a permit to attend the Pope's morning levee today. I was informed that I should have to comply with the "regulations" in kneeling and kissing the ring. In due time the invitation from "Santita" and with it many thundering blows of conscience. Was I to lend my tithe to this gross superstition? Was I to prostitute the honor of this man, the Pope, and my own, by performing an act of debasement which I loathed? I did not need to see this display of stupidity to learn the depths of ignorance and blind credulity to which the Church submits its poor communicants. I had seen enough of that already. I was heartily ashamed of myself and I did not go near the Pope or his Vatican. I went instead to the Terme (Baths) of Diocletian and the National Museum housed there.

Years later I came to terms with this problem and met Pope Pius XII on several occasions, with respect and affection — and with never a need to kneel or kiss his ring.

A new batch of letters awaited me in Naples. Ben had forgiven me or had acknowledged some measure of my independence, and I was overjoyed as I wrote him:

> Ben, I think for the first time we met as equals, and the divine thrill will always remain to me a symbol of the reward which awaits me if I achieve, and a revelation of your greatness and love.

During the next week I became the hungry tourist again, fascinated by the ancient customs revealed in the ruins of Pompeii and delighted to watch the "peasant girls in bare feet ... fresh, bursting with life and beautifully trim of figure." Awed by the natural splendors of the Italian coast at Sorrento and Amalfi, I wrote that "Ulysses needed no siren to draw him to this shore so that he must tie himself to the mast to resist the call. The beauty of the shore itself is enough."

As the journey neared its end my moods fluctuated wildly. From Paris, I wrote:

> I received all the mail you have sent in the last month. The joy and thrill of power which swept me then will be ever memorable. . . . Life has expanded. I have torn from me the mask of stodgy conservatism, of narrow vision, of fixed idea. I can live. The air I breathe is charged with new energy, the earth I walk on filled with life and divinity, the sky is high and wondrous blue, my soul ventures forth to meet yours unafraid. I was dead and I live, I was weak and I am strong, I was hungry and I am fed. My life may be empty from now on, it may be unfruitful, but I face it fearlessly, for God, how I soar today. I am free, love pervades my being, power thrills in every fibre of me, and I transcend myself.

On board the S.S. *Belgenland,* en route home, I continued to write: not letters to Ben but attempts to sum up for myself my emotional wanderings and my philosophic progress. These notes are full

of warmth and love for mankind, the conviction that "joy is a sufficient answer to all existence," and a determination "to find my joy
beyond myself in giving infinitely of myself, the surging freedom of
remaining self." I was still trying to resolve my personal conflict.

I was also assembling the elements of what was to become a code
of conduct, a foundation, for my public life, but even in these para-
graphs, perhaps without realizing it, I was struggling with the brother
I loved:

> The rule of the world has since time immemorial rested in the
> hands of an intelligent and capable minority. Its ancient psychol-
> ogy was self-serving, . . . an exploitation of the great and ignorant
> mass for the benefit and aggrandizement of the rulers. It had to
> be kept together and in fear to prevent utter chaos, and those who
> kept it together made it pay. All men are not fit to be rulers.
> All men have not the intellectual capacity, the force of will, or
> the desire, to accept responsibility or to rule. . . .
>
> I am concerned here . . . with the man who quite honestly feels
> a capacity for thought, for direction, or for administration, which
> raises him above the mean level. . . . What shall that man do with
> his life? Shall he spend it in acquisition, in observing the world,
> in commenting upon it, in smiling at it and in assuring his per-
> sonal happiness as best he may, or shall he go further afield to
> seek real joy?
>
> I wonder how many of the men to whom I am speaking realize
> how inextricably their own happiness is tied up with that of the
> world and every living being in it. I wonder whether they believe
> that it is possible, by building a wall of money or power or
> household affection, to shut out the pain, the anguish, and the
> universal suffering. I wonder if they believe it possible to be wise,
> when the world is ignorant, to be beautiful when the world is
> ugly, to love when the world hates. I wonder whether they do
> not find ugliness and misery creeping in at every crevice, over-
> shadowing every smile, soiling every emotion, discoloring every
> art. I wonder whether like the ancient kings they do not ride in
> a coach of gold through streets of mire, with the suffering and
> the sick to stare at, and a fearful stench to smell.
>
> I conceive of the new man of intellect as a worker determined
> to light the world . . . as a man whose credo is to learn to teach.
> To roll up his sleeves and to give to the people he is bound to
> live with some of the intellect, the spirit, and the beauty which
> animates him.

Having thus described the dedicated life I wanted to live, I turned
to what I considered to be the most pressing social issue of the time:

The conception of ... a war to the death between capital and labor stands as the sacred shibboleth of the professional radical and as his most reprehensible crime. ... He justifies his theory of violence and war with the thought that the greatest good must be done to the greatest number and that great good is built upon pain and blood which precedes it. He does not realize that the capitalists' atrocities against labor which occur from time to time are themselves that very blood upon which the new order shall be built. He does not realize that that rancor and hatred and fear which industrial strife and the class struggle kindles within him will serve only to perpetuate murder, rapacity, and hate. ... He does not realize that the capitalist lives in a world whose basic idea is plunder and that he must conform or die. He does not know that the capitalist possibly suffers as much or more than his meanest laborer, for lack of love in a cruel, practical world.

Capitalist and laborer are both men; let them but meet as men and they will soon realize how closely akin they are. Cutting each other's throats will bleed them both to death, ... it will bleed society in the process. What they need is love and science. They both want happiness and security, ... they lack only a system of economic organization which will give it to them. The system lies neither in the end of the hired gunman's blackjack nor in the clenched fist of the laborer. It lies in the laboratory and in the senate house, it lies with the economist and with the thinker. ... Research and experiment must replace collective bargaining and walkouts. Love and tolerance must replace hatred and fear. Class unconsciousness and not class consciousness is the hope of the world, organization and not murder its method.

When I returned home I was at once admitted to partnership with my brother in the law firm of Javits & Javits. For the next few years I honed the skills I would need if I were going to realize any of the ideals I had expressed on my trip. I gained experience researching law, writing briefs and pleadings, and trying cases, gradually becoming comfortable in the highly contested proceedings in which I engaged. Most of my cases in the first few years were minor matters of interest only to the litigants: I defended a client charged with indecent exposure in a park and another who contested a bankruptcy action filed against him by his creditors. (In that one I was defeated by the cleverest practitioner in bankruptcy at the New York bar, a man named Archibald Palmer, and learned a great deal about trial practice in the process.) I argued many cases of accidents, small claims, and technical legal procedure.

More dramatic and significant legal work lay ahead.

FOUR

Trial Lawyer

On March 12, 1932, Ivar Kreuger, the Swedish financial genius who controlled three-quarters of the world's match market, lay down on his bed in his Paris apartment and shot himself through the heart. The world mourned the financial tycoon as a victim of the Great Depression, but a few weeks later Kreuger was revealed to be not victim but victimizer, the biggest swindler of all time. He had forged bonds, stolen securities from his own companies, set up dummy banks and corporations in a number of countries, paid dividends out of capital, and lied brazenly to brokers, bankers, and government officials — all in order to increase the apparent value of his financial empire so that he could persuade more and more investors to buy his securities or lend him money. Kreuger's interlocking network stood exposed as a nearly hollow shell, most of its "assets" vanished, and as it came tumbling down thousands of investors discovered they had been fleeced.

For the eager young firm of Javits & Javits, established in offices at 165 Broadway, in Manhattan's financial district, the Kreuger scandal offered a perfect opportunity to demonstrate that it was ready for big things. Our instincts led us unequivocally to the side of the investors who had trustingly put their money into the Kreuger enterprises, and thus we immediately found ourselves in opposition to some of the big, established "white-shoe" law firms representing the banks and brokerage houses that had promoted and sold Kreuger's securities without adequately checking up on his assertions or monitoring his operations.

That was the pattern of our practice all through the depression. In the aftermath of the 1929 stock market crash there were many stockholder suits against corporate officers, banks, and brokerage houses that had acted dishonestly, as Kreuger had done, or merely incompetently and irresponsibly — in either case leaving investors out on a limb. Most of the time we turned up on the side of the stockholders against these established interests. We were not part of the clubby brotherhood of Wall Street lawyers who were retained to safeguard the reputations of brokers, bankers, and big financial institutions. Ben and I had no such responsibilities. We were outsiders, and our ghetto upbringing left us with a sense of duty about recovering damages for the misdeeds and errors of the establishment. The big firms called us "strike-suit lawyers" — a derogatory term that carried the connotation of ambulance chasers — but to the people who had been cheated, and for the times, which called for reform, we and others like us were a boon.

Ben's inclinations and activities in this direction had already earned him the enmity of some of the "distinguished" law firms, even before I joined him as a partner. When I applied for membership to the Bar Association of New York, I was blackballed by one of these establishment lawyers, on the ground that no partner of Ben Javits deserved to be a member of the association. Ben himself had not applied for membership and the legal fraternity was taking their resentment at him out on me. Whatever specific allegations may have been made against Ben at that time, I am convinced that establishment firms merely resented the fact that Ben was fighting their interests. I thought the association was unfair to deny my application, because no allegations had been made against me. (I have often been asked whether anti-Semitism was involved in their decision. I do not know. I am willing to fight my battles on their merits without introducing that note into them.) I withdrew my application and did not apply again for almost twenty years. Not until I had been elected to Congress was I invited to join the association, and I did so.

Through our efforts, and the efforts of other firms like ours, investors were able to recover some of their funds, and some individuals and corporations that had violated their fiduciary responsibilities were brought to book. Furthermore, the revelation of abuses had a great deal to do with the subsequent cleaning up of the securities business. We practiced a daring, aggressive — almost swashbuckling — kind of law; it was the *pro bono publico* law of its day and I am gratified by my part in it.

Hundreds of lawyers and accountants on both sides of the Atlantic spent years trying to unravel the tangled affairs of Ivar Kreuger, and Javits & Javits played a crucial part in this endeavor. The U.S. litigation began when Kreuger's U.S. firm, the International Match Corporation, was declared bankrupt; Kreuger, it turned out, had systematically looted it, taking the securities it held and using them for his own speculations. Soon after that case got started, Ben was retained to represent a committee of U.S. investors who held more than $80 million worth of stocks and debentures in Kreuger and Toll, the financier's Sweden-based parent firm. We soon learned that Kreuger had stripped that firm of most of its assets as well; and many of its subsidiaries, which were supposed to be operating match factories in dozens of countries, existed only on paper. We filed a petition in federal court to have Kreuger and Toll declared bankrupt in the United States and set about searching for assets that could be used to reimburse our clients and many others.

There were several fascinating and unusual aspects to this case. One of them was that with Kreuger's death nearly all trace of his U.S. activities had been wiped out. Kreuger had once attributed his success to a policy of "silence, silence, and more silence," and even his most intimate friends and associates knew little about what he was doing. To a shocking extent this was also true of his U.S. under-writers, the dignified Boston investment banking firm of Lee, Higginson and Company. The partners in that firm had been so impressed with Kreuger's reputation and so mesmerized by his glib assurances that all was well — even in the weeks before his suicide when his position was beginning to crumble — that they had failed to audit his books and were completely unaware that much of his edifice was a façade. Nevertheless, they had promoted and sold hundreds of millions of dollars worth of his securities and had bought $9 million worth themselves.

Because Kreuger had kept his manipulations so secret, it required a great deal of legal sleuthing to find whatever solid assets of Kreuger and Toll existed in the United States. I plunged into this search and soon discovered that $3 million of Kreuger and Toll funds deposited in the Chase National Bank had been transferred to several brokerage houses a little more than a year before the financier's death. That suggested that the funds had been used for stock market speculations, which ultimately turned out to be the case. Our investigation also indicated that $33 million in German bonds belonging to Kreuger and Toll had been appropriated by Kreuger for his own use, as had been done with similar securities belonging to International Match.

By July 1932, the case was becoming extremely complicated and controversial because of the suits against the two bankrupt companies, the disputes between different groups of creditors, and the mysterious relationships among Kreuger's three hundred or so companies. Ben and I realized that the case would attract major counsel, and we decided that we also needed an experienced and well-known lawyer to represent us in court. I was only twenty-eight, and although I had done the investigative work and had prepared and filed the bankruptcy petition, I was not ready to take a case of this magnitude before a judge or a bankruptcy referee. So Ben sent me to Samuel Untermeyer, one of the most brilliant and famed courtroom lawyers of his day, who was then in his seventies and semiretired.

At Untermeyer's upper Fifth Avenue apartment I found the old lion of the courts ill in bed, looking aged and tired. But he heard me out and questioned me in detail. The case had already become the biggest legal issue of the time and the prospect of getting into it seemed to revive Untermeyer. He agreed to act as counsel for us. When he appeared in court a week later it was hard to believe he was the same man. His eyes sparkled, his mustache bristled, and he wore a flower in his lapel; he looked refreshed and debonair and ready for a battle. The case had rejuvenated him and brought him back from death's door to his accustomed role as a keen lawyer.

All through that summer I sat at Untermeyer's side in the Federal Courthouse, preparing his material, assisting him — and learning a great deal about courtroom technique. He showed me that to become an authoritative presence in the courtroom a lawyer must always give the impression that he knows exactly what he is doing. He taught me the value of infinite patience in examination and cross-examination — to keep at it until you get what you want or are completely satisfied that it does not exist in the memory or conscience of the witness. In that he was a master: He could coo like a dove or roar like a lion, as the situation demanded. Untermeyer's technique of dealing with the judge, in this case the bankruptcy referee, was also refreshing. He was courtly, entirely civil, absolutely polite — but he stood his ground as a lawyer having full equality with the judge, making clear that he would not hesitate to make appeals or take other actions if he thought injustice was being done.

The most important lesson I learned from Samuel Untermeyer, however, was never to ask a witness a question to which you, the lawyer, do not know the answer. That way you leave little room for surprise, or for having your point twisted and used against your cause. This method requires detailed preparation and a very thorough knowledge of the facts — which is the first element of courtroom technique in the trial of any case.

It was fortunate that we did have Untermeyer at the counsel table. Our main opposition came from another committee of Kreuger and Toll stockholders. This committee had been organized by Lee, Higginson and other banking houses that had sponsored Kreuger's stock issues; it was represented by the very proper, prestigious, and conservative law firm of Sullivan and Cromwell, and the partner in charge of the case for them was John Foster Dulles.

This was the first of the many contacts — and confrontations — that I was to have with Dulles as a lawyer. Much later, when he was secretary of state, we clashed often over the question of Israel. We always respected each other as colleagues at the New York bar, but we fought like tigers over the issues. At the time of that first meeting he was forty-four, and already a prestigious international lawyer. I viewed him and his firm as the epitome of the Ivy League–Wall Street legal fraternity defending the prestige and the fortunes of the entrenched bankers and brokers whose activities had fueled the boom and helped to bring on the bust. Although Dulles and I were both Republican lawyers practicing downtown, we found ourselves on opposite sides of the fence — professionally, socially, and instinctively. I am sure he regarded Javits & Javits as upstart troublemakers.

For two months Dulles and his committee stubbornly opposed our attempt to have Kreuger and Toll declared bankrupt in the United States. Their motive, they told the court, was that since most of the assets of the company were in Sweden and most of the creditors were in the United States, the U.S. creditors should not unduly antagonize the Swedes, and a declaration of bankruptcy would do just that. We were certain, however, that the Dulles group was blocking our petition because it wanted to save the reputations of the bankers and brokers who had underwritten Kreuger. As the *New York Times* reported cautiously, our committee believed that Dulles's group "was more interested in banking considerations than in recovery for the investors." (During that summer I was playing tennis every morning with the *Times* reporter covering the case, so the press stories were kept very current.)

The Dulles group's argument fell apart when the Swedish liquidators of the Kreuger syndicate consented to the bankruptcy proceeding — they could hardly do otherwise, it seemed to us — and urged the two American committees to get together. Dulles was compelled to withdraw his objections and Federal Judge Julian Mack pronounced Kreuger and Toll bankrupt, as Untermeyer and I had been urging. I drew up the order and Judge Mack signed it on August 5, 1932.

We then had to find the Kreuger and Toll assets in the United States or at least find someone who knew something about Kreuger's U.S. operations. Eventually I ran down a Norwegian named Anders Jordahl, who had been a friend of Kreuger's for thirty years and was one of his confidential Wall Street agents. Jordahl held a power of attorney on several of the financier's brokerage house accounts, and Kreuger's New York apartment was rented under Jordahl's name. In his final months, in a desperate attempt to shore up his threatened empire, Kreuger had speculated heavily with the funds he took from his companies or got fraudulently from investors, and Jordahl had handled some of these transactions. We suspected this at the time, but were not sure, and in any case Jordahl was not anxious to be found.

I located Jordahl in Carmel, New York, and on August 23, with a retinue of process servers, I hurried up there. We found his house at the end of a long country road, and I watched while he was served with a subpoena to appear before the bankruptcy court and testify on the disposition of Kreuger's assets.

When Jordahl failed to appear before the bankruptcy referee at the appointed time I moved that he be held in contempt of court and told the referee that Jordahl "has to account for millions of dollars of transactions with the bankrupt directly and through various brokerage accounts. . . . We have a check dated August 29, 1930, for $1,100,833 paid to Jordahl's account from the account of Kreuger and Toll. . . . It is unexplained. There is also a check made out to Mr. Jordahl from Kreuger's personal account at Chase National. . . ."

Jordahl finally did appear but he was not very helpful: Like all the others with whom Kreuger had dealt he knew only of Kreuger's dealings with him and not much of his boss's other activities — or at least that's what he said.

Early in 1933, the two creditor committees, ours and Dulles's, agreed to cooperate to settle the case. Interestingly, however, the two committees did not merge, because the underlying difference of opinion between them remained. Our committee wanted to force Kreuger's underwriters to return the purchase money and take back the securities, leaving to them the task of recovering the funds from Kreuger and Toll. The committee represented by Dulles, in order to protect the banks and investment houses, argued for the usual routine of assembling the bankrupt's assets and dividing them among the creditors. Javits & Javits was no longer involved in the case when the final settlements were made, years later.

* * *

The year 1932 was significant for me politically as well as professionally, for it was then that I formally enrolled in the Republican Party. After leaving Brooklyn in 1919, I had gradually abandoned the socialist ideology — though not the idealism that sparked it. I came to realize, first, that socialism would never be accepted by the individualistic American people, at least in my lifetime, and, second, that stock corporations could apportion among the people the ownership of the means of production just as well as socialism could; therefore I felt we had to look to the established political and constitutional processes to solve the pressing problems of poverty and injustice around us. About this time also I first recognized that the preservation of freedom required the average individual to work in the private sector rather than for the government, so that his political and economic roles would be distinct. I became more convinced of this with every passing year.

In 1928, the first presidential election in which I could vote, I had cast my ballot for Herbert Hoover and his "progressive individualism"; that seemed to me far better than the Democrats, who were dominated, I felt, by political leaders from a still racist South and by corrupt machines, like Tammany Hall, in New York and other big cities. My views on the Democrats were derived from the memory of my father's experience as a small-time Tammany henchman and also from attending the famous 1924 Democratic Convention in New York's Madison Square Garden. That convention deadlocked for 102 ballots before nominating John W. Davis to oppose Calvin Coolidge, and one reason for the deadlock was the Southern Democrats' prejudice against New York Governor Al Smith, a Catholic.

Until 1932 I was too busy with my law practice to devote much time to politics. But while I was working on the Kreuger case, in the spring and summer of 1932, another scandal was rocking New York. Judge Samuel Seabury's investigation of corruption in New York City had unearthed an appalling saga of kickbacks, bribery, the buying of judgeships, and outright fraud — all for the pecuniary benefit of the political bosses of Tammany Hall. That spring the trail of graft led straight to City Hall, and in June, Judge Seabury sent to Governor Franklin D. Roosevelt a list of fifteen serious charges against New York City's flamboyant, wisecracking mayor, Jimmy Walker. Roosevelt, who was then seeking the Democratic presidential nomination, dared not offend Tammany at that point, so he sat on the charges for two weeks. Not until he had the nomination wrapped up did the governor call in Walker, listen to the mayor's lame explanations, and demand he resign, which he did.

The fact of Tammany corruption was nothing new to any New Yorker with eyes and ears, although the magnitude of the graft and the gall of its perpetrators was shocking indeed. What disturbed me was that even so distinguished an American as Franklin D. Roosevelt — the standard-bearer of the Democratic Party — in order to retain the support of the corrupt machine had to delay the investigation that led to its downfall. Such dealing finally condemned the Democratic Party in New York, as far as I was concerned. It was time to do more than just vote. I formally identified myself as a Republican and joined the Ivy Republican Club on Manhattan's Upper East Side, where I was then living.

From a national standpoint, the year of Roosevelt's first presidential triumph and the beginning of two decades of Democratic rule in Washington may seem to have been an inauspicious moment to join the Republicans. But it was by no means clear to me that Roosevelt knew how to get us out of the depression, and local issues of political integrity seemed paramount. The Republicans seemed to me to hold the only hope for an end to Tammany corruption in New York City, particularly because of the emergence of Fiorello La Guardia, the progressive Republican congressman who was then on his way to becoming mayor of New York.

Fiorello La Guardia inspired me as no other contemporary politician had done. He was more than a reformer. Not only did he insist on clean government and sound administration, as had many "do-gooder" reformers before him, but he also saw the need for city government to deliver to the poor essential social services such as housing, transportation, and medical care; he was a prolabor man, with a passion for social justice that I shared. La Guardia knew he would have to do much more for the people than previous reformers had attempted, or else Tammany, which had always posed as a friend of the hapless poor, would bounce right back.

In 1933 La Guardia was elected to the first of his three terms as mayor of New York City; as a member of the Ivy Republican Club I worked energetically in his campaign and subsequently, in his 1937 and 1941 campaigns, I met many of the future Republican leaders of New York. But most of my time was still devoted to Javits & Javits.

The experience I had gained in the Kreuger and Toll case and the courtroom lessons I learned from Samuel Untermeyer prepared me to manage our next major bankruptcy case pretty much on my own. This one concerned the reorganization of the Standard Gas & Electric Company, which was one of the largest public utility holding companies in the United States. Standard Gas & Electric was incorporated in Delaware, where the state laws were generally favorable to corporate power and where the federal judges tended to have more faith in corporate executives than they might in other districts. In 1935 Standard Gas & Electric got caught in the depression squeeze and found itself unable to pay its debts. A committee of the corporation's note and debenture holders was formed, and Javits & Javits, largely because of the reputation we had made in the Kreuger and Toll and other cases, was retained by the committee.

In April 1935 we petitioned in Federal District Court in Delaware to have the company declared bankrupt. That forced the company to go into bankruptcy voluntarily, and our petition was dismissed. At that point another committee of note and debenture holders appeared and demanded that the court appoint a trustee to run the company while the reorganization was being carried out. I went into court to oppose this, along with lawyers for the company, in the conviction that the value of our clients' securities would be restored most easily if the existing board of directors continued to operate the company. The judge upheld our view and we won our first victory in this long case.

For the next three or four years we were involved in a tremendous and complicated litigation involving many law firms, a number of committees, and countless banks and accountants. My work entailed many appearances before Federal District Judge John P. Nields and bankruptcy referees in Delaware, as well as long meetings of our committee, whose minutes I drafted, plus extended conferences and negotiations with many interests.

Our aim, naturally, was to preserve the value of the notes and debentures of which the committee we represented held more than $10 million. In this we succeeded, for the new capital structure that emerged from the protracted proceedings was identical to the one that existed beforehand, except for postponements of the due dates of some of the long-term debts — in other words, the securities were not devalued.

Judge Nields, however, criticized the reorganization plan we all worked out. It was not, he said, a "genuine" reorganization. In his decision on our petitions for fees and allowances, Nields claimed that the fourteen law firms, thirteen individual lawyers, twenty-eight committee members, and nine banks who had all been involved in the two-and-a-half-year process had duplicated services and wasted a great deal of time to little benefit for Standard Gas & Electric. Consequently, Nields drastically cut back the fees that we all applied for and actually denied some of them. Javits & Javits received only $35,000 of the $132,500 we asked for. The company's own law firm received a higher proportion of its request. In Delaware, in those days, the corporation was almost always right.

Justifying his slashing of fees, Nields said, "The evidence shows that an enormous amount of time was consumed by committees and their counsel in negotiating conflicting interests and claims of the various security holders. These negotiations were fruitless. The holders of securities came out of the litigation as they went in." Which was, of course, precisely my goal.

For a young lawyer, the legal essence of a judicial decision is often no more important than the judge's comments and summaries. Judge Nields's predilections compelled him to cut the fees of the New York lawyers, but his description of our activities did much to enhance my reputation within that small — but to me important — group of colleagues who took the time to read his lengthy decision.

Judge Nields pointed out that my argument carried the day on the question of whether the company should be continued in possession of its assets, that on several occasions my suggestions brought other committees around, that I had drafted many of the proposals during the negotiations. Nields reproached me, but he also paid me one great compliment. He said, "During the course of the reorganization of debtor many problems affecting its subsidiaries were presented. . . . In each instance Javits investigated these problems and conferred with the attorney for the debtor. However, it is nowhere shown that his services contributed to the solution of the problems of the subsidiaries or that counsel for the debtor was in any way assisted by him."

The compliment, I think, was much more important, because it touched on the fundamental skill that a lawyer — or a lawmaker — must have: "Certain holders of debentures filed a petition seeking an order restraining the debtor from making any further payments of interest on the ground that such payments would create a preference. The court denied this petition. The debenture holders took an appeal and obtained a stay of the court's order. . . . Javits undertook to find a means for paying interest on all issues of notes and debentures without the creation of a preference. He suggested a practical procedure for the payment of interest due which was adopted. The debenture holders withdrew their appeal. Since December 1, 1935, this plan for payment of interest was followed."

To devise a "practical procedure" that solves a problem and settles a controversy is, to my mind, the essence of the art of practicing law — or of politics — for without such a procedure no compromise and thus no democratic progress is possible. The training I was getting by untangling these complex corporate legal problems was to serve me well as a legislator.

My work on these cases consumed long hours and constricted the social life that a young bachelor lawyer about town might have enjoyed. I did most of the legal drafting and courtroom work for Javits & Javits, seldom with more than one or two assistants, while Ben brought in the business, negotiated fees, and determined the general direction of our work: He was our strategist and I was both tactician and operative. This meant that after spending all day in a courtroom or in conference with clients and opponents I would then have to devote the evening to planning the next day's events, deciding, for example, whom to subpoena, what motions to make, what questions to ask of witnesses — or merely reading and considering new information that may have come in.

Very often I would not finish this preparation until nine or ten o'clock at night, which was not difficult for me because I had become accustomed to working at my debt-collection business after my law-school classes and then studying after that. It did, however, limit my selection of dinner companions to those young women who did not mind dining at 10:00 P.M. (Eating earlier and then going back to work would have spoiled any date, of course.) Fortunately I was able to find such companions, and the habit of late dining has remained with me. I never get hungry in the evenings until at least 9:00 or 9:30, and I do not like to sit down to dinner — and I want to make every one a good one — when I still have work to do. I like to eat and have a drink and talk, with the feeling that the chores of the day are finished and that I can just relax or read until I go to bed.

So my social life during my early days as a busy lawyer consisted of these late dinners, usually at Sardi's or a French restaurant, and I was always on the lookout for women who would not find my schedule too outlandish. In 1932 or 1933, at a party that I did manage to attend, I met a very attractive, vivacious, and self-assured young woman who seemed to be intrigued by my lifestyle — and, I like to think, by me.

Marjorie Ringling was the adopted daughter of Alfred Ringling, one of the circus Ringling brothers. She was about twenty-one, an excellent pianist, studying music and living a somewhat bohemian and fun-filled existence in New York, supported by her uncle, John Ringling, who lived in Sarasota, Florida. (Her father had died.)

Marjorie and I dined together more and more often and became very fond of each other — and then we were in love. I liked her self-confidence, her sense of adventure, her willingness to meet the world on its terms. I had worked hard for so long — I was still working hard, with little opportunity for fun and relaxation. Marjorie not only gave me the chance to laugh and devote some time to pleasure, she virtually made it imperative to do so, and I was delighted.

In September 1933 we were married at New York City's Municipal Building marriage chapel. Ours was a civil ceremony because Marjorie was Catholic and I was Jewish. Our first home together was a small apartment on East Sixty-seventh Street, where I had been living for a couple of years, but we soon moved to a very elegant apartment

on East Seventy-eighth Street, where we had a living room big enough
to accommodate Marjorie's two grand pianos. Marjorie was very gre-
garious and liked to have guests in; we did a lot of entertaining of
her friends and mine. Ben's wife, Lily, kept us supplied with cooks
and other household help, and we ran a very active house.

For two years our marriage was like an extended honeymoon.
We visited her family's ranch in Montana — my first trip to the ranch-
ing West — and we went from time to time to see her uncle John at
his place in Sarasota, the winter headquarters of the Ringling Brothers,
Barnum and Bailey Circus. Uncle John had suffered a stroke, but
despite a withered arm and a speech impediment he was one of the
most lusty and vigorous men I had ever met. He was very fond of
Marjorie and wanted to see a great deal of her, and he did.

John Ringling was not only fabulously rich, he was fabulous. Before the stock market crash of 1929 he had been considered one of
the richest men in the United States. He had used a good part of his
wealth, an estimated $35 million, to build a black marble museum
next to his mansion in Sarasota and fill it with what is perhaps the
most extensive collection of Rubens paintings in the world.

My marriage to Marjorie Ringling was a recreation marriage, a
good-times marriage — and that was not enough. When the recreation
gave out the marriage gave out, and Marjorie became unhappy in it.
In spite of the fun we had when I had time, she found it difficult to
share the life of a hardworking young lawyer who was fighting to
succeed in a very tough profession and whose primary concern was
his career. She took very little interest in my cases — I suppose she
may have found them boring — and my habit of working late almost
every evening, while she was alone at home or entertaining guests
before I arrived, added to the strain.

There were other strains as well. I doubt that Marjorie ever became fully adjusted to the fact that we were of different faiths. Before
we married we had discussed the religious education of children, and
I had suggested that any children we had be brought up with the
knowledge of both the Jewish and Catholic religions so that they
could eventually choose for themselves. But later, although we had
not been married in church, Marjorie could not face the idea that her
offspring would not be baptized. As a result, although we both wanted
children — and I was more anxious for them than she was — we did
not have any. I am sure it troubled her, as it troubled me.

Another matter that may have added to the pressures on Marjorie
was my close relationship to Ben. At the time I was married to Marjorie, Ben and I still shared all our property in common — all our

funds were held jointly and neither of us had a private bank account. There was never any money problem in our marriage: Ben and I were doing well and we had just about everything we needed, and Marjorie herself could have called for financial assistance from her family if it had been necessary. Nevertheless, the close financial and family relationship of the Javits brothers may have been more than she could handle.

Marjorie and I spent more and more time apart. To escape from our problems, Marjorie started to travel frequently without me to visit Uncle John in Sarasota. I was often away, too, traveling to Washington helping clients who were setting up the new industrial codes under the National Recovery Act. Even when we were both in New York her state of depression made it difficult for me to deal with her sympathetically, and her trips to Sarasota decisively pulled us apart.

Ultimately Marjorie fell in love with someone she met in Florida, and she asked me for a divorce. Marriage should enable two people to live together in an orderly, communal existence, with at least affection and respect if not love; it should never bind them together with hoops of steel. So I could not object to Marjorie's request. I asked her to wait a week or so to be sure her decision was firm, and then I agreed. We divorced in 1936 after two and a half years of marriage. The divorce was by agreement, yet both of us felt we had lost something of life's happiness that might never be regained.

The joyous moment we had shared ended without bitterness or rancor, only with sadness, and Marjorie continued to count me as a friend. She married twice again. During the war she suddenly wrote to me from California. She had divorced her second husband and had heard I was an officer in the army. Plaintively and rather wistfully she said she would like to see me in uniform. A year later when I was out in California I went to Los Angeles to see her and we went dancing, but there was absolutely nothing left for us. She was ill after that, and when I was in Congress she communicated with me again; as the widow of an army officer, her third husband, she was trying to get hospitalization from the Veterans' Administration and she asked my help. I did all I could and we corresponded from time to time thereafter. A few years later she came to visit me in the Senate, this time — heartbreakingly — in a wheelchair. Until she died in the 1960s she knew she could call on me for whatever assistance she needed, and I would help; I cannot renounce, or cut out of my life, someone I have loved.

My divorce impelled me to take stock of myself. I was thirty-two years old, earning substantial legal fees and with a solid reputation as a trial lawyer. Yet my struggle for independence from Ben's domination, which had begun so poignantly during my trip to Europe in 1927, was not yet complete. We were not only loving brothers and a smoothly functioning law partnership: Financially we were one and the same.

I thought this situation over and finally decided that, much as Ben and I loved and trusted each other, the time had long since come for me to accept the normal financial responsibilities of adult life. Besides, Ben had his wife and, by then, his children to provide for, and I felt therefore that I should set up a fund to take care of our mother. It seemed fairer to everyone to divide things up, and I said so to Ben.

Ben was very upset at my request. We had always been so close that he believed I did not need anything of my own. He pointed out that everything he had was also mine, and that I would have much less if we divided it up. Strictly speaking, he was right, but he had not reckoned the value of independence. After much discussion between us I insisted and he agreed. I told him that he should decide how to allocate our property and that I would accept any formula he proposed. The details were not so important to me as the fact of the division. Reluctantly, Ben complied, and we carved up our holdings, two-thirds for Ben, one-third for me. Nevertheless, I don't think he ever got over my insistence on financial independence.

Ben's views and mine were then beginning to diverge in other ways as well. Together we had espoused socialism, together we had seen its flaws, together we had become Republicans. But from that point on we began to differ. Ben was becoming a fervent, single-minded believer in the power of business to solve all society's ills. It was the corporation, he believed, that made socialism invalid. In his view, the corporation, owned by hundreds of thousands of small shareholders, would socialize the means of production, spread ownership around into many hands, and retain the free-enterprise system. He believed this could eliminate economic and social injustice. He started an organization of shareholders and wrote a number of books on his theory, which he called Ownerism. Ben had tremendous faith in the corporate business system and believed that it could do away with poverty and lead the American people into a more stable, more successful era.

Eventually Ben's beliefs led him to a position that was very close to corporate statism, the original foundation of Italian Fascism, in which society is divided into workers, employers, and technicians. The essence of his system was his faith that the managers of business would do what was in the public interest. While I shared his view that the functioning of a corporation could invalidate much of socialist theory, I never shared his faith that business managers, standing alone, could be entrusted to operate business in the public interest. I believed that the will of the people could be best expressed through government and that government-business collaboration could encourage business to perform in the public interest. Although I felt that we could rely upon the U.S. business system to run the U.S. economy, I did not feel that we could entrust the economic well-being of the American people solely to the multitudinous transactions of the marketplace.

Our law partnership was unaffected by these emerging differences of opinion. In 1937 Javits & Javits entered another complicated, long-drawn-out stockholders' suit. The firm in this instance was the General Investment Corporation, a holding company that had been financed in 1929 by the Chase National Bank and Kidder, Peabody, one of the country's most distinguished banking houses. We charged that General Investment and some of its officers, for the benefit of those officers, had fraudulently, negligently, and illegally wasted and dissipated about $50 million of U.S. stockholders' funds by investing in a number of questionable railroad and utility companies in several countries. The 1929 crash practically wiped out these companies. And for the next five or six years the directors of General Investment and the banks and brokerage firms involved with them just sat hoping no one would sue them. By the time I got into the case, control of the company had been taken over by a group of Boston financiers, but there was only about $1 million left in the till — out of an original enterprise worth more than $100 million.

In 1937, on behalf of two stockholders, I tried to persuade the new management of General Investment to sue the former directors for the funds that had been so improvidently lost. The new management, unfamiliar with the case, refused, so, on behalf of the stockholders, Javits & Javits filed suit for $50 million against the corporation itself and a number of former directors, banks, and brokerage houses. Shortly thereafter, other stockholders and lawyers filed similar suits based on our complaint. The new management of General Investment soon realized our suit was justified and joined in with us, and the corporation became a coplaintiff instead of a defendant.

The case dragged on with court arguments, appeals, affidavits, and investigations for two years before coming to trial in 1939 before Justice Philip J. McCook of the New York Supreme Court. On our side was Mortimer Hays, of the firm of Hays, Podell and Shulman, and the firm of Szold & Brandwen. Arrayed against us once again was the white-shoe legal fraternity: Sullivan and Cromwell; Millbank Tweed & Hope; Mudge, Stern, Williams & Tucker. Often dozens of lawyers were present in the courtroom at the same time. In many court sessions extending over an additional two-year period, we endeavored to prove that the former directors of the firm and the brokerage houses had conspired to invest the company's funds in worthless enterprises, to their profit and the company's loss. Mortimer Hays and I led our team, but each of us specialized in particular sets of transactions and I handled the cross-examinations of many witnesses.

In April 1942, nearly five years after the first legal move was made, the case was finally settled for a negotiated sum. The seventeen defendants agreed to pay to the corporation $1,375,000, of which $350,000 was awarded by Justice McCook to the plaintiffs' four law firms, including Javits & Javits.

Although the defendants admitted no wrongdoing and settled for far less than we had demanded, I regarded the case as a victory for the rights of investors. In addition, the examinations and cross-examinations before and during the trial gave me valuable training for my future work on business and economic issues in Congress and taught me significant lessons about the inner workings of big corporations. The case proved to me that businessmen and bankers of good reputation, even those who have achieved tremendous financial success, are just as fallible and vulnerable to error and temptation as anyone else. I learned not to regard reputations as sacred and not to be intimidated by the name or fame of anyone. The bankers and brokers and corporate directors whom we faced in the General Investment case were all men of great standing. Yet it became clear to everyone that some of them had behaved very improperly.

Like other corporate scandals of the period, this case influenced the regulations that were later established by the Securities and Exchange Commission to protect investors. Up until the early 1930s, the securities business was generally operated on the principle of "let the buyer beware." That is ancient history now.

FIVE

World War:
A Turning Point

While I was engaged in the law courts with the General Investment case, the world was heading for a trial of a different sort. As early as 1927, I had seen and been deeply disturbed by the rise of Fascism in Italy. By the late 1930s, it was clear that Hitler was threatening the peace and freedom of the whole world. I was particularly sensitive, of course, to the Nazis' treatment of Jews — Kristallnacht hit me very hard — but it went beyond that: Hitler represented the apocalypse and struck at the essence of civilization. When the Spanish civil war offered a chance to fight this menace, some of my friends volunteered, but I was busy as a lawyer and did not get involved in Spain. I had regrets about this, and by 1939, after the Anschluss in Austria, the rape of Czechoslovakia, and the Nazi-Soviet pact, I no longer felt satisfied in the law courts. It was clear to me that Hitler had to be stopped and that we would have to go to war to do it. This was *my* war; I had to be in it, fight in it — and die if necessary. In the summer of 1939 I went to the secretary of war, Harry Woodring, whom I had met socially, and tried to enlist in the army air force. Woodring was sympathetic, but he said that at thirty-five I was too old.

Ben's attitude toward what was happening in Europe puzzled me. His worry about the threat to civilization was just as great as mine, but his original socialist views imparted to his thinking an element of pacifism that I did not share. Our disagreement about participating in the war was something of a strain on our relationship. I wanted to throw everything over immediately to do what I could to fight Hitler; Ben, who had a wife and two children to support, felt this was not a role for him. I did not expect him to put on a uniform and go into combat — he was ten years older than I — but I felt there were ways in which he could have served. I was to reproach him from time to time for this posture. There was no outright break: We were still closer than most brothers, we saw each other whenever I came to New York during the war, and he was a great help to me afterward. But it was never quite the same again between us. I could not approve of his role during the war, although he seemed to approve of mine.

It may be difficult for later generations who fought in unpopular and indecisive wars to appreciate the emotions and motivations of those of us who participated eagerly and with dedication in World War II. We were involved in a cause we knew was right, and the fact that most of the world was on our side confirmed this faith. The evil of the enemy was clear and his strength was awesome. As we saw it, our survival was at stake, and the only choice was between war and a surrender to slavery. Some of us realized this early; most did not recognize the threat until Pearl Harbor. But once we were in the war the vast majority of the people of the United States felt an uplifting surge of common purpose such as we had never experienced before — and that we have never shared since. For me, World War II was even more than that: It was to be the crucial turning point that set me on the path of public service.

My first opportunity to do something about the threat came in 1940. That summer a few prominent citizens had come together at New York's Century Club to persuade the U.S. government to give to the British — who were standing alone against the Nazi war machine — some of our overage destroyers. I was not involved in the inception of the Century Group, which was one of several related groups that recognized the menace, but I quickly volunteered to help it in any way I could. A New York advertising man named Peter Cusick, who subsequently became my lifelong friend, was running the Century Group's office on Forty-second Street when I appeared there. Peter had never heard of me, but as he put it, "Anyone who wanted to volunteer in those days was a great hero to us. Everyone thought we were nuts." The group, which subsequently became the Fight for Freedom Committee, needed lawyers; I helped in a small way on the legal memos that led to the treaty by which Britain got the destroyers in exchange for leasing naval bases to the United States.

At the same time, I was even more involved in another project that concerned the war effort in a very direct way. In 1940 Franklin D. Roosevelt was running, against Wendell Willkie, for an unprecedented third term. At first I was torn: My Republican loyalties were pitted against the obvious need, with war approaching, to have in the White House an experienced president clearly aware of the menace of Hitler to civilized values. Someone at the time said, and I agreed, that Roosevelt was worth two million men to the Allied cause. My mind was made up when Fiorello La Guardia, whom I had come to admire more and more during his terms as mayor, endorsed Roosevelt and formed with Senator George Norris a committee of Republican progressives and independents for Roosevelt. La Guardia remembered me from his 1937 campaign and asked me to join.

The Norris–La Guardia Committee made clear that it admired Wendell Willkie greatly but felt that a Roosevelt defeat would severely set back the international momentum of allies preparing for war; the negotiations with Britain and other allies would have had to start all over again if Willkie had been elected. The war issue was paramount in our minds. We felt that with Roosevelt the United States was already on the right anti-Nazi track, and we did not want to risk a derailment.

Ben did not share this opinion; he saw no reason to desert the Republican fold. He saw Willkie as an enlightened leader from the business world better able to support his, Ben's, ideas about the U.S. and world economy, so he actively supported the Republican candidate. We made an unusual bet on the outcome. On election night I gave a big party at my apartment on East Thirty-eighth Street and ordered several cases of champagne — to be paid for by the loser. We were drinking the champagne as the results came in, and Ben paid.

Soon after that I found another small way to help counter the Axis threat. We were aware that large colonies of Germans and Italians were becoming influential in Latin America and that many of the German "businessmen" there were active agents of Hitler. Few United States citizens lived in Latin America or understood the languages and culture of the area, and late in 1940 I dreamed up the idea of training young American college graduates to live and work there. Secretary of State Cordell Hull put me in touch with other people interested in the idea, we wrote to scores of colleges to recruit students, and we found excellent educators to run the program.

The upshot of this was the establishment of the Association of Committees for Inter-American Placement (ACIP). I donated $5000 to pay for the program, and Dean Halfdan Gregerson of Williams College, who had joined with me early, took charge of it. By June 1941 Dean Gregerson had rounded up a staff and found a building — a fraternity house at Williams — and we had selected seventeen graduating seniors from Yale, Harvard, the University of Chicago, Smith, Bennington, and other good colleges. For six weeks that summer our students were given an intensive course in the languages, civilization, culture, government, economics, history, and geography of the Latin

American republics. Businessmen, officials, editors, artists, musicians, and economists from Latin America also conducted seminars and discussions to give the group a well-rounded understanding of life in the other American republics. Some of the members of the group were then sent to Mexico for further study, and several of them were soon placed in positions and jobs where their new knowledge and understanding were of inestimable value in improving U.S. relations with Latin America.

Planning for a second ACIP summer was interrupted by Pearl Harbor, and no further sessions were held. But it was an imaginative and valuable project. As soon as the United States entered the war almost all of our students were snapped up by the State Department, which was anxious to expand its representation in Latin America. Dean Gregerson himself went to work in Washington for Nelson Rockefeller, who was then the U.S. government's coordinator for Inter-American Affairs, and so did one of our star students, Kingman Brewster, later president of Yale University and ambassador to Great Britain. For a while Gregerson and I shared an apartment in Washington: Finally, after all my searching for an active war role, I had found one almost by chance.

Late in 1940 or early in 1941, at a cocktail party in Washington given by a friend of mine who held a reserve commission in the service, I met Major General Walter C. Baker, who was then chief of the Chemical Warfare Service (CWS) of the United States Army. General Baker mentioned that his service was having a great deal of difficulty in procuring filter paper for gas masks and magnesium for incendiary bombs. I saw at once that I could help. One of the most important clients of Javits & Javits was the Crown Zellerbach Corporation, a large Pacific Coast paper manufacturer, and Harold and David Zellerbach were my good friends. Besides, through Ben, I knew Charles "Electric Charlie" Wilson, president of the General Electric Corporation, who was soon to become a member of the War Production Board. It required just a couple of phone calls to obtain from the Zellerbachs a promise to make the filter paper Baker needed, and, thanks to Wilson, it took only a little longer to find the magnesium.

My quick solutions to problems that had stymied the army's Chemical Warfare Service for months seemed miraculous to the military. Actually, all I had done was some fast troubleshooting, fairly common in the business world and not very difficult if you have good relations with the right people. But the Chemical Warfare Service did not have my business contacts, and General Baker was very impressed. Besides his immediate procurement headaches, he also faced the need to expand and reorganize the service rapidly for war, and he knew that my legal experience included reorganizing the administration of bankrupt corporations. So General Baker asked me to serve as a part-time legal consultant to the CWS. I readily agreed, and starting in January 1941, I spent two days each week in Washington as a "dollar-a-year man," advising the general and his staff on legal, procurement, and administrative matters.

I could not give the CWS more than two days a week because the General Investment trial was still going on. Moreover, in the summer and fall of 1941 I was again involved in New York politics, this time helping Mayor La Guardia's third-term reelection campaign. Early in the year La Guardia had expressed some doubts about running again and a citizens' committee was formed to persuade him that he should. Another lawyer, Percival Jackson, and I organized the collection of seventy thousand signatures on a petition urging La Guardia to run, and after he agreed I helped in his successful campaign. My job, with Percy Jackson, was to broaden and develop the citizens' nonpartisan effort that our petition drive had opened up. I spoke at meetings, helped establish many local headquarters around the city, and recruited volunteers to canvass voters by phone and in person. We also ran a very effective speakers' bureau. Immediately after the election, by prearrangement with the army, I started work as a full-time civilian consultant to the Chemical Warfare Service, and on December 2, 1941, I was appointed special assistant to the chief of the CWS.

The fateful Sunday of December 7, 1941, remains especially poignant in my memory not only because it marked the beginning of the war, which was such an important turning point in my life, but because of where I was when I heard the news: I was courting a beautiful and talented woman.

Hollace Shaw was a singer, a very fine coloratura soprano who had sung with Toscanini, on the Broadway stage, and on her own radio program. We had met sometime during 1940; I had already heard her perform when someone introduced us, and we started to see each other regularly — or at least when her busy life and mine would permit. That year Hollace sang in two Broadway shows; in *Very Warm for May*, starring Eve Arden, Hollace introduced that lovely American theater classic "All the Things You Are," which is still one of my all-time favorites. Hollace had a soft and responsive southern California speech and manner, long blond hair, green eyes, a sunny complexion, and a velvet voice. She liked to swim, as I did, and we enjoyed New York's simple pleasures, like riding on the open top deck of the

Fifth Avenue bus. We were very much in love with each other and had every intention of marrying.

On Pearl Harbor day Hollace and I were just finishing brunch in her New York apartment when at about two o'clock the telephone rang. It was the duty officer of the Chemical Warfare Service calling from Washington to tell me — quite calmly, I thought — that the U.S. fleet in Pearl Harbor had been attacked, that there was intelligence of a possible invasion of the West Coast, that all services had been ordered on immediate war footing, and that I should return to Washington immediately. Even the most peaceful of men can feel exultation on the threshold of a just war. As I dashed out to make the four o'clock Congressional Limited from Penn. Station, I was telling myself and Hollace that the moment of truth had arrived and I was lucky to have already found a slot in which I could do my part.

From that first euphoric moment on December 7 I immersed myself completely in my army job, working seven days a week and late into the nights until I could no longer keep my eyes open. What went through my head was the thought that, considering how other men were suffering and dying, it mattered very little how I expended myself as long as the job got done. The job was a big one. To put the Chemical Warfare Service on a wartime footing we had to expand its manpower and materiel, train thousands of men, many in secret, set up depots and posts and stations, and develop plans and procedures, many for unknown contingencies.

The big problem we faced was that we did not know whether we would have to use poison gas. We were sure that the United States would not take it up first, but we knew that if the Germans or Japanese employed it we would have to retaliate. So we had to prepare our own gas weapons and defenses. The basic CWS weapon for close-in infantry combat was the 4.2-inch mortar, which chemical warfare troops put into action in every theater of the war for the firing of high explosives and smoke and phosphorus and magnesium incendiary shells, all part of standard infantry tactics. The same 4.2-inch mortars would have fired poison gas shells if it had come to that, and so our CWS 4.2 crews, attached to every regiment, division, and army, all had to be trained in gas warfare as well as in the use of conventional weapons. In the first hectic months of the war my job as a civilian was mainly concerned with the procurement of the gas masks, shells, explosives, gases, and chemicals that the CWS needed — for its own units and for the gas warfare branches of the U.S. Navy and the Army Air Forces as well.

Around Christmas 1941, I got a few days off and Hollace and I flew out to San Diego, which was still blacked out every night for fear of a Japanese raid or invasion. Hollace was already wearing my diamond and ruby engagement ring; with the war taking people away from each other, we thought it best to marry quickly. She had met my family and we went to California so that I could meet hers. Her sister, Anne, and her brother Robert were also musicians; Robert Shaw later became a noted symphony orchestra conductor and choral director. Another brother, Jim, was a minister, soon to become an army chaplain. Hollace's father was a minister of the Christian Church — and I suppose that is where the problem arose.

Our reception by Hollace's father and mother was cordial enough; they were very nice people but they were reserved. Anne and Robert were very supportive, but Hollace's parents were worried about their daughter marrying a Jewish man. Indeed, my background and theirs were as different as day and night. Hollace herself did not have a bigoted bone in her body, but she loved and respected her parents and followed the religion they had taught her. When she realized the depth of their feelings — which were very sincere — I felt instinctively she would find it very difficult to flout their wishes. So I returned to Washington from San Diego quite saddened. Our love for each other was not diminished by her parents' disapproval and we continued to spend as much time together as possible during the next couple of years, but I think the glow of our romance began to fade when our marriage was blocked that Christmas season. For some time, however, I still hoped that the Shaws would change their minds or that Hollace would determine to marry me notwithstanding their objections.

For the first four months of the war I remained a civilian aide to the chief of the CWS. In addition to my work, I attended a chemical warfare civil defense course at CWS's Edgewood Arsenal in Maryland, so that I would have some direct personal knowledge of the equipment my office was dealing with. In March the U.S. Army (through Major General William Porter, the new chief of CWS) decided that I could better serve it in uniform; I was commissioned as a major and appointed assistant executive officer of the Control Division of the CWS. To celebrate this very big event for me, I invited all the top brass of the CWS to a party at Washington's Park Sheraton Hotel. Eight generals came, considerably more than normally toast a brand new major, but I had worked with all of them and they wished to show they appreciated my efforts. It was a good party and I had another reason to celebrate: Just a few weeks earlier the General Investment case had been settled and Javits & Javits had earned a good fee.

As is not unusual in war, I was now a chemical warfare officer who had made no special study either of warfare or chemistry — gaps that had to be filled at once. I went back to Edgewood Arsenal to take the five-week specialized course in chemical weapons techniques designed for army reservists coming into the CWS. At the same time, I went through an abbreviated version of army basic training. It was a tough grind. With a few other officers who shared my predicament, I got up at 5:00 A.M. every day for two hours of basic training under a tough sergeant who apparently had been told to forget our rank. The rest of the day was spent in chemical warfare training, in which we carried around mortars and shells, learned to maintain and fire the weapons, participated in field exercises, and sat through innumerable lectures and training films. In the evenings we had to read and master the chemical warfare training manuals — a stack as tall as I am.

Back at headquarters in Washington, the long hours continued. We were inviting officers from the Latin American armed forces to Edgewood for training in chemical warfare and we had few officers who could converse with them. Because of my ACIP work, I was chosen to handle this problem, and I took cram courses to improve my Spanish at the Latin American Institute in Washington.

The work of the Control Division was frantic and intense. The division was charged with organizing and keeping track of the world-wide administrative services of the CWS. When I joined it the Control Division consisted of Colonel Elliott, the executive officer, me, and a secretary. Six months later we had four commissioned officers and seven consultants in Washington and about two hundred fifty officers stationed all over the world. The division was also involved in the continuing reorganization of the service with its consultants and experts from scientific and business institutions.

My new commanding officer, Major General Porter, was a remarkable man who had a great influence on me. Everything General Porter touched seemed to turn into a negotiation, whether with other branches of the army, with his superiors, or with his subordinates — and he was a master negotiator. He was also very genial; he and I used to share a little champagne late at night in his office after one of our typical sixteen-hour days. I provided the champagne and he provided the refrigerator, and at about midnight or one o'clock in the morning I would go into his office and we would have a glass to help us relax.

My immediate superior during that time was Brigadier General Paul X. English. General English was a great big hulk of a man who had the voice and the manner and the physique of a master sergeant. He should have been commanding troops out in the field. An office was too small for him: He would move his elbows and the walls would fall away. But he was a very decent, outgoing, and warm-hearted Southerner, even though he was generally griping about the army and what it was doing to him.

Throughout my wartime years in Washington I took care to maintain my ties to my friends in the business and political worlds. The Zellerbach brothers and their friends came to Washington frequently — they were all involved in the war effort. I corresponded with them, saw them often, and helped them with their contacts in official Washington. I had become friendly with David K. Niles, President Roosevelt's adviser on minority affairs, and Niles and I dined together frequently all through the war. Niles was wealthy, Jewish, from Boston, and an ardent New Dealer with a deep social consciousness who had also become a very shrewd and influential Democratic politician. In a very subtle and civilized way we exchanged favors. He would never ask you to do something but would suggest it and hope you got the point. And it was unwise to ask him to do anything too directly; if you did, he would hedge. But you could leave a suggestion with him and something would get done. He was not a man to say yes or no. Through Niles my horizons were broadened, and I began to see that I could be part of history and help make it happen, not just sit on the sidelines. Niles introduced me to many of his friends and I introduced him to mine, particularly business leaders such as the Zellerbachs, who were very pleased to have a friend in the White House.

During 1942 I continued to spend what free time I could find with Hollace, who was becoming very well known. She had joined Phil Spitalny's All-Girl Orchestra and sang as "Vivian" on Spitalny's popular radio program, "The Hour of Charm." The show was broadcast from concert halls all over the country, and the orchestra performed at army bases, so she was traveling constantly, but we did manage a few weekends and dates and we sometimes could attend a play together.

But mostly those months were long hours of hard work. In July I wrote to Dave Zellerbach: "We are really in the work up to our ears now, and I have a strange feeling after working for fourteen or fifteen hours in a day that there must have been something wrong with another day in which I worked ten hours because our progress could not have gone as rapidly on the ten-hour day." In September it all caught up with me. One evening I passed out at my desk; another officer found me there with my head on my arms, and I was taken to Walter Reed Hospital. The diagnosis was atypical pneumonia, but the real problem was just complete exhaustion. I remained in Walter Reed for six weeks, frustrated that I was missing out on some of the planning for the invasion of North Africa.

Soon after my release from the hospital I was promoted to lieutenant colonel, and that winter I entered the army's Command and General Staff College at Fort Leavenworth, Kansas. General Porter had turned down my request for overseas duty as a line officer when he came to see me at Walter Reed — he said I was too old for that. But with more training, he thought, I could become a full-fledged staff officer, and he arranged for me to enter the Command and General Staff College. It was a red-letter day for me when the CWS personnel office cut those orders.

Ben came with me on the train trip to Fort Leavenworth. He had been very concerned over my illness and was worried that I was still weak. It may seem strange that I, a lieutenant colonel in the Army of the United States, on my way to study the higher arts of war, was accompanied by my elder brother, somewhat as if I were a youngster going to camp. But neither Ben nor I thought there was anything odd about it — that's how close we always were.

At Leavenworth I was enrolled in the Twelfth Command and General Staff course, designed to train staff officers for headquarters of army divisions and above. It lasted for two months and was one of the toughest experiences that I had ever had in terms of hard work, day and night, seven days a week. The instruction was given in lecture courses (field training was presumed to have been mastered), and it covered infantry, armor and air tactics, planning, logistics, and intelligence. The course requirement was to learn all that went into the writing of a field commander's five-part field order, a necessity for any operation large or small. Its parts were: (1) the information needed to carry out the mission; (2) defining the goal of the mission; (3) tactical missions for supporting units — that is, what each element or individual must do; (4) administration and liaison (who reports to whom); and (5) arrangements for communications, locations of headquarters, and so forth. The order and precision of this system have become a part of my life in the last thirty-six years. Another method of military planning I learned at Leavenworth was backtiming: deciding where you wanted to be at what date and hour, and with what forces and equipment, and planning back from that objective.

The practice at Leavenworth was to order off the base the night before graduation those officers who had not completed the course satisfactorily. This was such a traumatic experience that some failed officers committed suicide. The decision really was somewhat arbitrary because the passing grade was determined by deciding how many staff officers the army needed at that moment and then drawing a line under the corresponding number and eliminating the rest. In my class, the split was 80 percent accepted and 20 percent not needed.

Upon graduating successfully (and it was the most prized diploma I had ever earned), I was appointed executive officer to Brigadier General Alden Waitt, the chief of operations of the Chemical Warfare Service. Waitt was a very gifted officer who later became a major general. He was a professional soldier, and his main goal in life was to become chief of his service. Although Waitt valued greatly his army status, he was very democratic and earthy; he was good with the enlisted men because he did not make too much of his own authority.

I still have one of Waitt's pithy memos. It was attached to another document in which someone had suggested that the CWS cut down on reports and paperwork. Alden wrote, "Cutting down reports is like gentlemen jockeys and lady whores, you hear a lot about it but you never see one." After the war Waitt retired from the army and took up painting.

All my friends and colleagues knew about Hollace and teased me about her. In March 1943 she was chosen by the Fashion Academy as the "Best-Dressed Woman in Radio," and friends sent me clippings from the gossip columns about that — as if I had not been aware of the award and everything else about her. In April 1943 David Zellerbach was planning to come to Washington and I wired him that I would not be there. His reply, which I received later, said, "My secret service in New York advises me that Hollace Shaw is going down to visit in Florida so I assume that's where you are going to be. Give her my regards." (He was right.) Then there was the colonel from a CWS procurement office in Texas who wrote expressing disappointment that I would not be able to visit his command. He said: "There certainly must be plenty of field activities in the 8th Service Command that would justify your coming this way, particularly if 'The Hour of Charm' is broadcast from some one of the Texas training centers. See if you can fix that up."

My post in Washington, my access to people from many walks of life, and my frequent trips to bases around the country gave me the chance to perform many small kindnesses for my friends — which I have always liked to do. When I went to Florida with Hollace I sent baskets of oranges to several army colleagues. When Hollace was scheduled to sing in a city where I had friends I wrote to them in advance suggesting they meet her. Ben had an interest in a vitamin company, so I sent vitamins to many of my army friends who had gone to England. When the parents of Dave Niles's secretary had difficulty obtaining tickets for a sellout show, *This Is the Army*, I bought tickets for them through the show's manager, whom I knew. And I helped a number of my friends who were too old for regular military service get army commissions or other jobs where their skills could contribute to the war effort. One typical case concerned a young man, the son of a businessman I had worked with, who had been classified 4F, physically unfit for military duty; he desperately wanted to get into uniform and I tried to help him.

Courteous behavior had been taught me by my mother and by Mr. Mittleman of P.S. 20; by this time it had become a pleasant habit and later it would help me in politics. Fortunately the secretaries at the Javits & Javits branch office in Washington were available to handle the considerable volume of correspondence these activities generated. "I've got a friend in Washington" was the wisecrack of the time. For lots of people I knew, that friend was me.

My duties under General Waitt put me in closer touch with what was going on overseas. The British, who could not match our resources, were uncomfortable with the extent of our chemical warfare readiness. They worried that the United States, which was becoming thoroughly prepared to use gas in retaliation, might go off half-cocked and employ the weapon unnecessarily. Since they were within range of the enemy, their civilians would have suffered much more in a gas war than ours, so they were naturally more cautious. I attended many sessions of the British and U.S. chemical warfare committees that discussed the procedures governing the use of gas and that decided how much of each kind of agent and weapon should be deployed at various command-level depots. The U.S. policy was an early version of the nuclear-deterrent theory: We held that only a strong gas capability on our part would prevent Hitler from using gas first. We were always aware that the Germans had initiated the use of gas in World War I.

In August 1943 I got a chance, finally, to go overseas myself: General Waitt and I spent about two months in Europe and North Africa inspecting our CWS units and helping to plan future operations. We flew first to England, departing from a secret air force base in Massachusetts in a convoy, code-named Cossack, of four DC-4s carrying General "Hap" Arnold and his staff to open the U.S. Army Air Force headquarters in London. The flight took more than twelve hours and one of our planes had to make a forced landing on a Scottish beach. On my first night in London there was an air raid: Chandelier bombs lit up the sky and anti-aircraft guns were firing from Hyde Park.

Our primary mission at London headquarters was to discuss chemical warfare policy with the British committee, but what I remember most often about wartime Britain is a day spent at a U.S. air base in the Midlands.

Arriving at the field in the early morning, I ate breakfast with the crew members of a B-17 bomber, accompanied them to their briefing for a raid on a German fighter base in occupied France, and watched the squadron take off at midday — eighteen planes lumbering into the air at intervals of thirty seconds. Then came the seven-hour wait for their return at dusk. I saw the red flare from the lead plane indicating that there were wounded airmen in the flight, and I peered at the bombers with almost unbearable tension until I determined that "my plane," my friends, the men I had spoken with in the morning, had come through unscathed. But I saw the wounded from the other planes and learned at the debriefing that two of our planes had crash-landed elsewhere in the United Kingdom and that some, from other bases but on the same raid, had not made it back at all.

I had seen no combat and until the London air raid I had never heard a shot fired in anger; this was the closest I had come so far to sharing the essence of war. The calm, matter-of-fact heroism of the B-17 crews fired my own sense of mission. My war had consisted of meetings, administration, reports and paperwork: fundamentally the same tasks I had been performing all my life. That is why the drama of the air base made such an impression on me. Knowing that people get killed in war is one thing; seeing it happen, or seeing the people to whom it has just happened, is an experience of quite a different magnitude. As I watched the wounded airmen being gently lifted from their planes, the war was suddenly transformed from an abstract concept to a very palpable horror.

A few weeks later, in North Africa, this feeling was intensified. To get there, General Waitt and I took a long night flight from Scotland in a blacked-out transport, sleeping on bucket seats, with our briefcases for pillows. On board were a pair of young British officers: She was an air-ferry pilot and he was an RAF pilot. I do not know whether they had ever met before, but they obviously were awake all night in fond embrace, and the wonder was in the complete disregard of all the others in that crowded plane and the sweetness in their demeanor toward each other.

In the morning we found ourselves in Marrakech, Morocco, an exotic Near Eastern oasis with snake charmers and veiled women and orange groves. But at our next stop, Algiers, where General Eisenhower's headquarters were located, the wrecked ships in the harbor, the anti-aircraft guns and crews, and the swarms of dusty soldiers reminded us forcefully that we were in a war zone.

One afternoon, during a break in the chemical warfare conferences we were attending at Ike's headquarters, I wandered over to the railroad siding in Algiers, near our hotel. A hospital train had just come in, carrying wounded from the fighting in Italy, and I watched as the cars were unloaded. There were hundreds of wounded, a staggering accumulation of missing limbs, shattered torsos, damaged faces, and bandages covering what one could tell were empty eye sockets. I stood there for what seemed hours as this almost unbelievable scene of human destruction unfolded before me.

These pitifully hurt young men were by then a day or more from the battle; they had already received excellent medical care, including drugs to dull the pain, so there were no screams and few groans. The horror was in the numbers, the vast sum of carnage and agony and maiming contained in that day's awful harvest from the battlefield. As I stood there transfixed — unable to move except when I came close to throwing up — there began to grow within me a determination to help in some small way to arrange the affairs of the world so that tragedies like this one might not be seen again.

From Algiers, General Waitt and I flew to Tunis, then Sicily, and then Naples, which had been taken by our forces just two weeks earlier. It was hard to recognize the beautiful city, now mangled, chaotic, cluttered with blasted trolley cars and ruined buildings. Although there was no water or electricity in the homes and little food in the markets, the streets were teeming with joyous people walking about, talking and smiling. Children played in the streets, shutters were open, and laundry was hung out to dry. For the Neapolitans, a black cloud had receded and the sun was shining again. It was no longer necessary to peek from behind shuttered windows or keep the children indoors, because the heavy hand of Fascism had been lifted. The people almost blinked, as if suddenly released from the night. I remember a group of ragged kids who were watching some Signal Corps GIs string communication wire. Every once in a while a soldier turned around and made a wisecrack or a face at a kid. The kids did not understand, but they knew a friend when they saw one and they happily grinned back.

At a hospital outside Naples I was awed by the composure and bravery of wounded men fresh from the front, some of them still in pain. They spoke straightforwardly about where they got hit, where they were from, who were their buddies, and said that their outfits were the best in the army. Only rarely did we hear any criticism or sense any bitterness — either of which might have seemed natural under the circumstances.

Up near the fighting front we lunched at the command post of one of our 4.2 mortar battalions, and as German artillery rumbled in the background we heard from the colonel and his enthusiastic staff what a fine bunch of men were in *that* outfit. Several weeks later, on the Rapido River, that colonel and many of the men we met that day were killed instantaneously by a single German bomb.

Our eight-day return trip took us to Palermo, Bizerte, Algiers, Oran, Fez, Marrakech, Atar, and Dakar, across the South Atlantic to Brazil, and thence to Washington. What was really on my mind during that trip emerged in a long letter to Hollace written from Oran. Although it now was apparent that we would not marry, she had been very much in my thoughts. We had begun to discover that we did not see eye to eye on everything. Had we been married, or definitely planning to marry, perhaps these differences might have been resolved. Or perhaps we might not have been as happy together married as we were when our romance was new. I am not sure I ever sent this letter, but the draft of it, which I saved, says a great deal about my state of mind as I returned from Europe in October 1943:

My Darling Hollace. This is a confession of faith to you and at the same time a summation of this tremendous experience. . . . I have come to the conclusion that our generation, if it is not to be blind, cannot rest. There is no peace for us. . . . The task is . . . to assure to the humble people of the world, peace, security . . . and freedom. . . . It is fitting that I should write this to you, for I love you, yet our love has been constantly overshadowed by the ugly struggle of the forces of darkness to engulf the world. You want quiet, order, a nice retreat away from the roar of the conflict. You almost want that to the exclusion of justice and a better world. Yet somehow you cannot go that far, something in you shrinks from it. You know it is not right, for you continue to love me. . . .

Hollace, listen. . . . Your God and mine cry out for action. The place of a woman as well as of a man is on the ramparts in this epic struggle. They may rest only as a soldier rests, the better to undertake the next action.

Only on the ramparts, Hollace, will you find love; only there will you find life. The country needs you, religion — all ethical religion — Christian and Jewish alike needs you — I need you. But none can you help unless you open your heart and your purpose to those who need you, unless you work for them and not for self.

Back at our desks in Washington, General Waitt and I turned to the accelerated plan for Operation Overlord, the invasion of France, and the island-hopping campaigns in the Pacific. The tremendous increase in the size of the army meant that we were catching up with requirements, and although we still worked hard there was no need to work ourselves into exhaustion. Both the army and the business world were looking ahead to the end of the war.

In February 1944 I was invited to speak to the annual convention of the National Paper Trade Association, which I had served as counsel before the war. I took the opportunity to protest some of the business-as-usual attitudes that I had noted in wartime. I spoke frankly, as a man in uniform, to businessmen who had not been involved in the fighting and who were still concerned with profits. The youth of America, I told them, have

> deprived you of all right to self-seeking or to prejudice, and [have] dedicated you to the service of the nation. . . . It has been said that the soldier in the field is impatient of strikes in industry. May it not also be said with equal justice that he is impatient of strikes by management? Do you think that the soldier believes that the foundations of the republic are tottering because you have to file some extra forms and work nights to do it; or that free institutions are about to fall because of a provision in the tax bill about reserves? Do you believe that he will ever forgive you for sitting back and not planning for the day of his return because you think we are becoming too socialistic? Not at all. Not any more than you believe that the war is being lost because we are not in Rome today! You cannot fail to make plans and leave the field for government, and then complain about the fact that the government will be planning your economy.

Trying to awaken a social conscience within U.S. business, I told my listeners not to be afraid of going into partnership with the government and urged them to make binding commitments to give a specific number of jobs to returning veterans after the war.

* * *

Personal and national concerns were thoroughly entwined in my life early in 1944. Hollace and I could not be together often. The love was still there, but perhaps she could not accept the growing intensity of my commitment toward the war and world human problems. In a sense she was living in a dream world, the world of theater, music, and singing; she did not feel the burning sense of mission that I did. We drifted apart, and early in 1944 she phoned me and told me it was all over. She had met someone else and was getting married. She did marry very shortly thereafter.

I had seen it coming, of course, but it was a deeply unhappy ending. Hollace married twice, never had children, and died when she was about sixty. The failure of our venture in love may have unmade her life; I know it changed mine. Our love was genuine and it was not finally consummated, and what that does to one I really do not know, but I am sure it leaves a scar. Only with hindsight do I realize Hollace and I might not have been happy together. At the time I had no doubts that we could have made it. I was sure that Hollace, as a decent and caring person, would have listened to those voices that I urged her to hear. As I saw it, the real reason for our breakup was the fact that we had not been able to marry two years earlier, and the cause of that was the deep-seated sectarianism of her parents.

Despite the prejudices I knew to exist around me, I had never blamed prejudice for any of my losses. I had been educated, had earned friends and clients and a good living as a lawyer, and had won an army commission and post on the strength of my own abilities. Hollace represented the first time I had been thwarted because I was Jewish. It hurt deeply. The intolerable aspect of this experience was that the nation had sent the cream of its youth to die in the fight against the barbarous principle of racial superiority, while at home countless people who considered themselves good and religious Americans were not above practicing a polite, less lethal version of the same cruel principle. And I did not have to look far, of course, to see that discrimination against Jews was as nothing compared to discrimination against blacks.

In June 1944 I put these thoughts into a long article I hoped to get published. It was titled "Do We Mean It?" — that is, do we mean what we say about the freedom of religion and speech and the individual rights guaranteed in the Bill of Rights? The point of the article was that the "Nazi philosophy . . . had found some fertile soil in our country," that Jews and Negroes were not getting a fair deal, and that the essence of the United States is the constitutional guarantee of equal rights for all citizens regardless of race, creed, or origin. And I called on citizens who were Christians to be aware that rights to be enjoyed by any must be enjoyed by all, and to demonstrate that every citizen is valued by his neighbor regardless of origin or creed.

The article was too long, repetitive, and somewhat rambling; it was never published. I sent it to some of my friends for comment and was disappointed to find that many of them, Jews included, felt that it would be dangerous and divisive to publish such views in the middle of a war, especially with a presidential election about to take place. I never got around to rewriting or condensing the article, and it had no impact whatever. But it did help me clarify the thinking that led to my Senate civil rights work in behalf of blacks and other minorities. The gist of that thinking was the conviction that what happens to any minority happens to every minority.

After the invasion of Normandy the CWS focused its main attention on the Pacific, where General MacArthur was getting ready to return to the Philippines. We were worried that the hard-pressed Japanese might resort to gas warfare. To make sure that our own gas warfare policies were understood by our forces and that our depots and supplies were prepared for all contingencies, and also to help with the planning for the Philippines, General Waitt and I set out in September 1944 for a two-month tour of the Pacific. Our depots and bases and mortar battalions were spread out on scores of islands, and it seemed to me that we visited them all, pausing on occasion to look with mixed reverence and horror at the battlefields on Guadalcanal, Tarawa, Kwajalein, and Saipan.

On Bougainville, one of our 4.2 mortar battalions was still on a combat front. The heaviest fighting was over and our troops had "secured" the large beachhead area, but organized units of the Japanese army prowled the interior of the island and occasionally attacked our perimeter. As we picked our way among the dugouts and trenches of this jungled area, we found our soldiers casually reading and sunning themselves on top of their bunkers though they knew they might have to dive for cover at any moment. The casual way they risked death in order to relax a bit in the jungle mud reminded me of what peace meant and how men will try to find it even in the midst of war. When my general addressed an assembly of our battalion the men were grim and serious. There was no room for kidding on the subject of "the weapon."

Finschhafen, in New Guinea, was a major supply area where we had several chemical depots. It was ninety thousand men in a sea of mud miring a billion dollars in equipment. As we traveled for two days from unit to unit through an unceasing rain, each unit we visited was better prepared for the general's inspection than the one before. The first units were in only fair shape, but they passed the word that we were coming and by the time we arrived at the last one everything looked spick-and-span despite the mud. The proverbial army sergeants' grapevine was really functioning.

My private notes on this trip included some candid comments on the generals and admirals we met. At Admiral Chester Nimitz's headquarters in Pearl Harbor I noted that the officers of the naval staff were "cool, clear-headed Jap haters." Of General MacArthur's head-quarters above Hollandia, New Guinea, I wrote: "GHQ on the mountain top. MacArthur's staff.... It does get done though it looks cumbersome. The general sees few people. Everything goes through the chief of staff. Pentagon coolness and alertness to power in New Guinea. The generals have a private mess."

MacArthur's great air force commander, Lieutenant General George Kenney, however, made a cockily wrong prediction: The war against Japan will end first, he said, because the Japanese will know they are licked when we take the Philippines and they will sue for peace; then, he said, his air force boys will go to Europe to show them how to clean it up.

We spent two glorious weeks in Australia inspecting our depots and conferring with Australian army officers — who always made sure their Yank friends had a good time in their country. I was certainly in a position to appreciate it: I may not have been footloose, but in the wake of the breakup with Hollace I was certainly fancy-free, and the Australian women were a delight. My trip notes convey my mood and inclinations:

Melbourne ... the girls are so pretty with flaxen hair and delicate tint of the peaches bloom in clear white skin. They are so healthy and so happy.... Rosemary is very English.... We tear up the dance floor at the Embassy — we even jitterbug.... Jean is a very dear girl with all the best softness of touch of Australian woman-hood. She is kind and devoted.... There are no cabs after 12:30 and the trains are very intermittent. We take a horse-drawn cart — We rattle and clatter and creak. Jean and I are snug inside — she is such a dear. She lives in a cottage surrounded by flowers, the stars twinkle as we part. We do not like it at all but it is very late.

Sydney ... I come upon a vision while we are out shopping. She is a perfect beauty and I cannot rest until we arrange for supper.... Afternoon in the harbor and CO's boat ... we go up a fjord. Homes and gardens come right down to the water's edge, the whole inlet is deep blue water, the gardens are fresh with flowers, the hills green with trees and verdure — for a moment I wish for my vision, or Jean, and such a home and lots of children — so good and so unlikely for me ... supper and the vision. She is not only beautiful, she feels so good and dances so well. I'm afraid she's a little taken aback by my enthusiasm. Well, it is high time I had some....

Brisbane ... we have a supper party and we sing and sing and sing. . . . U.S. and WACS and Australia all arm in arm down Queen Street — why general! — to the tune of the strawberry blonde. . . . The moon is full and the sea and the world brighter than I ever have seen them — oh, for my love this night!

There were two moments of intense personal emotion on my Pacific tour. On the island of Biak I went alone to visit the military cemetery. Jim Shaw, Hollace's brother, who had served as an army chaplain, had been killed on the island a few weeks earlier. When I found the neat cross that marked his grave, my heart stood still: On the grave next to it was a Star of David. How sad, I thought, and perhaps how fitting, that Jim should be resting here beside a Jewish soldier. I could have been bitter, I suppose; I could have made a point of telling his parents that the Jews who were not good enough to marry their daughters were good enough to die with their sons. But I do not think I felt that. I picked up a few stones from Jim Shaw's grave and took them with me to send to his family. He had been a fine young man, dedicated to his beliefs, and I could only mourn him as I mourned his comrades.

Near Hollandia, I experienced another poignant moment. In a borrowed jeep I was driving alone from headquarters to Lake Sentani, where I had been told I could have a swim. It was a clear, crisp day on the plateau, there were many jeeps and trucks on the wide, hard-packed dirt road, and the blue waters of the lake reflected the mountain ridges. As I drove along I became aware of where I was and why, and I suddenly felt free, felt that finally I was doing what a man ought to do and what was right: In this remote place, knowing my job, having been through mud and privation, and having seen so much tragedy, I was joined with other men in a common effort for a just cause. As a sense of liberation surged through me, I knew this was right, that I was, at the mature age of forty, finding myself, perhaps for the first time, as an independent man in free association with others. I had finally broken free of the series of ties of love and control that had dominated me all my life.

To this moment of exultation and revelation there must be added a small anticlimax. I never did get to swim that day. The medics had declared the lake off limits because of harmful bacteria in the water.

When I returned to Washington in November 1944, I plunged into another series of high-level assessments of gas warfare. Although it was clear we were winning the war, we knew that our enemies had lethal gas available, and it was feared that in their desperation they might use it. Again we asked ourselves whether we should use it first, and again the answer was no: Gas would not be decisive, the moral offense to the world made it prohibitive, and if the enemy retaliated we could be hurt as much as he was. So we carefully investigated every alleged use of gas (no deliberate use of lethal gases was ever substantiated) and we maintained our readiness to retaliate. We even invented new techniques of gas warfare, just in case. I am convinced that the Japanese and Germans did not use poison gas because they knew our response would be powerful and effective.

In all of these cool and rational assessments, I always came down on the side of those who recommended that we not use gas unless it was used against us first. But there was one angry moment when my hatred of the enemy had conquered my reason and put me on the other side. It was in Guadalcanal, during my Pacific tour. General Waitt and I had just come from Bougainville and I had heard the men speak of the fanaticism of the enemy — particularly of a Japanese officer who, they said, had shot two of his own soldiers in order to use their bodies as shields. On the hallowed ground of Guadalcanal I picked up some of the soldier's fighting emotion that the lawyer in me would not have approved — and the thoughts that I scribbled that evening certainly do not represent my feelings today. I cite them here to show what war could do even to the thinking and civilized man I considered myself to be. I wrote:

> ... These Japs are an incubus. They think, if they do at all, in an equation we do not comprehend; their God is death and not life. We must break them and their power.... I am bitter clean through and consider the Great Design. I must strike from where I am, this powder puffing with the army will not do. If our stuff will do the job we must marshal world opinion to allow it. The Jap wants to lose millions in battle, we do not.... I tell Gen. W. something of this; he is not too sure, the conception is pretty powerful, there is time to let it sink in. My general will I am sure be convinced, for he believes in the weapon as decisive, but he wants to get in close — good.

I must have been beside myself at that point. That is what torn-up bodies and torn-up lands and all that misery can do. I regarded the Japanese then as incomprehensible beasts — but later I became the author of the bill establishing the U.S.–Japan Friendship Commission. I can understand why I had moments like that, even though it was my conviction not to use poison gas unless it was used against us; my considered judgment at that point had more to do with the practicality of our own defenses than with the moral element.

These sensitive questions led directly to my final military assignment. Early in 1945, we heard that at the founding conference of the

United Nations, to be held in San Francisco in April, an effort would be made to outlaw poison gas. Since we still had Japan to defeat, the Chemical Warfare Service was concerned that such a prohibition would tie our hands while leaving Japan free to use gas against us. We needed to be kept informed about any move to outlaw poison gas at the United Nations conference so that we could point out to the U.S. political leaders how such a ban might be dangerous to the United States.

It was generally agreed within the CWS that I was in the best position to observe the United Nations conference, since it had already been decided that I would be released from active duty early, in order to take on a special public-affairs advisory job. So on April 3, 1945, I went on terminal leave from the army and on June 13 I was released from active duty. During those two months, while technically on terminal leave, I attended the United Nations organizing conference and reported on it unofficially to the Chemical Warfare Service. As it happened, the ban on gas warfare was never seriously considered, but my reports earned me a special letter of commendation from my superior, General Waitt.

When I finally took off my uniform in June 1945, I knew I would never be satisfied again with just lawyering in New York. The war, my part in it, and the business and political friends I had made in the fascinating power center of Washington had broken my relatively parochial professional horizons and opened a much wider world to me, a world where individuals put their stamp on their times. I knew I would have to devote the rest of my life in some way to the larger issues that concerned mankind, the issues of peace and war, prosperity and depression, management and labor, and the welfare of the men and women whose sufferings I had seen. Just how I would do this, I did not know, but I was sure I would be effective. All I had to do now was decide which way to go.

SIX

Searching for a Role

Nineteen forty-five, the year of victory and new challenges for civilization, was a year of fresh opportunities for me. I felt I was at that stage in my life where maturity of experience and zest for living are in harmonious balance: I was old enough to know my own mind and young enough to act spontaneously.

Among the many friends and associates eager to give me advice or to invite me to work with them was Charles Wilson, president of the General Electric Company. It was Wilson's suggestion that I take on the special public-affairs advisory post with GE that led to my early release from active duty: My army superiors thought it would be useful to have someone with my wartime experience advising a great enterprise such as GE during the difficult transition from a wartime to a peacetime economy and were willing to release me for that job.

The General Electric project developed from Ben's ideas. I still had faith in his vision of shareholder democracy and "business in the public interest," and he began to see me as a spokesman who would disseminate his economic philosophy to the world. Ben's thesis was that the millions of stockholders in the United States, if organized and informed, could make business operate in the public interest and that then the business community, free of government interference, could be counted on to bring about economic prosperity and social welfare for all.

He and I were concerned about the trend toward government regulation, and we saw a threat to the free-enterprise system in the growing number of Americans who worked for government rather than for private business. We did not so much fear nationalization as we thought that excessive regulation of business by government might lead by degrees to nationalization even if nobody wanted it. I was not so certain as Ben was of the essential goodness of businessmen; but I felt — and still feel — that business could avoid excessive regulation by taking more responsibility itself for introducing such programs as health plans, pensions, in-plant manpower training to upgrade workers' skills, and profit sharing and stock ownership by workers.

My first attempt to do something with these ideas was to draft a proposal for a new business journal. The editorial ideas for it were not highly developed, but its philosophy was clearly expressed in a prospectus I wrote in January 1945. The private-enterprise system, the prospectus declared, is the key to the American system; if "the political power is joined with the power over jobs and the economy, the U.S. society as we know it will have ended"; but business managers can increasingly become trustees of the public interest through the widespread ownership of U.S. business.

The publication never got off the ground; we couldn't find sufficient financial backing. But Wilson seemed to offer another outlet for these concepts. I would organize a consulting firm that would help General Electric and a few other selected clients to pinpoint the areas and the projects in which they could do more for the welfare of the U.S. economy in general and for their workers in particular, acting in concert with government in a new way. Wilson had agreed, in theory. As soon as I went on terminal leave from the army, in April 1945, he asked me to present my ideas in written form for the benefit of the General Electric board of directors.

I sat in my room at New York's Ambassador Hotel and on hotel notepaper set down the outline for what I called the Bureau of Public Relations, Inc. The prospectus for the Bureau of Public Relations, which I sent to Charlie Wilson a week or so later, emphasized that the firm would serve only large corporations whose operations had significant effect on the national economy. Furthermore, the only clients would be companies that recognized "their public responsibility for the continuous and equitable operation of the economic system. . . . The idea is that business is the servant of the social order."

My bureau was to be like no other public-relations firm I had heard of. Starting from the premise that my clients would want to promote full employment, greater productivity, lower prices, higher real wages, and an expanding world economy — an idealistic premise, to be sure — my role as I saw it was to identify the specific areas and issues in which the corporations could make such contributions to the public interest. I wanted to shape my clients' policies regarding antitrust laws, labor, social security, and tariffs, and to influence their relations with the government, with consumer groups, with farmers, and with unions. I stressed cooperation between the various segments of the economy and underlined the need to educate and inspire youth with the realization of the possibilities of business. I did not neglect the more familiar public-relations activities — creating public awareness of "what makes the wheels turn" — but I was aiming much higher than that. "By retaining the bureau," my memorandum concluded, "our clients identify themselves with the proposition that the surest guarantee of the American constitutional system is an effective, successful and democratic private-enterprise system for our economy — side by side with our constitutional political democratic government." I was asking U.S. business to enter a new era of public responsibility leading to prosperity for everybody. It was to me an ambitious and dazzling concept.

My memo caused some consternation at GE corporate headquarters. Charlie called me and told me it might take some weeks or months before the corporation would agree to retain my firm. Wilson himself was receptive, but his company bureaucracy was resisting too strongly for him to try to push the project through on his own authority. Part of the objection may have stemmed from jealousy on the part of GE's own public-relations officials — although I had carefully explained that my activities would enlarge the scope of their job, not diminish it. The main objection was ideological: Too many people in the company saw a conflict between their traditional ideas of corporate profit and my philosophy of business in the public interest. These people would have to be handled with care.

I was impatient at the delay. I have always found that you solve problems by plunging into them — not by sinking your head in your hands and thinking about them abstractly. So on April 20 I wrote Wilson:

When we talked about clearing through your organization neither of us anticipated negotiations or months of a selling campaign. . . . Under the circumstances would you permit me immediately on my return to get started handling your *personal* public relations (assuming that GE will not then be ready to retain my firm itself)? Then at least I will be in business with one client, yourself. That is not the easy way, but it is the best. I have had this experience in the army where I started just that way with General Porter — and before. . . . Once this is done I'm sure we will all feel much better and begin to see daylight. . . . My organization could start by advising you upon and handling your personal speaking dates, statements, articles and broadcasts. . . . We would consult with GE public relations and coordinate with them. . . . Please think of that old and thrilling football yell, "Let's go!"

I wrote that letter from Chicago, on a layover between trains, and I put it out of my mind as I continued my journey. I was on my way to San Francisco for the founding conference of the United Nations, and I was exhilarated at the prospect of seeing history made. Here was the culmination of all our efforts and wartime bloodshed. Here the hopes for a peaceful world would be shaped, we all thought, into an effective and durable structure. My work in Washington had already infected me with Potomac fever, that obsessive attraction to the capital, to the center of important affairs. Now San Francisco, for a few weeks, would be the capital of the world. Government leaders from Washington and from fifty nations were gathering at the San Francisco Opera House. Representatives from dozens of U.S. business, labor, religious, educational, and veterans' organizations, all designated as consultants to the U.S. delegation, were also converging on the city for this portentous event. I had wanted very much to be there and was thrilled that I had found a means of going.

Unofficially, as an officer on terminal leave, I was observing the conference for the Chemical Warfare Service. My status at the conference was as a journalist. Leigh Danenberg, the publisher of the Bridgeport, Connecticut, *Sunday Herald,* had appointed me a special unpaid correspondent for his paper so that I could attend the sessions as a member of the press. On the train between Chicago and San Francisco I conscientiously wrote my first article for the *Herald.* President Roosevelt had died just eight days earlier, and my story applauded President Truman for going ahead with the conference. As journalism, it was not a very exciting or newsy article, and it was not published. It did represent another earnest attempt to communicate the theories about the relationship between government and the economy that were crystallizing in my mind.

The transcontinental train arrived in Oakland in the early evening of April 22 and I boarded the ferry for the ride across San Francisco Bay. It was a gorgeous evening. I stood on the forward end of the lower deck admiring the hills and tall buildings of San Francisco's skyline in the twilight and felt full of anticipation of the momentous events to which I would soon be witness. A young man stood next to me; I had a vague recollection of having seen him at some social gathering in New York and we had most likely exchanged some casual greetings on the train. We leaned on the rail of the ferry, admiring the view of the city and perhaps mentioning the UN conference. All I knew about him was that he was a pleasant young man whom I met on the ferry; we parted at the dock in San Francisco. Eleven years later, in a blaze of publicity, I would learn that his name was Fred Field and that he was a writer for the Communist Party newspaper *The Daily Worker.*

Good friends in San Francisco went out of their way to make my three-week visit to their city both pleasant and productive. I stayed with Harold and Doris Zellerbach on Jackson Street — remembering to bring along and give them some food-ration stamps, as all good house guests did in those days. I felt comfortably at home with the Zellerbachs. By California standards they were an old family. Harold's grandfather had come to California in the gold rush of 1849 and soon was selling the paper bags used to package the gold dust. His business developed into one of America's great pulp and paper manufacturing concerns, the Crown Zellerbach Corporation. The Zellerbachs' lifestyle was pure California: a great attention to life's pleasant details, a sunny and colorful house, good food, lots of sports, warm friendships, and a happy and sharing family. I spent a great deal of time with them and with two of their lawyers, Philip S. Ehrlich and Bartley C. Crum.

My conversations with Phil Ehrlich explored a new and intriguing professional opportunity. Phil was a San Francisco lawyer whose principal client was the Crown Zellerbach Corporation. We had come to know each other well when we settled an antitrust case for the company before the war, and during the war my continuing contacts with the Zellerbachs had kept me in touch with Ehrlich. Phil knew that I was not enthusiastic about a return to lawyering in New York, and he suggested that I move to San Francisco and become a partner in his firm, with a guaranteed drawing of $75,000 per year. It was a generous and attractive offer and I considered it seriously. I did not know what I was going to do if the Bureau of Public Relations foundered, and San Francisco would certainly provide a break from the past.

Ehrlich set about "selling" me San Francisco. We discussed not only his legal practice but the social and personal amenities that I would find in his enchanting city. He thought of everything. Like many of my friends, Phil knew of my disappointing experience with Hollace Shaw; he was aware that there was no important woman in my life at the moment but that I was thinking about marriage and a family. He suggested that I might find some interest in a young woman client of his who had just inherited millions. Phil was frankly trying to arrange a *shiddach,* a match. He described the woman in question, Louise Bransten, as bright, divorced, concerned with the political issues of the day, and attractive; her inheritance, he thought, certainly did not detract from her charm.

I was curious and intrigued, so I arranged to have a drink with

Louise Bransten in the cocktail lounge of the Mark Hopkins Hotel. She kept me waiting for more than an hour and I was annoyed. Perhaps her tardiness had upset me, or maybe we were both embarrassed by Phil's introduction and what it suggested. She was a slender and willowy woman who affected a plainness that was somehow disturbing and which I did not understand. I have a dim memory of her sitting in a high-backed chair in the cocktail lounge of the Mark Hopkins as we had a drink and tried to make intelligent conversation. She seemed to be knowledgeable about the issues of the UN conference and listened, I thought with interest, to my views. We did not make much of an impression on each other, however. I suppose it was in deference to Phil Ehrlich, and perhaps to get to know me a little better, that she invited me to a party at her home, and I suppose for the same reason I accepted.

I have no clear recollection of that party and no notes of any sort to confirm that I went to it, but, apparently, I did. I remember, vaguely, wood-paneled walls and I recollect also that something about that gathering — either the other participants or the conversation or perhaps just the awkward circumstances of how I happened to be there — made me feel very uncomfortable. I did not stay long. I do not believe I saw Louise Bransten again in San Francisco, and I know that I ran into her only once, years later, in a grocery store on University Place in New York. But that innocent, entirely unmemorable evening at her home in San Francisco would also come back to haunt me eleven years later.

Another old friend in San Francisco was Bartley C. Crum, a liberal Republican lawyer who was associated with Ehrlich in his law practice. In the 1930s Crum had represented the William Randolph Hearst organization and had worked with the famous trial lawyer Clarence Darrow; in 1953, in his most celebrated case, Crum won a million dollars for the actress Rita Hayworth in her divorce from Prince Aly Khan. But Bart Crum spent most of his time and energy as a firm supporter of civil liberties, altruistically supporting progressive — and often unpopular — causes. He had represented the leftist West Coast labor leader Harry Bridges in his successful fight to avoid deportation, and later he was to oppose the attempt to outlaw the Communist Party. On the latter occasion Bart stated his creed succinctly: "It is unconstitutional and utterly stupid for government to attempt to prevent people from thinking and believing as they wish. . . . As a non-Communist I think the most effective answer to the Marxists is to make our democracy work by providing equality and job opportunities for all." It was characteristic of Bart Crum that of all the friends to whom I showed my 1944 discrimination article — "Do We Mean It?" — he was one of the few who responded enthusiastically, "in wholehearted agreement with what you say and the need that it should be said."

In 1945, Harold Zellerbach and Phil Ehrlich were trying to help Bart by getting him appointed West Coast attorney for the Reconstruction Finance Corporation, a federal agency, and I had lobbied some of my Washington contacts on his behalf. But, as usual, Bart himself was more interested in a cause, one that became an abiding issue for me. He was dedicated to finding a homeland for the Jewish people; later he served as a member of the Anglo-American Committee of Inquiry on Palestine, which urged the British to honor the Balfour Declaration of 1917 promising that Palestine would become a Jewish state. Previously, I had supported a Jewish homeland, but my support became devotion to the cause as the result of what I heard and saw in San Francisco, and thanks to Bart Crum, a Catholic.

The failure of the United States and other countries to take in many of the Jewish refugees of Nazi persecution had deeply agitated many Americans, including me, who realized that if the Jews had had a homeland to which to escape, many of Hitler's victims would have been able to survive. The Jewish organizations of the United States wanted the United Nations to provide for a Jewish homeland — or at least not to block it. Through Bart Crum and David Zellerbach, I met two leaders of the American Jewish Committee who were involved in this endeavor. They were Joseph Proskauer, a leading New York lawyer, and Jacob Blaustein, the head of the American Oil Company of Baltimore. Proskauer and Blaustein were deeply involved in complex negotiations aimed at persuading the British to turn over some of their colonial territory in Palestine, which they held under a League of Nations mandate dating from World War I, to a new Jewish state. I, of course, was only an observer in these negotiations and conversations, but as I got an inside view of them I began to realize how important this effort was to the future of the harassed Jewish people. Proskauer and Blaustein succeeded in getting the United States to strongly support a declaration of human rights in the UN charter, and in warding off all attempts to block a Jewish state in Palestine. As I listened to these men I absorbed much of their zeal and dedication, and I began to see the power of their dream. Thus these meetings in San Francisco in the spring of 1945 helped to strengthen my support for the founding of the state of Israel. It has been an important issue in my public life ever since.

I spent my three weeks in San Francisco attending many of the sessions of the conference, sending back several reports to the Bridge-port *Herald* (none of which was published — notice that journalism was not my game), and informing the CWS that the poison-gas convention issue would probably not arise. I continued to be fascinated by the growing interest in the United Nations' Economic and Social Council, an interest matching my conviction that peace could only be guaranteed if the health of the world's economy was also assured. I was beginning to realize that I would be expending a great deal of effort on this issue in later years. But I do not think I would have dreamed at that moment that within two years, as a member of the Congress of the United States, I would be voting to send massive amounts of U.S. economic aid to Europe.

The conference also gave me a firsthand view of many political leaders, journalists, and diplomats, from the United States and foreign countries, whom I would come to know well. Many achieved prominence — or notoriety — of their own. John Foster Dulles was there as an adviser to the U.S. delegation; Nelson Rockefeller, then the coordinator of Inter-American Affairs, played host on a grand scale to many delegates from Latin America. (John F. Kennedy was also present, on a newspaper assignment as I was, but I do not think I met him.) The secretary-general of the conference, the man responsible for keeping all the wheels turning, was Alger Hiss, of the State Department. He struck me as a man very sure of himself, certain of his own position and social acceptance. My impression of Hiss made it hard for me to comprehend him as a Communist agent. As a lawyer I have learned that outward appearances can be deceptive, but I can understand those who could never bring themselves to believe the charges against Hiss: The impression he made just did not tally with the accusations.

The conference did not finish its work until the end of June, but I returned to New York in the middle of May. Away from the spell of San Francisco, I realized that my life was not there. My roots, my connections, and my experience were all in New York; I was a New Yorker inside and out, and I felt that I had to keep my base where it was. With regret, I wrote to Phil Ehrlich declining his very generous offer. And that was progress of a sort: At least I had discovered one thing I did *not* want to do.

Negotiations with Charlie Wilson were still at an impasse. Wilson had accepted my idea that I join him as his P.R. assistant, but his board of directors would not accept my conditions. I knew I needed some degree of autonomy from the board. I would be subordinate to Wilson, but I wanted the board to guarantee me a certain term of office. The point was that I foresaw many of the directors might not agree with my ideas, and I did not want them to be able to get rid of me as soon as I suggested something they did not like. I could not accept the idea of working for the corporation as another cog in their machine, and the whole idea of working for General Electric had to be dropped. Had I gone to work for Wilson I might never have entered politics.

Ben, of course, was anxious to have me continue to work with him. He was spending more and more of his time with the Investors Fairplay League, an organization of stockholders through which he hoped to turn business toward the public interest. When the General Electric project fell through, Ben suggested that I take control of Javits & Javits while he remained in the firm as counsel, which meant that he would be available for consultations but would not do any major legal work. As late as August 1945, after spending some time on the beach in East Hampton, Long Island, I was still giving this notion serious thought. But in the back of my mind I knew it would not work. At fifty-one years of age, Ben was still very vigorous; he would have tried to run the firm from the position of counsel and I would have been back where I started. So there was really no choice. I had to be on my own.

It was then that New York politics claimed my attention. Another mayoral campaign was beginning and the Republican Party had nominated Judge Jonah Goldstein, a friend of mine and Ben's. Goldstein also had the endorsement of the Fusion Party, which had supported Mayor Fiorello La Guardia in the past. Opposing Goldstein on the Democratic line was William O'Dwyer, the Tammany Hall candidate.

This was an interesting campaign because, on both sides, forces that had worked together in the past were split and new alliances were formed. The "good-government" anti-Tammany leaders represented by the Fusion Party were split by La Guardia, who was piqued because the Republican and Fusion parties had not nominated him.

La Guardia had long been an idol of mine. Dedicated to reform, believing in municipal help for the underprivileged, and aware of New York's new role as the world's premier city, he had accomplished a great deal in his three terms as mayor. But by 1945 he seemed to feel that New York had come to the point where it could not get along without him or his hand-picked successor. Everybody else, he said, was a "stooge" or a "phony." Instead of placing his influence and support behind Judge Goldstein, the reform candidate, La Guardia insisted on putting up his own candidate, Newbold Morris, who had served as city council president for eight years. Morris was a good man, but his presence as a third candidate in the race seriously divided the good-government forces that were trying to remove Tammany Hall permanently from control of New York City.

There was also a split on the Democratic side. The American Labor Party (ALP), which had supported Franklin D. Roosevelt, the New Deal, and the war, had moved sharply to the left and was accused of being under the control of the Communist Party. Certainly the ALP, which had little strength outside New York City, echoed the policies of the Soviet Union. In 1944, a group of moderate, non-Communist labor leaders and ALP politicians, led by David Dubinsky, president of the International Ladies' Garment Workers' Union, and Alex Rose, president of the Hatters' Union, broke away from the ALP to form the Liberal Party. (It is a mark of the good sense of New York voters that the Liberal Party is still with us, while the ALP has long since passed into oblivion.) In the 1945 campaign, the ALP supported the Tammany candidate William O'Dwyer; the new, much smaller Liberal Party endorsed Judge Goldstein. Thus the three candidates for mayor were the Republican-Fusion-Liberal, Jonah Goldstein; the Democratic–American Labor candidate, William O'Dwyer; and La Guardia's "No Deal" Party candidate, Newbold Morris, a late but important entry.

Despite my continuing admiration for La Guardia's achievements and for him, I could not support him. His obsession with having his own way, it seemed to me, was wrecking the chances of the good-government forces. I felt very sad that La Guardia seemed momentarily blinded to the real issues. My impression is that he came to regret 1945, too. Years later, I happened to run into him when he was visiting the House of Representatives, where he had once served. We greeted each other warmly and I asked him, "Well, Mr. Mayor, what do you think of this place now?" He looked around and said, "Well, Jack, I don't know why I ever left it."

I think it was Ben who first suggested that I work for Goldstein's campaign. We went to see Goldstein and his campaign managers at their headquarters at the old Astor Hotel on Times Square, and it was all arranged very quickly. My legal and army experience as well as my work in La Guardia's prewar campaigns certainly qualified me to take a role in this campaign. Goldstein needed a research director and I was immediately appointed to that post.

It was an ideal job for me; it not only trained me for the future, it gave me a chance to plunge into a cause. As research director it was my task to analyze the pros and cons of all the campaign issues, to help the candidate formulate his positions and platform, and to provide him with the information that he needed for his speeches.

It is with some nostalgia that I reread our campaign literature and note that we promised to preserve New York City's five-cent transit fare "because the subway is not a business but a public conveyance." Another issue on which I concentrated was our proposal to establish a city department of commerce that would promote economic development by bringing in more jobs and industry, creating full employment for the city's workers, establishing facilities for foreign trade, and enhancing the city's position as the center of culture, music, theater, and fashion. It is interesting to note thirty-five years later that New York City has as yet been unable to effectively unite its diverse interests — especially its business interests — to coordinate redevelopment, as smaller cities such as Boston, Philadelphia, Pittsburgh, Atlanta, San Francisco, Houston, and Dallas have done. New York, I suppose, may be just too big for that kind of civic development plan, and many of its businessmen and politicians necessarily think not in terms of the city alone but of the country and the world. But I am not ready to give up on this endeavor.

We ran a hard-hitting campaign attacking both of Goldstein's opponents. We urged the voters not to waste their ballots on Morris, "La Guardia's stooge and water boy," the "kamikaze candidate," who didn't have a chance of survival. But our biggest guns were trained on O'Dwyer, particularly on our charge that his ALP supporters were Communist-dominated. Most of the speeches of the Goldstein supporters — and I wrote a number of them — hit hard on the theme that O'Dwyer represented an unholy alliance between Tammany and the pro-Communist forces. The substance of our position became clear on September 18, when the Communist Party itself formally came out in support of the ALP and of candidate O'Dwyer. (It is ironic that years later I was accused of having worked *with* the ALP in the late 1940s; my accusers conveniently chose to ignore the fact that in 1945 I was working actively and energetically *against* the ALP and pointing out its pro-Communist affiliations.)

The Goldstein campaign marked my formal entry into New York politics and the inner circles of the New York Republican Party. As Goldstein's research director I met the important leaders of the Republican and Liberal parties. I sat in on the meetings of the top campaign staff and became well acquainted with all of them. Arthur Schwartz, who later became a New York Supreme Court judge, was counsel to the New York Republicans and served as the unofficial, backroom manager for the Republican side of Goldstein's organization. Years later, Schwartz commented on how the campaign affected me: "I could sense that Jack Javits liked this kind of life. Politics is like a disease, and he got infected with it in the 1945 campaign."

Two other men who attended those campaign strategy meetings at the Astor Hotel and who had a very significant impact on my later career were Alex Rose and David Dubinsky, of the Liberal Party. I had already met both of them, but during this campaign I got to know them on a first-name basis. The following year, when I came to them for assistance in my own first campaign, they quickly agreed to help.

Dubinsky and Rose were labor leaders, not politicians, but the requirements are similar and they turned out to be effective in both roles. Alex Rose became a master political strategist, manipulating the relatively limited manpower resources of the Liberal Party so brilliantly that he made the party and himself serious factors in municipal, state, and even national elections. David Dubinsky, whose union provided the Liberal Party's manpower and money, was the king who treated Alex Rose as his grand vizier.

Still another fateful meeting took place in Goldstein's campaign headquarters, one that had nothing to do with politics. On my first day aboard the campaign, I was given the number of a room down the hall and told to set up my office in it. When I got there I found the office already occupied — by a very attractive and spirited young woman who informed me she was the secretary to Judge Nicholas Pette (the candidate for city council president on Goldstein's ticket) and that this was *his* office. We chatted briefly as we waited for the mix-up to be straightened out and I learned that she was an aspiring actress working as a secretary just for the campaign. Her name was Marian Borris, and two years later she was to become Marian Javits.

Marian and I went out together several times during and immediately after the campaign. I took her to a concert to hear Artur Rubinstein, we went dancing at the Ambassador Hotel, and we found each other very congenial. She came from a poor family, as I had, and, although she was only a little more than half my age at the time, she had sufficient strength of character and self-assurance not to be intimidated by my years and experience. She had strong political ideas of her own, so she was not put off by my favorite topic of conversation, as many women might have been.

Toward the end of the campaign Judge Pette asked Marian to arrange a cocktail party for his campaign volunteers. She had worked for the Astor Hotel so she knew what to do; besides, she was — and is — an instinctively gifted hostess. It turned out to be an excellent party and I was very impressed by the way Marian managed it all. The food and drinks were just right and the guests — mostly campaign volunteers — blended together easily under the influence of her warmth and friendliness. I, too, was planning to give a party, on the eve of election day at my new sublet apartment on West Twelfth Street just off Fifth Avenue, and I asked Marian to take over. That occasion was also very successful, thanks to Marian's skill as a hostess. But soon after the campaign we stopped seeing each other. At the time Marian was as committed to her acting ambitions as I was to political and economic affairs, and I saw this as a warning flag.

During the campaign I was still pursuing other possible projects. The Bureau of Public Relations was not completely dead, even though it was now certain I would not be working with General Electric: In September we actually began the legal steps to set up the bureau. Harold Zellerbach and Dave Niles came to New York, I went to Washington once or twice, and we discussed my future and Bart Crum's. I find in my files a puzzling but amusing letter I wrote to Dave Niles. It was dated October 29, 1945, and was apparently written on a Goldstein-for-Mayor campaign letterhead. Niles, it must be remembered, was an ardent Democrat, and FDR's assistant.

> Dear Friend: Receipt is acknowledged of your campaign contribution of twenty cents in unused railroad ticket coupons and an empty envelope of Sen Sen.
>
> It is clear that it was your intention to be very helpful in the campaign of our candidate for the mayoralty and we appreciate your interest very much. We do hope that when it comes to backing a gubernatorial and presidential candidate, you will continue your support and perhaps by then events will make it possible for you to increase it.
>
> Faithfully yours,
> J. K. JAVITS
> *Director of Research*

Despite our efforts, Jonah Goldstein was defeated and Bill O'Dwyer was elected mayor of New York. As we had feared, La Guardia's "kamikaze candidate," Newbold Morris, had taken away votes that might otherwise have given Goldstein a victory. The campaign had been tremendously stimulating, but I was weary and needed to think, away from the city, from my brother, and from friends. As Arthur Schwartz has said, I had been seized by the political fever, but whether it would cure itself or become chronic was still unknown.

In December I set off, alone, on a four-week trip through Mexico and Guatemala, visiting the Mayan ruins at Chichén Itzá, and Chichicastenago. Considering all my options, I felt that I had done a good job for Goldstein, that my particular talents were congenial to politics, and that a political life was wide open to me. Here, I began to see, was the role I had been searching for; in no other capacity could I better serve my state, my country, my world — and peace.

I recognized the hazards of public life: risk of sharp criticism and stern opposition, diminished earning power, hard work, profound disappointments and frustrations, and limited personal life.

I saw the rewards: a chance to make an impact on my times and on history, self-fulfillment for my talents, the opportunity to do good for people, and the opportunity to make a name and a reputation for myself and my posterity. The rewards outweighed the hazards.

The time was right. The war was over and many returning veterans were getting ready to run for office. A new era was beginning and I wanted to be part of it. When I returned to New York in January 1946, my mind was made up.

SEVEN

On the Stump

On the. whole, luck was with me in my campaigns for public office. My first run for the House and my first for the Senate both took place in years of Republican success, and after I had established a reputation as a vote getter it became easier to attract support and contributions, even from Republicans who did not share my views. Getting elected and reelected earned me the tolerance and respect — if not necessarily the affection — of most of the party's professionals, who came to realize that my presence on a Republican ticket could often strengthen it.

But I started out against the odds, capturing a congressional seat that had been Democratic for a generation, and I won elections against the tide as well as with it. I never relied particularly on charisma, nor did I generally carry the banner for one burning, emotional issue that could bewitch voters into following their hearts instead of their heads. I did not have the backing of a well-oiled political machine that could turn out the vote for me, nor did I possess — or command — vast funds to finance campaigns.

I believe my success in nine consecutive campaigns derived from two factors. One was the capacity to work long hours on a campaign at the cost of almost every other consideration, never assuming that the battle was won or lost until the polls closed and the votes were in. Such doggedness requires complete dedication, which means loving the job, all of it: the crowds, the handshaking, the speeches, the debates, the need to stay on top of the events of the day, the duels of words and ideas — and even the heckling. I did not say "liking" all this, I said "loving"; there is a difference. The second factor was the ability to grasp, analyze, and explain the central point of a complex issue so that the voter could understand the issue and my position even if he disagreed with me.

When I returned to New York from Mexico in January 1946 I had decided that Congress was the place for me, where I could make my mark; for the next ten months my every waking moment was devoted to the goal of getting elected. An obvious first target was my own boyhood Lower East Side, where a special election for Congress was scheduled in February to fill the seat of a congressman who had been appointed to the bench. I did not think I could win in that Democratic area in such a short campaign; but I hoped that if I could get the Republican nomination and make a respectable showing I would have a chance to win in November.

Arthur Schwartz, who had been impressed with my efforts in the Goldstein campaign, enthusiastically endorsed my aspirations. He introduced me to Sam Koenig, the Republican Party leader of Manhattan, and pointed out to Koenig that I could raise my own campaign funds without depending on the party. Koenig agreed that I should have the nomination in the special election, which he knew no Republican could possibly win, but the November nomination, he said, was out of the question because he had already promised his support to someone else. So the Lower East Side was a dead end, and I decided to look elsewhere for another Democratic district where the chances of a Republican victory might be slight — and where I, a neophyte, might be welcomed by the local Republican organization. At the same time, I wanted a district where the Democratic incumbent or the likely nominee was vulnerable to a strong challenge, to give me at least a fighting chance. Finally, I hoped, it would be a district compatible with my background and my liberal philosophy, and with which I had some previous connection.

Joined in this search by Arthur, whose knowledge of Manhattan Republican politics was vast, I set about attracting some attention to myself. In the absence of a warm-up special election, I needed another means of making my name and my views known, especially to Republicans. With Ben's help, I worked out an arrangement with the *New York Herald Tribune* by which I wrote a series of letters to the editor setting forth my political and economic philosophy. There were six letters, and the *Herald Tribune* ran them all, one a month, from February through August. Together they represented a complete statement of my views and outlined almost all of my later legislative interests. They also made it clear that I was an uncommon type of Republican for the time — what was then called a liberal Republican but which, by my own definition, was a progressive Republican. For I harkened back to the days of the La Follette Progressives between the wars, when the problems created by age, ill health, unemployment, lack of educational opportunities, and discrimination on grounds of race, creed, or color were major concerns for Republicans, equal to their interest in sound business and sound money.

The first letter, "The Veteran Looks at the Republican Party," criticized my party for giving lip service to the rights of labor while simultaneously voting for antilabor laws. The only way for the party to attract the votes of the homecoming veterans, I wrote, was to work for full employment, profit sharing, fair employment practices, and the acceptance of international responsibility for peace. In the second letter I emphasized my Republicanism: I predicted a conflict between the private business system and the proponents of a state economy and declared that the Republican Party was the logical defender of free enterprise. But the letter also urged investors to exercise their responsibilities of ownership by protesting antisocial policies — especially unfair antilabor policies — by managers of their enterprises. Only by remedying the "grave imperfections" in the business system, I said, can greater production, lower prices, and full prosperity be attained.

Another letter warned that the pent-up wartime demand for consumer goods, coupled with a high level of consumer savings, posed a grave threat of inflation. I urged consumers to invest in industry instead of buying high-priced goods, and I called upon the Republican Party to support the extension of wartime price controls until "production is reasonably adequate for current demand." The party did not take my advice and price control became a major issue in the campaign.

The fourth and fifth letters spelled out my views on the rights of labor and the need for business to act in the public interest. The Republican Party, I wrote, should take the lead in establishing a tripartite organization of employers, employees, and government, to give labor a greater share of profits and to ensure greater productivity. I declared that business managers are trustees in the public interest and should act accordingly by making collective bargaining effective and by fulfilling their responsibilities to consumers and the national economy as a whole; I warned that their failure to do this "must inevitably lead to a state ownership and control of business which Americans do not want." Commenting on one of the major issues of the day, I wrote that "in our national housing emergency, normal profit-making considerations by business should be put aside."

The final letter suggested a Republican foreign policy based on the elimination of hunger and the improvement of living standards of the whole world. "Economic development," I wrote, should be "our permanent approach to a world solution and we must start on it with at least the intensity with which we work on the political side." This proposal foreshadowed the Marshall Plan and other U.S. programs of economic aid that were soon to be established, but my plan would have offered aid to all countries, not just our ideological allies. Specifically, I proposed "that we start by lending Russia a billion dollars now — not later — for the production or purchase of more consumer goods." The Soviet Union, I pointed out, was no economic threat to the United States and could not use any money lent to it for war because its steel-producing capacity was so far below ours. Had this startling proposal been implemented, the history of the postwar era might have turned out somewhat differently.

This series of letters brought me to the notice of many progressive Republicans who were as concerned as I was about the relationship of business to society and about the U.S. role in the world. Prominent among them was John Hay "Jock" Whitney, the public-spirited investment banker who later became ambassador to Great Britain and publisher of the *New York Herald Tribune*. As a result of the letters, Whitney got in touch with me through a mutual acquaintance, contributed generously to my campaigns, and became my close friend over the years.

Meanwhile, Arthur Schwartz had been busy. Early in the spring he called me to his office and introduced me to Samuel Lepler, one of the Republican leaders in Manhattan's Washington Heights, which was part of the Twenty-first Congressional District. Sam and I hit it off immediately, and it quickly became apparent that the Twenty-first District was the place for me to make my run. No Republican had been elected to Congress from the district since the Harding landslide of 1920, and Lepler had been looking for a respectable candidate willing to enter what everyone believed would be a losing battle. I had never expected the Republican Party to risk a district in which it had a chance of winning on an unknown newcomer, so that was fine with me. My ability to raise the money for my own campaign, which Schwartz carefully pointed out, helped convince Lepler and — through him — other Republican leaders in the district to pledge their support. The Twenty-first Congressional District had a special appeal for me, since I had lived there for a few years and had been in the first graduating class of George Washington High School, which was in the center of the district.

As I studied the district and the available support, I sensed an opportunity to break the long-time Democratic hold on it. At that time, the Twenty-first Congressional District encompassed the entire northern tip of Manhattan Island south to 159th Street, and a narrow strip along the Hudson River down to 114th Street, taking in congeries of great cultural institutions, including Columbia University. It was about equally divided among Protestants, including some blacks, in the southern end around Columbia, Jews in the central Washington

Heights area, and Catholics in the northern sections of Inwood and Marble Hill. So many Jewish refugees from Europe had settled in Washington Heights that the area was sometimes called the Fourth Reich. Many of these victims of Nazi persecution had already become American citizens and could vote, and I felt that my background, my war record, and my international outlook would appeal to them. Among the estimated ten thousand refugee families in the district was one named Kissinger. Henry Kissinger has told me that his parents were among my early supporters.

Columbia University and the other cultural, educational, and religious institutions in the district were also assets for me. Among them were the Union Theological Seminary, the Jewish Theological Seminary, Yeshiva University, Manhattanville College, the Juilliard School of Music, the Academy of Arts and Sciences, the Columbia-Presbyterian Medical Center, the Cloisters, and a number of important museums, churches, and synagogues. I believed that the students and staff of these intellectual and cultural establishments would prefer me to some Tammany Hall hack.

The Democratic Party forces themselves were in disarray in the district, which was another encouraging sign. The incumbent congressman, James Torrens, had made such a lackluster record in Washington that even the Tammany leaders were unhappy with him, so they were dumping him and putting up a local state assemblyman, Daniel Flynn. Torrens refused to take his ouster lying down and let it be known that he would enter the Democratic primary anyway, without the support of the bosses. It appeared likely that the American Labor Party would also field a candidate in the Democratic primary.

Despite Lepler's support, I was not assured of the Republican nomination until early May. My own rival for it was Johannes Steel, a popular radio commentator with American Labor Party connections who had announced his intention of running in three primary elections, Republican, Democratic, and ALP. If I had not shown up, the Republicans would probably have gone with Steel, despite his left-wing proclivities, because it was generally conceded that no one could win in the district on the Republican line alone. But I offered the Republican Party a much more palatable alliance, in addition to my overall qualifications: As Schwartz made clear to the local Republican leaders, I could almost certainly get the Liberal Party nomination if the Republicans chose me. Consequently, on May 6, the Republican Assembly district chairmen of the Twenty-first Congressional District voted to designate me as their candidate. The formality of the August

20 primary still remained, but the designation of the party leaders, announced to the press with appropriate fanfare by Tom Curran, the county chairman, was regarded as decisive. Soon thereafter Steel withdrew from all three contests.

My next order of business was the Liberal Party. The Republican Party could count on the support of only about three out of ten voters in the district, so I needed the Liberals to attract some of the remaining seven. I therefore called on Alex Rose, the Liberals' vice chairman and political mentor, whom I had met during the Goldstein campaign the previous year, and asked for his support. Alex, who lived in the Twenty-first District himself, was encouraging; but he could do nothing for me without the approval of the Liberal Party's district organization.

The Liberal leader in the district was Morris Shapiro, a well-known civil rights lawyer who became a great friend. Morris later described our first exchange:

> It was a Sunday. Jack called me and asked me to see him. He said he had the Republican nomination for Congress in the district and wanted to talk to me about Liberal support. I said I'd be happy to meet with him and he said, "Could I come over now?" Just like that. He came over and he spent a couple of hours. I indicated that I would consider supporting him if he gave me his pledge that he would not take ALP support under any circumstances. He agreed with that.

While the Liberals looked me over, I set about planning my campaign. As I look back on it thirty-five years and ten elections later, it is apparent that the task I was undertaking was a formidable one indeed. I was unknown in the district except perhaps for classmates at George Washington High School who might have remembered me — and might still own a copy of the yearbook with its prediction that I would become a "political boss." I had a lot more to learn about the district and I had to relocate in it; and I was to be the candidate of two minority parties, one of which, the Liberals, had not yet earned an automatic line on the ballot by gaining the necessary fifty thousand votes in a statewide election. Money had to be raised, campaign literature had to be written and printed, speaking schedules and committees had to be established, and I had to reach a hundred and fifty thousand voters.

To organize for these tasks I turned to the precise and orderly system of military planning I had learned at the army's Command and General Staff School. As I adapted this to political campaigns, in 1946 and afterward, the scheme worked out like this: (1) raising money; (2) gathering staff and volunteers; (3) marshaling my positions on the issues and my own qualifications for the office; (4) preparing pamphlets, ads, buttons, and so forth; and (5) intelligence — researching issues, voters, and opponents.

I had already begun making public my positions and qualifications with my *Herald Tribune* letters, and Ben got to work on the fund raising. Campaign literature had to wait until I was assured of the Liberal Party nomination. That meant my priorities had to be recruiting a staff and getting to know — and become known in — the district.

In the middle of May I put together a preliminary campaign staff: Shirley Storch, a very competent professional researcher; Dick Roffman, a public-relations man; Audrey Swift Newton, who had served overseas with the Red Cross during the war and who was to become executive director of the campaign; Louis Birk, a public-relations and political adviser; and my old friend from Fight for Freedom and Washington days, Peter Cusick. Shirley Storch prepared a tentative list of issues and campaign activities, and on May 22 we held our first staff meeting. We outlined a publicity campaign, drew up a list of names for an invitational committee to write letters to others to form a Citizens' Committee for Javits, and made assignments to cover some of the leading cultural institutions in the district in the search for more campaign workers. We decided to tap veterans' organizations for additional volunteers and to start scheduling lecture and speaking dates. Around June 1 I moved into the district, and my subleased apartment at 425 Riverside Drive became my first campaign headquarters.

To obtain all the information I could about the people of the district I developed two strategies. First, I commissioned Elmo Roper, one of the pioneers of public-opinion polling, to analyze the demographic make-up of the district and to find out what issues the voters were thinking about and what they thought about them. I was one of the first candidates anywhere to use the new polling techniques in a political campaign.

At the same time, I started meeting my future constituents. From the Republican and Liberal leaders in the district and from other friends I obtained a long list of influential citizens who might support me. They ranged from the president of Columbia University, Nicholas Murray Butler, to the heads of local civic organizations, and I went out to talk to them all. Generally, I would first call on the telephone, introduce myself, and ask for an appointment. In some cases, of course, this was preceded by an introduction from a friend or associate of the person I was calling and therefore I had some knowledge of the response I would get. But when I had to make a blind approach I took a more cautious and modest tack: Rather than ask for support, I said that I was running for Congress, was just back from military service, and wanted to hear that person's views about what the district, the city, and the country needed in the years ahead.

I had little trouble getting in to see everyone I wanted to meet, which is quite characteristic of political campaigns. Very few Americans are uncivil, or unwilling to listen and to exchange ideas. In my campaigns I have stopped thousands of people on the street, in retail shops, in factories and offices, and coming out at the end of the workday or going in at the beginning. In any single campaign I have generally encountered no more than ten or twenty people who would not shake hands or respond.

Even in some of these face-to-face talks in 1946 I did not feel it right to ask for support in the campaign. But the unspoken purpose of the visits was clear: to let as many influential people as possible get a close look at a candidate they might eventually support. The visits could help them too: "Jack Javits came to see me in my office the other day," one might say to attentive friends, "and he seems to be a decent guy." As a campaign activity these brief calls — which seldom lasted more than ten or fifteen minutes — accomplished the same purpose as shaking hands with voters on a street corner. Because of their position and influence, these leaders needed more than a handshake or a smile. They could be counted on to speak of me — and I to learn from them.

In the course of these encounters I forged some close political alliances and established some lifetime friendships. For example, I walked into the office of the president of Yeshiva University, Dr. Samuel Belkin, and introduced myself. We had a very extensive and wide-ranging discussion about morality and ethics in politics, about my views on our Jewish faith and what influence it would have upon my conduct if I were elected to Congress. Dr. Belkin and I, as a result of this auspicious beginning, became close friends.

Dr. Louis Finkelstein of the Jewish Theological Seminary and Dr. Henry P. Van Dusen, who headed the Union Theological Seminary, became friends and supporters in the same way. Another cleric whom I met at that time was Father George B. Ford, the Catholic chaplain of Columbia University and the pastor of Corpus Christi Church nearby.

Father Ford was one of the most enlightened Catholic clergymen I have ever encountered. He had a deep sympathy for the poor and the oppressed, he was a devoted civil libertarian with a passion for equal opportunity, and he was a strong advocate of government aid for housing the poor, especially the working poor. Father Ford and I were good friends for years.

One of the people I went to see in this round of visits was Dr. Bella Dodd, a lawyer and politician who had once been an official of the New York Teachers Union but who had become involved in other political activities by 1946. How Bella Dodd's name got on my list I have never been able to recollect for sure, but it did get on the list. Presumably she was on it because of her influence with New York's teachers, a great many of whom resided in the Twenty-first Congressional District. Even though it may seem a strange lapse, I am quite clear about the fact that I did not know at the time that she was a Communist Party official. At any rate, I spent fifteen or twenty minutes in her office on Forty-second Street, talking about teachers and their problems, and went on my way. Ten years later, that nearly forgotten meeting, like my chance encounters in San Francisco the year before, would give me much grief.

Except for these visits, my continuing meetings with Morris Shapiro's Liberal Party group, and my meetings with the organizers of an independent citizens' committee (mainly local retailers and mostly Democrats), I was still not reaching the district's voters. It was too early for that, and, besides, I did not want to distract the voters from the spectacle of the rivals for the Democratic nomination cutting each other up. Torrens, the incumbent who had fallen from Tammany grace, had decided not to buck the leadership himself but had thrown his support to a little-known local figure named Norman Rein. Together Torrens and Rein were pointing out to everyone how little Daniel Flynn, the Tammany designee, had accomplished in his thirteen years in the state legislature. Meanwhile, in mid-June, City Councilman Eugene P. Connolly had obtained, unopposed, the designation of the ALP after Steel withdrew, and had also entered the fight for the Democratic nomination. Connolly and his supporters charged that Flynn was allied with the Christian Front, a notorious anti-Semitic organization. Flynn retaliated by charging Connolly with Communist connections.

Connolly's presence in the race (he was the second-ranking leader of the ALP in Manhattan) was a mixed blessing for me. With the Democratic nomination as well as the ALP, he would be a very tough opponent. But if he lost the Democratic fight and remained as the ALP candidate, my chances would be enhanced in the resulting three-way race. Connolly provided me with one bonus: The Liberal Party, which was engaged in a desperate citywide fight against the ALP, would work even harder for me in order to defeat Connolly. Not only was Liberal support essential to me, but my emergence as a strong candidate had become essential to the Liberals' obtaining a line on the ballot and to their survival as a party.

Although most of my campaign activities during this period were organizational, events outside the district soon gave me the opportunity to get directly involved in the issues. The wartime Price Control Act expired on June 30 because President Truman had vetoed Congress's weakened version of the extension bill he had proposed. With controls gone, retail food prices shot up 14 percent in July, and the new control act to which Congress and the President finally agreed late in the month forbade any price controls on meat until August 20. The inflation that I had predicted in my *Herald Tribune* letter in May was suddenly upon us, and consumers were angry.

Most of the Republicans in Congress were voting against strong price-control measures, but I felt no hesitation in restating my opinion that any essential commodity still in short supply should remain controlled. By bucking the majority view of my party and establishing myself as a maverick within it even before I was elected, I was earning voter support in the district: Anyone in favor of price control and the Office of Price Administration (OPA) could vote for me on the Liberal line, and loyal Republicans would probably vote for me anyway. Furthermore, the issue was irresistible from a purely political standpoint, because Torrens was absent from Washington during the price-control fight and recorded not a single vote on it. Although he was not my opponent, I made sure that the voters recognized his dereliction of duty as a sign that Tammany Hall cared little about them. Also, with an issue such as control over a runaway cost of living, it is a mistake to think that a conservative Republican voter is not just as anxious as a liberal Democrat to get a fair break for himself as a consumer.

During those confusing weeks of the price-control hiatus, I set up scores of little "Save OPA" booths throughout the district. Volunteers wearing Javits buttons manned the booths and polled the voters on price control. Seven out of ten people we talked to favored the reestablishment of the OPA for a year, and most of those in favor signed a petition that we wired to all the members of the New York congressional delegation.

Through the price-control issue I was also able to capture the attention of the retail shop owners of the district, who were probably more concerned than anyone about prices. Later in the summer I started out on a time-consuming but highly effective campaign of personally visiting every single retail establishment in my district. I would walk in, introduce myself, shake hands with the proprietor and his clerks and customers, and hand out thin wooden pencils stenciled in red, white, and blue with my name. Many of the storekeepers agreed to place one of my poster cards in their windows and to keep a stack of my campaign leaflets on hand for their customers.

I could not always take the time in these visits to discuss the issues of the campaign in detail. But as I made my rounds I pointed out to the small-business community that if price control came off, and if wholesale price increases then compelled them to raise their prices above a level tolerated by the consumers, they would face the danger of a buyers' strike. Eventually, of course, the market would force prices down, but that would take time and retailers could be ruined in the meantime.

Around 149th Street and Broadway I found a group of retailers who, even before my arrival on the scene, had been looking around for a political leader to articulate and act on their concerns. They quickly decided that I was that person and organized a small-business committee in behalf of my candidacy. The leaders of this group were Morris Freyberg, a haberdasher, Sidney Loevin, owner of Loevin's, a ladies' clothing store, and Morris Kramer, a jeweler.

In my meetings with them and with similar groups, and in letters I circulated to retailers, I urged them as merchants to guide their customers away from scarce and expensive products and to help them purchase reasonably priced items still in plentiful supply.

In October, for example, a shoe retailers' association criticized the OPA for predicting a 30 percent rise in shoe prices and pledged to fight manufacturers' price increases on shoes. I immediately sent a telegram to the head of the association complimenting him on his statement, and then made sure that every shoe retailer in my district had a copy of the press report of the association's stand and of my encouraging telegram. These efforts were marvelously effective.

On August 4, the Liberal Party leaders announced their candidates for the fall elections. Only two Republicans appeared on their entire citywide slate, and I was one of them. There was no opposition to me, and I was therefore nominated. The next day I issued a formal statement of my program. Passage of a new price-control law had temporarily quieted the inflation debate, and I declared in my statement that peace and jobs were the major issues of the campaign. On the job front I called for a fair-employment-practices commission, an increase in the minimum wage to seventy-five cents an hour (from the then current forty cents), unemployment insurance, and a broadening of social security laws.

Regarding peace, I emphasized economic development and re-habilitation, open trade, and a stronger United Nations. And I called for "the complete elimination of the war industry and military poten-tial of Germany and Japan." The statement also mentioned several other issues that were to become vital elements of my legislative pro-gram in the future: housing, health research, aid to education, and the elimination of racial discrimination in schools.

Before I could appear on the ballot as a Liberal Party candidate, there was a petition campaign to be waged. The Liberal Party had no automatic line on the ballot, so it was necessary for me to collect three thousand signatures on a nominating petition in order to have the Liberal Party listed on the voting machines. The signers had to be registered voters of the district who had not signed any other petition for a congressional candidate. Other legal technicalities made it essen-tial that great care be taken with each signature. Both the Republican and Liberal Party organizations in the district provided many eager volunteers for this task, and I joined in personally, getting signatures on the petitions on the street and ringing doorbells myself.

I found an enormous source of volunteer help and general sup-port in my fellow veterans, among both those residing in the district and those enrolled in the district's schools and universities. Since the previous year I had been active in the American Veterans Committee (AVC), a new organization that differed from the older veterans' groups: Instead of seeking to dip into the public purse to reward veterans for their service by bonuses, the AVC paid attention to the national interest and worked to help veterans find housing, jobs, and medical care so they could catch up with those who had not served. In June I had taken a few days off from organizing the cam-paign to attend an AVC convention in Des Moines, Iowa, where I helped write the organization's liberal domestic platform and at the same time made valuable contacts with many veterans from New York.

During August I was invited to speak to the local AVC chapters and to other veterans' groups. I urged my fellow veterans to seek to improve their country by getting involved in the political process. Veterans must be ready, I said, to help candidates who will work for housing, jobs, education, and other veterans' needs, and this help means "doorbell ringing, speaking at meetings, raising campaign funds, and all the other jobs which go to make up a political campaign." The nonpartisan AVC itself could endorse no candidates, but follow-ing my appearance at the Inwood chapter of the organization the chapter chairman and many of his members formed an Independent Veterans' Committee to work for my election.

The Democratic primary on August 20 turned out well for me: Flynn just eked out a victory over Connolly. This assured the three-way race I had hoped for, and the narrow margin — less than a thousand votes — indicated that Tammany was not as strong in the district as I had thought. The support for Connolly and Rein represented an anti-Tammany protest vote that could be turned to my advantage in November. The day after the primary I challenged Flynn to "a good old-fashioned Lincoln-Douglass type of debate," in which we both could discuss the issues facing the country. Flynn declined to debate: another point for me.

On the morning of September 7, my campaign staff members and I proudly went down to the Board of Elections on Broome Street to turn in my Liberal Party nominating petition. We had collected about ten thousand signatures. We had sought more than were needed, because we knew some might be thrown out on technicalities. In a statement to reporters, I outlined my goals and programs and added something new: To bring about world development, I said, "we need not only money but thousands of young Americans who will serve overseas as engineers and technicians to give other people their know-how." (Fifteen years later something of that idea was embodied in President John F. Kennedy's Peace Corps.) Having filed my petitions and made my pledges, I hurried back uptown to carry on the campaign.

With two months to go, we shifted into high gear. Ben, with his usual energy and zeal, had tapped many of his friends and associates, and campaign contributions were coming in. I moved the headquarters from my apartment to a storefront on 158th Street just west of Broadway, and set up the Citizens' Committee for Jack Javits. The committee became the core of the campaign. The Republican and Liberal parties had their own campaign structures, but I was affirming that the candidate mattered much more than the party label, and I wanted a nonpartisan central headquarters that members of all parties could enter comfortably.

Dr. James P. Gifford, associate dean of the Faculty of Law at Columbia, was chairman of the committee, and many prominent residents of the community were on it, including Maxine Shaw, the wife of Robert Shaw, Hollace's brother, who by an odd twist of fate lived in the district.

One tireless campaign worker was Duane Faw, a Columbia Law School student who had served in the Marines with Joe McCarthy, who was then running for the Senate in Wisconsin. I had also enlisted the aid of a local Republican lawyer, Arthur Spielberg, who was to serve me loyally and intelligently for many years as the manager of my New York office. People such as Edith Willkie, Wendell Willkie's widow, Senator Wayne Morse of Oregon, and Governor Harold Stassen of Minnesota endorsed me. And even Newbold Morris, whose candidacy for the mayoralty I had opposed in 1945, supported me.

We prepared campaign literature to appeal — within my platform and principles — to all sections of the community. For the university people we reprinted my six letters to the *Herald Tribune* and distributed them as a pamphlet. They were heavy reading, but I knew there were voters in the district who were both well educated and concerned enough to read at least those parts that interested them. For the younger, less sophisticated voter we produced a comic book showing Jack Javits as the friend of John Q. Public, a "mighty giant" who smashed with his votes the monsters of greed and bigotry and inflation. We turned out more Javits comic books in the elections of 1948 and 1950. In one of the later strips, "fearless" Congressman Javits is shown fighting inflation, urging people to vote, and coming to the rescue of a disabled veteran being evicted from his apartment. I look back at the device with some embarrassment, but it was effective, and at least it reflected accurately my stand on the issues.

One of the most important campaign weapons was the Roper survey, which was completed in September 1946. It revealed a remarkable similarity between the views of the district and the positions I had set forth earlier in the *Herald Tribune*. Most of the voters were dissatisfied with Congress; they sought curbs on both unions and management; they favored government action to prevent or relieve unemployment; they favored price control on necessities; they wanted to see the national budget balanced; and they were strong believers in the United Nations. On Palestine, an important issue in the district, 17 percent favored a Jewish state, 29.9 percent wanted to see Palestine divided into separate Arab and Jewish communities, and 34.3 percent favored the establishment of an international trusteeship to be administered by the United Nations.

The survey helped me focus my campaign. Early in the summer I had stated that peace and jobs were the main issues, but I had to shift my emphasis, without abandoning my own sense of priorities, when the poll showed that the housing shortage and high prices were the two issues of greatest concern in the district. Third on the list was the control of atomic energy, followed by relations with the Soviet Union, unemployment, racial discrimination, and strikes.

The Roper poll encouraged me to hit harder on the national

housing emergency. New York, I said in September, needs two hundred fifty thousand housing units to deal with the immediate shortage. I called for increased tax advantages for new construction, government guarantees of construction financing, more government condemnation of land for public housing, and an increase in the construction work force.

The last two months of the campaign, the public part of it, I remember as a nonstop blur of speeches, canvassing, telephoning, and political discussions with practically everyone. It was hard work — sixteen or eighteen hours a day — but it was also a joy. I felt I was using every talent God gave me. All of my training came together. My early days on the pushcarts of Orchard Street and on the Socialist soapboxes in Brownsville had given me the confidence to address a crowd of strangers and to persuade them to listen to me. As a salesman and a bill collector I had learned how to walk boldly into a store, or up to a person or group of people who did not know me, and get their attention. My experience in trying cases in the law courts taught me how to think on my feet, how to handle interruptions (heckling), and how to marshal facts to win arguments. Now, in the campaign of 1946, it all fused into an exhilarating experience.

There were three kinds of public exposure. I spent many hours with my canvassers walking the streets of the district, climbing stairs, ringing doorbells. I led my "troops" at all times. We went from building to building, in a concentrated effort in a given area each night, saying, "Support Jack Javits, a new man, a veteran who will do something for this district instead of taking it for granted." I enforced a strict discipline in this operation, even on myself. We made a standard presentation with no deviation or debate or discussion. Our aim was simply to get across to every voter the fact that there was a new man running; street-corner meetings and the other activities in the district would then convey more information. We did make a tally of the voters in each building, but this was done quickly. The tally sheets noted the number of voters in each household and whether they were "rather favorable" or "interested" or "undecided" or "unfavorable but took literature." Almost everybody accepted a leaflet.

My mornings were devoted to the visits to the retail stores of the district. I learned quickly not to get bogged down in debate; it is essential to cover the ground, which takes time and does not allow for diversion. This is an important lesson I have passed on to candidates who seek my advice. When you are out shaking hands with voters you must accept the fact that some of them will not agree with you. You must go on to ride your strength rather than spend precious time trying to make up for your weaknesses by attempting to persuade voters one by one. If a voter is open-minded, you will reach him with a speech, along with hundreds of others; if not, you cannot take enough time to argue. The purpose of canvassing and handshaking tours is to establish a good impression with as many voters as you can so that they are receptive when they read the literature, see you on television, listen to you on radio, or hear you speak — or spoken of.

The high points of the campaign for me, and I think for the voters, were my nighttime speeches from the "Javits Dreamboat." This was a large flatbed loudspeaker truck flamboyantly decorated with posters and red, white, and blue bunting. At about 7:00 P.M. we parked it at a busy commercial corner — my favorite was 181st Street and Wadsworth Avenue — and after some music and a couple of warm-up talks by my aides, I stepped to the podium facing the sidewalk.

Even in the rather garish setting of the Dreamboat I preferred to speak from a lectern. I generally had papers to which I referred and I liked the formality, the suggestion of a legislative debate, that a lectern provides. Some politicians feel comfortable with an informal, shirt-sleeve approach in which the candidate acts like one of the boys, but that was not my style. I believe that as soon as a candidate begins a campaign for an office he must act as if he already holds that office. He must never appear tentative or uncertain: Once he has said something it is done, and it should carry weight. If you run for a seat in the House of Representatives you have to act like a congressman; when you start to run for the Senate, you are a senator. That was my theory, at least, and it worked for me.

This does not mean that a candidate should assume victory. I never said "when I am senator," even after four terms in the Senate. I always said "if I am reelected senator." The people owe the candidate nothing, and the candidate must always behave as if it were his (or her) first campaign.

One thing that always impressed me about the street rallies in all my campaigns was the length of time people would stand and listen. The meetings would often last an hour and a half — thirty to forty-five minutes while I spoke, and then another thirty or forty minutes while I answered questions. There was no place to sit down, but the crowd would stay and grow, so that often, by the time we broke to move on to another spot, we would have as many as fifteen hundred people around the Dreamboat. There were not many hecklers either, at least in 1946. The crowds were generally serious: They wanted to hear what I had to say, even if they disagreed with it, and they usually shouted down anybody who tried to interfere. There is nothing more effective against a heckler than an annoyed crowd. Hecklers are delighted if they can annoy the speaker, but if the crowd gets hostile to them they generally shut up.

But hecklers did show up later, and I developed a few techniques for handling them. I never let a heckler interrupt my speech. When I was talking about some issue and someone yelled "What about the price of bread?" or "What about Harry Truman?" I at first ignored him. If he became very persistent I would say, "Sir, we're having a meeting, people would like to hear what I have to say. Would you be kind enough to stand by a few minutes and you'll be the first one I turn to for a question when I'm finished." And I always kept that promise even though I had no idea what question would be asked. And, of course, a speaker must never surrender the microphone. I often encountered some joker who would say, "All right, let me have that microphone and I'll tell you how to run the country." To that I would answer, "You just stay right where you are, sir. I can hear you, and I'll repeat your question." And I always repeated the questions before answering them — which of course gave me time to think of my answers while pleasing the questioner.

I used a version of the Dreamboat in every one of my four House campaigns and only once, in 1948, did I ever face a hostile or ugly situation. My opponent that year was Paul O'Dwyer, Mayor Bill O'Dwyer's brother, and my running mates and supporters were convinced that the police, to gain favor with City Hall, were encouraging neighborhood roughnecks to give me a hard time, particularly in the heavily Democratic and Irish Catholic Inwood area. One evening in Inwood a gang of these rowdies showed up at the edge of my crowd, talking loudly, jostling people, perhaps even throwing something toward the Dreamboat. I kept on with my speech until one fellow yelled, "Jack, eh? Isn't your name Jake?" Everyone realized he was reminding the audience that I was Jewish, and the crowd tensed. I stared at the man for a moment and said, "That's right, my name is Jacob," and then I plunged back into my speech, making clear that I was not going to be intimidated by that kind of nonsense. Within a few moments I had the crowd's attention again, and when the hoodlums tried to make another disturbance the crowd shouted them down.

In the 1948 election I had my own two-year record in Congress to defend and build on, and as the incumbent I quite properly became a campaign issue and target. But in 1946 none of the candidates were incumbents; there were few personal attacks and I concentrated on the issues. I paid relatively little attention to what the other candidates were saying and doing, but I watched very carefully the events of the day and made a point of commenting on them and bringing them into my speeches and campaign publicity as quickly as they happened. For example, when a meat shortage was angering people all over the country, I composed a telegram suggesting that the farmers' organizations, the meat packers, the labor unions in the meat industry, and the leading national consumer organizations all get together in a conference with the Department of Agriculture to resolve the problem. I sent this telegram to the five leading meat packers, to the two leading meat packers' unions, and to the three leading farm organizations — and then I sent copies of it to the ten daily newspapers in New York and to the Associated Press and United Press. That well-intentioned telegram blitz earned me, as I recall, very little press exposure. That was probably because I was neither suggesting a solution to the problem nor blaming anyone for it. But I mentioned the telegram in my street-corner speeches for the next couple of days and it showed the voters that I was making an energetic attempt to help solve the problem from where I stood, even as a candidate. I was applying the adage of my boxing instructor at Columbia University: "Hit 'em from where you are!"

The so-called Jewish issues — I preferred to consider them human rights issues — helped me with the voters and also got me some press attention. During that summer and fall the question of persuading Britain to give up its Palestine mandate was one of the main foreign-policy matters facing the country. Related to it was an even more urgent problem. The Anglo-American Committee of Inquiry on Palestine, of which my San Francisco friend Bartley Crum was a member, had recommended in April that Britain immediately admit into Palestine one hundred thousand Jewish refugees, survivors of the Holocaust. Britain refused and in August started the notorious blockade of Palestine ports, diverting Palestine-bound refugees to detention camps in Cyprus. My strong stand in favor of the admission to Palestine of these displaced persons naturally sat well with the Jewish refugees from Hitler who lived in the district. But a complication arose. Congress was simultaneously debating a loan to Britain for rehabilitation and development, and someone had seized on the idea of making the loan conditional on the admission of the refugees. I could not endorse this tactic. As I saw it, the loan was not a favor to Britain but was essential to help a destroyed Europe recover from World War II and to restore the world's economy; and I felt it should be granted and that the displaced-persons problem was likely to be sooner solved that way. So when some representatives of Jewish groups who were on their way to Washington to petition the British ambassador called on me for a statement linking the two issues, I had to disappoint them. I gave them the following statement and also issued it to the press:

I deprecate the effort to join a great humanitarian endeavor like the admission of the 100,000 of my coreligionists into Palestine with the enactment of a loan to Britain of $3,750,000. Upon the verdict of this loan hangs the whole decision regarding a world of economic cooperation or a world of warring economies. . . . The British people are a justly proud people — we should not use the means of coercion upon them. The case of the 100,000 Jews is too noble to deserve such means. I hope the House will approve the British loan without delay, and I urge the people of the 21st Congressional District to send telegrams to their representative, Mr. Torrens, to go down to Congress and do his duty and vote for the loan. I urge also that all of us telegraph the President and the British Ambassador that we want the 100,000 people of Jewish faith admitted into Palestine as recommended by the Anglo-American Committee now.

In the final weeks of the campaign I took the refugee issue a step further by demanding that we "open the doors of our country to not less than a hundred thousand refugees — a drop in the bucket compared to the unused immigration quotas under our existing laws"; and I attacked the 1924 Immigration Act, with its restrictive quotas discriminating against southern Europe and by race, and urged its revision, thus beginning a struggle that would later occupy much of my time and effort.

The postwar handling of the Nazi war criminals also became a campaign issue. During October Senator Robert A. Taft, known throughout the country as "Mr. Republican," declared in a speech that the Nuremburg trials of Göring and other Nazis were "ex post facto" and "will be a blot on the American record that we shall long regret." Here, conscience and practical political reasons coincided, and I joined the angry protest that met his remarks. Although an unknown first-time Republican candidate perhaps should have deferred to the party's leader, I felt that Senator Taft's statement was both wrong-headed and offensive. On this issue, therefore, I was at odds with one of the most important men in the party even before my election. But it could not be helped. I did not doubt that many similar clashes would occur if I were elected. New York Governor Thomas E. Dewey, who was running for reelection that year, also had to take issue with Taft, mildly, and without mentioning him by name. My response, in a wire to Taft, was much stronger:

Your statement . . . is a disservice to all we fought for and to the
cause of future peace. . . . It must be repugnant to every veteran
and to the millions who suffered so cruelly at the hands of the
Nazis. . . . It would have been a travesty on justice if the Nazi
criminals could not be punished because there was no court in
which to punish them. . . . Your statement about the impending
trials in Japan is especially mischievous, for it proposes to dissuade us from meting out international justice to the Japanese
warmakers. The hell they imposed on so many thousands of our
troops cannot be so soon forgotten.

Throughout the campaign I received scores of letters and ques-
tionnaires from individuals and special interest groups seeking my
views on all the conceivable issues of the day; and they all had to be
answered. Among these was a letter from the National Women's Party
asking my position on an Equal Rights Amendment prohibiting denial
of rights on the basis of sex. I answered: "There can be little question
about the validity of an equal rights amendment in our day and age
and I [would] certainly support such an enlightened measure, were I
in Congress." Thus my position on ERA was established very early.
It is interesting to note, however, that in typing the letter to the
National Women's Party my secretary (female) used the salutation
then customary for a letter to an organization rather than an individual — "Gentlemen." We have all come a long way since 1946.

In the last days of the campaign I rushed down to the studios of
WQXR every evening to deliver a live, five-minute radio talk on one
of the major issues. These talks were broadcast just before the nightly
news program of WQXR, a "highbrow" station emphasizing classical
music, and through them I was able to reach another group of voters
who might not have wanted to stand around listening to a political
speech on a street corner. The broadcasts were especially useful in
enabling me to respond to the news. For example, on the day the first
UN General Assembly met in New York I broadcast on foreign affairs,
reiterating my view that we should not be afraid of sending economic
aid even to the Soviet Union, but that our aid should go only to
countries where human rights and information are assured. On the
day the OPA changed price regulations I took the opportunity to talk
about that, and called for a new national economic policy. "Vote with
courage," I told the voters on my last broadcast. "Vote your hopes
and not your fears."

The visible campaign ended with a mammoth Dreamboat rally
at 181st Street and Wadsworth Avenue. Wendell Willkie's son, Philip,
appeared and spoke in my behalf. Among other things, he said,

"America is at the pinnacle of her power, yet our national leadership is pathetic. The Twenty-first Congressional District could go a long way toward curing that defect by sending Mr. Javits to Congress and starting a man on his way who will have a notable career both in New York and the nation." I put everything I had into my final speech:

The times demand that men and women who normally do not go in for politics should go in for it now. We need those with ideas, character, and a program, to undertake to deal with the problems which face us. . . . Party politicians have their eyes constantly fixed on the next election and do not act with responsibility for the whole community. . . . By voting for me the citizens will be breaking the back of that kind of reaction, which does not understand what is going on in the world and has no ideas of what to do about it. . . . The actions of the next Congress on the four critical problems facing us — inflation, strikes, housing, and peace — are likely to determine the fate of the United States for a century.

A Republican tide swept through the polling booths on November 5. Governor Dewey was reelected by a wide margin, with the entire Republican state ticket, and nationally my party gained control of both houses of Congress. Although I had clearly dissociated myself from the Republican call for a quick ending of price controls, the party's overall success helped me. The voters wanted a change, and in the Twenty-first Congressional District a vote for change meant a vote for me. Even so, I would not have won without the Liberal Party, or if Connolly had not drawn votes away from Flynn. I received 37,029 votes on the Republican line and 9842 on the Liberal line, a total of 46,871. Flynn, the Democrat, got 40,740, and Connolly, of the ALP, got 14,378.

Despite the general voting trend, Manhattan remained in the Democratic column, so my victory in a strong Democratic district was regarded as an upset by all the newspapers. Therefore, when I came up for reelection after my first term in Congress, my opponents knew they would have to unite to beat me. Paul O'Dwyer received both the Democratic and the ALP nominations and came within eight-tenths of a percentage point of ending my political career then and there.

In 1948 again I had the support of the Liberal Party. My work in Congress, particularly my votes against the Taft-Hartley Act, had won me the enthusiastic backing of labor, and several hundred trade unionists of the ILGWU volunteered to canvass for me. The sight of these mature men and women traipsing through the district on Sundays carrying my leaflets made a strong impression on the voters —

and me. With such devoted supporters I felt that I did not dare to fail.

As the incumbent, I had to defend my record. O'Dwyer claimed to be a progressive (as did Henry A. Wallace, running for president that year as the candidate of the Progressive Party). O'Dwyer charged that I was a crony of Tom Dewey, the Republican presidential candidate, and that I had voted in favor of the wealthy on tax legislation and other bills. That was easy to refute, because it was not true; but I had to explain carefully to the voters how a vote for an unsatisfactory compromise bill, the best possible at the time, sometimes obscured a congressman's earlier efforts for a different measure. O'Dwyer had taken some of my votes out of this context to try to make the case against me.

A more troublesome attack came from some of the conservatives in Inwood, who claimed I was "soft on Communism" because I had voted against the dangerous and unconstitutional Mundt-Nixon bill. That bill, which passed in the House but not in the Senate, would have required the Communist Party and "Communist-front" organizations, and their officers, to register with the federal government, and it would have barred from federal government employment members of such organizations. The rub was in the determination of which organizations were "Communist fronts." This was to be decided by the attorney general under very fuzzy criteria; the bill would have left it up to the federal bureaucracy to decide who was to be disqualified from federal employment and — in the atmosphere of the day — who thereby would be ostracized and prevented from earning a living. O'Dwyer, had he been in Congress, would probably have voted against that witch-hunting bill too, but that did not deter some of his conservative Democratic supporters from attacking me on it.

To counter their argument I took to the Dreamboat with an argument of my own. In meeting after meeting on the streets of Inwood I read parts of the Mundt-Nixon bill. According to the bill, "any organization which engages in activity intended, or which it is reasonable to believe is intended, to further the objective of . . . bringing about acceptance, in the United States, of Communist ideology," was a "Communist front." I pointed out how easily you could substitute "Catholic" for "Communist" and with a similar bill punish Catholics — not for their religion, but for the social relationships that their religion created, such as attendance at parochial schools or membership in the Knights of Columbus. This was a potent argument. It took a while, but people began to realize that they were being lured into a situation that could be as harmful to them as it could be to Jews or blacks or any other minority. There is no way to know how many votes this argument won me, but I am sure there were many, and I needed every one.

Election night 1948 was a cliffhanger — a famous one for the nation and just as exciting for me. Early returns favored O'Dwyer; at about midnight he claimed victory, and the newspapers called me for a concession statement. I always judge early returns not by how well I am doing in the election districts I will probably win but by how badly I am doing in the election districts I am likely to lose. That night I could see that I was running behind my 1946 vote in Inwood, but not by as much as I had feared. I refused to concede. Nevertheless, with the radio reporting a Dewey victory nationally and an O'Dwyer victory in the Twenty-first Congressional District, Arthur Spielberg and I turned out the lights at headquarters about midnight and went home.

Marian and I had planned a party at our apartment and many of my supporters and friends were there when I arrived. But, with the bad news for me coming in, people drifted away. Then, at about 2:00 A.M., the tide began to turn. We phoned people to come back, and Ben and Lily rushed over, stopping at a delicatessen to buy more food. We called our poll watchers for late word from the election districts that were still counting, but the election was so close that I soon realized we would not be certain of the result until every vote had been tallied. So we finally went to bed, still unsure. When we awoke early in the morning the radio newscasters had a double surprise for us: It was Truman, not Dewey; and it was not O'Dwyer, but Javits — by a margin of 1873 out of 130,752 votes cast.

After that close call, the others should have seemed easy. But no election is easy.

EIGHT

Marian and Me

Our marriage works. It gives us intimacy, independence, and inter-dependence. But Marian has missed some of the romance, some of the attentions, and some of the continuity of emotional attachment that she expected to find over time with me. I recognize that my work in the Senate and my profound involvement in public questions has made Marian pay this cost, but after thirty-plus years we still have a marriage — and a quality of life — acceptable to both of us. Even now as we work together we are a remarkable team. We have produced three splendid children and we remain a close-knit family. We have established between us a congenial and stimulating relationship — and that does not happen often in marriages of long duration. Had I known how it would all work out when I wed Marian Borris in 1947 I would have married her just the same. We were much taken with each other.

Our wedding celebrations combined the solemnity of a synagogue service with the enthusiasm of a political rally in front of the temple. At the same time we contemplated a great event that had taken place that weekend: On the previous day the United Nations had voted to partition Palestine, a historic decision that would permit the establishment after two millennia of a Jewish state as a haven of security for all the harassed and persecuted Jews of the world. Congress was in special session, and I had to attend a vital meeting of the House Foreign Affairs Committee on the day following our wedding, so after the festivities we took the overnight train that ran from New York to Washington. The train departed about midnight, but passengers could go aboard at ten o'clock, get a full night's sleep, and arrive in Washington's Union Station in the morning. It must have been eleven o'clock or later when we boarded the train, Marian bedecked with pearls, in a form-fitting gray sweater set, I carrying my usual stack of morning newspapers. From the very beginning, work and world affairs were on a collision course with marriage.

* * *

About two years earlier, soon after the Goldstein mayoral campaign of 1945, Marian Borris and I simply stopped seeing each other. Much as I liked her and enjoyed our dates, much as I looked forward to marriage and having children, I had been put off by Marian's ambition for an acting career. I doubted that a woman with the goal of the stage in her mind would be able to mesh her life with mine, and I was not so smitten that I dared ask her to give up her dream. So when I kissed her good-bye and went off to Mexico and Guatemala for a four-week sightseeing holiday at the end of 1945, there were no promises or expectations that we would see each other again. Upon my return to New York I plunged into the maelstrom of the 1946 congressional campaign on Washington Heights and did not call her. I went to some parties and I gave some parties, I dated a few women friends, and I played a lot of tennis, but primarily I was working long hours and was not considering romance or marriage. I did think about Marian from time to time, but in the past tense, as an episode in my life.

Then, in April 1947, when I was a very busy first-term congressman, I received a note from Marian one day congratulating me on the rise in my career. While lying in bed with a cold, she wrote, she had heard me on the radio discussing some national political issue. She said she agreed with my comments, that I sounded intelligent and happily involved, that it reminded her pleasantly of our nice times together, and that she would like to see me again if I was interested in seeing her.

With that note a tide of pleasant memories came flooding back; I called her, she sounded as attractive as ever, and we arranged a date. That first date gave her a glimpse of what life with me would be like — but perhaps she did not even then grasp its significance. It was on a Saturday and I had arrived in New York from Washington late the night before. I asked Marian to come to meet me at my apartment at 150th Street and Riverside Drive, because I was to be busy with constituents all day and if I had tried to get over to the Bronx to pick her up I would not have arrived there until quite late and that would have spoiled the evening. She agreed, but took the wrong subway train from the West Ninety-sixth Street IRT station and arrived at about eight o'clock. I still had not finished my day's work: A delegation of Greek-Americans was talking to me about the Greek-Turkish aid bill, which was then before Congress. Marian waited patiently until I finished talking to the delegation and then we went out for dinner. It went pretty much that way every weekend. Marian met me where I was speaking somewhere or meeting with a group of constituents, and she had to spend a good deal of time waiting for me to get through with being a congressman before I could turn my attention to her. She did not seem to mind; maybe it pleased her that this congressman, whom all these people had to talk to, would be all hers for a while, afterward. Maybe she enjoyed listening in on political activity, in the expectation that she would become part of it one day. In any case, not until after we were married did she react strongly to the conflict between my work and her need for her husband's society.

The hours I spent with Marian in the spring and summer of 1947 were limited, but happy. We had dinners together and went to concerts and the theater and dancing — I could teach her the rhumba, conga, and samba, while she tried to teach me her generation's jitterbug. During the summer I took her up to Connecticut to visit Ben and Lily and to go swimming on the pebbly beach at Westport. My brother and his wife and my mother were all delighted with Marian. No one pushed me to marry or even mentioned it, but they all realized, with quiet approval, that my intentions were serious. On her part, Marian was touched by their personal generosity and the warm welcome they gave her; she was enchanted by the family warmth, the comfortable house, the fresh vegetables from Lil's own garden, their children, and the stream of guests and friends. It was a world she had never entered before, a very different lifestyle for her.

Marian was born in Detroit and came to New York as an infant to live in crowded tenements in Manhattan and the Bronx. She had not often been out of New York City until, at seventeen, she left for California with hopes for a Hollywood career. Her mother and father were immigrants from Odessa who had not broken out of their modest circumstances before the Great Depression caught up with them and intensified their economic struggle. They separated, reunited, and finally divorced when Marian was about ten, whereupon Marian and her mother and her chronically ill older sister moved in with Marian's grandmother, a sweet, wizened old lady who doted on Marian and was a bright spot in her existence. Marian's mother eked out a living doing electrolysis at home, and Marian, growing up beautiful and intelligent, became the hope of her family. She had to care for her sister and speak up for her in a series of public hospitals and clinics, and this taught her at an early age that she had to fight and persist if she wanted anything good to happen. She developed an iron determination to be independent and to overcome whatever difficulties and injustices she encountered, and she retains that drive to this day.

This difficult life and early responsibility molded Marian in the same way comparable circumstances had molded my brother, Ben. Instinctively I must have recognized this parallel, and among my feelings for Marian was the urge to protect her, to take her under my wing, to care for her. As Marian expressed her own feelings warmly and lovingly, she was a woman very easy to cherish.

Marian's determination to succeed on the stage had caused me to hesitate the first time around. But she was pragmatic, too, and having made too little progress in the theater she was beginning to look for other ways to direct her life. That was fine with me. I had enjoyed Hollace Shaw's fame and prominence during our wartime romance, but now I was in the public eye myself and I was not seeking another celebrity. At the same time I recognized that since I was so busy Marian could also have a profession that would absorb her. I offered to lend her the money to go to college and work toward a medical degree and a career in psychiatry, a subject that greatly interested her. But our marriage overtook that idea.

That summer I was appointed to a special congressional subcommittee to visit the displaced-persons camps in Europe. We sailed from New York on August 27 on the *Queen Mary*, and Marian came down to the ship for the bon voyage party. It was a gala leave-taking, the maiden eastbound voyage of the *Queen Mary* after the war, and there were dozens of congressmen and their aides aboard, members of several different committees. Some of my colleagues had heard a lot about Marian from me but this was the first time they had met her, and they were all charmed and impressed by the beautiful and exuberant young woman who came to see me off. When the "all visitors ashore" whistle blew I kissed Marian good-bye. Jim Fulton, a Pennsylvania congressman who was my best friend in the House, then claimed "congressional courtesy" and kissed her too, and some of my other colleagues did likewise. After which, of course, I came back and kissed her again to ensure that I was still number one. The departure was delayed several times and we went through it all again, with more kidding and high jinks each time. We finally sailed, to much gaiety and laughter and waving between the ship and the dock. As we moved down the harbor my obviously envious friends continued to tease me. I was very proud of Marian, and that night I called her up on the ship-to-shore phone, for the fun of making a call of that kind to her and because I wanted to let her know that although I was going off on a trip again, this time I was really interested and that my heart was very much with her.

During my trip, Marian stayed at my apartment with my niece Joan, Ben's daughter. (As I was on the other side of the Atlantic, Marian's mother approved.) I phoned Marian from all over Europe and bought her presents and souvenirs in every city. Whenever I called her or went shopping for her, Fulton and the others renewed their teasing, which I took as a compliment to her and to me. It was an arduous trip and my thoughts turned often to Marian. I realized that my future would be full of such hectic travel as well as the turmoil and pressure of politics, and I became convinced that Marian could provide a tranquil haven to which I could always come back for sur-cease and peace and contentment and the pleasures of family life.

On a Sunday evening soon after my return to New York in Octo-ber we were sitting in my apartment reading the papers — or rather, I was just looking at them because my mind was on the question of me and Marian. I had again been urging her to resume her education, but she had not enrolled for the fall term at Columbia as I had hoped she would, and I realized she was not going back to school. Suddenly I put down the papers and turned to her and said, "All right, I think we should get married." By "all right" I meant, "All right, as long as you're not going to school...." It was, I confess, a precipitous and rather unromantic proposal, but the thought was on both our minds and we were already very close and dear to each other — although I was obviously still so shy that I had to blurt it out like that. Marian accepted on the spot in a matter-of-fact tone that matched my own: I think she said something like "Yes, that would be nice." Neither of us was surprised at this decision.

At Marian's suggestion we took her mother to dinner. I had met Clara Borris before that, of course, but this time I was really being scrutinized, and although I was a congressman and was dining in my "territory," the Roosevelt Hotel, I felt stiff and uncomfortable under the appraisal of this pleasant and unassuming but romantic Russian woman. Marian's mother expressed great respect and affection for me, and the evening went well. But later she let Marian know she was worried about the great difference in our ages and the gulf that sep-arated Marian's world and mine. Early in my relationship with Marian, her mother had been concerned when I asked my secretary to tele-phone a message to Marian arranging a date instead of placing the call myself; she felt that was not the proper way to do things if ro-mantic feelings were involved. Marian's mother was thinking only of her daughter's happiness and it is a great credit to her that she voiced these misgivings despite the obvious advantages that the marriage might bring her family. Finally, having made sure that Marian under-stood her concerns, she gave us her blessing. My family, of course, was delighted that a dozen years after my divorce I was taking another wife.

We set the date for Sunday, November 30, which turned out to be a perfect day for our wedding: On the day before, the United Nations approved the Palestine partition plan that was the first step toward the establishment of the state of Israel; Jews everywhere were celebrating with us that weekend. We made quite a civic bash of our wedding at the Temple of the Covenant on West 180th Street, in my congressional district. Rabbi Joshua Loth Liebman of Boston, the spiritual counselor and intellectual leader of an important group of liberal Jews, whom I had met through David Niles during the war, officiated at the ceremony. We also had to have the rabbi of the temple, of which I was a member and which I attended on the High Holy Days and on Sabbaths when I could. That still left a number of prominent rabbis in the district who had invited me to speak about Palestine to their congregations and who had to be represented. We ended up with four rabbis as we said our I do's.

The guest list included all my campaign workers and contributors and all of the political figures I knew and whose support I would have for many campaigns, as well as many of the leaders of the Washington Heights community. The temple was filled to capacity — about five hundred people — with hundreds of invited guests overflowing into the streets and mingling with uninvited but enthusiastic constituents, all kept more or less in order by a police detail. It was more like an election-night victory party than a dignified rite of marriage. Marian was a stunning bride, the public loved her, and everyone was happy — but no one was happier than the bridegroom.

The special session of Congress had ruined our plans for a proper honeymoon — and we never had one. The closest thing to it was a trip to Havana a few weeks later — in the company of the same congressional subcommittee with which I had traveled to Europe that September. We were delegates to an economic conference in Havana that was supposed to draft the charter for a world trade organization, to be called the International Trade Organization (ITO), but the delegates of some of the smaller countries suspected that the United States wanted to exploit them and consequently the conference did not go well.

At one point Jim Fulton and I decided that the U.S. delegation should give a party for the other delegates in order to establish a more congenial atmosphere. Since Marian was with us and had already displayed her skills as a hostess, I asked her to arrange the festivities. This she did, and extremely well, although she had to transform a huge and barren hall in Havana's Nacional Hotel — you could smell the mothballs, she said — into a gala environment. The party itself was a great success and prevented the conference from breaking up altogether. Although few of the guests knew anyone else, Marian was able to generate an atmosphere of warmth, introduce delegates to each other, and make them all feel happy and at home. It was a remarkable social and diplomatic achievement. As far as the public could see, the Javitses were already an effective team.

But Marian was troubled and she let me know it. She considered the trip our honeymoon and she thought I was devoting too much attention to my official duties. Because the conference was in trouble, I had spent an evening hurriedly writing a previously unscheduled speech, in Spanish, that I was to deliver to the Americas over radio the next day, and she regarded that, too, as an unfair infringement on what should have been time for her. Just as the big cocktail party was about to begin, Marian for a moment wavered over whether she would or would not go to it. The crisis passed, but it was an omen for the future. Marian was discovering that my responsibilities as an elected official might compete with my responsibilities as a husband. One might think that our courtship evenings shared with my constituents would have shown her how I lived and worked, that she should have known what she was getting into. But the fact is that because of her romantic nature she had not accepted the situation, and she was hurt. Perhaps she relied on the idea that in the happily-ever-after of wedded bliss I would change, magically. More likely, she thought that if she set her mind to it she could change me even though I was twenty years older and filled with determination too. She tried to change me, on occasion successfully — and she is still trying.

The success of that Havana party encouraged Marian. Her abilities as a hostess had attracted me in the first place, and over the years she has developed and refined them. Her parties are always exceptional, often glamorous, and frequently of great practical value to me. She enjoys them too, particularly as she brings together stimulating, creative, influential people. I remain very impressed by Marian's skill as a hostess — to the extent, as she points out, that after a good party I will compliment her on it and thank her for it almost as if I were a guest and not the host myself. Eventually, however, Marian began to feel limited by the social role to which she felt I had confined her; she wanted to step out on her own into more intellectually stimulating and emotionally satisfying fields. This she has done with a great many work projects, usually connected with communications and the arts. On one occasion years later, her brief assignment with Iran Airlines, Marian's reaching out for a more meaningful work role caused trouble for both of us.

After the first few months of our marriage, Marian did not come to Washington often. It was an election year, I was spending a great deal of time in New York, and Marian was pregnant with our first child. Despite that, she worked hard in the campaign, accompanying me throughout that summer to local political clubs, veterans' groups, civic organizations, and synagogues and churches. Everyone liked her and she was a great political asset.

All through one day in the middle of September, Marian, though big with child, gamely stayed by my side as I hurried around to meetings and appearances. Late that afternoon we served tea in our apartment to about fifty ladies organizing a "Women for Javits" campaign committee. Everything was going well and I was about to make a little speech to the group when Marian excused herself and went into the bedroom. Not until I had finished speaking did I find out why: Her labor pains had begun and she thought we had better get to the hospital — quick. It was then about six o'clock. I took her down to our car and drove her the forty-five blocks to Jewish Memorial Hospital on Broadway and 196th Street, carefully stopping at every red light despite our urgency; after all, I *was* in my own congressional district, and it was election season. After Marian had been admitted, I waited, as nervous as any new father, until around midnight, when I was told it might take a few more hours and I should go home. So I went home and to bed and was no sooner settled than a phone call announced the birth of a baby girl. Back I dashed to the hospital as fast as I could, this time disregarding traffic lights. I felt guilty at my absence and wanted to join what now had become the majority of my family. We named our baby Joy Deborah, after Marian's maternal grandmother, Freda, meaning joy, and Deborah, meaning the prophetess, from the Bible.

In the spring of 1949, during a very busy session of Congress, Marian and Joy joined me in Washington. Jim Fulton very graciously moved out of the apartment on Q Street that we had shared, and my wife and daughter moved in. All went well enough until the summer. The session dragged on all through August and into September and I was involved as always with many different pieces of legislation. The apartment was not air-conditioned — few, if any, were in those days — and there was no swimming pool in the building. The only way to cool off was to go up to the roof. Marian, pregnant again, was suffering from morning sickness, and the baby, Joy, was quite ill with diarrhea. I remember that summer as a hot, messy, sticky time for everyone: nauseous mother, suffering baby, father changing diapers in the middle of the humid night. Marian remembers that I was helpful and considerate, but that I was away a lot and she was left alone in her own discomfort with the sick child and the stuffy apartment in an unfamiliar city from which most of the other congressional wives had fled for the summer. After some weeks of this, Marian felt that since I could not spend much time with her anyway she would be more comfortable in our airy apartment in New York, where her mother could visit and help her. We discussed the advantages of this, as another baby was coming, and we decided to see how that would work for us. So before the summer was out Marian and Joy moved back to Riverside Drive.

Up to then we had made our New York home in the apartment I had occupied as a bachelor. But early that fall, with our second child due to arrive around the end of the year, we found a new apartment that Marian could truly call her own. This one was at 450 Riverside, near Columbia University, in a building in which many of the university faculty members lived. The apartment was more ample and more suitable than our first one, and Marian happily went about the task of furnishing and decorating it in excellent taste and style. I went to Europe on another congressional study mission later that fall and Marian's warm, loving letters to me were full of home news about arranging the apartment, Joy's first steps, dinners with relatives and friends, and how much my wife missed me and awaited my letters and return. We lived at 450 Riverside for five years, the remainder of my service in the House of Representatives. It was a comfortable and pleasant apartment — even though I was never able to fully satisfy Marian's hunger for our being together — and it became a marvelous showcase for Marian's talents to make us a warm and delightful home.

Our son, Joshua, was born in January 1950, and with two small children to look after Marian was fulfilled and busy. My growing family gave me great pleasure and I slipped easily into the Washington official's commuter routine. Perhaps a memory of my mother traveling daily between Brooklyn and the Lower East Side to cook for my father made it easier for me to accept the split existence; or more probably it was just that I found as much satisfaction in my work at one end of the route as I did in my family at the other. In those days most House business was conducted from Tuesday through Thursday to accommodate the many congressmen able to return to their districts once a week. I had no social life in Washington at all: I was on the House floor or in committee all day, in my office in the evening for more work — and a phone call to Marian and the children — and then went to sleep in a succession of hotel suites and small apartments. I would be up early for a stop at the House gym for a game of paddle ball, which I rarely omitted, and then back to work.

Late Thursday I would return to New York to a warm welcome

from Marian. Friday was a day of work at the Javits & Javits law office, for we found it difficult to live comfortably on my congressional salary alone and I had to continue such law practice as was ethical and permissible. Friday night we usually dined quietly at home and caught up with each other; that was one evening sacred to the family, and I delighted in the joys of fatherhood. Politics returned on Saturday: As many as a hundred constituents streamed into my district office for help on individual problems of immigration, or government pensions, or the draft, or with landlords (I had set up rent-control clinics in the district, manned by a devoted corps of volunteer lawyers, and they required attention too). Saturday evenings Marian and I tried to go out together to the theater or a party or a dance; but as often as not those plans were changed by the need for me to attend a church or synagogue affair or a civic function in the district or a big anniversary or birthday party of an influential constituent; and Sundays were sometimes interrupted too. On Monday I usually put in another day of legal work, but Monday night was a fairly safe night for us to entertain, at least in the early days, even if Congress was in session. As the congressional workload increased, however, I often had to spend more days in Washington, so some Monday nights and even, though rarely, some Fridays were lost to Marian and my family.

Although Marian complained about my absences, particularly about the weekend evenings at district gatherings, which she thought were often a waste of time, those years at 450 Riverside were good years for our marriage. The children cemented our relationship and we enjoyed a measure of that happily shared living that marriage is all about. We entertained a widening circle of interesting friends, as diverse as Time-Life's Henry and Clare Boothe Luce and the Actors' Studio's Lee Strasberg. Marian took Spanish and Russian and English literature courses at Columbia, some painting classes at night, and some acting classes with Gertrude Lawrence. On important social occasions, such as some White House dinners and receptions, she would come to Washington. Several times we tried again to live in Washington with our children during a summer session.

As late as 1961, when I was already in the Senate, we were still trying. We sublet for the summer a large and luxurious house in McLean, Virginia, a Washington suburb. It had a swimming pool and plate-glass doors around a terrace looking out to a lovely country view. We had three children by then (Carla was the youngest, born in 1955) and they were thrilled at the prospect of living with Dad all summer. One day late in June we drove down in a station wagon from New York with the children and our luggage and arrived about six in the evening. It had been a hot drive, so Joshua, who was twelve, Carla, who was six, and I jumped into the pool for a swim while Joy, thirteen, stayed in the house to help Marian unpack. But Joy was so eager to join us in the pool that after a few minutes Marian told her to run along. Joy put on her bathing suit and ran out of the house toward the terrace — and failed to notice that the plate-glass doors were closed. The scene has frozen in our memories: the three of us bobbing in the pool, Joy bleeding from head to toe amidst the shards of glass, Marian screaming to get help. We thought of no doctors to call instantly, but the owners of the house had left emergency numbers near the phone; the McLean Fire Department responded with an ambulance and Joy was in the hospital within twelve minutes. She had nineteen stitches and for a while we thought she might lose an eye, but she recovered completely. That disaster almost marked the end of all serious attempts at Washington living — but we continued to try.

Marion's customary absence from Washington, where I have spent most of my post–World War II working life, has caused more comment than any other aspect of our marriage. It is often said that she finds the Washington scene not so interesting or so exciting as life in New York. Marian has said that Washington is in a sense a "company town"; it has only one business — government. But Marian's unhappiness with living in Washington originated in the unfortunate summer of 1949, and then deeper and more complex influences discouraged her from living there. Increasingly, my world became one of politics and government, and she turned to the artistic and intellectual side of life, which she felt she could find best in New York. Whether our physical separation was the result or a cause of this developing pattern of our marriage is difficult to say; it was probably something of both.

The core of the problem was Marian's growing disinterest in the demands of public life as it became clear that my priority was work. During her early visits to Washington she made friends with the wife of the French ambassador, Henri Bonnet, and complained to her one day about how difficult it was to tear me away from my work in Congress. Madame Bonnet tried to reassure her by saying, as Marian remembers it, "But isn't it better for you, his wife, that his work is his mistress?" Relationships change: Some years later, in a magazine interview, Marian turned the remark around and said that the *Senate* had become my wife and *she*, Marian, my mistress.

Marian was criticized for that one, but I understand what she meant. She is more than twenty years younger than I, and her expectations of marriage were so romantic: dinner together every night, little attentions, a complete sharing of emotions. She felt that I was more attentive to the Senate than I was to her and that I spent most of my time and thought with my "wife" — that is, my work — and came to my "mistress" Marian only when I could be spared from the Senate. This is something more than a joke: I think the point made is a fair one. Congress was my wife in the sense that my work there limited my marriage, rather than the other way around. I devoted to Marian and my family such time as I could take away from my work, to which I gave priority — except in family emergencies or on significant celebrations — and my relationship to Marian was constrained by my job, as a mistress's role may be limited by a man's obligations to his family. Marian feels that I had my priorities backward, that she should have been the most important element of my life.

It is not just a question of time and energy. Marian feels that I was so involved with my work that she was never able to catch hold of me emotionally. I did get my greatest satisfaction from the knowledge that what I did was affecting and helping the lives of millions of people, and it was not Marian's fault that marriage seemingly could not overcome my devotion and commitment to the public life I chose. Marian's view has been shared by thousands of women all through history who married men who went off to fight wars or conquer empires or write symphonies or paint masterpieces or achieve power, and who found an emotional satisfaction in those endeavors that they could not duplicate around the family hearth. Many such women were content to fit in with their husbands' work; in contemporary society, with so many options open to her, this clearly was not Marian's way. Her expectations of marriage were very high, romantic, and demanding. What she wanted of me was more than I could give.

In her concern with my emotions, Marian also felt that I was too caught up in intellectual process, too devoted to the nitty-gritty details of legislation and politics, to act even on occasion emotionally or impulsively — that is, by my definition, incautiously — in my public life. Interestingly, Ben had the opposite view: He considered me romantic and somewhat starry-eyed. Probably both of them were right: I fall somewhere in between the emotional expression Marian demands and the drive for security and success of which Ben tried to make me conscious. Marian points out accurately that whatever I was doing, whether it was work or playing tennis or attending a party, I did it single-mindedly and that I never enjoyed the "luxury" of wasting time. For me, even recreation is work.

I had married not only to raise a family, which we were quickly and happily accomplishing, but to find a tranquil haven in which I could rest from the conflicts and strains of political life. I did not expect my home to become another arena of controversy, and when it did, *I* was upset. Marian, when she was very young, had been influenced by radicals of the intellectual left, and their doctrine, added to the real injustices and privations she experienced, infused her with a spirit of rebellion and something of a distrust of the established political and social order.

In the beginning, these differences were not so apparent. Marian was rather awed by my position and did not seek to express or develop strong opinions of her own on public questions. But as she matured and digested my views on public affairs she started to pay closer attention to what I was doing down there in Washington; her own opinions evolved, and they tended on occasion to differ from mine. Essentially, I am devoted to the American system and to our society, not only out of patriotism but because I think it works better than any other governmental system yet devised; I feel most deeply that the best way to improve our society and eliminate injustice is by working within this system and using its apparatus for reform. Marian questioned some of the premises on which these beliefs were based; she was not necessarily opposed to them, and she did not lack patriotism, but she was impatient with the system's flaws, and she tended therefore to challenge the fairness of the system itself. I am part of the system, and even personally identify with it, and perhaps it is my fault that I did not want to be challenged that much at home.

She and our children were very vocal in opposition to the Vietnam War before I took a public antiwar position, and the many dinner- and breakfast-table debates we had on that subject contributed to the development of my own ideas. Marian and I could agree on civil rights and civil liberties and the efforts to improve health, education, job opportunities for minorities and women, welfare, and support for the arts. On these issues she was not only an effective ally and aide but frequently provided the spark that ignited my interest and activity. I am always anxious to have Marian's approval, as she is to have mine, and when we agree on something we complement each other very effectively.

Marian is a very substantial, highly intelligent woman with what is now enormous experience; she is hardheaded as a business woman and about financial affairs. She is also absolutely honest with herself and everyone around her. She always calls things as she sees them. This makes her intolerant of fakery and pretense, even when it is intended to avoid hurting other people unnecessarily. Also, her straight-forwardness made it difficult for her to accept the compromises that are central to the life of a legislator. She never quite felt entirely at home as a Senate wife. She dislikes the public's view of her as the "glamorous wife," rather than the contributing significant ally she has been.

So Marian seldom accompanied me to the hundreds of dinners and speeches and appearances I made over the years. Generally she came along only on the rather rare occasions when her presence was particularly required, but when she did attend she always performed graciously. I remember one evening at the Statler Hotel in Buffalo when Marian and I stood in line and shook hands with about two thousand constituents. Marian charmed everyone, but I never urged her to attend many of these functions.

Marian has always been extremely loyal to me. When I am not present and I am attacked or criticized in any gathering, she defends me like a tigress. I am much more tolerant of criticism than she is: Attacks are part of the political process and they do not bother me unduly. But Marian tends to regard criticism by others as an insult to me, and a criticism of me as an attack on her. To the world, there-fore, Marian has always been one of my staunchest defenders and explainers. Within our home, however, she has never hesitated to take me to task when she thinks I have transgressed. It is almost as if she believes that only she has the right to criticize me.

Marian clearly demonstrated her loyalty in 1954. A few years earlier, when she was complaining most about the demands on a congress-man's life, I sought to reassure her by telling her that when I was fifty I would leave elective office. It was not so much a pledge as it was a sincere statement of intention. Although I made that decision with her desires in mind, I was also aware that one could get stuck in the House of Representatives — there is only so much one can do there — and I calculated that after four terms I would be ready to move on to something that would be just as satisfying to me but would allow me to experience a more normal family life. Marian, of course, was delighted at the idea; she latched on to its promise and clung to it, and it enabled us to get through the next few years with our hopes intact.

Then, in 1954, I had the chance to run for attorney general of New York State. We discussed it and agreed that it was a political opportunity I could not forgo, even though I had just turned fifty. Although she concurred in my decision to make that run, Marian at that point almost despaired of ever having me as the kind of husband she wanted. Yet she turned to very loyally in a do-or-die campaign against Franklin D. Roosevelt, Jr.; she did a remarkable job in recruiting volunteers, getting tens of thousands of letters mailed, running my campaign office, and bringing in contributions and supporters I could never have attracted without her.

Her loyalty was rewarded, for my career then took a turn that drew us together for a time, as both of us had hoped it might. Soon after I was elected attorney general, Marian and I moved from Riverside Drive to an elegant apartment at 911 Park Avenue, much closer to the social and cultural world that Marian enjoyed. For the next two years I spent more time at home than during any period of our marriage before or since. Our daughter Carla, just born in 1955, added to the bliss of this high point of our marriage. We went on holidays; we had the use of an official car; we went to operas and plays and we entertained a good deal; life was so good that Marian and I ignored the promise that I would quit public life at age fifty.

When, in 1956, I ran into a personal political crisis and it became obvious that the only way I could vindicate myself was to get elected to the Senate, again Marian concurred — the decision was unavoidable — but she was not happy with it. And after I went to the Senate, although the honor was great and the prestige was enormous, and it drew great attention to Marian in so many ways as a bright and able and beautiful woman, the differences in our lives became more pronounced. For, in fact, I had not retired; the Senate demanded an even greater input of my time and energies — in Washington and on many overseas trips — and of course required less frequent election campaigns in New York. Marian observed that the senatorial routine tended to deprive a wife of much of her opportunity for individuality and to establish her more as an element of her husband's career. She contrasted that with the social and cultural life she was able to lead as a prominent and popular woman who moved with ease among brilliant and creative people — and she became less willing than ever to live in Washington. Slowly, with enduring mutual respect and loyalty, but not without some pain on both sides, we began to work out the modus vivendi of separate interests — two lives interacting and intersecting but not congruent — that characterizes our marriage to this day.

Our children remember the intense political discussions over the dinner table; Joshua believes they were of great value in developing his own abilities to think and argue politically. Carla has pointed out that these discussions at home made her realize that government is not some mysterious, remote entity but is made up of people who can change things — she is a reformer, intuitively and by proclivity. Joy was generally a listener but could come up with a burst of perspicacity that made us all realize how very thoughtful she really is. Here she showed what I hope is a hereditary instinct for getting the central point; for example, she asked whether Vietnam was a prudent commitment for the United States, without regard to its merits or morality.

We went on trips together: Christmas holidays to Mexico, Puerto Rico, Bermuda, and Jamaica; and the whole family went to Europe and to Israel for Joshua's formal entry into manhood according to the Hebrew faith, his bar mitzvah. In the winter I took the children ice-skating at Rockefeller Center (although these outings were sometimes interrupted for them when constituents came up to talk politics). Skating was a greatly cherished ritual because it also included hot chocolate and often lunch in the café. In the summer we went bike riding in Central Park or swimming in a friend's swimming pool in the nearby suburbs, and often we played tennis together. Joshua was the most athletic and the quickest learner. Carla was the most persevering, and Joy refused to get serious about sports, treating them as fun, as indeed they ought to be.

Even when I was away in Washington, the children recall, my values and my activities were very much a part of the family. They always knew where I was and what I was doing, and I telephoned every evening around dinnertime to talk to them. If any of the children had misbehaved, Marian told me about it so that I could exert some measure of parental discipline over the phone, sometimes quite effectively. Marian sometimes wished me to show a little anger or impatience, but generally we agreed on their upbringing. I wanted them to grow up as independent human beings, and so we listened to their opinions, even when they were little, and even then we gave their opinions serious consideration.

We took care never to use money as a sanction — as a reward or punishment. Remembering how my brother and I were financially tied together until I was in my thirties, I am particularly proud of how our children managed their money. We helped them through school, of course, but always through prearranged budgets for which they took responsibility. The children almost always came to me with their financial or educational problems and to Marian with their emotional problems and matters of personal relations. Obviously, they knew and understood their parents as well as we understood them.

In sum, I do not think that the children were damaged by my absences. They are very close to each other, and to us, and we are very proud of them. The girls are more like me in temperament, and Joshua is more like his mother; all three of them are sophisticated and wise. If there is anything about our children that dissatisfies me it is that none of them is yet married, and whether that has anything to do with their parents' lives I just do not know. There is no love like the love of a parent for a child, and I want our children to feel that love too — I hope I live to see it.

As the children grew up and went away to school Marian and I found less time to share. For example, it became progressively more difficult for me to manage to get to New York just for the opening night of a play for which we had tickets, or for a concert or a charity ball — which were so popular in the 1950s and 1960s. In the beginning I would arrange for some couple we knew to take her, and then perhaps an individual. Eventually she began to arrange these times herself. Moreover, my Senate responsibilities required me to make many trips abroad, and since Marian likes to travel too, it would have been good for both of us if she had come with me. We did try that a few times, but it did not work out, first because she became busier as a business and arts consultant, and second because she did not want to submit to the discipline of so many fixed appointments: the early breakfasts, and the lunches and dinners and meetings with ministers and parliamentarians and heads of governments. I was busy on these trips, talking to people and making notes, but she would have liked me to share more personal activities with friends or artists and writers, and join her at a museum, instead of the seemingly endless official business matters that took so much of my time and interests. To Marian, a trip abroad should be also something of a holiday. My view was that we could go to a museum or have lunch when I had nothing official on my schedule, or we could fit it in at, say, four o'clock, because the minister had postponed an appointment. So in later years she only accompanied me abroad on such very special trips as visits to the USSR and the People's Republic of China.

*　*　*

Marian has a keen intuition about people and character; she can assess a person's abilities and weaknesses and can determine who might be helpful to a particular cause and who should be avoided. Many times I have telephoned someone she selected who was indeed able to advance whatever issue I was working on at the moment.

I feel now that if I had been able to compromise more with Marian's views, I would have been happier. Paradoxical as it may sound, I might even have been more effective as a politician if I had taken her advice and devoted less attention to the endless paperwork and the details of congressional hearings, the conferences between House and Senate and among committee members and with colleagues, the marking-up of bills in committee and the floor debates — and if I had used that time to build personal and social relationships with the journalists, writers, educators, and politicians whose understanding support I needed and who could have given me an even broader base of political advice and assistance. For out of these relationships there develops a philosophy for action on many issues, and they tend to sharpen one's reasoning and purpose. When I had them I enjoyed them immensely, and that is proof of the fact that I needed more of them and always have.

But despite Marian's pleas I did not take that course often enough, because too frequently I felt I could not spare that time for evenings of dinners and parties and strictly personal exchanges. I suppose it was not my nature to do so. If it had been, if I had been able to utilize Marian's talents to their fullest, and had conditioned our relationships with friends, our social plans, and our journeys accordingly, I might have accomplished even more.

NINE

The Congressman in Domestic Affairs

Representative Leon H. Gavin was a conservative Republican from the most rural backwater of Pennsylvania. He had a distrust of city people, a gravel voice that sounded like coal running down a chute, and a belief that freshmen in Congress — especially Republican freshmen — should ask no questions and just vote the party line. On February 27, 1947, Leon Gavin welcomed me to the House of Representatives with a characteristic blast.

I had been a congressman for only six weeks, but I had just offered amendments to the portal-to-portal pay bill, which was on the verge of passage. The bill decreed that employers need not pay their workers for the time spent on the premises preparing for work — changing clothes, collecting equipment, and going from the mine entrance to the work face, for example — and my amendment sought to increase the protection for workers with rights to portal-to-portal pay already established in union contracts or by industry custom. "I am a Republican who was elected to come here and defend labor and employer alike," I had told the House. And I had reminded my Republican colleagues that our new majority "was created by men elected from the big cities, just like me, and it has lifted Republicans — many of whom have been here for years in the minority — lifted them into the majority. Let us not forget that. . . . Evenhanded justice . . . is all I ask be done."

Gavin made no comment on the substance of my amendment, but he rose a few minutes later to chastise me for my audacity in offering it and "taking up everybody's time." His voice rumbled through the chamber: "I listened with a great deal of interest to the distinguished gentleman from New York, who told us he represented the great metropolitan area. I might tell the gentleman that I represent a rural area of Pennsylvania and that the American people are sick and tired of the conditions that have been prevailing. . . . The hearings on the bill have been held. The committee, I presume, has given everybody an opportunity to present any proposals that they have had. . . . Most of the members are ready to vote on this legislation. Now amendment after amendment is being offered to muddy up the waters with the result that we are unable to take definite action and clean up this matter. . . . It is time for action and not talk."

Such, at least, is how the *Congressional Record* quotes Gavin's words. As I remember them, they were much stronger and more critical of the "gentleman from New York"; I believe Gavin exercised his privilege of "correcting and revising" his remarks and toned them down before they were inserted in the *Record*. At any rate, I confess I was somewhat taken aback for a moment, as Gavin had obviously intended me to be, even though I knew I had a perfect right to offer amendments. Then Chet Holifield of California came to my rescue.

"I am somewhat amazed," said Holifield, "at the remarks of the gentleman from Pennsylvania . . . who gave some of the new members on his side a tongue-lashing for presenting amendments. . . . I want the new members to know, if they do not already know it, that they have the parliamentary privilege of presenting amendments when in their good judgment and in their conscience they think an amendment should be presented. . . . When one of the older members gets up and gives you a tongue-lashing and implies you are reflecting on the judgment of the members of the committee which brought in the bill, it is just so much hogwash. . . . It is a grandstand play for the benefit of the gallery." As expected, my amendment was defeated and the bill was passed.

The Gavin tongue-lashing — which was reported in the New York papers and therefore did me more good than harm — contributed to my realization that I was unlikely to swim in my party's mainstream for a while, and that I would probably have to make my own way in the House. A similar lesson was administered to me at about the same time by Representative John Taber, who was the dean of New York's Republican congressional delegation. He was an ultraconservative from the western part of the state who had served in the House for nearly a quarter of a century and had become chairman of the Appropriations Committee. When his committee brought in a bill to cut the budget of the Office of Price Administration by $9 million, I respectfully questioned Taber about it on the floor of the House.

I said: "Do I understand the gentleman then to assure us — and the gentleman knows that I have very high regard for his assurance — that he is convinced that OPA can do the rent-control job with the funds which will be available to it after the passage of this bill?"

Taber replied: "I believe they can, if they do it honestly."

On the strength of his assurance I voted for the bill — only to learn a couple of days later that the cut would put the OPA out of business almost immediately. I began to hear from my constituents about it and, reversing my position, I did something that was very unusual but which in all good conscience I felt I had to do. I testified before the Senate Appropriations Committee, which was still considering the matter, and urged that it disapprove the bill I had voted for.

That embarrassing incident certainly taught me a lot about congressional advocacy and about how important it is to know who said what as well as what was said. In a political forum such as the House or Senate, one has to exercise eternal vigilance concerning every word and fact; everything in congressional debate is open to challenge, and the fine nuances are very important. It is essential to know the background and character of the other members, for every commitment and every expression must be taken in the context of the speaker's particular belief, record, and standing. Debate moves fast and it is almost impossible to retract something once said. To react quickly, it is necessary to develop a sixth sense about the opinions and the interests motivating the other members and the context in which they are speaking. In the case of the OPA appropriation, Taber was an avowed enemy of the entire rent- and price-control system; in his mind, the word "honestly" probably justified the answer that misled me.

* * *

Right from the beginning of my term in the Eightieth Congress, a combination of circumstances earned me a measure of notice, identified my prospective allies and opponents, and laid the groundwork for my future congressional career. As Congress convened, I found myself in a strange position: The Republican Party was in control of both Houses of Congress for the first time in fourteen years, which should have filled me with pleasant anticipation. But I was representing a district that was fundamentally Democratic, and I found that on most of the vital domestic and international issues facing the new Congress my own opinions were much closer to those of my district than to those of the House Republican leadership. In this clash of loyalties — loyalty to constituents, loyalty to party, and loyalty to myself — my constituents and I had to prevail. As I made up my mind on these issues one by one, I did not consider myself a rebel. Rather, I felt that my views were closer to the Lincolnian ideals of the party than were the views of the Republican congressional leaders who were frustrated by the long years of opposition in the minority (especially as a small minority in the Roosevelt years) and who seemed determined to put their stamp on the country and undo all they could of the works of the New Deal, which many of them considered oppressive and un-American.

Pragmatic politics and my own inclinations thus converged; again and again I had to make the kinds of speeches and offer the types of amendments that Gavin, Taber, and the old guard disliked. In my early House years, before I gained experience, found allies, and learned to sense the temper of my colleagues, my efforts must often have seemed quixotic and doomed to failure. But regardless of the prospects, I prepared carefully and stated my case as forcefully as I could. It would have gone against all my training as a trial lawyer to take a back seat in the legislative process and to let men no more honorable, patriotic, or intelligent than I tell me what to do so that I could go along and get along in the party. I was no wide-eyed "Mr. Smith" arriving in Washington from a strictly local background. I was forty-two years old when I entered Congress, and I knew how the world worked.

Nonetheless, I was always affected by the jitters just before any major action, particularly in those early days when I was about to cast a vote or take a position that I knew would be unpopular with my fellow Republicans, or which might be publicly unpopular. I used to walk from my office to the House, and on the way I knew full well that I would do exactly what I proposed to do when I got there, but I was nervous en route. I had felt the same way in my lawyering days in New York, when I walked from the Javits & Javits office to the Federal Courthouse, wondering whether I would perform up to par; I always had butterflies in my stomach until the moment I opened my mouth in court — at which point I was under way and had no more doubts.

The novelty of a Republican Congress intrigued the country, and because the American public loves to cheer a maverick, my activities attracted a great deal of press attention. In the first session of the Eightieth Congress, I spoke out on the floor more often — and on a greater variety of subjects — than any other congressman from Manhattan, and the New York papers ate it up. In March the *New York Times* remarked on the freshman speaking out for liberal measures, and the United Press noted that I was crossing party lines more often than any other Republican. By April, Drew Pearson had reported on my doings three times in his widely read column, "Washington Merry-Go-Round," and had praised my independent voting record. Independence, of course, cuts both ways: When I voted *with* the Republican leadership on a tax bill, a liberal newspaper expressed dismay and called me a "riddle." There was no riddle. I was, officially and in truth, a Republican-Liberal — and I had and have a hard head about money.

Despite my disagreements with Republican policy, I found understanding and friendship at the highest level of the party in Congress. Joseph W. Martin, Jr., of Massachusetts, led the Republicans in the House through all my four terms there. He served as Speaker of the House in the Eightieth and Eighty-third Congresses, when the Republicans were in the majority, and as minority leader when the Democrats were in control. There was no question of Joe Martin's conservatism, but he had a professional politician's pragmatic view of party discipline. "As long as you vote Republican for the organization of the House," he told me soon after I arrived, "from then on it is your job to get reelected and to do whatever it takes to get reelected." On such matters as the election of the Speaker and votes on adjournment or the calendar of House business — matters of leadership prerogative — the party generally could count on my vote; otherwise I felt free to act as I saw fit.

That meant that I tried to reflect the most rational judgment of my informed constituents on money matters — because when it comes to money I think a representative should follow what people think is best for themselves. But on matters of constitutional principle, individual liberty, or the care of the poor and the oppressed, I did my best to ascertain the need and respond to it. And when the moral content of the decision was great — for example, on the major issues of civil rights — my own conscience and training and experience determined the vote.

The Speaker befriended me in the House from the start, and for this I could thank my brother's contacts. Ben lived in Westport, Connecticut, and through him I met Sam Pryor, a powerful Connecticut Republican politician who had been one of Wendell Willkie's principal sponsors and mentors in 1940 and who was close to Joe Martin. Pryor personally introduced me to Martin and pointed out that I had been elected from a heavily Democratic district. Pryor's introduction gave me an immediate advantage over the other new Republican members knocking on the Speaker's door. As a result of it I was appointed to the Foreign Affairs Committee, as I had hoped to be, and that first appointment determined the direction of much of my future career.

Joe Martin and I voted differently on many important issues over the years, but I do not believe he ever regretted his early favors to me. Exactly ten years after we first met, on the day I was being sworn in as a senator, Joe Martin strolled over from the House (where he was still minority leader), put his arm around my shoulders as we stood behind the desks near the dark brown leather sofas on which senators' top staff members sit, and let his gaze sweep across the Senate chamber. "Jack," he said, "this is a very hard place to get to. Ask me, I have tried for years."

The domestic issue that marked me most indelibly as a maverick was labor-management relations, particularly the historic Taft-Hartley Act. A wave of major strikes had beset the nation right after the war as the unions sought to catch up with rising prices and to compensate for four years of wartime controls. Some of their strikes — on the railroads and in the automobile, coal, and steel industries — had threatened the whole economy, and the public mood had turned against the unions. Even the Seventy-ninth Congress, controlled by the Democrats, who were officially prolabor, had passed an antilabor bill and had come within five House votes of overriding President Truman's veto of it. Antiunion feeling had been partly responsible for the Republican congressional victory in 1946, and so it was inevitable that the Eightieth Congress would crack down on labor in 1947.

The Portal-to-Portal Act, on which Gavin had lectured me, was one harbinger of things to come. A week later the Supreme Court gave judicial sanction to the "punish-the-unions" mood by upholding the conviction of the United Mine Workers in an illegal-strike case. (The President had seized the coal mines under his wartime powers, which had not yet expired, and the UMW had defied an injunction ordering the miners back to work.)

My own labor sympathies alerted me to the dangers in this situation. On March 19 I wrote to Representative Fred A. Hartley, Jr., of New Jersey, the conservative chairman of the House Education and Labor Committee, who was conducting hearings on a tough new labor relations bill. In my letter, which I released to the press, I urged Hartley not to write legislation that would cause industrial strife. "Our country," I wrote, "has much more to gain from constructive legislation, yes, even moderate legislation, than from taking drastic action, which will inevitably have drastic reaction. . . . American workers and their families should be given no cause to harbor resentment for years to come."

The bill that emerged from Hartley's committee was anathema to labor on almost every point. Besides banning the closed shop, industrywide bargaining, jurisdictional strikes, secondary boycotts, and mass picketing, it forbade employer contributions to union welfare funds and made unions liable to damage suits for breaches of contract. Most important, it provided that whenever the President declared that a work stoppage would imperil the national health or safety, court injunctions could be issued to force the union to continue working during a mediation and cooling-off period.

During the debate on the bill I offered an amendment to do away with the injunction provision — which I described as "involuntary servitude and ineffective in the public interest." Instead of injunctions, my amendment would have authorized the President to seize any struck plant or mine in a national emergency and to operate it not for the profit of the private owners but only to the minimum extent required for public health and safety. The government, in my plan, would pay the workers the prevailing wages of the area and would pay the owners "just compensation" for the use of the facility. In this way, the facility could keep operating and both workers and management would have an incentive to settle their differences quickly. The Hartley bill, I argued, "trades on the very real fear of the American people that any labor group might paralyze the country by a strike." My proposal, I pointed out, could relieve that fear by providing an alternate — and more effective — means of preventing such paralysis "and in this way enable us to deal constructively with labor, free of the pressure of this legitimate public fear." The Hartley bill, I said, "is not statesmanlike legislation; it is legislation driven by fear and vindictiveness; it is legislation with a cutlass not a scalpel." I wound up my speech with a heartfelt appeal:

> I know what I am talking about in matters affecting labor, for I am myself a son of a working man.... Before the days when unions in the clothing industry amounted to much my father worked in a shop for fourteen hours a day during the season. He carried his own machine on his back, supplied his own thread and his own needles and for all of this he received just about a current living wage. But the season lasted just four months, and for the other eight months he had the privilege of starving to death. I say that what you are doing in this bill in the pulverization of labor unions, and in the destruction of gains made by working people for fifty years, is of a nature to bring back those sweatshop and substandard conditions. No American wants that to happen.

My amendment was voted down (the suggestion that the government seize private property, even in national emergencies, horrified many businessmen), and moderate amendments proposed by other members were likewise defeated.

The Hartley bill passed the House on April 17 with only twenty-two Republicans, myself included, voting against it. Taft's Senate version passed a few weeks later. On June 20 President Truman vetoed the Taft-Hartley bill, criticizing it as manifestly unfair to labor. On the same day, with no debate, the House passed the bill over his veto (two-thirds required) by a vote of 331 to 83. I was one of only eleven Republicans voting to sustain the Democratic President's veto, and as I called out my "Nay" and walked out of the chamber (I had taken a seat near the doors) I could almost feel the disapproving glances of some of my Republican colleagues stabbing me like arrows. Across the aisle, only seventy-one Democrats had supported their own President; one of them was John F. Kennedy. Three days later the Senate also voted to override the veto, and Taft-Hartley became law.

As we had predicted, Taft-Hartley was ineffective in curbing serious strikes — besides being repressive to labor. During the first two years of its operation, four injunctions were issued under its authority in national-emergency strikes, and in none of them did the cooling-off period provide any settlement.

A campaign for repeal, or at least significant revision, of Taft-Hartley grew in intensity, and when the Democrats regained control of Congress in 1949 we expected results. But the coalition of conservative Republicans and Southern Democrats who had supported the bill in the first place managed to substitute for the administration's repeal bill a new piece of legislation that was essentially a copy of Taft-Hartley with only minor prolabor revisions. Again I submitted my seizure amendment as a way out of the impasse brought on by national-emergency strikes — and again it was defeated. The House sent the false "repeal" bill back to committee, which kept the possibility of Taft-Hartley revision alive, but the battle between the prolabor and antilabor forces was then shifting to the issue of the minimum wage, and the Taft-Hartley law did not come up again in that session.

Despite its elemental humaneness, the proposal to raise the statutory minimum wage (then forty cents an hour) caused so much controversy that four successive bills went through the House Education and Labor Committee, each one weaker than the one before it, until the weakest one finally reached the floor. Finally, everyone agreed on seventy-five cents and the issue boiled down to how many workers would be covered. I fought against an amendment that excluded an estimated eight hundred fifty thousand workers from the minimum-wage system, but the amendment passed.

Even though the final bill contained a cut in coverage, I voted for it. The Senate had not yet acted on the measure and it was my hope that a better version would eventually emerge when the Senate and House bills were adjusted in conference. Such votes can sometimes be misconstrued, but I generally voted for the passage of a bill that I favored on the whole, even if it contained provisions with which

I disagreed. That way, it progressed into conference where it could be improved. In this case my hope was justified: The bill that finally became law excluded only five hundred thousand workers from minimum-wage coverage; at the same time, 1.5 million workers who had been earning less than seventy-five cents an hour gained immediate raises under the law. Since few, if any, of the workers removed from the system actually found their wages cut, the net gain was tremendous.

Labor legislation provided only part of the excitement of that 1949 session of the Eighty-first Congress, which for me was the busiest, most productive, and most significant of my eight years in the House of Representatives. I was constantly on the go, commuting regularly between New York and Washington, meeting with my constituents on Saturdays, trying to spend Sundays with Marian and our new baby, putting in a few hectic hours at Javits & Javits on Mondays, and then grabbing a train or plane back to Washington. My position on the Foreign Affairs Committee involved me deeply in many of the important decisions that marked the early stages of the Cold War. Simultaneously, I was engaged in the struggles for housing, rent control, health legislation, civil rights, and dozens of less momentous matters. I even introduced a bill to plan the establishment of national theater, opera, and ballet companies, a forerunner of my later Senate work on the National Endowment for the Arts.

I was learning, that year, how to be effective on my own, without being a favorite of many of my party leaders. I could not carve out a comfortable niche of expertise on one subject and expect my party to anoint me as its spokesman on that issue; I had to get involved in almost everything, become knowledgeable in just about every subject that affected my district, or else be crushed between the two parties. Most important, I had to join in to counter the powerful coalition of Southern Democrats and conservative Republicans who were blocking so much socially beneficial legislation and enacting repressive laws.

It was in the crucible of a long fight over housing that a liberal alliance of urban representatives of both parties emerged to challenge the dominance of the conservative coalition. The severe housing shortage of those years touched several chords in me: my slum boyhood, my constituents' needs, and my contacts with other veterans. The returning veteran who wanted to settle down and raise a family suffered most from the lack of housing. On the other hand, I had come to Congress believing that business could operate in the public interest; as I had suggested in one of my 1946 letters to the *Herald Tribune,* I had hoped that private enterprise would subordinate profit-making considerations to help solve the housing crisis as it had solved wartime production problems. In principle, I was opposed to government taking over any job business could handle.

It soon became apparent, however, that business was not going to be able to do an adequate job, that government efforts to provide decent housing for veterans were going to be necessary, and that government intervention was needed to remove the disgrace of the postwar housing crisis. Early in 1947 I introduced the bipartisan Taft-Ellender-Wagner bill, which had passed the Senate in 1946 but had then died in the House. It provided funds to build five hundred thousand units of low-rent public housing over four years and additional federal grants to aid urban redevelopment — that is, slum clearance. Research, farm housing, and liberalized federal mortgage guarantees were also included in the bill. Underlying this bill was the recognition that the nation needed a total of 1.2 million new homes every year for ten years in order to wipe out the shortage caused by the years of depression and war, and that two-thirds of the people needing housing could not afford to pay more than $40 a month in rent. When it became apparent in mid-June that such a comprehensive plan still had no chance of passing the House, I introduced a resolution calling for an investigation of the housing shortage.

My resolution was superseded by another one calling for a joint Senate-House study, and when that came up in July 1947 the debate degenerated into partisan wrangling. Charles Halleck of Indiana, our Republican majority leader, happened to be carrying the ball for the Republican side. He was a very tough, even slightly choleric, conservative politician, deeply devoted to the party and its policies, who measured his Republican colleagues by only one standard: whether they were voting with him or against him.

Debating the resolution for an investigation, Halleck rose and said, "If there is a housing shortage today it should be laid right smack at the door of the Democratic New Deal administration which controlled the government for fourteen years and which permitted this situation to come about. . . . As a matter of fact the papers carried the information that in the month of June more houses were constructed than had been built in years. That is what has taken place just from the fact that you have a Republican administration in Washington again and the people are beginning to get some things done." (Charlie Halleck was so pleased to find himself in the majority that year that he seemed to think a Republican administration was in control of the executive branch of the government too, which of course it was not.)

This partisan stance bothered me. I took the floor and said, "I trust I will be pardoned if I ask the members for a little less heat and a little more light on this trying subject." I cited figures to show that housing starts were only about half of what they should have been to solve the shortage and stated that the resolution for an investigation "is the very least that we must do at this time ... for I am by now most regretfully convinced that there is no chance of passing the Taft-Ellender-Wagner bill before this session ends." Then I summarized the essence of the dispute:

> There exists a basic difference of view between some members of Congress who sincerely believe that the private building industry ... will be able to fill our housing needs ... and those members, of whom I am one, who are convinced that the critical housing shortage is a liquidation of the war emergency and the government must help materially. ... If we needed any proof of that, the desperate plight of the two to four million veterans ... especially the newly marrieds living doubled up or in bad housing, would be an eloquent enough answer.

The resolution passed, and when the joint committee was established, Senator Joseph McCarthy of Wisconsin became its vice chairman. In those early postwar years McCarthy was a champion of veterans' rights and this brought him into the housing battle. He often invited the freshmen Republican congressmen who were veterans, like myself, to late-afternoon parties at the old Willard Hotel, where he served Wisconsin cheeses and a drink and we talked housing strategy. I had heard about McCarthy's egocentricity and his wartime prediction that he would go far in politics from Duane Faw, who was an early supporter of mine while he attended Columbia Law School. But I got to know McCarthy myself during these early struggles for housing and veterans' benefits. Although he worked hard for veterans' housing loan guarantees and other legislation to help veterans buy homes, Senator McCarthy did not favor the kind of public-housing programs for the poor and working poor that I felt were necessary, and so we diverged, even then.

* * *

Early in 1948 the new liberal bipartisan coalition began to take shape. At the start it centered around veterans, and the issue it focused on was housing. In February, under the auspices of the American Veterans Committee, Congressman John F. Kennedy and I, who had already cooperated on the Veterans' Housing Act the previous year, put together a National Veterans' Housing Conference in Washington. Franklin D. Roosevelt, Jr., who was elected to Congress himself the following year, and Robert F. Wagner, Jr., later mayor of New York City, joined us as principal sponsors.

The conference was intended to make Congress aware of veterans' housing needs, which we knew were critical, but as we started to organize the event it did not seem that we would attract many participants. The returns were slow in coming in, and as the date drew closer we got very nervous, knowing that a failure would discourage many of our congressional colleagues who were almost ready to support a strong housing bill. In one of our last meetings before the conference, as we went over the agenda and inspected the auditorium of the Department of Labor, where the gathering was to take place, we were very gloomy indeed, as it appeared then that only a few hundred people would show up. But on the appointed day at about 10:00 A.M. the crowd began to pour in, and we ended up with more than thirteen hundred veterans from all over the country. The exultation we felt that day, the backslapping and the happy congratulations we exchanged, have seldom been equaled in my career.

In April, after the Senate again passed the Taft-Ellender-Wagner bill and the House committee bottled it up once more, Jack Kennedy and I filed a discharge petition (which needed 218 signatures, a majority of the House, to be effective) to force the House Banking and Currency Committee to report the bill; with the petition we distributed a detailed explanation of how low-income federal housing worked. But when the bill was finally reported the Rules Committee prevented it from reaching the floor, and the House — and later the Senate — passed instead an emasculated housing bill containing most of the Taft-Ellender-Wagner provisions *except* the important parts, public housing and slum clearance.

So, not until that busy spring of 1949, with the Democrats again in control, did the showdown battle on housing take place. Lobbyists for and against the housing bill descended on Washington by the hundreds, and the atmosphere was one of intense and often acrimonious debate. Truman had made passage of a significant housing bill one of the main issues of his campaign, but the conservative coalition still stood in the way in the House and it became obvious immediately that the administration Democrats would not be able to enact a housing bill without the help of liberal — and moderate — Republicans.

To rally the prohousing forces on our side of the aisle, I teamed up with Representative Frances Bolton of Ohio, a woman of great determination and charm. We were both members of the Foreign Affairs Committee. In January 1949 Mrs. Bolton and I enlisted eight of our Republican colleagues to sponsor a new comprehensive housing bill that preserved the essence of the original Taft-Ellender-Wagner proposals. It provided for eight hundred thousand units of low-rent public housing to be constructed over a six-year period at a maximum cost to the federal government of $308 million per year; for slum clearance, the bill allowed a billion dollars in loans and $500 million in capital grants. Our bill was something of a compromise between a more ambitious administration plan and a more conservative measure introduced by Senator Taft in the Senate. There was one provision of our bill, however, that was new and unique: direct loans to cooperative and nonprofit corporations to build housing for the lower-middle-income groups — those families who could not afford private housing but who could not qualify for the public housing to be financed by the federal government.

I worked hard for this housing bill. I testified before both the Senate and House committees in favor of our direct loan provisions for middle-income housing, which I said would help 15.5 million families, "the solid foundation of our middle class." In May, I addressed the National Public Housing Conference, an organization of public-housing officials, emphasizing the bipartisan housing coalition emerging in Congress and urging the officials to police themselves against housing abuses. By June, the Senate had passed a bill similar to ours (but without the middle-income direct loans provisions) and the House battle was reaching a climax. The Republican leadership of the House, claiming that it merely wanted to avoid a federal deficit, had announced its implacable opposition to the administration's bill. My progressive Republican colleagues and I found ourselves holding the key to a compromise.

At that point I organized a congressional tour of New York and Philadelphia slums. Mayor O'Dwyer of course cooperated and took our group in buses to inspect some of the city's decaying neighborhoods. As I recall it, we went to Madison Street on the Lower East Side, not far from where I was born, and the first apartment he showed us was so much like the one I had lived in for the first thirteen years of my life that it gave me a chill. There I was, forty-five years old, and the slum conditions on the Lower East Side were exactly as I had experienced them thirty years earlier: the toilet in the hall shared by four families; no bathroom, just a sink and two washtubs; only one room facing the street; the kitchen doubling as dining room; and the dank, malodorous hallways lit by a dim electric bulb — the only "modern" improvement over the gaslight I remembered. The trip certainly impressed my colleagues from the wonderful, open faraway places like Illinois, Kansas, and Nebraska, and gave them — in some cases for the first time — an idea of the conditions public housing was designed to deal with.

On June 23, addressing the House, I showed my colleagues photographs of the slums we had seen and compared them to photos of public housing. I attempted to rebut the economic arguments against the bill by comparing the figures of $300 million a year to be invested in low-rent housing to the $15 billion a year spent for national defense. And I said:

> We are told today that private enterprise on the one hand is doing the job, but we know it cannot, because if it were, we would not have these urgent representations that are coming up from the leading national organizations, the cities and communities, the veterans and people generally, for this type of relief, a demand that comes from all over the country. . . . Somewhere there is a gap, and I submit that this bill is designed to fill up that gap.

Our attempts to add the middle-income housing loans to the bill failed, but other amendments brought the figures in the bill into conformity with the more modest Senate version, and with our January bill. Then, on June 29, the die-hard opponents of public housing made their last desperate effort to defeat it. The key vote came on an amendment to eliminate the public-housing title from the bill. Twenty-four Republicans joined 184 Democrats (and independent Vito Marcantonio) to defeat that amendment by the narrow margin of five votes (209 to 204) and thus save the bill. An amendment to recommit the bill was defeated by a slightly larger margin, after which the housing bill passed by a vote of 227 to 186. As they saw which way the wind was blowing, ten of my fellow Republicans changed their stand at the end; thirty-four Republicans voted for the bill. The Housing Act of 1949, signed into law by President Truman on July 15, would have been an impossible achievement without our twenty-four Republican votes on June 29. In this victory our small band of progressive Republicans, which was to increase in influence in the years ahead, won its spurs.

The housing shortage underlined the need for strong rent-control legislation, but my conservative colleagues did not agree with that proposition either. In 1947, in extending wartime rent controls for a year, Congress permitted a 15 percent "voluntary" increase in rents — that is, where tenants and landlords agreed to it — and what choice did the tenants have considering the woeful shortage of housing? With other representatives from the cities — where most voters were renters — I opposed the increase, arguing that tenants could be forced to sign a "voluntary" lease by the threat of eviction. When we lost this battle I urged my constituents not to be panicked into agreeing to rent increases, and to help them cope with the complexities of the law I established a number of "rent clinics" in my district.

Sam Roman, who represented part of the Twenty-first Congressional District in the New York State Assembly, cosponsored the clinics with me. On specified evenings, residents of the district could go to the Republican or Liberal clubhouses, where volunteer teams of competent and enthusiastic young lawyers gave free legal advice on the rent laws and suggestions on dealing with landlords who may not have been providing the services to tenants that they were supposed to provide. Over the years the clinics helped thousands of tenants — who of course remembered the congressman who had set them up.

On June 23, 1949 (the same day I addressed the House on the housing bill), I managed to give my constituents — and tenants everywhere — a new legal safeguard. This was a rent-control amendment requiring landlords to certify that they were maintaining all building services before they could get that "voluntary" 15 percent increase permitted under the legislation. The Javits amendment, as it came to be known, restored the balance of justice between landlord and tenant. In the first year of its operation, in New York City alone, more than seventeen thousand tenants successfully had their rents reduced or their services restored by recourse to this law.

Still another major issue of domestic legislation competed for my time and energy during that spring and summer of 1949. President Truman presented to Congress a comprehensive national health program, the Ewing Plan (named for Federal Security Administrator Oscar R. Ewing), which called for compulsory national health insurance to be financed by a 3 percent payroll tax. The American Medical Association criticized the plan as "socialized medicine" because under it the federal government would have paid the doctors and the hospitals directly. Trade unions and liberal and civic groups supported the scheme.

I knew we needed a fair, orderly, and economical way to deliver health care. As a child I had seen illness all around me on the Lower East Side. During the Eightieth Congress I had introduced a bill that eventually became the National Heart Act of 1948, establishing the National Heart Institute to coordinate and carry out research and training in heart diseases — my first legislative success, which won me friends and helped reelect me.

Despite this deep concern, I felt the Ewing Plan could create such a huge and sudden demand for medical services and raise expectations of help from the federal government so high that the whole health-care system would break down. So with six other House Republicans I introduced an alternative. We proposed that local, cooperative health plans and private insurers pay the medical bills for their subscribers, with federal and state governments making up the difference between the cost of the medical service and the money available to the local plan from subscribers' fees. The fees were to be set at 3 percent of the subscribers' income — up to an annual income of $5000. Our proposal envisaged the establishment of hundreds of non-profit health-insurance organizations, like Blue Cross and Blue Shield and the Kaiser-Permanente plan in California, each one locally controlled. Since membership in these plans would be voluntary for both doctors and patients, we hoped the AMA might eventually support our proposal, but it never did.

Both our bill and the Ewing Plan were buried in committee that year, and although I reintroduced our bill year after year, no action was taken during my service in the House. Little did I dream when I first introduced that bill in 1949 that eleven years later, as a senator, I would again be involved in a similar debate with Jack Kennedy, my House colleague, who would then be the Democratic Party's candidate for President — or that thirty years later the United States would still lack a comprehensive national health-care system.

* * *

The passage of a good bill does not always solve a problem; the Housing Act of 1949 provided for one hundred thirty-five thousand units of low-income public housing every year, but construction never reached half of that goal. The will of Congress was undermined by cuts in appropriations, a facet of the legislative process that seldom gets the attention it deserves.

The sabotage of the public-housing program began in 1951. Under the act, the President had the authority to cut housing starts down to as low as fifty thousand in any year if economic conditions so required. Citing shortages of construction material caused by the Korean War, Truman in 1951 cut housing starts to only seventy-five thousand units for 1952. Then the real-estate lobby and congressional opponents of public housing went to work and the Appropriations Committee cut that figure to fifty thousand. That was a move of doubtful legality and we fought against it. But the worst was still to come. The House, as the Committee of the Whole, debated the appropriations bill on a Thursday and Friday; that meant that no final vote could be taken until the Committee of the Whole (in which a quorum was only 100 members, less than one-fourth of the House) reported to the whole House (where a quorum was 218), and we were informed by the bill's managers that that would not happen until the following week. Consequently, twenty-one of New York City's twenty-four congressmen, myself included, as well as many housing supporters from other Eastern cities, went home to their districts for the weekend. We did not notice that the antihousing bloc was remaining behind.

Late that Friday, with only about one hundred fifty members in the chamber, Representative Ed Gossett, a Democrat from Texas, moved to cut the housing starts to merely five thousand, thereby gutting the Housing Act of 1949. Two Chicago Democrats desperately tried to block the coup, but after only about half an hour of debate the Gossett amendment was passed, 110 to 40. Contrary to our understanding, the committee then rose and a formal, record vote was called. The few prohousing representatives present scurried around looking for their allies, but most of us had been lulled — or gulled — into leaving town. The record vote showed 181 for the cut and 113 against it.

When we learned what had happened we were furious. The fight to rescue the housing program ranged from Capitol Hill to New York's City Hall. We immediately established an Emergency Committee to Save Public Housing, hoping to gather enough public support to reverse the cut in the Senate, which was still considering the bill. On the committee, besides myself, were leading religious, labor, and political figures, including the bishop of the Episcopal Diocese of New York, the Right Reverend Horace W. B. Donegan; Robert F. Wagner, Jr., who was then Manhattan borough president; and Roy Wilkins of the National Association for the Advancement of Colored People. New York Mayor Vincent Impellitteri called a protest meeting in City Hall, which was attended by three hundred public officials and spokesmen for civic organizations. President Truman, who was as outraged as we were, sent a telegram to the meeting, stating, "I hope the public meeting you have called will arouse the citizens of the largest city in the country, in the entire nation, to a realization of the danger which threatens us if the real-estate lobby succeeds in killing public housing." The national security was endangered, Truman added, by the lobby's attempt to kill the federal housing program.

In the House, I read to my colleagues a letter from the administrator of the Housing and Home Finance Agency, Raymond Foley, stating that seventy-five thousand units a year could be built with materials that were available. I said, "It now appears quite clear that the action taken was unwarranted by any requirements of defense mobilization, but was rather dictated by an effort to reverse on an appropriations bill a housing program which had been authorized by the Congress . . . after years of effort and consideration." The loud protest we raised helped rally the housing forces in the Senate. The Senate restored the fifty thousand–unit figure, and after another close fight over the conference report the Senate version prevailed in the House.

In order to salvage anything of the housing program we had to run through similar scenarios annually for the next three years. Through 1955 only about one hundred eighty thousand of the eight hundred ten thousand units of low-rent public housing authorized by the Housing Act of 1949 had been completed, because of the obstruction by the real-estate lobby and its allies in the Congress.

That public-housing struggle had a lasting effect on my attitude toward U.S. business. It taught me that there was a limit to the degree to which business could be entrusted to serve public responsibilities, and that the profit motive had to be considered. Profit is an entirely legitimate and proper motive for business, and it is a powerful stimulant to the construction of our society, the most productive the world has known. But private enterprise, I realized, could not be depended upon to supply all that might be needed socially; the social need in this case was for housing for the poor and low moderate-income families, which might not be built without government partnership or assistance, or government incentive through the tax system or otherwise. This was a critical lesson for me. It conditioned my thinking for the future and marked a definite point of departure from Ben's idea of entrusting private enterprise alone with the entire responsibility.

* * *

Of all the domestic matters I faced as a congressman, the twin issues of housing and rent control probably did the most for my popularity and my repeated successes at the polls. This remained true even after 1950, when New York State enacted its own rent-control law providing better protection for tenants than the federal law.

Just before the New York law became operative on May 1, the federal housing expeditor, Tighe Woods, authorized four thousand rent increases of 15 percent each — for a total burden on the tenants of approximately $1 million a year. These increases would not have been permitted under the state law that was about to come into effect, and I protested vehemently in well-publicized telegrams to Woods. I charged that Woods was making an effort to "circumvent the New York State law" and that he was not observing the Javits amendment requiring landlords who got increases to certify that they are rendering all services to the tenants. In a press statement released with my telegram I declared that "most of these substantial increases have been or are being awarded to properties owned by large insurance companies. Seemingly, Washington is signing off its New York rent-control program with a final 'pat on the back' to the large property owners."

I also reminded tenants that they need not pay increases after the New York State law came into effect unless the courts decided they had to.

This controversy went on for several months. Woods's responses to my protests were unsatisfactory, so I called for investigations of his decisions and introduced a bill in the House that would have invalidated his last-minute rent increases. I also endeavored to amend the new federal rent-control law that was then being debated so as to prevent the housing expeditor from taking any action inconsistent with a state rent-control law. My amendment and my invalidation bill were both defeated and my protest to Tighe Woods evoked nothing more than polite letters. But the voters realized that, on the issue of rent control at least, they were getting a better deal from the Republican Dewey Administration in Albany than from the Democratic Congress and administration in Washington.

Although nothing that happened in Congress on rent control would have a direct effect on the tenants in my district after the New York law took over, I continued to speak out in the House debates on the subject. At one point, Albert Cole of Kansas, a conservative Republican with whom I almost never agreed, became exasperated with me. Cole believed that rent control was an abridgment of constitutional freedoms; he had utter faith in the beneficial effects of the free market in housing. "We have been treated this afternoon," he said, "by an amazing spectacle of part of a delegation of a great state taking the major part in the argument in the consideration of a bill in which they are not interested. . . . I cannot understand . . . the great interest displayed upon this floor, particularly in general debate, by those members from the metropolitan area of New York who are not interested in the result of this bill. Cheap politics, the buying of votes, may or may not be the reason, but I would like to know why the people from the metropolitan area of New York want to wag this dog's tail today."

It was clear that Cole was referring to me, so I asked him to yield and replied:

> I am one of the representatives over here from the metropolitan area who is for this bill, and I should like to tell the gentleman why. In the first place it is not an appeal for votes as the gentleman wants us to believe, because we have rent control in New York. We are for it and for it very determinedly because New York, the greatest city in the world and the greatest city in this country, does the most business with the people of the United States. We feel that the economic situation of the whole country requires the continuance of rent control. Therefore, it is very

much a question of primary interest to the people of the city of New York and the people of the state of New York.

"We are deeply moved," Cole responded, "by the great sympathy of the people of the city of New York."

Eventually, perhaps inevitably, my concern with this issue raised the hackles of Republicans who were more important to me than those from Kansas: that is, the Republicans in New York. In 1953, Governor Dewey and the New York State Legislature enacted an across-the-board 15 percent rent increase applicable to all rentals that had not risen by that much since the first wartime rent freeze. This was a state and not a federal matter, so it did not concern me in any formal, legal sense. But by that time, in my fourth term in Congress, I had established myself as the leading Republican defender of tenants' rights, and I could not and would not look the other way.

In private and in public I spoke out against the increase. Housing, I insisted, was still in serious short supply — and therefore it should be regarded during the emergency as tantamount to a public utility. I said that landlords should be guaranteed a fair return on their investment and should be allowed increases if necessary to ensure that fair return; but a general increase not based on landlords' needs was unfair, I said, and would lead to a rapid upward spiral of rent. Also, I opposed the suggestion that vacated apartments be automatically decontrolled, because this would give landlords an incentive to evict tenants for one excuse or another. I made these arguments in a series of letters and telegrams and press statements, and I introduced a bill that would have enabled New York City to go back to federal rent control if the state law were not renewed. Finally, I publicly urged Governor Dewey to veto the increases. I believe that Dewey never forgave me for "interfering" in state matters that he considered out of bounds for a congressman.

While my constituents, and liberals generally, applauded my efforts on housing, on labor, and on foreign affairs, the ultraconservatives in my party were horrified by my consistent stand against the erosion of civil liberties that I strongly felt was taking place in the nation in the name of anti-Communism. To the right wing of the Republican Party, nothing certified my apostasy more than my opposition to the witch-hunt tactics of the campaign against Communist "subversion." In my first term, I was one of only eight Republicans voting against the Mundt-Nixon bill, which would have required the federal registration of all "Communist-front" organizations — whatever that meant. Repeatedly I voted against appropriations for the House Un-American Activities Committee (originally the Dies committee) — and in 1949 I introduced resolutions to abolish it and establish instead a Joint (Senate-House) Committee on National and International Movements, with explicit rules to protect the constitutional rights of witnesses. In 1950, a few months after Joe McCarthy displayed his list of alleged Communists in the foreign service and the State Department, only two Republicans voted against the McCarran Internal Security Act and to sustain Truman's veto of it — and I was one of them. (The act established a Subversive Activities Control Board to determine what organizations were "Communist-front," required such organizations to register, and barred their members from holding federal jobs or passports.) I had the "effrontery" to take on Roy Cohn, chief counsel of McCarthy's committee, in a debate on these issues sponsored by the Bronx County Bar Association. The debate topic was the role of the lawyer in congressional investigations. "We should insist," I said, "that congressional committees be bound by fair rules of procedure."

There was no question in my mind that to preserve our free society we had to pay attention to possible internal conspiracies, because there *were* Americans willing to lend themselves to Communist sedition. But this was a job to be handled by the courts, under constitutional laws, not by denunciations, or by affixing guilt by association; submission to these practices would nullify the individual's right to liberty, job, and privacy under the Constitution. The Un-American Activities Committee, and later McCarthy, tried to lump together as Communists, or "crypto-Communists" or "fellow travelers," everyone who held left-wing or even liberal views. The hysteria whipped up by these scare tactics damaged the reputations and livelihoods — and lives — of many individuals exercising their constitutional rights of freedom to speak and freedom to think. This was one of the great disgraces of our national life. In addition, it failed to uncover any significant number of spies who threatened our national security, or any of those who sought to overthrow our government by force, who would not have been caught anyhow by the normal judicial and law-enforcement process.

I do not pretend to have been a major opponent of McCarthy or his "ism"; I was not that important at the time. But in March 1951, as the anti-Communist hysteria raged, I called for the repeal of the McCarran Act in a speech to the National Civil Liberties Clearing House. The act, I said, places "serious disabilities on people because of what they believe in. That, I think, is very dangerous, because it can be extended . . . to any international movement . . . if a majority of the Congress feels like it. . . . As soon as the Congress . . . starts to define ideas it does not like and then punishes people for entertaining those ideas or belonging to organizations which entertain such ideas, instead of punishing people for acts which they commit . . . , a new and mischievous conception of our law has been created."

My efforts to establish a joint Senate-House committee to take over the job of investigating subversion were followed in the Senate by Henry Cabot Lodge, Jr., of Massachusetts. By 1950, Senator Lodge and I had become the principal congressional spokesmen for a growing movement of progressive Republicans in and out of Congress who were trying to replace Senator Robert Taft's conservative leadership with a spirit more in keeping with the times — and with the best of Republican traditions of fidelity to constitutional safeguards of individual liberty.

Much of our legislative research and many good ideas came from an informal Republican "think tank" run by Russell Davenport, an editor of *Fortune* magazine. His boss, Henry R. Luce, actively supported our efforts, and Jock Whitney and Nelson Rockefeller contributed some funds. This group represented the Willkie wing of the Republican Party; in 1950 we set up an organization called Republican Advance to persuade the party to espouse more liberal goals. The concept of Republican Advance was to present Republican alternative programs premised on the capability of the private-enterprise system to function more effectively in the economy. It was considered to be the Republican counterpart to the Americans for Democratic Action, and its basic philosophy survives in the Ripon Society of today.

In January 1950, in a speech to the National Affairs Committee of the National Republican Club, I explained our dilemma:

> There is a grave danger that a majority of Republicans in both houses is succumbing to a stand-pat negative opposition and to improvising coalitions with Southern Democrats. If this trend is permitted to go unchecked the two-party system is doomed. If the Republican Party is not to fulfill its historic role of either being the majority party or the effective single minority party, another opposition, rivaling both the Democratic and Republican parties for power, is bound to arise on the extreme left.

The outbreak of the Korean War and the deteriorating international situation caused us to postpone our ambitious plans for Republican Advance. But in 1952 most of us joined forces again to urge Dwight Eisenhower to run for president. Eisenhower's nomination was a defeat for Taft and the conservatives, and in the Eisenhower presidency some — but by no means all — of our hopes and ideas were to come to fruition.

TEN

The Congressman
in Foreign Affairs

The maverick congressman swam in the mainstream on foreign affairs. The liberal views that put me at odds with many of my Republican colleagues on domestic issues placed me much closer to my party when we were considering the broad range of complex and sometimes bewildering issues of foreign policy.

Even before I was first elected, in my 1946 letters to the *New York Herald Tribune,* I had enunciated some of the basic themes that were to become the cornerstones of our foreign policy: helping to feed the hungry people of the world, sending economic and technical aid to developing countries, encouraging international cooperation for peace, developing a world where goods and people may move freely, and assuring human rights. But I do not think that even I imagined then how active a role I would play in pursuit of these goals.

When I entered the House of Representatives in January 1947, Washington, D.C., was already the effective capital of the world. Because of the United States's economic and military power, our democratic ideals and free-enterprise system — and the fact that we had been relatively unscathed by war — we were in a position to work our will in the world to a great extent. Never before had any nation exercised such ideological, moral, economic, and military preeminence; and, it might be added, never may any nation again.

My interests and opinions matched the requirements and events of the era. I had run for office because of my concern for peace and justice; my boyhood as the son of immigrants in the cosmopolitan turmoil of the Lower East Side had made me aware from an early age of the world beyond our borders; the works of Henry Thomas Buckle had fascinated me with the dynamics of relations between nations; my 1927 trip had introduced me to Europe and its affairs.

And my exposure to the horrors of war had convinced me beyond any doubt that the United States had to play a major role in establishing peace. So it was no accident that I sought to become a member of the Foreign Affairs Committee of the House of Representatives. As the United States embarked on the vast foreign-aid program, the House, where all appropriations bills must originate, was about to assume much greater importance in foreign affairs, and the House Foreign Affairs Committee was to be at the center of governance as it had never been before.

I did not wait to be sworn in before I plunged into the issues that I knew would concern me as a congressman. It is practically a rule that representatives from New York City visit the European homelands of their ethnic constituencies. In November 1946, just a couple of weeks after my first election, and before Congress convened, I set out on a trip to Palestine, Greece, Italy, and London. Fortunately, I could pay for the trip myself, without waiting to go at the taxpayers' expense. I announced to the press that I was going "under nobody's auspices but my own," and that was so unusual in those days that the comment was picked up and repeated in just about every newspaper in the city. I also pleased my Catholic constituents by having a thirty-five-minute audience with Pope Pius XII. Nineteen years earlier, on my visit to Rome as a young man, I had not seized my first opportunity to see a pope because I feared unnecessarily I would have to "debase" myself by kneeling and kissing the ring. This time there was no thought or suggestion of the obeisance that had put me off in 1927. His Holiness shook my hand warmly and we talked about the social issues that concerned us both. He gave me a commemorative medal that had been struck to celebrate the naming of thirty-two cardinals, and I gave that to my good friend Father George Ford when I returned to New York.

My visit to Greece also had a political genesis (there were five thousand families of Greek extraction in my district), but that is not the only reason I went there. A guerrilla movement along Greece's northern border areas was causing concern that Greece's Balkan Communist neighbors might overrun the country or foment a revolution. Four hectic days in Greece, conferring with politicians of all shades of opinion as well as U.S. and British officials, demonstrated to me that the war-ravaged country needed substantial economic aid to get on its feet again. It was also apparent to me that the Greek people did not want to adopt Communism, despite the Communist-led insurgency, and that given a decent economic opportunity they would not choose it. Within a few weeks I was to be using what I learned in

Greece when Congress considered President Truman's request for $400 million to aid Greece and Turkey.

The situation in Palestine was of even greater concern to me. I was deeply interested in the establishment of a secure Jewish home-land for the persecuted survivors of the Hitler Holocaust. In the fall of 1946 Palestine was becoming a tinderbox. The British, still in control under their old League of Nations mandate, were refusing to let in more than fifteen hundred Jewish immigrants a month. They had also made it illegal for Jews to purchase land from Arabs, allegedly to protect the economic well-being of the Arab population of Palestine. Jewish extremists had already started their campaign of bombing and harassment against the British army in Palestine. The big question, of course, was what would happen after the British left: Would there be a partition of Palestine into Arab and Jewish states or a unified administration under a United Nations trusteeship? During my elec-tion campaign that year I had found that most of my constituents favored UN trusteeship for Palestine, and as I arrived there in Decem-ber 1946 that was my view too.

I spent ten days in the Holy Land; it was the first of many visits to that troubled region that I have made over the past thirty-four years, and it was the most memorable. I arrived in Palestine by way of Egypt, flying from Cairo on an Egyptian commercial airline called Al Misr. The pilot yanked the twin-engine Dakota around as if he were riding a horse, slamming it down hard on the tarmac at Tel Aviv in a landing comparable only to landings I experienced later on aircraft carriers. Not many months afterward, the air service be-tween Cairo and Tel Aviv was suspended, not to be resumed for more than three decades — but that had nothing to do with the flying style of my pilots.

In Tel Aviv, British tanks patrolled the streets to guard against infiltration by the Haganah (later the Israeli defense forces) and to suppress the activities of the Irgun, the Jewish extremist organization. One evening, as I was walking along a narrow street, a tank came rumbling toward me with its searchlight sweeping from wall to wall. I noticed other passers-by flattening themselves against the nearest wall and I quickly did likewise. I stood there feeling trapped as the tank clanked by, almost within arm's length of me. It was an eerie experience for me but one that the residents of Tel Aviv took as a matter of course: It was the way they lived under British rule.

The British were affected by the tension, too, as I learned in Haifa a few days later when the British commanding general invited me to dinner. At the appointed time a British major in a command car picked me up at my hotel for the trip up Mount Carmel to head-quarters. As I got in, he handed me a .45 pistol and said, "We might conceivably get into some trouble on the way. Do you know how to use this?" I assured him that the U.S. Army had taught me how to use a .45, put the pistol on my lap, and then said, "I appreciate very much your giving me this weapon for my protection, Major, but are you sure whom I'll use it on?" The major roared with laughter and when we got to the top of the hill he immediately told the general about my remark. The general also thought it was very funny, and I later heard it played back to me from other British officers as the story went the rounds. The appreciation of this grim joke was characteristic of British courage, British humor, and the British army.

Representatives of the Jewish Agency for Palestine showed me the whole country. I talked to Jews, Arabs, the British, and Americans; I visited agricultural settlements, schools, hospitals, and urban businesses. I had a very stimulating discussion with the president of the Hebrew University, Judah Magnes, who was devoted to the idea of a binational state in which Arabs and Jews would cooperate regardless of which was the majority; and I also spoke to more militant Zionists who were thinking in terms of a Jewish state.

One incident that has stuck in my mind was a four-hour conversation with an Arab high-school principal and his four strapping young sons. He could see nothing but doom for the Arabs in Palestine. He was sure that most of his people would leave or be driven out of the country and that the Jews would take it over and make a state of their own. But he did have some hope for eventual coexistence. His closing words to me were, "If the Jews can last long enough — if they can survive the next span of years — they will be the most useful people in the Middle East. In time, they will be welcome here."

At that time there were about 1.2 million Arabs living in Palestine and about six hundred thousand Jews. It seemed to me and to others that if the Jewish population were doubled the two communities, thus nearly equal in size, might live in peace. At the grassroots level Arabs and Jews were getting along well. But the Arab "notables" felt threatened by the Jewish influx, and the British, to maintain their strategic links to the oil lands of the Middle East, defended the Arab position. Although I pointed out to the Jewish press in Jerusalem that Jewish terrorism was alienating U.S. public opinion, I could understand the frustration of the Palestine Jews seeing their core-ligionists who had suffered so much turned away from the Promised Land by an alien occupier.

I put all this and much more into my maiden speech on the floor of the House, delivered on January 20, 1947. I urged the United States to grant emergency aid to Greece and I proposed the dispatch of a special U.S. mission to Palestine to supervise increased immigration and land settlement. I warned that "the situation of the Jews in Europe and in Palestine will grow worse on all counts the longer a solution is deferred and tension remains at a peak." The speech attracted a gratifying amount of attention and established me from the start as a congressman seriously concerned with the issues and able and willing to work hard to understand and deal with them. A *Washington Post* editorial commented, with mild surprise, that I had actually saved some substantive information for my colleagues in the House rather than exploiting it through press statements and headlines.

My speech also got me off to a running start on the Foreign Affairs Committee, where I served happily throughout my entire career in the House of Representatives. During regular working days I spent more hours in the meetings and hearings of the committee than I did in my own office and at least as many as on the floor of the House itself. In those days the committee staff was much smaller than it is now; congressmen, especially junior members of the committee, were expected to help out on many issues and chores, even those for which they were not technically responsible. That was especially true in those postwar days when the work of the committee was rapidly expanding, and it was fine with me, for I was curious about everything.

It was in the committee that I found my closest friends and allies in Congress. The closest of all was James Fulton of Pittsburgh, a liberal Republican like myself. We immediately took a liking to each other on ideological as well as personal grounds, and we shared many laughs over the eccentricities of some of our colleagues. Several times Jim Fulton and I traveled abroad together on committee business; it was Jim who teased me most persistently on that day in 1947 when Marian came to see us off on the *Queen Mary*. Fulton and I agreed on almost every important issue. He could always be counted on to support my positions on Israel and the displaced persons. Though his urban constituency contained a significant Jewish population, his help was not politically motivated — he truly believed in the justice of both causes.

As the Foreign Affairs Committee began its work in the Eightieth Congress, Jim Fulton, John Davis Lodge of Connecticut, and I found ourselves in an interesting balance-of-power position. This was highly unusual considering the fact that Lodge (who later became governor of his state) and I were both freshmen and Jim Fulton had served only one term. The eleven Democrats on the committee almost always voted with the Truman Administration; most of the fourteen Republicans were Middle Western conservatives who generally voted on the opposite side. The chairman of the committee during the Republican Eightieth Congress, Charles A. Eaton of New Jersey, was something of an internationalist, but he was already an older man and did not try to dominate the committee. Fulton, Lodge, and I, three moderate internationalist Republicans, could therefore make the committee majority. As far as the House of Representatives was concerned, Fulton, Lodge, and Javits were the core of the bipartisan foreign policy.

In February 1947 President Truman asked Congress to authorize $350 million to relieve starving people in Europe. Three weeks later he came before a joint session of Congress with his historic "Truman Doctrine" — a request for $400 million to help Greece and Turkey defend themselves against Communism. The two measures were very different, one for purely humanitarian relief, and the other a significant new departure in foreign policy. But they went through Congress almost simultaneously and evoked the same sources of support and opposition.

When the $350 million food-relief bill came before the Foreign Affairs Committee, conservative Republicans tried without success to cut the figure down to $200 million and to limit the effectiveness of the measure in other ways. Fulton, Lodge, and I worked hard to preserve the essence of the proposal. It was not just a matter of voting with the Democrats for the Truman measure. If we had done that, the bill could have been reported to the full House as Truman proposed it but it would have faced almost certain defeat. Our job was to take note of the opposition and to amend the bill in committee so that the House would accept it.

As we received it from the administration, the bill contained only three conditions limiting the expenditure of the money. First, that the supplies would be distributed without reference to race, creed, color, or political belief; second, that U.S. press representatives would be permitted to observe and report freely on how the relief was handled; and third, that the countries receiving the food and funds would inform the United States about what was being done with them. To these conditions, we in the committee insisted on adding three more: that the countries receiving the aid tell their people where the aid was coming from; that each such country make a maximum effort to reform and reconstruct its economy so that the aid would accelerate reconstruction; and most important, that U.S. representatives be permitted to supervise the distribution of the relief. The committee also assured the House that it would monitor the program as it went along — a process called "legislative oversight."

But our attempts to make the bill palatable to the conservatives of both parties failed. The humanitarian food measure included Hungary and Poland among the countries that would share in the aid; conservatives attacked it on the ground that the food would go to help Communism and that it would tend to cancel out the effects of the anti-Communist Greek-Turkish aid bill. On April 28, Mississippi's John Rankin wrapped himself in the Confederate flag and described how the veterans of the Civil War had come home and "tied their empty sleeves to plow lines and began making their own way." Since the Civil War veterans had received no assistance from anyone, why, Rankin wanted to know, did we have to help the war-damaged economies of Europe feed their people? To him, the relief bill and the Greek-Turkish aid measure were both examples of American giveaways. He said, "If we are going to fight Communism, let us begin on Capitol Hill. . . . We cannot afford to fight it at one place and feed it at another. . . . When you send this food into these Communist-dominated countries, the Communists take it and use it to suit themselves and let the Christian women and children starve to death."

Listening to this reactionary demagogue, it was difficult to remember that he was living in our century and our world. Although Rankin represented the mindless extreme of conservative chauvinism, he was not alone in his willingness to let Europe remain prostrate unless it could recover by its own efforts. Most of the opponents of these measures were sincerely worried and concerned about Communism, but they could not or would not see that the roots of Communism are economic and that if we pulled in our heads and let the world starve the Communists would surely triumph by our default. I therefore rose to try to answer these arguments and to defend the relief resolution against an attempt to cut the amount from $350 million to $200 million.

"No word has been spoken here this afternoon about the people who are waiting for this relief," I said. I told my colleagues what I had seen in Greece. "The roads are torn up and the railroads are torn up. There is no rolling stock on the railroads. The farms are denuded of the equipment with which to cultivate crops. . . . If the Greek people do not have this relief from us to look forward to . . . their despair would drive them into the arms of Communism, not tomorrow, but today. . . . The Communists tell them that . . . we are so selfish, so money mad, so generally egotistical and set on maintaining our own standard of living, that we will let them starve. The greatest thing in the world for Communism is this debate taking place on the floor of the House today. . . ."

Despite our efforts, the House cut the aid figure to $200 million and passed the bill with an amendment stating that the relief supplies were to be distributed by American officials, not by officials of the governments concerned. The Senate restored the full figure, however, and after a debate on the Senate-House conference report, we managed to beat back another attempt to reduce the aid amount.

I had two concerns about the Greek-Turkish aid bill as it came to the committee. The first was that in giving Greece military aid to withstand what was seen as a Communist insurgency we might be helping an undemocratic government preserve itself against the legitimate wishes of its people — for no one was satisfied that the Greek government was democratic and representative. My second concern was that the Truman Doctrine departed from the established U.S. policy of trying to solve international disputes through the United Nations.

This latter concern was shared by Republican Senator Arthur Vandenberg of Michigan, chairman of the Senate Foreign Relations Committee and the chief architect of the bipartisan foreign policy. Senator Vandenberg wrote into the Senate draft of the bill a provision that allayed these concerns to some extent. The "Vandenberg amendment," which was accepted by the House and survived in the final legislation, directed that the aid program be terminated if the Security Council or the General Assembly of the United Nations declared "that action taken or assistance furnished by the United Nations makes the continuance of such [U.S.] assistance unnecessary or undesirable."

Some of us in our committee wanted to go much further. I offered amendments that would have *required* the President to take the crises to the United Nations while furnishing military aid in the meantime. Helen Gahagan Douglas, a California Democrat, proposed to defer all aid to Greece and Turkey until the United Nations had been given a year to act on the crises. Representative Chet Holifield, also of California, proposed to turn the whole matter over to the United Nations and to grant merely $100 million for the rehabilitation of the Greek civilian economy. When the committee reported the bill out, Helen Douglas, Mike Mansfield of Montana, and I merely voted "present," to reserve our right to criticize or revise the bill. In my own addendum to the committee report I stated that the program "should have been undertaken through the United Nations if the

United Nations were in a position to carry the burdens involved. . . .
Unilateral action, whether of defense or offense, has inevitably led
to war."

I had still another suggestion, which I did not put in my remarks
appended to the report and did not offer formally, but in the light
of later history it is interesting to recall it. In an executive session of
the committee, as we were questioning Secretary of War Robert
P. Patterson, I proposed to insert words to guarantee that U.S. military
advisers in Greece and Turkey would be used "in an advisory capacity
only." I stated that "we are worried about the undertaking of tactical
aid . . . we are worried that one day an American captain will be found
in the mountains advising a Greek officer how to fire on a guerrilla."
Patterson insisted that the language of the bill — "instruction and
training of military personnel" — was a sufficient safeguard, and the
committee seemed to agree with him. Nothing further came of my
amendment and no such problem developed in Greece. Twenty years
later, however, military advisers in a foreign country did help us
stumble into a greater war in Vietnam.

When the bill got to the floor it provided an excellent lesson on
the politics of the House. The Democrats, except for thirteen "left-
wingers," supported their President on this key element of his foreign
policy. The Republican split — 127 for the bill and 94 against —
was almost completely geographic. The main Republican opposition
to the bill came from the Middle Western farm states, while almost
all the Republicans from New England, New York, and the East and
West Coasts voted for it — a classic proof of Henry Thomas Buckle's
theories about politics following geography and commerce. Coastal
Republicans, more involved in trade, were much more keenly aware of
U.S. relationships with other countries. This Republican split was
the key to the bipartisan foreign policy, and also to my own hopes
of becoming influential in Congress, but it marked a deepening of the
internal differences that would plague my party for years.

One dramatic exception to the geographic pattern was Representative Karl Mundt of South Dakota, whose repressive subversive-
activities plan I would oppose the following year. Mundt not only
voted for the bill — recognizing its anti-Communist thrust — he also
collaborated with my final attempt to assure that the aided countries
were democratic. My amendment would have directed the President
to withdraw aid, even if he were not asked to withdraw it, if he
found that the government receiving the assistance was "not representative of a majority of the people . . . or is not taking . . . the measures
essential for the reconstruction of such country." In support of the
amendment I said that I wanted Congress to give assurance to the

Greek people "that we are not giving this relief or assistance only if they keep this government," but that we would help any government of Greece that represented the Greek majority and that we would not help an unrepresentative government of the right or left.

Mundt was the only member to back me up on that amendment. He pointed out that it was our desire not only to stop Communism but "to help create conditions that will be resistant to the growth of Communism," and he pointed out that my amendment would also encourage both Greece and Turkey to assume all the burdens of their own economy and generally to create conditions that would eventually enable U.S. aid to cease. But my amendment was defeated — by the overwhelming vote of 104 to 6. I believe Helen Douglas and Chet Holifield, the two very progressive Democrats, and perhaps one more conservative, like Mundt, voted with me — as strange a collection of political bedfellows as one was likely to find.

Despite the defeat of my amendments I voted for the final bill. It did include the Vandenberg amendment, which held out some hope for United Nations action; nevertheless, the decision was a close one for me. The crucial argument was this: There might not be *time* for the Greeks to bring about democratic reforms with the Communists pressing on them. Once a Communist regime fixes its collar on a people it takes forever to undo it. As I said to the House, "Once seized, such power can be perpetuated by terror, propaganda, fixed elections, and the suppression of personal freedoms and become so firmly entrenched that it cannot be shaken off for years." Therefore I felt that whatever the faults of the Greek government — and they were many — they had a hope of being remedied only if Greece remained on the side of relative freedom. In the case of Turkey, which was under pressure from the USSR for control of the Dardanelles, I believed that we had to act in tandem with the United Nations.

During the roll-call vote on the bill on May 9, 1947, I walked across the aisle to the Democratic side and sat down next to Helen Douglas and tried to persuade her to vote for it. Helen was a gracious, intelligent, and beautiful woman — an actress by profession — with a warm heart, a deep sympathy for humanity, and a great devotion to peace and international cooperation. In those few months in which we had both served on the Foreign Affairs Committee I had already developed a deep admiration and respect and friendship for her. Whenever Helen spoke on any of the subjects close to her heart she was very eloquent and persuasive. But at a certain point, almost inevitably, her voice would sink to a lower register and she would begin to speak from her diaphragm and the emotion would come pouring out. At that point, all too regrettably, I thought, she became far less convincing. I knew she intended to run for the Senate, and I feared that her vote against this bill would be misunderstood. She was drawing a fine distinction between insisting on UN action first and proceeding in parallel with UN action — as the bill provided. I warned her that few people would appreciate the difference. Right up until the moment she voted I pleaded with her to vote for the bill, on every possible ground I could think of, but she finally answered the roll call "No." That vote indeed proved to be her undoing: In the race for senator from California in 1950, her opponent, Richard Nixon, repeatedly cited that vote to depict her as a "pink lady" who "has not recognized the menace of Communism" and who voted with "Communist party-liners" against measures "for the security of the country." Defeated by innuendo, Helen Gahagan Douglas retired from politics.

In recent years "revisionist" historians have criticized the Truman Doctrine as an unwarranted interference in an internal conflict and as a policy that intensified the Cold War. According to this view there never was a real threat that Greece would fall into the Soviet camp. In a 1976 summary of the 1947 debate, even the House International Relations Committee (successor to the Foreign Affairs Committee) embraced the revisionist theory, stating that the claims of Russian control over the Greek guerrillas were "rather dubious" and that we in the committee had not been sufficiently rigorous in questioning those claims. It was the Yugoslavs, it is now said, who most actively supported the Greek guerrillas, and Yugoslavia later broke with Moscow.

I reject this thesis. Yugoslavia had not yet broken away, and the evidence of outside help for the Greek pro-Communist guerrillas was clear. It was logical to assume then — as it is logical to believe today — that the ultimate authority came from the USSR. Furthermore, Greece remained in the democratic world — aside from the temporary aberration of the colonels' rule beginning in the late 1960s — and there is no way of knowing what might have happened had we failed to act.

Turkey's position as an anchor of the NATO southern flank can also be credited to our action in 1947. In my judgment, the validity of the Truman Doctrine was demonstrated when the Soviet Union used force in Hungary and Czechoslovakia, and the final proof came with the Brezhnev Doctrine of the 1970s, declaring that the USSR had the right to intervene militarily anywhere to protect a Communist political movement.

Meanwhile, I was devoting a great deal of time and energy to two interrelated issues of great concern to my district: the refugees in Europe and the Jewish homeland in Palestine that so many of them sought. In my 1946 election campaign I had pledged to do everything I could to help the one million "displaced persons" still living in camps under the care of the Allied forces. Early in my first session, I addressed the House on "the plight of these living dead, the walking casualties of World War II." About a quarter of the total were Jews; the rest were Poles, White Russians, Ukrainians, and other Eastern Europeans who refused to return to their native lands behind the Iron Curtain. I urged the House to approve U.S. membership in the International Refugee Organization, which was to take over responsibility for the displaced persons, and I pointed out that by doing so we would save some of the money we were spending in caring for the refugees ourselves.

That short but heartfelt speech brought me my first moment of national prominence. Columnist Drew Pearson picked it up and commended me in his popular "Washington Merry-Go-Round." I was very gratified, not only because it meant that people would listen when I spoke, but because it publicized from coast to coast a human tragedy about which I felt deeply. I was only a generation removed from the Jewish settlements of Europe; I might have had cousins in the displaced-persons camps, and if not for the immigration of my parents some sixty years before, I might have been in the same situation as those million people — if I had survived the Holocaust at all.

Because of restrictive U.S. immigration quotas, special legislation was needed to bring a significant number of displaced persons to the United States. Most of the DPs, as they were called, came from Eastern European countries for which the annual quotas were ridiculously small: less than 3000 a year for Czechoslovakia, for example, and only 869 for Hungary. Several attempts had been made in 1946 to permit the entry of large numbers of DPs, but the American Legion, the Daughters of the American Revolution, and other nationalist groups had successfully lobbied Congress to keep the doors closed.

Given the temper of the House, it was clear that if any urban Easterner were to introduce a refugee immigration bill, it would get nowhere. What was needed was a traditional Republican from the Middle West. William G. Stratton of Illinois turned out to be the ideal man. He was a downstate — that is, rural — conservative Republican with very decent instincts who, I thought, would be sympathetic to the refugees' tragedy. Moreover — and this was very important — I knew of his ambitions to become governor of Illinois, which he eventually realized; he needed to attract the favorable attention of the large Eastern European ethnic minorities of Chicago.

So I approached Bill Stratton one day in the House Republican lunchroom, a long, narrow windowless room at the rear of the Republican side of the chamber. Presiding over this emporium for eating, banter, and negotiation was a wonderful, motherly woman who prepared sandwiches and soup, and knew the tastes of every member. Only congressmen can use this lunchroom facility (the Democrats have one just like it on their side) and one never goes for lunch into the opposite party's room. The lunchroom was a place for a quick bite — for me, a cheese sandwich, a piece of apple pie, and coffee.

Bill Stratton and I sat down over coffee that day and I suggested displaced-persons legislation would be ideal for him. "You've got the right mixture in Chicago," I said. "You've got Poles, Lithuanians, Hungarians, you've got them all." He could become a hero of the ethnics, I suggested, if he introduced and fought for a bill to allow a large number of DPs to come into the United States. Stratton agreed, with enthusiasm. He asked me to work with him on it and I helped him draft the bill he introduced a few weeks later. It would have authorized the entry of four hundred thousand displaced persons from Europe over a four-year period, and with Stratton's name on it, the bill got the respect and the hearings it deserved. The Stratton bill never became law, but it started the ball rolling; many of its provisions, and certainly the basic thrust of it, made their way into later legislation.

Another displaced-persons bill I worked on that year, this one with Senator Irving Ives of New York, went through a similar process. Our bill would have admitted refugee orphan children beyond the quotas, but only if and when their adoption by U.S. "parents" had been arranged. Since the orphans would live with their adoptive families and would not compete with anyone for jobs, Senator Ives and I assumed it would pass with no trouble. But Congress was so frightened of fiddling with the immigration laws that no action was taken that year. In 1948 the essence of our bill, the admission of three thousand war orphans over and above the agreed-upon total of quota refugees, was incorporated in another act.

*　*　*

Although we could do something legislatively to help the DPs and Greece and Turkey, there was no way to legislate a Jewish state into existence. Congress helped and protected Israel after it was established, but during the vexing months of 1947 and 1948 Palestine lay beyond our formal powers. The British had turned over to the United Nations the decision on Palestine's future, but they blockaded the eastern Mediterranean, took "illegal" Jewish immigrants off blockade-running ships by force, and sent these unfortunates to detention camps in Cyprus — and sometimes back to Europe. Arab leaders, refusing to discuss any kind of Jewish state in Palestine, threatened to go to war if further Jewish immigration were permitted, and when a UN committee made a recommendation they did not like, Arab nationalists blew up several Western consulates.

Meanwhile, the United States was doing next to nothing. In fact, as the United Nations began to consider the subject, the State Department seemed to be retreating from the traditional U.S. policy of support for a homeland for the Jewish people.

In this frustrating situation a few of us in Congress who were committed to that goal hit upon an effective technique to marshal such influence as we had in the effort to redeem Britain's promise of a Jewish homeland. This technique was the round-robin letter, used frequently thereafter. Representative Robert J. Twyman, a freshman Republican from Chicago, and I rounded up twenty-eight of our Republican colleagues to sign a letter to Secretary of State George C. Marshall and to the United States' delegate to the United Nations, Warren Austin, asking for clarification of U.S. policy toward Zionism and Palestine. Marshall replied that it would be "premature" for the United States to enunciate its policy before the United Nations had acted — thus confirming our fears that the administration was abandoning the policy of favoring a Jewish homeland in Palestine. We released both our letter and Marshall's to the press, so that even though the reply was discouraging the exchange brought the issue into the open, gave us a basis for future action, and served notice that a congressional group sizable enough to get public attention and good press coverage was concerned about this issue and stood ready to call the administration to task over it.

I wrote and organized such letters again and again at times of crisis or tension for Israel. On that first one, in April 1947, Twyman and I recruited only Republican signers because neither of us yet felt confident enough to rally the Democratic minority. Later, the round-robin letters became bipartisan, with Emanuel "Manny" Celler of New York often enlisting the Democrats while I enlisted the Republicans. Isaiah "Si" Kenen, the information officer of the Israeli UN delegation in the early years of the new state, who later became executive director of the American Israel Public Affairs Committee (AIPAC), was often involved; he was a good, objective editor with a sound knowledge of Congress and a fine — and helpful — reputation for integrity among my House colleagues. Usually I would find a Democratic colleague to draft the letter with me and then we would buttonhole the others, having sounded them out first on the substance of it. Rather than risk embarrassing a colleague who might refuse to go along, we approached only those whom we judged to be sympathetic.

Other congressmen wrote similar letters on other subjects, of course, but the round robin was particularly apt for Palestine and Israel because the issue cut across all party lines and ideological differences; normal coalitions and caucuses based on party or economics or section had little bearing on what was fundamentally a moral and international question. Some of the most conservative Republican congressmen, whom I opposed constantly on other matters and whom I would not approach in another context, could be counted on to sign these round robins. They felt simply that after the Holocaust the Jews had to have a secure haven.

At the United Nations in the summer of 1947 a consensus developed for partition of Palestine into Jewish and Arab states. But the relative silence of the Truman Administration encouraged the Arabs in their intransigent opposition to any scheme embodying a Jewish state. The Arab leaders were rapidly working themselves up to the point where they would *have* to go to war once Israel was proclaimed a state or risk losing their credibility.

The U.S. silence was a symptom of the cleavage between the professional diplomats of the State Department — trained to preserve the status quo — who tried to maintain the U.S. relationship with the Arabs, and the politically sensitive officials in the White House who were more sympathetic to Israel. For thirty years — until the Camp David agreements of 1978 — this split from time to time tended to paralyze U.S. policy in the Middle East.

Harry Truman confirms in his memoirs that the Arabophiles in the State Department were urging his administration to do nothing to antagonize the Arab rulers of the oil-producing states. The department's Near East specialists, Truman wrote, "were almost without exception unfriendly to the idea of a Jewish state. Their thinking went along this line: Great Britain had maintained her position in the area by cultivating the Arabs; now that she seems no longer able to hold this position, the United States must take over, and it must be done by exactly the same formula; if the Arabs are antagonized, they will go over into the Soviet camp."

Britain's callous treatment of Jewish immigrants to Palestine led me at the time to rethink some of my views. During my 1946 campaign I had vigorously opposed an attempt to retaliate against Britain by blocking a British loan until more Jewish immigration into Palestine was permitted; Britain's economic recovery, in my view, was essential to the security of all free nations, including the United States.

By August 1947, however, I was declaring that it would be useful if, before seeking further U.S. aid, Great Britain would immediately admit into Palestine the sixteen thousand Jewish refugees held on Cyprus or being shipped back to Europe. I also hinted that Congress might want to consider economic measures against the British if the Palestine problem had not been resolved by the time we reconvened in January.

I still thought it was improper — theoretically — to threaten economic sanctions on the Palestine issue. But pragmatically, time was running out; the situation was becoming more urgent for both the Jews in Palestine and the DPs. The British attitude was becoming intolerable.

Meanwhile, Jim Fulton and I felt it was imperative that the United States do something about the displaced persons. We both had expected Chairman Eaton to appoint us to the Select Committee on Foreign Aid, which was going to investigate economic conditions in Europe in preparation for legislative work on the Marshall Plan. I had already started making plans for the trip and had written to several U.S. consuls telling them I wanted to talk about the visa problems that concerned friends and relatives of my constituents — so many of whom were refugees from Hitler. But my independent style probably kept me off the Select Committee. Not wanting to be left behind that fall, and realizing that none of the scores of traveling congressmen were planning to look at the displaced-persons camps or the International Refugee Organization (IRO) or the International Trade Organization, Fulton and I persuaded Eaton to appoint a special subcommittee of the Foreign Affairs Committee to study these matters. Fulton became chairman of the group; Joseph Pfeifer, a Brooklyn Democrat, and I were the other members. Pfeifer was unable to join us at the last moment, so we enlisted a congressman from outside our committee: Frank Chelf, a Democrat from Kentucky. Chelf was a member of the Judiciary Committee, which handled immigration bills, and his presence on our subcommittee was vital.

The Select Committee, under the chairmanship of Christian Herter of Massachusetts, sailed for Europe on August 27; we were attached to it for the journey. Marian Borris came to the ship to see me off. As the big ship, laden with at least two dozen members of the U.S. Congress, moved down the harbor, I glanced at the skyline of lower Manhattan. There, fluttering from the window of the Javits & Javits office at 165 Broadway, was an enormous white sheet that the secretaries in the office had hung out with a message painted on it for me: "Bon Voyage, Congressman Javits, and Good Luck."

We attended Herter's shipboard briefings on the European economy and we stayed with his group for a few days in London, conferring with U.S. and British officials, including Harold Wilson, then president of the British Board of Trade and later prime minister. The Fulton subcommittee then flew off to occupied Germany, and for ten days we shared the agony of the displaced persons. It was a profoundly heart-rending experience that remained in our minds long after we had returned home and fired each of us with the determination to end this great shame. We broke up into teams of one congressman and one aide; each team visited a different series of camps and we came together in the evening, or every few days, to pool our knowledge — and our outrage. Between us we visited two hundred displaced-persons camps, spoke to four thousand inmates and also to U.S. Army administrators and IRO officials.

Many of these homeless people were still living in what had been extermination camps, and others were in Nazi SS barracks. Usually their living quarters consisted of a wide open space in a warehouse, partitioned off into family cubicles by blankets or cloths pinned up on a rope strung five or six feet from the floor like clotheslines. Kitchen and toilet facilities were shared — and primitive. At one camp there were more than three thousand inmates, 80 percent of whom had been rescued from a Nazi concentration camp nearby. In two and a half years they had moved only two kilometers. One man in that group, however, had done a lot of traveling. We spoke in Yiddish, and he told me how he had escaped from a concentration camp in Poland, fled eastward through Russia, Siberia, and China, and found himself in Shanghai at the end of the war. There was little to eat in Shanghai and no chance of a settled life, so he worked his way back across Asia and ended up in a displaced-persons camp. I asked him how he had managed to survive, to eat and to travel. "It's easy," he said, "I was always in business for myself." What business was that? "I'm a barber." That was one of the few light moments.

One confusing and difficult aspect of the situation was the bewildering variety of displaced persons. Besides the Jewish survivors of the Holocaust, there were Russians who had been taken by the Germans as slave laborers and, under the Yalta agreement, were supposed to be repatriated but who refused absolutely to go back to the USSR. There were Jews who had fled from Russia and Poland after the war because of anti-Semitism or a dislike of Communism — or just because they wanted to go to Palestine. There were men, women, and children from Estonia, Latvia, and Lithuania, whose countries had been taken over by the Soviet Union and who feared persecution for their beliefs and the loss of any chance ever to emerge again if they returned.

Many of them were skilled workers who showed us their handiwork: I saw a beautiful Ukrainian altar made of tin cans, a neon sign and a loudspeaker system, and garments woven from parcel string.

Everywhere, the DPs crowded around to give me names and addresses of "relatives" in the United States. This was important because the United States granted priority visas, within the quota, to those whose relatives were already U.S. residents. I took back with me a lot of those names, and I am sure many of the names were not bona fide; they were people they thought *might* be relatives, or perhaps names and addresses they had received from someone else. They were desperate; they grasped at any straw, any means that would get them out of those camps where some of them had already wasted six years of their lives; I have little doubt that many of these imagined "relatives" generously sponsored and brought into the United States DPs they had never heard of before.

My ability to talk to the Jewish inmates in Yiddish had a great effect on them and on me. They still feared the Germans and wanted to get out of Europe to go to the United States or Palestine. A U.S. congressman who spoke Yiddish and understood their problems represented the brightest ray of hope they had seen in months, and they vastly overestimated my influence. This was especially true of the refugees from the infamous immigrant ship *Exodus*, to whom I spoke in Lübeck. Intercepting the ship within sight of Palestine, the British navy had captured the four thousand passengers in a bloody gun battle and forcibly brought them back to the British zone of occupied Germany. Once more they were Jewish prisoners — these were not classified as DPs — behind barbed wire on German soil, being guarded by German (and British) police. The whole world was watching the unfolding of this tragedy.

I visited the Lübeck detention camp the day after the *Exodus* prisoners arrived. I wanted to see this outrage for myself, and the New York newspaper *PM* had cabled me asking for an eyewitness account. The refugees in the camp were bitter, angry, and suspicious of all foreigners and officials, but as soon as I started speaking Yiddish they mobbed me. The men had been separated from their wives and children and this frightened them because it reminded them of Nazi camps. "We have been beaten," said one man. "We want to be returned to our families. We are being held for no reason. We are not lawbreakers. We don't want cigarettes or anything else. We just want to go back to our wives and families." In a brief cable to *PM* I told of the filth and darkness and confinement of the ships, the despair of the refugees, and the barbed wire and searchlights at the prison camp. I wrote: "They prefer death to Germany. They believe their only chance for life to be Palestine. . . . When we asked if anyone were sick they said, 'No, none outside, but we are all sick inside.' " The effect of these conversations on me was profound: These were my people, not cold statistics in an official report. I suffered with them and felt that there was no higher priority for me as a congressman than to work to eliminate this enduring wound of the war.

Frank Chelf, our Democratic colleague from a Kentucky farm district, was even more upset by the misery of the displaced-persons camps than I was. I, after all, was a Jew, the son of immigrants, and had a particular interest in European affairs; I had embarked on the trip with a pretty good idea of what I would find. Chelf, who had not more than fifty foreign-born people in his district, came with a more typical American outlook: That the DPs were certainly unfortunate but it was not our sole responsibility to solve the problem. But Frank Chelf was a sensitive and decent man and he was outraged by what he saw; the trip converted him into a staunch advocate of displaced-persons legislation. As he was on the Judiciary Committee, and since the House knew he had no ax to grind, his presence in our little group was a godsend. Seldom have I seen such clear evidence of the need for congressmen to learn firsthand about the places and people their legislation will affect. Some critics dismiss congressional travel as junkets — and some congressmen take ridiculous pride in never having traveled outside the United States — but this is a dangerous, know-nothing attitude. If anyone wants to know why congressmen should travel, I refer them to the case of Frank Chelf of Kentucky.

Frank himself made this point in an eloquent speech during our debate on the 1948 immigration bill a few months later. At the beginning, he said, he was a "doubting Thomas," opposed to the Stratton bill. "I was against any of this sort of legislation and I prepared to issue a press release condemning the whole business. I could have gone home, I could have got on the highest hilltop and shouted, 'Keep the bums out, keep all of them out.' " But instead, he said, he went to see for himself. And then he proceeded to describe what he saw and to answer the arguments that the DPs were illiterate, criminal, black-marketeering scum. He told of a conversation with a woman who was making exquisite linen handiwork, buying the raw material with American cigarettes — the only medium of exchange the DPs were allowed to use. He displayed to the House some exquisitely made albums and trays that DPs had fashioned from bits of war wreckage. "I have never seen," Chelf said, "a class of people in all my life who with so little did so much." He reported that "the vast majority were clean, orderly, law-abiding, and . . . America would be proud to have them as citizens. There were flowers blooming in profusion in and about their camps. They had their own churches, with beautiful lecterns and pulpits. There were homemade candles brought in to decorate their churches." He described what they had gone through — the loss of family, home, and possessions, the sadistic treatment by the German army — and then how the Russian NKVD "took these same, poor, pathetic unfortunates, these poor homeless people, these people the opponents of this bill called crumbs and the hard core, who were driven like cattle before the Russian hierarchy and charged with being pro-Nazi — and instead of being released, merciful God, they were tattooed on the other arm and slapped into a Russian concentration camp. . . ." In conclusion, he said, "I have had an opportunity personally to thrust my hand into the wound in the side of the problem, likewise to see the tattoos . . . and to feel the scars of the bayonets in the hands of these heart-rending, pathetic, miserable unfortunates of our DP camps in Europe. As a result, like St. Paul on the road to Damascus — I suddenly saw the light."

The light kept burning for Frank Chelf. A year later, when we were again debating a displaced-persons bill, he made many of the same points, and this time he added that in the intervening year a group of DPs had arrived in Lebanon, Kentucky, and that "these so-called terrible displaced persons . . . are fine, clean, erect, substantial, 'salt of the earth' people, and the folks of my friendly, neighborly, generous little community have taken them all into their hearts and their homes. . . . I'm happy to report that the DPs are making good citizens. The fact is you cannot tell one of them from one of our own folks, because now, thank God, they have a smile on their face and a song in their hearts in thanksgiving to a great nation."

On the way home from the displaced-persons camps I stopped in London. The comfort of Claridge's Hotel, after the mud and depressing conditions of the camps, almost overwhelmed me. Resting in that gorgeous hotel — the hall man having brought me a plate of chicken sandwiches and run my bath — being babied, practically put in the bath, gave me the greatest feeling of pure luxury I have ever experienced.

In the face of racist, isolationist, and conservative opposition, Congress in 1948 passed a law to admit to the United States two hundred thousand DPs, "our fair share," from camps in the occupied zones of Western Europe. But the law contained several blatantly discriminatory provisions and was hedged in with a number of restrictions that made it almost unworkable. It also "mortgaged" future European quotas, thus cutting off immigration from some countries for decades to come.

The most discriminatory provision of this law was inserted by the Senate. It stated that only DPs who had entered the camps before December 22, 1945, could be admitted to the United States. This excluded — and was designed to exclude — most of the Jewish DPs, who had fled from Polish Communism in 1946. In the House we had set a cutoff date of April 21, 1947. Manny Celler and I tried to restore this date when the bill came back from conference. We pointed out that under the Senate version only about six thousand Jews could be included in the two hundred thousand immigrants. Celler moved to return the conference report to committee, which would have killed the bill altogether for the moment. I voted for his motion, but we lost; the bill, combining, as I said at the time, "the worst features of the Senate bill and the most onerous features of the House bill," became law. Truman signed it with reluctance, commenting that "it mocks the American tradition of fair play and discriminates in callous fashion against persons of the Jewish faith."

The law indeed turned out to be unworkable; only 2507 DPs of all categories were admitted under it by the end of 1948. In 1949 we fought the battle in the House all over again. With the Democrats in control, Celler was chairman of the House Judiciary Committee and his committee reported out a good basic bill. But the Senate Judiciary Committee was headed by Pat McCarran of Nevada, one of the most implacable foes of more open immigration — and of foreigners in general — in the entire Congress, and that was an ominous portent.

In both the 1948 and 1949 debates the fear and prejudice expressed by some of my colleagues was appalling. It was not just the rejection of Jewish immigrants implied by their remarks, though that was bad enough; some of them spoke as if World War II had taught them nothing. They seemed to believe that we, as Americans, were better than anybody else and that we could shut our gates and our eyes and our ears to the misery and injustice in the rest of the world.

There was, for example, Democratic Representative Ed Gossett, a Texan who declared on several occasions that the DPs were "the refuse of Europe" and that the displaced-persons camps "are filled with bums, criminals, subversives, revolutionists, crackpots, and human wreckage." He was afraid that the refugees from Communism were actually Communist agents seeking to enter the United States to subvert it. There was Representative Robert F. Rich, Republican of Pennsylvania, who proclaimed with warped pride that he was "opposed to the opening of the doors of this country to everyone who wants to come to America from some foreign country." John Rankin chimed in with invective about spies and "Yiddish Communists" among the DPs. Representative William Jennings Bryan Dorn, a South Carolina Democrat, claimed to be an expert on DPs because he had been stationed as an enlisted man near a displaced-persons camp right after the war; Dorn said, "It was my personal observation that these men and women aren't fit to be American citizens."

Again and again Jim Fulton, Frank Chelf, and I, and other supporters of the bill, answered charges about crime rates, alleged Communism, and the skills and talents and human worth of the DPs we had seen. The objections to displaced-persons immigration were usually based on isolated reports of individual incidents or on emotional dislike of foreigners. The House in 1949 properly put more faith in our thorough and systematic reporting than it did on hysteria and anecdotes, and it passed a bill that increased the total of admissible DPs to 339,000 and advanced the cutoff date to January 1, 1949 (thus opening the doors to many more Jews). But McCarran in the Senate decided that no new legislation was needed, and that was that for 1949. Not until 1950 was the law revised to permit the entry of large numbers of DPs. To get the 1950 bill through McCarran's committee, some ingenious pork-barrel trading took place. McCarran had sponsored bills to admit several hundred Basque sheepherders who were needed by Nevada ranchers. Supporters of the 1950 DP immigration bill blocked McCarran's Basque bill until his committee reported out the DP bill. When the conference report on the DP bill was approved, both houses voted to admit McCarran's sheepherders.

By that time Israel had been established and had taken in one hundred ninety thousand DPs from the camps, thus relieving a great deal of the pressure. During the crucial months before and after the birth of the new state in May 1948, I was deeply involved with Israel. I was speaking, of course, on many subjects before the Congress, but at times of crisis in the Middle East it seemed that I was delivering two or three addresses every week on the subject of Israel. I found it hard to turn down these opportunities.

Speaking itself had always come naturally to me; I could arrive at a function, spend a few minutes talking to my hosts, and then, having jotted down a few notes — talking points — on the back of my place card, speak. I knew what I wanted to say. On more significant occasions I would speak from a press release, issued in advance, which made my main points, my "story line." A draft of such a release was generally prepared by a professional staff member knowledgeable in the subject.

I generally relied on these press releases when I spoke in the

House, always being careful to use the exact words contained in the release, and then adding to them. Later, in the Senate, where there was opportunity for longer speeches, I did prepare texts and distribute them to the press and to constituents. But my fundamental need in speaking is merely a set of talking points, and I find great satisfaction in the freedom of talking from a press release.

I had so many speaking engagements they sometimes conflicted. In May 1948, just a few days before the proclamation of the state of Israel, I had been invited to address the fourteenth annual meeting of the Jewish Federation of Delaware in Wilmington. But then, as the Israel issue heated up, I was invited to take part in a broadcast of the "Town Hall of the Air" from Lexington, Kentucky, on the same night. So I made a record of the speech for the Delaware group and was heard there at the same time I spoke to a national audience on the "Town Hall" broadcast.

When I could not show up for a speaking date at all, or when I had to decline an invitation, I always sent a telegram. These telegrams became a standing joke with my staff and my friends. It was said that the new definition of a *minyan* (the quorum of ten Jews needed to conduct a religious service) is nine Jews and a telegram from Jacob Javits.

* * *

On November 29, 1947, the UN General Assembly voted to divide Palestine into separate, independent Jewish and Arab states. The United States, the Soviet Union, and Britain all supported the resolution and I helped get some of the Latin American countries to vote for it. The happiness that greeted the outcome in the Jewish community — and especially in my district — contributed to the festive mood for Marian's and my wedding the next day. But the euphoria was short-lived. The Arab states denounced the plan and threatened to use force to block it. Bombings and violent disorders broke out all through the region, and Great Britain announced she would withdraw from her mandate occupation of Palestine on May 15, 1948. As Arabs and Jews geared for the now-inevitable war, the United States announced an arms embargo to the Middle East. While Britain armed the Arabs, the Arab states used the threat of war to cause the United States and the United Nations to back away from the partition the UN General Assembly had ordered.

Early in 1948 I met on several occasions with two future Israeli prime ministers, Moshe Sharett, who was the Jewish Agency's observer at the United Nations, and Golda Meir, who came to the

United States to raise money to pay for the guns the agency was buying in Europe. They warned of the precarious position of the Jews in Palestine and of the danger that the partition plan would be abandoned because of U.S. timidity and British devotion to the Arabs. In a major House speech on January 27, 1948, I attacked Britain for arming the Arab states and undercutting the UN decision that Britain herself had asked for. "I think the time has come," I said, "to call a decisive halt to Britain's double-dealing with the United Nations on Palestine, and it may prove necessary to cut her off from aid if she persists in acting so as to defeat the world's cooperative organization for peace." I called upon the U.S. government to lift its embargo and to insist that the Arab nations cooperate with the UN decision. The United Nations, I said, was at a crossroads: "If it is ineffectual, in the matter of a little country like Palestine, and permits itself to be successfully defied by a handful of small and recently created Arab states, then it, like the League of Nations, is finished."

We sent another round robin to Secretary of State Marshall, and with Representative Arthur Klein, a New York Democrat, I sent a bipartisan telegram to leaders of all the Jewish organizations in the country urging them to mobilize against the "conspiracy . . . to scuttle the United Nations Palestine decision."

Nonetheless, the pro-Arab faction in the State Department again seemed to prevail. On March 19, Ambassador (and former Senator) Warren Austin asked the Security Council to suspend partition and to call a special session of the General Assembly to restudy the entire issue and create a temporary UN trusteeship under which a Jewish-Arab compromise might be achieved. This sounded disastrous. I did not know that on the previous day President Truman had met secretly with Chaim Weizmann, the acknowledged leader of the movement for a Jewish state (and future first president of Israel) and had reaffirmed the U.S. commitment to a Jewish homeland; Truman was sincere in his intent merely to postpone partition in the hope of working out a peaceful settlement. However, the Arabs' supporters in the State Department were at the same time trying to use this delay to destroy the partition plan forever. I introduced a bill to lift the arms embargo, and I organized another round-robin letter, this one to Chairman Eaton, demanding a full committee hearing on Palestine and an investigation of the State and Defense Departments' handling of the situation. On April 4, with forty thousand other people, I marched in a Jewish War Veterans parade and rally in New York to protest what we regarded as the betrayal of justice for the Jews in Palestine. About two hundred fifty thousand people turned out to watch and cheer as we marched by the reviewing stand at Madison Square Park chanting "A Jewish state in '48" and "Lift the arms embargo."

A week later I rose in the House to castigate the change in U.S. policy. I said it was based on the idea that the Arabs would be a buffer against Soviet incursion in the Middle East and I expressed for the first time a view that I would reiterate many times: that U.S. security, not moral principle alone, demanded support for the Jewish homeland. "The administration was right the first time," I said. "American security and American interests are best served by the finality of partition in Palestine." This idea ran so strongly against the common wisdom of the time that I did not make much of it then. I called again for the lifting of the arms embargo and proposed that a volunteer force of Jews from the United States should be sent to Palestine to enforce the UN partition resolution. "To those who say this will increase violence in Palestine, I ask whether they mean that violence will be reduced and indeed eliminated by the slaughter of all the Jews there."

On May 14, as the British withdrew their troops, the Arab League declared war against the Jews in Palestine, and David Ben-Gurion and his colleagues proclaimed the establishment of the state of Israel. As soon as I was notified I rose in the House to urge that the United States recognize the new state. Then, with a few other congressmen, I rushed over to the Jewish Agency office on Massachusetts Avenue to celebrate. Israelis and Americans danced the hora around a large table laden with food and Israeli wine. In the midst of this happy party came President Truman's announcement that the United States had recognized Israel — the first nation to do so. This called for a great cheer, more dancing, and tears of exultation. Two thousand years of the Diaspora had ended.

The founding of Israel, the Arab attack, the Israel's successful defense made simpler the task of establishing mutually supportive U.S.-Israel relations. From that point on, military and economic aid for Israel was emphasized, and in Congress and the country at large there was a growing sympathy for Israel. Many Americans began to see Israel as a dependable ally essential to U.S. security. By 1949 I was making the keynote of my Israel position the statement that "balance in military capability is essential to stability in the Near East and . . . the Israelis have shown that they are doughty fighters for independence and freedom against any aggression from Communism." That was an answer to the argument that the shipment of British arms to the Arabs was essential to Western security.

The realization of Israel's importance to U.S. security became over the years a basic tenet of U.S. foreign policy, and I may have been the first U.S. national politician to express it. I even received a backhanded compliment from the Soviet Union on this point: In 1953, the Soviet newspaper *Izvestia* named me as one of the three prominent American Jews who had worked out plans to make Israel the major anti-Communist stronghold of the United States in the Middle East.

Increasingly I found myself attacking British policy on Israel. In House speeches I opposed additional financial aid to Britain because Britain had been caught red-handed aiding the Arabs; I exposed in detail Britain's military and financial aid to the Arab Legion, the military force of Trans-Jordan, and I called upon the House to investigate Britain's diversion of U.S. aid money to the Arab forces. Early in 1949, after Israel shot down five RAF planes, I introduced a resolution of inquiry calling upon the State Department to give the House all the information it had about British military aircraft fighting in the Middle East. These statements and speeches made it awkward for me to deal with the British on other matters. Late in 1949 I was a member of a subcommittee scheduled to visit Britain and other Western European countries to investigate the functioning of the European Recovery Program and the occupation of Germany. In order not to embarrass the mission, I found it wise to skip the British part of the trip. This situation was not the beginning of any anti-British posture by me; but it was the end of an era of British colonialism over which Ernest Bevin, British foreign secretary, presided.

In the course of many disputes involving negotiations between Israelis and Arabs, border clashes, the Arab boycott of Israel, attempts to solve the displaced-persons and refugee problems, and arms sales and embargos, I had many direct contacts with Secretary of State Dean Acheson and his successor, John Foster Dulles. Acheson, I think, viewed Israel and its problems as a domestic political nuisance and not the stuff of high-level diplomacy that he as a careerist and an American aristocrat ought to have to handle. He was not callous or unsupportive; he had no profound like or dislike of Israel. I got along quite well with him — I never found him arrogant, as some people did — but he considered himself a cut above the rank and file of the people whom it was his destiny to help govern. He did, in fact, help Israel in the long run because he knew that the Congress, speaking for the American people, would bring him up short if he did not.

John Foster Dulles, whom I had known for years, was a very different kind of secretary of state. Dulles belonged to the world of corporate business — which included the oil companies — and which

he regarded as an orderly influence that would bring the most satisfaction and opportunity to Americans and to friendly peoples. He
believed that Israel was lucky to exist at all and that it should be
content to remain as it was. He was especially uncomfortable about
Israel's ideas of what it needed for its military security. He could not
conceive of a Jewish state that was strong militarily. Dulles was not
anti-Jewish, but he thought that it was against the U.S. national interest to be so involved and — as he saw it — almost obsessed with Israel
in the face of the enormous Arab world of 100 million people with
its great strategic potential and oil reserves. Dulles's viewpoint — that
Israel should remain one of the world's smallest states and its military capability modest — contributed to President Eisenhower's ambivalence on the subject.

My first major confrontation with Dulles took place in 1953.
Dulles and I, of course, were old professional antagonists from
the 1930s. As lawyers in New York we had crossed swords, and although I was a member of Congress when he became secretary of
state I am sure he approached dealing with me again with some suspicion. As time went on I believe he acquired some respect for me
and my word and my ability to get things done, but it could not have
been easy for him.

My first major confrontation with Dulles took place in 1953.
Dulles and Eisenhower had initiated a new Mideast policy of "im-
partiality," which I had welcomed at the time because it seemed to
encourage regional development that would benefit both Arabs and
Jews. I made many speeches to anxious Jewish groups urging the
American Jewish community to support the new policy. (Later I was
to criticize it and warn that it was being considered appeasement of
the Arabs because it tolerated Arab refusal to cooperate in developing
the Middle East and resettling the Palestine Arab refugees in neighboring Arab lands.)

Although Israel and her neighbors were formally at peace during
1953 the area was tense; Egypt was blocking Israeli ships from using
the Suez Canal and Israel's borders were the scene of almost daily
armed skirmishes and incursions by the Arab Fedayeen, and other
cease-fire violations. On the night of October 14, 1953, in reprisal for
a series of raids that had killed more than four hundred Israelis in
the previous three years, five hundred armed Israelis stormed into
the Jordanian village of Qibya, killing at least forty-two Arabs and
destroying the village school and reservoir. Prime Minister Ben-Gurion
denied that Israeli army forces had taken part in the Qibya raid and
blamed the violence upon the Jordanian government for tolerating
"acts of murder and pillage against inhabitants of Israel."

Four days later Dulles let it be known that the United States would hold back $60 million in economic aid that had been allocated to Israel. Dulles was quicker than any secretary of state I have dealt with to use the hammer blow when something displeased him. On occasion, he had very little understanding of the sensitivities of other people and seemed to believe that the application of raw power would automatically solve problems. He also found it hard to understand the human ability to suffer and to sacrifice for an ideal.

I could not condone the Qibya incident, but I deplored the fact that in protesting the raid the U.S. had neglected to express sympathy for the Israelis who had previously been killed in the area by terrorism. I sent Dulles a telegram declaring that millions of U.S. citizens were "profoundly concerned" by the U.S. action, which had been taken before the UN Security Council had made any report on the incident.

Dulles's relations with the U.S. Jewish community reached a new low at that point. New York Senator Ives and I led a delegation of prominent Jews to call Dulles to task for his shoot-from-the-hip response to Qibya. Cutting off aid — which put Israel in far greater jeopardy than the Arabs — was completely uncalled for, given the fact that both sides were violating the border. We pointed out that the Arab states were refusing categorically to negotiate with Israel for a peace treaty, thereby immobilizing the United Nations commission on the subject. The way to halt tragic incidents on the frontier, we said, was for the U.S. government to address itself to the UN Security Council's attempt to establish a real peace; impeding or delaying Israel's economic development would only encourage Arab extremists to intensify hostilities.

Dulles was very much out of sorts during that visit. I think he resigned himself to the thought that in this case we would probably prevail because the politician in President Eisenhower would respond to us. And two days later President Eisenhower indeed announced the resumption of aid to Israel, whether because of our call I cannot say.

The aid bill involved in that controversy was the Mutual Security Act of 1953, the successor to the original 1948 Marshall Plan, or European Recovery Program (ERP). The ERP had set the pattern for U.S. foreign aid and an unusual situation within the Foreign Affairs Committee had given me an early opportunity to work closely on it. Chairman Eaton did not feel that he could take on the grueling day-to-day management of the weeks of hearings and the long floor debate that he knew was coming on this major piece of legislation. The number-two Republican on the committee was Representative Robert

B. Chiperfield of Illinois, a quasi isolationist who did not want any part of foreign aid and who voted against it. So Eaton appointed John M. Vorys of Ohio, the next Republican in line, to manage the bill. Since other Republican committee members senior to me were also less than enthusiastic about the idea, I was chosen to assist Vorys. Therefore, although I was only a freshman congressman, I became the assistant floor manager for the Economic Cooperation Act of 1948. This required me to help direct the long hearings, to work closely with Vorys on drafting the committee's version of the bill, and to work on the floor of the House almost constantly during the five days of debate in March of 1948 when the bill was considered and finally passed.

Because this debate began the week after the United States reversed its policy on Palestine partition, I found myself in an ambiguous position: One day I was denouncing U.S. government policy on Palestine; then for five days I served loyally as a key lieutenant of the United States bipartisan foreign policy by helping to shepherd the ERP bill through the House. This conflict taught me an interesting lesson in legislative discipline. Protests were raging in the Jewish community, of which I was very much a part, and yet my job as comanager of the ERP bill prevented me from dismaying the administration by expressing my protests about the Middle East. Everyone recognized my difficult role in this situation. And the day after ERP was passed I signed the letter to Chairman Eaton requesting an investigation of the government's Palestine policy.

One of the stickiest problems in drafting the ERP legislation was in finding a way to assure the Europeans that our aid would continue for three or four years, without, at the same time, committing future Congresses to authorize or appropriate funds — which we could not do under the Constitution in any case. The Western European nations' Committee for European Economic Cooperation had drawn up excellent plans for the efficient and productive use of the U.S. aid that George Marshall had outlined in June 1947. Clearly, these plans would come to naught — and any money we authorized would go to waste — if the program were to be abandoned after a year or two. President Truman had originally asked Congress to authorize $17 billion over a four-and-a-quarter-year period, much too large an amount for Congress to swallow at one gulp and beyond Congress's constitutional power to provide beyond its own two-year term. Therefore, at the suggestion of Senator Vandenberg, the administration bill that we began with requested an authorization of only $6.8 billion dollars for the first fifteen-month period. But the grand total of $17 billion, much closer to what Europe really needed, was in the back of everyone's mind, and we had to find some way to let the Europeans know they could rely on approximately that much aid over the entire life of the program.

The task of incorporating this assurance was complicated by conservative congressmen's insistence on, first, cutting the authorization for one year to $4.3 billion and, second, on adding,a provision stating that the law implied *no* commitment for future authorizations. John Vorys and I worked out an unusual formulation to bridge this gap. If the participating European countries continued to cooperate and remained eligible to receive assistance, our phrase said, "such funds shall be available as are hereafter authorized and appropriated to the President from time to time to June 30, 1952, to carry out the provisions and accomplish the purpose of this title." Following that came the statement about no expressed or implied commitment of future aid. This was intended as a clear signal to the countries of Europe that although we could make no binding promises, Congress expected to stay in the aid program for the long haul if the Europeans did their part.

I have on many occasions in the House and Senate worked on such minuscule but tremendously significant bits of legal draftsmanship, but I am no prouder of any of them than I am of that 1948 work on the original Marshall Plan.

Another aspect of the Marshall Plan that interested me was a provision authorizing the government to guarantee $300 million worth of private investments in approved development projects. This reflected my belief in the importance of private enterprise in the operation of the reconstructed European economies. An investment guarantee program was included in the original administration bill and in the Senate version, but we put a specific dollar figure on it and added detailed provisions as to how it would work and be administered. In future years, particularly when I served as chairman of the subcommittee on Foreign Economic Policy of the House Foreign Affairs Committee, I worked continually on increasing the participation of private enterprise in the whole fabric of foreign aid.

My encouragement of private investment was based on two concepts: one, that private enterprise is more efficient than government in producing and delivering goods and services; and two, that private enterprise develops a middle class, which provides stability and leadership and an ultimate balance to government power, thereby helping to assure individual liberty.

The debate on the Marshall Plan brought out all the expected opposition from conservative Middle Western Republicans and from Southern Democrats. We heard charges that the Marshall Plan money would be better spent for military rearmament and that the European Recovery Program was a "glorified global WPA in Europe," and that it would "prop up all the socialistic dictatorships in Europe." Ralph W. Gwinn, a white-haired upstate New York Republican who looked more like a congressman than most of us, introduced a substitute bill to replace the entire program by private charity. Gwinn was an Ice Age man; his ideal economy would have been eight people living on a prairie exchanging gold coins for goods in one store. He said foreign aid was "devil Statism" and that the ERP was unconstitutional.

More interesting and significant, however, was that many conservatives and even isolationists came to understand the bill's necessity and eventually supported it. One of these was Everett Dirksen of Illinois, who later became the Republican leader of the Senate. In a moving speech, Dirksen confessed that "I voted against many things here, ten, eleven years ago that I would not vote against today. I freely confess . . . that in courage, vision, and conviction I failed on occasion, and others failed with me; the inevitable and inexorable result was a costly conflagration that must be measured in terms of blood and treasure." Perhaps the most startling turnabout was that of John Taber, the upstate New York chairman of the Appropriations Committee. Taber, whose assurances on OPA had misled me the previous year, had strongly opposed the early attempts to bring the ERP bill to the House. But events in Europe and opinion in his own district had made this ultraconservative change his mind. He took little part in the debate and we all assumed he would vote against the bill. But on March 31, in the final roll call, John Taber startled the entire House of Representatives by voting aye. Even he had realized the ERP was no giveaway but a measure vital to the security of the free world, and thus to the security of the United States itself.

By encouraging the countries of Western Europe to cooperate on economic matters, the Marshall Plan provided the fundamental underpinning for the present-day European Economic Community and NATO. Not the least of the benefits that have come from a more unified Europe has been the means of revitalizing West Germany as a strong, democratic, and peaceful nation. In the immediate aftermath of the war there was considerable concern about whether we could ever trust the Germans again. But, as we perceived a new threat from the Soviet Union, many people tended to forget the Nazi crimes and the threat of German aggression. In the search for allies against Communism, Americans wanted to move too fast — in my opinion —

to rearm and revitalize Germany. My own convictions, and the views of my constituents who had suffered personally from Nazism, persuaded me to oppose this trend.

Late in 1948, during the election campaign, I began speaking out about the U.S. occupation policies in Germany, which appeared to me to be too soft on former Nazis. I was planning to introduce legislation calling for Congress to legislate for the occupation of Germany rather than having it done by the administration, but the Democratic victory that fall, which carried the House and the Senate as well as the presidency, made such a plan unworkable and I dropped that specific idea. I was opposed to the "Morgenthau plan," which would have reduced Germany to a pastoral economy, but I did not want to see Germany rearmed just yet; only within the framework of a united Europe would it be safe to allow Germany to arm once more.

By March 1949 I had become concerned enough to write a letter to General Lucius D. Clay, the U.S. military governor, questioning his appointment of former Nazis — and industrialists who had worked closely with the Nazis — to positions of responsibility. I followed this up with a speech on the House floor, warning of the "revival of the Nazi spirit" in Germany.

In the fall of 1949, I was a member of a four-man study mission from the Foreign Affairs Committee that traveled to Germany and held a series of hearings there to investigate U.S. occupation policies. My concern was the de-Nazification and democratization of Germany; this was shortly after the Berlin blockade, however, and some of my colleagues were more interested in seeing how soon Germany could be brought into the Western military alliance. Arriving in Berlin, I declared publicly that I opposed German rearmament under any circumstances, a view that did not go down too well with the other committee members. When we returned to Washington they let it be known to the staff that they were not too anxious to have a report published, and so our report was buried.

The trip confirmed my own concerns about Germany. I found Germans still organizing themselves in totalitarian ways, and I came back to Washington convinced that the United States had to plan on a long-term occupation. I estimated it would take ten years before we could safely turn the Germans loose to run all their own affairs. I did not expect that we would have to maintain large numbers of occupation troops in Germany, only that we would have to maintain overall policy control. In press interviews upon my return, I stated that Germany should not be rearmed, and I expressed the concern that reunification of the two halves of Germany might lead to a new alliance with the Soviet Union. In one press statement I tried to deflate the newly fashionable idea that Germany could become some kind of a buffer state between the West and the USSR. "I can't think of a bulwark more unreliable than Germany, considered in that way," I said. "There are still plenty of Germans alive who believe that they should lord it over Europe and who have no qualms of conscience about their original alliance with Russia."

Administration officials, noting East Germany's military forces, seemed to me to be insufficiently concerned about continuing evidence of a Nazi — or at least an ultranationalist — revival in West Germany. The U.S. high commissioner for Germany, John J. McCloy, who still wielded considerable power over the new German government, was delaying the disposition of several war crimes cases, and General Omar Bradley, chairman of the U.S. Joint Chiefs of Staff, had told our committee that a West German army would be desirable from a military point of view. Early in 1950, as a means of calling attention to these disturbing trends, I opened a polite but pointed public correspondence with McCloy, asking whether Congress might "help" him by investigating the occupation administration.

A few weeks later I joined a bipartisan group of eight senators and eleven representatives who introduced a resolution calling upon the President to appoint a commission to inquire into the "conduct and status of American policy in Germany," particularly in reference to cartels, anti-Semitism, de-Nazification, war potential, and progress toward democracy. Public rallies supported this call and protested U.S. "coddling" of ex-Nazis. I addressed one in New York on the fifth anniversary of V-E Day, and another one in Philadelphia in June. Warning that the Communists were trying to goad the United States into rearming West Germany in order to create conditions to make Germany their ally, I reiterated my basic belief: "The German people can be given hope not by a military policy but by American efforts to integrate Western Europe economically, and then to bring about a confederation of which Germany may be a part."

The outbreak of the Korean War in June 1950 reinforced the pressure for German rearmament. Concerned that President Truman would now succumb to it, I requested an appointment with the President and on July 12 I discussed Germany with him. We talked about the Morgenthau plan — which he also had opposed — and the delicate task of rebuilding German industry without at the same time encouraging German militarism. The President listened with interest to my description of latent Nazism in Germany and to my appeal that he block German rearmament, now. He made no commitments, but he did seem to agree with me that Germany could only be redeemed in the context of Pan-Europe.

This was my first conversation alone with Truman, and I was very impressed. He was sophisticated about Europe and he displayed a thorough grasp of the facts and policies. Instead of the crude political hack that his detractors proclaimed him to be, Harry Truman turned out to be attractive, well informed, and direct.

In the next twelve months significant progress was made toward joining West Germany with the economy and defense of Europe. But no broad. inquiry had been conducted, and I remained unconvinced that West Germany should be released from three-power control or that she was ready to graduate from the course in democracy that the Western Allies had tried to give her. Former Nazis were working in the ministries in Bonn, war criminals' sentences had been commuted, the holdings of the fabulously wealthy munitions maker Alfred Krupp were being restored, neo-Nazi political parties had organized, and polls showed that most Germans might not oppose a Nazi return — while, with the Cold War in full swing, most Americans had stopped worrying about German rearmament and were encouraging it instead.

In July 1951 Truman asked Congress to declare an end to the state of war with Germany. A formal peace treaty could not be signed as long as Germany was divided, but the U.S. administration found it awkward to cooperate on economic and military matters with an "enemy" government. When the resolution terminating the state of war came up before the House on July 27, no one uttered a word against it. But I was deeply troubled. During the roll call I paced back and forth at the rear of the chamber listening to member after member vote aye. I did not wish to oppose the overwhelming sentiment of the House in favor of encouraging West German democracy, but neither could I vote aye in view of my profound concerns and reservations.

I did not respond the first time my name was called; I just continued my pacing back and forth at the rear of the chamber. I was hoping that the roof would fall in or that I would break a leg, or that something would make it unnecessary for me to vote at all. Even at the last call, as I walked down to the well of the House to vote, I did not know whether I would say aye or nay when I finally had to open my mouth. I was the last member to vote, and what I said when the clerk called my name was simply "present." Three hundred seventy-seven members had voted in favor: I was the only one not to vote aye — my vote was considered a dissent.

Over the years since then I have had the opportunity to know well every West German chancellor and the leaders of the opposition, men of a very high level. Konrad Adenauer, Willy Brandt, and Helmut Schmidt stand out especially in my mind. Adenauer brought Germany into the context of Europe; Brandt is memorable for his courageous leadership as mayor of West Berlin; and I consider Schmidt to have one of the finest minds in Europe.

Although I never mentioned to the German leaders my vote on the resolution terminating the state of war, I think all of them knew my record. I made clear to each of them that I was still worried about the dangers latent in the German psyche — worries that some of them shared. My frankness and wariness about Germany, and my determination to help the German people develop their creativity through European unity, helped me to deal effectively with the successive chancellors. I believe I have been of help to them and that my candor has served them as a reliable sounding board: They felt that if they could convince me, then the policy they were adopting would be satisfactory to the United States.

In 1976, when the Federal Republic of Germany awarded me the Badge and Star of the Order of Merit — a decoration for those who have contributed to peace and to the reconstruction of Germany — I declared that although my relationship with Germany had grown into one of warmth and mutual respect I adhere to my view that a unified Europe is the best framework for the German future.

ELEVEN

Adventures in
New York Politics

In 1953, after I had served in the House of Representatives for three
terms, I began to suspect that I would not want to stay there forever. The House is an excellent training ground for political leaders,
but there comes a time, usually after the fourth or fifth term, when
it is necessary to break out into a higher, or at least different, office.
Members who do not make this break find it increasingly difficult to
give up the perquisites and committee positions that come with seniority and that are often very important to their communities, so they
are likely to get rooted in the House for their entire careers. In my
own case, the strains on my marriage caused by my presence in Washington while my family lived in New York added another incentive
to seek an office that would enable me to enjoy a more normal family
life.

I had, of course, always maintained my close contacts with the
"good-government" forces of New York City, the civic-minded anti-
Tammany leaders and voters whom Fiorello La Guardia had managed
to weld together into an effective "Fusion" movement that governed
the city with minimal corruption and in the interests of its citizens.
That coalition had fallen apart in the election of 1945, in which I
worked for the Republican-Liberal candidate, Jonah Goldstein. In
1949 some Young Republican Clubs began to mention me as a possible mayoral candidate to bring the good-government elements together again, but it was too early and nothing came of it. That year
William O'Dwyer was reelected mayor.

In 1951 an opportunity to run for city office was offered to me.
Mayor O'Dwyer, whose administration was accused of corruption, resigned in 1950 when President Truman conveniently appointed him
ambassador to Mexico. City Council President Vincent Impellitteri,
an independent Democrat with no machine ties, running on the Ex-

perience Party ticket, defeated the Tammany candidate in a special election for the mayoralty. That left the city council presidency vacant, and in the spring of 1951 both the Republican and Liberal parties offered me the nomination for the special election to be held that November.

That seemed to be a good moment for a Republican who had always attacked Tammany Hall to seek city office. The Senate Special Committee on Interstate Crime (the Kefauver committee) had been investigating the underworld's connection to politics and business for nearly a year; Bill O'Dwyer had just admitted to the committee that he had visited the apartment of underworld boss Frank Costello and that he had appointed to office some men connected with organized crime. In a report on May 1, the committee declared that O'Dwyer had "contributed to the growth of organized crime, racketeering, and gangsterism in New York City." The connection between corrupt Tammany Hall politics and crime was now out in the open for even the doubters to see, and it seemed likely that in this new climate of public awareness the good-government forces could win. So, in offering me the nomination for city council president, the Republican and Liberal parties were giving me an opportunity to get in at the beginning of what looked like the wave of the future.

But as a congressman I was dealing with the momentous national and international issues of peace and war, economic development, health, and housing, and I was engaged in attempting to move the Republican Party to a more liberal and progressive stance. Although the Republican Advance had been put aside after the outbreak of the Korean War, those of us interested in its principles hoped that the presidential election of 1952 would help us — as indeed it did. It seemed to me that I could be more effective in Congress than I could as president of the New York City Council. So I wrote to Tom Curran, chairman of the New York County Republican Committee, and to Adolph A. Berle, Jr., the New York City Liberal Party chairman, respectfully turning down the offers.

That decision antagonized Curran and some of the other Republican leaders in the city. They thought I could win and they wanted for Republicans the patronage the office carried in those days. And I doubt the Republican leadership then in Washington would have considered my withdrawal from Congress a great loss. Frank Kenna, the Queens County Republican chairman, who was even more conservative and more opposed to my policies than was Curran, had agreed with Curran on my selection, and both of them found it hard to understand my refusal. The city council president earned a high salary, had the use of a city car and driver, and enjoyed prestige second only to the mayor's. Curran and Kenna assumed that I thought the job was beneath me and that I had already set my sights on the mayoralty, which was not the case. I told them I thought the public interest demanded my remaining in Congress, despite the personal advancement the council presidency might have given me — and that was indeed my reason.

During the next two years, however, the situation changed significantly and I became intrigued by the challenges of New York City. Many of the postwar issues I had been working on in Congress had been solved, at least temporarily, and the moderates in the Republican Party had nominated and elected Dwight Eisenhower to the presidency. Early in 1952, when Eisenhower was still undecided about entering politics, I had been one of nineteen congressmen who wrote him a joint letter urging his candidacy, and this had been one of the influences that convinced him to run. Although I experienced some disappointments and difficulties with his administration, I was confident as he took office in 1953 that the country was on a good course, and I thought the time had come for me to consider leaving the House.

A mayoral election was coming that fall and City Hall appeared to be a reasonable goal. Mayor Impellitteri had been elected with the hope that he would be as efficient as he was honest, but he had not been able to break Tammany's grip on the levers of power and it was obvious that if he did choose to run again, which was doubtful, he could be beaten. Early in the year I was approached from a number of directions to see if I would be interested in the mayoralty. I was indeed, and I began a seven-month period of intense political activity that was to end in considerable disappointment for me — and for many fine people who supported me — but which laid the groundwork for a successful campaign for attorney general of New York State the following year.

On February 15, 1953, I cautiously tossed my hat into the mayoral ring. On a radio program sponsored by the nonpartisan Citizens' Union, I declared I was "ready to serve," if the good-government forces of the city wanted me. I emphasized that I was not yet a candidate and would not be one until and unless it was indicated that a broad range of anti-Tammany forces could unite behind me. The essence of my thinking was that only a broad coalition of good-government groups could beat Tammany and overcome the traditional inclination of the majority in New York City to vote Democratic.

My broadcast elicited many statements and gestures of support from friends who had helped in my congressional campaigns and from civic leaders who had been close to La Guardia. The tiny City Fusion Party, heir to the name but not the political strength of La Guardia's movement, prepared to nominate me if I would formally announce my candidacy — but it would have been foolish to accept that nomination before obtaining the support of the major parties. More significantly, a new group calling itself the Citizens' Non-Partisan Committee (CNPC) was organized a few days after my broadcast: Its 195 civic-minded members, among them David Rockefeller and Marie La Guardia, were dedicated to the cause of a good-government coalition.

Of course, what we meant when we said "good-government coalition" was an alliance between the Republican and Liberal parties, with the splinter groups joining in. As a Republican-Liberal congressman I was an obvious choice as the nominee of such an alliance, but it was not that simple. Although many Liberals supported me for the mayoralty, some of them felt so great an animosity toward the Republican Party that they could not bring themselves to send a Republican to City Hall even though that was the only way to defeat the Tammany machine. Besides, the Liberals had what they regarded as another strong candidate, Rudolph Halley, who had made a name for himself as counsel to the Kefauver committee. In 1951, when I declined to run, Halley had been elected city council president by running on the Liberal line alone and defeating the Tammany man. Now he wanted to be mayor, and his Liberal Party backers imagined he could repeat his triumphs and capture the top city post in a run against both major parties. (As Halley was a Democrat, though independent of Tammany, he was completely out of the running for the Republican nomination, so no true coalition was possible with him.)

In the Republican camp I had a friend and supporter in John Crews, the Brooklyn leader, but Tom Curran and Frank Kenna were distrustful of my liberal views and still peeved about my spurning of their offer in 1951. In March, Curran listed me and eight others as Republicans he could back; that was not much of an endorsement, but coming from Curran it was better than nothing and I appreciated it at the time.

An even greater obstacle to the Republican nomination was Governor Dewey. We were not enthusiastic about each other and we each knew how the other felt. Three times I had run for Congress when Dewey was on the ticket: In 1946 and 1950 he was elected governor, and in 1948 he ran for President. As I was in a normally heavily Democratic district, I had to play down my party connection, and if voters asked me about Dewey I generally answered, "I'm a Republican and I support the ticket," a proper and respectful comment that indicated I did not agree with all of Dewey's policies. I am sure Dewey learned of this caution — and remembered it.

To make matters worse, as far as the campaign was concerned, I had angered Dewey by "interfering" in what he regarded as state matters of no concern to a U.S. congressman. Earlier that year, 1953, the Republican-controlled state legislature, with Dewey's backing, allowed an across-the-board 15 percent rent increase on rent-controlled apartments. Governor Dewey had also proposed a transit authority to take over New York's buses and subways and increase the fare from ten cents. These two measures were very unpopular in the city, and I criticized them publicly. By attacking these Dewey policies I was of course risking my quest for his political blessing, but if I had said nothing I would have, in my opinion, disqualified myself as a serious candidate for mayor of New York City.

So I spoke out, both before and after the new rent-control bill was passed. On April 24, addressing the Young Republican Clubs of New York, I combined an attack on Tammany and the inefficient city government with an explanation of my views on rent control, housing, and transit fares. A complete overhauling of the city government is required, I said; to put the city on a sound financial basis, I declared, it would be necessary to establish a "blue-ribbon" team of civic groups, the Republican Party, the Liberal Party, and the City Fusion Party, a "team . . . distinguished by its integrity, character, and record, composed of men and women who have not been implicated in the failures from which New York is suffering." On several matters I took issue with Dewey: I proposed a city administrator, to be appointed by the mayor, in preference to the city manager Dewey had suggested; I criticized the transit-fare increase embodied in Dewey's proposals; I reminded my listeners that I had opposed the across-the-board rent increase; and I came out against a city payroll tax Dewey had suggested. On the other hand, I offered Dewey and the Republican regulars a good reason to support me. I declared that state aid was not the answer to New York's financial problems and that the city had to manage its affairs more efficiently. Finally, I hinted at the benefits that would accrue to the city if city, state, and federal governments were all controlled by the same party. "The people's will can perform miracles," I said. "Look what happened to General Eisenhower at Chicago." At that point my volunteers began to distribute "I like Javits" buttons to the audience.

The press response to this speech was even better than I had expected. Each paper emphasized the points appropriate to its reader-ship. The *Times,* for example, ran the headline JAVITS OFFERS FOUR-POINT PLAN FOR A CITY COALITION REGIME. The *Daily News,* a more mass-oriented paper, headlined, JAVITS, IN MAYORAL BID, SLAPS RENT-FARE RISES. In an editorial, the *Times* said I was "among the most eligible possibilities for mayor" and that I had given the city a "well-rounded program for restoring the city's political health, financial stability, and position and respect in the eyes of the world."

The *New York Post,* however, commenting as a Liberal Party paper, declared that Javits's "major misfortune at this moment is that he and Thomas E. Dewey belong to the same party." I had said some "sensible things" in my speech, the *Post* conceded, but it added that I had run into trouble when I tried to "explain why New York should elect a Republican mayor in the light of the things Dewey has done to us in recent months. Javits does not bless the Dewey high fare, higher rent program but neither does he condemn it in fighting terms." The truest remark in the *Post* editorial was that "the life of a liberal Republican [is] a complicated one."

An added complication was the question of timing. As I saw it, my campaign and the campaign for a coalition were practically the same thing. No one else stood much chance of getting both the Liberal and Republican nominations, and I could probably not get either one unless I was assured the other. It was in my interest to push for an early decision from the Republicans, before the Liberals got impatient and decided to go it alone with Halley. But the Republican leaders wanted to wait to see what the Democrats would do — and the Democrats were involved in even more complex maneuverings. Curran and Kenna would have been just as happy if I lost the Liberal nomination in the meantime, for that would have removed their most compelling reason for nominating me. Every day of delay worked against me.

I had plenty of grassroots support within the party, particularly among young Republicans who had worked in the Eisenhower campaign. To speed up the decision-making process I organized these enthusiastic volunteers into a citywide group called Young New York for Javits, with headquarters on Park Avenue. The group started holding rallies and meetings, put out press releases, and generally began beating the drums. At the same time, a growing number of more senior civic leaders, particularly those in the CNPC, were coming to the conclusion that a coalition ticket with me at the head of it could win the election and rescue the city from Tammany.

For my own part, although I had still not declared myself a candidate, I spoke to dozens of Republican groups throughout the city, trying to sell the good-government coalition idea and urging the rank and file of the party to push their local leaders and candidates to talk about the issues. In a speech on Staten Island, I took the risk of criticizing the city's Republican leaders — who were not jumping to my side anyway. I challenged them to give leadership to the good-government forces and asked the questions: "Why has New York been since 1945 . . . a one-party city in municipal affairs? Why have we [the Republicans] failed to elect a mayor for New York City for so long, despite the fact that the voters of New York have shown that they are not one-party voters?"

On May 17, the day before my forty-ninth birthday, twenty-five hundred of my friends and supporters gathered in the grand ballroom of the Waldorf-Astoria Hotel for a Javits testimonial dinner. We made no secret of the dinner's purpose: to attract attention to me as a sound, able, well-organized candidate around whom the anti-Tammany forces could rally. Weeks of meticulous planning had gone into the dinner. My friends Sam Roman, Peter Cusick, Arthur Goldsmith, and Herbert Malkin had begun the arrangements late in March, and then we had brought in Jock Lawrence, an experienced and politically astute P.R. man, to organize the festivities with a full-time professional staff. From the dinner-committee offices in the old Marguery Hotel emerged an endless stream of memoranda covering every detail: the cost of the flowers on the tables; the selling of tickets; the delicate selection of the special guests invited to the cocktail party beforehand; accommodations for out-of-towners; the timing of each speech and each course; advance texts of speeches; and even a corps of volunteers assigned to help the reporters and photographers at the press table identify the people on the dais. It was not a fund-raising dinner; at $15 a plate the event did not even pay for itself. But it was an unqualified success.

The stars of the evening were two colleagues of mine from the House Foreign Affairs Committee who were now governors of their states: John Davis Lodge of Connecticut, who served as toastmaster, and Christian Herter of Massachusetts, who praised me for having the courage to speak out openly, "whether my conclusions were popular or unpopular" — an apt comment at the moment. President Eisenhower sent a nice message, but no endorsement, and even Tom Curran rose to the occasion in a limited way. Noting that I was one of "several outstanding citizens" the Republican Party could nominate for mayor, he chided the Liberals for hesitating to name me. "The time has come for the Liberal Party," he said, "to emphasize the cause of good government in its deliberations. . . . Just how 'liberal' does one have to be to be supported by the 'Liberal Party'?"

According to the next morning's newspapers, I had become the leading contender for the mayoralty. One paper, the *Daily Mirror*, ran a headline saying that Curran "backs Javits," a statement that was helpful, though not entirely true. A *Post* editorial noted that the dinner "caused Javits's stock to climb several points" and added that "there probably has not been such a well-organized and smoothly functioning political affair around here in years . . . a meeting carried off with such efficiency meant one thing to political leaders — a strong, well-led organization that could function in a primary." *That* was what I wanted to hear.

But all the papers also took note of Tom Dewey's conspicuous absence. DEWEY PUTS THE BITTERS IN JAVITS CUP OF JOY, the *Post* headline read. An editorial in the *Daily News* sarcastically pointed out that "the state's most powerful Republican neither attended the Javits dinner nor sent a telegram. The Governor certainly has $15 or the price of a wire, and it is inconceivable that he did not know about the party ahead of time. So the only logical inference is that Mr. Dewey is not backing Mr. Javits as of now . . . highlighting the fact that a considerable block of GOP opinion around town likes Javits as a congressman but dislikes the idea of him as mayor." And that was precisely my problem. To win the Republican nomination I still had to make peace with Governor Dewey.

Early in June, after I had made another speech or two pressing the coalition issue, an official Republican committee got together with Liberal and CNPC representatives to explore the coalition possibilities. I was encouraged but by no means reassured, and I began to consider the possibility that I would have to wage a primary fight for the Republican nomination. So in the middle of June, to increase my visibility among the voters in the city who did not pay much attention to testimonial dinners, I set up a new organization called New York for Javits, with Edith Willkie as honorary chairman.

As the coalition conferences dragged on, the *Daily News* published the result of a straw poll that put Halley far ahead of all other candidates. The sampling had little real significance (the eventual winner of the mayoral contest, Robert F. Wagner, Jr., received 4.9 percent and I polled 4.3 percent), but it gave Halley's supporters a psychological lift. He received such an emotional ovation at a Liberal Party dinner that I sensed a go-it-alone stampede in his favor. To head it off, I called a press conference on June 24 and formally announced my candidacy for a coalition nomination. I warned that "tremendous divisive forces" were threatening to break up the coalition plan, and I identified these forces as the Republicans' delay and the "renewed activity in the ranks of the Liberal Party to go it alone."

My announcement precipitated the necessary showdown. When the interparty conference met for its third session on the twenty-sixth, the Liberals asked the Republican delegates pointblank whether the Republican Party would endorse me for mayor as part of a coalition ticket. The request was urgent: On the following Tuesday, the thirtieth, the Liberals were to meet in an informal convention to name their candidate, and only an assurance from the Republicans that I would be nominated could stop the Halley boom and save the coalition. But the Republican delegates, although they knew the request was coming, reported that they could not give the Liberals that assurance because they were "uninstructed." Another meeting was scheduled for the thirtieth.

On a hot and sultry afternoon, just a few hours before the Liberal convention, the good-government coalition faced the crucial test. The Republicans produced a list of twelve names, mine included; any name on the list, they said, would be acceptable as a coalition mayoral candidate — but only on the condition that a complete coalition slate for all city and borough offices could also be agreed upon. As the Liberals had only asked them about me, the submission of a long list of alternatives — few of whom had much chance for a Liberal endorsement — merely confused the issue. The Republican offer also had the effect of delaying a decision, because it obviously would take many more meetings to work out the complexities of a citywide coalition slate. Since the Liberals were publicly committed to choosing their candidate that evening, the suggested delay effectively scuttled all prospects for a Republican-Liberal alliance. That night, lacking assurance that the Republicans would nominate me, and unwilling to consider a package deal, the Liberals selected Rudolph Halley as their mayoral candidate.

Both the *New York Times* and the *New York Herald Tribune* next day rebuked the Liberals' hasty move and suggested that I would have been the best candidate. Most of the newspapers considered the coalition idea dead, but I had invested too much time and effort and had gathered around me too many supporters to give up at that point. There was still a glimmer of hope that a coalition of sorts could be put together with the Republican Party and the CNPC, and that I would then stand a fair chance of coming out ahead in a three-way or four-way race.

For the next two weeks I managed to keep this hope alive with speeches and statements, while Curran and Kenna continued to put off a decision. They were still waiting for the increasingly bitter Democratic Party infighting to resolve itself, and I suspect they also wanted to delay until it would be too late for me to gather petitions for a primary fight. To break the logjam I went to see Governor Dewey on July 15.

We met for lunch in his suite at the Roosevelt Hotel and talked for several hours through the afternoon. I tried to make clear to him that, despite our past disagreements, he should have no qualms about me. I did not pledge to support his every policy, but I promised that I would be friendly and respectful to the governor and that I would not surprise him with some embarrassing statement without notice. Dewey was still unhappy about my "interfering" in rent control, but I reminded him that in New York City that was the only reasonable political line to take and that it was because of such stands that I was the most electable Republican. Our conversation covered a broad range of issues and we worked out many details of what I would do, what the state legislature would do, what I would advocate for the city, and how we could reconcile the differences that might arise between us.

We explored in depth the traditionally antagonistic relationship between mayor and governor (La Guardia had once called Governor Herbert Lehman a *gonif,* which is Yiddish for *thief*). I told Dewey that I would be an independent mayor but that just as when I practiced law I never offered an opposing lawyer a settlement I would not accept, so I would never, in any confrontation between governor and mayor, offer a proposition I would not take myself, and that therefore in the financial bargaining between city and state I would be much more realistic than a Democratic mayor.

In that meeting Dewey and I got along much better than we ever had before. He seemed to accept my reasons for opposing him on the rent increase and my assurances that I understood the landlords' problems, too. I think I convinced him that I was a resourceful and level-headed person who could work with him, that I was not a maverick just out for the publicity, and that I understood business and finance. When I left him we shook hands with great cordiality, and I went home and told Marian that the long fight was ending in success after all, and that I thought I had a deal. I was confident that, if nominated, I could outpoll Halley; and the Democrats were in such disarray that I was pretty sure I had a chance of beating them also and getting elected.

At nine o'clock in the morning two days later, the phone rang on Riverside Drive. It was Tom Dewey. As nearly as I can remember the conversation, Dewey said, "Jack, I'm very sorry to tell you, but Curran and Kenna were in and they just won't have it. . . . They'll put up someone against you in the primary and that's the kind of fight the party cannot undertake." I was dumbfounded: not that Curran and Kenna opposed me, for that I knew, but to hear that Dewey would give in to two county leaders who I knew did not have that much power while Dewey was governor. As I recall, I said something like "Governor, it's the first time I ever heard that you would yield to Curran and Kenna, but if that's what you want, O.K."

And that was it. I could have — and perhaps I should have — taken Dewey on, then and there. I was organized, there were still three weeks to the petition-filing deadline, and I might just have made it and won the nomination and the election. But political conflicts involving my own personal advancement were always difficult for me; I could get involved in legislative combat on a bill, an issue, or a matter of principle and fight it through all the way almost joyously, but I stepped back from the brink of all-out political war. I accepted Dewey's verdict. Five days later, the Republican county chairmen announced that they would nominate Harold Riegelman (a lawyer who had also served in the Chemical Warfare Service during the war). Later, I came out for Riegelman too — and loyally campaigned for him.

I am still not sure what caused Tom Dewey to reverse himself in such a startling and sudden manner. He was a complicated character with a Byzantine side to his nature, and one could never be sure of his motive. I find it hard to believe that if he really wanted me he would have given in to Curran and Kenna; many times before and after, Dewey ran roughshod over local political leaders as powerful as they were. I suspect something else changed his mind and that he found it convenient to blame them. I think he must have had some residual suspicion that I might not really cooperate with him and that I might become too big a figure as mayor of New York. Nevertheless, on the record, the opposition of Tom Curran and Frank Kenna was fatal to my cause.

Despite their conservative views, I feel there was no fundamental reason for these leaders to blackball me as they did. If I had been able to make peace with them, if I could have enlisted the aid of a strong political agent to meet with them frequently, to keep me in touch with their thinking and them with mine — if I had, in other words, cultivated them — they could have permitted my nomination, though not necessarily with enthusiasm. As I wrote to Ben a week or two later, "In the final analysis the local leaders were just concerned to go along with me, indeed to win with me. Life is like that and I'm sure for some reason I have not dispelled their concerns. . . . I really think it is my fault for not knowing them much better, working with them and getting them to know me, for in truth there was no reason for their action out of any concern about me and, on the contrary, every reason for giving me the designation. I understand that at the very last Governor Dewey found me acceptable too, but it just did not work out even then."

As it turned out, my organization and my favorable publicity were not to be wasted, for the election enhanced my political stock. Republican leaders were grateful because I campaigned hard for Riegelman, and the Liberals had cause to regret abandoning me: Halley ran a disappointing third in the November elections, receiving only a little more than four hundred thousand votes, and thereupon passed from the political scene. Robert F. Wagner, Jr., the Democrat, was elected. The following year, 1954, I was given another opportunity to break out of the House of Representatives, and this time I succeeded.

In September 1954, Governor Dewey announced he would not run for reelection that year, and his attorney general, Nathaniel Goldstein, declared he would step down as well. Letting it be known that I was interested in state office, I increased my contacts with party leaders upstate. I was better known in New York City, of course, but as a liberal Republican congressman I was somewhat of a rarity, and I had therefore already attracted the attention of those Republicans around the state who were interested in progressive goals — Willkie, George Norris, and La Guardia people — and who had found little support within the party until I started getting noticed in the newspapers. Upstate Republican leaders of urban counties began inviting me to speak, as did business and civic organizations around the state. These people wrote letters to me and dropped in to see me in Washington, and I slowly gathered a small but loyal upstate following.

One of my earliest and most enthusiastic upstate supporters was Billy Hill, owner and publisher of the *Binghamton Sun-Bulletin* and the Republican leader of Broome County. Already elderly at the time, Hill was considered the dean of the New York State Republican county chairmen, and he exerted a great deal of influence over his neighbors in the southern shelf of counties along the Pennsylvania border. Hill had taken a shine to me — and I to him. Despite his age and his innate conservatism, he was astute enough as a politician to see how the party had to move with the times in order to win elections; I could always count on his support for my candidacies and almost always found him in my corner when it came to platforms and issues. Harry Marley in Syracuse, Manuel Goldman in Rochester, and Ray Lawley in Buffalo were among my other early upstate backers. Closer to home, John Crews, the Brooklyn chairman, and J. Russell Sprague of Nassau County in Long Island were more than supporters: They were my friends and worked actively in my behalf.

I would not have had the opportunity to utilize this support, however, were it not for a bitter fight in the Democratic Party between Congressman Franklin D. Roosevelt, Jr., and Carmine DeSapio, the powerful leader of Tammany Hall. Roosevelt looked and talked like his father; he believed that his name and popularity could win him any elective office he desired — and that was almost true, then. Early in 1949, in a special election following the death of Representative Sol Bloom, Roosevelt defied Tammany and the Democratic regulars, ran as a Liberal, and was elected to represent the Twentieth Congressional District, just south of my own. He won again in 1950 and 1952 (on those occasions with Democratic Party support). And in 1954 he wanted to run for governor of New York, an office his father had once held.

DeSapio would not have it. He had apparently not forgiven young Roosevelt for the 1949 rebellion and probably felt that his leadership would be invalidated unless he could punish such behavior. Besides, the Tammany boss had a better candidate for the governorship: Averell Harriman, a wealthy railroad and shipping executive and loyal Democrat who had served Presidents Roosevelt and Truman in many high-level diplomatic and cabinet roles, including ambassador to the Soviet Union, director of the Mutual Security Agency, and secretary of commerce. Harriman had very little experience in New York State politics or government, but his prestige was great, he had very briefly contended for the Democratic presidential nomination in 1952, and his wealth was an asset to any campaign.

The younger Roosevelt carried his fight for the gubernatorial nomination to the Democratic state convention, but DeSapio prevailed and Harriman was nominated. Then, as a sop to Roosevelt's supporters and to preserve party unity, the Democrats offered Roosevelt the nomination for attorney general. At first Roosevelt spurned this nomination, but later, citing his duty as a loyal Democrat, he accepted. All the Democrats — and most Republicans, too — judged that Roosevelt would strengthen the Democratic ticket and that he would probably run ahead of Harriman. The Republicans faced a problem.

Governor Dewey, though retiring, remained the undisputed leader of the New York Republican Party, and he had picked Senator Irving Ives to succeed him. Ives was the most prominent Republican in the state after the governor, and he had a well-earned reputation as a champion of civil rights and other liberal causes. As a member of the state legislature he had coauthored the 1945 Ives-Quinn bill, the first law anywhere in the United States to prohibit racial discrimination in employment, and then he had come to the U.S. Senate in 1947, the same year I entered the House. Ives and I did not always agree — he voted for the Taft-Hartley Act — but on housing, civil rights, foreign aid, and Israel we cooperated regularly, and we frequently called on Secretary of State Dulles together to urge some point of Middle East policy affecting the security of Israel. Ives was straight, honest, dedicated, and had fine humanitarian instincts. There developed between us a profound regard and deep affection, which included his wife, Marion, as well.

Running Ives for governor was Dewey's idea, not Ives's, and I do not know what induced Irving even to consider the governorship. He did not seem to me to be hungering for the office. But my support for him was unequivocal and complete; he would have made one of our best governors. He knew New York like the back of his hand.

The rest of the ticket was still in question when our state convention opened in Syracuse on September 22, just as the Democratic convention in Buffalo was winding up. Having had no response to my earlier feelers, I arrived in Syracuse without expectations — and in fact I had already started my campaign for reelection to my House seat. Nor, obviously, did the State Committee have any hint of what was to happen: They assigned me what must have been the smallest room in the Hotel Syracuse, a tiny cubicle with one bed and just enough space to get up, turn around, and step into the bathroom. But even before I saw that room the action began. John Crews and Russell Sprague met me at the top of the steps of the hotel entrance before I checked in, took me aside to a corner of the lobby, and told me they wanted me to run for attorney general. Frank Roosevelt had just been nominated by the Democrats, and the newspapers were reporting that Frank thought he was doing his party a favor in making the run. Crews and Sprague declared with conviction that I was the only Republican who had a chance against FDR Junior and that they were trying to sell Dewey on the idea.

Some hours later, Dewey summoned me to his spacious suite on the top floor of the hotel. Remembering how he had taken me up the hill and down again on the mayoralty the year before, I entered his rooms warily but expectantly, with the feeling that I had better be on the ball in mind and spirit, and with the knowledge that I was facing a major test as a politician. Dewey was reclining on a day bed with his back against the wall, his arms folded, his feet up, and his shoes on. Without even shaking hands, he motioned me to a chair at the bedside. Then, looking me straight in the eye, he said, "Jack, why should we nominate you for attorney general?"

I waited perhaps thirty seconds before replying, "Governor, you should nominate me because I'm the only Republican who can beat FDR Junior." And then I gave him my reasons. Frank Roosevelt was notorious as an absentee congressman. He did not treat his congressional duties as seriously as I — and other members — thought he should, and although he had shown interest in some worthy issues and was generally decent and well motivated, his lack of involvement was so striking at times that even when he did espouse a good cause he might fail to show up on the floor of the House when it was being debated or when it was necessary to support or oppose amendments. As the congressman from the district next door, I had occasionally helped his constituents when he was not to be found, so I was in a better position than almost anyone else to expose his sorry absentee record. Besides, I told Dewey, I could point to my own more extensive legal experience as a reason for the voters to choose me over Roosevelt as the state's chief legal officer.

The governor apparently was persuaded and announced his decision to a closed meeting of the Republican State Executive Committee late that night. There, my old nemesis, Frank Kenna of Queens County, objected bitterly and threatened to resign if I was chosen. "Who else have we got?" Dewey is reported to have said. He called Kenna's hand this time and I was duly nominated the next day. It all happened so fast that my staff had to scramble to find kids to hand-letter Javits posters for the requisite "demonstration" on the convention floor.

Since I was from New York City and Jewish, I "balanced the ticket" geographically and ethnically. Republican conservatives undoubtedly regarded my nomination as a no-lose situation for them: If I won, I would dispel forever the specter of another Roosevelt in New York politics; if I was defeated, that would be one less maverick to worry about. I doubt there were more than fifty delegates among the three hundred fifty accredited to the convention who had the remotest idea I could win that election. Dewey probably considered it a throwaway nomination that might give Ives some extra votes in New York City.

That election campaign for attorney general was the shortest I ever waged: less than six weeks from nomination to election day. Indeed, my posters for reelection to Congress were already on display in the Twenty-first Congressional District. When I got back to the city from Syracuse, I rushed to the Javits & Javits law office in Rockefeller Center and started banging away on the telephone to line up a new campaign staff and arrange finances, headquarters, and materials. Ben dropped everything else and went to work raising money; we spent several hundred thousand dollars in that campaign and he found it all, single-handedly, in a few weeks. Marian worked hard to recruit volunteers, and before election day we had five thousand campaign workers throughout the state.

On the recommendation of Nat Goldstein, the outgoing attorney general, I had a talk with an able young lawyer named John Trubin and immediately engaged him as my campaign manager. Trubin was a liberal Republican who shared my views and who had worked closely with the Republican organization; he was an active member of Tom Curran's own district Republican club in Greenwich Village and thus bridged the gap that had often separated me from the New York County chairman. John performed miracles of organization in that campaign. Finally, I was able to reactivate many of the organizations that had helped me on the mayoralty the year before. This saved a tremendous amount of time; the members knew each other and often just one phone call could bring a whole group back to life.

We spent about a week organizing and then we got going. Right at the start I made two overall strategy decisions. One was that I would run an independent campaign focused against FDR Junior instead of tagging along on the Ives state ticket. The other was to concentrate on the New York metropolitan area, particularly the city itself.

I have always believed that a political candidate must ride strength — give first priority to the areas where voter support is greatest in order to increase the percentage of support. The city was a natural constituency in which I could do the most good for myself and the ticket. Upstate — where we could count on traditional Republican majorities that I could do less to enhance — the ticket would have to help me. To win the election we had to cut deeply into the normal Democratic vote in the city, and that, I thought, I could do better than any other Republican.

Because time was so short, John Trubin and I also decided to rely heavily on the telephone. We set up large telephone banks all around the state and had hundreds of volunteers making phone calls to voters every day and evening. By insisting that the volunteers stick to a set presentation from a written manual and not get diverted by the arguments of some voters, we were able to use relatively inexperienced volunteers to contact hundreds of thousands of sympathetic voters. Of course we got many turndowns, but by avoiding debate and moving rapidly along, the volunteers placed my message where it counted and identified ardent supporters who could then be called for further volunteer effort.

We also contrived a more sophisticated version of the old Javits Dreamboat. This was a bus, not a truck, and we called it the Javits Bandwagon. Plastered with posters and stuffed with leaflets, it carried relays of volunteer speakers to every neighborhood of the city. Like the telephone volunteers, the speakers on the bus were precisely instructed. The speakers' kit included detailed outlines for several speeches — a general one for the whole ticket, a general speech for me, and a series of specific talks contrasting my legal qualifications, my legislative record, and my ability to handle the attorney general's job with Roosevelt's. There was no time for sloppiness; I knew I had a good case and I had to get it across — fast — to counter the Roosevelt name and charisma.

Basically, my message was that FDR Junior had neglected his district and shortchanged his constituents, and that he had only three years of law practice and almost no trial experience. In contrast, I pointed to my own attendance record (one of the highest in the House, even while I was involved in the mayoral campaign); to the large number of bills I had introduced and amendments I had offered while my opponent was doing little; to my conscientious weekly servicing of constituents' needs; to my general congressional effectiveness; and to my long years of legal experience in all the courts of the state. Thanks to the rent and housing struggles, the Israel and displaced-persons and civil rights issues, and the mayoralty try, all of which had earned me extensive press coverage, I was already well known to the voters of the city and suburbs as a hard-working congressman sympathetic to their needs. Roosevelt, despite his charm and the autograph seekers who mobbed him wherever he went, was beginning to be regarded as something of a disappointment by people who expected him to be like his father. So my message began to take hold.

At first, Roosevelt was supremely confident of victory and campaigned against Republicans in general. He and the other Democrats took great delight, for example, in bringing up Defense Secretary Charles "Engine Charlie" Wilson's notorious comment comparing the unemployed to "kennel-fed dogs" who sit around and howl, in contrast to "bird dogs . . . who'll get out and hunt for food." That one did not bother me too much, for I immediately and repeatedly repudiated it. Early in the campaign, in an upstate speech, Roosevelt referred to me scornfully as "that bumptious lawyer from New York." Two weeks later, as my attack on him began to erode his support, he tried to explain away his lack of courtroom experience by saying that his firm does not practice criminal law — as if he had never heard of civil cases. And he repeated the old white-shoe establishment sneer that Javits & Javits was a "strike-suit" firm engaged in "somewhat questionable minority stockholder actions." That was just about the only charge that Roosevelt could make about my record — aside from my being a Republican — and it just did not wash.

Besides his absenteeism, the biggest single blot on Roosevelt's record was a federal slum-clearance and housing project that he helped obtain for his district — and which was under investigation by the Senate Banking and Currency Committee and other government agencies. It was a shocking story, which I explained to the voters in some detail. In the two years since the project had been authorized only about one-sixth of the site had been cleared and nothing had been built — yet the backers of the development corporation had already made a profit of more than $600,000. FDR Junior had been involved as a congressman, and his law partners had represented the corporation. There was never a suggestion that young Roosevelt had profited from the mess or had done anything illegal, but his incompetence and his neglect had clearly contributed to the project's utter failure. On my campaign TV broadcasts I showed pictures of FDR Junior's vacant lot and the successful low- and middle-income project completed in my district during the same period.

Generally we bought our TV air time on local stations in fifteen-minute chunks, a practice that would be prohibitively expensive today; I broadcast live and sent kinescopes (films of the broadcast) to stations upstate. At first I just sat at a desk and talked to the camera, but I quickly discovered that no matter what you were saying the viewers would switch off after a few minutes if you did not provide visual variety. With the help of an advertising agency and a talented television producer named Sheila Kelley (who later joined my staff and married my principal legislative aide, Bob Kaufman), I started using projection screens, photographic blowups, and other visual techniques to hold the viewers' attention.

Probably the most effective of these was the empty chair. I called it Congressman Frank Roosevelt, Jr.'s chair and focused the camera on it while I or a narrator addressed pointed questions to the "congressional delinquent" who was absent not only from Congress but from the debates that I repeatedly challenged him to join. On one memorable broadcast, an unseen narrator, playing the role of the clerk of the House and calling the roll on specific bills, called out "Javits." I answered, "Aye," and then the narrator called "Roosevelt." Silence — with the camera on the empty chair — after which I came on to explain the significance of each vote FDR Junior had missed. Roosevelt was furious. He challenged my statistics and claimed that his vote had been recorded when I said it had not. The argument became very convoluted: I had made an error in my original listing of his voting record, but rechecking revealed that he had been absent on even more roll calls than I had charged. Furthermore, I pointed out that he was trying to confuse the issue by counting votes on which he had been "paired," which is often merely a way of letting the record show how a member would have voted had he been there. There was no doubt about Roosevelt's absenteeism, and the empty-chair broadcasts nailed him on it.

The turning point of the campaign, however, was a dramatic charge, by Ives, that Harriman had been guilty of corruption and dishonesty twenty-five years earlier. Ives's campaign had been going badly and Dewey had urged him to get rough, but that kind of campaigning was not Ives's style and it backfired on him. The charge involved a bribe that someone in Harriman's shipping company had allegedly paid in 1930 in order to secure the lease of a pier, but the story had all come out years before; Harriman had denied authorizing or even knowing about the bribe and he had been completely exonerated of any wrongdoing. When Ives showed me the "bombshell" that he was about to drop on Harriman, I looked the material over as a lawyer and told him I would not go along with it because it contained no evidence to implicate Harriman. But Ives persisted; after first building up public suspense with advance promises of startling revelations, he went ahead. When the reporters asked me about Ives's charges, I made it clear that I was not joining in any attack on Harriman's integrity, and while I questioned the Democratic candidate's qualifications to be governor, I said that "I am not personally charging Mr. Harriman with dishonesty."

Ives's allegations strained the public's credulity. Harriman had been confirmed by the Senate for five federal posts and his background had been thoroughly investigated; it was unreasonable to suppose that he could have hidden such malfeasance from that kind of scrutiny. The voters have brains too. No matter what partisan stresses a candidate may be laboring under, he should never try to sell the public a story reasonable people will find hard to believe. The chances are the public will not buy it, and then the accuser will be in worse trouble. Ives's attacks on Harriman's integrity (there were several, besides the pier scandal) cost him the election — and my disavowal of them saved me.

On the Sunday before election day, I televised a mock courtroom proceeding to drive home to the voters my opponent's failures. Roosevelt — represented by the empty chair — was on trial. The presiding judge was played by Frederick VanPelt Bryan — a prominent New York lawyer whom I subsequently recommended for the federal bench — and I was the prosecutor. I made an opening statement to the "jury" (the audience could see only the railing of the jury box), cross-examined the absent defendant, and appealed to the judge, who made rulings on the evidence. I then summed up for the "jury," indicting my opponent. The "trial" was broadcast in the fifteen minutes preceding a Sunday afternoon opera program; as viewers tuned in for the opera, my audience kept building and a tremendous number of New Yorkers saw and heard my "summation." That broadcast and my disavowal of Ives's blunder were the highlights of my campaign and explain what happened two days later.

The true-life drama of election night was more exciting than anything Sheila Kelley could have devised for the cameras. In the early returns the whole Republican ticket was running far behind and the *New York Times* first edition went to press with a story headlining Roosevelt's "substantial lead" over me. At a little before 10:00 P.M. I was sitting in my headquarters office at the Roosevelt Hotel with my campaign staff; we were watching the bad news on television and making and receiving telephone calls from and to local clubs and county headquarters to get returns ourselves. Suddenly a grimfaced Tom Dewey entered the room. With all my aides about, he could not talk privately, so he pulled me into the bathroom and closed the door. Then he told me that we had lost and that the whole ticket should concede. I thought it was much too early, for the bulk of the upstate precincts had not yet been heard from. So I refused to concede and Dewey marched out, grimmer than ever.

Apparently he had better luck with Ives. A few minutes later there was a big commotion in the hall. I went to the door and there was Irving Ives rushing down the corridor with all his assistants. "Irving, where are you going?" I asked him.

"I'm going to concede the election," Ives said.

"Are you crazy?" I said. "It's only ten o'clock."

"Well," he replied, "I'm behind two hundred thirty thousand

votes and I think it's all over and I might as well be a good sport about it."

So at 10:16 P.M. we saw Ives on TV conceding the election to Harriman. This was just about the time that the newspaper and TV statisticians were revising their projections on the basis of new returns. Harriman's lead began to diminish, to ninety thousand at 10:30, to seventy thousand at midnight, then to twenty-six thousand. It began to look like a very close election, but it still seemed unlikely that Ives would make it. In the general gloom around headquarters no one paid much attention to me, although my staff and I had noticed that I was running ahead of Ives in some districts.

It must have been around 2:00 A.M. when I was called upstairs to Dewey's office. All the Republican candidates were there, sitting in a semicircle around Dewey's desk: Ives; J. Raymond McGovern, the candidate for lieutenant governor; Frank Del Vecchio, the candidate for controller; and myself. Harriman's lead was being whittled down with each new batch of returns, and Dewey, as governor, was ordering that all the voting machines and ballot boxes be impounded and guarded for the official recount. Every fifteen minutes or so, Dewey hopefully called the *Times* for the latest score, but Harriman's narrow margin held. Then, during one of those calls, Dewey suddenly turned to me with a look of stunned surprise on his face. "Jack," he said, "you're ahead."

Shortly after 3:00 A.M., FDR Junior conceded, and I soon found myself refusing another Dewey directive — this one that I go out and claim victory. I could not quite believe what had happened, and remembering Ives's unwise gesture, I did not want to make any rash statements until all the votes were counted. So, in the predawn confusion of our headquarters, the reporters were treated to a bizarre situation: Ives, who it appeared had a slim chance of winning, was still insisting that he had lost, while I, although my opponent had conceded, refused to say that I had won. I went off to bed — "feeling good" I told the press — although the *New York Post* reporter wrote that Javits "acted like he still expected to wake up and find himself a loser."

But I woke up a winner — the only Republican winner. While Ives was losing to Harriman by just 11,125 votes out of more than 5 million cast — the narrowest gubernatorial margin in New York's history — I was defeating Franklin D. Roosevelt, Jr., the man everyone thought could not be beaten, by 172,899 votes. The *Post*, which had backed Roosevelt, called that "a sensational figure for a man running on a losing ticket."

The key to the outcome was New York City, as I had hoped it

would be. The normal Republican majorities upstate of course helped me, but I ran thirty-one thousand votes behind my ticket out of the city. FDR Junior did not get many of my lost votes, however, because, upstate, he ran slightly behind *his* ticket. That is the normal "drop-off" effect caused by people who vote only for the top of the ticket — generally President or governor. Therefore, in that close election I would probably have been defeated by a greater margin than Ives if my campaign had not brought about a remarkable phenomenon. In heavily Democratic New York City, which his father had carried by huge margins time and again, and in which he was expected to run well ahead of his ticket, FDR Junior received one hundred twenty-three thousand *fewer* votes than Harriman. This was not just drop-off, for most of his "lost" New York City votes were cast for me. I polled more votes than Ives did in every borough of the city (and in all five suburban counties as well). Instead of dropping off, I added on and ran eighty-five thousand votes ahead of my ticket in the city. I did not carry the city, of course. That, for a Republican without third-party support, was considered impossible — until I did it eight years later. But the Harriman votes I took away from Roosevelt in the metropolitan area, added to upstate Republican majorities, provided a solid victory for me while my running mates were going down to a narrow defeat. Even my old congressional district, the Twenty-first, was reverting to its Democratic voting tradition.

There was a sad note to this triumph. In 1947, seated in the gallery of the House of Representatives, my mother had witnessed my swearing-in as a congressman — and with that she had seen her passion for my advancement fully realized. But she was not destined to watch me being sworn in as attorney general in the governor's ornate red and gold hearing room in Albany, for she had passed away the previous spring.

* * *

In many respects, attorney general was the best job I ever had. Certainly it provided a personally pleasurable interlude. Compared with what I had been accustomed to in Washington, the workload was light and the prestige was great: I was the highest legal officer of the state, not one of 435 representatives. A staff of more than two hundred lawyers worked under my direction and I was driven to my offices in Albany and New York City in an official car. Generally I had to spend only about three days a week in Albany when the legislature was in session and two days otherwise, which meant only one or two nights a week away from home — and no long lines of constituents on the weekends. So the job allowed me more time with my family than I had ever had before as an elected official. We moved from Riverside Drive to a more spacious and comfortable apartment at 911 Park Avenue. There, my new prominence as the man who beat FDR Junior and as the highest elected Republican in the state combined with Marian's brilliance as a hostess to open up many glamorous new worlds to us. We entertained a lot, we took trips together, we went to the theater and to concerts, and I played tennis regularly. Our third child, Carla, was born in 1955, and it was a happy time all around.

The job itself was lawyering, which I have always enjoyed. Constitutional issues involving federal-state matters or controversies with other states — power lines that crossed borders, for instance — were often fascinating. I had to interpret state law and issue opinions on whether laws being considered by the legislature were constitutional. The governor's office and state government departments frequently had to refer matters to me, and since the ones that actually reached my desk were the most complex and controversial, I found the handling of those, too, a very stimulating intellectual experience. I also took pride in bringing the attorney general's office into the field of consumer protection, and in setting up a committee to develop a youth program to halt the rise of juvenile crime. To my delight, I even once managed to appear in court myself to represent the state of New York, which attorneys general rarely do — the solicitor general is the trial lawyer in the attorney general's office. The complex case involved constitutional law, commercial rent control, and Tammany politics, so I could not deprive myself of that treat.

A good deal of my time, however, was taken up with bureaucratic details and routine cases of property or money claims against the state. We always had a large number of "Article 78" appeals, in which citizens take the state to court to contest some administrative decision, such as the suspension of a driving license. There was also a huge practice in the writs of habeas corpus sued out by prisoners claiming some illegality in their convictions or sentences. These were all essential matters, but not of the kind to challenge me.

I derived great satisfaction from my associates, however. I had appointed John Trubin, who had managed my campaign, my first assistant attorney general, and he turned out to be a superb lawyer and administrator. He ran the New York City office of the attorney general with a strong hand but extraordinary sensitivity, alertness to pitfalls, and professional skill. My solicitor general was James Moore of Buffalo, another fine lawyer and advocate, who later became a New York State Supreme Court judge; when I became a senator and was able to practice law in a limited way, Jim Moore joined me and John Trubin in the law firm I organized, Javits, Moore and Trubin.

Sam Roman, my running mate in Washington Heights who had been elected to serve in the New York State Assembly while I was in Congress, had lost his Assembly seat in the 1954 election, when Tammany regained control of the Twenty-first Congressional District. So he came with me, too, as executive assistant of the attorney general's New York City office.

With such a competent staff I really had little to do in the way of administration and routine, except to keep an eye on it all. Yet I continued to prefer an arena where I could fight for a national issue or a national principle.

All through 1955 I maintained my franchise as a spokesman on the issues that had concerned me as a congressman. I addressed Jewish groups around the state on the troubling events in the Middle East, and I made speeches to many audiences on labor, education, immigration, foreign policy, the economy, and other matters beyond the formal jurisdiction of the attorney general. One of these matters was the future of the Republican Party.

Early in 1956 some liberal "Eisenhower Republicans" who were unhappy with Richard Nixon were mentioning Massachusetts Governor Christian Herter, my old friend and ally from Congress, as a possible vice-presidential candidate. To help Herter gather some quiet support, I invited about twenty of New York's most prominent Republicans to meet him over dinner at our apartment. Among them were Nelson Rockefeller, John Loeb, Sr., and Jock Whitney. The talk at dinner concerned the dangers of war and Soviet expansion, the structural problems of the U.S. economy, and the need to accelerate economic and social development in the less-developed countries. The Herter movement died at the convention that summer, but that dinner marked my entry into the upper echelons of Republican politics.

These activities represented an attempt on my part to remain involved with political challenges and with the critical issues facing the country. I did not know that I would soon be facing the most critical challenge of my life.

TWELVE

The Lie That Failed

Nineteen fifty-six stands out in my memory as a year of threat and crisis. Suddenly, in the waning phase of McCarthyism, half-forgotten incidents of the past were dug up and distorted in an effort to destroy me as a public man.

There was no logic, no orderly progression of cause and effect, to the events that suddenly enveloped me. The threat did not emerge as criticism of anything I had said or done during my four terms in the House of Representatives or during my year and a half as attorney general. Nor was it expressed as an attack on my philosophy as a progressive Republican — although certainly my views had antagonized some members of the party. Instead, it surfaced first as a whisper, a vague innuendo regarding people I had met and talked with more than a decade earlier. Soon it was a rumor rampant, intended to cast doubt even on my loyalty to the United States, discussed behind my back by politicians and journalists and thousands of puzzled voters.

How does one fight a lie? Ignore it, scorn it, and hope it goes away? Perhaps, but suppose it refuses to go away? That was the dilemma I faced early in June 1956 when an official of the American Jewish Committee forwarded to me a letter from a friendly rabbi in Binghamton. The rabbi stated that Bella Dodd, a former Communist, was spreading the charge that Javits in 1946 "was a Communist and moreover she [Dodd] was instrumental in bringing him to New York so that he might bore from within."

Although I had met Bella Dodd when I first ran for Congress in 1946, this story was so patently false and nonsensical that I ignored it at first. Of course I had never been a Communist, and no one had to "bring" me to the city where I was born and had lived all my life. But a week after I saw that letter the attack escalated. On June 14, Bella Dodd, who had apparently been a Communist until expelled from the party in 1949, testified before the Internal Security Subcommittee of the U.S. Senate's Committee on the Judiciary, of which James O. Eastland was chairman. My name did not come up in the public part of her testimony, in which Dodd charged that several other New York politicians — Republicans and Democrats — were Communists. In an executive (closed) session, however, Dodd apparently testified about me. That testimony has never been made public; at that time I was not even aware of it. But months later the committee counsel, Robert Morris, confronted me with it at an open hearing called at my request.

According to Morris, Dodd testified that in 1946 some West Coast Communists who were "interested" in my political future had contacted Dodd — who was the Communist Party official in charge of political activity in New York — and asked her to see me; that she had discussed with me my first run for office; and that the Communists had supported me in that 1946 campaign. In this more sophisticated — and thus more dangerous — version of the charge, Dodd did not state that I was a Communist. But in suggesting that I had sought and received Communist aid in my first congressional campaign and that I was a protégé of some unnamed Communists, Dodd implied that I was a tool of the Communist Party, a "Manchurian candidate" diabolically planted by Moscow in the body of the Republican Party.

At that time — June 1956 — no one dared to utter these charges in public or in print. But this was juicy gossip, which has its own way of getting around, especially in an election year, and the juicier gossip is, the more fun it is for malicious tongues to spread it. I have no doubt that some conservative members of my own party took pleasure in repeating Dodd's charges — and they may have included the people who invited Dodd to speak in Binghamton in the first place. At any rate, the rumors and whispers had begun to get about and were feeding on themselves by the time Marian and I and the children moved out to a summer cottage on Fire Island in July.

It was an agonizing summer. I was for the moment confounded, uncertain of how to handle the situation, and I wanted some privacy and time to think, so we did not encourage visitors. I played some tennis; we went clamming in the bay. Carla, our youngest, was just an infant, born the preceding August; I remember pushing her baby carriage in the sunshine along the pathways of Seaview (no autos allowed), sitting on the great wide beach a block from our pleasant cottage looking out at the horizon, and wondering whether I was going to be destroyed as a public man and whether I might even have to resign as attorney general.

Marian and I speculated about what I might do — teach, go into business, practice law quietly. Marian's loyalty, her passion for integrity, and her sober thinking and philosophic determination to see us through our trials gave me a solid base of support; only Marian's encouragement and Ben's inestimable support during those days prevented my anguish from becoming despair.

I was outraged that those ridiculous charges had been made against me — much as a victim of a robbery may experience anger far out of proportion to his actual loss. At one point, Len Hall, who was then chairman of the Republican National Committee, phoned me from Washington to find out what I was going to do. I have only a dim recollection of the conversation, but Len later remembered that "it was one of the few times Jack Javits was at a loss; the whole thing shocked him and he didn't come out punching as he usually did. I think he was crushed."

Looking back on that crisis a quarter century later, it is difficult to imagine that anyone could examine my record in Congress, listen to my speeches, consider a full roster of my friends and associates and activities — and then react to the suggestion that I was secretly a Communist ally with anything but scornful laughter. But this was happening in 1956. The country had not yet recovered from the McCarthy madness — and, indeed, Senator Joseph McCarthy, though not a member of the Internal Security Subcommittee, had attended the session at which Bella Dodd testified publicly, and he had praised Dodd for her "courage."

Scores of innocent people in government, in the arts, and in education, people better known than I was then, had found their names blackened, their careers ruined or sidetracked, by charges as baseless as these. The notion of guilt by association was still current, and in the peculiar illogic of the times a vigorous anti-Communist record was sometimes cited as proof of Communism, on the ground that Communists were known to cloak their views and identities in respectable guises. Therefore, despite the absurdity of the whispered charges against me, I was deeply troubled.

During those lonely days on Fire Island, where the bright sunshine and the laughter of children contrasted so starkly with the gloom of my thoughts, I traced in my memory the slim thread of events out of which this false fabric had been woven. I *had* met Bella Dodd in 1946 during my first run for Congress. As I have related, she was one of the scores of people with whom I had been urged to talk as I started my campaign. I did not — and do not — remember who put Dodd's name on my list, but I recalled that I had spent ten or fifteen minutes talking to her in her office.

I also remembered that at one point in the 1946 campaign it had been suggested to me that I seek the support of the American Labor

Party, and I had discussed this with Liberal Party leaders. This, too, was being dredged up ten years later. Many other New York candidates for public office, Democrats and Republicans, ran with ALP endorsements in 1946, even though the ALP was considered to be under strong Communist influence. (Bella Dodd, I learned later, was one of the principal Communist functionaries within the ALP.) I knew I had not sought the ALP nomination; I had run on the Republican and Liberal Party lines, and the ALP had fielded a strong candidate against me in a three-way race. I recalled an editorial in the *New York Daily News* just before election day, 1946. This is what the *News* said: "Javits has been smeared by Communists and fellow travelers, who have put up their favorite, Eugene P. Connolly, against him as a separate ALP candidate — an excellent reason why Javits should be elected." Yet here I was, ten years later, under attack for having sought ALP support in the same election. Despite that bitter irony, I began to sense that if I could not somehow "clear" myself I might not survive as an elected official even until 1958, when my term as attorney general would expire.

There was another element that I suspected might add to my problem. In her public testimony on June 14 Bella Dodd had named as Communists, or as close allies of the Communist Party, a number of people whose paths had crossed mine at one time or another. One was a New York Republican lawyer who had run for office; another was the brother of a Republican leader in my old Washington Heights district; another was the woman Phil Ehrlich had introduced me to socially on the West Coast in 1945; still another was a union official in New York; and a fifth was an assistant to an elected Republican official.

These people may well never have been party members or sympathizers. But Dodd had *said* they were, and under the prevailing doctrine of guilt by association, anyone who had met them, however briefly or innocently, was automatically suspect. Moreover, in a busy life as a lawyer, army officer, and five-times elected official, I had undoubtedly met many other people who might later have been accused of Communist Party connections. Which of these chance encounters, I wondered, were about to be exhumed and displayed as "evidence" of Jack Javits's "connections"? Should I try to clear myself? Or would that be giving in to those who believed that an American had to prove his "loyalty"? And if I did try to clear myself, would my word be credited against the innuendos of some shadowy "informant" whom I could not confront or cross-examine?

Gradually, through a fog of indecision, I began to analyze the motives behind the attack on me. Early in the year, my name had cropped up in the press as a potential Republican candidate for the U.S. Senate. Although a run for the Senate presented a number of problems for me, I had done nothing to stop the speculation. Such talk never hurts; it keeps your options open, smokes out the opposition, and reminds the voters that you're around — essential considerations for a politician. On March 4, I had declared my availability for the Senate nomination in what I thought was a carefully worded statement:

> The Republican Party's job in New York now is to pick the strongest senatorial candidate, one most likely to succeed at the polls to assure that New York will be again in the Eisenhower column — and one who can do the best job for all the people of the state in the Senate. I want to participate ... with all Republicans in the state, toward making the choice. If we should together determine — considering also my present post and responsibilities — that I am the best able to help in this way to carry the New York State campaign for the Eisenhower ticket and to implement the President's policy in the Congress, then it would be my duty to run. This is consistent with the position I have taken in this matter since it was first raised early in 1956.

There grew in my mind that summer a thought that my tentative interest in the senatorial race may have triggered the smear campaign against me.

It was not just that some conservative Republicans regarded my brand of Republicanism with such antipathy that they would have preferred losing an election to having me win one. I was aware of that attitude and had learned to live with it. The year before, one guest at a White House dinner remarked that "Javits among Republicans is as popular as a skunk at a summer picnic." That was only a few months after I had emerged as the only statewide Republican winner in the 1954 elections.

Some inner fortitude sustained me in the face of such attitudes. I believed in vigorous private enterprise and in democracy. And I felt that the Republican Party — when following Lincolnian principles — was the party most capable of fulfilling our mission as a nation. Therefore I was not fazed by the opposition of Republican ultraconservatives.

But something more than conservative pique was involved in the smear campaign. Another more specific issue mobilized against me those who might have been seeking to build their careers by turning the anti-Communist crusade into individual character destruction. I cannot claim that as a junior congressman I had been a leader in the effort to thwart their methods, but I had voted against the Mundt-Nixon bill, against funding the House Un-American Activities Committee, and against the McCarran Internal Security Act. Profoundly disturbed by Joe McCarthy's irresponsible tactics, I had on several occasions sponsored legislation to protect the rights of witnesses before congressional committees, and I had debated Roy Cohn, McCarthy's counsel, on that issue. "I do not believe," I had stated to the House in 1950, "that it is either necessary or wise to weaken and impair our constitutional guarantees and our freedom here at home in order to root out subversives from our midst or to fight the 'Cold War.' "

And here I was, in 1956, a proven vote getter in what was shaping up as a good Eisenhower-Republican year, talking about running for the Senate. It should have been no surprise at all that the smear weapon appeared to have been picked up and brandished in order to keep one of its opponents out of the Senate.

There is another irony here, for it is not at all certain that I would have run for the Senate that year if I had not been threatened suddenly with political extinction. I still had two years to serve in the comfortable job of attorney general, and until the rumors started I had no compelling reason to jump headlong into the Senate race in 1956. In fact, there were good reasons not to: One good reason was Herbert Lehman, the respected, liberal Jewish elder statesman of the Democratic Party. Lehman had served New York well as governor and senator for seventeen years. It was his term that was expiring in 1956, and although he was then seventy-eight years old, no one was yet sure whether he would retire or run again. Obviously, as a Jew and a liberal myself, I shared a great part of my constituency with Senator Lehman. Running against him had always seemed to me politically unwise as well as personally unthinkable. As a congressman I had on many occasions passed by his door in the Senate Office Building. The simple sign, MR. LEHMAN, NEW YORK, impressed me; he had accomplished so much and enjoyed so much prestige and influence. "God," I would say to myself, "will I ever make that?"

I have never been accused of false modesty, but I could not consider seriously a run against Herbert Lehman. That was one reason I had proceeded so cautiously early in the year: If Lehman had decided to run again, I am sure I would have bowed out at that point; but if he was about to retire, as I thought possible, then I was ready to go after the seat. Evidently, I was not cautious enough. A few days after I had conditionally tossed my hat into the ring, in March, a Brooklyn weekly newspaper, the *Jewish Examiner,* denounced my temerity. My offer to run, an editorial in the paper said, was "shockingly ill-advised." And it continued:

> Mr. Javits has a good record as a Congressman, but Sen. Lehman is one of the greatest legislators in the history of the Republic.

There is no earthly reason why any voter would want to replace Sen. Lehman by Jacob K. Javits — or anyone else. . . . The removal of Sen. Lehman in the present critical period would be nothing short of a catastrophe. Mr. Javits can succeed, perhaps, in splitting and confusing the liberal vote, but what will his candidacy accomplish? What, pray, will he talk about during his campaign? Will he attack Mr. Lehman's unassailable record on civil rights, his courageous opposition to McCarthyism, his stirring championship of aid to Israel, his humane leadership in the fight to extend social welfare legislation? Or can the Attorney General honestly tell the voters that he, Javits, can do it better? No one can do it better! . . . We have always thought of Mr. Javits as more than a mere politician. . . . [He] should be astute enough to shun a political scheme which can only result in damaging his career.

I did not have to bow out at that point, of course; I still thought — and perhaps even hoped — that Lehman might retire. But I was "astute enough" to take a hint. Thereafter, every time I addressed a gathering that could be considered even remotely political, I took the precaution to open my remarks by stating that I would only be a candidate for senator if Lehman was not. And I meant it.

By mid-July the situation was changing on a number of fronts. First of all, the rumors about me, probably aimed at blocking my run for the Senate, were threatening to drive me out of public life altogether, and I was determined not to let that happen. Besides, six other candidates for the Republican senatorial nomination had emerged; they did not have the statewide appeal I had demonstrated two years earlier, but they were not to be belittled, either. Another unsettling development, from my point of view, was that Sherman Adams, President Eisenhower's top political adviser, was urging New York ex-Governor Tom Dewey to run for the Senate. Dewey, I knew, was happy in his law practice and not inclined to seek office again. But I also realized the nomination was his for the asking; if the White House insisted, he might decide to go for it while I dithered on the sidelines fretting about the rumors and waiting for Lehman to retire.

I was still brooding, however, when on July 10 I received a piece of good news for a change: Senator Lehman had declined to serve on the Platform Committee of the Democratic National Convention. To the political reporters — and to me — that seemed a signal that he was not going to run. Certainly the chances of his retirement seemed good enough to gamble on.

There comes a time in any crisis when one has to act — to do *something*. I am not the kind of man who can come to a decision by sinking my head in my hands and cerebrating. I must be in motion, talking to people personally and on the phone, trying out ideas, and weighing the ideas of others. Conversation can stimulate anyone, but political talk is essential to a public man. Only in the crucible of talk and action can he find solutions to problems.

My family was still on Fire Island when I started to make phone calls. As I did so, it became clear that the two issues bedeviling me that summer had become one: The best way to silence the rumormongers would be to get nominated by my party for the Senate and ask the voters of New York to give me a new mandate. And if I wanted the nomination, I could no longer afford to wait for Lehman's decision. I had to intensify my campaign immediately — despite the real though diminishing possibility that Lehman would run for reelection after all and that I would then withdraw. It was a gamble, but I took it.

Proceeding quietly and privately, I began to talk with Republican leaders around the state who had helped me in the past. Within a few weeks, my associates and I had lined up eleven county chairmen who were prepared to vote for me when the Republican State Committee convened on September 10 to choose a candidate.

It also seemed wise, considering Sherman Adams's preference for Tom Dewey, to send a message to President Eisenhower. I was Ike's representative in Congress when he was president of Columbia University and living on Morningside Heights, and I had urged him to run in 1952; I felt he would be favorable to my candidacy. Tex McCrary, the television talk-show host, was a good friend to both Ike and me, and as soon as Tex had been filled in on the situation he wrote to Ike:

> ... the fact that Sherman has expressed to several people, even to Javits, that he would like to see Dewey run, has not helped Javits here. If Dewey were to run, it might once and for all prove my point that he understands everything about politics but people. But I don't think you can afford to take that chance; not this year. Only Javits could beat Lehman, and even that would be tough. I hope somehow you can again lend a helping hand to the man who was once *your* Congressman; it could win you one more seat in the Senate, and it would be the beginning of the reconstruction of the Republican Party in New York State and city. ...

Two weeks later McCrary sent me a copy of his letter with the comment that "the Boss's reaction on all points was highly satisfactory."

I do not remember who among the people I spoke to during this period had heard the rumors about me. Those who knew me and had worked with me were appalled by the smear, and although they gave no credence to the substance of the rumors, some of them were worried for me and wanted to know how I was going to handle it. By the time I returned to the city in the last week of July, still mightily concerned, I felt it was time to try to find out precisely what Senator Eastland's Internal Security Subcommittee had been told and just what Bella Dodd or other informers might have said about me to anyone else. I went to see another friend, U.S. Attorney General Herbert Brownell. I told him of the rumors and asked him to find out if the FBI files contained anything relevant.

Brownell called me a few days later and told me that the information the FBI had came from what it called "raw, unevaluated" data, which meant that each bit had probably come from just one informant and that no effort had been made to check it. There were three principal charges in the file. The first was Bella Dodd's puzzling tale that in 1946 West Coast Communists had suggested she see me and that I had come to her for support. Dodd, apparently, had given the FBI the same story long before testifying to Eastland's committee, and the FBI files had probably inspired the committee's questions.

The second and third charges were even more ridiculous, but they were menacing because they purported to give the background to Dodd's story. Both of them related to my trip to San Francisco in 1945 for the founding session of the United Nations. One charge was that I had been seen on the Oakland–San Francisco ferry (presumably by an FBI agent) talking to Frederick Vanderbilt Field, a writer for the Communist *Daily Worker*. In fact, I had talked to the young man on the ferry, as I have described. But I did not know he was a Communist (if indeed he was), and our conversation was totally unrelated to anything except the beauty of the San Francisco skyline. I certainly had no business or social relationship to him before or since.

The third item in the files was somewhat more worrisome. It alleged that during the UN conference I had been a guest at the San Francisco home of a "'Communist sympathizer," a woman who had also entertained Soviet diplomats — including one who was accused of being an espionage agent — and that I had met in her home several other people who were later reported to have Communist connections. That alleged "Communist sympathizer" was Louise Bransten, the heiress who had kept me waiting in the cocktail lounge of the Mark Hopkins Hotel and who had, apparently, invited me to that awkward party at her home.

In saner times, the "accusation" that I had gone to a party could have been dismissed with a "So what?" It was not alleged that I had expressed sympathy for Communism: Talking to Communists was — and is — no crime; our government officials were talking to the Soviet delegation every day. But if I wanted to survive as a public official in 1956, I had to explain my 1945 social life. Bella Dodd had told the committee, in her public session, that she knew Louise Bransten and regarded her as a "Communist," thus leading to the inference that Bransten and her friends were the "West Coast Communists" supposedly "interested" in my career.

At about the same time I was learning of this flimsy bill of particulars, I went to see Tom Dewey. Some columnists were writing that a nomination battle was raging between us, and I wanted to obtain his endorsement before anyone talked him into making the run himself. I thought I could count on Dewey's support: I doubted that he wanted to be a senator and I was sure he knew by now that I could win. As I had expected, Dewey made it clear that he did not want the nomination. But he doubted he could use his influence in my behalf for the nomination until I could clear up those rumors. He suggested that I go straight to the Eastland subcommittee and answer the charges under oath. And then the old crime-busting D.A. said something like this: "Jack, make damn sure you don't say anything that directly contradicts anything they may have in the files. If you do, they'll nail you."

On August 3 I telephoned Bob Morris, the committee counsel, and asked for a hearing "to set the record straight on certain matters." Since the charges were still just unpublicized rumors, I suggested an executive session. Senator Eastland was off fishing in the Gulf of Mexico and couldn't be reached for several days. After that, he and the committee's other Democrats had to go to Chicago for the Democratic National Convention, and then I was due at the Republican National Convention in San Francisco. Finally, after more than a week of calls and telegrams back and forth, we settled on a date. I find in my files a memo in my own handwriting: "At my request, committee has granted me a hearing Sept. 5. Whether open or exec depends entirely on the committee, which I assume will decide entirely in the interests of national security."

From my standpoint, September 5 was cutting things close. The New York Republican State Committee was scheduled to choose a senatorial nominee on September 10.

With a feeling of rising tension and excitement, I flew to San Francisco on August 16 for the Republican National Convention. My quiet campaign to line up support for the Senate nomination was proceeding, but Lehman had made no announcement and Tom Dewey had not fully shown his hand. The newspapers were still speculating that Ike might ask Dewey to run, and all Dewey himself was saying was that he couldn't imagine a situation that would induce him to become a candidate. Moreover, in commenting on the results of the Democratic Convention, Dewey declared that "someone" had taken away the vice-presidential nomination from John F. Kennedy. This statement was being interpreted as a hint that New York Republicans should make a bid for the disgruntled Irish Catholic vote by nominating an Irish Catholic for senator, and there was one in the field. The rumors about me had not surfaced in public and it seemed likely that the nomination would be decided, unofficially, while we were all in San Francisco. Certainly, with the renomination of Eisenhower and Nixon a foregone conclusion, the New York delegation had little to do but politick on the Senate issue.

Then everything seemed to happen at once. On August 21 Senator Lehman announced in New York that he would retire at the end of his term. It was the break I had been waiting for all summer; I had won that gamble. Only Dewey, I felt, could take the nomination away from me, and I knew he really didn't want it. I scheduled a press conference for the twenty-third; it was time to shift my campaign into high gear.

But that press conference never took place, for the smear masters escalated first. On the afternoon of August 22, as I was contentedly nursing a drink in Phil Ehrlich's penthouse suite in the Palace Hotel in San Francisco, the telephone rang. One of Phil's aides answered it and called to me. A reporter, Lucian Warren of the *Buffalo Courier-Express,* was on the phone, and his words hit me like a thunderclap. He said that Jay Sourwine, a member of the staff of Senator Eastland's Internal Security Subcommittee, who was running for the Democratic State nomination in Nevada to replace Pat McCarran, had issued a statement concerning me:

> ... the Justice Department has evidence showing Javits to have been the protégé of important Communists who helped push him up the political ladder. [Javits] had been associated with one of the most important woman Communists in the country, who had lived with the top NKVD agent on the West Coast and had been seen with top Comintern agent Dimitri Manuilski.

There it was, out in the open, and at the worst possible time — as I had feared. Warren wanted my comments. His story, which appeared in the *Courier-Express* the next day, quoted me as saying that Sourwine's "scurrilous smear is beneath contempt in view of my life's record," and that if the charges had been true they certainly would have been aired long before by New York Democrats. Within hours, the Sourwine story had become the number-one topic of conversation at the convention. But now, at least, I knew how to fight the attack: openly, publicly, and with every resource at my command.

The Sourwine statement triggered a frenzy of politicking in the New York delegation at San Francisco. The supporters of J. Raymond McGovern of Westchester, who was by then my most serious rival for the nomination, redoubled their efforts and probably made some progress at my expense. My own friends and supporters rallied around — though some of them were worried. Herb Brownell told the press that the Sourwine statement sounded like a "straight smear job." Russell Sprague and John Crews, the Republican chairmen of Nassau and Kings counties respectively, both members of the party's Executive Committee, and Billy Hill, the Broome County chairman, as well as Oswald Heck, the Republican Speaker of the New York State Assembly, all offered support and advice.

The atmosphere was made to order for the political orchestrations of Tom Dewey. He did not want the nomination himself, but the press speculation that Eisenhower might ask him to run enhanced his influence, and he let it continue. He had carefully declined to back any candidate, so everyone courted him. He had shown sympathy to me and given me good advice in July — but then he had quietly urged both Herb Brownell and Len Hall to try for the nomination, too. These machinations annoyed me at the time, but Dewey probably believed he was merely protecting the party and himself: If I could not erase all the doubts about me, Tom Dewey, without a shred of embarrassment, would simply engineer the nomination of someone else. In this respect, Tom Dewey was a very interesting man and politician. He was capable of great warmth and human feeling, but at the same time he could make a ruthless political decision if he considered it necessary to advance or protect his interests as he saw them. I had experienced the implacable side of his nature in 1953, when he abruptly dropped me as candidate for mayor, and I was worried that he might make the same decision again on the Senate nomination.

The New York State chairman of the Republican Party was L. Judson Morhouse, who generally followed Dewey's instructions. Immediately after the Sourwine statement, Morhouse summoned Sam Roman, who was at that time my executive assistant, and told Roman unequivocally that I did not have a chance to get the Senate nomination unless I cleared up "that matter before the Eastland committee." I took that as a message from Dewey; what it really meant was that Dewey would not support me until the cloud was lifted.

I had less than two weeks between my return to New York and my appointment with the Eastland subcommittee; if I was to clear myself, I could not afford to waste a moment, and I plunged right into it. I called friends and former colleagues who knew my views and frankly asked them for statements of support. I set a staff member to work compiling my voting record in Congress and going through my speeches, so I could offer evidence of my anti-Communism. I urged the committee to hear my testimony in a public session. I called Alex Rose, senior political strategist and coleader of the New York Liberal Party, and asked him for his recollection of the ALP discussion in 1946. And I immediately started drafting a letter to Morhouse to put before the state Republican Party my denials of the charges and my record as a loyal public servant.

These were not pleasant tasks. The more deeply I became involved in the effort to clear myself, the angrier I felt. I was being forced to participate in an insulting process that was unhealthy for orderly, constitutional government.

Digging up proof of anti-Communism, the commentator I. F. Stone wrote of the case a few weeks later, "is to play into the committee's hands. It is to seek 'clearance' as one seeks clearance for government employment, a job in a defense plant, or a passport. It is to concede that the committee has the right to act as a censor of politics, to determine who may or may not safely be allowed to run for public office . . . Candidates are not to be judged on their record by the voters themselves, but must first pass the muster of the committee. What McCarthy was trying to do toward the last is what Eastland and Jenner are now attempting — to make their committee a kind of fourth branch of the government with power to pass on Congress itself."

The lawyer in me recognized this problem — and the man in me felt humiliated — but the practical politician had no choice. As far as I was concerned, it was too late for constitutional niceties. The Eastland committee had already established itself as a censor, and if I did not refute these charges, the voters would get no chance to pass judgment on me — that had been made clear by the Dewey-Morhouse edict. Were I to stand on the principle that the committee had no right to investigate my past associations, I would merely sacrifice my career; I had no desire to be a martyr to that cause.

Besides, there was another issue of principle involved. I did have influential friends and my record was indisputably anti-Communist. If I allowed my career to be destroyed by unsubstantiated rumors, what chance would there be for those similarly attacked who did not enjoy my political advantages? I was fighting the good fight for others as well, and I was determined to win.

For several days my staff and I sweated over the text of the letter to Jud Morhouse. I hoped he would circulate it to every member of the State Committee and I knew it would put them on the spot; with the charges and my record juxtaposed and out in the open, a vote against me would put the Republican Party of New York in the position of knuckling under to a prime example of McCarthyism. Someone suggested the letter take the form of a sworn affidavit, but I rejected that idea as demeaning for the attorney general. Tex McCrary came up with a piece of sound advice, and I still have his memo. It said: "In your letter to Jud ... you should *quote* Sourwine and then nail it as a *lie*. It is easier to nail a quote than a vague reference to undefined 'rumors and innuendos' — *define* and *destroy!*"

The letter went to Morhouse on August 29. It stated that "rumors and innuendos have been sedulously spread about me, apparently as an eleventh-hour technique to try to block that serious consideration which, together with every other appropriate candidate, I should have for the senatorial nomination." I then went on to quote Sourwine's charges that Brownell was backing me despite Justice Department "evidence showing Javits to have been a protégé of important Communists." And then I wrote:

> The point of the whole statement is of course untrue and libels not only me but our Republican Party in New York. Attorney General Brownell has already labelled this statement "a straight smear job." Perhaps there are some elements in the country ready to go to any lengths to try to stop me from going to the Senate, even to uttering contemptible and scurrilous falsehoods. . . . I cannot hope to keep up with a variety of rumors; therefore let me say categorically for now and all time that I am not and never have been associated in any way in any Communist activities or organization or knowingly sought the help or aid in public or private life of any person or organization engaged in such activities. Innuendos and rumors to the contrary are just false, and my whole life, career and public record give the lie to any such contentions. . . .
>
> I have been to hundreds of meetings, known, encountered and interviewed thousands of people and received scores of delegations. I have run for office four times in the 21st Congressional District and once statewide. . . . Yet never once in all this time were any such charges as I am discussing here made or even intimated. Indeed, I have been reviled by the American Labor Party and denounced by Communist publications in and outside the USSR.
>
> This is not the first time and unhappily probably not the last when scurrilous falsehoods might be spread about one in public life on the threshold of a nomination for high office. It is my duty and that of others similarly situated to set an example and to deal with such smears as they come up, on the facts, in this way encouraging others to do the same. . . .

I have dedicated my life to the people and they know it. I have great faith in their judgment and good sense.

Morhouse did not make the letter public right away, but it did succeed in prodding him to stand up and defend me. On August 30 he told the press that the Sourwine charge "sounds like something cut from a familiar pattern of smear." Sourwine, Morhouse declared,

has made a severe accusation but has not supported it with any facts. If he has any provable fact he should produce it immediately; if he can't he impeaches his own integrity, completely discredits what he has said, and owes an apology to Jack Javits, Attorney General Brownell, and to the people for an ugly offense against their sense of decency and fair play.... I cannot speak categorically for the entire State Committee of 300 members, but I am confident they would not allow any unsupported allegations, smacking strongly of smear, to influence their decision, one way or another, in selecting a senatorial nominee....

On that day, August 30, I suddenly found my problems the center of a national controversy. The Democratic margin in the Senate was 49 to 47, so a Republican victory in New York and in the nation (which was clearly indicated) could give us a 48–48 tie and a Republican vice president to break it, which would mean Republican control of the Senate. Bob Wagner, who was then mayor of the city of New York, had announced his candidacy for the Democratic nomination, which he seemed certain to get. So, with the famous Wagner name in the race, with the outcome so potentially significant for the nation and the leading Republican contender accused of Communist sympathy, newspapers and politicians all over the country were taking notice of the New York Senate race — and of what I said and did. When I issued my first formal press statement on the smear, it received front-page coverage in New York and was widely reported elsewhere. The statement said: "This is campaign time and these things happen during political campaigns. There is of course no truth in any of the vicious rumors being spread about me. They seem to be nothing but devices brought out at the eleventh hour to seek to block a Senate nomination...." A reporter from the *New York Times* also asked me bluntly: "Were you at any time a member of the Communist Party?" It was a humiliating question for a man in my position, with my public record, but I swallowed my pride and answered forthrightly: "No. Not in any way, shape, or form. Nor have I ever had any sympathy with the party or its ideas or been associated with Communists in any way."

If I still harbored any doubts about my outspoken tactics, they were dispelled forty-eight hours later when I picked up my copy of the

New York Times of September 1. In an editorial, the *Times* reprinted its reporter's blunt question and my denial of Communist affiliations, and then went on to say:

> We had such confidence in Mr. Javits that we felt we didn't really need to ask him this question, but we did. Our confidence in him, our respect for his integrity, our appreciation for his usefulness in public office and in leading the Republican Party to a more liberal philosophy remain unshaken. We thought that on this day when these ugly whisperings began to reach print more widely we would like to say a good word for Jack Javits and tell him that, as far as we are concerned, nothing has changed.

Those words stirred me profoundly. An elected official lives on trust, as an actor is nourished by applause. Rarely is that trust and confidence expressed so directly at a time of adversity as it was, in my case, in that *Times* editorial. All at once I knew I had a fighting chance to win; and more important than that, I knew I could hold my head up even if I lost.

It was not just the *Times*. The *New York Daily Mirror,* which had often criticized me in the past, wrote that I had "done exactly the right thing in facing the strange 'smear campaign' . . . we do not believe that Jack Javits has or ever had any sympathy whatsoever with Communist aims. He has the applause of decent people for facing the innuendos and scotching them in the open." The *Long Island Press* commented that the smear charges were "ridiculous"; the *Baltimore Sun* stated that "Mr. Javits' public record is entirely inconsistent with pro-Communism."

The *New York Post,* which generally supported Democrats, pointed out that the whispering campaign against me was being "promoted most actively" by members of the Republican Party. The *Post* continued:

> There is a certain irony in the spectacle of Republicans using the tactic of furtive slander to destroy their most effective vote getter in the state. But the stakes in this affair go far beyond any political contest. Javits' career as a public servant is a matter of record. . . . In Congress he steadfastly supported all those programs of economic and military aid designed to check the post-war Communist thrust. This personal history is hardly consistent with the portrait of a Communist collaborator. If Javits can nevertheless be ruined by anonymous informants, no man is safe. . . .

On that same Labor Day weekend an editorial in the *Washington Post* echoed my own feelings:

Mr. Javits' long and honorable public record provides a compelling refutation of the smear. It is a pity in a way that he has felt obliged to respond to it by offering a categorical declaration that he has not been a Communist in any way, shape or form and has never had any sympathy with the party or its ideas. The disclaimer is not only a personal humiliation for Mr. Javits but a degradation of the political process; in a real sense it humiliates all Americans. We hope that the national leaders of both parties will condemn this kind of campaigning and do what they can to put a stop to it. The country has had its fill of McCarthyism. . . .

During the next few days, telegrams and letters and phone calls of support came pouring in, some to me, others directly to Senator Eastland. Of all these heartening and helpful messages, three were particularly effective in demonstrating to the smear masters that they had picked the wrong target.

Jim Fulton, congressman from Pittsburgh, wired Senator Eastland:

HAVE KNOWN JACK JAVITS PERSONALLY AND WELL THROUGHOUT HIS ENTIRE SERVICE IN CONGRESS . . . AND KNOW OF HIS STRONG CONVICTIONS AGAINST COMMUNISM AND HIS DETERMINED EFFORTS TO COMBAT COMMUNISM. . . . WISH TO EMPHASIZE MY ABSOLUTE AND COMPLETE CONFIDENCE IN HIS PATRIOTISM AND INTEGRITY.

Congressman James P. Richards, of South Carolina, chairman of the House Foreign Affairs Committee, sent me this telegram:

WHILE YOU ARE A REPUBLICAN AND I AM A DEMOCRAT, AND A SOUTHERN DEMOCRAT AT THAT, AND WHILE WE VOTED DIFFERENTLY MANY TIMES . . . I MUST IN ALL CANDOR AND HONESTY SAY AS CHAIRMAN OF THE FOREIGN AFFAIRS COMMITTEE UPON WHICH I SERVED WITH YOU FROM 1947 TO 1954, THAT AT ALL TIMES YOU WERE ENERGETIC AND CONSTANT AS A FOE OF COMMUNISM AND THERE HAS NEVER BEEN ANY DOUBT IN MY MIND AS TO WHERE YOU STOOD ON THAT ISSUE. IN FACT, YOU WERE ONE OF THE BULWARKS OF OUR COMMITTEE IN FIGHTING THE COMMUNIST MENACE.

And there was this one from Congressman Walter Judd of Minnesota, whose anti-Communism was already legendary:

SHOCKED TO READ CHARGES THAT YOU HAVE BEEN ASSOCIATED WITH COMMUNISTS. IF ANY COMMUNISTS SUPPORTED YOU POLITICALLY IT CERTAINLY WAS BAD BARGAIN FOR THEM BECAUSE I KNOW FROM MY LONG AND CLOSE ASSO-

CIATION WITH YOU IN CONGRESS THAT NO ONE HAS BEEN
MORE INTELLIGENTLY AND EFFECTIVELY ANTI-COMMUNIST
THAN YOU. . . .

The day before the hearing, I held a press conference at my office
in New York City. I was still not sure whether the committee would
take my testimony in open session, as I now wished, or whether the
doors would be closed, leaving the public in doubt as to what I had
said. As emphatically as I could, I told the reporters that I would refute the falsehoods and would remain a candidate for the nomination
regardless of what happened in Washington. I considered it a good
omen that Morhouse released my letter the same day.

On the morning of September 5, I flew to Washington with Ben.
Jim Moore, my solicitor general, had come down the day before and he
met us at the airport with a telegram in his hand. The wire was from
Phil Ehrlich in San Francisco, and it relieved me of one lingering concern about the charges I might face. Phil's telegram said:

CONFIRMING OUR CONVERSATION IT IS MY BEST RECOLLEC-
TION THAT FRANCES AND I INTRODUCED YOU TO LOUISE
BRANSTEN . . . PROBABLY IN SAN FRANCISCO OR POSSIBLY
IN NEW YORK. IT WAS AROUND THE TIME I ACTED AS ONE
OF HER ATTORNEYS. . . . I AM PREPARED TO SO TESTIFY.

Phil Ehrlich and I had discussed the Bransten matter and he had given
me his recollections of it. His telegram was the evidence, should I need
it, of the innocent, social character of my acquaintance with Louise
Bransten.

Encouraged by the events of the past few days but by no means
certain of what lay ahead, I returned to Capitol Hill. During eight productive and stimulating years in Congress I had always approached the
inspiring dome of the Capitol with eagerness and anticipation, proud
that I was privileged to serve there and ready for the struggle. I would
not have relinquished a day of it. But on this fresh September morning
the dome gleamed chill and aloof in the sunshine; it had been my home
but now it was to judge me. I knew I should still feel proud of my ac-
complishments, and my briefcase bulged with testimonials, but I was
going on trial for my political life and the inquisitors were not noted
for their sympathy for liberal politicians. A queasy feeling gnawed at
my innards.

We went first to Senator Eastland's home, a block or so from the
Capitol, for an executive session. Senator Eastland and Bob Morris listened to my response to the rumors and asked a few questions. At my
urging, they agreed to an immediate public session and we all trooped

over to the Senate Office Building for an open hearing, which took place in Room 318, the Senate Caucus Room. That august paneled chamber had been the scene of many climactic committee hearings and political pronouncements, including the Army-McCarthy hearings two years earlier; two decades later the entire country would know it as the site of the Senate's Watergate investigation. Room 318 seemed to breathe history, and on September 5, 1956, I was at the center of it.

To my surprise, Senator Eastland was the only member of the Internal Security Subcommittee present to hear my testimony. I felt slightly encouraged by the absence of the other eight members, particularly Senator William Jenner of Indiana, whom I guessed might have egged on the "investigation"; perhaps Jenner and the other absentees realized by now that the charges were ridiculous and wanted to dissociate themselves from the whole affair. But Bob Morris was very much present; now he was armed with every snippet of gossip and half-truth that could possibly embarrass me, much of which I was to hear for the first time at this open hearing. The press tables were full.

After summarizing Bella Dodd's story of the 1946 election, Morris promptly tried to link it to my San Francisco trip in 1945. To a question about getting off the train "in the company of Frederick V. Field," I replied:

> ... I did not get off the train in the company of Frederick V. Field. My recollection ... is that I met a young man on the ferry who said something about the scenery or some ordinary expression of that kind, who was a college-boy-looking type of chap and described himself as Fred Field and said he was going to cover the UN conference for some newspaper work. And we exchanged some pleasantries. . . .

Morris pressed on: "But you will deny, will you not ... that you got off the train with Fred Field?" And I answered:

> Well, whether I met Fred Field on the train or not ... I really could not tell you, but ... I did not leave New York with Fred Field — I had no business with him — he was not my traveling companion.

Morris then attempted to suggest that I had made several other trips on the Oakland ferry with Field "at an early hour of the morning," which I denied unconditionally. As a parting shot on that subject, Morris pointed out that Field at that time was "UN editor to the *Daily Worker*." "I am glad to get that information," I responded, "but I can say flatly that that is something I did not know when he encountered me." Round one to me, I judged.

Next came the Bransten matter, and in this Morris and his research director, Benjamin Mandel, provided a living definition of the
word *innuendo.*

Morris began by asking Mandel to "put in the record at this time
what evidence we have about Louise Bransten." So far nothing whatever had been said linking me to Bransten. Mandel read from an FBI
memorandum reporting that during the UN founding conference in
1945 Louise Bransten had entertained in her San Francisco home the
representative from the Ukrainian SSR "who was more widely known
as a long-time official and spokesman for the Communist International." The memorandum also claimed that later she had "established
contact" with the Soviet acting consul general in New York "who has
been reported . . . as the head of the Red Army intelligence espionage
activity."

Mandel then started listing background details about another Soviet official. Like the others, this man had nothing whatever to do
with me, but unlike the others, nothing was said to link him even with
Bransten. He was just another ominous Russian name brought up, it
seems, merely to add some kind of bogus verisimilitude.

Morris finally directed Mandel back to the subject of Bransten.
Citing as authority some testimony before the House Un-American
Activities Committee, Mandel said that "many social affairs were given
in [Bransten's] home . . . for the purpose of entertaining and bringing
together Communist Party members, including members of Communist
espionage rings. . . ."

Finally I had to point out that "there is no implication that in-
volves me in that very long and seamy description"; Morris agreed —
and then mentioned "information and evidence to the effect that you
did know Louise Bransten." I said that Phil Ehrlich had introduced us,
that she kept me waiting at the Mark Hopkins Hotel, that we didn't
seem to like each other, and "from my recollection, that is the last I
saw of her until some years ago, five, six, seven, when I ran into her in
a grocery store on University Place in New York."

Before Morris could refer to it, I mentioned the dinner. I told the
committee that I had spoken to Ehrlich to refresh my recollection and
that he remembered a dinner either at his home or Bransten's. "That
is his recollection," I said. "It is not my recollection. That is all I know
about Louise Bransten."

For the next fifteen minutes or so Morris hammered away with
questions about several dinners and meetings at Bransten's home, naming people I was alleged to have met there. And for each name, Morris
or Mandel supplied the particulars of that person's Communist connections. As I had already stated that I had no clear recollection of

visiting Bransten's home, this gratuitous recitation of Communist activities moved me to complain to Senator Eastland.

"Mr. Chairman," I said, "if I may, I would like to make this observation. It is not charged that I had anything to do with these people. And I think we can assume that those Judge Morris would ask me about have some kind of a Communist record. And yet, in a public hearing it seems to me that, as all of this stuff goes in the record, I do not know who might get some impression that I did or did not have anything to do with that. I put that up to the chairman."

Eastland agreed, and Morris then asked a direct question: Had I met two of these people at Bransten's home? This gave me a chance to restate my position, which was essentially this: that I did not remember going to Bransten's home or meeting those people; that because of Ehrlich's recollection I had to accept the possibility that I had been there; that I had no close association with any of those people; and that if I did go to Bransten's home "it was certainly not more than once, because, as I say, Mrs. Bransten and I just did not take to each other." And that was as close as I could come to an outright denial, for I obviously could not remember the name of every person I might have met at a social gathering eleven years earlier, or what they might or might not have talked about.

Morris then turned to the main point: the Bella Dodd story and the 1946 campaign. I spoke about it in some detail: I said that I had been given "a long list of people that I ought to see to get educated about what is going on in New York," that I saw Dodd "as one of the people on that list to get educated about teachers," because of her connection with the Teachers Union, and that I spent ten or fifteen minutes with her talking "about teachers and what they wanted."

I stated then that Alex Rose had recently reminded me of another 1946 incident, which, I said, "may and may not have any connection with my visit to Dr. Dodd." I related the incident as follows: "In a meeting when we were talking about the Liberal Party designation I told him [Rose] that some friends of mine were talking about the fact that I ought to try to get an American Labor Party designation . . . that many Democratic candidates and some Republican candidates had taken the ALP designation. . . . That when I told Alex that, he says — now he refreshes me on this, and I accept and state it as a fact — he said, 'Don't you know, Jack, that this ALP crowd, we have just broken off from, and they are Commie dominated?' And then I said, 'I want no part of them. I would rather lose the election. I will not go in for deals like that.' And that was that."

I knew Dodd was reported to have said that I discussed with her which district I should run in, so I explained in detail how, with

Arthur Schwartz, Bill Groat, Sam Koenig, Sam Lepler, and other Republican leaders, I had decided to run in the Washington Heights area rather than the Lower East Side of Manhattan. Morris brought me back to the meeting with Dodd: "Is it your testimony you did not know that she was, you might say, openly and notoriously a member of the national committee of the Communist Party?"

"I have no recollection of knowing that," I replied. "I do not know what the newspapers showed at the time, either. I can only tell you this: that it is inconceivable to me that I would call, for any reason, on a person who was an open and avowed Communist. That is all I can tell you about it."

Morris thereupon produced and inserted in the record two 1945 clippings from the *New York Times* that mentioned Dodd as a Communist Party official — which I did not remember ever seeing — and a *Life* magazine photograph of Dodd with other top Communists. That photo had appeared *after* my meeting with Dodd, and I pointed that out to the committee.

The subject of ALP support was then brought up again. Morris asked:

> Did you not tell Murray Baron [then an official of the Liberal Party], in connection with the 1946 election, that you could have either the secret support of the ALP or they would remain neutral, depending on what you wanted? Mr. Baron has told us that.

And I replied:

> I wouldn't challenge Murray Baron because I have the highest regard for him. I have no such recollection, and I would like to point out to you that the ALP candidate, a man named Connolly, tried to win the Democratic Party nomination in an election.... They did their utmost to knock me off in 1946 and 1948, when they ran Paul O'Dwyer, and he almost defeated me.

There were several more questions along this line, but I insisted I did not remember discussing ALP support beyond that first conversation with Rose. I said: "I am very clear, aside from the muddle I may have been in in the 1946 campaign, when I was new on the job, in a sense. I had no doubts about the ALP thereafter. By 1948 I had served two years in Congress, and I had encountered ALP doctrine in the shape of its congressmen here."

At the end of the hearing I asked permission to insert in the record a file of my congressional letters and reports to my constituents, because, I said, "it represents an effective anti-Communist struggle ... of which I am very proud." Eastland agreed and the hearing adjourned.

Outside, I told the waiting newsmen that it had been a "rough experience." But I made clear to them that I remained a contender for the Senate nomination. One of the reporters gave me a piece of news that seemed like a good omen: The previous day, in the primary election for the Nevada Democratic senatorial nomination, Jay Sourwine had come in last in a field of five. The Nevada Democrats had rejected a smear master; certainly, I thought, the New York Republicans would reject the smear.

I returned to New York that afternoon, the eve of Rosh Hashanah, the Jewish New Year. It was a night for thanksgiving, for reminiscing, for taking inventory of the year: the perils avoided, the benefits received, experiences undergone, the love and warmth of family. I felt these all with special poignancy. I was not yet out of the woods, but I could see a light in the distance.

My optimism was short-lived. Senator Jenner had not bothered to attend the hearing, but he immediately said there were "clear inconsistencies" in my testimony and asked Eastland to investigate further. Morris kept the issue alive by intimating to the press that the committee could recall Dodd, Baron, and other witnesses whose testimony might conflict with mine.

So the fight went on — with just four days to the nomination. The *New York Times* reported that upstate Republicans felt my chances of winning the nomination had been damaged and that downstate party leaders thought my chances were still good — which meant, probably, that no one had changed his mind. Alex Rose issued a statement on Thursday, the day after the hearing. Rose took a pot shot at my support of Nixon — whom he called "the father of the Communist-smear technique" — but he praised my "clear-cut anti-Communist record" and corroborated my testimony. Referring to 1946, Rose said:

> I found Mr. Javits, who had been in the army for a number of years, quite naive and uninformed.... On one occasion ... Mr. Javits asked us whether, besides the Liberal Party nomination, he should also try to get ALP support. I told him then that the ALP was Communist-dominated and that if he took their support he could not be the Liberal Party nominee. Mr. Javits quickly accepted our judgment.

That day I wired Eastland, complaining that the Jenner and Morris statements were an underhanded way of keeping the issue open. I offered to appear again immediately to answer any further queries, "so that there cannot be any question left over in the minds of the Republican State Committee that I am just as clear of any Communist taint, impulse, or connection as I believe you are."

Even as I sent that telegram, I realized I could not depend on the Eastland committee to "clear" me — at least not in time. I would have to take my case directly to the people — and to the politicians. Tex McCrary helped out by putting me on his program that Thursday night. I arranged to appear on the nationwide network program *Meet the Press* on Sunday. On the Friday before that, I bought television time in New York and spoke for fifteen minutes, denouncing the smear campaign, reaffirming my anti-Communism, and once more rebutting the charges. This was one of the hardest-hitting speeches I have ever made. I said:

> . . . There is no doubt that I have talked to Communists, as has every public man of our time. But Communists don't walk around wearing badges with neon lights proclaiming their secret political affiliation. . . . No man in American political life, no matter how distinguished or dedicated his career of public service, could stand immune to the most vicious and violent form of character assassination if the standards that have been applied here are applied equally to all. . . . I tell you that Joe McCarthy and William Jenner — and when I speak of Jenner I speak of Mr. Jenner of Indiana, who stood on the floor of the U.S. Senate and called . . . George Marshall a traitor — have cost this country more good will . . . than any group of political hatchet-men in my memory. . . .

On Friday I also went to see Tom Dewey again. He had still not tipped his hand, and the press was still speculating that he might run. I am sure that as a lawyer he knew the charges against me were nonsense, and I felt it was time for him to start making phone calls in my behalf. I have no notes of our conversation, but I told him something like this: "Look, Governor, you know that if you wanted to be senator I certainly would rally to your support and rally all my supporters to help you. But if you don't want it, I think it's best to quiet the speculation, because I *am* interested and certainly have proven that I can win in this state, and it is something that would realize an ambition I've had ever since I went to the House. Though I thought I was on a state track when I was elected attorney general, as the situation shapes up now, coupling my interest in the Senate with the need for vindication from the party and the voters on the Internal Security Subcommittee inquiry, it makes an irrefutable case for me that I ought to run for the Senate if you're not interested. And I would hope you would support me as I would support you if you wanted it." To that, as I recall, Dewey said something like "I'm not interested in it, Jack, and I'll certainly help you."

This was encouraging to me, for Tom Dewey still exerted a strong influence on the New York Republican Party even though he was no longer governor. Despite our previous differences, I knew he wanted to nominate a winner. Having beaten a Roosevelt, I thought I was the candidate most likely to beat a Wagner and take the Lehman Senate seat, and Dewey's remarks indicated that he now thought so too.

Hoping that Dewey would act quickly, I went to Washington again on Saturday. *Meet the Press* was to be telecast live from there on Sunday afternoon, and I needed a day away from the maelstrom to relax and unwind. Len and Gladys Hall graciously invited me to stay with them for the weekend at their apartment in the Sheraton Park Hotel, and their warm friendship and calm, wise advice were a tremendous encouragement. At one point, referring to the Bransten matter, Len said to me, "You know, Jack, none of us ever used to ask a girl if she had a Commie card in her pocket before we invited her out."

Meet the Press went on the air at 6:00 P.M. Sunday, September 9. The members of the New York Republican State Committee were already gathering in Albany for the next day's meeting that would decide the nomination, and I knew that in every one of their hotel lounges they would be gathered around the TV sets to hear me, watch me — and judge me. As Ned Brooks, the moderator, introduced me and told the audience I was "the central figure in a free-swinging political controversy now occupying the front pages," I knew this was my last chance. I had better be convincing — and good.

And I think I must have been. Once more I went over the matter of ALP support and Bella Dodd and tried to explain the so-called inconsistencies of my testimony. I pointed out that in 1946 the ALP supported "practically the whole Democratic Party ticket" as well as five Republican candidates, and that "I was the fellow that didn't get it." I remarked on Jenner's unfairness. I corrected a panelist who had misread my testimony on one point, and explained why I would not contradict Murray Baron, although I had no recollection of discussing ALP support in 1948. When I was asked why this attack had been let loose against me, I replied that "there are some people who just don't want me . . . to get this Senate nomination."

As the minutes went on I kept searching for an opportunity to send a telling message to those pragmatic men and women clustered around the TV sets in Albany. At length it came: Murray Davis of the *World-Telegram* asked me, "How can a person with your intelligence and background get involved in a thing like this?"

"Mr. Davis," I replied, "that's the best question I know of, and the answer is I'm not involved . . . If Bella Dodd is the only Communist I've ever met — I just don't believe it, with the thousands of people I've met . . . I'd like to tell you something about the Dr. Dodd thing which is very interesting. The legislators up in Albany tell me she was a lobbyist for years. The testimony is I saw her once, but they saw her twenty or thirty or forty times. Who can anticipate what she might or mightn't say about any conversation with anyone?"

Later, Richard Clurman of *Newsday* asked if I expected to get the nomination. "I never try to predict the results of a nomination or election," I replied. "I have done my best. I believe I deserve the nomination."

I don't know if the *Meet the Press* panelists were entirely satisfied by my answers to their questions, but I was determined to present my case as convincingly as possible, and if I had to pass over minor matters to get the main issue across I was not going to worry about it. For I had truly been the victim of an unscrupulous assault and I was truly innocent of any taint of Communism. When you are attacked by a mugger in a dark street you don't fight back under the Marquis of Queensberry Rules.

That night a reporter for the *Chicago Tribune* reported from Albany: "Opposition to New York Attorney General Jacob K. Javits as the Republican nominee for U.S. Senate virtually evaporated tonight on the eve of party conventions here." By the time I arrived in Albany the next morning, I knew that Tom Dewey and *Meet the Press* had finally, after that long, agonizing summer, provided the margin of victory. I arrived with my acceptance speech in my pocket. When the Executive Committee met that morning, I received seventeen votes and Raymond McGovern got eight. That afternoon the full committee nominated me unanimously.

It was with almost unbearable joy that I addressed the committee members at the Ten Eyck Hotel. "It is a tribute to our party," I said, "that it stood fast by the proposition that it would not tolerate rumors, innuendos, smears, and political character assassination; that we would respect facts and willingness of a member of our party to meet the facts in the most public way — no matter how uncalled-for the ordeal. I am proud of our party. This is the true spirit of Lincolnian and Eisenhower Republicanism, in the highest American tradition."

There still remained, of course, the worry that Jenner, Morris and company would keep the charges alive, perhaps with a full-dress investigation that could cost me the election. But Bob Wagner, the Democratic nominee, quickly buried the smear. "I won't bring up the Communist issue in the campaign," Wagner said. "I have known Mr. Javits a long time and I have always found him a decent American." The mayor said that the voters were interested "not in mudslinging but in the issues of the campaign."

I thanked Wagner publicly for that. It was an honorable, decent thing to do, characteristic of Bob, and of his father. The issue disappeared and Bob Wagner and I have been friends ever since — even though we had some tough things to say about each other in the campaign that followed.

THIRTEEN

Victory and Vindication

The press reported that Robert F. Wagner, Jr., was not eager to run for the Senate in 1956. Despite his Tammany connections (which he severed a few years later), he appeared to be doing well in his first term as mayor of New York City; his popularity was high, and at the age of forty-six he still had plenty of time to attempt to follow in his father's footsteps to the Senate. Besides, with President Eisenhower running for reelection, the prospects were not encouraging for a Democrat in New York. But every race for the Senate that year was regarded by both parties as vitally important; the Democrats held an edge of only two seats, so a small net shift could have given the Republican Party a Senate majority, with all the power of selecting committee chairmen and controlling the legislative calendar. Even a shift of just one seat could have had that effect if a Republican vice president were presiding to break the tie. Therefore the Democrats needed the strongest candidate they could find to hold on to Lehman's seat and retain Senate control, and that candidate, they agreed, was Wagner. Both Lehman and Adlai Stevenson, the Democratic presidential candidate, personally urged Bob to run, and he agreed. Wagner and I received our nominations as Senate candidates on the same day.

There were several ironies in that state of affairs. As a Republican I have rarely supported a Democrat for high office. Yet in 1940, when we were on the verge of war, I supported Franklin D. Roosevelt for President; fourteen years later I defeated his son and namesake in the election for attorney general of New York. In 1944 I contributed $100 to the reelection campaign fund of Democrat Robert F. Wagner, Sr., because his liberal prolabor philosophy was close to my own and because party labels meant little in the middle of a war; twelve years after that, I found myself running against *his* son and namesake for *his* Senate seat. (The elder Wagner retired in ill health in 1949; Herbert Lehman, after defeating John Foster Dulles in a special election to serve the unexpired portion of the Wagner term, was reelected in 1950 for a full six years.) A final irony emerged twenty-three years later when

I broke the senior Wagner's record for the longest service as senator from New York.

Bob Wagner was a much more formidable opponent than young Roosevelt had been. He had the advantage of his name — almost as well known in New York and as widely respected as Roosevelt's — and he had the platform of New York's City Hall, from which he could get good coverage for almost any pronouncement, at least in the city. Like young Roosevelt, he had inherited the automatic support of the Liberal Party, but unlike my opponent of 1954, Wagner did not offer any easy or obvious targets; he had no shocking or clearly recognizable vulnerabilities comparable to Frank Roosevelt's absenteeism. Wagner was liberal and able, and his decency had been underlined by his announcement that he would not bring up in the campaign the charges regarding Communism that had been made against me earlier in the year. I realized that Wagner would be difficult to attack. Moreover, as the campaign began I had to assume that a significant number of conservative Republicans would deny me their support and their votes. Some of them still harbored doubts about me as a result of the smear attack, and others could not reconcile their beliefs with my progressive record. I had to expect a "drop-off" from the Eisenhower vote in the Republican areas upstate.

I did have some advantages. I was running on the ticket with the most popular Republican President in half a century. Also, I had been thinking about the campaign for months, and while Wagner, a relative latecomer to the contest, was still organizing, I could plunge into full-time campaigning immediately. (Just a few days after my nomination, in fact, on a wet Yom Kippur — the Jewish Day of Atonement, on which it is forbidden to ride in a vehicle — I walked miles in a driving rain all across Manhattan's Upper West Side to visit six synagogues.) As the New York legislature was not in session, I also had more time than did the mayor to travel and campaign. My startling victory over FDR Junior two years earlier was still fresh in the voters' minds, and my activities as attorney general had kept my name before the public all around the state. Finally, compensating for any defection of conservative Republicans upstate, I was expected to capture some of the traditional Democratic vote in New York City, as I had done in 1954 — or at least that was the hope until international events upset everyone's strategy in the last week of the campaign.

Putting together a statewide campaign organization was much easier the second time around. John Trubin took a leave of absence from his post as first assistant attorney general to become my campaign manager again. Sheila Kelley came back on board as my television consultant. Marian, although she knew that if I was elected to the Senate I would again be spending less time at home, loyally set to work once more rounding up volunteers. My activities as attorney general and my frequent speeches on Israel and other issues had helped me develop an active "Javits network" of bright and concerned people around the state. My lifelong habits of courtesy, of writing letters and returning small favors, had a cumulative effect; growing numbers of people who might have had merely a brief encounter with me nevertheless remembered me and counted me as a friend because I followed up with some gesture — even if only a one-paragraph note.

By the beginning of October a statewide Citizens for Javits organization was functioning. Oren Root, a lawyer who had been prominent in liberal Republican politics since setting up the Willkie clubs in 1940, shared the chairmanship with another lawyer, and later judge, Mrs. Caroline K. Simon, who was noted for her work in civil rights. Upstate, local chapters in Binghamton, Rochester, Utica, Buffalo, and other cities were operating under the direction of corporate executives, former Republican legislators, lawyers, bankers, and businessmen; the New York City vice chairmen of the group included such Republican notables as Edith Willkie, Newbold Morris, Arthur Schwartz, and Paul Warburg, as well as other well-known individuals representing the ethnic diversity of the city.

Ben, with his indefatigable energy and verve, took over the fund-raising job again. Contributors like to back a winner, and most of those who had helped me in 1954 were eager and willing to contribute again. This time Ben added some new wrinkles: He organized a group of rabbis to seek contributions in their congregations; and even Nelson Rockefeller, in addition to making a significant contribution himself, was persuaded to ask his wealthy friends for further financing. John Loeb, Henry Luce, William Paley of CBS, and Thomas J. Watson of IBM were among those who contributed generously.

Since Bob Wagner and I respected each other and were not so very far apart ideologically, it was clear from the start that we would wage a dignified and properly senatorial contest — the kind I like best. I based my campaign on two main points: my own qualifications and the Eisenhower Republican record. The difference between us, I told the voters, was that I had experience that suited me for the job of senator and Wagner did not. Early in the campaign, editorials in both the *New York Times* and the *New York Herald Tribune* emphasized the fact that Wagner's experience had been confined to state and city matters while I, in the words of the *Times,* had spent "eight recent years as a congressman engaged in national problems and intensely occupied with foreign affairs." Both papers also pointed out a circumstance that became something of a joke during the campaign: Many people thought that Wagner was doing too good a job as mayor to be sent to the Senate, because the city council president would then succeed him in City Hall. As the *Herald Tribune* put it, "A vote for Wagner is a vote for Abe Stark, the amiable but undistinguished heir apparent to the mayoralty."

In attempting to gloss over his lack of international and national background, Wagner made a few unwise statements that gave me just the opening I needed. When he was asked at a press conference about his experience in these matters, Wagner replied that he had become familiar with national and international problems in two ways: First, as mayor of New York he had discussed world problems with many leaders from abroad; second, "I was very close to my father during the twenty-three years he was in the Senate — I was with him often after my mother died. I worked with him and I sat at his feet." Contrasted to my eight years on the House Foreign Affairs Committee and my many congressional trips abroad, this was a ridiculous argument. "We cannot afford to have a senator . . . who has to get on-the-job training," I retorted. "The mayor has been president of the Borough of Manhattan, an assemblyman, and commissioner of the Department of Housing and Buildings. Admittedly he is a nice fellow, but it takes more than affability and a desire to fill his father's shoes to qualify to serve in the U.S. Senate. I don't come to United States foreign policy, as my opponent does, as an apprentice. . . . My experience is based on performance." Commenting on Wagner's boasts about being close to his father and meeting free-world leaders in New York, the *Herald Tribune* declared:

> Surely not even Mr. Wagner can seriously contend that these are suitable credentials for tackling great global concerns in the United States Senate. There is no comparison between him and Mr. Javits on skilled knowledge and long performance. As the Republican nominee says, "Our state is entitled to more than an apprentice Senator." The issue is whether New York wants a highly qualified Senator or an amateur.

To discuss the issues of the campaign, Wagner and I faced each other in two lively and intensive televised debates. The first one covered civil rights, and for most of it my opponent and I traded claims about which party had done the most to end discrimination and racial segregation in the past and which candidate could do more in the future: I pointed to the racist Southern Democrats and to the Republi-

Above left: Morris Javits, JKJ's father

Above right: JKJ at three and a half

Right: Ida Javits, JKJ's mother, with JKJ (left) and his brother, Ben

JKJ (wearing bathing suit) as a young
bachelor, with friends in Hollywood,
Florida

JKJ, just promoted from major to lieutenant
colonel in the Chemical Warfare Service,
with chief of the service, Major General
William N. Porter (holding cigar)

JKJ bringing nominating petitions
to the Board of Elections, 1946

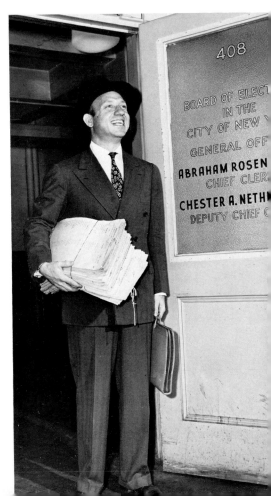

JKJ and the former Marian Ann Borris as they prepare to cut
their wedding cake, November 30, 1947 (Associated Press)

Two young congressmen, JKJ and John F. Kennedy, look over the Veterans Housing Bill of
1947 (Press Association, Inc.)

Left: JKJ with the Javits Jets (his office team) gets a hit in the annual baseball game

Below: A Javits campaign tool, comics for constituents

THE GENTLEMAN FROM NEW YORK ...and THE GIANT!

AS YOUR CONGRESSMAN, I SHALL WORK FOR THE HAPPINESS AND SECURITY OF OUR PEOPLE, AND THE PEACE AND FREEDOM OF THE PEOPLES OF THE WORLD.

JKJ announces candidacy for mayoralty of New York City (Interstate Photographers)

JKJ with Adlai Stevenson at Alfred G.
Vanderbilt's estate, 1954

JKJ with Pope Pius XII at the Vatican,
1956 (Associated Press Photo)

Senator Javits with his wife,
Marian, and their children,
Carla, Joshua, and Joy, 1956

Left: JKJ with David
Ben-Gurion in Israel, 1956

Below: JKJ with Congressman
Adam Clayton Powell, who
supported JKJ's senatorial
campaign, 1956 (Wide World
Photos, Inc.)

JKJ with his fellow
senator from New York,
Kenneth B. Keating, 1956
(AP Wirephoto)

Left: Marian and JKJ
(Copyright © 1966 by Henry
Grossman)

Below: Playing tennis in
Florida

Nelson Rockefeller and JKJ in
a television studio after the
election of 1958

JKJ with "Der Alte," Konrad Adenauer, chancellor of West Germany, in the late 1950s

JKJ with Bernard Baruch at the Rotunda in the Capitol (Henry Grossman)

JKJ with President Dwight D. Eisenhower

JKJ with Helen Hayes (Bill Mark)

JKJ's staff gathers for his birthday, circa 1960

JKJ and Nelson Rockefeller campaigning together in a store in Flushing, Long Island, 1962. The lady wanted him to buy a shirt. (Associated Press Photo)

JKJ being hugged by an enthusiastic constituent in Washington Heights, 1962 (Morris Warman, *New York Herald Tribune*)

Above: JKJ and Rockefeller in a 1962 campaign photo

Left: Dressed for winter and the first trip to the USSR in 1962

Below: Vice President Lyndon B. Johnson swear JKJ in to the Senate, 1962, as Marian looks on

JKJ at the civil rights March on Washington, 1963

Senators celebrating the passage of the Civil Rights Act, 1964 (left to right): Kenneth Keating, Everett Dirksen, JKJ, Leverett Saltonstall, John Pastore, Hubert Humphrey, Warren Magnuson, Hugh Scott, and Philip Hart (*Life* magazine)

Herblock cartoon from the *Washington Post*, 1964: "Don't Jump" (Copyright © 1964 by Herblock, the *Washington Post*)

Cartoon by Hy Rosen: the hawk-dove debate on Vietnam

JKJ with marines and Congressman Ogden "Brownie" Reid in Vietnam, 1966 (U.S. Marine Corps Photograph by Sergeant F. A. Markham)

JKJ in Brooklyn with Rabbi Sherer, executive director of Agudath Israel, examining an ancient scroll

JKJ proposing a toast at a friend's birthday party in Katonah, New York, 1967

Above: JKJ, former Vice President Richard Nixon, and Governor Nelson Rockefeller at the building of the mall in Albany, 1967

Right: JKJ and George Romney: a chance for national office, 1967

Senators Edmund
Muskie, JKJ, and
Hubert Humphrey at a
committee hearing

Right: Reelection to the
Senate in 1974: JKJ with
Joy, Marian, and Joshua

Below: President
Richard Nixon, JKJ,
and Secretary of State
Henry Kissinger confer
in the White House

Above: Senator Edward Kennedy and JKJ sit on the Committee on Labor and Human Relations, 1975

Above right: JKJ with Golda Meir, prime minister of Israel, in Israel, 1970 (Photo— Emka, Ltd., Jerusalem)

Right: JKJ with President Anwar Sadat of Egypt, 1976

Senator Henry "Scoop" Jackson, JKJ, and Senator Abraham Ribicoff with President Gerald Ford in the White House.

Above: JKJ and Senator Frank Church with Deng Xiaoping in China, 1979

Left: JKJ and Senator Abraham Ribicoff watch as President Jimmy Carter signs a bill for civil service reform

Below: JKJ leaving the Capitol after a long day (Thomas Stiltz Studio)

cans' desegregation of the District of Columbia; Wagner claimed that Eisenhower was "neutral" in the fight against discrimination and that Roosevelt and Truman were responsible for most of the progress that had been made. The debate merely proved my argument that civil rights was a bipartisan issue.

In that debate, however, Wagner attempted to depict me as less than diligent on civil rights. I had declared earlier that if elected I would not be sworn in as senator until a few days after the congressional session opened on January 3. The purpose of this delay was to wait until New York's Republican-controlled state legislature could convene and appoint another Republican attorney general; if I were to resign my state office when the legislature was not sitting, the governor would have the power to choose my successor, and Harriman would of course appoint a Democrat. I owed it to my party to make sure that the office of attorney general stayed in Republican hands for the remainder of the term to which the voters had elected me. (If the Republican Party increased its strength in the Senate, making my presence on opening day necessary to form a majority, then, of course, a higher party priority would have required my taking the oath on January 3.)

The controversial element in this procedure was the biennial attempt by liberal senators to amend the Senate rules so as to limit the segregationists' filibusters that had stymied civil rights legislation for years. Such rules changes could be made, if at all, only on the opening day of each Congress. Wagner asserted that if elected he would be there on opening day to vote for such a change, and he claimed that if I were elected my absence might jeopardize a chance to silence the filibusters.

That accusation was just a debater's point without substance, but it had to be answered. I said there was no evidence that the Senate liberals had nearly enough votes to change the rules that year, and I explained how I felt about the attorney general's job: The voters had elected a Republican and one was needed to keep check on the Democratic state administration. To drive home my rebuttal, I challenged Governor Harriman to announce that if I were elected he would not appoint my successor before the legislature convened. If the Democrats were really concerned about the Senate rules change, I said, Harriman would do that, and "I will take his word for it and I'll be there on January 3." Harriman made no such pledge, and although Wagner repeated his claim, I do not believe anyone took it seriously.

Toward the end of that debate Wagner suddenly pulled from his pocket a photo of Vice President Nixon campaigning with me, and as he held it up to the cameras he listed some of the conservative and repressive causes, such as the Mundt-Nixon bill, that Nixon had espoused in the House of Representatives and in the Senate. But it was futile to try to make the voters believe that Nixon and I were great pals who saw eye to eye; my record was too well known and I simply replied that I had voted against the Mundt-Nixon bill. Nevertheless, I was supporting Nixon, because he came with Eisenhower, and Wagner continually brought this up before liberal audiences. (Eisenhower's heart attack the previous year particularly worried those who distrusted the vice president.) In May I had expressed some dissatisfaction with Nixon and had played a role in the consideration of substituting Christian Herter as the candidate for vice president. But in October I was backing the ticket. I declared during the campaign that Nixon had matured, that he seemed completely devoted to the Eisenhower philosophy, and that, in the event that the vice president might have to take over, "the people have the right to assume that Nixon would be in the image of Eisenhower."

A week later Bob Wagner and I debated before the television cameras again, this time on foreign affairs. The Korean War had ended during Eisenhower's first year in office and peace was a major Republican asset in the campaign. I had already emphasized in my speeches that Eisenhower's foreign policy had shifted the struggle with the USSR from the military to the economic arena, and that the Geneva summit meeting of 1955, at which the President had put forward his famous "open skies" proposal for aerial inspection of military installations, had relaxed international tensions. However, Adlai Stevenson, the Democratic candidate, was behaving as if all threat from the Soviets had ended; Stevenson wanted to end the draft and was calling for a unilateral U.S. suspension of hydrogen-bomb testing. I accepted the administration's position that the best way to halt testing was by a mutual inspection agreement with the Soviet Union. I had charged Stevenson with giving the American people "false hopes" that the H-bomb tests could be ended with a "paper treaty" that lacked inspection provisions.

Bob Wagner and other Democrats clearly had doubts about Stevenson's H-bomb pronouncements, which became a major campaign issue in the middle of October. Everybody on both sides took positions — except my opponent. In our foreign-policy debate I made an issue of Wagner's "inability or reluctance to make the tough decisions." Two weeks had gone by since Stevenson had spoken of an "instant necessity" for stopping the tests, I said, but we had yet to hear from Wagner on the subject. Wagner rebutted by saying that his responsibility for the health and safety of New York City residents made him "unwilling to jump into any purely political conclusions on the H-bomb tests. Mr. Javits has probably no such compunctions. He talks fast and loose without knowing the facts, and I have been studying the facts and the opinions of the outstanding defense experts and scientists."

"Mr. Mayor," I replied, "your failure to take a position on this H-bomb matter demonstrates . . . either your unwillingness or your inability to take a stand upon a great issue, and I think that is a real weakness. . . . You were asked on October 17 what you thought about this matter. . . . You haven't answered yet, and from what I hear now you don't intend to answer at all before the campaign is over." Then I named many people who had discussed the issue, including many people not running for nearly as high office as the U.S. Senate. "Mr. Mayor," I said, "when you are on the floor of the Senate and there is a vital amendment . . . before the senators, you might have an hour or you might have two, or you might not even have that much. You're going to have to vote and you're going to have to decide, and you can't consult experts at that time. You have got to have some background or knowledge. In addition to that, you can't appoint commissioners, you can't even send out the whole police department to find out about it."

Wagner tried to get off the hook by insisting the issue was too important "to jump to conclusions," and he promised to make his position clear before the election. I had the opportunity for the last word in that debate and I came back to the point again. I said I was glad he would announce his position on the H-bomb, but "you owed it to the people today, when you were facing me, and you could debate it now; you are going to make some statement and I'm going to say something else about it, and it is going to get lost in the muddle. Now, Mr. Mayor, you cannot do that on the floor of the Senate of the United States if you are going to represent sixteen million people." I think my argument came across clearly to the voters and helped me significantly on election day. Although Bob Wagner was seriously interested in coming to the right conclusion, he did not have the background to reach an opinion or make a statement without consulting extensively, and at short notice, with whatever experts he could find.

At about the same time, a bizarre new element was suddenly injected into the campaign. As I was taking part in a television program that invited viewers to telephone questions, several callers asked whether I had abandoned my Jewish faith. "This is a complete lie," I replied. "I hate that word, but really there is no other way that one can put this. I am Jewish. My father and mother were immigrants. I have always been Jewish. I am proud of my Jewish faith. I cannot for the life of me see where one could possibly have gotten any other notion."

I suppose I was fortunate that I had the opportunity to answer that canard in a public forum where it was obvious I was not prepared. It proved once more that the best way to handle such scurrilous falsehoods is to let them come out and nail them immediately.

The high point of the campaign as far as I was concerned occurred late in October, when President Eisenhower came to New York to address a campaign rally at Madison Square Garden. If anyone still entertained any lingering doubts about my integrity or about the smear attack that had been made on me that year, Eisenhower's ringing endorsement must surely have put those doubts to rest. As soon as he had quieted the thundering ovation that he received when he was introduced, Ike told the crowd he wanted to "say a special word about Jack Javits." Then he went on:

> I know that some people have tried to impugn his loyalty, some have called him a wild-eyed radical, and others lately, I see, have said he was a stick-in-the-mud reactionary. . . .
>
> I've known him for some years. I have served with him in Washington. I have found him a man dedicated to his country, devoted to his duty, and wrapped up in his public service. So I would hope that everybody who believes as he does in good clean government will turn out and give him such a blazing majority that he will go to Washington inspired by your action, uplifted in spirit to do a job for you, for the country, and for peace. . . .

At that point, with everything going well for me and my party, the fabric of peace, so carefully woven and of which we had been justifiably proud, was suddenly rent by armed conflict. In the last days of October, Hungary rebelled against Soviet domination and the Russians sent troops and tanks to suppress the revolt; Britain and France and Israel, in secret alliance, made war on Egypt and attempted to capture the Suez Canal.

Adlai Stevenson tried to capitalize on the simultaneous crises; he charged that Secretary of State Dulles's "blunders" had given the Soviets a foothold in the Middle East and that the administration had been "caught off guard" in Eastern Europe. But the sudden flare-ups disproved his earlier contention that weapons testing and the draft should cease, and most of the electorate seemed to feel that with war threatening in two places the country needed Eisenhower.

Although the crises may have helped reelect the President, the invasion of Suez, and Eisenhower's denunciation of it, presented me with the most agonizing dilemma I have ever had to face during an election campaign. I was torn between my loyalty to Eisenhower and my approval of his policies on the one hand and my deep sympathies for and identification with Israel's cause on the other. Such a dilemma would have been troublesome at any time, but arising in the closing days of a crucial campaign, it was a political nightmare. In the end I put aside loyalties and sympathies and supported what I believed to be correct policy, which is to say that I made the decision as if I were the senator I was attempting to become, not as a man attempting to become a senator. That decision brought me some very unpleasant moments in the final hours of the campaign.

The Suez crisis grew out of rising Arab nationalism, diminishing British and French power in the Middle East, and Soviet attempts to exploit both of those developments. By failing to recognize consistently the importance of Israel to the security of the region, Secretary of State Dulles had allowed the situation to deteriorate. For several years, the Egyptians had prevented Israeli cargoes from transiting the Suez Canal and had blockaded Israel's Red Sea port of Elath, thus closing off Israel from any eastward commerce. In 1954 the new nationalist Egyptian government of Premier Gamal Abdel Nasser negotiated an end to the seventy-year British military occupation of the canal zone, and in June of 1956 the last British troops left. By then, the Soviets and their satellites had started supplying military arms and economic aid to Egypt, and Egypt had signed with Syria a mutual defense pact that was clearly aimed at Israel. All during this period Israel was subjected to an escalating series of Arab border raids and incursions, especially from Arab Fedayeen operating out of Egypt's Gaza Strip.

Faced by these threats and attacks, Israel repeatedly tried to buy sophisticated arms from the United States to offset the Soviet military assistance to Egypt. I had made a number of speeches endorsing that request, but Eisenhower and Dulles, who were still trying to win Arab confidence and were fearful of triggering an arms race, refused to sell weapons to Israel. They consented only to France selling twenty Mystere jet aircraft to Israel.

Disturbed by the Egyptian-Soviet arms deal, however, the United States and Britain in July 1956 withdrew their offer of economic aid for Egypt's Aswan Dam on the Nile. A week later, on July 26, Nasser retaliated: He nationalized the Suez Canal Company, which was owned mainly by Britain and France, and sent Egyptian troops and officials to seize the company's facilities. Canal revenues, Nasser said, would be used to finance the Aswan Dam. The seizure of the canal made little practical difference to Israel, which could not use it anyway, but Britain and France received all their oil through the canal, and they reacted sharply to the idea that Nasser, increasingly linked to the Communist bloc, could control the waterway. After two months of intense international diplomatic activity failed to reach any agreement between the Western powers and Egypt over the ownership and operation of the canal, Israel, Britain, and France secretly began to plan joint military action to resolve the impasse.

On October 29, Israeli forces attacked Gaza and advanced across the Sinai toward the canal. Using this as a pretext, Britain and France issued an ultimatum demanding that Israeli and Egyptian troops pull back ten miles from the canal so that they, Britain and France, could occupy the canal to protect it and keep the peace. Egypt rejected the ultimatum, and on October 31 British and French planes and ships began bombing and shelling Egyptian ports and airfields around the canal.

A furious President Eisenhower appealed to the British and French to call off their invasion, which commenced on November 5, and he referred the matter to the UN Security Council, where a U.S. cease-fire resolution was vetoed by Britain and France. That was the first time Britain had used her veto and the first time the United States and the Soviet Union lined up against Britain and France on a major issue.

Eisenhower's condemnation of the attacks and his attempts to solve the crisis peacefully, through the United Nations, were criticized by many of Israel's friends in the United States as simply "anti-Israel." I was torn. On the surface it certainly appeared that the war would give Israel the secure borders she needed. On the other hand, in addition to the risks of a wider conflict, it seemed to me that in the long run Israel's future could best be secured by alignment with the United States; I suspected that Britain and France, Israel's allies at the moment, might very well abandon Israel when it suited them to do so. I briefly considered putting the blame for the crisis on Dulles, and I actually drafted a statement asking the President to relieve the secretary of state of responsibility for the Middle East and to appoint Tom Dewey as a special envoy with powers to negotiate a settlement. But I never issued that statement, for I realized it would look like an attempt to straddle the issue. I had told Bob Wagner that senators must vote one way or the other on tough questions, so I had to make up my mind on this one. Fully aware of the political risks, I took a stand for peace — and against the military action of Britain, France, and Israel.

There was no point in trying to find a friendly audience for what I had to say. On October 30, at a rally on Delancey Street in the still heavily Jewish Lower East Side of Manhattan, I told a stunned crowd of several hundred people that the United States could not and should not condone Israel's military operations. I carefully avoided using the word *aggression* and I mentioned the "tremendous provocation" that

Israel had suffered. But, I said, "No matter how great Israel's provocation, and it couldn't be greater, we have to insist on no crossing of
borders. It can't be done." To soften the blow, I offered the hope that
"we can use this hour" to solve all of Israel's difficulties with the Arab
states. I told a hostile questioner it was unfair to call the administration policy "anti-Israel," reminding him that the administration was
committed to preserving Israel's territorial integrity; and I confessed
that I, too, was "not satisfied" with the administration's refusal to sell
arms to Israel. The crowd was not appeased, nor was another group at
a synagogue community center uptown any friendlier to a similar talk
a few hours later. "The unthinkable happened last night," the *New
York World-Telegram and Sun* reported the next day. "Mr. Javits, a
Jew and a warm supporter of Israel, was booed and hissed by an audience of 300 persons in a Manhattan synagogue as he tried to affirm his
support of the Eisenhower-Nixon ticket."

All through the final, awful week of the campaign the "unthinkable" continued to happen. Eisenhower pledged that "there will be no
U.S. involvement in these hostilities," and he declared: "We will not
condone armed aggression — no matter who the attacker and who the
victim. We cannot . . . subscribe to one law for the weak and another
law for the strong, one law for those opposing us, and another for
those allied with us." I picked up his points in several speeches I made
around the city that week. I emphasized that his "no-involvement"
policy would bring peace to the Middle East and that no American
blood would be shed. I said that the main U.S. goals should be an end
to hostilities, an end to Arab incursions into Israel, the opening of the
Suez Canal to Israeli ships, and a United States–Israel mutual-defense
agreement. My main point was that if the United States were to support the three-power attack, the Soviet Union would have been compelled to react militarily as well. "Every move we make," I said in one
speech, "must have as its objective the prevention of any large-scale
war." I am sure that many thoughtful Jews agreed with me, but those
who did not were more vociferous — and their attitude hurt.

Bob Wagner took a popular and partisan line in a bid for the Jewish voters who seemed to him to be falling away from me. He accused
the administration of having "double-crossed" our allies, charged that
the Eisenhower-Dulles policies had "aligned America on the side
of the Kremlin," and said that the United States should be cooperating
with Britain and France instead of voting with the USSR in the United
Nations. He finally came out with an ambiguous statement on H-bomb
tests, calling for a halt but also conceding the need for inspection or
"guarantees"; his statement was so hedged as to be almost meaning-

less, and I said it proved his "incompetence" in foreign affairs. By then, in the closing days of the campaign, Wagner and I had both slipped just a bit from the high level of discourse on which we started. Wagner was calling me a "Hoover Republican" and saying that Javits was "talking out of both sides of his mouth." I was calling him a "political hack."

On the last Sunday, I campaigned in Coney Island. As I walked along the boardwalk shaking hands with those who were sitting there in the autumn sunshine, some Jews not only refused to take my hand but spat upon the boardwalk. On the last day, at my final rally at Eighty-sixth Street and Broadway in Manhattan, I got the same treatment: As I walked through the crowd I stuck out my hand, saying "I'm Javits," and people turned away and spat. That had never happened to me before that week and it never happened again. I think the Jewish community has learned that even though I do not automatically approve of every Israeli action I generally espouse policies on Israel that can be accepted by Americans of all faiths and all parties; and I think most Jews understand that by helping to define and explain those policies I helped Israel survive in a hostile world. But I certainly took my lumps in that campaign.

That night, with the campaign over, I gathered my hard-working staff together at headquarters to tell them of my gratitude. Win or lose, I said, they would always have my appreciation. It was a very emotional moment and all the troubles and strains of that year of crises caught up with me, particularly the stresses of those past few days, the insults I had endured from people for whose cause I had labored so hard. I am told — I do not remember it — that tears came to my eyes and that I slammed a table with my hand. I seemed to be on the verge of letting go, which I have never done. Just then, someone — I think it was John Trubin — said, "Jack, we know how you feel." And at that, knowing they understood, I walked out of the room and went home.

On November 6, Eisenhower was reelected by the largest popular vote in history up to that time and a plurality of 9,560,000, second only to FDR's 1936 victory. The President carried forty-one of the forty-eight states, took New York by a margin of 1,590,000, and came close to carrying Democratic New York City. Wagner ran about half a million votes ahead of Stevenson; I ran behind Eisenhower's huge total by about six hundred thousand votes, losing quite a few in the Jewish districts. But enough Eisenhower votes stayed with me to elect me by a plurality over Wagner of four hundred sixty thousand.

These figures alone might suggest that I was carried to victory by

Eisenhower. But it must be pointed out that the presidential "coat-tails" were singularly ineffective that year. The Senate seat I captured was one of only four Democratic seats that swung to the Republican column while four Republican seats were going the other way — leaving the Democrats in control. Eisenhower's immense personal triumph also failed to influence the voting for the House of Representatives, where the Democrats actually *increased* their majority. It was the first time in more than a century that a triumphant President had been unable to carry at least one house of Congress for his party. In New York, despite Eisenhower's 60 percent of the vote, the party line-up of the state's delegation to the House of Representatives remained precisely as it had been. Certainly I was helped by Eisenhower, but the Senate race was largely independent of the presidential contest, and I felt my victory was my own. It was also my vindication.

Marian and I realized that my election to the Senate would change our lives; two and a half years after my fiftieth birthday I was embarking on a new and more demanding public career, and we knew we would be spending less time with each other. So at the end of that anguished year of 1956 we set off together on a month-long trip around the world. The journey combined recreation and sightseeing with some serious study of remote and exotic nations, such as India, that were new to me. Marian and I shared the excitement of these visits. My glimpses of Asia reminded me of the diversity and the complexity of the problems with which I would soon have to deal and assured me that I had made the right decision. The United States Senate was where I had to be.

FOURTEEN

The Most Exclusive
Club in the World

For twenty-four years the United States Senate was my home. I know its rules and traditions and moods, and I could often sense what action it was about to take. My seat on the aisle in the Senate chamber became as agreeable to me as a favorite living-room easy chair, and I was familiar with the voices, the quirks, the foibles and inclinations of the ninety-nine other senators. I was thrilled when a team of senators enlisted in a cause worked smoothly, like a well-drilled football backfield, each senator knowing the others' moves, and communicating by a sixth sense based on shared knowledge and skill. I was stimulated by the ebb and flow of debate and the philosophic tensions of the work we did — balancing lofty principles against sectional or selfish interests, welding together antagonistic human and economic and ideological forces into the coherent schemes of governance that we call laws.

Despite my familiarity with the Senate, I am still impressed and sometimes awed by the institution and the ineffable hold it has upon its members. The Senate has its own life that everyone in it, with but rare exceptions, feels constrained to honor and protect. Many representatives regard the House of Representatives as a way station to higher office, but being a senator is reward enough, and no member takes the institution for granted. Senators are always concerned that the institution should appear correct in the eyes of the public, that it be an effective instrument of democracy; and the most successful Senate leaders are those who can utilize the institution's self-image to curb some of the Senate's excesses and emphasize its strengths. Even senators like the late Jim Allen of Alabama, who knew the rules so well that he could twist the Senate into complete frustration, or Howard Metzenbaum of Ohio and James Abourezk of South Dakota, who invented new ways to stymie the Senate, were nonetheless ultimately subject to a fundamental respect for the Senate as an institution.

From the very beginning I savored the privileges of being a senator, particularly the privilege of debate. Having served eight years in the House, where speeches were sometimes limited to forty-five seconds and where, if you were lucky, you generally got five minutes to package all your arguments on a complicated issue, I was delighted with the Senate's tradition of speech and debate. If a senator has the floor, he can go on as long as he wishes — except when time for debate has been limited by unanimous consent or a cloture vote — about almost anything. Even when cloture has been imposed — which means debate has been limited to stop a filibuster — each senator may speak for another hour, and that is usually enough even for the most long-winded.

When I first came to the Senate we spoke without microphones or a public-address system, and when I got impassioned on a subject I used to love to prowl all over the chamber, up and down the aisles and around the desks, while I was talking. Later, we were limited by the length of our microphone cords, but I could not complain because I submitted one of the first resolutions for a public-address system myself.

Normally, the Senate is a very informal and intimate place that goes about its business without strict adherence to rules until, in the midst of some critical dispute, somebody invokes the rules — and then it can get very technical indeed. Generally that is not done. Senators defer to each other, and honest persuasion is the preferred means of battle. Senators believe they can rely on a colleague's word — and woe to the senator who promises something and fails to deliver. Unless the issue truly warrants such action, it does a senator no good whatever to raise an objection when another member asks unanimous consent for some point or other, because that member will surely remember and retaliate in kind against a senator who violates the code unnecessarily. It is this atmosphere of mutual dependence and trust — and privilege — that gives the Senate the reputation of a club — the most exclusive club in the world.

I discovered quickly that the Senate committees provide a more stimulating forum for individual creativity because they are so much smaller than those in the House: about fifteen or sixteen members compared to thirty-five or forty or more. I am most proud of what I accomplished in the Senate in the committee mark-up sessions, and in the House-Senate conferences. I had rarely been a conferee during my eight years in the House; House appointments to conference committees depended strictly on seniority, and there were so many ahead of me. In the Senate, with its smaller committees and more casual system, I found myself serving in conferences almost from the day I began.

I cannot deny that from the start I also enjoyed the modicum of real individual power the Senate confers on its members. Eisenhower was President when I came to the Senate, and as a Republican senator I had a great deal to say about federal appointments affecting New York, as I did again in the Nixon-Ford years. Moreover, almost anything a senator does or says attracts attention. In later years, as I came to be recognized as someone who could express coherent and reasonable opinions on a wide range of domestic and foreign issues, I got media exposure occasionally even when I was not looking for it. Newspaper and television reporters called me up at almost any hour of the day or night for comments on any governmental subject they happened to be working on, whether I had recently been involved in the matter or not, and I tried to oblige them — when I could. A New York television talk show was discussing gun control one morning when the host decided to get a congressional opinion. He phoned me in Washington and interviewed me live, on the air, about the need for antihandgun legislation. On the more frivolous side, a *New York Times* reporter once phoned me the day before the Superbowl to find out if I was going to watch the game and which team I was going to root for.

Because I savored also the prestige and honor of membership in the Senate, I was immensely gratified early in 1980 when a national magazine polled senators and reported that I was ranked by my colleagues as the third most persuasive in debate and one of the four most respected overall. I mention this accolade, at the risk of appearing immodest, merely to mark off the stages of my Senate career. Such a finding would have been impossible during my early years in the Senate. I was not always the Senate "insider" whose views and advice were sought on a variety of subjects. Far from it. When I arrived in the Senate, I was looked on with suspicion by the conservative leadership of my own party and with an even more hostile attitude by some of the Southern "barons" of the Democratic Party who controlled the Senate. For a time I was an outsider with little power or influence in the Senate beyond my one vote and my ability to get quoted and thereby to influence public opinion. Often, in those early years, when I rose to speak on some hotly contested issue, such as civil rights or labor organization, the chamber went deathly still and I could feel a chill of hostility. Sometimes the senior Southern senators walked out, leaving one of their new boys to answer my arguments; only gradually, as the media picked up my remarks, did they begin to participate in debates when I was speaking on subjects that affected them.

I am frequently asked whether anti-Semitism played a role in my initial cold welcome to the Senate. It is possible, perhaps even likely, that such prejudice did exist in the Senate — as it exists elsewhere in our society. But if it did, I have never been aware that it got in my way; I never attributed anything that happened to me to anti-Semitism. In fact, I make that a point of personal policy: I find it easier to handle any difficulty or opposition I encounter as directed against me personally and not against me as a Jew. A personal snub or problem can be dealt with, but if you succumb to the paranoia that your opponent is fighting you because of your religion or ethnic background, then you might as well give up entirely, because there is no way to change your identity.

Besides, there were other reasons for the coldness and hostility of the early years. Many senators already knew me as a maverick Republican in the House, and there was no secret about my differences with Tom Dewey and other New York Republican leaders on rent control and similar issues. Joe McCarthy was still in the Senate when I arrived in 1957, and even though he had been censured and was dying of cancer, he still had friends and allies who may have believed the wild accusations that had been hurled at me during the previous election year. Furthermore, I made it clear from the outset that although I respected the Senate leaders I would not bow down before them; as I had done in the House ten years earlier, I spoke out when I felt the need to, always with civility but without worrying too much about whether I was embarrassing or stepping on the toes of one of the patriarchs. Frequently, to establish a point of principle, or to build a record for the future, I made waves by fighting for some bill or amendment on which it was abundantly clear from the start that I would be defeated — which is not the accepted way of making friends quickly in the Senate club.

Social circumstances also hampered my access to the inner circles of Senate power. In those Eisenhower years a lot of government business was transacted informally on the golf course. I could play golf, but I was never very enthusiastic about it; my sports were tennis and swimming, which are much less conducive to the kind of conversation that builds business or political alliances. Tex McCrary had astutely pointed out this obstacle a couple of years earlier, in a letter to Eisenhower urging the President "to find some way to draw Javits into your circle of valued friends." McCrary wrote: "I realize that Jack does not . . . play golf or bridge nor does he enjoy freshwater fishing. This is said not in sarcasm, but only in realistic appraisal of the differences between Jack and all the other men who have earned your close friendship." Although Eisenhower replied that "I have never felt for Javits anything other than friendship," McCrary's point was valid, and it applied to the Senate as well.

Furthermore, I do not really enjoy idle social chitchat, and so I did not seek to be included in that group of Republican senators who gathered at the close of a day, usually in the office of the secretary of the minority, for a relaxing drink. At those times I would be reading up on a bill or an issue, or signing mail, or meeting with constituents, and when I did get together for a meal or a drink with other senators it was most often with a group that was planning strategy for some specific legislative goals, not just passing the time of day in collegial camaraderie.

Finally, another social obstacle to my quick acceptance was the fact that most of the time we did not live in Washington. Marian came to the capital when I suggested she join me at what I considered to be a particularly important event, but during her absences I passed up many social activities, and my work took priority. When Marian did come to Washington we invited senators and cabinet officers and their wives to dinner — and those were enjoyable and useful occasions. When she was not there, I arranged working suppers at my apartment; at Marian's direction, Helen Hager, our Washington housekeeper, cooked broiled chicken or a marvelous beef stew for those evenings. (I introduced Henry Kissinger to a group of senators at one such supper, and we negotiated a good deal of the War Powers Resolution of 1973 at others.) I went to embassy dinners and receptions from the beginning, but not nearly as many as I would have attended had Marian been there.

None of this would have amounted to much had I not, upon my arrival in the Senate, become a leading spokesman and activist for the cause of desegregation and racial justice. This struggle could not be carried on without antagonizing the Democratic Southern barons of the Senate and some of the conservative Republicans as well. It threatened not only what Senator Richard Russell of Georgia called the "social order" of the South (by which he meant simply the second-class status of blacks) but also the senatorial prerogative of unlimited debate, which these Southerners had extended and abused to filibuster repeatedly against the majority will of the Senate and the Congress.

A key battleground in the struggle for racial equality was the biennial attempt to amend Senate Rule XXII — the means by which the Senate can invoke cloture and end a filibuster. The cloture issue was technical and complex, and it involved many points of constitutional law as well as Senate rules and traditions. It was therefore an issue that I enjoyed sinking my teeth into, not only because the elimination of racial discrimination depended upon it but because it called upon my legal and debating skills.

The original Rule XXII, adopted in 1917, had allowed two-thirds of those senators actually present and voting to close off debate on a legislative matter. Cloture could not be used to stop filibusters on *procedural* matters, however, and that loophole had been used in 1948 to block the *consideration* of an anti–poll tax bill. The following year, under postwar pressure, Southern Democrats and conservative Republicans agreed to a compromise change in the rule; cloture was extended to procedural matters, but it thenceforth required the vote of two-thirds of the entire Senate, not just two-thirds of those voting. Moreover, the 1949 rule specified that cloture could not be invoked to change the rules. This was a fortress within a fortress — really a "Catch-22." Rule XXII as so amended protected itself against the will of the Senate to change it, for no filibuster against a rules change could be stopped. As the rule could not be changed while operating under it, further liberalization of the cloture mechanism seemed hopeless; it appeared that one-third of the Senate membership would be able to block civil rights legislation forever.

The attempt to get around this impasse brought up a constitutional nicety: Is the Senate a continuing body whose rules remain in effect from one Congress to the next, until amended by procedures established under those very rules? Or does it become a brand-new Senate every two years with the right to adopt new rules by normal parliamentary procedure, that is, by majority vote? At the opening of each Congress a small group of Senate liberals, of which I quickly became an active member, fought to establish new rules. We argued that the Constitution gave each house of Congress the power to make its own rules (which the House of Representatives did every two years) and that the power could be exercised by a simple majority because there were no rules in existence at the beginning of each Congress.

In 1957, 1959, and 1961, Vice President Nixon, as president of the Senate, supported our stand. He gave it as his "advisory opinion" that the Senate could not be bound by any previous rule "which denies the membership of the Senate the power to exercise its constitutional right to make its own rules." Opposed to us, essentially under Southern leadership, was the majority of the Senate, which held that because only one-third of the Senate was elected every two years it was a permanent body with rules that carried over automatically. The Senate had generally operated with that interpretation, so tradition was against us too; we never did get a majority to go along with us, and the constitutional issue was not really tested. Nevertheless, we kept at it, on the opening of the new Congress every two years, and each time the rules carryover was confirmed by one parliamentary means or another we introduced resolutions to amend the existing Rule XXII.

I missed the opening round of the rules struggle in 1957 because

I had delayed my swearing-in so that the New York State Legislature could choose my successor as attorney general. But I quickly had the chance to catch up. Assigned to the Rules and Administration Committee of the Senate, I was appointed to a special two-man subcommittee that was established just to look into all the proposals to change Rule XXII that had been introduced at the beginning of the session. The other member of the subcommittee was Herman Talmadge of Georgia, then an ardent supporter of Senator Russell's. We were cochairmen, but as Talmadge was senior to me, he controlled the subcommittee, and the whole procedure was slowed by scheduling what I considered to be lengthy and unnecessary hearings. Senator Talmadge brought in a parade of Southern senators and other witnesses to explain that it would be a violation of "States' rights" to "take a senator off his feet" and make him stop talking. For the record, I therefore had to provide witnesses to expound our view that it is a "fundamental weakness of our governmental system that a small minority can paralyze a majority for action on the protection of vital constitutional rights for millions of Americans."

Obviously, Senator Talmadge and I were not going to agree, and our seven long sessions of hearings in the summer of 1957 merely succeeded in postponing action for a year. But the work of the subcommittee was a valuable experience for me. The discussions with witnesses, the careful study of the history of Senate debate and Senate rules on cloture, and the analyses of the many proposals to change the cloture rule all combined with my legal training to give me a thorough understanding of the cloture issue; I was to use this expertise in future debates — to the even greater annoyance of the Southerners.

When Senator Talmadge and I submitted our separate views, I recommended that the Rules Committee report favorably Senate Resolution 17, of which I had been a cosponsor. Resolution 17 would have permitted cloture to be imposed by two-thirds of the senators present and voting two days after a cloture petition was filed, and, more significant, by a simple majority of the full Senate fifteen days later. It also eliminated the restriction on using cloture against a filibuster on rules changes themselves. In 1958, to my immense gratification, the Rules Committee accepted my view and reported Resolution 17 to the full Senate with the recommendation that it be passed. But from the "fortress within a fortress" came the threat of an unstoppable filibuster, and no further action was taken.

In 1959, Democratic Senators Hubert Humphrey of Minnesota and Paul Douglas of Illinois and Republicans Clifford Case of New Jersey and I mounted another major effort to amend Rule XXII. This time Majority Leader Lyndon Johnson, perhaps the most skillful tactician ever to manage the Senate, outmaneuvered us by devising some minor revisions of Rule XXII and persuading his Southern friends to accept them as a compromise without filibustering. With the support of the Republican leadership, under the new minority leader, Everett Dirksen of Illinois — a conservative and a master at persuasion — Johnson's scheme passed easily. Lacking the votes to win with our more drastic proposals, my allies and I had to be content with the knowledge that nothing would have happened at all if we had not been fighting. Johnson's 1959 revision breached the inner fortress by once more applying cloture to debate on motions to change the rules, including Rule XXII, and it restored the cloture power to two-thirds of the senators present and voting. However, it declared that "the rules of the Senate shall continue from one Congress to the next Congress unless they are changed as provided in these rules." That was a bitter pill to swallow, but we had to pay for what we got.

Despite this latter proviso, we continued our campaign to convince the Senate that it had a constitutional right to change its rules by majority vote at the beginning of each session. We failed each time (and, having failed, we sometimes used the filibuster ourselves, notably, on one occasion, to prevent the conservatives from passing a bill to delay the enforcement of the Supreme Court's one-man–one-vote reapportionment decision). Not until 1975 was the cloture rule changed to allow three-fifths of the full Senate to cut off debate. But our efforts finally persuaded two-thirds of the Senate to take action against a Southern filibuster. In 1964, cloture was invoked by a 71-to-29 vote, and the most far-reaching civil rights act since the Civil War was passed.

Our most formidable opponent in these civil rights struggles, and the source of most of the coldness directed against me in the early years, was Senator Richard B. Russell of Georgia. Russell was deeply committed to the "social order" of the South, which was based on the proposition that the segregation of the races was essential to public tranquility and economic stability in that region. As the last great Southern "baron," he was one of the most important figures who ever served in the Senate, and had already been in office twenty-four years when I arrived. He was chairman of the Armed Services Committee and was in line to become chairman of the Appropriations Committee, a post he assumed a few years later. Intelligent, able, and skillful in debate, he had mastered the rules of the Senate and applied them ruthlessly to cut down any senator he considered hostile to his point of view. It was believed, when I came to the Senate, that Russell could make or unmake Senate leaders at will, and he seemed to get his way almost all the time. He had amassed so much power and was so highly regarded that he had become something of a sacred cow: Few senators dared to oppose him, even though he was completely wrong in his belief that the Constitution permitted racial segregation as long as the separate facilities for blacks were "equal."

But I was experienced enough when I came to the Senate not to stand in awe of Richard Russell, and I took him on over the issue of civil rights. For a long time he had much the better of me. Although, strictly speaking, Democrats had nothing to say about the Republicans' committee assignments, Russell may have had a hand in keeping me off the Foreign Relations Committee for twelve years. When I was appointed to the Appropriations Committee in 1962, to fill the place of a Republican who had died, Russell and I clashed frequently: I was usually urging more funding for health research, aid to education, and anything that could further desegregation, and I voted far more liberally than Russell did on foreign aid. At the beginning of the next Congress, Russell arranged to have the committee reduced in size by one member on each side, I think just to eliminate me, as I was the most junior Republican on the committee. I could not get back on the Appropriations Committee for four years thereafter.

Senator Russell was defending a social order that seemed to him as natural and God-given as the beat of his pulse, so it was to be expected that he would fight any threat to that order with every weapon at his command. A further cause of his hostility to me was that I had taken a Senate seat away from his party. Although he disagreed with the Northern liberals, Russell never forgot for a moment that his power depended on the election of enough Northern Democrats, liberals included, to provide a Senate majority. He had to tolerate Democratic liberals and even help them get reelected, but Republicans who sought to upset his Southern social order could expect from him only a minimum of senatorial courtesy, which barely masked his determination to thwart their objectives. Richard Russell played for keeps — and ultimately he lost the game. Ironically, for many years my office in Washington was in the Senate office building named after him.

Not all of the Southerners were so adamant about the South's "social order" as Russell; many of them adjusted to the times — and even to me. Senator Sam Ervin of North Carolina, who won the nation's respect for his wise and eloquent conduct of the Senate's Watergate investigation, was one of these. Ervin had started his career as a circuit lawyer traveling through the rural areas of North Carolina, where the Biblical quotations and the folksy humor that endeared him to television audiences in 1973 were a necessary part of a trial lawyer's professional equipment. Later, as a judge of his state's highest court of appeal, he was a serious student of the law who read his cases carefully.

His erudite references to Supreme Court cases interspersed with his marvelous stories made him very convincing and effective as an advocate, but I thought he was just plain wrong in his anticipation of how the Supreme Court would rule in the civil rights cases. The quip of the day had it that Ervin was an expert on the Constitution — up to the Fourteenth Amendment. I came to believe that on civil rights cases Ervin's views represented wish fulfillment rather than the sound legal thinking of which he was so very capable.

So I fought Ervin, just as I took on Russell, on the ideology, the national policy, and the law respecting civil rights. I turned out to be right and he turned out to be wrong at just about every point. But he and I eventually developed a warm friendship based on mutual admiration for each other's legal skills and political integrity; when he retired in 1974 I paid a tribute to him on the Senate floor, praising his conduct of the Watergate hearings and his dedication to individual freedom. "He has been to me," I said, "both a staunch and effective ally and a respected and honorable adversary." Later Sam Ervin returned the compliment to me. It was a fine demonstration of the best of the Senate that two diametrically opposite "foes" on legislation could become true friends, and that a Democrat and a Republican could exchange such compliments in the full but tacit understanding that neither would use them politically.

Friendships with such ideological opponents take a long time to develop. In the early years I was naturally closest to senators who agreed with me, and foremost among them was Paul Douglas, Democrat of Illinois, my partner in the cloture fights for a decade. Douglas was a truly noble American and a durable and powerful reformer. He had been an economics professor and a Chicago alderman before enlisting in the Marine Corps in World War II at the age of fifty, and he was the author of the 1957 Senate Resolution 17, which, in its various forms over the years, served as our civil rights battle flag.

Paul Douglas and I had a lot in common and we made a good team. My input was primarily on the lawyering side, on drafting, rules, and tactics on the Senate floor; Douglas, as a Democrat who had been around the Senate longer and knew our colleagues better than I did and had some influence at least with the majority leadership, directed strategy and persuasion. He and I put together a bipartisan task force of a dozen pro–civil rights senators (generally six from each party) — which came to be known as the liberal group. He ran it on the Democratic side and I on the Republican. We met periodically, and even daily when a civil rights measure was before the Senate; we would divide up the list of senators on both sides, and members of our group would then spread out to solicit votes. During a Southern filibuster, one or two members of our group were always on the floor of the Senate to monitor the proceedings.

When Douglas was defeated for reelection in 1966, Senator Philip Hart of Michigan became my partner in this effort. The major battle had already been won in 1964, but we were still trying to change the cloture rule and eventually succeeded. Phil Hart was one of the kindest men in the world, but beneath his soft manner lay a flint-and-steel dedication to principle. Everyone in the Senate understood that he was a man of his word who would carry out any obligation he undertook. Sadly, we watched him die. He grew weaker and weaker as his cancer progressed, and just a few weeks before he passed away in 1976, a large number of his Senate colleagues gathered together to say a good word and present him with the framed resolution by which the Senate had given its new office building his name. Phil was so weak by then that he could barely thank us, but we could read his feeling and appreciation in his eyes as we shook hands with him and said what we all knew would be our final farewells.

Another reliable ally was Senator John Pastore of Rhode Island, a very clever debater who would speak passionately and even loudly when he was exercised by an issue and who compelled attention by the emotion — and conviction — in his voice. In one civil rights debate he took on Senator Russell Long of Louisiana, who told the Senate that he loved blacks because his "mammy" had rocked him in her arms and was like a mother to him. Pastore tore him to bits, exposing what he was doing to the self-respect and humanity of this "mammy" and her family, who lived like slaves in the segregated South even though they might have been treated well and were technically free. It was one of the greatest Senate speeches I ever heard, and it was pure Pastore.

Pastore could get almost as passionate about wanting to recess and go home when it got to be six or seven o'clock on a Friday evening and his wife was, he said, waiting for him with dinner. Here were men tearing their hair in debate, fervently engaged in an issue, ready to go on for days and risk heart attacks in the process, so deeply were they convinced about the rightness of their respective causes. And then John Pastore, about five feet two, would get up, counseling sweet reason and delivering a homily about how we should wind it all up because dinner was on the table — and many times we did.

On the Republican side, the friendships and alliances of those years soon coalesced into a loose-knit but influential Senate group known as the Wednesday Club — because it met every Wednesday for lunch, on a round-robin arrangement, in the office of one of its sixteen members. All the members were Republicans, and most were progressives. They included, from time to time, Ed Brooke of Massachusetts, who could closely anticipate the vote on a given issue; Charles Percy of Illinois, who brought to us a very intimate understanding of the U.S. business community; Mark Hatfield of Oregon, now chairman of the Appropriations Committee; James Pearson of Kansas, an enlightened conservative who played a very useful role in reviewing policy matters from a Middle Western point of view; and after 1970, Lowell Weicker of Connecticut, the Senate's most stalwart independent.

The Wednesday Club came into existence about 1964 and operated as a nonbinding caucus within the Senate Republican Conference framework. We exchanged ideas at those luncheon meetings, solicited cosponsors for measures we wanted to launch as individual senators, and sometimes undertook assignments to work on some subject and report on it to the others. The group achieved a great deal, particularly on the antipoverty program, on foreign aid, on matters relating to the United Nations, and on dozens of other issues of common interest to its members. I did not always agree with all my Wednesday luncheon companions — far from it — but the group was very helpful in my later efforts on pension reform and the War Powers Resolution.

*　*　*

The dominant figure in my early Senate years was unquestionably Lyndon B. Johnson (with Everett Dirksen right on his heels). Johnson was fundamentally a Southerner, but of a different kind. His sympathy went to people who work and sweat and worry, and that overwhelmed his lingering regional attitudes. Eventually his instinct for the underdog prevailed, and he played an indispensable role in the passage of the early civil rights bills.

Lyndon Johnson never gave up on anybody. If he wanted you to vote his way, he would keep after you doggedly, no matter how firm in your disagreement you might seem. I always stood up when he approached my seat, as he was the leader of the majority. He would reach across my desk from the next lower row of seats, grab the lapels of my jacket and pull me toward him until we were looking at each other almost nose to nose, and then he would talk with great sincerity and conviction about why I was wrong about the vote that he knew, or I had said, I was going to cast on some measure.

He could be a redoubtable foe. In 1957 Arthur Larson, the Eisenhower-appointed head of the U.S. Information Agency, declared in a speech that the Roosevelt and Truman administrations had been in the "grip of an alien ideology." Johnson was incensed at this partisan and impolitic comment and proceeded to cut the USIA's budget to ribbons. The administration had asked for $144 million, and at one point Johnson had it down to $90 million. I was a brand-new senator and perhaps I should have kept my head down, as most Republicans did on this issue, because it was obvious that the majority leader was going to have his way. But I fought him tooth and nail, pointing out how his cuts would hurt our country by crippling the agency's overseas information programs, which were needed to counter Soviet propaganda. Johnson crushed me like a steamroller. I had only fourteen other senators with me voting nay when the Senate approved the cuts; even most of the Republicans voted with the majority. When the conference committee report on the appropriations bill was approved, allowing $96 million for the agency, Richard Neuberger of Oregon and I were the only senators in opposition. Johnson really tried to teach me my manners as a freshman senator, but I still feel I was right: It took the USIA ten years to recover from those Johnson budget cuts.

But Johnson never let a senator's opposition or even defiance on one issue affect the next. A year after the USIA episode, Johnson came to me for assistance when Southerners and conservative Republicans, angered by Supreme Court decisions on civil rights and civil liberties cases, tried to curb the powers of the Court. We worked closely together on that, and the attempt — the Jenner-Butler bill — was defeated by a narrow margin.

During a rules-change battle in 1963, at the opening of the Eighty-eighth Congress, when Johnson was vice president, I had another memorable run-in with him. As president of the Senate, Johnson had just declined to make a ruling that a motion to cut off debate on a rules change, by majority vote, was in order; instead, he said he would submit the question to the Senate. Such a ruling was essential to our strategy, and his refusal to make it meant that our efforts to change Rule XXII were defeated once again. I rose to remonstrate with him and to try to explain how he should exercise his authority. I said that "the chair does not by law have to submit a constitutional question to the Senate." And then I added: "The vice-presidency is not a hollow shell."

Johnson took that very badly and he never forgot it. I did not intend to call him a hollow shell — it just came out that way because I became very passionate on the subject. Passion does not make me lose my reason, but it sometimes makes me indignant, and that is what I was in that case. Actually, what I was saying was true: that the vice president of the United States does have power, as Nelson Rockefeller, in almost identical circumstances, demonstrated a dozen years later.

In the early years I could not get the committee assignments I wanted, so in order to make an impact I had to work with any tool I could find. I made myself an expert on a great variety of subjects, and I was willing to take on unpopular and obscure subcommittee assignments within the committees to which I belonged. In the Banking and Currency Committee, for instance, I served on subcommittees dealing with housing, securities, and financial institutions. In the Judiciary Committee I was a member of five subcommittees: immigration, constitutional rights, refugees, Trading with the Enemy Act, and juvenile delinquency. To make up for not getting on the Foreign Relations Committee, I sought appointments to almost every subcommittee that had anything to do with foreign issues: for example, the Intergovernmental Relations Subcommittee of the Government Operations Committee, the International Finance Subcommittee of the Banking and Currency Committee, and the Foreign Economic Policy Subcommittee of the Joint Economic Committee. And I accepted, willingly, a place on the Labor and Public Welfare Committee, which interested few other senators but gave me the chance to push for legislation on labor, health, education, and other issues that concerned me and my constituents. In this way I attempted to cover almost the entire work of the Senate and to prove what I could do.

Perhaps I took on more than I needed to, and I am sure that at times I was more abrasive than I needed to be. I know I stood up and spoke out on occasions when perhaps I should have held my peace. I never hesitated to step out on a hostile stage and lead an attack on principle, or on an issue I felt deeply about. That was not the traditional way for a senator to behave, especially when success seemed a long way off. But on issue after issue, by persisting, by badgering, by slowly piling up in my colleagues' minds a realization of the need for this or that piece of legislation, I was rewarded with eventual success — though not always with recognition. The secret of legislative achievement is to let as many people as possible take credit for a good law. Very often my groundwork paid off when someone else or some event lifted an issue into the national consciousness, and I never complained when others took the credit, as long as the job got done.

In the beginning, some of my senatorial opponents doubted my sincerity; they thought a liberal Republican was a contradiction in terms and they accused me of pandering to the New York electorate. But eventually they became convinced that I meant what I said, that I believed in what I was doing. And as I accumulated legislative knowledge and my debating points struck home, the Senate as a whole began to take more favorable notice of me.

Much as I might like to think that my ability and wisdom eventually turned my colleagues around, I cannot claim all the credit for my metamorphosis from cold-shouldered outsider to respected insider. Nor did I change my ways or try to ingratiate myself with the leadership. The march of events was on my side; by the mid-1970s many of the battles I fought were won. On civil rights primarily, but also on labor, education, aid to the arts, youth and antipoverty programs, many of the "unpopular" views I had espoused had been accepted by the Congress and by the nation and had become the laws of the land. The watershed event for the nation and for me was the passage of the Civil Rights Act of 1964. After that there was no reason to freeze me out.

In 1969, at the beginning of my third Senate term, I was finally appointed to the Foreign Relations Committee, and eventually became the ranking Republican member. Even before that I had become chairman of the Economic Committee and then of the Political Committee of the North Atlantic Assembly — the NATO Parliamentarian's Conference — and was actively involved in issues of trade and free-world security. My constant attention to Israel and the Middle East, and my continued insistence that U.S. interests demanded support of Israel, also were redeemed; I was recognized by the Senate not only as an authoritative spokesman for the Jewish community but as someone who understood the issue in terms of U.S. security.

Finally, the new Republican administration of 1969 put a seal of approval on me. For two decades in Washington I had made repeated calls on secretaries of state to press my views; the first time the secretary of state took the initiative to *ask* me what I thought, I knew I had arrived in the inner circle.

If politics is the art of the possible, the U.S. Senate is one of its grandest studios. Only by finding a common denominator of purpose that enables conflicting forces to fuse for an instant can meaningful legislation be passed and step-by-step progress made. Senate leaders such as Johnson or Dirksen achieve their goals by persuasion, cajolery, and the careful trading of votes and favors. But the Senate also needs members who can define the possibilities — and that was one of my major roles.

I was generally able, on hearing two apparently conflicting points of view, to find a formula that expressed the area of agreement they shared — or could share — and then to get it adopted. I did this not by "papering over" the differences between two opposing positions but by defining the essence of their common ground and getting them to see it, thus enabling a committee or the Senate itself to move forward. Even in my early Senate years, for instance, when I was on the Labor and Public Welfare (now the Labor and Human Resources) Committee, Barry Goldwater and John Kennedy, feuding over some conservative-liberal issue, could turn to me to draft a provision or a phrase they both could accept.

Sometimes these formulas were almost absurdly simple, as was the health warning that the Senate in 1979 voted to place on all bottles of hard liquor. Senators from Kentucky, a whiskey-producing state, objected to the wording proposed by two of the Senate's teetotalers. The original warning read: "Caution: Consumption of alcoholic beverages may be hazardous to your health, may be habit forming, and may cause serious birth defects when consumed during pregnancy." My compromise, accepted by both sides and adopted by the Senate, simply dropped the last part, and thus read: "Consumption of alcoholic beverages may be hazardous to your health." More often, the solutions to these puzzles were exceedingly complex. Most of the time they were somewhere in between.

If I was floor-managing a bill or otherwise closely involved in a debate, finding common ground came as a matter of course. But if I was not one of the contending parties I had to be more cautious. I might have been just listening to a debate, trying, as always, to pick up the main point at issue. And then someone asked a question or asked someone else to yield — something clued me in to the heart of the matter, which may have eluded the senators locked in combat. A solution to the difficulty often presented itself to me at the same time, and then I had to decide whether to intrude with an amendment of my own, at the risk of appearing to meddle in someone else's domain, or stay silent. One way I handled that was to scribble out a suggested amendment and send it to the senator who needed it so he could offer it himself. Consequently, senators of both parties and their aides came to me on occasion to help them find a way to draft part of a bill so that it would pass. I was referred to by both foes and allies from time to time as the lawyer of the Senate, a job description that pleased me in either case.

A key element in the senatorial art of the possible is the ability to sense the mood of the chamber. The Senate may react one way at a given moment and quite differently only a few hours later. On many occasions a measure has failed in the morning and passed the same afternoon without any alteration in the facts or arguments. In 1975, on the eve of the Christmas recess, we advised Secretary of State Henry Kissinger that if the Ford Administration insisted on an immediate vote on a pending amendment to a defense appropriations bill, the administration would lose — the amendment would pass; if the leaders waited until after the recess, I advised, it could probably be defeated or effectively compromised. But the President insisted on a vote before the recess and, as I predicted, the amendment passed (I voted for it): It barred the United States from sending any military aid to any of the factions then fighting in Angola.

Kissinger has bitterly described that vote as a tragic failure of U.S. will that enabled the Soviet Union to get a foothold in Africa through its Cuban surrogates. The real issue was whether Angola would trap the United States into a situation comparable to Vietnam. I believed — and expressed my belief to Kissinger — that the thirty-day recess would give senators an opportunity to become more acquainted with the Angolan situation and the way in which the administration proposed to handle it; a delay and more discussion could have quieted the Senate's fears about another Vietnam and produced a compromise that I and others might have supported. The failure was not of the Senate's will but of the White House's willingness to compromise with the Senate.

Determining what can be done and when to do it is a talent not shared by all senators in equal measure. There were times when even good friends and long-time allies accused me of abandoning a cause because I chose a pragmatic course that could succeed instead of an idealistic stand that would have led to defeat. Democratic Senator Abraham Ribicoff of Connecticut, with whom I had had a long and warm friendship dating back to our days on the House Foreign Affairs Committee, once made this misjudgment of my motives, too.

In 1971, during debate on a bill to aid school desegregation in the South, Senator Ribicoff introduced an amendment that would have required Northern metropolitan areas to end their de facto segregation within ten years by mixing suburban and inner-city pupils. I thought his idealistic plan flawed because it blurred the distinction between de jure segregation resulting from deliberate government policy, which existed in the South at the time, and de facto segregation caused by the white flight to the suburbs that was taking place in the North. More important, I believed the adoption of his amendment would have killed all chance of the main bill passing the Senate (and in fact some of the Southern Democrats favored it for just that reason).

When I opposed his amendment, Senator Ribicoff took the floor to deliver an unusual, blistering personal attack on me. He accused me of "hypocrisy" for being "unwilling to accept desegregation for [New York] though . . . willing to shove it down the throats of the senators from Mississippi." Looking right at me, he declared: "I don't think you have the guts to face your liberal constituents who have moved to the suburbs to avoid sending their children to school with blacks."

I was stunned and embarrassed, because here was an attack from a good friend and a friend of civil rights who questioned my good faith and my commitment to that issue. All my life I have been blessed with my mother's ability to endure abuse and to avoid angry confrontations by simply ignoring unpleasantness. This trait saved me as I rose to reply to Ribicoff, in a hushed chamber. "The senator from Connecticut is my friend and has been for years and will continue to be after today," I began. And then, as calmly as I could, I explained again why I opposed his amendment: "This idea of the senator from Connecticut may be good and it may be bad. However, I know that it would sink this bill." A few minutes later, my contention was borne out as Southern senators, who opposed the bill, voted with Ribicoff to defeat a motion to table his amendment.

Abe Ribicoff promptly edited his remarks in the official transcript, as every senator is entitled to do, so the *Congressional Record* does not show exactly what he said. But a competent *New York Times* reporter, David Rosenbaum, had been in the gallery, and his account of Ribicoff's words, from which I have quoted here, appeared on the front page of the newspaper the next day. As debate on the Ribicoff amendment resumed, I pointed out to the Senate the discrepancy between the *Record* and the *Times* story. Ribicoff, I said, had made "a most reprehensible charge," and I went on:

> I speak only in sorrow and not in anger. I hope very much that these vestiges, this fustian kind of debate, we will be spared in this body. I would hope the record had not been cleared up. . . . I know that the motivation for whatever revisions were made was friendly and not unfriendly. . . . But I wish it had not been done. . . . We learn from these passages not to play with fire, and to legislate under the cover of epithet in a free country is playing with fire.

The Ribicoff amendment was defeated and we passed the bill, and Senator Ribicoff (who retired from the Senate in 1980) and I became better friends than ever. The U.S. Senate proceeded on its stately way.

* * *

Even after nearly a quarter of a century in the Senate, I still made mistakes. In 1977 my Republican Senate colleagues objected strenuously to a House Democratic bill regulating campaign expenditures. I favored most of the bill because it would have provided federal matching funds for Senate and House elections, but many Republicans claimed that the Democrats had designed it to cripple Republican fund raising. I was impressed by the strength of the Republican feeling, so I advised Minority Leader Howard Baker that if the Republican Party wanted a chance to debate the bill I would not vote for cloture for a while.

Normally a week of debate before the filing of a cloture petition is not considered excessive, but in this case the Democrats forced the first cloture vote four days after the bill came to the floor. This looked like a Democratic attempt to roll over the Republicans with raw power.

Many Republicans argued that if the Democrats could easily silence the minority party on this partisan issue, then the Republicans would no longer be able to function: The Democrats would know that they could impose their will on the Senate at any time without paying attention to the minority.

So I voted against cloture at first, but I told Senator Baker that when the last cloture vote was taken I would vote for it: I wanted to make it difficult for the Democrats to silence my party, but I also wanted the bill to pass. And with me were four or five other Republicans who felt very much as I did. Two cloture votes failed, and just before the third one, I went to Senator Robert Byrd, the majority leader, and asked him if this was the last cloture vote. He did not answer, and I took that to mean it probably was *not* the last cloture vote, and so — unwisely, as I now see — I voted against cloture once more.

But when that attempt failed, Byrd took the bill down; that is, having been defeated on cloture three times, he abandoned all effort to pass it — much to my surprise. I could have won it for him, because probably most of my group would have gone with me — if he had only shared the information that this was the last chance. I may not have made it clear to him that I would vote for cloture on the final try, but in any case he was a little too secretive for the bill's good, and, as it turned out, for mine.

Common Cause, the citizens' lobby, had backed the bill and it excoriated those of us who favored the bill but had let it be defeated. The organization would accept no explanation of any kind but simply attacked us, week after week. So I just forgot about it and let it go. But it had been a mistake, because my Republican colleagues, who wanted to filibuster the bill to death, had exploited my willingness to help the party.

Two years later, we faced a similar situation. In 1979 we were debating the windfall profits tax on oil, and again some Republicans had profound objections to the bill. Again I was urged to vote against cloture and give my Republican colleagues a chance to debate it and get a fair break. Remembering my experience with the campaign-financing bill, I said, "Not on your life. I vote for cloture first crack out of the box, and I keep voting for it." And so in this case I voted three times for cloture, each time helping to build up the cloture vote to within four votes of the needed sixty. Eventually, although cloture was not actually imposed, the bill was passed because its opponents realized that cloture was imminent and they had to compromise.

I may still make mistakes, but I learn from them.

FIFTEEN

The United States
and Israel

When Israel was still young and I was in the House of Representatives, I stated on several occasions what was then a radical proposition: that Israel was the "anchor and bastion" of democracy in the Middle East and was vital to U.S. security. At the time, few people agreed with me — or even paid much attention. The fledgling nation surrounded by hostile neighbors seemed too small, too weak, and too precarious ever to be worth much as an ally to its all-powerful benefactor half a world away. The generous U.S. aid and support that Israel received in those early days was given not with much expectation that the United States itself would benefit but out of a genuine humanitarian desire to help the Jews, the victims of Hitler's Holocaust, establish a national homeland where the survivors — and those who might be threatened again — could live in peace.

I too was moved by this humanitarian impulse, of course, but in addition I can look back with satisfaction to the part I played in the House and the Senate in convincing other U.S. leaders that by helping Israel we were helping ourselves. The gradual acceptance of this concept underlies the history of the development of U.S. policy toward Israel. As Israel proved its mettle in war, as it prospered economically and progressed technologically, as it endured through vicissitudes as the only freely functioning democracy between India and Italy, increasing numbers of Americans recognized its value as an ally. At the same time, the volatility and instability — and frequently the unreasonableness — of some of Israel's neighbors tended to undercut the view held by some professional diplomats that Arab friendship was more important to the United States in the overall power struggle with the Soviet Union. Although there are thoughtful Americans who still believe that the United States would be better off in a close alliance with the oil-producing countries of the region, the concept that

Israel is our most reliable ally in the Middle East has become a basic tenet of U.S. foreign policy, consistently supported by a majority of both houses of Congress. This has occurred notwithstanding some irritating policies of Israel itself — some of its settlements on the West Bank, for example. But Israel's strength is that it is a democracy and a free society, and most Americans realize that we, as its principal supporter, have to pay a price for that, even if the price is Israel's occasional defiance of our wishes.

In 1978 a group of 177 retired U.S. generals and admirals endorsed a view that they could not have expressed publicly while on active duty. They said that "the ability of the U.S. to protect its security interests in the Middle East is closely linked, if not dependent on, the maintenance of a potent Israeli military capability." Pointing out that Israel alone could deter the intervention of Soviet combat forces, the military men declared: "No other society in the area can be counted on to mobilize reliable, battle-tested ground and air units, or to make available secure access points. . . . If not for the proven capability of the Israeli armed forces, we would be forced now to station a significant number of men and substantial materiel in that region." Everything I had said and done in support of and occasionally in criticism of Israel had been founded on that belief.

My direct involvement with the issue of Israel began in 1946 with my trip to Palestine a few weeks after I was first elected to Congress. Almost exactly ten years later, a few weeks after I was first elected to the Senate, I visited Israel again. I had made a number of trips there in the interim, had often conferred with its government leaders, and knew the country well. Just the year before, in 1955, I had investigated a report that the Soviet Union had offered to sell arms to Israel, and after talking to Israeli Prime Minister David Ben-Gurion, I had been able to assure President Eisenhower that the idea of a Soviet-Israeli arms deal was a fiction.

Late in November 1956, as a senator-elect, I set out with Marian on a round-the-world trip, and Israel was our first important stop. In the immediate aftermath of the Suez war U.S.–Israel relations were at a low ebb; I found my Israeli friends resentful of President Eisenhower's condemnation of their invasion of Sinai and unhappy about my support of Eisenhower's policy. The morning after I arrived I was taken by plane to the two strategic places for which Israel had gone to war and that her forces still occupied. The first was Sharm el Sheik, the fortress at the southern tip of the Sinai Peninsula; from there, Egypt had closed the narrow Strait of Tiran at the mouth of the Gulf of Aqaba, thereby blockading the port of Elath, Israel's only outlet to the Red Sea and points east. At Sharm el Sheik I saw the Egyptian guns and the captured armored cars with dashboard labels written in Russian.

The second strategic point was the Gaza Strip on the Mediterranean coast. Originally part of Britain's Palestine mandate, Gaza had come under Egyptian administration after the 1949 armistice that ended the first Arab-Israeli war. Nearly three hundred thousand Palestinian Arab refugees lived in Gaza, most of them under the care of the United Nations Relief and Works Agency (UNRWA), and it was from these refugees that Egypt had recruited Fedayeen guerrillas who had been raiding across the border into Israel for years. The strip was peaceful when I saw it, and the Israeli commanders were sympathetic to the refugees' plight. Most of the refugees seemed too stunned by the recent fighting to realize they were under Israeli occupation; one fiery youth I talked to reiterated the Arab demand that the refugees be repatriated to Israel — but only under Egyptian control.

That afternoon I had a long conference with Prime Minister Ben-Gurion and delivered a personal note to him from President Eisenhower. With his mane of white hair, his burnished complexion, and his twinkling eyes, David Ben-Gurion was a commanding and authoritative figure despite his small physical stature. When he spoke there was no doubt in his mind whatsoever that his listeners would try to accommodate him, that the world would try to do whatever he asked it to do, and that any other president and any prince or king would try to do likewise. If you said no to him, he just did not hear you — he just went right on as if you had said yes. That aura of authority came from an extraordinary determination and faith in himself. He was sure that he could persuade you or that events would persuade you and that somehow you would find a way.

On this occasion, in 1956, Ben-Gurion spoke to me about what he saw as the errors of the Eisenhower policy. The United States, he said, had failed to understand what was happening in the Middle East. "Why does the U.S. build up Nasser?" he asked me. "Does it not know that its policies are doing just that?" He pointed out that Nasser had become an ally of the Soviet Union. Israel's existence is only possible in the free world, he said; Israel would be eliminated and its people sent to Siberia or exterminated if the Communists were to take over in Africa and Asia. He insisted that even if only the surrounding Arab states went Communist, Israel could not survive.

The principal message Ben-Gurion wanted to convey to Eisenhower through me was that Egyptian troops should not be permitted to return to the Sinai. The Sinai, he said, is not important to Egypt's economy, but Egypt's presence there would again threaten the Israeli border. Israel, he said, would be willing to withdraw its troops, as a

UN resolution had demanded, but he insisted that there should be no discrimination against Israel. Why, he wanted to know, is the resolution's point about opening the Suez Canal to Israel not being pressed with Nasser? And he insisted on guarantees of free navigation of the Gulf of Aqaba, so that Israel could use Elath port.

Through the U.S. Embassy, I immediately cabled to the White House a report of my conversation. "There are deep misunderstandings as to the effect of U.S. policy here which ought to be dispelled urgently.... The prime minister equates Nasser directly with the Communist penetration of the African continent and the Middle East. Our policy is being read as building up Nasser so as to enable him to realize all his ambitions and to dominate the Arab and perhaps the Moslem world...." Other Israeli leaders elaborated on Ben-Gurion's grievances and I left Tel Aviv feeling utterly convinced that the United States had to listen to their case.

From Israel, Marian and I went to Pakistan, India, Thailand, the Philippines, Hong Kong, Taiwan, and Japan, and I met with leaders of all those countries. Everywhere I heard a willingness to accept U.S. leadership; but as our distance from the Middle East increased the intensity of interest in international affairs diminished and the concern with domestic matters expanded. In my trip notes I wrote that "it is almost as if the Cold War is a luxury that only the U.S. and the USSR can afford.... Most Americans would probably be shocked by the serene view taken in leading Asian countries about the Communist threat of aggression or subversion." But I also noted a general opinion that "if we continue our policies and the Communists continue theirs the Communists will come out on top in Asia and the Middle East." The lesson was clear to me: We had to do a better job with our allies and we had to persuade many more of the developing countries of the free world to understand democracy.

Back in Washington, as my first Senate session began, I was immediately involved in debates about U.S. policy toward the Middle East. President Eisenhower had asked Congress to authorize the use of military force as well as economic aid to prevent Communist aggression in the Middle East. This was the "Eisenhower Doctrine"; like the Truman Doctrine of 1947 and the Carter Doctrine of 1980, it opened up the possibility of U.S. military action in a region that had not previously been considered of vital strategic significance to the United States. Declaring that the danger in the Middle East was that "power-hungry Communists ... might be tempted to use open measures of armed attack" if they believed the region was inadequately defended, Eisenhower asked for authority to give military aid to countries requesting it, and also "to employ the armed forces of the United States against overt armed aggression from any nation controlled by international Communism."

Eisenhower's request represented a shift from his Suez position that there would be "no U.S. involvement in these hostilities." It reflected, I thought, a greater acceptance of the Israeli view of the situation that I had brought back from my meeting with Ben-Gurion, and I was heartened by this evidence that Eisenhower and Dulles now recognized that the security of Israel and the security of the United States were linked in the Middle East. Therefore I spoke out in favor of the Middle East resolution backing Eisenhower's request when it was debated in the Senate late in February and early in March. Amended by the Senate to state that the United States "is prepared" to use armed forces, instead of authorizing the use of forces, the resolution passed on March 5. It also pledged that the United States would support the United Nations Emergency Force (UNEF), which had been dispatched to the Sinai to police the truce between Egypt and Israel.

Meanwhile, negotiations to establish a firmer peace between Israel and Egypt were approaching a climax. Israeli forces had withdrawn from most of the Sinai Peninsula in December 1956, and the UN Emergency Force was in place. But the Israelis were refusing to relinquish Sharm el Sheik and the Gaza Strip until they were guaranteed that Gaza would not be used for hostile actions against them and that the Gulf of Aqaba would remain open to their ships.

Most members of Congress recognized the justice and common sense in the Israeli demand: A withdrawal without that assurance would have restored the conditions that led to the Suez war. Late in January, seventy Democratic members of Congress urged Secretary of State Dulles to work out some way to provide such guarantees, and I joined a bipartisan group of six other senators in introducing a resolution calling for United Nations guarantees to Israel. Our resolution suggested that in the meantime the UNEF be ordered to prevent the resumption of guerrilla attacks and the interdiction of international shipping through the strait. At the same time we were arguing against a new UN resolution that would have imposed economic sanctions on Israel for failing to comply completely with the United Nations' withdrawal order. In a long letter to Dulles, Senator Irving Ives and I pointed out that Egypt was also in violation of UN resolutions and the UN charter by refusing to allow Israeli (and French and British) shipping through the Suez Canal and by insisting on the right to blockade the Gulf of Aqaba. "Impartial justice," we wrote, "dictates that our government should not back sanctions against Israel. Our government should insist that there be appropriate and effective guarantees against the interdiction of shipping . . . and against new guerrilla raids."

During this period a great deal of private, backstage negotiation was going on between Egypt on one side and U.S., British, and Canadian diplomats on the other, with UN Secretary-General Dag Hammarskjöld serving as a conduit. Backed up by the strong public statements that I and others were making, these conversations eventually produced an apparent resolution of the problem. Nasser made some conciliatory gestures, and U.S. and UN officials began to come forward with the assurances and promises that Israel had demanded.

First, Henry Cabot Lodge, the U.S. ambassador to the United Nations, declared that the UN Emergency Force would remain in place until peaceful conditions were established. A few days later, a United States memorandum to Israel declared that "the U.S. believes the Gulf of Aqaba comprehends international waters and that no nation has the right to prevent free and innocent passage through the straits giving access thereto." Then came a speech by President Eisenhower promising that the United States would use its position in the United Nations to deploy the UNEF so that "the Gaza Strip could no longer be a source of armed infiltration and reprisals." Hammarskjöld also joined the chorus, asserting his understanding that Egypt would observe the terms of the 1949 armistice — that is, would not mount raids against Israel or try to block shipping through Aqaba.

Although these statements did not have the force of treaty or law, they seemed to me to add up to the assurances that Ben-Gurion had demanded, so I urged our Israeli friends to accept them as reliable promises. On March 1 Israeli Foreign Minister Golda Meir announced that Israel would take these statements on faith and, assuming that they would be carried out, would withdraw the remainder of her forces from Sharm el Sheik and the Gaza Strip.

The Israelis, I told the Senate the next day, are relying on "moral responsibility, not upon bargains and conditions." The responsibility was ours, I said, adding: "Our test now will be whether we allow ourselves to be influenced in carrying out these and other moral responsibilities essential to world peace by the opposition and bitterness of any state because that state can muster support . . . of the Arab nations or of the Arab-Asian bloc." This was indeed a crucial test. Israel, on the solemn assurances of the United States, was giving up territory vital to her survival as a state.

The test came quickly. A few days after the Israelis withdrew, Egypt's Nasser proclaimed that he would not go along with an interim plan for the opening of the Suez Canal to all nations; furthermore, he insisted on Egypt's "right of belligerency" to close off shipping at the Strait of Tiran. At the same time, he sent in Egyptian officials to reestablish his authority in the Gaza Strip, despite the presence of UN troops and officials who were administering the territory. Nasser contended that the mission of the UNEF was solely to supervise the Israeli withdrawal and that the UN troops should themselves withdraw, since the Israelis had left. In the wake of this backtracking, Golda Meir flew to Washington in an effort to bring U.S. pressure to bear on Nasser, and another round of intense diplomatic activity began. The upshot was a "compromise" that may have been precisely what Nasser was aiming for in the beginning. The UNEF remained in Gaza and at Sharm el Sheik, so the Gulf of Aqaba remained open to Israeli ships. But Nasser kept complete control of the Suez Canal. France attempted to contest this control and even boycotted the waterway for a time, but Britain and the United States began using the reopened canal and thus, by acquiescence, enabled Nasser to keep it closed to Israel. Nevertheless, a shaky peace was established.

This narrative demonstrates the responsibility that the United States assumed by inducing Israel to withdraw from territory won in the Suez war. Linked to the Eisenhower Doctrine — which was approved by Congress only after an amendment had been added in the Senate promising U.S. support for UNEF — the responsibility could not have been assumed without the growing awareness that the security of Israel was important to the security of the United States. Moreover, as was often the case with Israeli matters, U.S. congressional and public opinion led the way to the solution. The congressional outcry against the plan to punish Israel, and our insistence on guarantees instead, forced the administration to put together the assurances and the shaky compromise that gave the Middle East ten years of relative peace.

My role in these matters had changed when I entered the Senate. As a member of the House from a district with a one-third Jewish population, I took positions quickly and reacted firmly to every event that concerned Israel. To represent my constituents and to make my voice heard among the congressmen competing for attention, I did not let pass any opportunity to speak out for the cause of security, development, and justice for Israel.

As a senator, however, I was able to embrace a more global and more deliberate view. I did not have to leap to the barricades at every news bulletin. My constituency was broader, my influence was greater, and I had to consider and account for a much wider range of interests and events. Since I could get attention for my views much more easily as a senator than as a representative, it was not desirable to keep up a drumbeat of speeches and statements. But my views and convictions on Israel were unchanged.

Besides, there were other ways for a senator to exert influence besides making a speech or putting out a press release. Even at the beginning of my senatorial career, and certainly later on as I became more of a Senate insider, it was frequently more effective for me merely to pick up the phone and speak to someone privately on some point of policy than to make a speech about it. State Department officials, ambassadors, UN delegates, and even, informally, officials of foreign governments were ready and willing to listen to the comments of a U.S. senator. I gradually became recognized as an independent and relatively objective thinker on Israel and the Middle East.

Parallel to my view that it was — and is — in the U.S. national interest to aid Israel was my firm determination that if it had ever come to a choice — and it never did — my responsibilities as a U.S. senator would have had to outweigh my sympathies as a friend of Israel. During one of my early trips to Israel I had the opportunity to make this point clear to the Israeli government. I had an appointment to see Walter Eytan, the director-general of Israel's foreign office, and when I arrived Walter was talking in English with three or four of his assistants. As they continued their conversation I realized they were discussing Israeli defense matters that I, as a foreigner, should not have been privy to.

"Walter," I said, interrupting them, "I'd like you to know that notwithstanding my devotion to Israel's security I am an American senator and I do not wish to hear any of Israel's secrets or anything that might become a secret. I have to make it clear that in the event of any conflict between my country and Israel, which Heaven forbid, I would feel it my duty to reveal anything that I know which is of significance to my country. I do not wish to have any weight upon me of information that I have no business to know."

Eytan and his associates seemed to be startled. They had apparently taken for granted that they could talk about confidential matters in my presence. Eytan responded characteristically that he felt exactly the same way about his country; he apologized for not having considered my presence in those terms and assured me that the mistake would never be repeated. The story must have been told to other Israeli officials, because after that, in all my conversations with Israeli leaders, the problem never recurred.

Although the Israelis never discussed secrets in front of me again, the possibility that they might forget my prime loyalty was never far from my mind. On one occasion, a few years after the incident in Eytan's office, I was talking to Foreign Minister Golda Meir in Tel Aviv. The conversation was a bit tense — I think we had been discussing the Suez war — and after some remark of mine Mrs. Meir said, teasingly, "Oh, Jack, you're talking just like an American." Peter Lakeland, my foreign-policy aide, was with me, and he remembers that I bristled at that and said, "Madame Foreign Minister, I *am* an American and I hope you'll always remember that." In retrospect, I do not believe Mrs. Meir had meant that I, as a Jew, should be expressing anything other than a U.S. opinion; but I was obviously determined that the Israelis always deal with me as a U.S. senator.

On occasion, I have disagreed with the Israeli government and some of the Jewish organizations in the United States. Sometimes we have differed on policy — such as my public support of the Eisenhower stand on Suez — and sometimes on tactics. Delegations of American Jewish leaders sometimes urged me to take a specific public position and then criticized me when I decided I could be more effective working without publicity, in the Senate or with administration officials. That is what happened in 1974 on the Jackson-Vanik Trade Act amendment, which barred most-favored-nation trade status to countries such as the Soviet Union that put unreasonable restrictions on the emigration of their nationals.

The original form of the Jackson-Vanik amendment, which a number of my friends wanted me to support, would have required all countries to list the religion of their emigrants so the United States could determine whether Jews were being allowed to leave freely. This would have been thoroughly counterproductive, because some countries, such as Iraq, were letting Jews out quietly and could not have done so if they had had to acknowledge the fact officially. I worked to change the wording of this amendment so I could support it, but some supporters of Jewish emigration from the Soviet Union criticized me for not taking the amendment as it stood. Then we got into a complicated negotiation with the USSR, which is detailed in Chapter 26.

A wide range of Jewish organizations in the United States concern themselves with government policy on Israel. The most important in the early days were the Zionist Organization of America, which sent funds and immigrants to help Israel get started, and the American Jewish Congress and the American Jewish Committee, which were also active in the civil rights struggles of the 1950s and 1960s. Educational, charitable, and service organizations such as Hadassah and B'nai B'rith and the National Council of Jewish Women also make their views known publicly, and, since their memberships are large and politically aware, they are listened to.

The American Israel Public Affairs Committee (AIPAC) is a registered lobbying organization. For many years it was under the direction of Isaiah "Si" Kenen, who won the confidence of members of Congress because he operated dependably and responsibly, always on the basis of facts. He never approached a member of either house before carefully evaluating the significance of his suggestions to the individual congressman and his district, or senator and his state, and he knew the states and districts well enough to make intelligent judgments consistently. In 1951, when I was in the House, Kenen and I worked closely together in obtaining for Israel a significant grant of economic aid from the United States. It was the first U.S. economic aid for Israel.

That 1951 effort illustrated how Congress works, and it explains the enduring support for Israel among members of Congress. After a bill to grant Israel $150 million in aid had been introduced in both the House of Representatives and the Senate, I wrote a bipartisan congressional "declaration" favoring aid to Israel and citing the fact that Israel had absorbed hundreds of thousands of displaced persons from Europe. The statement went on to say that the aid would help Israel become a "military, economic, and ideological bastion for the free world in the Middle East."

Veteran Representative Manny Celler helped me circulate the declaration and 155 members of the House signed it. Nevertheless, the reaction of the House Foreign Affairs Committee, on which I was serving, was in doubt. The committee was considering a Mutual Security Assistance bill, which earmarked $125 million for the Middle East, including a $50 million contribution to the UN Relief and Works Agency to help care for the Arab Palestinian refugees. That bill provided Israel only about $13 million in technical assistance.

We therefore planned to offer the larger Israel aid bill as an amendment to the MSA legislation. The night before the committee was to take up the appropriate section of the MSA bill, Si Kenen and I dined at Hammel's Restaurant in Washington. We were both concerned that the committee would quickly vote down the ambitious $150 million aid-to-Israel proposal and that it then would become difficult to offer a reasonable amount later. So Si and I came up with the idea of an amendment for $50 million specifically labeled as aid for the Jewish refugees; that would balance the $50 million that was going to be granted for the Arab refugees and it sounded like a reasonable proposal the committee might accept. But I was obviously not the person to introduce it. So the next day, before the committee meeting, I suggested to Representative Walter Judd of Minnesota that he put in such an amendment after the higher ones were defeated. Judd was noted as a leading figure in the China Lobby, but his admiration for and devotion to Israel were also strong, and he agreed to help.

So after amendments to grant Israel $150 million and then $125 million were voted down, Judd, to the surprise of almost everybody but me (and Christian Herter of Massachusetts, who cosponsored Judd's amendment), suggested adding just $50 million for Israel to the MSA bill and earmarking it for economic aid for the Jewish refugees.

That was the crucial moment. If the committee did not add this item to the MSA bill, aid for Israel would have no chance on the floor of the House later. Many members were unsure that Israel would survive. They seemed willing to provide aid for Israel's security, for they recognized the heroic struggle that Israel had put up in its own defense. But they felt that aid for resettlement and development would have to come from private sources and they did not know if that would be forthcoming. If it were not, any aid the U.S. government provided might be wasted — if Israel, then only three years old, could not make it as a state.

Most of the committee members came from districts with few Jewish families, but I asked them to consider those few. "Isn't it a fact," I said, "that each of those Jewish families would give their last dollar to preserve Israel, and isn't that the surest guarantee that Israel will last and survive — with the help of the absolute and unqualified support of the Jewish people of the United States?"

The silence that greeted my question was an acknowledgment that I was correct. Even those members who had only five or six Jewish families in their district knew that American Jews would not let Israel die. This might not have been the final, convincing argument, but the Judd amendment was approved, and Israel received for the next fiscal year a total grant of about $65 million (the $50 million for the refugees and the rest from the general fund for the area for technical assistance).

I have also worked with a number of distinguished individuals instrumental in galvanizing public opinion and working for harmony in the relations between Israel and the United States. Among these was Rabbi Arthur Hertzberg of Englewood, New Jersey, a most enlightened, erudite, and able statesman-rabbi who for six years headed the American Jewish Congress. Hertzberg's strength lay not only in his understanding of Judaism but in his ability to discuss Israel rationally and persuasively with Americans who are not so passionately devoted to its cause as he. Another figure was former Supreme Court Justice Arthur Goldberg, who was appointed ambassador to the United Nations by President Johnson and served in that post during the very difficult period of the Six-Day War in 1967. Justice Goldberg remained true to himself while skillfully and objectively sustaining the U.S. position on Israel in the United Nations; it was an extraordinary achievement that won the admiration and respect of all sides.

Two other people of outstanding importance in regard to U.S.–

Israel relations are Max Fisher of Detroit and, of course, former Secretary of State Henry Kissinger. Kissinger himself was a refugee from the Holocaust, and he is deeply grounded in the history, the philosophy, the sensitivity, the passion for justice, and the tradition of independent thought of the Jewish people. It is these qualities, as well as his intellectual brilliance, that gained him such high repute.

Max Fisher, a Detroit civic and business leader, is perhaps the single most important lay person in the American Jewish community; he is certainly the most successful fund raiser for Israel. He has held the highest offices in key organizations active in U.S.–Israel relations, including the chairmanship of the board of governors of the Jewish Agency, which disburses most of the private money raised in the United States for settlement and development in Israel. Max Fisher is a Republican, and during the administration of Presidents Nixon and Ford he had a greater influence regarding Israel than any other American not in public office. His intercessions have always been made with an eye to the highest national interest of the United States, which he, too, feels is so often parallel to the interest of Israel. I met him years ago when I went to speak to a fund-raising gathering in Detroit, and we have been friends ever since.

Soon after the Middle East situation settled down in 1957, the Arab League intensified its boycott of Israel, a policy that included blacklisting U.S. firms that did business with Israel or even employed Jewish managers. This had begun several years earlier. When I was a member of the House I brought to the attention of the State Department several complaints from Jewish firms whose contracts with Saudi Arabian importers had been canceled suddenly as a result of the boycott decree. The Saudis admitted they were boycotting Israel, a stance with which we could not quarrel because legally a state of war still existed, but they denied they discriminated against U.S. firms with Jewish directors. As a senator from New York, I was especially outraged by the fact that Jewish construction workers from the United States could not get jobs on U.S. Army construction projects in Saudi Arabia, since the Saudis refused to issue visas to Jews. New York State's Fair Employment Practices Act forbade discrimination in the recruitment of workers, so the army engineers and American construction companies seeking workers for Saudi Arabia simply stopped hiring in New York altogether when they found that Jewish employees could not be sent to that country. Therefore the whole state of New York was being discriminated against.

In 1957, at Saudi insistence, the United States renewed an agreement not to assign airmen of the Jewish faith to the U.S. Air Force base at Dhahran. The administration was so eager to keep the base and so pleased that Saudi Arabia was breaking out of the Nasser sphere of influence that it was willing to make a mockery of American principles. In speeches and in exchanges of letters with the State Department, I repeatedly urged the government to correct the situation.

At one point the State Department wrote me that they had "expressed their concern" to the Saudis and that the Saudis had explained "that their regulations were not intended to discriminate against citizens of another country on the basis of religion, but were related to the tension deriving from the Arab-Israel dispute. . . . The Department will continue to take every appropriate opportunity to emphasize the continuing concern of the U.S. over the existence of these restrictions." In my reply, which I made public, I asserted that to allow such discrimination was a "grave retreat from the highest American traditions and principles. It is an intolerable situation." I wrote that I did not get the impression from the department's letter that they would make a determined and continuous effort to undo those injustices. The State Department, I said, "should be taking much firmer steps than apparently are being taken or contemplated." To that, Assistant Secretary Robert C. Hill promised that the department would continue pressing the Saudis and pointed out that "Saudi Arabia has given and is giving us important support to help combat the menace of international Communism." On that point, of course, he was in effect probably correct, which was why the issue was so difficult for me.

In 1959, as the blacklists became more onerous, Senator Wayne Morse and I tried to amend the Mutual Security Act to prohibit assistance to any country discriminating against Americans by race or religion. We failed to enact such a prohibition, but we did get into the Mutual Security Appropriations Act the statement that such discrimination was "repugnant" to our principles. It was not a binding law, but it gave the President the authority to apply it if he wished, in negotiating aid.

For about two years after the 1957 "compromise," Nasser had allowed Israeli cargoes — though not Israeli ships — through the Suez Canal. Then he started blockading Israel's cargoes, too. The UN Emergency Force remained in the Sinai, so Israel could use her port at Elath, and the Israel-Egypt border was more or less protected. But after Syria joined Egypt to form the United Arab Republic, Israel's border with Syria was violated by new guerrilla raids and by Syrian artillery firing from the Golan Heights on Israeli settlements around the Sea of Galilee. A series of coups in the Arab countries tended to unify the Arab world against Israel. Even Jordan, which in the late 1950s seemed

to be ready to make peace with Israel, joined with the other Arab countries to block Israel's development of the Jordan River. Nasser's propaganda kept the Palestine refugees in a high state of excitement, and
the Arab states blocked resettlement efforts, preferring to keep the refugee issue open as a grievance against Israel. All the while, the Soviet
Union continued to send arms to the Arab states.

In the early 1960s I proposed — several times — that the United
States, Britain, and France join in a mutual defense treaty with Israel.
I protested the presence in Egypt of German ex-Nazi scientists who
were helping Nasser to develop advanced weapons. Repeatedly, I urged
the administration to redress the military balance by allowing Israel
to purchase more arms in the United States. In 1963 Senator Ernest
Gruening of Alaska and I managed to get through the Senate a Foreign
Aid Act amendment that authorized the President to cut off U.S. aid
to any country committing or preparing aggression against any other
recipient of U.S. aid. It passed the House, too, but it was not enforced:
Despite Nasser's clear preparations for war against Israel the United
States continued to send the United Arab Republic millions of dollars
worth of food aid and other financial assistance.

By 1966, a full-fledged arms race was under way in the Middle
East and the border violence was escalating. Gruening and I put
through another such amendment, which had also been approved by
the House, this time naming the United Arab Republic. But no action
against Nasser was taken. By then, the U.S. government was too busy
with Vietnam to develop a strong policy for the Middle East.

In 1967, the years of appeasing Nasser and his allies — on the
canal, on the boycott, on the border raids, and on other violations of
international law and UN decisions — finally bore their bitter fruit. In
the middle of May 1967, Egyptian and Syrian troops massed on Israel's
borders. On May 18, Nasser demanded that the UN Emergency Force
be withdrawn from the Sinai, and UN Secretary-General U Thant
quickly complied — a decision that was unwise and precipitate. Four
days later Nasser announced that the Gulf of Aqaba was closed to
Israeli shipping and to all ships bound to or from Elath. Then the
Egyptian president called for a "holy war" against Israel and signed a
mutual defense pact with Jordan and Iraq. (He already had one with
Syria.)

Thus, in a matter of days, all the pledges that had induced Israel
to withdraw from the Sinai in 1957 had been violated, and it was up
to the United States to face the moral responsibilities assumed at that
time. Since I had played a part in eliciting those pledges and had urged
Israel to accept them and withdraw, I felt a personal responsibility as

well. With a heavy heart, but determined to do everything I could to prevent the approaching war and help save Israel from destruction, I plunged into an intense and frantic period of activity.

I was not yet a member of the Foreign Relations Committee, but as I was already recognized as one of the Senate's authorities on Israel, I was invited to join the committee's meetings on the crisis. Secretary of State Dean Rusk and other officials of his department met with us repeatedly, with the conferences sometimes continuing almost around the clock. In speeches on the floor of the Senate, I and other senators criticized U Thant for pulling out the UNEF; I called for a Security Council meeting to override his decision, and I reminded the Senate several times of the series of pledges made to Israel ten years earlier. I was gratified to hear President Lyndon Johnson reiterate U.S. policy by declaring that the Gulf of Aqaba was an international waterway and that "a blockade of Israeli shipping is illegal."

Within the Senate and in the upper levels of the Johnson Administration there was near unanimous agreement that Nasser's actions were illegal and dangerous and that the United States had to do something about them. Our main worry was that if something was not done quickly Israel would be forced to take military action, which would brand her as an aggressor. "It is constantly being asserted [in the United Nations]," I pointed out to the Senate, "that if Israel acts to ensure its survival by launching hostilities, it would be the aggressor. No account whatever is taken of the closing of the Strait of Tiran, which could strangle Israel. . . . Is it aggression to strangle a nation, or is it aggression only if you fire a shot?" Senator Stuart Symington of Missouri, who had the floor and to whom I was addressing my rhetorical question, agreed. "The longer this latest move is allowed to continue," he replied, "the greater the possibility of Nasser achieving his goal. . . . If this status quo continues hour after hour, day after day, possibly week after week, then he will be able to portray any resistance to this closing as aggression on the part of the state of Israel."

The plan that emerged was that the United States and its NATO allies should form an international convoy to sail through the Strait of Tiran to Elath. Egypt would not dare to fire on such a convoy; the blockade would be broken and Israel would not have to start a shooting war. President Johnson was willing to send U.S. Navy ships with such a convoy, but he dared not act unilaterally because the United States was already so heavily involved in Vietnam. I remember the President's messages to the committee pleading for "just one ship from the British or the Dutch to go with us to force the Strait of Tiran." But our NATO allies declined to help. Because of the war in Vietnam, most of them lacked confidence in U.S. leadership and feared that by joining us they might get involved in a similarly frustrating conflict. No ships were sent to Aqaba. As we could not save Israel, Israel had to save herself: On June 5 the Six-Day War began.

I could not criticize Israel for firing the first shot in that war. A large country can wait until it is actually invaded before fighting back; a small and vulnerable country like Israel could be overrun in days by a major invasion. Besides, as Senator Symington and I pointed out, the 1967 war really began when Nasser went back on his promises and illegally closed the Gulf of Aqaba and denied Israel the use of Elath.

Israel captured a vast amount of territory from the Arabs in the Six-Day War — including strategic Sharm el Sheik, all of the Sinai up to the Suez Canal, the Gaza Strip, the old city of Jerusalem, and the West Bank of the Jordan River — and the Israelis intended to hold on to it to protect their vulnerable borders. The Soviet Union mounted a great effort in the United Nations to condemn Israel as an aggressor and to demand that she withdraw immediately from all the occupied land. Throughout that long summer and fall I was on the phone constantly — to Arthur Goldberg at the United Nations, to the State Department, to Jewish organizations, to Israel's ambassador, and to every other ambassador of any UN member country I knew — to help the United States defeat the Soviet campaign. In November, after dozens of debates and draft resolutions and votes in both the General Assembly and the Security Council, the Soviets were defeated and a British resolution was adopted unanimously by the Security Council.

This was the historic Resolution 242, which calls on Israel to withdraw its armed forces "from territories occupied in the recent conflict" and states that the Arabs must simultaneously recognize Israel and acknowledge its "territorial integrity . . . and political independence and right to live in peace within secure and recognized boundaries." It also calls for free navigation through the Suez Canal and the Gulf of Aqaba and for a settlement of the refugee problem. Resolution 242 still expresses the fundamental requirements for a comprehensive Middle East peace — but among the Arab states only Egypt has really accepted it, and that did not happen for more than a decade.

The Six-Day War made profound changes in the politics of the Middle East. France had supported Israel with aid and arms — including fighter planes — since the Suez war, but shortly after the 1967 fighting ended, French President Charles De Gaulle declared that "France condemns the opening of hostilities by Israel." De Gaulle blamed the Mideast conflict on the war in Vietnam, and indirectly on U.S. policies there, and he used that as an excuse to cut off all further military supply to Israel. That put an even greater burden on the United States, and particularly on Israel's friends in Congress, to provide Israel with the military hardware it needed to defend itself. Fortunately, Israel's lightning victory in 1967 enhanced overnight the U.S. public's image of Israel. The Israelis were seen as heroes, as the supermen of the Middle East, and as reliable and effective allies; this view of the Jewish state made our task much easier in the years to come.

Frustrated by their failure to eliminate Israel in war, and unwilling to negotiate with Israel or to recognize her right to exist, as Resolution 242 required, the Arab states encouraged extremist Palestinians to embark on a campaign of bombings, hijackings, and terror. Travelers to Israel were gunned down, planes blown up in the air, Olympic athletes held hostage and killed in Munich. One of my own foreign-policy assistants, Hal Rosenthal, was killed in a terrorist attack on tourists standing in line in Istanbul for a plane to Tel Aviv.

Thereafter, I redoubled my efforts to find some way to resettle the Arab refugees, whose homeless plight — so much due to the unwillingness of their neighboring Arab brethren to accept them — helped to inspire terrorism and to cause wars.

In 1968, with the Carnegie Endowment for International Peace and its devoted and wise president, Joseph E. Johnson, I organized and raised much of the money for the Middle East Commission, which attempted to devise economic development plans that could eventually integrate Israel and the Arab refugees into the Middle East. The idea was to develop separate but parallel and compatible projects for the Israelis and the Arabs without trying to join them at first, but of course aiming at ultimate coordination. Senator Edward Kennedy was my partner in organizing the commission, and we enlisted a stellar international membership, including Herman Abs, Eugene Black, Reginald Maudling, Gunnar Myrdal, Lester Pearson, Sir Eric Roll, and Sir Eric Wyndham White. The commission operated under the Carnegie Endowment, and it wrote some good reports on development possibilities for Jordan and the West Bank. But a new president of the Carnegie Endowment, Thomas L. Hughes, succeeded Johnson; he did not favor the commission and in 1975 he let it lapse by failing to support it.

At about the same time, I began developing contacts with Arab leaders in the Middle East and their ambassadors in Washington and at the United Nations. As early as 1962, during one of my visits to Israel, U.S. Ambassador William B. Macomber, Jr., had arranged for me a very unusual side trip to confer with him in East Jerusalem. I passed through the Mandelbaum Gate in divided Jerusalem and spent several hours in Jordan with the ambassador. The Mandelbaum Gate was the only place one could cross the no man's land between the Israeli and Jordanian sectors, but generally the traffic was all the other way: The Jordanians normally permitted no one to enter their country from Israel — which they were boycotting and refusing to recognize. Later, I got to know Jordan's King Hussein; he came to the United States for medical check-ups and I had several visits with him at the U.S. Army's Walter Reed Hospital, in Washington.

After the Six-Day War, Marian and I began to invite some Arab diplomats to our homes in New York and Washington, and other Arab ambassadors began to call on me. Through their good offices, I was enabled to visit Egypt, Syria, and Saudi Arabia in the 1970s, and accompanied by the U.S. ambassador in each country, I had long talks with the heads of state and foreign ministers of those countries. I could only do this and preserve my usefulness because, while I was already recognized as a firm friend of Israel and its leaders, I was known as a U.S. senator who retained his objectivity.

I have made it my business over the years to get to know well the important leaders of Israel. In my estimation, David Ben-Gurion remains the most outstanding leader and Golda Meir the most distinctive character. Ben-Gurion was a man of contrasts, a zealot devoted to the Zionist cause. He never fully understood why every Jew in the world would not want to migrate to Israel. Every time I saw him he would ask, "Why don't the Jews from the United States settle in Israel? Israel needs them; they have no business remaining in the Diaspora."

On the other hand — and this may surprise some people — the cofounder of the Jewish state was not all that strict about the orthodox rituals of the Jewish faith. In December 1962 Marian and I took our family to Israel to celebrate our son Joshua's bar mitzvah there. During our stay, Ben-Gurion invited us to visit him at his country home at Sde Boker, an agricultural kibbutz in the Negev. The kibbutz was exposed to Fedayeen raids; we noted when we got there that a tractor driver plowing a field kept a submachine gun handy beside him on the seat.

We had brought with us a friend from New York, a young man, very orthodox, very observant of the Jewish dietary laws of *kashruth*. He and Marian and I and our three children were eating at a large common table in the mess hall with about twenty members of the kibbutz, including Prime Minister and Mrs. Ben-Gurion. Hamburgers were served, and our orthodox friend apparently felt that in the kibbutz of the prime minister of Israel the food must be kosher. We were well into the meal, all of us happily eating and talking and having a wonderful time, when Marian, thinking of our friend, asked Mrs. Ben-Gurion about the food: "I assume, Mrs. Ben-Gurion, that all of this is kosher?" And the wife of the prime minister replied, "Kosher, smosher, what difference does it make?" Our young friend heard that, froze in the middle of a bite on his hamburger, then leaped from the table and disappeared. We did not see him again until he quietly rejoined us at the airstrip as we were about to depart that evening.

In the handling of Israel's external affairs, and particularly in relations with the United States, Golda Meir surpassed all her colleagues. Her directness, her vigor, her candor, and her single-minded devotion to the main issue at hand were tremendously effective with Americans of all parties and at all levels.

Although I met with Mrs. Meir on several visits to Israel, I remember best an urgent trip she made to Washington at a time of crisis for Israel in the early 1970s. Senator Ribicoff and I, with the majority and minority leaders, Senators Mike Mansfield and Hugh Scott, invited all our colleagues to meet with Prime Minister Meir on the morning of her arrival. More than half the Senate attended the gathering in S.207, the Senate reception room — a remarkable turnout on short notice. Golda Meir sat down, plunked her pocketbook on the table beside her, took out her ever-present package of U.S. cigarettes — she was a chain smoker — and lit up. Then she said, "We are in terrible trouble. We need your help. We need it now. Any questions?" There were lots of questions, and she answered every one in a straightforward, colloquial, and folksy way. She managed to transform that international-crisis meeting with half the U.S. Senate into something that felt more like a family discussion around a kitchen table. Later she also met with President Nixon and probably handled him as she had handled us.

*　*　*

Early in 1979 (after the Camp David accord), when negotiations between Israel and Egypt were stalled at a very delicate stage, I dipped into the reservoir of good will that I had accumulated within the U.S. Jewish community and made an effort to nudge the talks forward. Prime Minister Menachem Begin was in Washington, and the U.S. had just made a proposal designed to eliminate a last-minute snag in the talks. On a snowy Sunday night President Carter called to the White House a few congressional "leaders," including Senators Jackson, Ribicoff, Stone, and myself, and Representative Sidney Yates of Illinois. The President explained the situation to us and asked us to see if the U.S. Jewish leaders might be able to persuade Israel to agree to this final step.

It was clear to me that we were on the verge of a historic peace settlement. From the White House I rushed back to my apartment in Washington and started telephoning all the top Jewish leaders of the United States. I explained that I was not trying to make a judgment of what would or would not jeopardize Israel's security; I was putting up a standard against which to test how serious that jeopardy would have to be to warrant forfeiting the treaty. I told the U.S. Jewish leaders that Israel and Egypt were very close to signing an agreement, that Israel had to make the final decision, and that I thought that would be it — there would not be another chance. Whatever may be the deficiencies of this agreement, I said, if Israel could sign it without believing that she was absolutely undermining her own security, then every argument of policy respecting Israel's standing with the Congress and the American people dictated acceptance and signing. "This is the moment of truth," I said. "I call you because I hope you will, in every way that your organization has open to it, ask your members and those affiliated with you to urge the approval by Israel of this agreement and to urge those you work with and help in Israel to urge their government to do that."

Every one of the leaders I called, even those I did not know very well, promised to help. They all understood the immediacy of it. And I believe that as soon as we hung up they picked their phones up again and starting calling their people. I am sure they did everything they could and that the message reached the Israeli government loud and clear. A few days later, Israel's cabinet agreed to the final point and the historic peace treaty between Israel and Egypt was signed.

SIXTEEN

The Nation's Health
versus the Nation's Politics

My critics on occasion sought to write me off as a "phony" liberal, a politician pandering to the New York electorate to win votes. The charge was leveled against me by Senator Russell of Georgia for my advocacy of civil rights laws while he was the Senate's powerhouse. Even friends in the heat of debate sometimes made or implied that charge. Why?

These critics saw me as a Republican, formerly a New York trial and corporation lawyer, sophisticated, hardheaded about money and taxes, dedicated to the preservation of free enterprise, and dealing on equal and comfortable terms with leading bankers and business executives — and they wondered how I could simultaneously work so hard for the oppressed and the depressed and the people who must labor for a living, and for the people who *want* to work but cannot find a job. These two sides of my public personality may have appeared contradictory, and so my detractors said that my liberal concerns were a sham.

But my personal commitment is rooted in my boyhood on the Lower East Side of Manhattan, and it has lived with me all these years; that commitment and my belief in a world rule of law to replace the rule of force were my reasons for being in public life. I escaped from life on the Lower East Side because of Ben and luck and my own efforts, but I cannot forget those who could not or did not escape soon enough. It is not altruism that has motivated me, but the call for social and economic justice for those still trapped in the figurative and literal ghettos of today. My work in their behalf was the price of admission to the world that I am privileged to live in and it made my life compatible with my conscience.

One of the basic problems for the underprivileged is the issue of health. Almost everyone around me in the Lower East Side ghetto was concerned with health — and the lack of it. I listened to stories about my brother's primitive lung operation. I watched from a back window across a garbage-filled alleyway while a poor woman, stretched out on a wooden table, suffered a clandestine abortion. I saw the endless waiting and often grudging treatment dispensed in the charity wards of the ghetto hospitals of those days; and I was a witness to my father's early death caused by illness and overwork. Like others around me, I venerated our own local doctor, Michael Katz, and for a while I wanted to become a doctor too. I chose another path, but I feel I have helped a much greater number of the sick poor and near-poor by my legislative activities on health than I could have if I had gone into medicine.

In 1959, two years after I entered the Senate, I was appointed to the Labor and Public Welfare Committee, now called the Labor and Human Resources Committee, and I served on it for the rest of my Senate career. (In 1979 I gave up my post as ranking minority member to assume that position on the Senate Foreign Relations Committee.) As a member of the Labor and Human Resources Committee and its subcommittees on health and alcoholism and narcotics, I helped to get enacted almost every piece of health legislation to pass the Senate over those twenty years. I tried to push Congress toward greater financial commitment to health research and to the recruitment and training of doctors, nurses, and other health personnel. My legislative drafting included laws establishing community health centers and health maintenance organizations, safeguarding workers exposed to industrial health hazards, and regulating clinical testing.

But the single most important health challenge that has faced our nation is the need to provide reasonably equal medical care for all our people without regard to any particular individual's ability to pay. Although much progress has been made, the health care that any individual American receives, and his life expectancy, are still too largely determined by his financial capacity.

Furthermore, very little is done in preventive health care: Our health-care system still concentrates on curing people who get sick rather than on helping them to stay healthy in the first place. There is also a great inequity in the location of medical skills and facilities. On fashionable streets such as Park Avenue and Fifth Avenue in New York, or Lake Shore Drive in Chicago, we find far more doctors than are needed, and they are backed up by a corresponding concentration of health facilities and allied personnel. But in many less-settled areas of the country — and in poor neighborhoods in larger cities — there is neither adequate personnel nor often even equipment to provide a nondiscriminatory standard of health care for the people. As a nation we spend $245 billion a year for health care, and at that price we ought to do it right. A comprehensive national health-care system would not cost us much more than that, and even if it did, we would be repaid many times over in the work effectiveness and the satisfaction of living of our people and in reduced welfare costs and dependency.

My first attempt to legislate a national health-insurance system had been buried in committee in 1949 when I was still in the House of Representatives; the Truman Administration's Ewing Plan for compulsory health insurance had met the same fate. Both plans were politically premature: They tried to guarantee medical care to the entire U.S. population at one legislative stroke, and neither the public nor the health profession was ready for such an ambitious departure. As all such bills continued to fail in Congress, proponents of national health care tried to work out a piecemeal approach that would cover one segment of the population at a time. It seemed clear that the first group to be protected should be the elderly. Older people could not easily buy private health insurance, many of them suffered from chronic or long-term illnesses, and those living on pensions and fixed incomes did not have the money to pay their doctors' bills.

By the time I entered the Senate, some liberal Democrats were proposing that the Social Security system's Old Age and Survivors' Insurance (OASI) pay the hospital bills of retired people on Social Security. With the support of labor unions and liberal groups, Democratic Representative Aime J. Forand of Rhode Island repeatedly sponsored bills to that effect; President Eisenhower and the American Medical Association and most Republicans opposed Forand's plan. I opposed it too: It was compulsory, to be financed by an increase in the Social Security tax; and it provided for direct federal payments to hospitals and doctors, an arrangement that was damaging to the patient-doctor relationship and anathema to the AMA as "socialized medicine" — and that was therefore likely to abort any national health-insurance scheme before it could get off the ground.

In 1960, with a presidential election in the offing, health care for the aged became a partisan political issue. Unfortunately, my Senate debate on the issue with Senator John F. Kennedy, who had just been nominated as the Democratic candidate for the presidency, resulted in the defeat of both his national health-insurance proposal and mine, and the problem that both of us wanted to deal with was left unsolved. The entire cause of a national health program may have been set back for some years by that political confrontation alone. On the other hand, the events of that session showed the majority of my party that in order to compete realistically for political support Republicans had to endorse feasible and progressive programs — a Republican enlightenment that was later translated into new initiatives on housing and education. Health care, however, fell victim to electoral politics.

The politicking on health began in January when Senator Kennedy, running hard for the nomination, introduced in the Senate his own version of the Forand bill — hospitalization for the aged paid for by Social Security. The House Ways and Means Committee, however, under the conservative chairmanship of Representative Wilbur Mills of Arkansas, refused to endorse the Forand bill. The moment was perfect for a Republican initiative — but the Eisenhower Administration was not up to it. The President stated that he was opposed to the kind of compulsory health insurance proposed by Kennedy and Forand — he called it a step toward socialized medicine — but his administration had not come up with any realistic alternative.

I believed that it was essential to block the Forand proposal. If enacted, it would have immediately placed a tremendous burden on the nation's hospitals, possibly causing them to break down under the increased patient load. What we needed, I thought, was to provide more health care for elderly citizens without forcing them to inundate the hospitals to get it, and that meant more ambulatory and preventive care. So in April 1960, with seven other Republican senators, I introduced a Health Insurance for the Aged Act. My plan, not linked to the Social Security system, provided for federal aid to states that offered health-insurance coverage to all residents aged sixty-five and older; federal and state funds would make up the difference between the cost of health-insurance premiums and what each subscriber could pay. The bill provided not only for hospitalization insurance but for the doctors' visits that could keep subscribers healthy enough to stay out of hospitals if at all possible. No one would have to join and the patients could choose any qualified doctor they pleased.

My bill was in keeping with the Republican principles of federal-state cooperation and the encouragement of private enterprise (the private health-insurance companies that would cover the subscribers). It also avoided the compulsory aspects of the Forand approach, to which Eisenhower was opposed. But the administration did not back my bill. Vice President Nixon, however, who already had the Republican nomination all but sewn up — and who had cosponsored my first health-insurance bill in the House — saw the political realities more clearly; he knew that if the Republicans did not do something on this issue the Democrats would gain the whole initiative.

At one point in the spring of 1960 I went to see Eisenhower to urge him to let Dick Nixon take the lead on this issue, since he was the one who was going to be running on it. Finally, early in May, the administration came out with a bill of its own.

The administration plan was attacked by both Democrats and conservative Republicans; Barry Goldwater called it socialized medicine and liberal Democrats said it was confusing and inefficient. Although it incorporated some of the federal-state features of my bill, the administration plan would not have offered any significant preventive care because it carried a $250 deductible provision: you had to be very sick before you could collect. Furthermore, not everyone over sixty-five was eligible, only those below a certain income level. Nevertheless, I was encouraged by the administration bill because it showed that all sides recognized the need and that significant legislation was obtainable. "Let us work on the basis of the things we agree on — not our differences," I said in a speech that spring. "We are agreed that health care for the older citizen is essential, that its solution calls for federal assistance because most persons in this age group cannot meet medical costs. . . . I want a law, not a political issue, and I deeply believe that this is the way to get it."

What we got, however, was a political issue. My bill, sponsored only by Republicans, was not scheduled for hearings in the Democratic-controlled Senate. The House Ways and Means Committee, having killed the liberal Democrats' Forand bill, turned down the administration's plan too, and produced instead a very modest alternate plan geared to help only those aged poor who would become completely indigent if they had to pay their medical bills. It was not in any sense a substitute for a broad health-care program.

The House passed that inadequate measure and sent it to the Senate just as Congress was about to recess for the political conventions; the Senate was to consider the matter in a special session to be held after the conventions, when we knew the atmosphere would be even more partisan.

When we returned to Washington in August, after the Nixon-Lodge and Kennedy-Johnson tickets had been nominated, the battle lines on health care were quickly drawn. The Senate Finance Committee sent to the floor the House bill, amended to include more generous provisions but still offering aid only to those aged people at the bottom level of the economic scale. This satisfied neither Senator Kennedy nor me. Kennedy declared that health care for the aged through Social Security was a vital part of his program for the nation — as it was for his campaign; together with Democratic Senator Clinton P. Anderson of New Mexico, he introduced a floor amendment that revived the significant features of the Forand and Kennedy bills. Vice President

Nixon, not to be outdone on health care, threw his support to a modified version of my bill I then offered as an amendment to the Kennedy-Anderson amendment. Nixon came up behind me one morning on the Senate floor and whispered in my ear, "Jack, I'm going to endorse your bill."

In the long run it was unfortunate that the Republican campaign so quickly became identified with my amendment, because I still believe that Kennedy and the liberal Democrats might ultimately have been persuaded to support my approach. But once it had been endorsed by Nixon, they of course opposed it, and I had to oppose *their* plan.

So, as the issue came to the floor in late August, there were three plans before us: The first was the Senate Committee's version of the House bill, which provided health-care aid only for the needy. The second was the Anderson-Kennedy amendment, providing assistance through a compulsory Social Security payroll tax. And the third was my government-private plan, endorsed by Nixon.

In the debate on my amendment, I emphasized that my plan, financed out of general revenues (insofar as government funds were involved), would require all taxpayers to share in its cost, whereas the Social Security method would put a greater burden on people with lower incomes — as Social Security taxes are taken only from the first tier of an individual's annual earned income. I noted that Anderson himself had recognized that his plan would strain the nation's hospitals, because his amendment postponed benefits until the age of sixty-eight. "Nothing would be more tragic," I said, "than to compel old folks to go on a long waiting list to enter a hospital already subject to overcrowding. We hope to lighten that burden by enabling our older citizens to get preventive care before they fall seriously ill."

My amendment was voted down on a partisan roll call. Every single Democrat, sixty-two of them, voted against it — as did five Republicans. Voting for my amendment were twenty-eight Republicans. I then said that, since both presidential candidates favored strong health plans, our elderly could expect to get one in the next session regardless of what happened in the Senate or in the elections.

With that thought I announced my position on the Anderson amendment: "I have concluded that at this time, under the intensely political circumstances of this brief session — which I would be blind not to see, and so would the American people — I must vote against it." I repeated my critique of its flaws and warned that if it were attached to the committee bill President Eisenhower would probably veto it, and if that happened, an entire package of Social Security improvements and the basic plan for medical assistance to the aged indigent would go down the drain too. I suggested the possibility that we might find "a proper meeting ground" between the Anderson-Kennedy plan and mine, but added that "after looking at the vote on my proposal, I think all the country can see what is happening here. This will be a straight political issue — Democrats against Republicans — with very little chance of anything else happening. I do not wish to be a party to seeing our elder people caught at those swords' points. I do not think it is necessary."

Looking back at that speech with the perspective of twenty years, it seems clear to me that even then I was regretting that such an important issue had been caught up in the political wars, and that I was trying to justify in some way my vote against the Anderson plan. But I had no choice. The Anderson plan of that year *was* inadequate; and the dangers in it that I warned of were real. Whatever its merits, it was clearly not good enough to persuade me to break with my party on an issue on which both presidential candidates had so firmly committed themselves. If I had known that our votes that day would set back the cause of health insurance by a number of years, however (it was five years until a reasonable Medicare proposal was enacted), I might have decided differently, but not even senators can foretell the future.

It was, after all, an exciting and historic moment: A long legislative struggle was about to be decided on an issue that everyone could comprehend and that was being described as the first round in the presidential electoral battle. Kennedy and Johnson were both in the chamber throughout the debate, and crowds of summer tourists were lining up for hours to spend a few minutes in the Senate gallery to see Jack Kennedy sitting in the rear row. Vice President Nixon did not take the presiding officer's chair that day, which he could have done as President of the Senate, but he was present and visible, talking to senators and lining up votes. The press galleries were full and ninety-four of the one hundred senators answered a quorum call after my speech.

In this spotlight's glare, Jack Kennedy rose to answer me. He was anxious to get out of Washington and start his campaign, but he also needed a few legislative victories to give him a boost to the presidency, and the special session so far had not been kind to his proposals. As Kennedy and I looked across the aisle at each other, it was hard to remember that thirteen years earlier we had been sworn in together as freshmen congressmen, both of us veterans, both committed to humane, social legislation like the health-care bills before us. Now he was trying to become President and I was seemingly getting in his way. Politics may make strange bedfellows, but it also makes uncomfortable antagonists.

"I listened," Kennedy said, "with great interest to the speech of the senator from New York, whom I regard as one of the most constructive members of this body. He did state a political truth — that this Congress meets in highly political circumstances. He did suggest it appears that on this issue there may be a party-line vote." And then, looking at me again, he made the kind of bipartisan appeal that we both used to make in the House of Representatives in the old days:

> I believe it would be impossible [Kennedy said], for us to secure the passage of this amendment ... unless we can receive the support of at least five or six of the senators on the other side of the aisle. If the senators on the other side of the aisle vote a straight party vote on this issue, I would say we shall have an uphill fight. ... It may be that the senator from New York is correct. I do not in any sense criticize him. ... If we cannot pass the Anderson amendment, in my judgment, I think it means we are going to have an extremely difficult time passing any progressive legislation in this session of Congress. ... Then I think we should take the matter to the people. ...

A few minutes later I responded to his challenge. "The senator from Massachusetts has appealed for some Republican votes," I said. "But I should like to explain why he faces this difficulty today." I reminded him that on a minimum-wage bill six Republicans had helped him because we were working together on a program in which our ideas were represented. In the present case, I said,

> I happen to think that my health bill is more liberal than the Anderson proposal. ... But now the senator from Massachusetts asks us to endorse the Anderson-Kennedy amendment. I am sorry, but this is not the season for that. ... Unhappily, the senator from Massachusetts cannot ask liberal Republican senators just to "sign here," when their ideas and their views and their deeply held convictions are not reflected in the paper they are asked to sign.

The roll-call vote on the Anderson-Kennedy amendment was climactic. The other Republican liberals were expected to follow my lead, which is why Kennedy had made his appeal to me, but we were not sure what would happen and we knew the vote would be close. As a clerk started calling the names of the senators, Vice President Nixon entered the chamber and came to my desk. He hovered over the tally sheet that I was marking as each senator's vote was recorded, and several times he moved about the chamber, almost as if he were the party whip, talking to Republicans who had not yet voted to make sure they would stay with us and vote nay to the Anderson-Kennedy proposal. As Tom Wicker wrote in a front-page story in the *New York Times* the next day, "the Republican lines held remarkably fast on the politically potent vote. . . . One by one the senators whom the Democrats had sought to lure to support of the Social Security amendment — Senator George D. Aiken of Vermont and Margaret Chase Smith of Maine, for instance — voted 'nay.' " The final tally was fifty-one nays and fourty-four yeas. Nineteen Democrats (mostly Southerners) joined thirty-two Republicans to defeat the Anderson-Kennedy amendment. Only one Republican, Clifford Case of New Jersey, broke ranks to vote for it.

The outcome was seen as a reverse for Kennedy (not that it hurt him in the long run), as he had been identified with the Social Security approach to health care for a long time. But more than Kennedy, more than Nixon, more than me, the real losers that day were the elderly people of the United States, who had to wait another five years for Medicare. The only thing we accomplished was the passage of the main committee bill, which became known as the Kerr-Mills Act, a worthy but totally inadequate program that was to have practically no impact, especially in the regions of the country that needed health care most.

My optimistic belief that health care for the aged would be quickly passed in the following session was not justified. In 1961 President Kennedy asked Congress for a new law based on Social Security, but his administration failed to push hard for it and it never got out of committee. By 1962, however, the administration did launch a major drive for such a program, and this time I went along. I had always seen room for accommodation between the Democrats' Social Security approach and my insistence on using private and nonprofit insurance plans. Certainly the 1960 results indicated that the only way to pass a health-insurance plan for the aged that could lead to health insurance for the entire population was to combine the two methods.

That spring, Senator Anderson and I got together to work out such a compromise. It retained his basic proposals: the financing of medical care for the aged through an increase in the Social Security tax with OASI paying the hospital and medical bills. But it enabled individual patients to pass up the direct federal payments and arrange private health insurance for which the government would reimburse the insurers. That provision, plus an extension of benefits to several million people over sixty-five not covered by Anderson's earlier plans, removed my basic objections to the Social Security approach.

Four other liberal Republican senators (Case of New Jersey, John Sherman Cooper of Kentucky, Kenneth Keating of New York, and

Thomas Kuchel of California) joined me in cosponsoring the Anderson-Javits amendment (to a public welfare bill); all the liberal Democrats in the Senate supported it, and President Kennedy wagered his prestige on the measure. But the AMA lobbying power was tremendous. On July 17, after two weeks of debate, Senator Robert Kerr, Democrat of Oklahoma, moved to table — that is, kill — the Anderson-Javits amendment. In one of the most stunning and significant defeats of the Kennedy Administration, the motion to table was carried — by just four votes (52 to 48). No Republicans beyond the cosponsors joined me in voting against the motion.

During the next two years I kept hammering away at the issue. I was a member of the Senate's Special Committee on Aging, which in 1963 issued reports analyzing the inadequacies of the 1960 Kerr-Mills program. Senator Barry Goldwater was on the committee too, and he filed a minority report supporting the Kerr-Mills Act as sufficient. During the same period I organized and raised funds for a private National Committee on Health Care of the Aging, of which former Secretary of Health, Education and Welfare Arthur Fleming was chairman; the committee reported its findings to President Kennedy in November 1963, just a week before his assassination, and recommended a dual public-private insurance program to cover the greatest part of the total health care needed by older citizens. In 1964 I introduced a new bill incorporating these recommendations. That one, at least, passed the Senate, as part of the Gore-Anderson-Javits amendment to a House bill, but it died in a House-Senate conference.

Our many years of efforts finally bore fruit in the "Medicare" Act of 1965, a direct result of the Republican Party debacle of 1964. The Democrats gained enough seats in Congress to pack key House committees with liberals and thus overwhelm their own conservative wing. President Johnson made health care for the aged his top priority for the 1965 session, and even House Ways and Means Committee Chairman Wilbur Mills listened to the voice of the President and abandoned his long-standing opposition to a meaningful health-insurance plan. Despite the continued opposition of the AMA, Congress passed Medicare, a health plan for the elderly that was much more ambitious and comprehensive than anything we had thought possible just a year or two before.

As enacted, the law established hospitalization insurance through Social Security for almost every citizen over sixty-five, and in addition — and this was the gratifying surprise — an inexpensive, voluntary, supplemental insurance plan to cover doctors' bills and out-of-hospital diagnostic costs, with the voluntary choice of doctor that I had been advocating for so long.

I had relatively little to do with shaping the final form of the 1965 legislation because the Democrats did not need my support. One principle that was important to me did not get into the law: the use of private and nonprofit insurance organizations, such as Blue Cross, to provide the voluntary part of the coverage. (Medicare, even the supplemental part, is administered by the Social Security agency.) Despite what in my view is an imperfection, the act was an outstanding piece of legislation and I voted for it and supported it with enthusiasm.

This process repeated itself many times in my career: I worked hard for a cause, often with very little support or public awareness, and then some outside event or new circumstance — in this case the Democratic election victory of 1964 — lifted the issue to the national consciousness. Thereupon others with a more inside track in the Congress on that issue took over. I confess it would be nice to have more laws with my name on them, but since my party was in the minority through most of my career, that would not have been likely in any case. I do not mind the absence of such memorials. For me, all those committee meetings, all those speeches, all those times that the people seemed not to be listening paid off when a significant piece of legislation was passed. I had helped to articulate a need, and while others got the credit for filling it, as in Medicare, I had done my part to bring it to fruition and I felt fulfilled.

One unexpected result of the Medicare program was a sharp increase in medical costs for all Americans, which led to a revival of interest in a comprehensive system of health insurance to cover us all. President Nixon at first encouraged this idea but later, because of the cost, retreated. In 1971 Senator Edward Kennedy became chairman of the Health Subcommittee of the Labor and Human Resources Committee, and began to introduce a series of new bills to broaden health-insurance coverage, and I was introducing bills for the same general purpose. It then occurred to me that the next step on this still-to-be-traveled road to comprehensive national health care should be to provide special benefits for people on the opposite end of the life cycle from those being helped by Medicare: that is, pregnant women and small children.

In every session between 1976 and 1980, I introduced the National Health Insurance for Mothers and Children Act, which would set up a system like Medicare for all children up to the age of eighteen and for all pregnant women. This "Kiddie Care" bill, which was sponsored in the House by its originator, Congressman James H. Scheuer, a Brooklyn Democrat, would also utilize all the private health-insurance means available. The cost would be relatively low (because children and mothers are generally healthy) and the effort could demonstrate the value of a national health-care scheme and enable us to expand the coverage to other segments of the population as we gained experience administering it. Furthermore, we did not expect that taxpayers could raise serious political objections to a health program for mothers and children.

I believe we will have some kind of national health-insurance plan before the 1980s are too far along (even though at this writing — in 1980 — all such plans have been shelved by the effort to cut the federal budget). Senator Ted Kennedy's 1979 comprehensive health-care proposal included for the first time my plan to use existing private and non-profit health-insurance agencies. And President Carter adopted the idea of "Kiddie Care" as the first step in his administration's approach to national health care.

* * *

My initiatives on health matters often originated with doctors or health organizations who approached me with ideas. But not always. One unusual exception was the legislation that I originated and pushed through to passage to control venereal diseases. Marian and I were on a flight to California one day in the early 1970s, when she noted a newspaper story about the rising incidence of VD among young people. Always independent-minded and not highly enamored of "politicians," she turned to me and said, "Why are you politicians so afraid to touch an unpleasant subject like VD?" I replied, "That may or may not be true of politicians in general, but it is not true of me. I'll look into it." She teased me a bit and warned me that any senator getting up on the floor to talk about VD might be accused behind his back of having an indiscreet personal reason for urging such legislation. But having been challenged, in a sense, I became more determined. Marian and I realized that I was the ideal person to get such legislation started, because I was the ranking minority member of the Senate committee handling health and because few would question my serious interest in the issue.

As soon as I got back to Washington, I started putting together a bill. Many members of Congress were indeed timid about pursuing the subject, but most of them recognized the problem and were willing to go along if they did not have to take the lead role. The administration opposed my bill on the grounds that the Department of Health, Education and Welfare, not Congress, should decide which particular diseases should be attacked. I argued that since the federal government was spending huge sums to combat diseases like cancer, for which no cure had been found, the government should also do something to make sure that the known cures for other diseases were properly applied. In 1972, my law authorizing $62.5 million a year for the detection, control, and treatment of venereal diseases passed the Senate by a vote of 70 to 0, and the House by 386 to 2. As appropriations fluctuated in the years since then we discovered that the incidence of VD, especially in the young, always goes down when the federal programs are intensified, and goes up when the budgets are cut, thus demonstrating the need for such targeted campaigns.

Another health related subject on which my family lobbied me successfully was marijuana. In the late 1960s, through my children, I became aware of and alarmed about the widespread use of marijuana among young people. I also noted that many young lives were being ruined by indiscriminate arrests in some states of high-school and college youngsters, some of whom, under barbaric state laws, were sentenced to long prison terms for the use or possession of very small quantities of the drug. Our children were in their teens and they and their friends were close to the situation and very adamant about it. (I have little doubt that my older children smoked now and then — though I had not seen evidence of it — as did many of their contemporaries.)

We had several long discussions about marijuana over dinners and Sunday brunches at home. The children and Marian set out to convince me that to smoke pot was less harmful than to drink a gin martini — which I loved. All three of the children were convinced that marijuana should be decriminalized — that is, that the penalties for smoking or giving away small quantities should be eliminated. (Legalization would be another matter: That would entail making the cultivation and production and commercial sale of marijuana completely legal and I remain opposed to that.) I listened carefully to my children on this issue — they obviously knew more about it than I did; my talks with them prepared me for later Senate debates and also gave me an understanding of the impulses that drove children of good families to violate the law and to use a mood-altering drug that could only be harmful to them.

What intrigued me from the start was the controversy over whether marijuana was addictive. If it were not, it seemed to me there was little reason for drastic punishment. But if it was addictive, if it could lead to a craving for more powerful drugs that could only be satisfied by expensive purchases and in turn by a wasted life or a life of crime, then it seemed to me that penalties would be justified. In 1970 I introduced and got passed legislation that established a National Commission on Marijuana and Drug Abuse. Former Governor Raymond P. Shafer of Pennsylvania was appointed chairman of the commission, on which I also served. Among the other members were Senator Harold Hughes of Iowa, Representatives Tim Lee Carter of Kentucky and Paul G. Rogers of Florida, and several doctors and law-enforcement experts.

The commission made a thorough medical and social evaluation of the uses and effects of marijuana and concluded that it was not addictive and that possession of small quantities, in private, for personal use should not be a criminal offense. (But more recent research has challenged this conclusion.) The commission majority recommended that *public* possession of more than an ounce of marijuana should still be regarded as a crime.

Senator Hughes and I wanted to go further and permit public possession of "some reasonable amount" for personal use; we also recommended that all not-for-profit sales be decriminalized. In 1972 we introduced a bill removing all penalties from the use, possession, and transfer without remuneration of small quantities of marijuana. That made me a hero to my children and their friends but not to Congress, which has not yet passed — or even seriously considered — such a law.

The "drug" problem of alcoholism has also concerned me for a long time. I have always found it difficult to deal with the irrational conduct of people who are drunk. Starting in 1966, following a federal court decision specifying that an alcoholic cannot be punished for public intoxication, I urged legislation to treat alcoholism as an illness (rather than a crime) and to establish research grants for the treatment and prevention of it. Although six million Americans were reported then to be afflicted by alcoholism, no action was taken in Congress until 1968. In that year the U.S. Supreme Court, in the case of *Powell* v. *Texas,* upheld the conviction of an alcoholic for his public drunken behavior, but declared that alcoholism itself was not a crime.

That decision helped. Congress amended the Community Mental Health Centers law to treat alcoholism as an illness and to authorize grants for treatment and rehabilitation. The passage of the appropriations for these grants we owed to a conservative Democrat, John McClellan of Arkansas, the chairman of the Senate Committee on Government Affairs, of which I was also a member. Two years later I teamed up with Senator Harold Hughes of Iowa to pass a comprehensive alcoholism law. Senator Hughes, long before, had been an alcoholic himself and had passed through that phase to become a teetotaler, governor of Iowa, senator, and lay religious leader. He is a very colorful figure. I, as the lawyer of the team, wrote the legislation, but Hughes deserves the credit for giving it the drive that carried it through. The administration opposed the bill, however, and as the final step it proved necessary for me to win President Nixon's signature to the law by persuading the White House that it was sound legislation. The law established a National Institute on Alcohol Abuse and Alcoholism, which now oversees a $600 million program — a major attempt to solve a problem that does tremendous damage to our society.

SEVENTEEN

Endowing the Arts

The effort to improve the physical health of the American people was matched by a simultaneous attempt to nourish their minds and spirits. Two months after the enactment of Medicare in 1965, Congress established the National Foundation on the Arts and Humanities, which represented for me the culmination of a dream — and of another long, uphill struggle. Every time I go to the theater or a concert — which is not as often as I would like — I feel a deep satisfaction at the knowledge that I have helped bring the beauty and inspiration of drama, music, dance, and the visual arts to a widening public and to parts of our country that rarely enjoyed them before.

I grew up with an awareness of music and theater. Even though we were poor on the Lower East Side I was taken occasionally to the Yiddish theater, and all through my childhood I heard tales of Jacob Adler and David Kessler and Boris Thomashefsky, the great Jewish actors. My mother even managed to bring music into our tenement home: Ben learned to play the violin — and stayed with it until it became a fixture in his life; I tried the piano for a short time, but work and study did not permit me to practice enough. When I was in high school, Ben brought us records and a phonograph, and when I was in law school I studied the law cases listening to classical music with those early radio earphones clamped to my head. Saturday-night students' concerts at Carnegie Hall were a highlight of my week.

As an adult I was therefore naturally attracted to people in the worlds of art, theater, and music. My first wife, Marjorie Ringling, was a pianist; Agnes De Mille was — and remains — a close friend; Hollace Shaw, the girl I almost married during World War II, was a singer. And Marian had trained for a career in the theater and was seeking acting parts when I met her. It is sometimes assumed that it was Marian who interested me in the arts, but that is not the whole story. I introduced her to the art and some of the music of the past, and she, in turn, brought me into the contemporary art and theater world for which she had great talents and in which she had many friends who were to help me in the campaign for what became the National Foundation on the Arts and Humanities.

It was in England during the war, however, that I found the prime inspiration for that campaign. Even while the bombs were falling, an organization called the Council for the Encouragement of Music and the Arts (CEMA) was sending theatrical troupes and musicians to aircraft and other defense factories all around the country to entertain the workers. CEMA, which later became the British Arts Council, was funded by the British government, and it made a very significant contribution to British morale in the war. I looked into the British Arts Council when I went to England as a congressman, and I realized that if democratic Britain could support the arts there was no reason to fear state control of the arts, and that the United States could develop a similar program. But there were more pressing problems facing the country, and it was not until a remark by Marian pushed me to it that I became significantly involved.

As I recall, the conversation with Marian took place late in 1948; like the talk that goaded me to do something about venereal-disease legislation, the discussion was airborne. As we looked out over the landscape — I think it was over Utah — Marian remarked that the United States was really very backward in one respect: Here was this great beautiful country of ours, she said, with just about everything in it; but, unlike the older nations, we had no program to aid the arts. And that was true; at that time the United States was almost alone among the developed nations of the world in its lack of funding and support for a national arts establishment. We discussed my observation of the British Arts Council, and I determined then to start the ball rolling and submit a bill.

In 1949 I introduced in the House a bill that would have prepared the way for the establishment of national theater, opera, and ballet companies. Most of my colleagues simply ignored the suggestion — or laughed at it. In the view of most members of the House it was another "artsy" New York idea; at that time the only other senators or representatives interested in doing anything for the arts were my fellow New Yorkers, Representative Emanuel Celler and Senator Herbert Lehman. The House in general was so antipathetic to the arts, and so uninformed about them, that one antediluvian congressman delivered a long speech in which he claimed that modern art was nothing but a vehicle that the Communists had invented to subvert the United States. Modern art, he said, "contains all the 'isms' of depravity, decadence, and destruction."

The resistance in Congress to government support of the arts was a holdover from days when theater, music, and dance, other than folk, were regarded as effete activities that had nothing to do with the more vital and virile concerns of the population. The European nations, by contrast, were still influenced by a tradition under which kings and princes patronized art and music. It was not that support of the arts by the United States had been completely unknown. The Smithsonian Institution was created in 1846; Congress established the Commission of Fine Arts in 1910; President Franklin D. Roosevelt set up a Section of Painting and Sculpture in the Treasury Department; and the State Department was subsidizing overseas tours by U.S. arts groups, to a limited extent. But such efforts were few, and little had been done for the performing arts.

Despite the ingrained opposition to my national theater bill, I plugged away at it. It was not the first priority in my legislative work, but it was a constant interest. I sought out groups and individuals who would help me, and my Washington office became an information center for those people and organizations who were interested. In 1950 I sought the help of the National Music Council, a private organization. "Almost alone among modern nations," I told the group, "the United States gives no government assistance to theater or music. More than forty governments, all smaller and poorer than the United States, are today actively aiding the theater." I pointed out that 90 percent of the U.S. population had never seen a professional theatrical production, and that even in New York City there were less than half as many professional theaters as there had been twenty years earlier. Music, too, I said, "shows equal areas of barrenness" — thousands of musicians are unemployed, thousands of towns and cities in the country lack creditable music performance for the public. I assured my listeners that government subsidy of the arts in a democracy would not bring about government or authoritarian direction, any more than federal aid to education meant centralized control of the classroom.

These ideas had made little progress while I was in the House, and I started immediately to introduce bills to establish a United States Arts Foundation as soon as I arrived in the Senate in 1957. Also, I joined with Senators Hubert Humphrey and Paul Douglas in sponsoring a bill calling for the establishment of a Federal Advisory Council to advise the President on the arts, but not even this modest approach — which would have cost the government virtually nothing — was passed by either House in the Eighty-fifth Congress.

Very slowly, however, Congress was becoming more enlightened — although by today's standards the "victories" we won seem minor indeed. In 1958 Congress donated some federal land near the Potomac

River for a National Cultural Center. No funds were authorized to build the center — that money had to come from private sources within five years — but that 1958 act created what is now the John F. Kennedy Center for the Performing Arts.

Another small step was taken the following year, after Marian called my attention to an archaic tariff law regulating the duty-free import of works of art. Way back in 1927 a court case had arisen from a customs inspector's attempt to charge duties on an abstract sculpture by the Rumanian artist Constantin Brancusi; since the piece, *Bird in Space,* did not look like a bird, the customs officers said it was not art and therefore was subject to import duty as a manufactured article. Brancusi appealed to the U.S. Customs Court, which upheld his insistence that an artist's work does not have to imitate nature to be art. "While some difficulty might be encountered in associating it with a bird," the court said of Brancusi's sculpture, "it is nevertheless pleasing to look at and highly ornamental." Therefore it was art, and entitled to be imported free of duty.

But that landmark legal sanction for abstract art applied only to that one work, and I discovered that the old laws were still on the books. Unless an importer wanted to go to court each time, only art made from traditional materials, and sculpture in "imitation of natural objects ... in their true proportion of length, breadth, and thickness," could be imported duty-free. Artists and museum authorities were therefore delighted when I introduced a bill to amend that old law. I explained to the Senate that collages made of paper and cloth and even manufactured articles, a technique developed by Picasso and Braque in 1921, were still, forty-seven years later, subject to a 20 percent customs duty because they were not made of traditional materials, while paintings by the same artists could be imported duty-free. That regulation and the rule about abstract sculpture "tend to expose us to ridicule in other advanced countries," I said, adding that any revenue lost by changing the rules would be made up by an easier interchange of art between the United States and other countries.

My colleagues were not much interested in this matter one way or the other, but with the aid of the Junior Council of New York's Museum of Modern Art, which Marian enlisted and inspired, we drummed up support from thousands of people who were members of museums all around the country and urged them to write to and call on their senators and congressmen about it. This campaign was very effective and other senators began to call me: "Listen, Javits," they said, "what is that damn arts bill of yours and when is it coming up? I'm being inundated with mail on it from my constituents." After getting some pressure from the Virginia art museum, the late Virginia Senator Harry

F. Byrd, Sr., who was chairman of the Finance Committee and a conservative on financial matters, agreed to incorporate my bill into the tariff amendments of 1959, and it passed in that form. The successful mobilization of the cultural community in behalf of a minor but meaningful piece of legislation was an encouraging practice run for the arts-foundation struggle that lay ahead.

Early in 1961 I introduced a new version of my arts-foundation bill, which included the visual arts as well as the performing arts. The foundation I proposed would have been authorized to make loans and grants to nonprofit professional and educational groups, to help them to put on theater productions, concerts, and art exhibits in places where they would otherwise have been unable to do so. Senator Joseph S. Clark of Pennsylvania, a former mayor of Philadelphia, put in a bill to accomplish the same purposes by means of matching grants to the states, and Senator Hubert Humphrey again introduced a measure to set up an arts advisory council. "Now is the most strategic moment," I told a press conference at Actors' Equity, the actors' trade union, in New York, where I had gone to discuss my bill with the leaders of the union. I was greatly encouraged by the establishment of an arts council in New York State — the first in the nation — under Governor Nelson A. Rockefeller, and by the new President's appreciation of the arts. John F. Kennedy had spoken favorably of an arts establishment during the 1960 campaign, and he had invited writers, artists, and composers to attend his 1961 inauguration — at which Robert Frost recited a poem he had written for the occasion.

In the same mood of optimism I wrote an article for *Art in America* magazine: "The mood is right, the climate appropriate for the final push that will place the United States at last alongside Europe, which long ago . . . acknowledged the fact that the arts represent an essential element of national life." I pointed out that new theaters and cultural facilities were being built all over the United States, reflecting "the ever-growing needs of Americans for creative fulfillment, and the growing awareness that in a free society, cultural pursuits are not a luxury but a necessity." Taking note of the fear that government subsidy might corrupt the artistic climate, I listed some of the world-famous performing groups — such as Britain's Royal Ballet and France's Comédie Française — supported by their governments "without any hint of lower artistic standards." Government support of the arts, I wrote, "is a widely accepted method of stimulating artistic enterprise. . . . Only through the cooperation of both government and private initiative can we give our artistic pursuits the continuity and national outlook they need to serve the artist and the community."

But it was not to be so easy. Despite President Kennedy's support of an arts establishment and the glittering White House dinners for Pablo Casals, Igor Stravinsky, and several Nobel Prize winners, the federal bureaucracy responded but slowly. The Treasury Department, the Bureau of the Budget, and the Department of Health, Education and Welfare all opposed the idea. They recommended to the Senate's Labor and Public Welfare Committee that an advisory council be formed first and that the council should then decide how the government should support the arts. Even that modest idea was too radical for the House of Representatives. At our suggestion, Representative Frank Thompson of New Jersey and Representative John Lindsay (later mayor) of New York, had introduced bills similar to our Senate bill, and a special House subcommittee under Thompson's chairmanship held extensive hearings and received widespread support. But the only bill Thompson dared report to the floor, given the temper of the House, was the modest one for a council and a nominal budget to set it up. The House quickly voted that down, 173 to 166, in September 1961. One senior member of the House, trying to ridicule the whole idea, asked Thompson, "Is poker playing an art?"

That fall a threatened strike almost blacked out New York's Metropolitan Opera and underlined the financial problems of all artistic organizations. I joined others in urging Arthur Goldberg, then secretary of labor, to intervene in the Met dispute, pointing out in a letter to him that "the Met is a national institution . . . as fully identified with the United States as the Bolshoi is with the Soviet Union." Goldberg arbitrated the dispute, enabling the Met to open on schedule, and in his report he made an eloquent plea for government aid to cultural institutions. He wrote:

> The American artistic scene today is alive and vibrant. At the same time, some of the foremost institutions of American culture are in grave difficulty. The Metropolitan Opera is not alone. . . . The artists, moreover, are generally underpaid. The problem, of course, is money. The individual benefactors and patrons just aren't there as they once were. Just as importantly, as we become more and more a cultural democracy, it becomes less and less appropriate for our major cultural institutions to depend on the generosity of a very few of the very wealthy. . . . We must come to accept the arts as a new community responsibility. The arts must assume their place alongside the already accepted responsibility for health, education, and welfare.

Addressing the worry that federal support for the arts would lead to political interference, Goldberg expressed faith in the independence and integrity of the American artist. The best way to avoid government control of the arts, he suggested, is to make sure that federal funds, in matching grants, represent only a portion of the total monies involved. He listed six sources from which financial support for the arts had to come: the public, enlightened patrons, private corporations, the labor movement, local governments, and the federal government. "An artist may be well fed and free at the same time," Goldberg said. "That an artist is honored and recognized need not mean he is any the less independent." Goldberg's statement received the wide attention it deserved; it was cited often in congressional hearings and remains a landmark in the struggle for official recognition of the arts.

In 1962, Senator Lister Hill of Alabama, chairman of the Labor and Public Welfare Committee, set up a special subcommittee to consider the three arts bills before the Senate. Senator Hill, a benign conservative (known as a devoted advocate of medical research and as the protagonist of the National Institutes of Health), gave us a break: Most of the senators who had sponsored or cosponsored the arts bills were named to the new subcommittee. Senator Claiborne Pell of Rhode Island, whose ensuing partnership with me on this issue led to a long and deep friendship between us, was appointed chairman. We took testimony from theater and musical administrators, representatives of theatrical and music unions and guilds, art educators, and directors of philanthropic foundations active in the arts field, as well as from other members of Congress. I reported to the committee that I had received expressions of support from a great many people in the world of theater, dance, and opera, including Helen Hayes, Ralph Bellamy (who was then president of Actors' Equity), Richard Rodgers, Katherine Dunham, Erich Leinsdorf, conductor of the Metropolitan Opera, Rise Stevens, Mimi Benzell, and Sol Hurok.

Frank Thompson and John Lindsay, somewhat discouraged by the defeat of their bill in the House the previous year, reported to us that the outlook there was still bleak. They felt that a bill for an advisory council might be able to pass the House under different parliamentary circumstances, but that their colleagues would not support any expensive funding of the arts for years to come. Therefore they both felt, regretfully, that we should put aside the foundation goal for the present and concentrate first on establishing an advisory council.

I felt this was the wrong way to go about it. "May I suggest to you gentlemen," I said, "that it may be that this bill has been defeated because its objectives are somewhat limited, and that if you are going to be defeated, if you are going to have a frustrating struggle, you might just as well try for the grand prize." I believed that we should go all the way for federal funding, that a spectacular failure might galvanize the public, and that public opinion was ahead of congressional opinion on this issue. If we set up a council and stopped there, I felt, we would be sidestepping the issue and missing a great opportunity for a decisive breakthrough.

My belief that we should act to get immediate federal support for the arts was borne out by other testimony. The American Guild of Musical Artists, which represented opera, concert, dance, and ballet performers, reported that 60 percent of its members earned less than $1000 a year from their profession and that less than 6 percent earned more than $5000. A representative of the American Federation of Musicians reported that half of its members could not make a living in music, and that "serious music cannot survive much longer" without government aid. "The American pool of career musicians is fast drying up," another musicians' union official said, and "the trend will continue so long as the economics of the profession are so bitterly unrewarding." Senator Humphrey testified and pointed out that "governments with far fewer financial resources have come to the aid of American art. It is worthy of note that in recent years the Italian government has granted a subsidy to the Chicago Lyric Opera Company, and the West German government has pledged $2.5 million for the new Lincoln Center Opera House in New York."

The subcommittee reported out a bill combining the features of my bill and Senator Clark's, but the Senate had no time to act on it before adjourning for the 1962 elections. I was up for reelection myself and I found that my work for the arts helped me immensely, particularly in New York City. Indeed, I ran ahead of Nelson Rockefeller, who was reelected governor, and I carried the city — the first Republican to do so on the Republican line alone since 1914.

When the new Congress convened we reintroduced the arts bill that the subcommittee had written the previous year. But Senator Humphrey was not completely satisfied. President Kennedy was about to establish a National Arts Council by executive order and Humphrey wanted Congress to make such a council permanent, by statute. Humphrey also wanted to broaden the arts foundation to cover not just the visual and performing arts, as Clark and I were proposing, but "the arts" in general, including literature, architecture, painting, photography, motion pictures, and television. I agreed — with the proviso that costume and fashion design, so important to New York, be included too. So Humphrey put in a new bill, which Clark and I cosponsored.

The new bill represented a significant widening of our purpose. Everything was in it: my proposals, Clark's, the council, and Humphrey's expanded list of the arts. It was far more comprehensive than my original 1949 suggestion that we establish national theater, opera, and ballet companies and more ambitious than the bills that had failed to be passed for two years. We were casting our net more widely, but we still had not caught any fish — nothing yet had been accomplished. By taking in all of "the arts" we were making the bill attractive to greater numbers of people, and perhaps to their senators and congressmen as well, which is why I went along with it. On the other hand, I began to worry that we might be defeating our purpose by attempting too much. But we persevered.

We worked hard to get that bill passed. To arouse public support, I made speeches to the American Academy of Dramatic Arts, to museum members, and to other interested groups, and my partners in Congress did likewise. Marian did some effective buttonholing of key senators and representatives, and she also enlisted Robert Rauschenberg, Andy Warhol, Jasper Johns, and other artists, as well as stage personalities, to organize committees and lobby members of Congress. The publicity on the opening of New York's Lincoln Center for the Performing Arts helped our cause, and August Heckscher, President Kennedy's special consultant on the arts, issued a report calling for an arts foundation.

Not until the fall of 1963, after the great civil rights march on Washington, could the Pell subcommittee meet again. We held five days of hearings and received support from all over the country. By this time the administration had lined up behind us: Even the Bureau of the Budget endorsed the foundation idea. To allay some of the fears that were still being expressed, the committee added to the bill a statement prohibiting any agency of the federal government from controlling or directing the work of the foundation (which was to be run by knowledgeable private citizens under a chairman appointed by the President and confirmed by the Senate). Otherwise, the bill sent to the Senate was almost identical to what Clark, Humphrey, and I had written.

But that session of Congress was one of the longest and slowest in history; the Senate failed to act on many vital bills, and the arts foundation was buried in the stack. Even some appropriations bills were not passed until long after the new fiscal year had begun, and a major civil rights bill had to be held over until the following year, 1964.

And then came the tragedy in Dallas, on November 22. I was having lunch with my brother at the Gloucester House restaurant in New York when a busboy called me to the telephone. My Washington office was on the line with the paralyzing news that President Kennedy had been shot and that it appeared the wound was mortal. I went back and told Ben and we left the restaurant at once, too stunned to talk.

After the shock and the mourning, everyone reordered priorities, and the arts bill seemed to be low on every list: It had failed to pass so many times. Furthermore, the long session and my consequent absences from New York had increased strains at home. My children needed to see their father and I needed a holiday. So in the middle of December, Marian and I rented a house in Acapulco, Mexico, for two weeks, and we flew down there with the children to rest in the sun, adjust to the awful national events, and put our own lives in order.

We had no sooner settled in, however, than President Johnson decided that the country and the Kennedy loyalists in the government needed reassurance that the slain President's ideals would not be forgotten. The arts bill was a fitting vehicle for this gesture, and since there was no significant opposition to it in the Senate, Johnson arranged with Senator Mansfield, the majority leader, to bring it up for passage on December 20. As I recall it, I got a phone call in Acapulco on the afternoon of the eighteenth informing me of this sudden development. After fourteen years of fighting for this bill I could not pass up the moment of victory. Senator Pell was managing the bill, and I sent him a message that I would get there somehow and asked him to delay the vote until I arrived. Then I got the first plane I could and flew north, musing, as I left the sunny beaches below me, that victories never come cheap.

Mansfield called the arts bill up as my plane was approaching Dulles Airport. Pell described the bill and urged its passage. Senator Kenneth B. Keating, the junior senator from New York (he had replaced Irving Ives in 1958), filled in for me and made the first speech in favor from the Republican side. Senator Strom Thurmond of South Carolina then rose to oppose the bill. He argued that the Constitution gave Congress no power to legislate on the arts and that the national debt was already too great for us to be spending money on such projects. No one joined Thurmond in opposition, but Pell took plenty of time rebutting him. Pell invoked the name of the late President for the "extraordinary impetus" he had given to cultural progress and pointed out that support for the arts would help the United States in its competition with the Soviet Union, which was dispatching musical and dance groups all over the world. He went on to name and commend all the senators who had worked for the bill, complimenting me as the "most illustrious pioneer in the field of cultural endeavors in the Congress" — but I had not yet shown up to hear it.

Claiborne Pell was beginning to repeat himself when I arrived —

out of breath but exultant. "The first thing I should do," I said when I took the floor, "is to thank so many senators for 'holding the fort' on this bill until I could reach the chamber. I'm especially grateful to the majority leader and to my beloved colleague, the senator from Rhode Island, who has so graciously done this." I returned Pell's compliment, summarized all the reasons for passing the bill, and gave the Senate a rundown on the many state arts councils that had been formed in anticipation of receiving federal aid from this bill. I emphasized that for every dollar we appropriated an estimated eight dollars would be generated in matching funds from state and private sources to encourage and support the arts.

With no real opposition and no roll call needed, the arts bill passed by voice vote. Senator Thurmond could have given us trouble, by demanding a roll call or by offering amendments or by speaking at length, but he chose not to and I was very grateful. When Senator Pell was again complimenting our allies on the bill, I walked across the aisle to thank Thurmond. When I had the floor again, I said that Thurmond "if he had chosen to do so, could have made it much more difficult than he did to pass the bill. I have just told him personally, and I would like to tell him publicly, that personally I feel a great responsibility to the Senate. . . . We shall be very vigilant, especially with respect to the problems which he has pointed out." Thurmond courteously reiterated that he thought the bill a mistake, and he added, "I hope I will be proved wrong, and that my colleagues will be proved right." Later that day I got on a plane again and flew back to Acapulco to rejoin my family; I really enjoyed the rest of that vacation.

I believe Senator Thurmond probably would agree today that we *were* right, but for the moment his side had the last laugh. In 1964 the House of Representatives, as Frank Thompson had predicted, removed the arts foundation from our bill and passed only the title setting up the National Council on the Arts, with no federal grants whatever. Conservative House Republicans opposed even that, one of them warning that the government "will soon be called upon to subsidize everything from belly dancing to the ballet; from Handel to Hootenanny; from Brahms to the Beatles; from symphonies to the strip tease." But Thompson managed to get the council measure through, 213 to 135. By the time it got back to the Senate it was late in the session, we were all exhausted after a monumental civil rights struggle, and a presidential election was coming up. We decided to accept the House bill rather than try to fight it out in conference. With the National Council on the Arts established, "at least," I said, "we have made some progress."

In 1965, as we began the struggle again, a new element was added: a proposal to create a foundation to promote the humanities just like the one we were trying to establish for the arts. The president of Brown University, Barnaby C. Keeney, had suggested the humanities foundation the previous fall; then Lyndon Johnson had picked it up during the election campaign and Senator Pell had embraced the idea. Early in the 1965 session, Pell introduced a bill to establish a humanities foundation to support the study of language, literature, jurisprudence, archaeology, and some of the social sciences.

At first I was not at all convinced that we should confuse the issue that way. I thought the colleges and the universities were doing enough for the humanities at the moment and that there was no need for Congress to do more than continue its support of higher education and libraries. For a minute I even thought seriously of opposing Pell on this issue, even though we were close friends and had been through a lot together in this field. But Claiborne Pell is tenacious. He is not a combative senator, but he has great force when he gets his teeth into an issue. He insisted that if we were to continue to cooperate on the arts bills, as he really wanted to do, his humanities bill would have to get equal treatment. The two together, he argued, would attract much wider support than either one separately and would have a good chance of becoming law, especially since President Johnson had put his seal of approval on both.

I had to consider the politics as well, namely the Democratic sweep in the 1964 elections. Just as the strengthened Democrats were able to pass the Medicare bill without paying too much attention to my views, they might shape the arts legislation, too. With President Johnson and Senator Pell wanting to enact both the humanities and arts foundations as a package, I decided not to try to dissuade them. So I agreed to cooperate with Pell on the two proposals; it was the only way to get aid to the arts finally enacted into law.

Since the administration and the majority leadership were committed to the concept, we were able to work on the foundation bills early in the session. In February, our subcommittee opened hearings, and shortly thereafter the Johnson Administration put in its own bill — the first time any administration had formally committed itself to an arts foundation.

Out of this welter of new proposals and the congressional history that I had set in motion so many years before, the final shape of the legislation emerged in Senate Bill 1483. It established the National Foundation on the Arts and Humanities, which consists of a National Endowment for the Arts and a National Endowment for the Humanities. A seven-member federal council coordinates the work of the two endowments, but each endowment is run by its own national council. (The National Council on the Arts that had been established the previous year became the Arts Endowment's council.) The Arts Endowment, essentially identical to the arts foundation in our earlier bills, was authorized to provide matching grants to states and to nonprofit groups, as well as to aid individuals engaged in the creative and performing arts. The Humanities Endowment was authorized to provide grants and loans for research, to award fellowships and grants to institutions for training, and to support the publication of scholarly works. Each endowment was authorized to spend $5 million a year in the next three years, with additional funds available to match gifts, bequests, and expenditures by states.

Forty-three Senators were listed as cosponsors of the measure when it came up before the Senate on June 10, and the entire administration was backing it. We had statements of support from HEW, the Department of State, the Smithsonian Institution, the Library of Congress, and even the Atomic Energy Commission. Virtually the entire academic community of the United States was clamoring for the bill as well. This time not even Strom Thurmond saw fit to oppose, and the bill was passed. It was, I said, "a monument to the Eighty-ninth Congress."

The Republican Policy Committee of the House declared that the arts and humanities were thriving and would continue that way "so long as the deadening hand of the federal bureaucracy is kept from the palette, the chisel, and the pen." But the enlarged Democratic majority in the House made passage there seem likely — though not before the conservative curmudgeons had had their "fun" with the bill. Representative H. R. Gross, an Iowa die-hard who possessed more wit than understanding on this matter, tried to kill the bill with ridicule: He proposed amendments to add belly dancing, baseball, tennis, pinochle, and poker to the list of arts eligible for financial aid. With the joke out of the way, the House approved the bill. The margin of victory was only twenty-three votes.

On September 29, 1965, Marian and I attended at the White House when President Johnson signed into law the National Foundation on the Arts and Humanities Act. In recognition of Marian's tireless efforts in behalf of the legislation, the President gave her personally, in recognition of her help, one of the pens with which he had signed it.

*   *   *

As it turned out, one of the most important elements of the act was a minor exception to its general "matching fund" rule that the federal government pay no more than half of the cost of any state arts or humanities project. The exception granted a state lacking an arts council up to $25,000, free of any matching requirement, to plan and establish such a body. Every state that had not already done so was therefore induced to create some kind of arts agency, thus stimulating an enormous grassroots arts movement all around the country. The states were helped in setting up their new arts councils by an organization called the American Council for the Arts, which was partially financed by the Rockefeller Brothers Fund and was directed by a dynamic, sensitive, and creative woman named Nancy Hanks, who later played a vital role in the growth and development of the Arts Endowment.

The first chairman of the endowment was Roger Stevens, a New York real-estate executive, theatrical producer, and patron of the arts. His term expired in 1969, and the search for a successor consumed almost a year. I took a hand in the search myself; much to my regret, a number of candidates the President wished to appoint were not, I thought, equal to the task, and I was compelled to reject them.

Then one day when I was in Scotland attending the Edinburgh Festival with our younger daughter, Carla, I got a phone call from Len Garment, special consultant to President Nixon, and a musician himself. Garment said the White House wanted to appoint Nancy Hanks to head the endowment — a choice I enthusiastically endorsed because I had become aware of her abilities in working with the state arts councils. But Garment said the President also wanted to get Michael Straight, another outstanding patron and devotee of the arts, to work with Hanks, and that he had been told that Straight would only come aboard as chairman. The team of Hanks and Straight seemed ideal to me; I promised Garment that I would try to persuade Straight to accept the post of Hanks's deputy and then try to work out an arrangement between the two so that they would operate in tandem. And that is what happened. It gave me great pleasure to persuade Nancy Hanks and Michael Straight to come in together.

Under their dedicated stewardship, the Arts Endowment spread its influence throughout the country, distributing wisely and widely the grants it is able to make. It has encouraged the better state arts councils to do outstanding jobs that inspired the others to improve. The appropriations for the Arts Endowment increased from the original $5 million to, most recently, $140 million, without any breath of scandal, and with nothing but the utmost approval from practically every member of Congress — a fine record that has confounded all the predictions made by the opponents of the idea.

The Humanities Endowment developed more slowly than the Arts Endowment because so many great institutions of higher education were already in existence, but it has grown steadily and is making a major contribution to the culture and literature of the United States. One of its finest moments was the production on public television of *The Adams Chronicles,* which was of enormous benefit and interest to the American people. Claiborne Pell has given his constant and patient attention to the Humanities Endowment, which represents his own creative contribution to the National Foundation. Recently, the Humanities Endowment established an Institute of Museum Services to assist art museums in managing their collections more effectively and more efficiently, by profiting from the best museum practices.

All told, this arts and humanities experience has probably been as worthwhile an example of the value of federal assistance as one could find in any field to which the U.S. government has given its aid. The Arts Endowment has become everything this founding father ever hoped for.

EIGHTEEN

The Struggle
for Civil Rights

I began my long struggle against racial discrimination when I chose to become a Republican. In my early years the political phenomenon of the "solid" Democratic South was virtually synonomous with the national shame of Jim Crow, or racial segregation. Even had I not been repelled by the corruption of Tammany politics in New York City, I doubt that I could have allied myself with the party whose national power depended to a great extent on a regional political and social system that kept black citizens in a state of subservience and often fear. As I saw it then, Northern Democrats who castigated Southern racism while reaping political benefits (such as congressional committee chairmanships) from the Democratic majorities provided by the solid South were not entitled to the mantle of liberalism they claimed as their right.

Then, World War II brought home to me the terrible irony that while our young men were dying in the fight against the Nazi concept of Aryan superiority, many otherwise upright Americans were maintaining a social order based on white supremacy. I realized that discrimination against any minority leads inexorably to discrimination against every minority. In 1944, I had put these thoughts into a long article, never published, in which I called on Americans of all faiths and all colors to recognize that our Bill of Rights reflects the intellectual and spiritual essence of the entire Judeo-Christian tradition, and that these constitutional rights must be enjoyed by all citizens if they were to be truly enjoyed by any.

My World War II army experience also made me keenly aware of the effect of discrimination on the morale of black troops, most of whom served then in segregated all-black units and many of whom were assigned to menial tasks. These men could just as well have lived and fought in mixed companies.

I have never believed that racial discrimination can be eliminated by legislation or by government order alone. But I believe that a society can be established in which discrimination against individuals will not significantly affect their way of life or their economic well-being. In the Constitution and the Bill of Rights, the United States possesses a unique instrument for creating such a society; the attempt to employ that instrument for that goal occupied a large part of my public life.

Immediately after the war, the executive and judicial branches of government took the lead in this campaign. President Roosevelt had started the trend by establishing a wartime fair-employment committee in a modest attempt to eliminate racial discrimination in defense plants. President Truman carried on by desegregating the military in 1948 and then, in the same year, asking Congress to enact civil rights legislation. When that failed to pass, Truman issued executive orders barring racial discrimination in federal employment and in work done under government contracts, and eliminating segregation in the District of Columbia and in railroad dining cars.

During the same period the U.S. Supreme Court was doing its part by abandoning in stages the classic 1896 doctrine of *Plessy* v. *Ferguson,* which held that racial segregation was acceptable under the Constitution as long as the separate facilities provided for blacks were equal to those provided for whites. In 1950, the Supreme Court declared segregation on interstate railroads to be unlawful, and found that segregation itself was a "prejudice or disadvantage." Four years later, in the historic decision in the case of *Brown* v. *The Board of Education of Topeka, Kansas,* the Court went all the way and repudiated the "separate but equal" doctrine, holding that separate public educational facilities are "inherently unequal" and that segregated education violated the Constitution because it deprived black children of benefits and rights. Although it took many years for the Court's decision to be implemented (and de facto segregation is still with us in many places), the *Brown* case set the stage for a momentous transformation of the relations between the races — a transformation that has taken place largely through the legal process and, considering the extent of the changes, with only a relatively small amount of violence.

Congress, however, did not play its part in the early years of this movement. When I was in the House of Representatives, I worked diligently, year after year, with a bipartisan group of Northern Democrats and moderate Republicans, to enact several kinds of civil rights legislation. I became party to the effort to pass an antilynching bill. We passed legislation to outlaw the poll tax, which had disenfranchised the vast majority of black citizens in the South, only to have it die in the Senate. I worked hard for the House passage of a mild fair-employment bill in 1950, but that was defeated by a Senate filibuster.

All through my years in the House the stumbling block to progress on civil rights was the Senate. We did not pass all the civil rights bills in the House either, of course, but we did pass some — only to have them buried or defeated in the Senate. The Senate was intrinsically no more conservative or racist than the House; it was merely that the constitutional structure of the Senate — two members from each state regardless of population — gave the South greater power proportionately than it had in the House; and the Senate tradition of unlimited debate allowed a few members to tie it up with a filibuster. Therefore the civil rights effort focused on the attempt to amend Senate Rule XXII so that cloture could be applied to shut off Southern filibusters.

When I arrived in the Senate, the politics of civil rights were changing. In the 1956 election, blacks all over the country had voted for candidates who promised action on civil rights — instead of automatically voting Democratic as they had done overwhelmingly since the beginning of the New Deal. That meant that many blacks had voted Republican, particularly where Republican candidates had made a campaign issue of the Democrats' sorry record on civil rights. Furthermore, blacks were going to the polls in increasing numbers — even though only about one-fourth of the blacks in the South were registered.

Northern Democratic senators who may have thought they were protecting their party by refusing to vote for cloture on Southern filibusters soon realized that their tactic had been a mistake, and they began lining up to sponsor civil rights bills. For Republicans, the fluid black vote represented a great opportunity. Many Republicans sympathetic to the black cause had failed to work for civil rights because they did not want to disturb the easy and fruitful partnership they had developed with conservative Southern Democrats on taxes and economic issues. Moreover, they saw no political advantage in trying to attract black voters who were likely to vote Democratic anyway. But when the solid black Democratic vote began to erode, Republicans recognized that if they could lead Congress to legislate voting rights for blacks the party would reap a double harvest: It could gain a larger proportion of the black vote at the same time that the black vote itself was growing. Therefore, just as I was entering the Senate in 1957, my party was finally adopting positions like mine on civil rights.

Clarence Mitchell, the director of the Washington bureau of the National Association for the Advancement of Colored People (NAACP), who was the principal Washington lobbyist for the black community, summed up what had happened. Both parties, he said in April 1957, had been jolted out of their complacency by the 1956 election: "The Democrats learned they will have to do something to make up for their anti-Negro Southern committee chairmen, while the Republicans found out they can win Negro votes away from the Democrats."

The historic civil rights movement grew out of this fusion of forces: blacks, aware for the first time of their political power, unifying behind a strategy that depended on nonviolent demonstrations and on the political and judicial processes; Northern Democrats, forced by electoral arithmetic to abandon support of their Southern wing; and Republicans, for whom ethics and political opportunity had come together at last. Backing up this coalition was a broad segment of the American public that not only found segregation and racial discrimination abhorrent but was getting angry at Southern defiance of the Supreme Court order to desegregate public schools. I enlisted in this movement as soon as I could. "I am signing up in the civil rights effort for the duration," I declared a few days after I was sworn in.

Taking advantage of this situation, President Eisenhower in his State of the Union address in January 1957 put forward a four-point civil rights program. It called for the formation of a bipartisan commission to investigate alleged violations of civil rights; establishment of a civil rights division in the Department of Justice; new laws making it a crime to interfere with a citizen's right to vote; and authorization for the U.S. attorney general to go into federal district courts to seek an injunction against anyone depriving — or planning to deprive — a citizen of voting rights or any other civil right.

The issue was quickly joined. Senator Richard Russell of Georgia declared almost immediately that "a resolute group of senators" would vigorously resist passage of the Eisenhower program — that is, he was openly threatening filibusters, and since we had failed to change the cloture rule on the first day of the session (see Chapter 14), this threat was very real indeed. Russell went on to say, "I will not compromise in the slightest degree where the constitutional rights of my state and her people are involved."

On the other hand, Majority Leader Lyndon Johnson was very much interested in compromise. He realized that the Senate and the Democratic Party had to pass some civil rights legislation or else his party would lose many black votes and the Senate would look bad in the eyes of the nation. He was determined to find some formula that would satisfy us — the Northern liberals — but which would at the same time represent a step so small that Senator Russell and the other adamant Southerners would allow it to be enacted without literally talking it to death.

Thus Johnson shuttled back and forth between the two groups, talking to us about the need to compromise to achieve some meaningful civil rights legislation, while at the same time promising his Southern friends that if they gave up the idea of a filibuster he would arrange things so the bill that passed would not be all that lethal.

Early in the session my civil rights activities were concerned with the fight to change the cloture rule. As a freshman senator (and, in fact, the most junior senator of all, as I had been sworn in a week late), I did not expect to be listened to very much on the substance of civil rights, but there was one aspect of it that not many other senators were talking about, so I felt I had to bring it up. The world trip I had taken a few months earlier had made it clear to me, I told both House and Senate committees, that

> the great contest between freedom and Communism is over the approximately 1.2 billion people, largely Negro and Oriental, who occupy the underdeveloped areas of the Far East, the Middle East, and Africa. One of the greatest arguments used against our leadership of the free world with these peoples has been that if they follow the cause of freedom they too will be held in the subjection of segregation. . . . These people are, therefore, watching with the most profound concern our present internal struggle on civil rights. . . . We need now . . . to convince them of the meaning of freedom.

To me, civil rights was not just a regional or national issue; it was a burning international issue as well.

The Southern Senators, however, were not listening either to the times or to reason: They were manipulating the rules. Well-organized, fired by a powerful emotional commitment, and enjoying a mastery of Senate procedures gained from many years of seniority and committee chairmanships, they wielded much more power than their numbers deserved. In my first session of the Senate their goal was delay. We had lost the fight to amend Rule XXII in the opening days, and therefore the threat of a filibuster hung over us constantly. The Southerners knew that they would eventually have to let a civil rights bill come to the floor, but if it were to come up late in the session, when the calendar was crowded with unfinished business, then the Senate majority would be more likely to give in to the filibuster threat and accept a weakened bill in order to stave off chaos and deadlock; and that was the essence of Lyndon Johnson's "compromise" strategy. For Lyndon Johnson, though a Southerner, had started as a populist and was devoted to equal opportunity. But he was even more devoted to making the Senate an effective instrument, to pass the bills the Democratic majority programmed, and to build up the Democratic Party — and Lyndon B. Johnson, its Senate leader — for future elections.

The principal roadblock was the Judiciary Committee and its chairman, Senator James Eastland of Mississippi. The Senate bill, in effect the Eisenhower program, was being managed through its committee stages by Senator Thomas C. Hennings of Missouri, chairman of the Judiciary Committee's Constitutional Rights Subcommittee and a real friend of civil rights. Hennings's subcommittee held thirteen days of hearings in February and March, listened to seventy witnesses, and then tried to report a bill to Eastland's full committee. But there — in the words of New York Times Capitol Hill reporter Cabell Phillips — Eastland "unblushingly laid one snare after another to box in the civil rights report and prevent action being taken on it."

Senator Eastland, supported by Senator Sam Ervin of North Carolina, insisted that Hennings's report be printed — and that took a month. Then Eastland, using — and misusing — his prerogative as chairman, declined to recognize Hennings when the Missouri senator sought the floor in the committee meetings to bring up the bill. Eastland scheduled only the legal minimum of committee meetings during that period; he made sure they never ran overtime and he sometimes arranged things so that the committee could not muster a quorum. Not until May could Hennings bring the bill before the committee.

These dilatory tactics angered and frustrated the bipartisan group of civil rights activists that was beginning to coalesce around Illinois Senator Paul Douglas and myself. We knew that the longer we were forced to wait the more likely it was that the Senate might give in to some discreditable compromise. Late in May, before the Senate, Senator Douglas in effect accused Senator Eastland of conducting a filibuster within the Judiciary Committee. An involved, tense — but extremely courteous — debate ensued, with Douglas and Senators Case and Humphrey meticulously going over the details of the Judiciary Committee's obstructions. Rules and the procedures, Douglas said,

> have all been nicely interlaced to delay and to impede any effective vote on the civil rights measure . . . This bill has been before the committee since January. Hearings were started in February. The hearings were concluded in March. It is now nearly the end of May. If we do not get a bill on the floor very soon, we know exactly what will happen. . . . My patience is running out and so is that of tens of millions of Americans.

Senator Humphrey pointed out that it was only four Southern Senators on the Judiciary Committee who were holding up the bill and he urged the other eleven members to force it out. "If four Southern Senators are so smart that they can bottle up the other eleven senators, then, believe me, the other eleven ought to be doing some thinking." Senator Eastland and his colleagues, Humphrey said, "are like the Spartans at the Pass of Thermopylae. They certainly 'mow 'em down.' All I ask them to do is to relax for a day or two, and give us an opportunity."

To all this Senator Eastland responded blandly that he was merely following the rules of the Senate and giving everyone a chance to be heard. He was just "the errand boy of the committee," he said, and he denied that he could dictate anything. But the press was already commenting that because of the delay and the threat of filibuster the civil rights bill of 1957 would be written, in effect, not by its proponents but by its opponents.

Paul Douglas was not going to let this happen without a fight. "I will not accept," he told the Senate, "a civil rights bill which is stripped of its teeth and rendered ineffective." He pointed out that the bills under consideration were already inadequate to the need, providing only a "bare minimum" of protection of the right to vote, plus the establishment of a study commission and a new civil rights section in the Justice Department. As a new senator, I had not felt it wise, in the interest of my state, to join Douglas's criticism of the Judiciary Committee's procedures, but I did add my voice to his determination to withstand the pressures for compromise.

Much of the 1957 civil rights debate centered on a Southern attempt to guarantee jury trials for anyone accused of contempt of court orders under the new civil rights bill. This struck at the heart of the bill, which provided that court injunctions would be used to compel compliance with the law. The only way to enforce injunctions is to punish violators for contempt of court. By insisting that these contempt-of-court proceedings be decided by jury trial instead of by a judge, the Southerners were taking the teeth out of the law: Southern juries were unlikely to convict anyone for depriving a black of his civil or voting rights.

Southerners in both the House and the Senate tried to justify this move on the basis of the constitutional right to trial by jury, but in truth there is no constitutional right to trial by jury in cases of contempt of court. Civil contempt (where the violator can go free as soon as he complies with the injunction) is never decided by a jury. And in criminal contempt cases (in which a violator is punished further, generally by imprisonment, for defying the court), legislation already in effect stipulated that if the United States is a party to the suit — as would be the case under the proposed civil rights law — no jury trials for contempt were required. The Supreme Court, in fact, had declared that the courts should be able to "vindicate" their dignity "without . . . calling upon a jury to assist" them.

The Southerners expected to pass a jury-trial amendment when the bill came to the House floor in June, but the Eisenhower Administration recognized that jury trials for contempt of court orders could make the bill worthless. As the debate in the House began, U.S. Attorney General Herbert Brownell declared that the jury-trial amendment "would permit practical nullification" of the proposed law and would undermine the authority of all federal courts "by seriously weakening their own power to enforce their lawful orders." The administration used its influence on wavering Republican representatives, and the jury-trial amendment was defeated in the House.

On June 18, the House passed the administration bill, virtually unchanged, by a vote of 286 to 126. Considering the obvious need, the bill as passed by the House was modest and moderate. There was nothing in it about fair employment practices, nothing about discrimination in housing or education or National Guard service or any of the other areas in which a number of states — notably New York — had already legislated successfully. It was concerned only with the right to vote and other basic rights of the kind taken for granted in civics textbooks but long denied to the black citizens of the U.S. South. Nevertheless, even this mild bill was to prove too radical for Senator Richard Russell and the Southern phalanx in the Senate.

On June 20, 1957, the civil rights bill that had been passed by the House was transmitted to the Senate. The normal procedure would have been to refer it to Eastland's committee, but as the committee had already tacked a jury-trial amendment on to its version of the bill, and was still stalling on the whole enterprise, we wanted to get the House bill to the Senate floor directly. When the routine motion to refer the House bill to the Judiciary Committee was made, Senator William Knowland of California, the minority leader, objected. Senator Douglas supported Knowland — they had worked it all out in advance — and so did the majority of the Senate. Senator Russell tried to block the move with a point of order, upon which a complicated series of parliamentary maneuvers began. We won that round: The Southerners were outvoted and the House-passed bill was put on the Senate calendar, which meant that the Senate could vote to consider it at any time, by-passing Eastland's Judiciary Committee.

On July 8, Knowland moved to take up the bill, and for the next eight days, through sixty-six speeches, the Senate debated — not the bill, but the question of *whether* to debate the bill. Russell, threatening a filibuster, declared that he and his friends were "prepared to extend the greatest effort ever made in history to prevent passage of the bill in its present form." Russell's real motives, and the depth of his antagonism to the bill, had already emerged when he declared that the bill was "cunningly designed to vest in the attorney general unprecedented power to bring to bear the whole might of the federal government, including the armed forces if necessary, to force a commingling of white and Negro children in the state-supported schools of the South." This was more than rhetoric aimed at the folks at home or at his colleagues in the Senate: Racial segregation was so deeply ingrained in the "social order" as Senator Russell saw it that he felt the bill was a threat to everything he lived for and believed in. "My intention is to amend this bill if possible," Russell said, "but to defeat it in any event."

The emotional commitment on the part of Senator Russell and his Southern colleagues was soon to put us at a tactical disadvantage: While Russell, Ervin, and other Southerners pledged absolute opposition to any thought of compromising on the bill and threatened to filibuster against it, Senator Knowland and other moderate supporters of the bill began talking about ways to soften the proposed legislation in order to help make it more palatable to the South and thus prevent the threatened filibuster. Senator Joseph C. O'Mahoney of Wyoming announced that he would introduce a compromise jury-trial amendment to help get the bill passed; we started hearing disturbing reports that even President Eisenhower was willing to accept a compromise; Republican Karl E. Mundt of South Dakota offered a weaker substitute bill that he said the Southerners could live with. This, of course, is exactly what the Southerners had hoped would happen. Although Johnson would vote to take the bill up, he too was opposed to it in the form that it came from the House and joined those who wanted to weaken it with the jury-trial amendment.

But I regarded it as my role to do what I could to prevent the pro–civil rights forces from giving in to the drift to compromise. "Contemplation of compromise now," I said in the course of the debate on Knowland's amendment, "only tends to divide and fragmentize those who favor a civil rights bill at this session, for there can be no legislation of any kind unless the bill comes before the Senate, and this has not yet been decided." Senator Douglas joined me in a pledge not to compromise, and Senator Pat McNamara, a Michigan Democrat, a great bear of a man who had been a plumber and a trade-union leader, pointed out that "the die-hard opponents of this legislation will vote against it" regardless of any compromises; he promised to support the bill "word by word and section by section."

So the sides were quickly chosen: the Southerners, threatening filibuster and expressing absolute opposition to the bill; Douglas, myself, and a few others equally determined to defend the bill as it stood; and the majority of the Senate in between, led by Lyndon Johnson, willing to compromise on a weaker measure in order to get something passed and prevent a filibuster. And with this line-up the Southerners held the stronger hand, for they were privately willing to compromise too, if they could really gut the bill.

I was able to play a larger role in the debate than I had anticipated, thanks to the Senate's decision to by-pass the Judiciary Committee. A bill of this significance normally is brought to the Senate floor by committee members who know it backward and forward, who are committed to its passage, and who stand ready to explain and defend it. These champions of the bill are armed, moreover, by a committee report that all interested senators will have read and studied before the debate begins. But this House civil rights measure, H.R. 6127, was an orphan in the Senate; there was no Senate committee report on the bill and no one was assigned to look after it. Of course, most senators had read the House report and hearings, and Senator Hennings and the members of the Judiciary Committee who favored the legislation could speak knowledgeably about it — but that was not quite the same thing: They were not specifically or officially prepared to explain its provisions to their colleagues.

This was a happy accident for me, and I quickly grasped the opportunity it offered — an opportunity rare indeed for the Senate's most junior member. As a supporter of the bill, and as a lawyer who understood its legal ramifications — particularly on the thorny issue of jury trials — I suddenly emerged as its prime legal protagonist. Paul Douglas, of course, remained the able and inspiring leader of the pro–civil rights forces, and Hubert Humphrey, Thomas Kuchel, and other liberal senators carried the general debate. But none of them had the desire or the legal experience to become entangled in the abstruse and intricate lawyers' debates that this provision demanded, especially when confronting the legal acumen possessed by many of the Southern senators. When it came to taking on Sam Ervin, an acknowledged constitutional expert, or Senator John C. Stennis, who had served as a judge in Mississippi before coming to the Senate, my allies in the civil rights fight were only too pleased to toss the ball to me.

When the debate began I was still getting the chilly treatment with which some Southern senators had greeted me when I arrived, and indeed, all through that debate Richard Russell never once deigned to engage me in a colloquy on the Senate floor. But his fellow Southerners were forced to, and when the debate was over — although we

failed to preserve all that we wanted to preserve of the bill — I found
that I had made a mark. Not all of the Southerners regarded me with
affection, I am sure, but they realized that they had to pay attention to
me when I rose to debate a subject in which they had an interest. And
while many Northerners may still have considered me an outsider, they
had to admit I was a useful one. In that 1957 debate I began to acquire
a reputation in the Senate as a lawyer and as a forthright debater who
had to be reckoned with.

The Senate galleries were always packed during this debate and
the atmosphere was electric. Senator Ervin opened his attack on the
bill by calling it "a queer concoction of constitutional and legal sins
[that] masquerades under the beguiling name of civil rights." Dipping
— selectively — into his vast storehouse of historical facts and legal
precedents, he sought to create the impression that the South would
endure "tyranny" if the bill were passed. He invoked the founding
fathers and even went back to the Magna Carta to claim that liberals
"who will vote for a bill which denies any man the right to trial by
jury [are] as reactionary as King John was before Runnymede."

Ervin's main target was Part III of the bill — the authorization for
the attorney general to seek injunctions where civil rights had been violated. He asserted that Part III gave the U.S. attorney general the right
to proceed that way in hundreds of different types of cases, and that this
was entirely too much power to vest in one official. And he declared:

> The only reason advanced by the proponents of the bill for urging
> its enactment is, in essence, an insulting and insupportable indict-
> ment of a whole people. They say that Southern officials and
> Southern people are generally faithless to their oaths as public
> officers and jurors, and for that reason can be justifiably denied the
> right to invoke for their protection in courts of justice the consti-
> tutional and legal safeguards erected in times past by the found-
> ing fathers and Congress to protect all Americans from govern-
> mental tyranny.

He went on in that vein for hours, citing a great many legal precedents and giving technical explanations of the law.

When I had my chance to reply over the next few days, I pointed
out that the federal powers Senator Ervin was concerned about were
not new ones created by this bill; "they have been in the law [for gen-
erations] and the idea that they will suddenly be misused is only a
hobgoblin in the closet."

At one point during the debate on the motion to take up the bill,
I found myself engaged alone against three Southern senators, William
Fulbright of Arkansas, Ervin, and Eastland, discussing jury trials in

contempt cases and the provisions of the old 1866 law that permitted the use of federal troops to uphold judicial decisions. At another point I went through it again with Senator Stennis, who claimed that the authors of the bill had deliberately given the attorney general the authority to get into these cases just for the purpose of denying jury trials to Southern defendants. But I responded:

> The bill does not repeal anything by simply making the United States a party to the suit. . . . If those of us who are the proponents of the bill can carry the burden of the fact that the United States ought to be a party, then we proceed to the point that it is not unfair, it being the established law, and nothing is being changed and nothing is being repealed. We have to prove that the United States ought to be a party.

I then reminded Stennis that in his own state of Mississippi a county board of supervisors "has the power to punish for contempt" without trial by jury.

The Southerners were also trying to insinuate that because Part III went beyond voting rights the authors of the bill were trying to put something over on the South. I reminded them that in the House hearings administration spokesmen had fully explained the attorney general's authority to move against the deprivation of any civil right. It was true that the compromise moves under way were aimed at stripping the bill of everything except the right-to-vote section, but we were determined to keep the broader protections in the bill. "I stand by Part III," I declared. "I see nothing to apologize for in seeking to gain for all our citizens the rights given to them under the equal-protection clause of the Constitution."

After eight days of preliminary debate and sixty-six speeches, the Senate finally voted, 71 to 18, to take up H.R. 6127. Thereupon Senator Russell took the floor to renew his filibuster warning. He and his fellow Southerners, he said, were "prepared to extend the greatest effort ever made in history to prevent passage of this bill in its present form." The filibuster never materialized: The threat, repeated on a number of occasions, turned out to be sufficient.

Majority Leader Lyndon Johnson voted with us to take up the bill, but he was not yet supporting most of the substance of the bill itself. Part III, he said, was "intolerable," and he declared that he "could not in good conscience vote against a jury trial for American citizens." That, it became clear, was the "compromise" that he demanded as the price of persuading the Southerners to refrain from a filibuster. An amendment was immediately offered to eliminate Part III from the bill and a number of otherwise liberal Senators, both Democratic and Republican, supported the amendment — in order, they said, to get the bill passed. I regarded the rights protected by Part III to be just as important and fundamental as the right to vote (which was covered in another part of the bill); so it was largely up to me to explain and defend it and to carry the ball for those of us who wanted to keep it in the bill.

This was my first major role in a Senate debate — and it was a heady and awesome and thoroughly fascinating experience. For two long July afternoons I held the floor of the Senate, arguing, persuading, citing statutes and cases, answering questions. I yielded for questions, according to the tradition of the Senate; most of my interrogators were opponents of the bill asking "questions" that were really opposing arguments — which is the way Senate debate works. In those colloquys, all cushioned with courteous compliments for the "distinguished and able" senators, and "my good friend and colleague," we confronted each other sharply and in deep legal detail over the ramifications of Part III, court procedures in the various states, the different kinds of injunctions and classifications of contempt of court, and dozens of other legal fine points involved in the proposal to let the United States bring suits to protect the individual's civil rights.

Sometimes Senator Douglas asked a question to help me bring out a point I had overlooked or left insufficiently explained. Once he intervened when Senator Spessard Holland of Florida, whom Douglas called a "living jumping box," kept asking interminable and often repetitious questions for nearly an hour.

I debated not only with Southerners making emotional (and sometimes misleading) attacks on Part III but also with senators from other parts of the country who were concerned that the bill might indeed, as some of the Southerners claimed, violate the civil rights of some citizens in order to protect the civil rights of others. One of my basic arguments for Part III was that it created no new laws or violations of laws, but merely introduced new procedures to enforce laws that had long been on the books.

In the course of those two days I took on several of the leading Southern senators. Senator Russell Long of Louisiana contended that Part III would force an individual or a local agency — a school board, for instance — to get involved in a lawsuit even if it did not want to; I responded that it would enable those agencies to proceed in court, through the U.S. attorney general, where they had been intimidated from doing so on their own. Senator Holland, among other things, tried to prove that the attorney general could work his will on the South by choosing to sue only before favorable judges; I reminded him that all federal judges in the South had to be approved by the senators from their states and that almost all of them were Southerners. Sam Ervin, after trying to get me to answer a leading — or, rather, a misleading — question, told one of his long funny stories about a stubborn witness in a court case in North Carolina. After the laughter, which was at my expense, I responded: "This is an illustration of why our problem is made more difficult. Those who oppose the bill, with very deep conviction, are very charming human beings and know such good stories."

Behind all the senatorial courtesy and the legal technicalities was the Southern fear of federal interference in local law enforcement, which of course was the heart of the whole question, the substance of the bill. In response to allegations of how dreadful federal participation would be, I was moved to turn away from legal arguments to remind the Senate of what was going on:

> I cannot understand [I said] how we can stand here and argue as if there were no gravamen to this case. Why are we here? Are we here because the law is being obeyed, because the law is being carried out, because there is no discrimination, because there is no violence, because everyone is receiving equal protection under the law; or are we here to correct a situation which we on our side of the argument consider to be a national shame, and that the federal government, therefore, must do something about it, because the local agency will not . . . ? What about the bombing in Montgomery, the shooting of the minister, the bombings in Florida? What are we here for? Why do we listen to all these arguments all these days? . . . Somebody has to press the button. Somebody has to defend rights which are not being defended. We are asking the United States to do it. That is what it comes to.

Sometimes, as Senator Humphrey remarked a few days later, it seemed that the debate was more concerned with protecting violators than with redressing grievances.

There were twenty-four specific civil rights that the attorney general could have protected under Part III, all of them well established in the law and many being violated daily in the South. They included the rights to serve as a juror, to testify in court, to be free of mob violence while in federal custody, to be secure from unlawful searches and seizures, to assemble, to be free of discrimination in public employment — as well, of course, as the basic freedoms of speech, religion, and the press. As Paul Douglas and I brought out in a long colloquy before the Senate, five Southern states had recently passed laws forbidding any individual or group, such as a legal defense committee, from paying anyone else's legal fees. That meant, we said, that poor blacks in those states who could not afford to hire a lawyer had no legal means whatever of securing those twenty-four rights — unless the attorney general was authorized to sue on their behalf. They would thus be virtually helpless without Part III of the bill.

When I had done all I could I relinquished the floor and other senators took over. The debate on the amendment to strike Part III went on for a week. Senator Wayne Morse of Oregon declared that Part III "breathes light, substance, and liberty for the individual into the Fourteenth and Fifteenth Amendments. It is time that we implement those great amendments granting equality of rights, in legal theory, to the Negro people of America." John Kennedy stated that Part III "creates no new civil rights, provides no unprecedented judicial procedures, and is based on no radical principles of constitutional law, but simply offers civil procedures as a supplement to criminal procedures now available. It is a moderate provision in a moderate bill lending itself . . . to intelligent implementation. . . ."

But many senators seemed obsessed with the need to compromise. The amendment to strike the operative section of Part III was sponsored by Clinton Anderson of New Mexico and Senator George D. Aiken, Vermont Republican, who ordinarily voted on the liberal side and who were certainly no Southern white supremacists; both claimed they were doing it because they wanted to see a civil rights bill pass the Senate. By a vote of 52 to 38, their amendment was accepted on July 24, effectively limiting the bill to the enforcement of voting rights only.

How did twenty-two Southern senators get thirty more senators to join them in eviscerating the 1957 civil rights bill? The vote revealed a new alliance that had emerged in the Senate. Regardless of party, sixteen of the twenty Senators from the Rocky Mountain states voted with the South, as they would again and again on civil rights issues. These were the economically developing states that needed large infusions of government capital for dams and roads and major public works. The Southerners, with their control of Senate committee chairmanships, had a lot to say about where federal funds for these huge water-development projects or airfields or military bases were spent, so they had a happy hunting ground in the mountain states and wherever land was politically as important as people.

The Westerners were not racist, but they had few minority voters among their constituents, and with some exceptions, they felt their states had more interest in federal law on land and water management than in civil rights for minorities. This alliance gave the Southerners of 1957 about one-third of the Senate — just enough to withstand a cloture vote. And that was what made their filibuster threats so credible.

With some variations, we met the same fate on jury trials as we did on Part III. We fought hard against that amendment — the other half of Lyndon Johnson's compromise. A group of law-school deans and law professors declared that the lack of jury trials would not violate due process and that the Senate debate was creating an "erroneous impression" of the need for jury trials in contempt cases. Proponents of the amendment tried to get labor-union support for it on the grounds that it would protect union members in labor strike injunctions — but that, I said, was a "cleverly laid trap" because labor injunctions are usually the final moves in a labor dispute whereas injunctions in voting rights cases had to continue. "The power to destroy a union ought to be impeded," I said, "but the authority to protect the vote ought not to be."

To my mind the jury-trial amendment was more than a blow at civil rights: As a lawyer I was deeply concerned about what it might do to our legal system. It imposed jury trials on all civil rights cases of criminal contempt where the United States was a party and it also applied to at least thirty statutes where jury trial for contempt did not exist. As I told the Senate, the amendment

> would impair the entire range of government activities in . . . antitrust, fair labor standards, atomic energy, security laws, and the National Housing Act. . . . How strange it is that we who seek to safeguard the equal protection of the right to vote guaranteed by the Constitution should be not met on the merits but by a challenge to . . . the whole traditional field of equity and the power of the courts to enforce their decrees. I urge that we be neither coerced nor intimidated by the latent threat of a filibuster. . . . There is no guarantee that we will not have a filibuster in any case. Having come so far with this bill, and the jury-trial amendment being such a negation of the whole bill, we can do nothing in justice to the historic opportunity before us other than reject any such implied threat of a filibuster as the basis for Senate decision.

On August 2, the Senate adopted the jury-trial amendment by a vote of 51 to 42. There was still some good in the bill, however, and despite my qualms about jury trials for these contempt cases, I voted for it, hoping that perhaps the House conferees would be able to restore their version. The Southerners, having gutted the bill, refrained from a filibuster, and the voting rights bill passed the Senate, 72 to 18, on August 7.

The effort to salvage the bill from the conflicting House and Senate versions took several weeks of meetings with leaders of both parties and with the White House, complicated by a Southern attempt to use the opportunity to kill the bill outright. I took an indirect hand in this by going to the press and the public with an explanation of the harm the jury-trial amendment would do to our legal system. In a memo I sent to Rowland Evans, a columnist for the *New York Herald Tribune*, I insisted that the failure to limit the jury-trial amendment to civil rights cases only would "command a jury trial in contempt cases resulting from equity decrees where the United States is a complainant, [and] would thereby work havoc with the federal administration of justice."

Fortunately, this warning, by me and others, took effect. The compromise eventually worked out between Johnson, Russell, and Knowland and their counterparts in the House limited the jury-trial amendment to voting rights cases and also gave the judge the option of trying minor criminal contempt cases without a jury; if the penalty imposed was more than $300 or forty-five days' imprisonment, the defendant could demand a jury trial.

Thus revised, the bill came back to the Senate for final approval late in August, with all sides agreed that it would pass. Senator Russell and his friends of course would vote against it, but having weakened it sufficiently they were keeping their promise to Johnson not to filibuster; they were well aware that a filibuster at that point would anger the nation and alienate the South's allies, that it would lead to cloture, and that as Senator Herman Talmadge of Georgia expressed it, it would bring about "the passage of new, radical civil rights legislation, with FEPC [Fair Employment Practices Committee] provisions." The fix, as they say, was in. Only one man refused to go along: Senator Strom Thurmond of South Carolina, the 1948 presidential candidate of the States' Rights Party.

Thurmond could not reconcile himself to the thrust of the bill. He rose on August 28 to conduct a symbolic, one-man filibuster. All day and all night, for twenty-four hours and eighteen minutes, Thurmond held the floor alone to denounce the bill and its backers, creating a record for the longest Senate speech in history. Throughout that day and night, Thurmond's wife, Jean, sat in the gallery directly above him, keeping a watchful eye for signs of collapse, silently communicating her moral support. Her solicitude and loyalty made a remarkable impression on all of us, even though almost every other senator disapproved of what her husband was doing. When she died not many months later, we all remembered with awe her long vigil at her senator's futile stand.

When Thurmond finally ran down, the Senate agreed to the revised bill, 60 to 15, and on September 9, President Eisenhower signed into law the first civil rights legislation in eighty-two years. That was followed by a wave of unrest in the South, and within two weeks events in Little Rock, Arkansas, demonstrated the real need for Part III. Governor Orval Faubus ordered out the National Guard to prevent nine black students from entering the previously all-white high school that the courts had ordered desegregated, and President Eisenhower was obliged to send federal troops to Little Rock to escort the children to school. If Part III had remained in the act, the attorney general would have had authority to deal with the problem in the courts before the use of the armed forces became necessary. Therefore we renewed our efforts to get Part III or something like it enacted into law.

For a while, however, we found ourselves on the defensive. In Congress, the coalition of Southern Democrats and conservative Republicans tried to punish the Supreme Court for its school-desegregation decisions by stripping the court of much of its power and authority. And in the South die-hard white racists bombed churches and synagogues and schools to protest the fact that religious leaders of many faiths had combined forces across the nation to work for civil rights laws. Douglas and I and the bipartisan liberal group in the Senate worked closely with Lyndon Johnson to defeat the punish-the-court bills in 1958. But our attempts to make dynamiting of buildings a federal offense did not get anywhere until 1960.

In 1958, Representative Kenneth Keating of New York ran for the Senate (to replace Irving Ives, who had decided to retire from politics after his gubernatorial defeat in 1956). In the course of his campaign, Keating promised to visit the South if he was elected. He won, and I accompanied him on a quick trip through the heartland of the segregated and troubled South to get a feel for what was going on and to see what we, as senators, could do about it. We visited Jacksonville, Atlanta, and Birmingham, and conferred with community and religious leaders of both races and all faiths. We came back convinced that federal laws were needed to deal with bombings and hate mail that incited people to violence, and that such legislation would be supported by many Southern leaders. "One of the underlying causes of this wave of terrorism," we said upon our return, "is the atmosphere of lawlessness rampant in many Southern communities as a result of open resistance by officials to compliance with the Supreme Court's decision ordering desegregation in the public schools."

We had asked the mayors of the cities we visited to arrange meetings with law-enforcement officials and community leaders of both races. After the Birmingham meeting began, however, we discovered that only whites were present — a fact we immediately protested. Nevertheless, our attendance at a segregated white meeting caused us a little embarrassment until we set the record straight.

In Atlanta, we were in the middle of a meeting with civil rights leaders and the police chief when the phone rang. The chief answered it and we heard him say, "No, they're perfect gentlemen." Apparently,

Senator Richard Russell had called to check up on how the two Northerners were behaving in his state. I do not know what he expected to hear.

All through 1959 the Senate Judiciary Committee again bottled up a variety of civil rights proposals. They included an administration bill to strengthen the 1957 voting rights act and to make bombing or burning a school or a church a federal crime; bills introduced by Senator Douglas and myself to enact a "Part III" law; and even a modest bill from Lyndon Johnson, establishing an agency to conciliate civil rights disputes. Similar bills in the House also were mired in committees. As the 1959 session came to a close in September, Douglas and I were still trying to get a bill to the floor. In order to mollify us and let Congress adjourn, Lyndon Johnson and the new minority leader, Everett McKinley Dirksen, promised us that civil rights would come up on the floor of the Senate early in the 1960 session.

Johnson himself opened the civil rights debate in February 1960 by saying, "We are going to do what is right in this matter, even though we do not satisfy the extremists on either side." To this "extremist," the timing could not have been more opportune. Just two weeks earlier, on February 1, 1960, a group of black college students in Greensboro, North Carolina, sat down at a "whites only" lunch counter and asked to be served. The peaceful "sit-in" movement spread rapidly through the South, demonstrating the determination of black citizens to achieve their civil rights, and thereby lending a sense of urgency to our efforts to do the same thing in Congress.

As no civil rights bill had been reported by the Judiciary Committee — or was likely to be — Johnson invited senators to attach civil rights amendments to a minor bill that had been passed by the House. Senator Dirksen offered the administration's 1959 proposal (which was finally getting to the House floor at about the same time), and the stage was set for another small but significant step for the cause of civil rights.

This time, right from the start, we knew we were going to get a filibuster. After a flurry of procedural motions by which the Southerners tried and failed to postpone the debate, they started delivering lengthy speeches in opposition to all the civil rights proposals. To break the filibuster, or at least limit its duration, Johnson announced that the Senate would remain in session "all night around the clock . . . until a vote is obtained." Senator Russell warned that he and his friends would use every parliamentary device at their command to hold things up; and Spessard Holland declared that the Senate leadership would be responsible for the "health and the lives" of any members who might not have the stamina for all-night sessions.

On February 29, the filibuster and the round-the-clock sessions began. From then until March 8, with only two short breaks, the Senate met continuously. All committees suspended their activities. The sergeant at arms borrowed forty cots from the U.S. Army and distributed them through the cloakrooms and the senators' offices. Policemen and doorkeepers and pages went on special schedules, so some were always at hand. The Capitol doctor arranged for medical personnel to stand by, and the Senate restaurant had a chef and waiters on duty day and night to provide short orders.

Richard Russell commanded the Southerners' forces. He divided his eighteen senators into three "platoons" and made sure that one platoon was always in or near the chamber while the reserves were resting or asleep or attending to other business. Each Southerner was required to make one four-hour speech every three days while his teammates sat by to ask him helpful questions. Late at night there were usually only four senators on the floor: two Southerners, plus two senators from our side attending in rotation, each side making sure that the other did not try to put something over on it. The Southerners made long speeches (most of them, surprisingly, relevant to the subject); they asked each other long questions so that the senator who held the floor could take a brief rest; they made complicated hypothetical parliamentary inquiries of the chair, to take up more time; and they smothered us with quorum calls.

The quorum call was the Southerners' primary device to wear us down and test our resolution. Calling the roll and waiting for fifty-one senators to answer to their names took up time and gave the senator holding the floor a rest. Furthermore, if a quorum could not be mustered the Senate would have to adjourn and a new official "legislative day" would begin, with all the time-consuming formalities entailed in that. So it was to our interest to prevent adjournment and force the Southerners to keep talking until, out of weariness, they yielded the floor or allowed a vote on the civil rights bill.

I slept in my office every night during that period. The Southerners made a practice of calling for a quorum along about 11:00 P.M., and we would all rush to the chamber to answer to our names. Then they would demand a quorum again sometime between two and four in the morning and again at about dawn — and fifty-one of us would have to pull ourselves awake, throw on our clothes, and shamble over to the chamber. The Southerners themselves lost no sleep, except for those on duty, because they were perfectly willing to let the Senate adjourn if it could not get a quorum. But most of the rest of us had to nap as best we could between those quorum calls. The quorum bells became so much a part of our lives that Clifford Case of New Jersey one night dreamed that he heard one and rushed to the chamber to find just a couple of Southerners droning away.

One of the most remarkable sights in those night sessions was the constant attendance of Senator Theodore Francis Green — who was not only the senior senator from Rhode Island but the oldest senator of us all. He was ninety-three years old during that debate, but he always entered the chamber fully dressed and looking well groomed and fresh as a daisy and ready to conduct Senate business as well as any younger member — if not better. Senator Margaret Chase Smith of Maine also retained her style, showing up for one 4:00 A.M. quorum call in a red dress and then appearing in a green dress two hours later. But most of us paid little attention to our attire. Lyndon Johnson was spotted by reporters wearing pajamas in his office, and Senator Winston L. Prouty of Vermont shuffled about the Senate chamber in bright orange bedroom slippers.

During the nine days of round-the-clock filibuster, we went through thirteen roll-call votes, answered to fifty quorum calls, and stayed in session for 157 hours. I consumed some of that time myself, although in a way it was aiding the Southerners, because they had all been talking against the civil rights bill and I felt strongly that the record should contain the arguments in favor of it. Only twice during that time did we recess (not adjourn), once for fifteen minutes and then again over the weekend when Johnson said, "Every man has the right to a Saturday night bath."

Meanwhile, Senator Douglas and I had been gathering signatures for cloture, and on March 8, when we had the necessary sixteen names (we had eight from each party), we offered the petition and moved to close debate. Lyndon Johnson opposed our move; he said he wanted to wait until two-thirds of the Senate could agree on what a civil rights bill should contain. Everett Dirksen was also against cloture, although the filibuster was holding up the bill *he* had introduced; Dirksen wanted to wait for the House to pass its civil rights bill. I declared that we should not wait. "The people of New York," I said, "sent me here on the constitutional principle that it took a majority, not two-thirds, of the Senate to act." And Douglas predicted that if we did not vote cloture we would be told we would have to drop strong measures because of the continued threat of filibuster.

We needed sixty-four votes to invoke cloture and we could not get them. On March 10 the Senate rejected our motion, 42 to 53. The South had won a battle, and a little later they won another: The Senate voted to table an amendment Douglas and I had sponsored that would have added a "Part III" provision to the bill.

The debate went on for another month, but from that point we resumed normal hours and began talking about and voting on specific proposals. A key issue that year was the plan to appoint federal registrars or referees to help disenfranchised blacks in the South register to vote. Under the administration's plan, a federal district court could appoint voting referees to register voters and observe at the polls in districts where the court had established that a pattern of racial discrimination to bar voting existed. That was fine, but Douglas and I proposed stronger legislation. Our proposal gave the federal government the authority to appoint federal registrars who would assist blacks to register wherever the U.S. Civil Rights Commission had certified that racial discrimination existed — regardless of whether the issue had been brought up in the courts. Once these registrars certified a voter's registration, it would become a federal crime to prevent that person from voting. We wanted the Senate to decide between the two plans before the House bill arrived, but our motions to introduce the registrar plan were tabled and therefore killed.

When the House passed its bill on March 24, the Senate abandoned the bills it was working on and turned to the House version. This time the House bill was referred to the Judiciary Committee — but (our triumph) with instructions by the Senate to report it out within a week. Then, in committee and later on the floor of the Senate, the familiar process of whittling away at what was already only a moderate bill took place. At that point we had about thirty senators in favor of a strong bill, and the Southerners who wanted practically no bill at all numbered about twenty. But the fifty senators in the middle, led by Johnson and Dirksen, were getting impatient, for the filibuster and the many weeks of civil rights debate had delayed other Senate business. In the end, the "moderate" majority prevailed over the "extremists" on both sides.

Senators Keating and Douglas and I made some last-ditch attempts to restore to the bill two of the administration's original provisions, namely, equal job opportunity and technical aid to school districts that were attempting to desegregate; but Dirksen, who had sponsored the original bill containing those provisions, backed down. Claiming that the two amendments would jeopardize the whole bill, he moved to table our motions, and we were defeated. A similar fate befell another amendment I offered, to give the attorney general "Part III" power to intervene in private suits for school desegregation.

As finally passed in April, the Civil Rights Act of 1960 specified penalties for the obstruction of federal court orders; it made bombings and burnings of any building, or possessing or transporting explosives across state lines, federal crimes; it required local registrars to retain voting records for twenty-two months and gave the attorney general the right to inspect them; and it authorized federal courts to appoint referees to help blacks register to vote. It was a modest enough accomplishment, we thought, but Senator Russell declared that it "flies in the face of the Constitution [and] absolutely destroys due process."

Civil rights became a major issue in the election campaign that year of 1960, and the Democratic platform promised to eliminate all forms of discrimination — in jobs, in schools, in housing, in public facilities. So when John Kennedy was elected President we expected that he would help us pass some truly significant civil rights legislation at last. But nothing happened. Kennedy's first two State of the Union messages barely mentioned civil rights. His administration took several praiseworthy executive actions against racial discrimination, and the Justice Department, under his brother Robert, did move more vigorously to enforce the voting rights laws we had already passed, but the Kennedy team gave no support to any new civil rights program in Congress.

The liberal Democrats could not attack Kennedy for his failure to live up to his principles on racial segregation because they were so closely identified with him, but a Republican could, and I did. There were murmurs of disbelief in the Senate in 1961, when I, a Republican, rose to complain that our liberal President was doing nothing about civil rights. But I and others continued to prod him on the issue, and in 1963 President Kennedy did, finally, submit to Congress a package of civil rights bills that eventually became the monumental Civil Rights Act of 1964.

By 1963, of course, the public pressure for civil rights action could no longer be ignored by anyone. Frustrated by the slow pace of the progress they were making toward full integration into our national life, blacks all across the country were demonstrating and boycotting and protesting — and many white liberals from colleges and church groups in the North were joining them.

The rising tide of pressure for federal civil rights legislation culminated in the mammoth March on Washington in August 1963, at which the Reverend Martin Luther King, Jr., delivered his famous "I Have a Dream" speech. Two hundred fifty thousand Americans thronged Washington's Mall for that stirring event; Marian and our children marched, and I attended the rally and sat on the Lincoln Memorial steps, which served as a dais. I was inspired and awed by this mighty, visible manifestation of the words in the Bill of Rights: "The right of the people peaceably to assemble, and to petition the government for a redress of grievances."

Marian and I were renting a house on Massachusetts Avenue in Washington that summer, and notwithstanding the warnings that right-wing forces might attempt to disrupt the rally, we decided to give a buffet dinner party for Roy Wilkins, A. Philip Randolph, and other civil rights leaders who came from all over the country to march in the rally. Marian also worked with those who were enlisting New York and Los Angeles writers and movie stars to participate. Ever since the McCarthy era, movie stars and directors had been reluctant to support political causes, but the civil rights cause brought them out — and many of the celebrities also came to our dinner, which was one of the few social events in Washington that night.

* * *

The outpouring of the thousands of men and women who marched that day, the orderly way they conducted themselves, and the deep sense of conscience that the event expressed, all had a great deal to do with creating the national and congressional state of mind that enabled us to pass the Civil Rights Act the following year. The American public *can* and did make the difference.

The new civil rights bill, which President Kennedy had finally requested in June 1963, was making its way through House committees at the time of the march. Strengthened and broadened, it was reported out favorably just two days before he was assassinated. No action was taken on it that year in the House or Senate, but it passed the House early in 1964 and came before us in February.

It was the legislation I had been waiting and working for during all my years in Congress. It broadened the laws protecting voting rights; provided for assistance to public-school districts wanting to desegregate; allowed the federal government to file suits to desegregate public schools and to cut off federal funds from any school district where racial discrimination was practiced. It outlawed racial and sex discrimination in employment and established the Equal Employment Opportunity Commission (EEOC), with some enforcement powers. But the heart and soul of the measure was the public-accommodations section, which banned discrimination by race, color, religion, or national origin in any restaurant, lunch counter, hotel, theater, sports arena, or similar public facility. Furthermore, the bill authorized the U.S. attorney general to go to court to sue where these accommodation rights were being violated.

The legislative history of this bill was even more complicated than that of its milder predecessors. Again we voted to by-pass the Judiciary Committee; again we spent weeks debating whether to debate the bill; again the Southerners arranged themselves in platoons and readied their filibuster. But this time we had more support from the public at large and from the highest levels of government. President Johnson in the White House put his persuasive powers behind the bill and exerted quiet pressure on wavering Democrats. Senate Majority Leader Mike Mansfield was committed to the measure, and the majority whip, Senator Hubert Humphrey, became the floor manager for the bill on the Democratic side. Senator Thomas Kuchel of California, the minority whip, managed the bill from our side of the aisle.

Paul Douglas and I and the senators who had once been considered extremists worked closely with and within the leadership group, but this time we had no significant differences within our parties. The leaders had come around to our way of thinking and were advocating some of the very same provisions they had fought hard to defeat just four years earlier when we had proposed them. We refrained from gloating over this welcome change, but toward the end of the 1964 debate I did make the happy observation that "it is now clear that the mainstream of my party is in support of civil rights legislation and, particularly, support of this bill."

The Democratic leadership took a much milder attitude toward their Southern colleagues than Johnson had done in previous filibuster situations. Mansfield declined to put the Senate through another ordeal of all-night sessions, saying he was concerned about the members' health and that he did not want to turn the proceedings into a "circus." Humphrey made a point of treating the Southern senators with kid gloves, accommodating them courteously on small matters whenever he could do so without sacrificing principle or strategy. Humphrey also realized early in the game that he could not win this fight without Republican support — and that meant more than just the handful of Republican liberals like myself. He had to win over the majority of the thirty-two Republicans in the Senate, starting with Minority Leader Everett Dirksen. "Everything is going to be talked over with the Republicans — strategy, tactics, and timing," he said. "We have obligations not only to the Republicans in the Senate but also to those of both parties in the House who were so faithful and effective" in passing the bill there.

Formal debate — and thus the filibuster — began on March 30. Humphrey and Kuchel spoke for the bill, and then Russell and his team took over, holding the floor, preventing any substantive voting from taking place (except, by agreement, a vote on another jury-trial provision early in May). As the debate dragged on, Dirksen let it be known that he had serious reservations about the fair-employment and public-accommodation sections of the bill. Late in April he submitted a list of some seventy changes he wanted to see made. But the question in everyone's mind was precisely which of those suggestions Dirksen regarded as important and which were the ones that, if accepted, could secure his support for the bill and the Republican votes for cloture that he could control.

Although not at all bigoted, Dirksen was a conservative, and he made us pay a price for the support he eventually gave the bill. For a long time we did not know where he really stood — until it finally became clear that he was just playing hard to get in order to corral more votes. I believe he was just as determined as we were to enact a comprehensive civil rights bill, and on only one point did he make us pay a price.

The negotiations with Dirksen on that point I regard as one of the highlights of my career. At various times Attorney General Robert Kennedy, other Justice Department officials, and leading senators from both parties joined the discussions. It took a long time to find out what Dirksen really wanted. We kept talking and talking, sitting in his office as the filibuster was going on, and finally, when he thought the time was right, he said to me, and I believe to other senators that same day, "Well, I might go along with this if there was no coercion in efforts to correct discrimination in employment."

Whether Ev Dirksen felt beholden to employers or merely was expressing his own innate conservatism, I do not know, but to get his support and pass the act we had to water down the sections dealing with job discrimination. We gave local agencies more authority to settle disputes before the federal government stepped in, and we removed from the EEOC the power to seek court injunctions against job discrimination. The U.S. attorney general was given that power instead, and he was authorized to sue only where a "pattern or practice" of unlawful discrimination existed. In other cases an individual could bring suit against an employer who had discriminated against him, but in the absence of a "pattern or practice" of discrimination there was no way for the federal government itself to enforce the job-bias provisions of the act until 1972, when Congress finally gave the EEOC the authority to sue employers who discriminated unlawfully.

That was the big compromise with Dirksen, and when he was satisfied on that issue, he took the whole bill and ran with it. From then on he became the champion of the Civil Rights Act of 1964. He was persuasive enough to bring to the bill a great many Republican senators who would not have supported us otherwise. We did not have enough votes for cloture, but he produced them after that compromise. He cashed in a lot of credit with Republicans, and even with some senators on the Democratic side; in the end, I believe he had even more to do with the result than did Lyndon Johnson, who exerted his great influence from the White House.

Once the deal was made, it was embodied in what became known as the Mansfield-Dirksen substitute bill, which was introduced late in May. Dirksen called in reporters and told them that "civil rights . . . is an idea whose time has come. . . . Let editors rave at will and let states fulminate at will, but the time has come and it can't be stopped." Some members of the original civil rights liberal group were suspicious of Dirksen's amendments; he had the reputation of being a wily fellow and they did not like the idea of weakening the EEOC. But I carefully analyzed the substitute bill and helped to allay the fears of my allied Democratic colleagues. "No title has been emasculated," I said, "and the fundamental structure of the bill remains."

Early in June, Mansfield and Dirksen introduced a cloture petition, which I and more than fifteen other senators had signed, and on June 10, 1964, the Senate for the first time voted to limit debate on a civil rights bill. Senator Russell saw defeat coming, but he reacted too late. The die was cast. He had made a strategic error in refusing to compromise early in the debate, when he might very well have succeeded in having some provisions of the bill changed. By June, after debating civil rights for three months, the Senate was no longer in a mood to compromise. Everett Dirksen had done his work. President Johnson called up some wavering senators, and church and labor groups in a number of states lobbied senators whom we had identified as unsure. By a vote of 71 to 29, with all one hundred senators present and voting, the cloture motion was passed. Angry at his defeat, Senator Russell declaimed that "we're confronted here not only with the spirit of the mob but of the lynch mob" — a strangely ironic remark.

After that, all that remained to be done was to patiently vote down, one by one, the ninety-nine amendments that the Southerners introduced in a desperate and futile effort to delay the bill once more. Then the House, in order to avoid a conference that might have sent the bill back to the Senate again, agreed to the Senate amendments; on July 2 President Johnson signed the monumental and historic Civil Rights Act of 1964, beginning a new era of civil rights guaranteed to Americans by law. It was a great victory and each of us who had had a hand in it, including Dirksen and Mansfield, treasured that final tally sheet as a precious symbol of morality and perseverance.

NINETEEN

Republicans Divided

In June of 1964, after twenty-seven of the thirty-three Republicans in the Senate had voted to impose cloture on the Southern filibuster, I breathed a sigh of relief. A month later, my satisfaction with Republican attitudes in Washington gave way to disappointment and defeat in San Francisco. Having knuckled under to the persuasiveness and power of Ev Dirksen on civil rights, the ultraconservatives of my party struck back with a vengeance. At the Republican National Convention in San Francisco's Cow Palace, which nominated Senator Barry Goldwater for President, they well nigh sank the party with an ugly display of convention tactics more appropriate to a totalitarian state than to our democracy. The result was division and disaster for the party and a time of great difficulty for me.

As any reader of these pages is aware by now, conservative Republicanism and progressive Republicanism (which the media insist on calling "liberal") had been in opposition for a long time, and I had always been active on the skirmish line between the two forces — often to my own political detriment. On housing, health, labor, civil rights, and foreign aid, I had generally opposed the ultraconservatives in the party and had gone against them even when a clear majority of the party itself supported them. And the ultraconservatives, as we have seen, had hit back at me.

At the start of my career I generally accepted as a premise that my ideological views would be different from the views of the majority of my Republican colleagues, and I acted on the proposition that both were acceptable within the spectrum of the party. Hence, I tried only to win them over to positions on specific issues, one at a time. But after I gained experience and some prominence, it was no longer enough for me to work for and argue for and vote for the bills I supported. Long before the 1964 convention in San Francisco, I became aware of the dangerous and politically suicidal direction in which some of the party's leaders were trying to steer it. I realized I could no longer ignore or merely deplore the general ideological tone of the Republican Party; I had to try to alter the tone itself.

So when Senator Goldwater emerged around 1960 as a national figure and the hero of the conservative Republicans, I was one of the few ranking Republicans willing to meet his challenge head-on. Barry Goldwater personally was high-minded and dedicated — and most likable (and in later years we forged a warm friendship). But the movement he led was reactionary in terms of the social issues of our time. I wrote a book, *Order of Battle,* to answer his *Conscience of a Conservative.* In magazine articles and in speeches I criticized the ultraconservative Republican ideology. I warned that if Republicans wanted to win national elections consistently again they had to revitalize the party and make it reflect the concerns of urban America — which already constituted more than 70 percent of our population in the early 1960s.

Those concerns were with the economic viability and security of the great cities, with racial problems, with housing, education, and poverty, with mass transportation, and with the quality of working life. The solutions to these problems were not to be found in the free-enterprise system alone or in rugged individualism alone as espoused by Barry Goldwater.

Goldwater believed that government should not be permitted to touch those matters lest it undermine our freedom. Such generally accepted government functions as relief for the poor, subsidies, and regulation of commerce and industry may be desirable in themselves, Goldwater conceded, but they deprive the citizen of the power to handle his own problems with his own money and his own resources. When that power is taken away by an omnipresent government, this philosophy holds, freedom is lost. Leave us alone, Goldwater was saying in effect, just look after foreign policy, coinage, the army, navy, air force, and FBI, and we will take care of ourselves; if anybody falls in that battle, he's falling for freedom, he's a martyr, and we should do nothing about it except practice philanthropy. Any suffering caused by those policies, Goldwater said, would be unfortunate, but there had to be casualties for freedom, as there are casualties in war.

That was where Goldwater and I disagreed fundamentally. I do not believe that people have to suffer privation in order to remain free. I accepted instead Abraham Lincoln's dictum: "The legitimate object of government is to do for a community of people whatever they need to have done, but cannot do at all, or cannot so well do for themselves, in their separate and individual capacities." I have always insisted that government and business together should be able to provide all our citizens with economic security without destroying their freedom and that the government must step in where free enterprise cannot or will not do the job. To me, that is the essence of "progressive" Republicanism, reflected in the ideas of La Follette, Norris, and La Guardia: that the government steps in when — and only when — private means are inadequate to do the job. "Liberalism," as exemplified by President Franklin D. Roosevelt's New Deal, calls on the government to deal with the vicissitudes of life from the start. And ultraconservatives such as those Goldwater led would keep the government out of the equation entirely.

In 1961, I took part in two very lively televised debates with Barry Goldwater on the ABC network program *Issues and Answers*. I charged Goldwater with espousing policies that — by ignoring those urban concerns — would turn the Republicans into a permanent minority party; I challenged him to support the amendment of the Senate's cloture rule to allow civil rights legislation to be passed. He responded with the characteristic ultraconservative statement that "the only civil right that is mentioned in the Constitution is the right to vote" — thereby ignoring the Bill of Rights and the Fourteenth Amendment. He was not against the filibuster, he said, because it was "a desirable thing to protect minorities." When I urged one of my favorite themes, that only the government could coordinate the efforts of private business to provide such programs as health care, he countered with the statement that too much government interference in the 1930s had slowed down recovery from the depression. It was a classic confrontation, with neither of us convincing the other, of course, but together providing the listeners with an illuminating comparison of the Republican conservative and progressive views.

When we turned to foreign policy, Senator Goldwater complained that our foreign-aid program, since the Marshall Plan, "hasn't produced any good for our side; we have lost more people to Communism than we have gained people to our side. . . . I haven't seen any evidence of new friends that we have bought with foreign-aid money." To which I replied that if we had not aided the developing nations, more of them would have entered the Soviet orbit. Goldwater had the advantage of hindsight in that argument: He and his conservative friends wanted to do nothing, so it was easy for them to point to our past failures and ignore our past successes. I was trapped in that discussion into debating foreign aid on his terms, on the question of whether it could buy us allies, instead of on the more fundamental grounds that foreign aid was essential to alleviate the poverty and underdevelopment that could lead to war or to Communist or other totalitarian takeovers, and that it was essential to trade and the adequate supply of raw materials.

In the following year, when President Kennedy sent federal marshals and troops to the University of Mississippi to enforce the registration of James Meredith as the school's first black student, Goldwater argued that the federal government had violated the Tenth Amendment to the Constitution, which reserves to the states all powers not delegated to the federal government. In a letter to Goldwater and in public statements, I reminded him that the Fourteenth Amendment authorizes Congress to enforce equal protection of the laws and that the Tenth Amendment was therefore irrelevant on the school-desegregation issue. Furthermore, I pointed out, the issue in the federal government's intervention at Ole Miss was "not school desegregation under the Fourteenth Amendment but, instead, the supremacy of law itself — an order of the court — in our society."

I also became embroiled in a public controversy with Representative William E. Miller, of upstate New York, who was destined to become Barry Goldwater's running mate in 1964. Miller at the time was chairman of the Republican National Committee, and in that capacity he declared that Republicans were opposed to financing medical care for the aged through Social Security. He issued that statement immediately after I had announced I would introduce a medical-care bill that would do precisely that, but which would also "contain basic Republican features," such as coverage of people not under Social Security and options for individuals to buy private insurance if they wished. I guessed that Miller, who was as conservative as Goldwater, was trying to undercut my bill; I challenged his definition of the official party position and referred him to the 1960 Republican platform, to which my bill conformed in every respect.

* * *

By the time we gathered for the national convention in San Francisco in 1964, in the aftermath of the civil rights struggle, Senator Goldwater had won control of the Republican Party. For eighteen months his people had been quietly and efficiently lining up support among conservative Republicans all across the country, and they were unstoppable. Goldwater was opposed by Governor Nelson Rockefeller of New York, who was my choice but whose candidacy was complicated by a recent divorce and remarriage. When it became clear on the eve of the convention that Rockefeller would not prevail, he released all his backers, including me, to transfer our support to Governor William Scranton of Pennsylvania. Scranton is a fine and able man, but he seemed not to have the stomach for the internecine fight that would have been required to wrest the nomination away from Barry Gold-water. Accordingly, his candidacy came to naught.

The Goldwater platform spoke of the "moral decline and drift" in the country, yet it repudiated a number of the traditional Republican positions on civil rights and foreign policy. Rockefeller was our chief spokesman as we carried the platform fight to the floor, but when he rose to address the convention he was hissed and booed and drowned out by Goldwater supporters in the galleries. I spoke later that night and got similar treatment.

Never before had I experienced such an ugly example of mob rule at a political gathering — in the United States. These Goldwater supporters — in gold shirts and cowboy hats and boots — had organized sections of the gallery. A shout, "We Want Barry," would come from one corner and the response — "Olé" — would resound from the other, completely drowning out the speaker. There were bells and horns and drums to add to the din. It seemed to be a deliberate, organized attempt to prevent any opposing voice from being heard, and it chilled me with the thought that I might be seeing the beginnings of an American totalitarianism. Theodore White's *The Making of the President 1964* says that the managers of the Goldwater team tried to quiet the demonstration. I accept that statement — but the effort was certainly not successful.

I could not support Barry Goldwater for President. His willingness to give the NATO commander, as well as the President, the right to order the use of nuclear arms, his position on the Social Security system and other fundamental safeguards for the worker upon which our society was built, and his attitude toward the Civil Rights Act, which the country needed so badly and to which I had devoted so much effort, forced me to sit out the 1964 presidential election. It was not a decision that had to be thought through carefully, weighing all the various alternatives. I simply could not endorse any candidate who advocated those positions, as much as I might like the candidate personally and despite whatever inducement I had to give him some support in the interest of party harmony. I just could not do it.

Consequently, a week after the convention I called a press conference in New York and announced that "I am and will remain a Republican, and will not bolt the party, and will not support President Johnson, but I must in conscience withhold my support from the national Republican ticket." The Goldwater position, I said, threatens to recast American politics "along sharp ideological lines" and "could wrench the social order out of its socket." And I added that "there have been ominous indications that structured into my party's campaign strategy may be an effort to exploit the 'white backlash' in the

North and to appeal to the dying, old social order of segregation in the South — two prospects which are alien to the principles for which I have fought all my life."

* * *

I predicted at the time that the Goldwater campaign policies would decimate the Republican Party and thereby lessen its strength and usefulness, as indeed they did. The sweeping defeat of the party in 1964 was a debacle that brought the party to the brink of ruin, a situation from which it is not completely recovered, even today. Republicans lost State Houses and county seats, governors and legislators and local officials in droves; everything went down the drain. From a relatively good position we found ourselves flat on our backs. We emerged from the election with only 32 senators and 140 members of the House of Representatives.

In the aftermath of this crushing defeat a new liberal group, called Republicans for Progress, was organized in New York, led by many of my friends in the progressive wing of the party. But it never accomplished much. The entire party realized that the Goldwater campaign had been a disastrous mistake; with everyone willing to turn to something else, it seemed a bad time for a Republican splinter group. Although I agreed with its principles, I kept a polite distance from Republicans for Progress. Having broken away by not supporting Goldwater, I did not want to remain too far from the mainstream, so I was not anxious to affiliate with any breakaway group unless it was very substantial, which this was obviously not going to be.

Within a few weeks of the 1964 disaster, however, I started agitating for a program that would somehow rebuild the Republican Party. In an article in the Sunday *New York Times Magazine* two weeks after the election, I bluntly declared that the leadership of the party, the Republican National Committee, had to be changed, that more young people had to be brought in, and that "the Republican Party must adopt and develop a new and inspiring mission. It must provide an alternative both to President Johnson's 'government first' approach and to Barry Goldwater's 'no government' approach." Goldwater's Southern strategy, I wrote, had created for the party an image of a "lily-white" party appealing to the old order of the South and "driving away and alienating . . . millions of Americans for years to come. How ironic it would be for the party of Lincoln to move full circle in one hundred years to take on the look of the Dixiecrat party in 1964 . . . The road back for the Republican Party is long and will require a struggle of enormous magnitude."

The Republican train had "left the tracks" in the 1964 convention, I wrote, and I pointed out that the Goldwater philosophy was not conservatism at all. Conservatives such as Taft, Vandenberg, and Eisenhower "took on strangely liberal hues when confronted with the so-called conservative philosophy advanced by Senator Goldwater." The issue before the country and the party was not, I insisted, socialism or private enterprise, as Goldwater had tried to make it, but "how we can strike the right balance between government's presence in the economic system and the enlargement of freedom, opportunity, security, and dignity for the individual."

By early 1966, rank-and-file Republicans all across the country were looking beyond the party's conservative wing for a new standard-bearer. They realized that the party could not get anywhere sticking to outmoded nineteenth-century concepts that were based on a vanished ideal of a small-town America and that ignored racial discrimination and the problems of urban America. Rejecting the Goldwater philosophy, these Republicans began paying more attention to the party's liberal wing, and especially to Governor George Romney of Michigan. Governor Romney's brief and ill-starred attempt to obtain the Republican nomination for President was to involve me directly, for the first and only time, in the quest for national office: I was Romney's choice for a vice-presidential running mate.

George Romney was the front-runner for several reasons. Refusing, as I had refused, to endorse Goldwater, Romney had won reelection as governor of Michigan in 1964, although his state voted overwhelmingly for Johnson. Romney was a personable figure with excellent Republican credentials whose administrative experience had been proven by a successful business career in which he had risen to the presidency of American Motors, the country's fourth-largest automobile manufacturer.

Furthermore, his potential rivals were hanging back. Nixon, who lost to Kennedy in 1960 and then lost the California gubernatorial race in 1962, was deep in eclipse — although he quietly scored points with Republican congressmen by helping out in their 1966 election campaigns. Rockefeller at that time had taken himself out of contention for 1968. Having failed to get the nomination in 1960 and 1964, the governor of New York was biding his time; he had, in fact, encouraged Romney to throw his hat in the ring — either because he really thought Romney might make it or because he wanted someone else to carry the moderate banner until he, Rockefeller, judged that the moment was right for him to pick it up himself.

I first met Romney through Max Fisher, the Detroit business executive whose role as a leading member of the U.S. Jewish community I have described. Max was a backer and a friend of Romney's, and through Max I was invited to a rather ceremonial lunch at Governor Romney's summer mansion on Mackinac Island in Lake Michigan. Max and I and our wives cruised out there from Detroit one day, in Max's boat, and we spent a full afternoon with the governor. We talked politics and shared our concern that the Republican Party would never recover unless it evolved new policies and a new direction; and of course we discussed Romney's chances for the presidency. The idea that I would be his running mate evolved naturally from that meeting. Besides our ideological affinity, we could offer a ticket well balanced not only by geographic and ethnic backgrounds (Romney was a Mormon), but by our differing governmental experience. Visiting my Washington office one day, Governor Romney noticed the gallery of photos of me in the company of foreign leaders and commented on how well my considerable experience in foreign affairs and in national legislation would balance his domestic record of excellent business and state administration.

Romney's status as the most visible Republican candidate gave his words great weight, and when he mentioned to reporters that I was his vice-presidential choice, the press was suddenly beating on my door. The nominating convention was still two years away, but that did not seem to matter — and I certainly did nothing to quiet the talk. In May 1966, *Time* magazine wrote of the Mormon-Jewish ticket; in June *U.S. News and World Report* weighed in with a story declaring that Rockefeller had not only urged the Republican Party to nominate Romney and Javits but was pledging the ticket all kinds of support. A couple of weeks later I was on the cover of *Time,* the subject of a favorable story that commented on the idea of my becoming vice president: "Audacious, perhaps. But preposterous? Not really."

From a practical political standpoint, two years in advance of a convention was much too soon for such high-powered exposure focused so sharply on one's candidacy. But I made no attempt to cool down the campaign. I would have been mightily pleased to be nominated for vice president, as my prime desire was to help revitalize and modernize the Republican Party. But at the time I did not really believe I would be nominated, and it was not until years later that I realized that if I had done things a little differently I might have had a real shot at national office, either then or later.

But I did believe that my candidacy was the best means of bringing about the changes in the party that I thought were necessary, and for that I needed all the exposure I could get. As I told *Time,* "Even

Harold Stassen had a bigger voice than I did [in 1964] simply because he was a candidate. You have to be a candidate to be heard . . . I'll be any kind of candidate for anything to carry this cause — or I'll be no candidate, if that's the best way to get the Republican Party back into the mainstream of American life."

Time was sympathetic to my brand of Republicanism, so I took advantage of the excellent forum the story gave me. "Those Republicans who are not willing to make a fight for the big cities," I told the magazine, "are in effect saying that they mean never to win a presidential election in modern times." Eisenhower, I pointed out, had carried twenty-five of the nation's biggest cities in 1956, and Kennedy had taken twenty-two of them in 1960, but Barry Goldwater took only six. "Republicans can indeed win in the cities," I argued, "if they are forceful, energetic, and imaginative enough to offer programs to tackle and solve the problems of the cities. . . . The struggle within the Republican Party is between a type of conservatism which can disable the party from being really national and a progressive viewpoint which can make the party eligible for a national mandate." I defined that disabling conservatism as meaning "in practice denouncing the federal government for trying to do too much — while in effect sustaining the right of the status quo to do nothing at all."

I was very pleased and proud to be mentioned for a national ticket, and I believe I would have helped Romney very significantly had we been nominated. I do not believe that I would have suffered any handicap from my religion. Although some politicians and people with whom elected officials have to deal may harbor anti-Semitic feelings, I have never felt that such prejudice has blocked me politically. I was always able to assure my colleagues and the electorate that I was and would be objective regardless of my personal feelings on an issue. Besides, Jack Kennedy had dispelled the notion that a member of a religious or ethnic minority was somehow less trustworthy in national office than a white Anglo-Saxon Protestant. In some ways there was probably a greater reluctance to elect a Catholic than there would be to elect a Jew, because many people feared all kinds of horrors from the "Church of Rome." As one result of Kennedy's presidency, and of the general growing up and sophistication of America, the door is now open for anyone, regardless of race or origin or religious belief — or sex — to become President. I believe the country is ready for it.

Unfortunately, that Time cover represented the high point of my vice-presidential foray. It was probably too early, for both Romney and me, to appear to be so far ahead of the pack — we had too much early foot, as they say in horse racing. Everything a front-runner says and does is scrutinized microscopically, and Romney, a highly moral man, was regarded by the reporters who followed him around as somewhat "square"; he was never really understood by the press and never learned how to use the press effectively. Although he won reelection as governor that fall by a resounding margin, Romney's national popularity, as measured by the polls, went steadily down all through 1967. As Ted White pointed out in *The Making of the President 1968*, when Romney tried to attack Lyndon Johnson's Vietnam policy his statement came out sounding so much like the President's policy that Johnson praised it — thereby wiping out Romney's attempt to create an independent position for himself.

Then, in the summer of 1967, at the end of a hectic day of campaigning, Romney uttered those few casual, careless, and now historic words that changed his image — and ultimately destroyed his candidacy. Arriving late for a television taping on a local Michigan station, with no time for briefing and none of his advisers with him, Romney was asked whether his current position on Vietnam had not changed since an earlier statement. And he replied:

> Well, you know when I came back from Vietnam, I just had the greatest brainwashing that anybody can get when you go over to Vietnam. Not only by the generals, but also by the diplomatic corps over there, and they do a very thorough job. And since returning from Vietnam, I've gone into the history of Vietnam, all the way back into World War II and before. And, as a result, I have changed my mind . . . in that particular. I no longer believe that it was necessary for us to get involved in South Vietnam to stop Communist aggression. . . .

It was a throwaway line, not a major statement, and Romney did not even stay to listen to the playback of the tape. Even the interviewer, according to White's account, did not realize the import of the remark until he read over the transcript a couple of days later. But then, wrote White, he alerted the *New York Times*, which picked up the story. The networks borrowed a film clip from the local station, and the entire nation heard and saw a man who aspired to control all our destinies, who wanted to be the one with his finger on "the button," assert that he had been "brainwashed" by U.S. generals and diplomats.

Romney's candidacy, already in trouble, never really recovered from that gaffe. That one word, *brainwashing*, destroyed his chance for the presidency — as if someone had pushed him off a cliff. Almost any other word would have been all right. The American people were getting disenchanted with Vietnam; they wanted a President who could lead them out of the war and who could not be swayed from that purpose by the military. Romney had been a responsible, honest businessman and an able governor, but people thought he was not enough of a politician either to see through the misleading briefings he may have been given in Vietnam, or, if he did feel he had been brainwashed, to talk about it in some way less destructive to himself. He was an honest man giving an honest answer to a fair question; but the bare statement, with no attempt to use it to teach a lesson to the country or to others, seemed to many to show insufficient preparation and sophistication to be President of the United States. He might have survived as a candidate if he had dropped the matter — but he spent weeks trying to prove that he was not unsophisticated politically, which just underlined the charge. He later served effectively as housing secretary in the Nixon cabinet, but the presidency was closed to him.

Romney's sudden fall helped give the nomination to Richard Nixon, who was seen as a decisive man. He, too, had come to the conclusion that we should get out of Vietnam — "with honor," he said — and he had a reputation as a tough anti-Communist.

The demise of the Romney candidacy ended my attempt at higher office as well. When Romney formally withdrew from the race in February 1968, in the middle of the New Hampshire primary campaign, I gave my support to Nelson Rockefeller. Governor Rockefeller shared my hopes and views about what the Republican Party should become, but, even had he wished to, he could never offer me second place on *his* ticket because of the constitutional prohibition against President and vice president coming from the same state.

I had another campaign to think about in 1968. I was up for reelection as senator, and my persistent attacks on Barry Goldwater and his policies had made me the favorite target of all the ultraconservative forces that New York State could muster — and that is saying a lot. As soon as it became apparent that Romney's candidacy was doomed and that I would not be running on a national ticket, I turned my attention to my Senate race. I faced not only the normal challenge from the Democrats but a powerful, well-financed threat from a relatively new entity, the Conservative Party.

It was no coincidence that the New York Conservative Party had first appeared on the scene in 1962, the only time when Governor Rockefeller and I were running for reelection together. Its founders were J. Daniel Mahoney and Keiran O'Doherty, right-wing Republicans to whom Goldwater was a hero. They were irked by the success and popularity Rockefeller and I were enjoying as progressive Republicans, and they were determined to remove us from our jobs. The only ideological premise in their party's early years was the thought that since liberal Democrats were at the helm of the Democratic Party, progressives should not be permitted to head ours. The Conservative Party was simply out to wreck or take over the Republican Party of New York State.

O'Doherty, the Conservative Party senatorial candidate in 1962, received only about 2 percent of the vote. But the Goldwater movement inspired the Conservative Party, and the anti-Vietnam ferment and protests of the 1960s provided new targets for its wrath. In the ensuing years the party grew in strength, attracted to its banner some sincere if misguided conservatives (such as James Buckley), and developed its own ultraconservative philosophy: against government aid to education and housing, against antipoverty programs, against basic protections for labor, against any real effort to help or to train the chronically unemployed. The Conservative Party campaigned on money issues — balance the budget — and paid no attention to the human consequences that would follow any government failure to rescue innocent victims of ill health, unemployment, or other economic and social catastrophes. The Conservative Party was against the United Nations, too, and in recent years it has come out against the right of poor women to have federally funded abortions.

I opposed the Conservative Party because I saw it as a wrecking operation — and it opposed me because I was working hard for many of the programs it was most against. As time went on, Rockefeller, as governor and head of the Republican Party in New York, had to open some channels of communication with the Conservative Party in order to reach many of the local Republicans who were taking endorsements from them. But they campaigned bitterly against me every time I ran, and finally contributed heavily to my defeat in 1980.

My concern, late in 1967, was not that the Conservative Party could elect a senator but that it might draw enough Republican votes away from me to let the Democrats win. I needed some way to keep those conservative Republican votes while maintaining my progressive principles. Presidential politics brought me a solution to this dilemma in the person of Richard Nixon.

I had kept in touch with Nixon during his years in the political wilderness. Having moved to New York after his 1962 defeat in California, Nixon was practicing law with a Wall Street firm, and he lived not far from us. My family still recalls the afternoon Nixon came to our Park Avenue apartment for a talk with me. I had somehow completely forgotten the appointment and was at my office in midtown.

My son, Joshua, who was then about sixteen, let him in to our apartment. The two of them, expecting my arrival at any minute, began what turned out to be a fascinating conversation for my son. Finally Joshua phoned me and said, "Dad, Vice President Nixon is here waiting for you. He's been here for an hour. We've had a marvelous talk about politics, about his life, about his family, and about everything in the world. Now we've run out of talk, so you better hurry on home." Which of course I did, marveling at this little-known side of a complex man who chatted uncomplainingly with teenagers in the middle of a busy day.

I was never a strong ally of Nixon's. Although I had campaigned for him in 1960, I was backing the campaign of George Romney in 1967, and Nixon was aware that if Romney fell by the wayside I would line up with Rockefeller. I regarded Nixon as somewhere more toward the middle of the Republican spectrum, between the progressive wing represented by Rockefeller and myself and the ultraconservative forces that had given us Goldwater in 1964. Certainly, as he began to emerge from his temporary eclipse, Nixon shared my keen desire to rebuild the Republican Party along more progressive lines.

Late in 1967, Nixon's desire for more political exposure and my need to thwart the Conservative Party gave us a chance to help each other. To kick off my senatorial campaign, I was planning a fund-raising dinner for more than two thousand people at the New York Hilton that December. Governor Rockefeller, ten Republican senators, and a number of other high-ranking Republicans were all scheduled to attend and to speak in my behalf. Nixon had not yet appeared on the political scene in New York, and it occurred to my brother, Ben, that it would be a political "ten-strike" if he attended my dinner. So I invited him; he accepted eagerly and agreed to speak, too. It did not matter that I was not about to endorse him for the presidential nomination: Neither he nor Rockefeller had yet announced their candidacies. I felt that my dinner, bringing Rockefeller and Nixon together in a political context, could help everyone; it would put Nixon in the political limelight once more, and his presence and kind words would spike the ultraconservative guns that were already being aimed at my reelection bid.

And that is just about the way it turned out at the fund-raising dinner and in the general election the following fall. The Conservative Party ran James Buckley against me, and he got 1,139,000 votes — a powerful showing for a third-party candidate but not enough to unseat me. I received a total of 3.3 million votes (running on both Republican and Liberal lines once more), giving me a plurality of 1.1

million over Paul O'Dwyer — the Democrat I had defeated in that cliff-hanging House race in Washington Heights twenty years earlier.

In that election and in 1974, and between elections as well, I was the main and constant target of the Conservative Party. The Conservative Party attacked Rockefeller because of his prominence, but they did it without the sense of derring-do they displayed when they took after me. They attacked me directly, frontally and by name, and in every conceivable way. And they also attacked me indirectly: In 1974, for example, their allies, the right-to-life groups, picketed with signs calling me a "murderer of infants" as I was entering a dinner of the Catholic Charities in Nassau County, where I had been invited to speak. For a while they even advertised a special telephone number one could call to listen to a hate-filled diatribe against me. They raised a lot of money by naming me as the villain they were out to beat — and I once wrote them, asking for my cut of the contributions they were getting through use of my name; needless to say, they did not reply.

Jim Buckley made it to the Senate as a Conservative in 1970, defeating Charles Goodell, the liberal Republican whom Rockefeller had appointed to fill out the term of Robert Kennedy. The conservative-liberal split within the Republican Party reached a new level of bitterness in the Buckley-Goodell campaign. Vice President Spiro Agnew, the number-two Republican in the land, showed up at a dinner for Buckley and called Goodell the Christine Jorgensen of the Republican Party. Buckley won a three-way race that year with 39 percent of the vote.

I served alongside Jim Buckley in the Senate for six years, and I came to know him well. I exclude him from the charge that his party was simply a "spoiler," for he was sincere about the policies for which the Conservative Party stood; the Republican Party was simply not conservative enough for him. The extremes to which Buckley's conservative beliefs carried him, however, were demonstrated during the New York City fiscal crisis in 1975, when he briefly opposed federal aid and implied that bankruptcy for the city would not be a catastrophe.

The divisions within the Republican Party, which became so acute in 1964 that the party almost destroyed itself, have never fully healed — and perhaps it is too much to expect that they should. Sometimes, however, I get a sense of déjà vu. At the Republican National Convention in Kansas City, in our bicentennial year of 1976, I sensed that history, if not repeating itself, was perhaps standing still. Ultraconservatives in the California and Texas delegations and their allies from other states enacted a chilling replay of the mob-rule tactics of some of the Goldwater forces at the Cow Palace in San Francisco in 1964.

This time the television audience, at least, was able to see me and hear what I had to say — a strong plea for the new directions that I thought the Republican Party had to take — but the hall was a hostile mob scene as far as I was concerned. The demonstrators were apparently infuriated by my presence, and their noisemaking drowned out most of my remarks in the hall. As someone who has spent years attempting to understand and reconcile opposing viewpoints, I was saddened and frustrated by the narrow-mindedness of the people who refused even to listen to another view in our party. As they blew their automobile horns and mechanical whistles — devices that must have required a great deal of planning and forethought to bring into the hall — I was struck by the realization of how dangerous was such an attitude, and I was inspired to a stronger sense of resoluteness to overcome this manifestation of the greatest evil of our time — intolerance of opinion and denial of free speech. For I realized that, indeed, it *can* happen here — and to prevent it calls for eternal vigilance.

TWENTY

The Governor
and the Senator

In my view, Nelson Aldrich Rockefeller was one of the most extraordinary figures to surface in U.S. politics after World War II. Central to all his policies and never very far from his consciousness was his breathtaking vision of a world in which interlocking economic relations would become the decisive force for peace, a world in which all countries would work together for development and mutual support because of their economic interdependence. He saw the possibility of such a world in the 1940s, when he was coordinator of Inter-American Affairs, and he worked toward it all his life. He was a remarkable man and the world is a poorer place now that he has left it.

Nelson (I never heard him called Rocky by a personal friend) and I generally agreed on policy and issues, but he was not always easy to get along with, and I probably encountered more of his suspicion, his stubbornness, and what I saw as his intolerance of dissent than anyone. His value to the nation and the world far outweighed these personal idiosyncrasies, but we were involved in a series of recurring, sometimes stormy arguments and confrontations over politics and our own political relationship. One reason for this was his reluctance, it seemed to me, to accept many people outside his family as equals. His whole life's training gave him the feeling that he was superior: because of the Rockefeller family tradition, because of his real and demonstrated ability and vision, and also because of his connections and wealth, which he used decisively to enhance his authority and power.

Furthermore, Nelson was very deeply committed to his own views, which were quite hard to change once he had come to them. Like Franklin D. Roosevelt, he felt he was right and that anyone who disagreed with him was not only likely to be wrong but might be trying to exploit him. I am convinced he sincerely believed that. But his certainty on policy was not matched in politics. He was indecisive in matters affecting his own political career and future, and that made him a difficult ally.

In many ways, my feelings toward Nelson Rockefeller were like my feelings toward my brother, with whom I also experienced periods of tension and misunderstanding. Nelson and Ben were similar on some points of character. As Ben sometimes tried to dominate me, Nelson sometimes attempted to have me do his bidding, and when I went my own way each of them felt betrayed. Both of them resented slights, real or imagined.

Like my fraternal bond with Ben, however, my link with Nelson was indissoluble. Despite moments of frustration and sometimes even anger, we stuck with it, and as late as 1974 Rockefeller made a generous contribution to my reelection campaign. I felt we were close friends.

* * *

My first distant contact with Nelson Rockefeller took place about 1941, when Dean Gregerson and I were setting up the ACIP program at Williams College to train young Americans for jobs in Latin America. Rockefeller, as the U.S. government's brilliant coordinator of Inter-American Affairs, quickly recognized the importance of the project; his office assisted us, and Rockefeller himself wrote to Brigadier General Lewis B. Hershey, the director of the Selective Service System, to request draft deferments for a few of our graduates who had already found positions in Latin America. I saw Rockefeller on occasion in Washington during the war, and later when I was a congressman, and he contributed to some of my congressional campaigns. But I did not get to know him well until 1958, when I was already in the Senate.

Early that spring, Jock Whitney, who was then ambassador to Great Britain and publisher of the *New York Herald Tribune,* invited me to a breakfast meeting with Rockefeller at the Mayflower Hotel in Washington. Nelson told me that, having served in several high-level positions in the executive branch of the federal government, he was now interested in elective office and he wanted to run for governor of New York. He said that he thought his ideas about the Republican Party were parallel to mine, and that, as I had been the sole successful Republican in the 1954 election, in which Averell Harriman had been elected governor, he wanted me to work with him and help him gain the nomination and the election.

I was delighted. I told Nelson that I thought he would be a great boon to the New York Republican Party and that he could help make it the most progressive in the nation. Having already chosen the route of national rather than state office, I was giving nothing away in supporting Rockefeller's bid — except that I was welcoming a potential rival for power within the state party.

Early in Rockefeller's first campaign, I arranged a rally for him and his three running mates in the garment district on Seventh Avenue in Manhattan, normally a stronghold for the Democratic and Liberal parties. After Rockefeller, Louis Lefkowitz, Malcolm Wilson, and James Lundy had made their speeches, I called all four candidates back to the platform, lined them up behind me, and said to the audience, "Now that they have made their presentations, they are ready to answer your questions."

Nelson later recalled that moment as his first lesson in practical politics and the point at which he began to gain self-confidence in campaigning. He had not expected to confront the electorate that directly, but he proved he could do it, and very capably too. Someone asked him how a man as rich as he was could expect the people to elect him governor. As I remember it, he replied, "The same kind of providence that has made me and my family what we are, an object lesson on how to use vast sums of money wisely and in the highest public interest, will make me a good governor." His opponent, Averell Harriman, was not so poor either, so the issue of wealth could not become a serious issue in the campaign; but this was one of the milestones in Rockefeller's development as a public man.

From that point on, Nelson's native talents as a campaigner emerged with full force. He soon became a master at persuading the electorate. He usually started a campaign far behind in the polls but gained dramatically as the voters listened to what he had to say and became convinced. He had a dashing and effective campaign style, which was, of course, helped by the glamour: When a Rockefeller shakes your hand and looks you in the eye and says "Hiya, fella," that is pretty intoxicating stuff. And he meant it; he was very genuine, warm, and human, and it came through to the voter.

Rockefeller's ambitions aimed beyond Albany, of course, and everyone knew that from the start. Ever since he was a boy, his eye had been on the White House. "When you think of what I had," he once said, "what else was there to aspire to?" Having proven himself by winning the 1958 gubernatorial election by half a million votes, Nelson immediately began running for the 1960 Republican presidential nomination as the candidate of the progressive wing of the party. It was an effort I enthusiastically supported and which was typical of Rockefeller. He set up a large "exploratory" campaign staff in 1959 to sound out Republican leaders all across the country — and when he discovered that they were almost all committed to Vice President Nixon

— and that the business community would not contribute significantly to a Rockefeller campaign — he announced in December that he would not be a candidate. (He could have financed a presidential campaign himself, but political success can seldom be "bought" with personal funds.)

Six months after his "definite and final" withdrawal from the race, Rockefeller was back in it, propelled by the U-2 incident and the collapse of the East-West summit meeting, and by what he saw as a crisis facing the country and the Republican Party. But it was too late, of course. In his famous "Fifth Avenue Compact" with Richard Nixon on the eve of the 1960 convention, Rockefeller did succeed in reshaping the party's platform to conform more closely to his progressive and activist ideas, but the nomination went to Nixon.

In 1962, Rockefeller and I were both up for reelection — the only occasion when we faced the voters of New York together. That was the year of the second big congressional battle over health insurance (see Chapter 16), when Senator Clinton Anderson of New Mexico and I devised the Anderson-Javits amendment. I had been working hard on that issue and had introduced a bill that emphasized the role of private health insurers. Then Rockefeller came up with a health-care-for-the-aged proposal of his own. Representative John Lindsay introduced it in the House and Rockefeller asked me to sponsor it in the Senate. His bill was a good one, similar to mine in all its important aspects, but it made no sense from a tactical standpoint and I declined to introduce it. Many Republican senators and representatives were ready to vote for a good health plan, but I knew they would refuse to back any legislation with Rockefeller's name on it because that would appear to be taking sides in the expected fight for the 1964 presidential nomination. It would have been more productive for Rockefeller to have supported my bill, which already had attracted some important Senate backing and which in fact reflected some of Rockefeller's thinking. But that was not Nelson's way. He was running for reelection and he had to have his own proposals.

The newspapers were always looking for disagreements between Rockefeller and me, and when the reporters learned of my refusal to introduce his bill, newspapers all over the state headlined ROCKY, JAVITS SPLIT. Those stories may have made good reading, but they were not true, for we continued to agree on the issue of medical care for the aged. It was just that he wanted to have a health plan to campaign on and he was heedless of the legislative realities in Washington. As I recall it, he was annoyed at first, but when I explained my reasons he understood, and little more was heard about his bill.

There were few policy matters on which Rockefeller and I disagreed. In 1962 we tested each other out. Each gave the other a detailed questionnaire covering all the substantive issues of the day we could think of, and the remarkable outcome was that on more than 90 percent of the issues facing the country and the state, the janitor's son from the Lower East Side and the grandson of the richest man in America saw eye to eye.

Our policies of progressive Republicanism were vindicated by the electorate. Although our party lost four seats in the Senate and failed to make any significant midterm gains in the House or in the total number of governorships, Rockefeller and I were reelected. The victory was somewhat embarrassing to me: Nelson defeated Robert Morgenthau by a little more than half a million votes, but my margin over James B. Donovan was nearly double that, 983,000 votes (the biggest plurality in the nation that year), and I carried New York City, which Nelson failed to do. Rockefeller had expected to win by a million-vote margin, which would have enhanced his chances for the presidency, and he was clearly disappointed at running so far behind me. Reporters covering our headquarters on election night wrote that I was "abashed" and "uncomfortable" at outracing Rockefeller; I worried that the result might cause him to resent me — as unreasonable as that might sound.

As *New York Post* columnist Murray Kempton described the situation, the governor

> had expected to win by 1,000,000; having been somewhat surprised to find that anyone dared to run against him, he was now confounded to find that there were even people who would vote against him. What is more, he found himself running nearly 450,000 votes behind Jacob Javits, a humble man, who was terribly embarrassed at this gaffe. Poor Javits, always apologizing, always explaining; in his most thundering triumph he stood there and said that he was sure that, if the Governor had run for the Senate, he too would have won by a million.
>
> "My family and I," the Senator said, "are full of gratitude." But the unspoken thought fairly cried out: I thank you for filling our cup, but did you really have to make it flow all over the Governor's carpet?

How many of our later difficulties can be traced to that disparity in our election totals of 1962 I do not know, but the returns made clear to Nelson that I was not and might never be beholden to him politically. Since he was on his way to dominating Republican politics in New York State, that might have been difficult for him to accept.

It must be pointed out that Rockefeller's 1962 divorce may have cost him votes in some of the conservative upstate counties. His remarriage, to Happy, the following year may have complicated his 1964 presidential bid, but it brought him so much peace of mind and confidence that it strengthened him as a person and a politician.

Toward the end of Rockefeller's second term as governor, we had one of our most serious misunderstandings. He was very low in the public-opinion polls; I recall that one poll gave him a favorable rating of only 28 percent. Mindful of the diminished plurality he had won in '62, I and some other Republicans became worried about the party's prospects in the gubernatorial election coming up in the fall of 1966. So I took a trip around the state to see for myself what it was all about and to find out whether Rockefeller could make it that year.

To Rockefeller, that was treason. Nelson's sometimes suspicious mind got the better of his good judgment. He became convinced that I was planning to run against him and that I was checking the state for my own candidacy.

I could understand his feeling that, as he was the dominant factor in the party, the question of whether he could win or lose the governorship should be no business of mine. On the other hand, I was the senior Republican officeholder in New York, and I had helped to bring Nelson into elective politics in 1958; so I felt that it was very much my business how the party fared, even though I would not be running in '66.

We met in Syracuse after my spring trip, and he accused me point-blank of trying to undermine him. He seemed to have forgotten completely how I had helped him in 1958. I got very indignant about his accusations, for I was not interested in the governorship: If I had been, I might have remained in state office and not run for the Senate in 1956 in the middle of my term as attorney general. I told him that and said that, despite his low standing in the polls, I thought he could win the election; to show him I meant it, I offered to become chairman of his campaign. That surprised him tremendously, and it took him a while to realize I really was in his corner.

Eventually he recognized that he was indeed in electoral trouble and appointed me his campaign chairman. Concentrating on his gubernatorial race, he put aside his presidential aspirations for the moment and encouraged the campaign for the Romney-Javits ticket, which is described in Chapter 19.

In retrospect, I am not sure of the reasons for Rockefeller's support of Romney. Given his own political and personal problems, it was certainly wise for Nelson to let someone else carry the ball for the progressive Republicans in 1967 while he tended to New York State. But I doubt he would have been happy if the Romney-Javits ticket had succeeded and I, another New York Republican, had taken the national limelight. He felt, like FDR, that the presidency properly should be his and that he was the best man for the office.

But, considering what happened in the later stages of the 1968 presidential campaign, it would be unfair to Nelson to accuse him of setting up Romney and me for his own ends: Nelson just could not make up his mind about waging a campaign to attain the presidency — which was something quite separate from his belief in his fitness for the job. In any case, he expected all his friends and associates to go along with whatever position he was taking at the moment.

This became apparent early in 1968, as the Romney drive was sputtering out. During the New Hampshire primary campaign, just a few weeks before Romney withdrew from the race, I declared in a series of interviews that if Romney failed to make a good showing in the early primaries I would back Rockefeller for the nomination. I pointed out that the moderate, progressive Republican movement "went down the drain" in 1964 because it arrived at the convention without a strong candidate. I said we could not allow that to happen again — though I acknowledged that Rockefeller was not about to announce his candidacy.

Rockefeller felt that the strength of his candidacy at that point depended on his *not* being a candidate, and he was furious at me for mentioning in public what everyone assumed, that he was preparing to run for the nomination again. He told the press that he was "sorry" about my statement and repeated his support for Romney. But I was not "switching" from Romney, as Rockefeller implied. I was trying to face the political reality: To counter Richard Nixon, the progressive wing of the party needed a stronger candidate than George Romney appeared to be.

When Romney withdrew from the race at the end of February 1968, even before the balloting in New Hampshire, the eyes and the hopes of moderate and progressive Republicans all around the country turned to Rockefeller. Volunteer Rockefeller organizations started working in many primary states, and his name was entered on the primary ballot in other states where no formal declaration of candidacy was required.

On Sunday, March 10, two days before the New Hampshire primary vote, Nelson, his top staff people, and a group of prominent Republicans — all supporters of his — gathered for a strategy session at his Fifth Avenue apartment. There must have been fifty of us altogether, including seven governors, three senators, five congressmen, and

Mayor Lindsay. For several hours we sat around a huge dining table in a beautiful room with Glarner murals on the walls and ceiling, and we discussed Rockefeller's political future and his chances for President. As the meeting began, it was clear that Nelson was uncertain whether he should become an active candidate or stay out of the primary battles and concentrate on discussing the issues. No formal decision was made and no statements were issued. But we all came away from that March 10 meeting convinced not only that he would run but that he would enter the Oregon primary, the next important event on the campaign trail.

Within the next few days, the presidential campaign heated up. In New Hampshire, Nixon won the Republican primary as expected; but Senator Eugene McCarthy came close to defeating the incumbent President, Lyndon Johnson, in the Democratic primary — whereupon Senator Robert F. Kennedy entered the Democratic contest. At about that time I called together in Washington a group of major business leaders who were all Rockefeller supporters. We wanted to plan a presidential campaign for Rockefeller, but the businessmen needed further assurance that he was really running. I telephoned him from the meeting, and I said, "Nelson, we're here, ready to organize for you throughout the country and raise a lot of money, and all these gentlemen want to know if you are running." And his answer, while not a flat commitment, satisfied all of us that he was in the race.

Our urgency was related to the calendar. Romney's washout in New Hampshire left progressive Republicans with no spokesman in the early primaries, and we felt it was essential that Rockefeller enter the May 28 primary in Oregon. The filing deadline for Oregon was only about a week away, and all it took was a declaration of intention by the candidate. I was prepared to enter the Oregon primary myself if Rockefeller declined to do so — not because I had any chance for the nomination but as a surrogate, in order to make a showing for the progressives and perhaps to win some delegates who could later be released to Rockefeller. But Rockefeller *was* running — or so we had been led to believe — and that was even better.

What we did not know as the clock ticked away was that Nelson had not made up his mind at all. He had several long meetings with his staff the following weekend, March 16 and 17, and his closest advisers were split. Nelson himself, I have been told, said he was prepared to go either way, but he did not like to be forced so early into a political fight where he would have to expend his energies going into every Oregon county; he wanted to pay attention to the national issues and to his own New York legislative program. At least one of his advisers told him bluntly that Nixon had the nomination all but locked up, and that Nelson should either give up or plunge into the Oregon primary for a full-scale battle.

Within another day or so, the Rockefeller staff reached a consensus and Nelson endorsed it. Although a public statement announcing his candidacy was in his pocket on Monday, March 18, by Wednesday afternoon, March 20, he and his staff had decided that he could not win without a long and bruising and difficult campaign — the kind he obviously did not want to wage — and that he should withdraw as an active candidate.

None of this leaked to the press. When Rockefeller called a press conference for Thursday, March 21, the entire Republican Party, as well as the nation at large, was convinced that Nelson was running; the *New York Times,* in fact, reported flatly that Rockefeller would announce his active candidacy. Governor Spiro Agnew of Maryland, who was a Rockefeller supporter, was so sure that Nelson would run that he invited friends to watch the Rockefeller press conference on TV in his office. All across the country, and especially in Oregon, the temporary volunteer organizations that had been beating the drums for Rockefeller prepared press statements and started looking for larger offices. And I started rearranging my schedule so that I could campaign in Nelson's behalf.

And then Rockefeller went before the TV cameras and the reporters at the New York Hilton and dumbfounded us all by stating in unusually definitive terms that he was *not* a candidate for President because the majority of the Republican Party's leaders "want the candidacy of Richard Nixon." He did not say that he would refuse a "true and meaningful call" from the Republican Party, but he emphasized that he expected no call and added: "I shall do nothing in the future, by word or by deed, to encourage such a call." It was the clearest, most unequivocal disavowal of candidacy I had heard.

His decision was terrible, for at the moment he spoke, the Oregon filing deadline was only hours away, and there was no time for any other progressive Republican to enter.

Six weeks later, Nelson jumped back into the race. The circumstances had changed drastically: President Lyndon Johnson had withdrawn from the contest; Martin Luther King, Jr., had been assassinated; and the country was in turmoil with race riots and student demonstrations against the Vietnam War. Furthermore, some of Rockefeller's supporters had continued to urge him to run. But many other Republicans were utterly disenchanted by his vacillation. It was too late. Although he campaigned energetically in May and June, he amassed fewer than three hundred convention delegates, and Nixon was nominated on the first ballot in Miami that August.

There is no question in my mind that, if nominated, Rockefeller would have been elected that year. He would have made a great President. He would have brought first-rate people into the federal government. His foreign policy would have been enterprising, and he would have done wonders with heads of state. With the Russians he would have been stunningly successful, because he understood money and business and they have shown that they are impressed by both. And he knew how to persuade people.

A Rockefeller presidency would have given me an unparalleled opportunity to be of service. As the senior senator from the President's home state, I would have become a major factor in the government. Yet I would have turned down, if offered, a cabinet post or executive appointment, because, notwithstanding our personal friendship, I would not have wanted Nelson, as President, to be my boss and to be able to ask for my resignation. I am very chary of appointive office: Except in the army, I have rarely had a boss, and I do not want one. A senator can be removed only by the people.

*　*　*

My reluctance to serve under anyone who had the power to remove me from office may have affected my decisions about running for mayor of New York City: Theoretically, the mayor can be removed by the governor. For twenty years after Tom Dewey blocked my attempt at the mayoralty in 1953, the possibility of becoming mayor of my native city ran through my career like a subterranean stream, surfacing almost every four years. And all during his tenure as governor, Nelson Rockefeller tried to get me into City Hall.

Nelson started urging me to run for mayor early in 1961. He hoped that a Republican win in the city would help recoup the political losses suffered by the party in the 1960 national election. I did not close the door on the idea, but I was not enthusiastic about it: I was already deeply immersed in national issues and I was looking forward to my reelection as senator the following year.

By May, the entire Republican hierarchy of the state, from Rockefeller on down, had consolidated in favor of my candidacy. They even got Richard Nixon to issue a statement saying that "the party and the country would best be served" if I ran for mayor. A special ten-member Republican Campaign Planning Committee, formed with Rockefeller's blessing, came out for a fusion ticket with me at the head. The committee pledged the Republican Party "to join and work with all political and citizens' groups in a nonpartisan spirit to select and elect candidates with the single purpose of giving the people of the City of New York the best government humanly possible." And in a comment on my known reluctance to run, the committee added that "no political, personal, or business considerations should be allowed to stand in the way of accepting nominations that are a call to civic duty."

The Liberal Party, the nonpartisan good-government forces, and many of my personal and political friends — including Jock Whitney — were all urging me to run. It appeared that for the first time since the days of La Guardia, New York had a chance for a good-government fusion administration.

Thus I faced a very difficult decision indeed when I flew up to New York from Washington on May 10, 1961, for a meeting at the Roosevelt Hotel with the five Republican county leaders of New York City. The *New York Post* that day declared that "pressure on Senator Javits to head a fusion ticket for mayor today was reaching the dimensions of a draft."

The Liberal Party publicly asked me for an immediate decision, and the Republican county leaders, backed up by Rockefeller, also insisted that I decide forthwith. They felt that if the decision were to be delayed and then I were to decline, the ultimate Republican nominee would have to start out with the handicap of being an obvious second choice.

The pressure on me and the demand for an immediate answer, there and then, forced me to say no. I told the county leaders that my inclination was to stay in the Senate and that if I were going to run for mayor I needed more time to think it over. They refused me that, and I turned them down. If they needed an immediate answer, I said, the immediate answer was no. And I stuck to that decision through several hours of intense conversations. Whenever I am not sure of what to do and I am forced to give an answer on the spot, my answer is no. If you press me, my instinct is to say no. And they pressed me.

The eventual Republican candidate that year, Louis Lefkowitz, my successor — and a great success — as attorney general, was defeated, and Bob Wagner won another term. By 1965, Wagner's popularity was waning and it had become clear that a Republican would have a good chance to be elected mayor. So once again Rockefeller and other Republican leaders asked me to run. Having carried the city in my 1962 reelection, I was an even more logical choice than I had been four years earlier, but the timing was not right for me. I was midway through my second term in the Senate and just hitting my stride, and a number of important initiatives I had taken there, such as the Arts Endowment legislation and the civil rights measures, were beginning to bear fruit.

Besides, in the aftermath of the 1964 Goldwater debacle, I judged that I could have a greater influence on reshaping my party from the Senate than I could as mayor of New York — where I might have become bogged down in the thousands of day-to-day details of city administration and not had the chance to give thought to national issues.

So I suggested to Nelson that the nomination go to John Lindsay, who was then an effective, active, and promising young Republican congressman from Manhattan. Nelson was disappointed, but he eventually agreed — provided I could induce Lindsay to run. John was as reluctant to leave Congress as I was, for similar reasons. After some discussion, John and I told Nelson that one of us would run, but the decision had to be made by March 1. We regarded three-term Mayor Bob Wagner as a strong opponent, and we knew we would need a lot of time to put together a campaign that could beat him.

A few days before the deadline, Rockefeller flew to Washington for a breakfast meeting with New York's congressional delegation. He praised both Lindsay and me as potential mayoral candidates, but he insisted that March 1 was too early to make a decision. He needed Mayor Wagner's cooperation to help pass his program in the state legislature, and he thought a campaign starting in March might unravel his delicate threads of contact with the Democrats.

According to *Newsweek*, which somehow obtained a fairly accurate account of that breakfast meeting, Nelson's argument

> infuriated Javits. "All right, then," he snapped at Rocky, "why don't *you* run for mayor?"
>
> His face flushed, Rockefeller first eyed Javits and then Lindsay. "Why don't you announce for mayor and do it right now?" he challenged. "You can win your argument for an early date that way."
>
> "Nelson," Javits retorted, "if you continue in that attitude, you can scratch my name off the list."

At the deadline I announced I would not run for mayor. Subsequently, I talked with Lindsay several times, explaining to him how much help Rockefeller and I could be to him if he made the run. I promised to campaign actively for him, and I did so when he later entered the race. He was elected, and I campaigned for him in 1969, too; at that time he ran successfully for a second term on the Liberal line alone, the Republican Party having denied him the renomination and given it to State Senator John Marchi.

The New York City mayoralty has compromised the reputations of fine politicians, and John Lindsay is one of them. By 1973 he was clearly out of favor with the electorate, and Rockefeller again tried to get me to take on the bruising job. He invited me to breakfast at his apartment and assured me of his whole-hearted cooperation if I became mayor. Together, he said, we could really redeem the city. I think he was serious about that — he felt he could work better with me in that job than he could with me as senator. By then I was too deeply involved in the Senate and in national issues. So I held him off.

At that point, perhaps just to smoke me out, Rockefeller let it be known that he, as the leading Republican in New York, and Liberal Party strategist Alex Rose were planning to nominate Bob Wagner for mayor. I came out strongly and publicly against that on the ground that the Republican Party in New York would be crippled for years to come if it endorsed so prominent a Democrat against whom it had campaigned energetically on four occasions.

Rockefeller was very upset — at my refusal to run or my statement about Wagner, or both. I was in Paris and he phoned me at the embassy residence and raised hell with me about my statement. I put him down pretty hard myself; I said that I had expressed my honest judgment, that I had done as much for the Republican Party as he had, and that I meant what I said. I have never had such a difficult conversation with Nelson as I did then. He ended up in complete rage and frustration. The Republicans nominated John Marchi again, the Liberals went their own way with Al Blumenthal, and Democrat Abe Beame was elected.

On all those occasions, I refused to run for mayor primarily because I felt I would have a greater impact nationally than I could in the city. I do have some regrets: My family and I might have had a better life had I gone after the mayoralty and won. Considering what I achieved in the Senate, however, I believe I made the right decision every time.

*　*　*

Despite all our difficulties and disagreements, I had an enduring respect and a deep affection for Nelson Rockefeller — and I still do. I got the chance to show it when he became vice president under President Ford. Rockefeller took his duties as president of the Senate seriously. I was his most ardent advocate in the Senate and I gave him a great deal of knowledge and information from my own experience there. While he presided over a body in which he had had no previous experience, Rockefeller's self-confidence and boldness had a chance to be displayed in a historic setting. He made rulings that no vice president, not even Lyndon Johnson, had dared to in the past — but he got into trouble, too.

Rockefeller faced his first test as vice president as soon as the 1975 session opened, and in his characteristic fashion he met it head-on. Once more we were fighting a battle to change the cloture rule. Although the filibuster was no longer the formidable Southern weapon it had been in the past, liberal and progressive senators of both parties were again taking the position that the Senate, as a new body at the beginning of a new Congress, could adopt whatever rules it desired. Our ultimate aim was to amend Rule XXII to allow cloture by a majority vote of the whole Senate — fifty-one votes — but we were willing to accept any meaningful compromise. To make progress, we needed a series of favorable rulings from the chair, and Rockefeller could provide them if we could show him what to do and that it was lawful.

During a month-long filibuster against a rules change, I helped to work out with Senators Mansfield, Mathias, and Mondale a detailed bipartisan strategy to bring the Senate to the point at which the vice president could make the rulings we all wanted. The parliamentary situation was very intricate; it involved motions to consider a change in the rules, points of order against that motion, and motions to table the point of order — all written out in advance in a word-for-word script. Nelson's aides had a copy of our script; the trail we proposed to blaze through the jungle of parliamentary technicalities was so tortuous that even we, the senators, might have lost our way without that road map — and Nelson was new to the game.

Our strategy succeeded because Nelson simply persisted. Following our plan, he held that a motion to take up the rules at the beginning of a new Congress could be decided without debate, that it could be tested by a point of order brought against it, and that if the Senate voted down the point of order — thus confirming the propriety of the motion — the motion would then have to be put to an immediate vote.

That master parliamentarian from Alabama, the late Senator James Allen, managed to delay our carefully prepared program for a few minutes. He insisted that the original motion had no effect until it was passed and that therefore it should be debated before being voted on — which would have opened it up to a filibuster. But Rockefeller held fast. In the context of the complex parliamentary situation, Rockefeller's ruling in effect upheld the position we had been advocating unsuccessfully for nearly twenty years: that the Senate could change its rules by majority vote at the beginning of each new Congress.

In the midst of this nerve-wracking and momentous session, Senator Allen became aware of how closely Vice President Rockefeller was following the script. At one point, as I was leading Rockefeller along with parliamentary inquiries that were all in the scenario, and to which I knew the answers in advance, Allen rose. To the laughter of the Senate, he addressed me and asked, "Will the vice president yield?"

Then he accused me of putting words in the vice president's mouth, and a few minutes later he declared, "The senator from New York — of course, it is a tortuous course — was aided ... by answers of the presiding officer that were numbered, as he called off one number."

Further parliamentary maneuvers later muddied the waters of Rockefeller's rulings. Yet a compromise was reached: The decision that the Senate could change its rules by majority vote at the beginning of a new Congress was buried in ambiguity; but in exchange we were able to pass an amendment to the cloture rule itself. On March 7, 1975, the Senate voted to allow cloture to be imposed (on any matter except a rules change) by sixty votes (three-fifths of the Senate) instead of by two-thirds of those present. That change, which made filibusters and the threat of filibusters less potent, could not have been achieved without the boldness of Vice President Nelson Rockefeller.

But Rockefeller's boldness got him into trouble with the Senate during that same controversy. Senator Allen continued to fight after Nelson's ruling. He was making dilatory motions and requests and inquiries — using all the rules he could think of to upset our applecart. Rockefeller got exasperated, as we all did, and when Allen rose yet again, Nelson just refused to recognize him, just "did not see him." That was an unforgivable breach of Senate tradition. The presiding officer can sustain a point of order against a senator, and he is under no obligation to respond to a senator's parliamentary inquiry, but he must recognize a senator who rises and asks to speak — and in this case we all saw and heard Allen ask for the floor.

Rockefeller had to apologize to the Senate for that one. "Every senator," he announced to the chamber a few weeks later, "has, at all times, the right to be heard and it is the responsibility of the chair to see that that senator or those senators have that opportunity." He admitted his mistake and said that it was "in no way meant as a discourtesy." The Senate applauded Nelson's apology — it was refreshing to find a vice president who admitted an error — and the issue was closed.

Almost exactly one year later, Nelson had to ask the Senate's forgiveness again, this time for uttering some sharp criticisms of one of a senator's staff members. "I would like to apologize ... for my remarks in an off-the-record meeting," Rockefeller told the Senate. "There is no question that it was a mistake." This apology, too, was accepted. Nelson was discovering that the Senate is a special place where the rough-and-tumble of the political and business worlds is not always tolerated and that senators have a way of calling the vice president to account — by their dissatisfaction — even though it is not a remedy specified in the Constitution.

Nelson may have had these experiences in mind when he told me one day that he could never do what I did, that he could never be a legislator. "It suits you," he said. "You like to debate and read and think." He said he would not have the patience to endure the hours of waiting for a turn to speak, of sitting on "duty" as a floor manager of a bill, or the interminable debates of weeks and even months. Besides, he said, "I like to see some tangible result of what I do. I go out and see a housing development or an office building or a ski run, as a result of something I have done; I can see it and touch it. But in this Senate business you don't see one hundredth of the things you do, even the things you do personally." That was his answer to my suggestion that he succeed me in the Senate.

Nelson Rockefeller made his own rules and they were sometimes misunderstood — promising to do something, he might say "Trust me," which meant "I'll do it my way for you." Nelson and I on occasion seemed to be political rivals, but we were not. Perhaps we were testing each other, testing our friendship and loyalty, and sometimes we both failed the other's test. One difficulty may have been my idea — and I may have been wrong — that to be his friend you had to think as he did and act as he wanted you to. I wanted to be his friend, yet I refused to buy his friendship with automatic agreement, and perhaps I leaned too far the other way.

* * *

Just a few weeks before Nelson Rockefeller died, I spoke to him about what he could still do for the country. He had retired from politics completely; he was refusing to show up for anything political and, as far as I know, was not even making campaign contributions to anyone. He was devoting his time and attention to his family, to his art collection, to his new business of selling art reproductions, and to other business and private pursuits. I respected that stance, but I disagreed with it: I felt he was too valuable and experienced for the country to be deprived completely of his services, and I told him so. I suggested that we invite him to appear as a witness before the congressional Joint Economic Committee, of which I was a member, to testify on the national and international economy, and to testify on Latin America before the Western Hemisphere Subcommittee of the Foreign Relations Committee. He said he would consider the idea, and he seemed receptive to it — but I never spoke to him again. A few weeks later he was gone.

I never thought I would outlive him. He was one of the country's most gifted sons of the time.

TWENTY-ONE

Winning and Losing for Labor

In two decades on the Senate's Labor and Human Resources Committee (formerly Labor and Public Welfare), and as its ranking member during most of that time, I had a hand in shaping almost all of the labor legislation that has come before the Senate, including fair minimum standards for workmen's compensation, occupational safety and health, child labor laws, minimum wage, and the expansion of job training and job opportunities for youths and minorities.

Of all these legislative struggles, the achievement that gave me the greatest satisfaction in the labor field is the Pension Reform Act of 1974, properly known as the Employment Retirement Income Security Act (ERISA). It represents the successful culmination of a seven-year campaign to reform and regulate the private pension plans in which an estimated 30 million U.S. workers were enrolled. My staff and I originated this idea, and I pushed and tugged and nagged at the Congress to get it enacted into law. It took hundreds of hours of committee sessions and meetings with other senators and staff and experts to work out the complex web of details and standards and requirements embodied in the law.

This massive legislation was necessary because the nation's private pension system was deceptive, unsafe, and unjust. Private pension plans had grown dramatically since World War II, when wages were frozen but pensions and other "fringe benefits" were not. Unions demanded pensions for their members, and Congress encouraged the trend by allowing greater tax advantages for employers' contributions to workers' pension funds. (These private pension plans are not necessarily connected to Social Security, although some of them deduct from pension payments whatever the retired worker receives from Social Security.) Between 1940 and 1960 the total assets of private pension plans in the United States grew from $2.4 billion to $52 billion and the number of workers covered grew fivefold. By 1960, 21 million workers confidently looked forward to a retirement made more comfortable by a private pension.

But in the early 1960s, as more and more of these workers reached retirement age, it was discovered that many of the pensions that looked so good on paper were illusory. Some of the plans could not pay the promised benefits because the employer had not set aside enough money to do so; other firms went bankrupt, leaving their pensioners out on a limb. Workers who switched jobs lost their pension rights almost as a matter of course. Even worse, there were thousands of instances in which the unread — and sometimes unreadable — fine print in the pension agreements disqualified workers who thought they were entitled to receive a pension and who then discovered, when they retired at the age of sixty-two or sixty-five, that because of some technicality they would get nothing or next to nothing from the company pension plan.

The most notorious and tragic example of pension failure took place in 1963, when the Studebaker automobile company in Indiana halted production and laid off almost all its employees. Approximately forty-five hundred Studebaker workers who had been with the company for an average of twenty-three years were informed that they had lost 85 percent of their pension benefits overnight. Some of them committed suicide.

We designed ERISA to prevent such tragedies. It did not require that pension plans be established, but it regulated any that were. Most important, it established elementary rules regarding "vesting," the employee's right to receive his pension regardless of whether he is still working for the company when he reaches retirement age. Under one of the vesting formulae that an employer can choose, for example, the law provides that after five years on the job an employee is "vested" in 25 percent of his earned pension benefit; he then becomes entitled to an increasing percentage with every year of service until, after fifteen years of employment, he is completely vested: Even if he resigns or is fired or changes jobs, he will receive upon retirement all that he has earned of his pension. This is only just, because the employee regards such plans as part of his emolument and to deprive him of it is unfair indeed.

The law sets up actuarial standards to assure that each pension fund has enough money to pay the pensions as they come due. (Originally, many large firms did not put aside pension funds at all; it was assumed that they would always have enough money to pay their pensions, and their workers took the obligation as a matter of good faith.)

ERISA also established the government-supervised Pension Benefit Guarantee Corporation, which functions like an insurance company: It collects premiums from companies offering pension plans and then pays the pensions to the workers if a company goes out of business leaving insufficient funds to pay its pensions.

My attention was first called to the seriousness of the pension problem by Frank Cummings, who was then minority counsel of the Committee on Labor and Public Welfare and who later became my administrative assistant. As a practicing labor lawyer Cummings had dealt firsthand with tragic cases of workers deprived of pension benefits for one reason or another. As I was the ranking minority member of the committee, Frank came to me some time in 1966 with the idea that a comprehensive law was needed. I agreed with him at once. Together we outlined what the bill should contain and Frank immediately went to work drafting it. Early in 1967 I introduced it in the Senate. It was the first bill to deal with the entire pension problem and in many respects it was similar to the ERISA law passed seven years later. It would have established federal reinsurance of pension benefits, minimum standards for vesting, funding, and administration, and a "pension bank" through which a worker could transfer his pension credits from job to job. My bill also would have established a U.S. Pension Commission, analogous to the Securities and Exchange Commission, to supervise the complex and technical aspects of pension plans.

The only action Congress had taken on the subject had been to require pension administrators to disclose the structure and operations of their funds. The Johnson Administration was proposing another law to tighten those accounting regulations at the time I introduced my bill in 1967. I pointed out to the Senate the inadequacy of disclosure alone. The administration's bill, I said:

> continues to rely . . . on the now well-nigh discredited technique of requiring more disclosure — on the theory, I suppose, that if you can only get the plan administrator to disclose enough, the beneficiaries will figure out what is wrong. I doubt that they will. It is hard enough for lawyers and actuaries to read annual reports, balance sheets, and other financial statements. I doubt that we can expect the average pensioner to absorb, let alone to have the expertise to see all the implications of, a complex pension plan.

But no serious hearings were held on my bill that year or for several years thereafter. In fact, not until Senator Harrison Williams, Democrat of New Jersey, became chairman of the Labor and Public Welfare Committee in 1971 did we make any progress whatever on pension reform.

"Pete" Williams is a prolabor senator. As soon as he took over the committee I suggested he join me in sponsoring this legislation, but there was substantial opposition to the bill and it took some months to convince him that this was the way to go. Eventually he agreed, and as he was chairman, we put his name on it first — that was the way to enact something. He promptly got a professional assistant in the pension field, and thereafter he and I and our staffs worked closely together in refining the various aspects of the legislation.

As we started drafting a new bill I began to hear from trade unions, pension trustees, banks, insurance companies, actuaries, and people who set up pension plans. Most of the business people advised me to stay out of the issue; they said it was a can of worms that would cause me endless trouble and alienate my friends and supporters, and I should just lay off. Some unions took the same position, but the more progressive union leaders came early and enthusiastically to our aid; Leonard Woodcock, president of the United Auto Workers (and later U.S. ambassador to the People's Republic of China), and I. W. Abel, president of the United Steelworkers of America, were very effective allies. They testified for a strong bill and they brought to our hearings many individual workers who had been victimized by pension failures. But with business groups opposed, and organized labor divided, the most important support came from the people and the press. We received thousands of letters from victims who volunteered to testify. In one two-week period in 1972 my office received twenty thousand letters of support for pension reform.

Our hearings, in Washington, New York, Newark, Philadelphia, Cleveland, St. Louis, and Minneapolis, were heavily covered by the press and revealed the full story of the misrepresentation, disappointment, and default that had deprived so many workers of their hard-earned pension rights over the years. It was heart-rending to hear these men and women recount how they had depended on their pensions, had worked hard to earn a comfortable retirement, had lived for that day in many cases — only to find the pension snatched away almost at the last minute of the last hour, for some reason that most of them really did not understand.

Some workers lost their whole pensions because they had been discharged shortly before they were entitled to receive them. One New Yorker named Robert Pratt had worked forty-seven years for the Gifford-Wood Company, an old and well-established firm manufacturing coal-mining equipment. Poor business conditions forced the company to lay him off in 1971, when he was sixty-four years old. The following year, just three months before his sixty-fifth birthday, the company was sold and its pension plan terminated. Funds were available to pay only the pensions of workers who had already retired. When

Mr. Pratt applied for his pension upon reaching age sixty-five, he was told he would get nothing at all.

Another case I brought to the Senate's attention was that of the Hickok Manufacturing Company of Rochester, New York, which sold out to a Fort Worth corporation and moved its operations to Texas. Although Hickok was increasing its profits at the time, its pension plan was canceled; employees already retired had to take a 12 percent pension cut, and four hundred fully vested but not yet retired employees, many of whom had worked for the company for twenty-five years, were deprived of all pension rights.

These cases were by no means unusual. A study by our committee had demonstrated that for every pension plan participant who earned vested rights in his or her pension, five employees with more than fifteen years of service forfeited all pension rights for one reason or another. The release of these statistics caused a sensation in the press and was a significant factor in directing public attention to the flaws in private pension plans.

We also found that in some unions, such as the Teamsters, trustees had used pension funds for their personal profit; some of the funds granted mortgages and loans to "insiders" or to businesses connected with organized crime. That created quite a scandal, and in one case, the Central States Pension Fund of the Teamsters union, the funds trustees were ousted after ERISA was passed; new trustees, pledged to carry out their responsibilities, were installed. But in 1980 the Central States Pension Fund and the government were still in litigation over loans and administrative arrangements made by the fund.

On September 15, 1972, after two years of hearings and investigation, the Labor and Public Welfare Committee unanimously reported out a bill that Pete Williams and I and our staffs had drafted. It provided fair vesting standards, set up a system to transfer pension rights from one job to another, required that plans be adequately financed and benefits federally insured, tightened fiduciary standards, and provided that the entire machinery be supervised by the Department of Labor. The bill, Williams and I told the press, will for millions of workers "make pensions a reality, rather than the myth that so many now prove to be." House committees had also held hearings on similar — though milder — measures. We confidently expected that our bill would pass the Senate that session and the House would come along with us the next year.

But ten days after we reported out our bill, the Senate Finance Committee, under the chairmanship of Senator Russell Long of Louisiana, dashed our hopes. Our bill had been referred to Long's committee because of its tax implications: The contributions to a pension plan by an employer are tax deductible as a business expense. The Finance Committee quickly stripped our bill of all the pension regulation and reported it out as an empty carcass, containing only a few new requirements regarding pension-fund administrators. The deleted provisions, Long's report said, "have historically been handled through the tax laws. . . . The committee believes that the coverage, vesting, funding, and related provisions should continue to be dealt with by the tax committees of Congress."

Finance Committee fears that its jurisdiction was being usurped may have played a part in the gutting of our bill, but the real issue was substantive. Senator Long and Senator Carl Curtis of Nebraska, the ranking Republican on his committee, simply thought our bill was unfair to employers. Long's mixed philosophy of populism and business opposed our bill from two directions: First, much of the business community opposed our bill because it required business to do more; second, populism demanded that government, rather than private pension plans, assume prime responsibility for retirement. Senator Curtis, on the other hand, was simply a very conservative Republican, and the Williams-Javits pension-reform bill offended all his political instincts. He just did not believe that the federal government should meddle in such matters.

At any rate, I was indignant over the actions of Long and Curtis and the Finance Committee. Indeed, I have rarely been so moved by a legislative event. Usually I am philosophic about legislative reverses, but the Finance Committee's emasculation of our bill seemed to me to be so unfair, so blatant a display of insensitive conservatism, that I could not let it pass. I took to the floor of the Senate to denounce the Finance Committee for what it had done. I spoke of the hearings we had held and the unanimity of the Labor Committee in reporting the bill. "Then," I said,

> in the fifty-ninth minute of the eleventh hour, along comes the Committee on Finance . . . [and] after one week, in a closed-door session, on a voice vote, and without any hearings, the Committee on Finance sent the bill back to the floor with the recommendation that every key provision in it be stricken. It will take a magician to demonstrate how the action of the Finance Committee is a service to our country and the American workingman. . . . What has happened is not unusual. It has happened before in American history, where a rather myopic point of view on what is best for this country has dictated some reactionary opposition to a given measure.

I challenged Senator Long, who walked into the chamber as I was speaking, to let the issue be fought out on the Senate floor. He responded with his familiar argument about the tax responsibilities of his committee. I rebutted that and added:

> I have no objection to the Finance Committee considering the matter. . . . All that I argue is, "O.K., that is fine, you have seen it." I do not want to see it stripped of everything meaningful. Now, while it is a hot issue, let us get to work at it and let the Senate decide whether it wants a meaningful pension-reform bill or wants to throw it into the ash can.

But the Finance Committee action had deprived our bill of any chance for Senate consideration at that time — and Senator Long and I both knew it. Nevertheless, my indignation was effective, for it aroused the ire of thousands of workers in dozens of unions. They complained to their senators, and the Finance Committee had to come around to a different view the following year. Pete Williams and I also went to work with two members of the Finance Committee, Senator Gaylord Nelson of Wisconsin, a liberal Democrat who was also our colleague on the Labor Committee, and Senator Lloyd Bentsen of Texas, a business-oriented senator who recognized the public-interest aspects of pension reform.

We conferred with Nelson and Bentsen at great length, and they eventually got their teeth into the bill and persuaded their colleagues on the Finance Committee to cooperate with us. Under the prodding of Nelson and Bentsen, the Finance Committee wrote its own bill, which paralleled ours in most major respects, and in September 1973 we worked out a compromise. The Senate, in an unusual vote, passed the compromise bill unanimously and, to force House action, tacked it on as an amendment to a House-passed tax bill.

But the House had jurisdictional problems too, and not until 1974 did the House pass a bill comparable to ours. Finally, between May and August 1974, in a very complicated House-Senate conference in which representatives of two Senate committees and two House committees all took part, we hammered out the final ERISA bill. Senator Williams and I both served on this conference committee, as did Senators Long, Curtis, and Bentsen, but the basic work, the detailed negotiation of the endless fine points, was carried out by Larry Woodworth, staff director of the Joint Committee on Internal Revenue Taxation, and by Mike Gordon, my staff aide whom our committee minority had engaged as a special counsel on pensions because of his professional expertise. Gordon was so devoted to this bill that he wore himself out during the conference and fell quite ill. Woodworth, who later became assistant secretary of the Treasury, died at an early age, his life shortened, I believe, by his labors on ERISA. Both of them were indefatigable in moving us all toward compromise, step by step, through the intricate pathways of this massive law. I consider them both great patriots in the cause of pension reform. Their efforts, and ours, were rewarded when both House and Senate passed the conference version of ERISA; the Senate vote was unanimous and only two members of the House voted nay.

President Ford signed the ERISA bill into law on Labor Day, 1974. That was an election year for me, and I found that ERISA was a great help in my campaign. As I traveled around the state, workers everywhere knew about ERISA and my role in getting it through, and they considered it a real blessing.

After the law was passed, some five to six thousand pension plans (out of six hundred thousand) were terminated. The opponents of the law claimed that the plans were closed down because of the excessive paperwork required by the legislation. This complaint threatened the whole structure of ERISA: Business people, especially the owners and managers of small firms, were honestly exasperated over all the forms they had to fill out.

We investigated and found that although there *was* too much paperwork (and we have since eliminated a great deal), it was not the reason the plans had been canceled. Rather, the small and weak pension plans that could not comply with the standards of the new law simply folded up or were converted into profit-sharing plans that did not require the employer to follow any specific funding rules. That did not discourage us. We felt that if the promise of a pension to a worker was not going to be kept, then it was better to terminate the plan or adopt a more limited one so that the worker at least knew where he stood. Then he could either negotiate with the employer for a plan based on the standards we had enacted, or he could go out and get another job where there was a better pension. We certainly would not have been doing the worker any good if we kept him in a job with a pension plan that was inadequate or unlikely to be realized.

The detail in ERISA makes it one of the major pieces of legislation with which American business is contending. But in any such major reform — analogous to Social Security in the 1930s — complaints are to be expected. I believe that we have successfully defeated the effort to identify the reform with excessive paperwork and that ERISA is now a permanent part of our legislative structure — as it should be.

Over the next few generations ERISA will prove to be one of the greatest benefits American workers have ever received. When it took effect in 1974 it covered 30 million U.S. workers enrolled in plans with $194 billion in assets. Pension assets totaled $362 billion in 1979 and they continue to accrue by about $40 billion a year.

Besides establishing security in retirement for the U.S. worker,

ERISA also benefits the economy by holding down Social Security taxes. In order to keep the Social Security system viable, these taxes have been increased to the point where employers and workers are now paying the government more than 12 percent of the wage package for Social Security taxes. If there were no ERISA, no insured private pension plans, we would have to pay about 20 percent of our income to the government to provide an adequate income for retired persons. If we allow the government to support the system of retirement benefits to such a degree, the state will become too large a factor in our lives. To the extent that ERISA helps prevent that from happening, it fulfills one of the great themes of my political and economic philosophy: the need for the private sector and government to work in tandem for the welfare of the citizen and for social justice.

The ERISA fight was one of a number of confrontations I have had with Senator Russell Long over the years. A powerful senator who can be a charmer, he operates with a combination of cajolery, toughness, and horse trading. When he wants you to vote his way, he drifts over, drapes an arm around your shoulder, and whispers very earnestly and persuasively in your ear. But when he is against you, little that is done comes out clear and simple, and even if you have the votes the result is often left so confused that it is hard to know who won. I like Russell Long and I believe he likes me, but too often we have passed each other on legislation as ships in the night, without hearing or understanding each other.

*   *   *

After we overcame the Finance Committee's objections to ERISA in 1973 and passed the bill in 1974, the country entered a recession. In late 1974 we were trying to make it unnecessary for unemployed people to go on welfare; by keeping them on unemployment compensation for as long as possible, we hoped to keep up their morale and keep them out of the poverty syndrome so that they could get back to work quickly as soon as the economy could absorb them. Therefore we tried to build up the unemployment compensation system.

At that time, the federal-state unemployment compensation system covered the first twenty-six weeks of unemployment, plus an additional thirteen weeks of federally subsidized payments when state or national unemployment reached certain levels. We were endeavoring to add still another thirteen-week period, on an emergency basis, so that the jobless would be covered for fifty-two weeks.

Senators Ribicoff, Nelson, and I introduced an emergency bill to provide those extra thirteen weeks of payments. The unemployment rate had reached 6.5 percent nationwide and almost everyone was in favor of the measure. The Ford Administration was behind it and the House passed a similar bill. Senator Long, the populist side of his nature in the ascendancy, not only agreed to let the House bill come directly to the Senate floor without going through the Finance Committee, but spoke in favor of it. He told the Senate that his committee had no objection to the House bill and added, in a burst of generosity:

> The substance of the bill is virtually identical to a measure recently introduced by Senators Ribicoff, Nelson, Javits and a number of other senators. I want to commend these senators for having worked out this measure, which has achieved such a wide degree of support and which so expeditiously and effectively addresses the pressing problem of rapidly rising unemployment.

That bill passed the Senate unanimously on December 16, 1974, and the following June, with unemployment approaching 9 percent, we passed another one, extending unemployment compensation payments to sixty-five weeks. Those measures took care of the immediate emergency. But when we tried to make more lasting reforms in the unemployment compensation system, so that such repeated emergency laws would not be necessary, we again ran into the opposition of Senator Long and the Finance Committee. A bill that Senator Williams and I introduced in 1977 would have established a standby program for additional emergency federal assistance, to be activated whenever unemployment goes above specified levels; the bill would also have set up a federal reinsurance grant program to help states out of the financial difficulties caused by their extraordinary compensation payments during periods of high unemployment. The bill died in the Finance Committee.

In fact we have retrogressed. Pension payments to workers are now deducted from unemployment compensation in some cases, and after state unemployment compensation has been paid for twenty-six weeks an unemployed worker — even an engineer or an executive — must be willing to accept any job, even at the minimum wage, or forfeit any federally aided additional unemployment payments.

*   *   *

My support for labor was steady and consistent during my Senate career, but I was not always successful in what I tried to do. On specific labor matters such as ERISA or unemployment compensation, I did, I think, make significant and lasting contributions to the well-being of the working men and women of this country. But on at least two occasions, one near the beginning of my first term in the Senate and the other near the end of my fourth, I and my like-minded allies lost important battles on significant, broader bills covering labor's rights and labor-management relations. The first of these two defeats was the passage of the Landrum-Griffin Act in 1959, and the second was our failure to reform the labor-relations laws in 1978.

The 1959 struggle grew out of the disclosures of corruption and racketeering in certain unions, particularly the Teamsters. Everyone agreed that legislation was needed to protect union members and the public from dishonest union officials. To this end, Senator John F. Kennedy introduced a bill aimed at keeping unions honest. The bill, which I supported too, required public disclosure of union finances, provided that union officials be elected by secret ballot, and specified criminal penalties for bribery, extortion, or misappropriation of union funds. The AFL-CIO supported the measure.

At the same time, however, a conservative coalition was attempting to exploit the public's fear of corrupt unions. The Taft-Hartley Act was still in effect, but the conservatives wanted to make it even tougher on unions. To my regret, President Eisenhower joined this antiunion move. The legislation he asked for would have placed tight controls on unions' secondary boycotts and on picketing for organizational purposes (that is, for the right to organize a union), and it would have given the states jurisdiction over "no man's land" labor disputes — those that the National Labor Relations Board refused to handle because they involved too few workers. With a handful of other moderate Republicans, I joined with the Northern liberal Democrats in an attempt to defeat the administration's bill (which had been introduced in the Senate by Barry Goldwater) and to prevent Kennedy's bill from being loaded with restrictive provisions unfair to the labor movement.

In the Labor and Public Welfare Committee we prevailed; we rejected the administration bill and reported out what was basically Kennedy's anticorruption bill with a few Taft-Hartley amendments the unions had asked for added to it. It was probably a tactical mistake to attach those prolabor provisions, because they made it difficult to separate the issue of corruption from the issue of labor relations. On the Senate floor our committee bill faced a barrage of antiunion amendments, some of which went even further than Eisenhower's recommendations. Led by Kennedy, the Northern Democrats were able to beat back most of these amendments — but only because that handful of Republican moderates voted with them. (Besides myself, the core of that moderate Republican band included Clifford Case of New Jersey, Margaret Chase Smith of Maine, John Sherman Cooper of Kentucky, and George Aiken of Vermont.) One major amendment that the unions — and I — opposed was approved, by a one-vote margin. That was a so-called bill of rights for labor, regulating unions' internal relations with their members.

In the House, however, the conservatives succeeded in adding on to the bill the first significant changes in Taft-Hartley. The resulting legislation is known as the Landrum-Griffin Act (for Representative Phil M. Landrum, Democrat of Georgia, and Representative Robert P. Griffin, Republican of Michigan). The Senate softened these measures slightly in conference, but, as enacted, many were still hard on labor. The act prohibited employers from agreeing with their unions not to do business with another firm that was on strike, barred picketing in secondary boycotts or for organizational purposes in many situations, and made it an unfair labor practice for a union to coerce an employer (by threatening to strike, for example) to get him to recognize a union or to stop doing business with a struck firm. I voted for the bill on final passage because of the vital anticorruption provisions that we had originally passed.

There was little I could do as a new senator to prevent the passage of the antiunion portions of that 1959 bill. But in 1978 I was one of the managers of the labor-reform bill — yet I had to acknowledge defeat again.

In 1978 we attempted to amend the 1935 National Labor Relations Act because some companies were denying their employees the rights to organize that were guaranteed under that basic law. The leading example of this was the J. P. Stevens Company, which, by clever lawyering, had blocked for more than a decade the unionization of their textile plants in the South. Another company, Farah, a pants manufacturer in Texas, had gone through a very long strike to hold off the organizing efforts of the Amalgamated Clothing Workers' Union.

Our bill really was not very ambitious. The House had passed a similar measure in 1977, but I knew that the bill would face strong opposition in the Senate and that it had to be reasonable if it was to have any chance at all. At my urging, the Labor and Human Resources Committee toned down the original bill. For example, there was a provision that if the employer stopped production to lecture its "captive audience" of workers about the dangers of unionism, then a union that was attempting to organize the plant would also have the right to talk to the work force during working hours. If the employer campaigned against unions without stopping production, then union organizers could enter parking lots or lunchrooms to talk to employees on their free time. To make the bill more palatable to management, I amended it to say that this could only be done after the union had given the employer written notice that an organizing drive was beginning.

The bill also increased the size of the National Labor Relations

Board, in order to expedite the handling of cases brought before it; gave the board more power to enforce its decisions; added protections to workers who might be fired for trying to organize a union; and allowed the board to award workers back pay if an employer refused to bargain seriously.

The committee reported the bill out in January 1978. Leading the opponents was a member of the committee, Senator Orrin G. Hatch, a Utah Republican. Hatch had been a labor lawyer in Salt Lake City, and as far as I could see, he started out prolabor and ended up as something of a hard-liner on unions. He feels he is very objective. He is, in fact, very bright, very likable, and he knows labor law backward and forward — but he is very conservative on labor.

The lobby against the bill hit on the idea that they could kill the bill if they could get small businessmen all over the United States aroused against it (and they turned out to be right). They started putting out propaganda that this bill would be a triumph for the labor "bosses." They said small businessmen would be forced to unionize, that their lives would be made miserable with organizing drives, that they would be buried under paperwork and would find themselves in constant litigation before the NLRB. These arguments were made despite the fact that about 80 percent of the businesses in the United States were not covered by the bill at all, because they were too small or did too little business in interstate commerce.

Business interests organized a tremendous, well-financed lobbying campaign against the bill. (Unions were lobbying for the bill at the same time, but the business lobby was unusual.) The campaign was concentrated on what the bill would do to small business — the potential that it allegedly had for victimizing the small businessmen, who were unprotected by the teams of labor lawyers that the large corporations could deploy. The small businessmen are workers, really, like those they employ, and the campaign was really a disservice to the people in the communities, with whom the small businessmen should have identified the most. There was no reason for the defeat of that bill on its merits; the hoopla — and that's what it was — brought that about. The impartial *Congressional Quarterly Almanac* had this to say about it:

> Millions of letters and postcards for and against the bill swamped Senate offices. Planeloads of business people, and hundreds of union members, stalked the halls searching for uncommitted votes.
>   Business groups were particularly effective in bringing out small-business representatives to oppose the bill. . . . Senators were impressed when small businessmen who seldom lobbied for anything came to Washington to express their concerns. "It's a dif-

ferent type of lobbying," said an aide to an uncommitted senator. "I'm seeing people on this bill that I wouldn't ordinarily see."

During the weeks of debate and filibuster on the bill, the Senate Reception Room was filled day after day with labor union leaders and representatives and by small businessmen from all over the country — many of them wearing construction-worker hard hats — importuning their senators with zeal and conviction.

A majority of the Senate favored the bill, but Hatch and his allies launched a filibuster. There were about fifteen or twenty confirmed opponents of the bill and they organized themselves into three teams of five or six each. They also prepared about a thousand amendments in order to further stymie the Senate, in case we were able to invoke cloture to close off debate.

In order to demonstrate his commitment to the bill, Senate Majority Leader Robert C. Byrd of West Virginia decided not to use what is called the two-track system; that is, no other Senate business was transacted during the period of the filibuster. And Senator Byrd earned my respect for his remarkable role in that struggle. He is a relatively conservative man and I believe that, psychologically, he might have been more in sympathy with the small businessman than he was with us. But he felt it his superior duty as majority leader to cooperate to the utmost on a measure to which his party's administration was pledged, and that is just what he did. Rarely have I seen such devotion to a duty that might run counter to a senator's political interest. Almost every day that this bill was before us, we met in Bob Byrd's office to plan strategy, to go over the names of senators who had not yet voted for cloture, and to discuss how they might be approached and persuaded. I am sure Bob Byrd had to do a lot of explaining back home as a result of that fight; even I got in trouble with small businessmen in New York, who had no grounds for complaint, as I was upholding prolabor policies on which I had campaigned and been elected.

Our prime task was not so much to argue the merits of the bill — although we did that extensively during the debate — but to try to round up the necessary sixty votes to impose cloture so that a vote on the bill itself could be taken. On June 7 and 8, 1978, three weeks after debate began, we held our first cloture votes — and turned up eleven votes short.

At that, Bob Byrd, Pete Williams, and I brought out a compromise proposal that we had prepared in advance for just such a contingency. The compromise softened several of the most controversial aspects of the bill without changing their basic thrust. In the next few days, four of my Republican colleagues were persuaded to vote for

cloture, and on June 15, for the fifth attempt, we had fifty-eight senators voting to end debate. But that was our high-water mark. On the
sixth cloture vote, on June 22, the supporters of cloture were reduced
to fifty-three, and we were beaten. The bill was sent back to our committee with instructions to rewrite it in forty-five days. "We will stream-
line it, harden it up, make it lean and tough, and bring it back," I
told the Senate. But although we did write a new version, we never
could get it back to the floor. Labor-law reform was dead for a while.

This was a tragic conclusion. It made organized labor resentful
of business and thereby damaged further our hopes for improving industrial productivity. U.S. productivity was already growing more
slowly than that of any of the other leading industrial nations — an
ominous portent for the future of our economy. A different outcome
to the struggle over the relatively simple and negotiable labor-law reform bill might well have helped reverse that slide. The employers
could have made some changes — and we offered many such opportunities — but this was economic war to the death, and the small-
business opposition was so heated that apparently no other outcome
was possible.

* * *

I do not always see eye to eye with labor, as any union leader can confirm. I believe, for example, that the danger of immobilizing the nation's economy or a substantial part of it must be avoided, even if that
requires a temporary limitation of labor's right to strike. In 1966, for
example, when a long strike by airline mechanics grounded 60 percent
of the country's commercial air traffic, I sponsored and comanaged a
Senate joint resolution ordering the strikers to accept arbitration and
go back to work. The bill passed the Senate but the strike ended before the House acted on the measure, so the effectiveness of such legislation was not tested. Nevertheless, it took a while before the International
Association of Machinists, and organized labor in general, forgave me
for that. Senator Wayne Morse of Oregon, who managed the resolution with me, attributed his electoral defeat two years later to his work
on that bill, which the unions perceived as antilabor. I survived the
1968 election because I had a broader constituency.

My fight for the labor-law reform bill of 1978 strengthened my
labor support. Union leaders realized that, although I might argue
with them and try to persuade them to compromise — sometimes
against all their instincts — and although I put the public interest
above even theirs and voted accordingly, my reputation as a prolabor
senator was well founded.

TWENTY-TWO

Vietnam and the Power to Make War

Like most Americans, I was an ardent supporter of the Vietnam War — in the beginning. The cause was idealistic — preventing a small nation from being overrun by an aggressive neighbor — and none of us dreamed it could become a major war that would traumatize our own country and end in failure.

In the summer of 1964 I voted for the Tonkin Gulf Resolution because, as I told the Senate, I thought "we must defend freedom in that area, or else see the balance of a large segment of the population of the world tipped against freedom." I was uneasy about the absence of our allies from the struggle, and I was already concerned that the South Vietnamese government could drag us more deeply into the war than we intended; during the debate on the resolution I closely questioned Senator William Fulbright, chairman of the Foreign Relations Committee, who was managing the resolution in the Senate, on both those points. I wanted to know whether our allies in the Southeast Asia Treaty Organization (SEATO) were being consulted and whether the administration would press for allied support and strive to utilize the United Nations and other international peace-keeping agencies. Bill Fulbright's replies were carefully worded, but I accepted them as assurances. I believed that the cause of the conflict was Communist China's desire to dominate all of Asia and that the United States had a moral duty to prevent that from happening — especially as a "hate Americans" campaign was then raging in the People's Republic of China.

So, with 87 other senators and 414 representatives (only 2 senators opposed), I voted for the resolution supporting "the determination of the President, as commander in chief, to take all necessary measures to repel any armed attack against the forces of the United States and to prevent further aggression." Armed with that congressional grant of authority and emboldened by his sweeping electoral triumph three months later, President Lyndon Johnson took the final steps to war.

Considerable doubt has arisen over whether the attack on the U.S. destroyers in the Tonkin Gulf, which was the immediate rationale for the resolution, took place exactly as the U.S. Navy said it did — a point on which I remain personally unsatisfied. It may be that we had not been paying close enough attention to what was going on in Southeast Asia. Most of us were concentrating on civil rights and elections and racial disturbances in the United States. Certainly Congress did not intend to surrender its war-making powers by passing that resolution. Looking at it as a lawyer, I feel that we were giving President Johnson a power of attorney, and when you give such an instrument, even to a trusted representative, you must expect that you could find your bank account and the contents of your safe-deposit box used for purposes you never anticipated or which you would never have authorized.

Not until 1973, with the passage of the War Powers Resolution, did Congress regain some of its power over presidential war. Meanwhile, our nation — and Vietnam and Laos and Cambodia — had paid a high price, and I and millions of Americans had come to the conclusion that our part in the Vietnam War, for all the high ideals that had inspired it, was clearly improvident.

As the war escalated through 1965, I continued to support the administration. But I was becoming increasingly concerned about where we were heading. In March, as the administration was preparing to send in U.S. combat troops (only "military advisers" had been in Vietnam up to that time), I introduced a resolution asserting congressional support for the administration but calling for "honorable negotiations." In May, I urged President Johnson to come to Congress for another resolution of support before he committed a U.S. division. In June, I warned of "a massive bog-down land struggle in Asia without any consent by Congress or the people for that kind of war," and I introduced a resolution seeking three items: a joint congressional and presidential statement of objectives, including our willingness to go back to the 1954 Geneva agreement (which had ended French colonial rule of Indochina); a statement of our willingness to negotiate even with Viet Cong representatives; and a declaration of our readiness to use the United Nations to end the war. None of my resolutions was adopted.

These efforts to bring Congress back into the decision-making process did not yet reflect any opposition to the war itself; I was still convinced of the morality and the necessity of U.S. military aid to a small country threatened by an aggressive neighbor, and after my first visit to Vietnam, in January 1966 — accompanied by Representative

Ogden R. Reid of New York, former publisher of the *New York Herald Tribune* and later ambassador to Israel, and Richard Aurelio, who was then my administrative assistant — I became more convinced than ever.

There were about one hundred ninety thousand Americans in Vietnam at the time, and the U.S. military was clearly in charge; they snapped you up as soon as you landed at the airport, and made arrangements for briefings and travel and accommodations — and as to these they were the only game in town. I was quartered in a rather sleazy hotel run by the army for officers and visitors. It was in the heart of Saigon, and so I got a view of the corruption, the prostitutes and black markets and clip joints dealing in illicit drugs. This looseness of moral and ethical standards was inevitable in a war-torn, divided country overwhelmed by the enormous inflow of Western money and soldiers, but most of the Vietnamese people seemed to hold themselves aloof from it. The Vietnamese managed well even with all the new-fangled mechanical marvels that the Americans had brought with them — the telephones and radios and motor-driven rickshaws. All the while the Vietnamese women in their flowing *ao dai* bicycled gracefully through the streets, presenting a vision of coolness and detachment in startling contrast to the hustle and griminess of a capital at war.

We traveled throughout the country, from the Mekong Delta in the south to the northern border area near Da Nang. I spoke to Americans and Vietnamese: General William C. Westmoreland, Ambassador Henry Cabot Lodge, and Prime Minister Nguyen Cao Ky in Saigon; military commanders in the field; village chiefs; and many others. We spent a day and a night at an artillery base in the north, near Da Nang, where the cannonading was almost continuous, and from there went further north, almost to the Demilitarized Zone, where a village mayor — probably carefully selected for our benefit — expressed his gratitude for U.S. help and gravely told horror stories — undoubtedly substantially true— about killings and torture practiced by the North Vietnamese.

On the same trip we flew to a Montagnard outpost near the Laotian border, deep in Viet Cong territory. To evade snipers as we descended, our helicopter plummeted to the landing pad and machine gunners stood by their weapons at the open doors. The outpost was about seventy miles from the nearest U.S. or South Vietnamese base, and it was subject to repeated raids by the Viet Cong. I was deeply impressed by the courage of the Montagnards themselves and of the U.S. troops — Special Forces in their green berets — who were a tiny island in the midst of these semiprimitive people yet spoke about them rhapsodically as reliable comrades-in-arms.

A Christmas bombing pause, coupled with a peace offer, was in effect during my trip, and the bombing of North Vietnam had not yet resumed when I reported to the Senate on January 28, 1966. But, as I pointed out, "the peace offensive seems to have failed.... Hanoi has had thirty-five days to consider coming to the peace table.... Instead, Hanoi has publicly vowed to intensify the war, has urged the destruction of U.S. 'aggressors' and has called for the annihilation of the South Vietnamese 'puppets.' " Therefore, I said, "the President would and should have the support of the overwhelming majority of the American people if he decides to resume the limited bombing." (The large population centers of Hanoi and Haiphong had not yet been attacked.)

At that point I had no criticism of the military conduct of the war. "Militarily," I told the Senate, "the situation is at least encouraging." Although the enemy is no weaker, "the impact of our build-up is just beginning to be felt." I reported that the Viet Cong had been strained by the increasing mobility and firepower of U.S. and South Vietnamese forces and that the size of the U.S. commitment was "justified by the nature of the struggle." I saw no prospect of getting bogged down in an endless Asian land war as long as major operations were confined to the Mekong Delta and the Saigon area. I reported that General Westmoreland and his officers recognized that the war was political — for people, not for real estate — and that they knew that the goal was to establish the security of the major population areas and begin the process of economic and social reconstruction. I said that the morale of our troops was high and they understood why we were in Vietnam. "I wish I could say the same," I added, "with respect to parlor conversations I have had in the U.S. about the understanding of the reasons we are in Vietnam and what it is about."

I was not a "hawk," although that speech may sound hawkish in the perspective of history (the hawks wanted to "bomb Hanoi into submission"). I acknowledged, however, that my conclusions differed from those of many liberals and "doves." I said I had studied their point of view but could not agree with it because "the struggle in Vietnam is worthy of the United States. I believe it is worthy of the cause of freedom. I believe it needs to be waged and I believe it deserves the support of the liberals." The issues of Vietnam, I said, are as vital to the United States as those involved in our aid to Greece in 1947 and our opposition to aggression in Korea. "Today," I added,

> whatever may have been the errors of commission and omission in our policy in Southeast Asia in the past, the incontrovertible fact is that the confrontation between freedom and totalitarianism in Asia is now in Vietnam. We did not choose this battleground; history chose it for us. It is clear to me ... that the Viet Cong is directed, supplied, and controlled by a Communist state — North

Vietnam — that seeks to expand Communist-controlled areas, to destroy the chance for freedom, and to humiliate the United States, freedom's most effective defender in Asia. Even if the action began as a local insurgency, which is questionable, it certainly is not one now.

On the other hand, I was not so optimistic about the political, social, and economic struggle for Vietnam. "Much needs to be done to identify our country more dynamically with the social revolution which the people of South Vietnam so fervently desire ... [and] to win the people over to democratic ideals ... to bring about truly representative government through free elections, to shake up the vested interests which for so long have exploited the peasants. ..." South Vietnam has great potential, I said, but the realization of it depends on the will of the South Vietnamese people, which I saw as impossible to determine at that time. "If the South Vietnamese were to vote today," I pointed out, "they would vote in whatever manner they believe would be the least likely to get them injured or killed. ... That is our challenge. We must see to it that South Vietnam, with our assistance, brings about a substantial change in conditions that will give freedom an honest chance."

"We have never," I said in conclusion, "labored under the illusion here that there is a representative government in South Vietnam. Therefore we must accept the fact, and live with it, that the United States is likely to be the dominant influence in South Vietnam for a considerable period ..."

That speech was my personal peak of support for the war. I continued to vote for military appropriations and I voted against an attempt to repeal the Tonkin Gulf Resolution. (Bill Fulbright, already a dove, frankly supported repeal of the measure he had urged us to pass.) But President Johnson sent more troops to Vietnam and started bombing oil facilities at Hanoi and Haiphong; antigovernment riots and demonstrations, by Buddhists and other protestors, threatened to dissolve Prime Minister Ky's Saigon regime, and in July Ky called for an Allied invasion of North Vietnam to help him out of his difficulties. Disturbed by these dangerous developments, I began reevaluating my stand; late that summer, in a series of four major speeches, I emphasized that force alone would not win the war; that reforms and free elections in South Vietnam were necessary to defeat the appeal of the guerrillas; that the Vietnamese themselves, and their neighbors, should bear a greater burden of the war; and that the United States must come forward with realistic peace proposals.

The U.S. and North Vietnamese governments, both claiming that they wanted to end the fighting, had exchanged a number of public and secret peace "signals." But their proposals were too far apart for any real hopes to be raised — until the end of 1966. At that time a real opportunity arose for talks, in Warsaw, based on a reasonable and valid accommodation between the two sides. But the United States killed those hopes early in December by suddenly bombing within an area of central Hanoi that had previously been a sanctuary.

Prime Minister Harold Wilson of Great Britain, whom I had known for twenty years, had been aware of the behind-the-scenes moves, and I soon learned something about them. I concluded that President Johnson had rejected a pretty fair deal that would have ended the war, gotten us out of Vietnam, and allowed some self-determination and some self-government for the people of South Vietnam — which was all we were fighting for in the first place.

This was a culmination of all my rising doubts and worries about how President Johnson was using the authority we had given him. When I came to believe that the President had turned down that deal, I concluded that the Vietnam War, regardless of whether it was desirable for strategic or other reasons, had ceased to be a prudent effort to prevent the South Vietnamese from being taken over by North Vietnamese forces against their will. It had become President Johnson's own war; his personal pride was now involved. It was my belief that President Johnson, facing what the Communists called a war of national liberation, had decided that he would become the savior of the world and earn a place in history by showing that American power could smash this Communist effort. Well, he was wrong, and I knew at the time he was wrong and that we had no business continuing the Vietnam War with that as its rationale. Johnson had missed the chance to end the war and he was preparing to escalate further. I could no longer support such a war.

I declared my break with the Vietnam War on February 12, 1967, Lincoln's Birthday, in a speech in Buffalo. President Johnson, I said,

> has become locked into the mistakes, illusions and overoptimistic predictions of his own policies. He is so busy defending himself, making excuses, and changing facts and figures that he appears to many to have lost the initiative and credibility to make peace on his own.... President Johnson made the mistakes and he feels he has to defend them. He may be defending them even at the price of extending the conflict. The Republican Party is not bound by his mistakes or his policies.

I argued that a further escalation would only "reunify the warring factions in Communist China, heal the breach between Peking and Moscow, and probably even involve us in a major Asian land war with global dangers." Even then, I said, the guerrilla war might go on, because wars of attrition take time. I insisted that we had to find a negotiated way out of the war and proposed that the United States cease bombing the north, declare that it expects the bombing halt not be exploited by the North Vietnamese for further infiltration, and at the same time present a realistic negotiating package.

Specifically, I urged that our government make clear to the North Vietnamese that the National Liberation Front (Viet Cong) could be permitted to participate both in peace negotiations and in a future government of South Vietnam. That meant guarantees by the Saigon government of political amnesty, a proposal that was not very popular at the time. But I pointed out that Hanoi and the NLF believe they have been betrayed by the Western powers in the past, and that they will not negotiate without assurance that our peace move can lead to something for them. "They cannot lay down their arms," I said, "until they believe that the people in the NLF can participate in the political and governmental life of South Vietnam." And I declared that the Republican Party must show that it has learned the lesson of Vietnam: "that the American people cannot afford and are not interested in being the policemen of the world."

I was certainly not the first senator or politician to come out strongly for a peace settlement, but I was by no means the last. Senator Robert F. Kennedy followed me by a few weeks, but such was his celebrity that in the ensuing months, as we both spoke out increasingly against the war, some people got the impression that I had followed *his* lead and had only taken my stand to compete with him for the liberal constituency in New York. In fact, we were both glad to have the other's company on this issue.

As the war continued, taking its toll in lives in Vietnam and disrupting our society at home, Marian and our children and many of my liberal friends pressed me to demand immediate unilateral U.S. withdrawal. But I saw that could lead to even greater casualties. My daughter Joy has noted that I was always cautious and practical. I would not emphasize that the troops should come out when I believed that we could not get them all out fast enough to avoid a massacre of the last units. I would say instead that I was not for pulling out of Vietnam until the troops could be safely removed — a statement that satisfied my own conscience but scored me no points with the doves. Nor could I condone the lawlessness or the burning of draft cards or the violent demonstrations, even though I shared the frustrations of the young people who thought they had no other means of expressing their opposition to the war.

The emotions tugging at the nation became very apparent to me one evening in November 1969. Marian and I were at our apartment in the Watergate when we heard on the radio that some demonstrators were trying to break into the Department of Justice and that there might be violence and arrests as the police tried to stop them. Our children were in Washington, too, and they were out, so we were somewhat concerned. Marian and I drove down to the area, parked near the Washington Monument, and proceeded on foot to Fifteenth Street and Constitution Avenue. There we saw a formation of about a hundred policemen wearing plastic masks and carrying shields and billy clubs, marching ten abreast down Constitution Avenue with a great many young people scattering before them in all directions. We heard the explosions of tear-gas shells that the police were lobbing into the crowd and we caught a whiff of tear gas ourselves. Covering our eyes with our handkerchiefs, we made our way back to the car. It was just one of many incidents taking place that year, few of which were violent, but it gave me an insight into the intensity of the passions running loose and the threat to the peace and tranquility of the nation. I realized how deep a wedge had been driven between the United States government and the youth of the country by this terribly vexing and frustrating Vietnam War.

At the beginning of 1970 the war seemed to be winding down. President Nixon had started to withdraw American troops, the "Vietnamization" program was proceeding, and the antiwar protests were losing some of their steam. But we were not yet out of the "tunnel." When I returned from a second trip to Vietnam in January 1970, I warned the Senate that although the United States now had the opportunity to disengage rapidly from Vietnam, "there also exists a very real danger that U.S. policy — unwittingly — may again be directed in ways which will keep us deeply enmeshed for an indefinite period."

Then, on April 30, President Nixon proved me right. He shattered the calm by announcing that U.S. and South Vietnamese troops had crossed the border into Cambodia to destroy Viet Cong "sanctuaries" there. All across the country the antiwar protests erupted again, and four students were killed by the National Guard on riot duty at Kent State University in Ohio. Congress was besieged by citizens demanding that we reassert our authority and end the conflict. Hurriedly organized busloads and trainloads of businessmen, lawyers, academics, and housewives descended on Washington; a large percentage of them came from New York and wanted to see me. I was deluged with so much antiwar mail that my other office letters were buried and lost in the pile; it took my office two months to open and sort one week's mail and we had to hire scores of students to do the job.

It was a time of outrage because Nixon seemed to be extending the war just as the U.S. public thought it was finally on the way to solution. Many people rejected his assertion that the Cambodian "incursion" would shorten the war: The revelation a few weeks earlier that a secret air war had been carried on over Laos for several years had cost the administration a great deal of credibility.

On May 9, more than sixty thousand protesters, mostly students, converged on Washington for a massive demonstration at the Ellipse, between the White House and the Washington Monument. I wanted to identify myself with this movement, and I also felt that the presence of a senator or two might help keep the gathering peaceful. So Senator Edward Brooke and I went down to it; we were the only senators there.

Unlike some of the other antiwar rallies and demonstrations I had witnessed, this one was extremely orderly, sober, and serious. The speakers were all determined to bring an end to the war, but they were looking toward the constitutional process to do so. It was a marked change in mood, which I attributed to the fact that the students and professors were getting in to see their senators and representatives; even some members of the administration met with the demonstrators. Knowing they would be heard, and that about half of the Congress, according to one poll, also opposed the widening of the war and wanted to end the conflict, the demonstrators were obliged to be more reasonable and less violent. That put a greater burden on their elected representatives: Now more than ever it was clear that it was up to Congress to take a hand in ending the war.

The immediate attention of the Senate and the country was focused on two important pieces of legislation, one of them offered by Senators John Sherman Cooper of Kentucky and Frank Church of Idaho, and the other by Senators George McGovern of South Dakota and Mark O. Hatfield of Oregon. The Cooper-Church amendment to the foreign military sales bill sought to bar all funds for military operations in Cambodia; it passed the Senate on June 30, 1970, but did not get through the House until the following year. The McGovern-Hatfield amendment to the defense procurement bill would have cut off all appropriations for U.S. combat activities in Vietnam at the end of 1970; that one was defeated.

I supported and worked hard for both these measures, but I did not regard them as sufficient: Cutting off funds was not a sure way to end the war, because there was so much money already in the pipeline. Furthermore, although the two amendments aimed at getting us out of the war, they did not address the question of how we got into it; they did nothing to prevent such tragedies in the future. For some time

I had been disturbed about the growth of presidential power to wage war without any real decision making by Congress. The Cambodian incursion had been undertaken without consultation with the Senate Foreign Relations Committee (of which I had become a member) and I considered that a grave breach of the "advice and consent" relationship between the President and the Senate. So with Peter Lakeland, my foreign-policy aide, and Frank Cummings, my administrative assistant and an excellent lawyer, I tried to design a law by which Congress could regain its constitutional power to control the use of the armed forces.

At dinner one night, Peter and Frank and one or two others of my staff sketched out some ideas on the back of a restaurant menu. They brought them to me as a memo, and we went on from there. This was the genesis of the War Powers Resolution, which was finally passed over President Nixon's veto three years later.

The issue of presidential war powers (about which I wrote a book, *Who Makes War*) was much more complicated than the simple fact that the United States was engaged in hostilities without a declaration of war by Congress. Beginning with Thomas Jefferson's dispatch of U.S. naval forces to fight the Barbary pirates of Tripoli, Presidents had used their constitutional power as commander in chief of the armed forces to commit the nation to combat. We recognized from the beginning that such powers and actions, essentially of an emergency or temporary nature, are often right and proper; we did not want to force a future President to come to Congress for a declaration of war every time he had to defend some U.S. citizen or interest or ship. But without a declaration of war and with only a sketchy congressional resolution, Presidents Kennedy and Johnson had deployed, step by step, half a million men and committed the United States to a full-scale war that was continuing under President Nixon and that Congress could not stop. Clearly, we needed a new law to draw the boundaries between presidential and congressional powers.

So we turned to the clause in the Constitution that authorizes Congress to "make rules for the government and regulation of the land and naval forces." The National Security Act of 1947, based on that authority, had never been challenged on constitutional grounds and had always been obeyed by Presidents. We drafted our first bill as an amendment to that act. Recognizing that there are times when the armed forces must go into combat in the absence of a declaration of war, my amendment defined those occasions. It declared that the President could commit troops to action only under one or more of four conditions:

1. To repulse an attack on the armed forces of the United States in its possessions or territories;

2. To repulse an attack on the U.S. armed forces on the high seas or lawfully stationed on foreign territory;

3. To protect the lives and property of U.S. citizens;

4. Pursuant to a national commitment resulting from an action taken by the executive and Congress, such as a treaty or convention.

The amendment required the President to report to Congress when he made such a commitment. Thereupon — and this was the essence of it — unless Congress specifically endorsed his move, the combat action would have to terminate in thirty days.

I introduced this amendment on June 15, 1970, and I stated that "because the Congress has not heretofore established rules for the initiation or continuation of military hostilities . . . in the absence of a declaration of war, it has fallen upon the commander in chief to exercise his executive discretion on an ad hoc, case-by-case, basis. This, in its cumulative effect over the years, has now led to great confusion and dissension in the nation, and has given rise to an anomalous and doubtful legal and constitutional situation."

Similar bills, some based on mine, were introduced in the House at about the same time, and the House that fall passed one that merely required the President to report to Congress if and when he sent troops into combat. The Senate, concentrating its antiwar fervor on the Cooper-Church amendment, took no action on my bill in 1970.

When the new Congress convened in 1971, however, the Senate and the country were beginning to recognize the need for stringent restraints on presidential power; the mood was accentuated early in February by the announcement that South Vietnamese forces were conducting a sweep through the border areas of Laos. On February 17, 1971, when I introduced a new bill based on my 1970 amendment, the issue had become major news and my bill received wide coverage in the press. Writing in the *Los Angeles Times*, Ernest Conine summed up the emerging consensus: "There is something wrong when the President needs congressional authorization to deepen the harbor at San Pedro . . . but not to involve the United States in a conflict which has cost us thousands of lives and many millions of dollars."

Shortly thereafter, Senator Thomas F. Eagleton of Missouri, who was building the national reputation that would earn him the Democratic nomination for vice president the following year, suddenly came up with a war powers bill of his own. Eagleton's bill was similar to mine, and some of my staff assistants were annoyed that instead of just jumping on my bandwagon he was trying to take over the driver's seat. But I welcomed his efforts because I did not regard my bill as perfect, and I knew we would need input from many allies if we were to pass a war powers bill at all.

By that time I had acquired an ally who was even more remarkable — and certainly more unexpected: John Stennis of Mississippi, chairman of the Senate Armed Services Committee. Senator Stennis came to the war powers issue at his own behest early in the game. I never would have thought of seeking the support of such an ardent Southern conservative. His years on the Armed Services Committee had made him a devotee of military power, and I assumed that he would be 180 degrees removed from me on the war powers bill.

So when he asked if he could join me on the war powers bill, it was like striking the Comstock Lode. I told him I was delighted and that I would cooperate to assure that the resulting legislation accorded with both our views. Although his overture had surprised me, there was nothing illogical about our alliance. Stennis, like most Southerners, is a strict constitutionalist; he recognized that Congress had a vital part to play in war and it troubled him deeply to see the power of Congress eroding to the point where we had little control over what a President could do to start or continue a war.

I had many talks with Senator Stennis about this bill, and never did our ideological differences get in our way or undermine the trust we placed in each other. We both knew we would remain opposed on other matters, but on this issue he was with me and I was with him. It is a great credit to our country that a man as conservative as Stennis would feel that he could ally himself with me for a given cause without contaminating his conservatism, and that I should feel the same way about him in regard to my liberalism. Neither of us shied away from the alliance for ideological reasons. And that was fortunate, for Senator Stennis's support was the key break in the whole situation. I doubt very much that it would have been possible to pass the War Powers Resolution had John Stennis not been party to it.

Senator Stennis publicly made his position clear in a speech in Jackson, Mississippi, early in January 1971. He said he had "totally rejected the concept advocated from time to time that the President has certain inherent powers as commander in chief which enable him to extensively commit major forces to combat without congressional consent." Drawing on my original bill (as his staff aides later told my assistants), Stennis declared that Congress should exercise its constitutional power "in a more vigorous fashion," and declared that Congress should develop "a more realistic method ... in providing explicit authority for the President to repel an attack, but requiring congressional authorization before hostilities can be extended for an appreciable time."

On May 11, Senator Stennis introduced his own resolution limiting a President's ability to go to war without a congressional declaration. "The decision to make war is too big a decision for one mind to make and too awesome a responsibility for one man to bear," Stennis said. The Founding Fathers, he pointed out, had wisely distinguished between the President's power to repel an attack and Congress's power to declare war, and he urged that Congress "design a mechanism which will restore to Congress the power to declare war without impeding the due exercise of presidential authority."

"We are witnessing a miracle," I told the Senate, and I went on:

When I first broached this subject last year, the senator from Mississippi electrified me by expressing an interest. He has pursued that interest diligently and carefully, and he has now come up with his own prescription.... With Senator Stennis now joining those of us who feel that it is essential to our nation that the Congress reassert its constitutional powers respecting war, there can be no doubt left as to the seriousness and earnestness of the Senate sponsors in this respect.... It would be demeaning of what I consider to be a historic moment ... if I now tried to analyze differences.... Suffice it, for the moment, to express one of the deepest satisfactions I have ever felt, either in or out of this chamber.

There were now three major war powers bills before the Senate — mine, Eagleton's, and Stennis's. All of them provided that hostilities must cease within thirty days unless Congress endorsed the President's action. There were some variations in the definitions of the emergency situations in which the President could act: Eagleton's bill permitted use of forces to evacuate U.S. citizens from danger; only mine included protection of property and compliance with a national commitment. Stennis's version, while closer to Eagleton's, authorized action to forestall an attack and to prevent or defend against imminent nuclear attack, neither of which were mentioned in my bill or Eagleton's. Stennis specifically excluded Vietnam from the terms of his bill, whereas Eagleton and I kept Vietnam out of the issue by stating that the resolution would not apply to hostilities under way at the time of enactment.

The weaker bill that the House had passed in 1970 was reintroduced by Representative Clement Zablocki, a Wisconsin Democrat. Zablocki, who later became chairman of the House Foreign Affairs

Committee, was chairman of the Subcommittee on National Security Policy and Scientific Developments, which was directly responsible for this legislation on the House side. Zablocki's bill, which passed the House again in August, required the President to submit a written explanation to Congress if he sent troops into combat without prior congressional consent. It urged him to consult Congress but recognized his authority to defend the nation. The House bill lacked any kind of congressional veto of or control over presidential actions, and was therefore completely inadequate from our point of view.

Senate Foreign Relations Committee hearings on our bills began in March 1971 and continued intermittently through the summer. We heard testimony from such eminent historians as Henry Steele Commager and Richard B. Morris, and from government officials past and present. Not surprisingly, the administration opposed the bills. Secretary of State William P. Rogers, who at first was reluctant to testify at all, at length came before us to oppose all three bills because they attempt "to fix in detail, and to freeze, the allocation of the war power between the President and Congress — a step which the framers in their wisdom quite deliberately decided against." Rogers also claimed that our bills would "narrow the power given the President by the Constitution."

On the other hand, McGeorge Bundy, president of the Ford Foundation and national security assistant to Presidents Kennedy and Johnson, supported my bill, as did a number of lawyers and historians. Bundy declared that Congress "can and should" set conditions for the use of armed forces and put limits on any hostilities that are authorized. "This is what we have not properly understood in the past," he added.

One of our most persistent and articulate opponents was Senator Barry Goldwater. In his view there was no need for any war powers resolution. It was not true, he said in a letter he circulated to the Senate, that the President had "led this nation blindfolded and solely on his own authority" into the expanded war, because "Congress is and has been involved up to its ears with the war in Southeast Asia. It has known what has been going on from the start and has given its approval in advance to almost everything that has occurred there."

Goldwater cited the SEATO treaty with its threat of retaliation and went on to point out that the Tonkin Gulf Resolution expressly recognized the U.S. obligation under SEATO to take "all necessary steps . . . including the use of armed forces" to assist any member in its defense. He also reminded us that Congress had appropriated billions of dollars for the Vietnam conflict after the Tonkin Gulf Resolution passed in 1964. If Congress were in recess and the United Nations bogged down, he claimed, the war powers bill could prohibit an immediate U.S. response to forestall an attack on NATO or an Arab conquest of Israel. Much of what he said indicated that the sponsors of the war powers bills had a big job — to educate our colleagues about what the bills said and did.

We had originally intended to mark up my bill and get it to the Senate floor that spring, but with Stennis and Eagleton proposing versions of their own, we decided that instead of rushing the issue it would be better to agree in advance on one bill that we all could put our names to and that would thus have a better chance of passage.

The three-way negotiations to work out a final bill took from May to December 1971, and they were very delicate and difficult. (Senators Charles Mathias, Maryland Republican, and William Spong, Virginia Democrat, also had to be consulted every step of the way because they had cosponsored my bill.) Stennis wanted Presidents to be free to "show the flag" in a crisis area — for example, by sending an aircraft carrier to stand offshore to demonstrate U.S. concern — so we agreed that the resolution would only come into effect when our armed forces are "introduced in hostilities, or in situations where imminent involvement in hostilities is clearly indicated by the circumstances." In cases where armed forces are dispatched to protect and evacuate endangered U.S. citizens from a foreign country, Stennis suggested we insist that the President seek the consent of the foreign government, and Senator Eagleton added a proviso that the President make every effort to avoid using armed forces in such a situation. Eagleton brought up the possibility of U.S. forces helping another nation's irregulars or guerrillas in combat, so we wrote a provision requiring specific statutory authority for the assignment of U.S. military personnel to "command, coordinate . . . or accompany the regular or irregular military forces" of a foreign country in a situation involving hostilities.

I went a long way to satisfy these two very creative and important new adherents to the War Powers Resolution, and they were very reasonable, too. For example, Stennis's original bill seemed to authorize preventive nuclear war, but after I pointed out to him that his language might imply that the U.S. was adopting a "first-strike" nuclear policy, he agreed to change his wording; the combined bill acknowledged the President's authority to "forestall the direct or imminent threat" of attack — without specifying nuclear attack.

Much of the negotiation was conducted on the staff level, where the arguments could be tougher and where exploratory suggestions could be made without committing a senator. (A staff aide could say he *thought* his boss would like a particular idea.) After Eagleton and I had agreed on a joint bill in September, Peter Lakeland held a series of meetings and lunches with Eagleton's and Stennis's aides; Professor Alexander Bickel of Yale University Law School took part in some of those meetings and helped hammer out the final bill.

One of those final meetings of the three staff aides and Bickel took place a day before I was scheduled to discuss the bill with Eagleton and Stennis. Lakeland found himself in agreement with Stennis's aide, but Eagleton's assistant was balking on several points. After their lunch I got an urgent message from Lakeland advising me to postpone the next day's meeting and keep Tom Eagleton out of it until what Lakeland called the rigidity of Eagleton's aide could be overcome on the staff level; I of course agreed, and it was all ironed out. On December 7, 1971, the Foreign Relations Committee unanimously voted to report out S. 2956, a war powers bill written and jointly sponsored by conservative Democrat Stennis, liberal Democrat Eagleton, and progressive Republican Javits — and cosponsored by Senator Spong.

As far as the Senate was concerned, that was an unbeatable combination. When the bill came up early in the 1972 session, the Senate's eagerness to pass a strong measure was immediately apparent: The Senate's doves, led by Bill Fulbright and John Sherman Cooper, criticized our bill as too weak. Fulbright stated that our conditions under which the President could act in emergencies "may have the unintended effect of giving away more power than they withhold"; Fulbright preferred a general statement of emergency powers that would "place the burden of responsibility squarely upon the President." Fulbright and Cooper also wanted to make the bill applicable to the Vietnam War. "To exempt any war from the bill's provisions," Fulbright said, "is, in effect, to exempt it from the Constitution." I had to take issue with Bill Fulbright on that score: I knew he would vote for the bill anyway, but if we had made the bill retroactive, to cover Vietnam, we would have lost the support of John Stennis and other conservatives.

As we expected, the Nixon Administration objected to our bill as unwise, unconstitutional, and unnecessary. Administration supporters within the Senate moved to commit the bill to the Judiciary Committee to study its constitutional questions, a move we thought would be tantamount to consigning it to the graveyard.

After several days of debate — with Senator Spong and me managing the bill and Barry Goldwater leading the opposition — I introduced a few perfecting amendments to which no one objected. They spelled out the President's authority to protect citizens endangered on the high seas; permitted U.S. military officers to continue to participate in joint headquarters operations such as NATO; and allowed the President to exceed the thirty-day action limit if "unavoidable military necessity" required him to do so "in the course of bringing about a prompt disengagement." Then, after voting down both the attempt to refer the bill to the Judiciary Committee and Fulbright's attempt to include the Vietnam War, the Senate passed S. 2956 on April 13, 1972, by a vote of 68 to 16.

Less than two weeks later, almost as if to defy us, President Nixon escalated the Vietnam War by ordering the bombing of Hanoi and Haiphong, and shortly thereafter he announced the mining of North Vietnamese ports. I criticized Nixon's "reversion to the Cold War jargon of the fifties," and pointed out in speeches that the President's moves underlined the need for the war powers bill. Despite this evidence, however, the House was holding back. Representative Zablocki took the position that his chamber had already acted on war powers (by passing the weak bill requiring only that the President report to Congress), and he therefore blocked House consideration of a real war powers bill.

Representative Zablocki seemed anxious to get some kind of war powers bill passed that year, but I felt he wanted it a House bill. Through our staff assistants, he suggested we compromise by making the bill a "concurrent resolution" that would not require the President's signature and would not have the force of law. When we refused this, Zablocki in the House Foreign Affairs Committee took the bill we had passed, amended it by substituting the terms of his bill in its entirety, and got it through the House. That opened the way for a Senate-House conference on S. 2956. We held one meeting of the conference committee, but the House still refused to accept the essence of our bill: the thirty-day cutoff. Compromise was impossible and the bill died for that year.

So we had to start the process over again with the new Congress, in 1973 — in vastly changed circumstances. For one thing, the signing of the Vietnam peace treaty in January 1973, and the later agreement between Congress and the White House to end bombing in Cambodia in August, permitted the issue of war powers to be considered rationally, without the emotional overtones of an ongoing conflict. Even more important, as it turned out, was Watergate. As the revelations of scandal kept popping up in every quarter, President Nixon's prestige deteriorated, and the notion that Congress should limit presidential authority became more palatable to many people who had rejected it in the past. If there was any silver lining to the terrible cloud of the Watergate affair, it was that it enabled the War Powers Resolution to be enacted.

In the Senate, the passage of our new bill, almost identical to the 1972 measure, was a foregone conclusion. We had sixty-one cosponsors this time and — since President Nixon had promised to veto the bill anyway — the small band of opponents made only perfunctory speeches against it. Senators Eagleton and Fulbright again attempted to make our bill even stronger, but their amendments were defeated and the Senate passed the bill, 72 to 18, on July 20, 1973.

The big change had taken place on the House side, where Representative Zablocki's subcommittee, clearly affected by Watergate, finally accepted our idea that the President's authority to deploy troops in combat be terminated automatically after a specified time unless Congress voted otherwise. Zablocki's new bill, which passed the House on July 18, gave the President 120 days to conduct hostilities without congressional authority; our bill granted only 30, but numbers are negotiable — the principle was what mattered. Besides, the House bill also provided, as ours did, that Congress could terminate hostilities at any time before the automatic deadline.

The House bill, however, lacked our carefully wrought delineation of the circumstances under which the President could act on his own, which we felt was just as important as the cutoff. Instead, the House simply evaded the issue; Zablocki's bill urged the President to consult Congress "in every possible instance" before a commitment of U.S. forces to hostilities and required him to report to Congress on such commitment within seventy-two hours after it occurred. The House bill appeared to recognize an independent presidential war-making power; we contended that the president had no power to make war except as defined by Congress. It seemed that the House wanted to give the President a blank check for 120 days — or until Congress told him to disengage.

As House and Senate conferees held a preliminary meeting in August 1973, we were helped immeasurably by a letter from the administration opposing both the House and Senate bills and claiming that the President had an almost unlimited "inherent" authority to dispatch U.S. forces to combat as he saw fit. This hard line proved that there was no point in trying to fashion a compromise to win President Nixon's approval: He was not going to sign a meaningful war powers bill in any case. (In threatening to veto the war powers bills, Nixon had stated that he would welcome "appropriate" legislation on the subject, but the White House was so overwhelmed with the Watergate crisis that it never got around to suggesting just what kind of bill it would accept.)

Previously, House members had tended to look upon themselves as allies of the President in a confrontation with the Senate. But the adamancy and rigidity of the White House on war powers swung the House around to a feeling of partnership with the Senate. By September, as the conference prepared for the first real bargaining session, a House staffer indicated to Peter Lakeland that the House was ready to modify its positions.

Lakeland urged me to stand fast in defending the Senate view. "You may have a tendency to underestimate the strength and prestige which you bring to the conference for bargaining purposes," Lakeland wrote me in a memo. "Our bill is a meticulous, finished product which has been reviewed and vindicated in the crucible of extraordinarily extended and high-level scrutiny. It *is* the Senate position and no part of it is lightly to be discarded or compromised. By way of contrast, the House bill is a hasty, jerrybuilt structure. (And, in their hearts, the House conferees are aware of the contrast.)" Lakeland reminded me that Representative Zablocki was even more eager than I was to get a bill that year, and he reported that Senator Eagleton's aide had said that Eagleton would oppose any conference bill that abandoned our definition of presidential powers. "You are the spokesman and attorney for a powerful and prestigious coalition," Lakeland said.

As I had expected, the House-Senate conference turned out to be a battle royal between Zablocki and me. From the start, Zablocki adamantly opposed spelling out the President's powers. I was faced with a grave dilemma. In a sense, part of our battle had been won months earlier, when the House accepted the principle of automatic cutoff; that was a historic breakthrough that I did not want to jeopardize. I had labored three years on this matter and I was determined to get something out of it. So I was prepared to compromise, too.

But some kind of definition of the President's powers was essential. I believed, as did most of the Senate, that by specifying the four circumstances under which the President could act — temporarily — on his own, we were excluding all others and assuring that no additional powers could be claimed. The House bill had finessed this issue completely and left the matter up in the air, and I could not accept that.

Zablocki and I argued for several days on this point, and eventually we hammered out a compromise that was by no means an exclusive definition but was better than nothing. It appears as Section 2(c) of the War Powers Resolution, and it states:

> The constitutional powers of the President as Commander in Chief to introduce United States Armed Forces into hostilities, or into situations where imminent involvement in hostilities is clearly indicated by the circumstances, are exercised only pursuant to

(1) a declaration of war, (2) specific statutory authorization, or (3) a national emergency created by attack upon the United States, its territories or possessions, or its armed forces.

On first reading, that definition may seem to be even more restrictive than the Senate's. But we had to write it into the act as a mere recital or declaration, without statutory force and not directly linked to the sections of the bill terminating hostilities and requiring presidential reports to Congress. I hoped that Section 2(c) would be accepted nevertheless as the basis of the whole resolution; perhaps it would have been if it had stood alone and not been squeezed out of a reluctant House, which wanted no such definition at all. Compared to the binding definition in the Senate bill, this one seemed weak indeed, and most commentators and officials have taken it as simply precatory and therefore ineffective.

There were other flaws in the compromise bill, from the Senate viewpoint. As we wrote it in conference, the resolution requires a President to report to Congress in three situations: (1) sending armed forces into ongoing or imminent hostilities; (2) sending armed forces equipped for combat into a foreign country; or (3) substantially increasing the numbers of armed forces already equipped for combat in a foreign country. But only the first of these conditions (hostilities or imminent hostilities) triggers the provision that the operation must cease if Congress says so or if Congress does nothing before the automatic cutoff (which we compromised at sixty days). That means that the President can send combat troops abroad with no real congressional restraint — except into imminent hostilities. Of course, if these troops are later attacked and the President were to send more men to reinforce them, the power of Congress to halt the operation would be triggered.

Clearly the law, the result of the give and take of the conference procedure over two quite different pieces of legislation, is not as strong as the Senate wanted. Nevertheless, I had to be content with the survival of our key point, that in the most dangerous circumstances, hostilities or the imminent danger of hostilities, the President loses the power to act after a stated period unless Congress declares war or acts affirmatively to back him up.

To my great regret, Tom Eagleton did not see it as I did. He refused to accept the conference version when we brought it back to the Senate. He called it "worse than no bill at all, . . . an open-ended blank check for . . . war making anywhere in the world by the President." Section 2(c), he claimed, was no more binding "than a 'whereas' clause in a Kiwanis Club resolution." I admitted that we had not won all points in conference, but I defended the result as a very real, active, substantive check upon the President. I could not convince Eagleton; my former ally joined Barry Goldwater (whose reasons for opposing were quite different, of course) and eighteen other senators in voting against the conference report. But seventy-five senators voted for it, so it passed, and the House approved it too.

As he had threatened, President Nixon vetoed the War Powers Resolution on October 24. He said it would "seriously undermine" our ability to act decisively at times of crisis. He called it unconstitutional and dangerous and said that its provisions "purport to take away, by a mere legislative act, authorities which the President has properly exercised under the Constitution for almost two hundred years." But Watergate had removed any credibility Nixon might have had on the proper exercise of presidential power; the "Saturday Night Massacre" (the removal of Special Prosecutor Archibald Cox and the two top officials of the Justice Department) had taken place four days earlier.

We had known all along that we had the votes in the Senate (two-thirds) to override a veto, but the House gave us a cliffhanger. A group of House liberals, who believed as did Tom Eagleton that the bill gave the President *more* power than the Constitution did, threatened to vote against it and sustain the veto, but at the last minute eight of them were persuaded by an intensive lobbying campaign to vote for the bill. On November 7, the House passed the bill over the President's veto, 284 to 135, with just four votes more than the necessary two-thirds. Four hours later we overrode the veto in the Senate, 75 to 18, with Tom Eagleton again opposed.

The passage of the War Powers Resolution over President Nixon's veto was a moment of high exhilaration for me. The resolution is one of the proudest of my legislative achievements and one of the best. It was the first limitation of the power of the President as commander in chief in two hundred years of U.S. history. I think it will have an enormous effect in the future; I think it will prevent future Vietnams because it does draw a line (although not as clear a line as I would have liked) between presidential and congressional power. Admittedly, some future President might defy it, and that could lead us into a constitutional crisis if the President and Congress differ sharply. But it is better to risk such a crisis than to have nothing at all on the books.

The resolution has already been invoked several times, primarily by President Gerald Ford in the *Mayaguez* incident and in withdrawing U.S. forces from Vietnam and Cambodia, but it has not yet been truly tested. In May 1980 President Jimmy Carter abided by part of it when he attempted to rescue the U.S. hostages in Iran. He reported to Congress within forty-eight hours because he was introducing forces equipped for combat into a foreign country. What he failed to do was consult us in advance; he claimed that he had no obligation to do that because he was not introducing forces into a situation where hostilities could be imminent. He was asserting, in other words, that the provisions for termination would not be applicable. Of course, it was all over so quickly that the resolution was not tested, but my point is that he should have consulted Congress. If an action deserves a report it deserves consultation, and since Carter had been planning the raid for months, there was certainly time to consult. If he had done so, perhaps the failure would have been averted.

Critics of the War Powers Resolution point out that in the seven years since its passage it has not prevented any military action by the United States. But I state it the other way: No major military action by the United States has taken place since the bill became law. Furthermore, the dire predictions of President Nixon and Barry Goldwater that the resolution would undermine the nation's ability to act decisively have simply not come true. Those who criticize the resolution for not stopping wars should also note that it has not "handcuffed" the President, as Nixon said it would. It has simply imposed on the presidency the necessity to stop, look, and listen, and to take prudent counsel when a military operation is suggested. As I argued time and again when the bills were before Congress, it is right that members of Congress should realize that if we go to war the blood is on their hands as well as on the President's. That is a remarkable antidote to jingoism — and a very sobering thought.

TWENTY-THREE

Watergate and After: The 1974 Elections

Nineteen seventy-four was a bad year for Republicans. Three months after a president resigns in disgrace is obviously an awkward time for any member of his party to face the voters; but, as luck would have it, that was an election year for me. I found myself as a man in the middle, attacked by both conservatives and liberals, criticized simultaneously for doing too much and not enough about the national trauma of Watergate, about Vietnam, and about other issues. And more than at any other time in my career I found that my instincts as a lawyer and my instincts as a politician were in conflict. The fact that I survived the year and was reelected to a fourth term in the Senate proved to me once more that hard campaigning and the record can mean more than party labels or conservative or liberal labels.

As the 1974 campaign season approached, my main threat seemed to be from the conservative side, particularly from the Conservative Party of New York. In 1970 I had supported the campaign of Charles Goodell, the progressive Republican Governor Rockefeller had appointed to the Senate in 1968 to serve out the term of Robert Kennedy, who had been tragically assassinated. When Goodell lost to James Buckley, the Conservative Party candidate, in a three-way race, I had opposed — unsuccessfully — Buckley's admittance to the Republican Conference in the Senate, thereby further antagonizing the Conservative Party. Two years later I angered them again by trying to block the renomination of Spiro Agnew as vice president. It seemed very likely that the Conservative Party, which had always found particular pleasure in attacking me, would spare nothing in its attempt to unseat me and that I would face the same kind of gutter tactics it had used against Goodell.

The Conservative Party made a strong showing that year, winning 823,000 votes despite the inexperience of its candidate, Barbara Keating (no relation to former senator Kenneth Keating). My Democratic opponent, former attorney general Ramsey Clark, also had a reputation as a liberal — Barbara Keating called us both ultraliberals — so voters who wanted to cast a conservative ballot were given a clear choice. Most of Keating's support came from voters who might otherwise have voted Republican.

At the same time, I was not too popular with the liberals either, although the Liberal Party supported me. Many liberals felt I had not taken a strong enough stance against the Vietnam War, that I had been too lawyerly and cautious in seeking a safe and honorable way out of the conflict. Rightfully, the passage of the War Powers Resolution over President Nixon's veto in the fall of 1973 should have earned me unqualified liberal support. In my mind it was a legislative triumph. But there were liberals, such as Senator Thomas Eagleton of Missouri, who believed that the compromises necessary to enact the resolution had taken the teeth out of it. Furthermore, Watergate revelations were breaking out all over the place and it was becoming difficult to credit any Republican with high statesmanship.

For a time I even gave some thought to retiring from the Senate that year. I had served twenty-eight years in elective office and I was approaching my seventieth birthday. I had accomplished, I thought, most of what I could accomplish as part of a minority within a minority, and it was clear that the Republican Party was not going to become the majority in Congress that year — and perhaps for some years to come. Furthermore, my brother had passed away in the spring of 1973 (at noon on May 18, my sixty-ninth birthday). We had not practiced law together for twenty years, and he had made some serious errors late in his career and had suffered because of them; but we remained very close and I knew I would miss the personal and fund-raising support he had given me in every one of my previous campaigns.

Nevertheless, I put those misgivings aside and on June 3, 1974, announced I was running again. I said I was "deeply troubled by the erosion of public confidence in our institutions," and that I felt it my duty to help deal with the causes of that erosion "and to start us on the road back."

The cause of that erosion, of course, was the unfolding tragedy of Watergate, which had occupied a great deal of my attention and concern in the preceding year and a half. Watergate indicated, I said, that "there has been something seriously, perhaps basically, wrong with the moral climate of our country when the perspective of so many in high places is so distorted as to countenance stooping to crime and mendaciousness in the waging of a political campaign and the search for political victories at any price."

Watergate was also a symptom of what had come to be called the imperial presidency, the accumulation of power in the White House at the expense of the other branches of government and to the detriment of every citizen. I had already been active in trying to eliminate some of these abuses. I had not reacted politically, by seeking headlines with bombastic denunciations of wrongdoers, but by striving to enact legislative remedies. There were a number of bills of that nature that I cosponsored, helped draft, or worked actively to get passed; like the War Powers Resolution, all of them sought to restore to Congress or to citizens in general the powers and rights the executive branch had usurped. To my mind, the assault on the institutions of government and on our constitutional procedures was as dangerous as the specific crimes of Watergate, appalling as those were, and I considered the defense of our institutions just as important as the investigation and punishment of the Watergate criminals.

One of the first of these bills was the Congressional Budget and Impoundment Control Act, of which I was a principal architect. It restored to Congress some of its constitutional power of the purse, which the White House had usurped by impounding funds Congress had appropriated, thereby frustrating the will of Congress. I had also helped formulate a congressional-right-to-information bill, which was our response to the White House claim that the President had an absolute executive privilege to withhold information. With Senator Edmund S. Muskie of Maine, I introduced two related bills: one designed to reform the system of classifying secrets, which had been used improperly by the executive branch to hide its mistakes, and the other requiring the President to report to Congress on the steps he had taken to carry out laws passed by Congress. I also cosponsored Senator Charles Mathias's Bill of Rights Procedures Act, to require warrants for wiretapping. Not all of these bills were enacted in the form in which they were presented, but many of their provisions and principles found their way into the range of legislation by which Congress put up new bulwarks against the abuse of presidential power.

The nation at large, however, was more interested in the guilt or innocence of Richard Nixon. On numerous occasions I had called upon the President to comply with the requests of the Senate investigation committee and the Watergate special prosecutor for tapes and other information, and I had warned that his continued refusal to do so could lead us to a constitutional crisis. There was no legal basis for Nixon's refusal to honor the subpoenas for information that he subsequently received; I stated this forcefully and I urged him to comply with the law.

But what I did *not* do as the trials and tapes and testimony piled up was call for the President's resignation. I had good reasons for this, but they were a lawyer's reasons, not a politician's, and therein lay a conflict.

The idea that Nixon might or should resign was first discussed openly after the "Saturday Night Massacre" of October 20, 1973, when Attorney General Elliot L. Richardson and his deputy, William D. Ruckelshaus, were forced out of their jobs because they refused to fire Special Prosecutor Archibald Cox. Spiro Agnew had resigned just ten days earlier in the face of an unrelated bribery scandal and the nation was without a vice president. It was my opinion that Nixon's resignation was completely out of the question until a new vice president had been named. If Nixon *had* resigned during that period, Speaker of the House Carl Albert, a Democrat, would have become President, and that would have repudiated the electorate's overwhelming choice of a Republican President in 1972. But on December 4, with Gerald Ford's confirmation as vice president assured, I declared, "By tomorrow, consideration of resignation or any call for resignation will come properly to the front and in such a context I and others will have to give every thoughtful consideration to that possibility."

In his State of the Union message in January, however, President Nixon said that he had "no intention whatever" of resigning, and added that "one year of Watergate is enough." But of course, Watergate was not finished. The House Judiciary Committee began impeachment proceedings; John Mitchell and H. R. Haldeman and other high administration officials were indicted in March for hindering the investigation of the original Watergate burglary; and a new conflict between Congress and the President emerged when Nixon refused to turn over to the House Judiciary Committee information that the committee needed to consider impeachment.

At this juncture, on March 19, 1974, Senator James Buckley publicly called for Nixon to resign. Declaring that resignation was the only way to solve the crisis, Buckley expressed the fear that the impeachment process would tear the country apart. If the President resigned, he said,

> self-evidently the impeachment process would end. Congress would be automatically discharged of the Watergate affair and could devote itself to the legislative business. A new President would be at the helm with the capacity to inspire and to restrain the Congress. ... We need the balance wheel that alone can be provided by a President able to exercise the full authority of his office or we run the risk of a runaway Congress that could commit us to new and dangerous programs from which we may never be able to extricate ourselves.

Buckley's statement got big headlines and put me in a tough spot. If a conservative Nixon loyalist like Buckley was urging the President to resign, why, everyone suddenly wanted to know, was Javits not suggesting the same course?

The problem was that I looked at the question as a lawyer representing a client, and I felt that if I had demanded that Nixon resign I would have been demanding that he plead guilty; no lawyer can advise his client to plead guilty if the client says he is not. No one under our system of jurisprudence — no matter how pat the circumstances look — is guilty· until proven guilty at a trial based on the facts, and given an opportunity to defend himself. I believed President Nixon had a right to stand trial — by impeachment — if he wished. Furthermore, as a senator I would have had to vote in the trial of the President if the House impeached him; to call for his resignation beforehand would have been prejudging the issue, and I regarded that as improper.

Had I been Nixon's lawyer I would have been right, but as a politician my lawyer's outlook trapped me in an untenable position. I found it very awkward not to demand Nixon's resignation when I was ready to vote for his removal. I was taking the position of Nixon's counsel, although I was not his counsel, I was a politician and a senator. In the conflict between the lawyer and the politician in me, the lawyer won that round.

As I faced the press and my liberal constituency in the aftermath of Buckley's statement, I could take only small comfort from the possible political benefit my lawyer's decision might bring me from pro-Nixon Republicans, for I believed that the Nixon presidency was ending.

At a news conference the day after Buckley's statement, I explained that I was not joining his call because I thought such demands were "sterile" and would "drain away the resolution of Congress to proceed with impeachment and a Senate trial." Buckley, I said, "is essentially a believer in the presidency and is the President's man. He's made that very clear ... And his particular leader has let him down, so he says, 'Mr. Leader, I want you to quit.'" Not sharing Buckley's fears that impeachment would imperil our governmental system, I expressed my "faith in the Congress as an independent instrument of government" and declared that I therefore wanted Congress to handle the issue through the constitutional impeachment process. "I'm not just saying that I won't ask for his resignation," I told the reporters. "What I'm saying is that I want to press forward with impeachment and trial."

Nevertheless, the press kept after me on the subject and my friends and my staff urged me to reconsider. I did reconsider — I thought about it constantly — and on one sunny day in May, shortly after the House Judiciary Committee began formal impeachment hearings, I came very close to joining the clamor for President Nixon's resignation.

Marian and I were spending the weekend at Quiogue, Long Island, at the summer home of Richard and Shirley Clurman. Clurman — a former chief correspondent and then an executive of *Time,* a former *Newsday* reporter, and an astute public-affairs consultant — had given me sound advice concerning public statements and he had helped me see myself as others see me — which made him a good friend indeed. The four of us sat around the Clurmans' living room that Friday night, agreeing on how terrible the situation was. I repeated my reasons for not wanting to ask the President to resign, but Dick — and I think Shirley and Marian agreed with him — thought I was wrong.

Dick argued that my lawyer's reasons were not sufficient, that as a senator I had to take a stand on this most vital issue facing our country. I had felt that Nixon *should* resign; it was just that I had not thought it my right to say so. But I had been appalled by the recently released tapes of the President's conversations, which — in addition to more deeply implicating the President — were laced with such crude and vulgar expressions as to demean the office and the man; and I was also indignant about the President's defiant refusal to release all the tapes. Clurman was very persuasive and I finally agreed that the time had come for me to state my opinion publicly. He suggested that I put out a statement by noon the next day, Saturday. There was no major Watergate news expected on Saturday and Dick made much of the point that I would have a clear shot at the front page of the Sunday *New York Times.*

So on Saturday morning I sat in the Clurmans' breakfast room, in the sun, and wrote out on a yellow legal pad a short statement, about one page long, that included the words "Nixon should resign." I explained why I had not said this in the past, and why it was justified now. Dick read it and thought it was perfect; he urged me to call it in to my press aide immediately so it could be issued in time for the Sunday papers.

But I was uneasy. I thought the statement was terse and inadequate; it was too important to write in haste. I told Dick I wanted to work on it some more. The second time it came out to about two pages. Dick liked the first version better, so I asked him to try to combine the two, which he declined to do. So I produced a third version.

It was now near noon, and, as Dick kept reminding me, it was getting late for the early deadlines of the Sunday papers. Marian and Shirley were awake by then and they had suggestions too. It then occurred to me that Barry Goldwater, who was as disgusted as I was with the Watergate developments, might want to sign this statement with me. If both the conservative and the progressive wings of the Republican Party called for his resignation, Nixon would have to listen. And I knew that anything I did with Senator Goldwater could not be used against me by the Conservative Party in the elections. I tried to reach Goldwater by phone, but he was out of touch with his office for a few hours; we waited until midafternoon for him to call back, and then we decided to put the whole thing off for a few days.

Back in Washington, I decided that my original position was still the best for me. That Wednesday, when a newsman at a press conference started a question by saying, "As I recall, you have been against the President's resignation..." I interrupted him to explain myself again: "I have not been against the President's resignation, and the country may well be better off without him. But I am not one of those who would ask for it.... A request for resignation is a confession of an inability to act and I have no feeling of inability to act. I don't think our country is going to come apart if we have impeachment and if we have a trial.... On the contrary, I think if we go through this trial by fire we'll be a better, freer, stronger nation."

And that was the way I left it — until August, when the "smoking gun" tapes showed that the President had indeed been involved in the cover-up of the Watergate burglary from the beginning. By then, a special steering committee of Republican senators, of which Goldwater and I were members, was meeting every day to deal with the situation. The new tapes made it clear to us not only that Nixon would be impeached (the House Judiciary Committee had already voted the first article of impeachment), but that the Senate would convict him and remove him from office. An angry Barry Goldwater declared the next day that Republicans could not support this situation any longer, that the party could be lied to only so many times, and that the best thing Nixon could do for the country would be to get out of the White House that day. We all felt that way. Nixon was informed by House Minority Leader John Rhodes and by Senators Hugh Scott and Barry Goldwater of our steering committee that he had not enough support left in the Senate to prevent his removal from office; two days later he resigned.

Under those changed circumstances it was best that the Nixon presidency ended quickly. Had Nixon been forced to resign earlier, however, before impeachment was imminent and without unmistakable proof of his guilt, millions of Americans might have been left to wonder whether he had been hounded from office, and that would certainly have damaged the country. The formality of impeachment and a Senate trial might still have been of value, but when those last tapes were released it was clear to me that the process of impeachment and removal would have been just that — a formality.

The Nixon resignation did not help my own reelection campaign. For one thing, my party was grievously wounded. For another, I knew that many voters would now consider my refusal to urge resignation an excess of caution. I had been concerned about the threat from the conservative side, but it now seemed likely that a liberal Democrat could give me even more trouble at the polls.

With renewed determination I turned back to the final stages of the long struggle to enact ERISA, the pension reform bill. The complicated House-Senate conference on ERISA had been going on all through that traumatic summer, and we finally issued our report the week after Nixon resigned. Later that month both the House and Senate passed the compromise version and President Ford signed ERISA into law on Labor Day, 1974. That turned out to be a big help in the campaign, because workers all around New York were aware of the benefits of ERISA — and of my role in bringing it about.

That September a new and unpredictable element was suddenly thrust into the campaign. I was given the opportunity to travel to Cuba — which no elected U.S. official had visited in fourteen years. The train of events that led to this trip had started early in the year. When the State Department authorization bill came before the Senate Foreign Relations Committee, Senator Claiborne Pell proposed an amendment calling for a review of U.S. policy toward Cuba. I joined Pell in this suggestion, the committee unanimously approved our amendment, and the bill containing it passed the Senate in April. To prepare for hearings on Cuba policy, the committee authorized Senator Pell and me to go to Cuba to examine the situation.

Contact with the Cuban government had to be made through the Swiss and Czech embassies, and it took some time to get visas and set up appointments. Furthermore, the State Department was by no means enthusiastic about the trip. As travel to Cuba by U.S. citizens was restricted, the department had to validate our passports, and the process seemed inordinately slow. We were all set to leave on September 6, with appointments in Havana arranged. But Secretary of State Henry Kissinger asked us to delay our visit, and someone in the State Department leaked to a columnist a story that the department had "torpedoed" our trip by refusing to stamp our passports — which was not true. (I believe Kissinger merely wanted to discourage us from going or to delay our trip until President Ford had a chance to state a new U.S. policy on Cuba.) Finally, in late September, the State Department gave clearance to us and to the U.S. reporters who wanted to cover our visit.

I had no idea how the New York electorate would react to stories about their senator talking and dining with Fidel Castro. But I felt a special solicitude about our relations in the Americas and I believed that we should, if possible, come to better terms with Cuba. I was deeply concerned about the political prisoners in Cuba, the Soviet military presence there, Cuba's influence in Central and South America, the problems of compensation for seized U.S. property, and the future of the Guantánamo naval base. Not long before, Raul Castro, Fidel's brother, had declared that normalization of relations was possible, and Fidel Castro's willingness to see us lent weight to that remark. With a new president in the White House, the time seemed right to open a dialogue with Cuba. I certainly did not know that Cuban troops would later be fighting in Africa in opposition to our interests, but if I had I might have been even more eager to go in order to try to head off that action. At any rate, I felt I could not say no, regardless of the election; I had to hope my constituents would have confidence in me despite their obvious hostility to Castro.

So Senator Pell and I went to Cuba for a weekend at the end of September. A small, twin-engine chartered plane — a puddle-jumper normally engaged in island hopping in the Bahamas — took an hour and a half to fly us the two hundred miles between Miami and Havana. Pell and I paid for the trip personally; the twenty-nine reporters flew over in a chartered jet and met us in Havana.

Upon our arrival, on Friday, September 27, we told Castro's representatives that first we would just like to look around. So after we checked into the clean but run-down Riviera Hotel, we strolled through a downtown shopping area — accompanied by the officials, of course. In a dimly lit department store, and in a Woolworth's that had a soda fountain but little else to remind one of its U.S. origins, we noted the crude and elementary merchandise that few people seemed to be buying — because ration coupons were needed to purchase most of it.

But word had spread that we were in Havana and a crowd had lined up in front of Woolworth's to applaud us when we arrived. Inside, we were greeted with smiles, handshakes, and even embraces. By the time we walked out, the crowd was huge and exultant. Although the government undoubtedly had its agents around, I doubt they could have had time to set up this welcome. These Habaneros seemed genuinely overjoyed and reassured by the sight of two U.S. senators in their midst.

Dinner that night at the El Bodequito del Medio restaurant, which had been a hangout of Hemingway's, cost Pell and me $500: Everyone in our entourage, including drivers, invited himself to dine with us. Block parties were going on all over Havana that night in celebration of the founding of the revolutionary committees that function as the Communist apparatus in every neighborhood, and we were taken to a few of them. We found music, strings of lights, and food and drink, but not much dancing or gaiety — rather a sweet and gentle enjoyment of the occasion. The sobriety of the participants contrasted to the exuberant nature of the Cubans I had known before the Communist takeover. We ended our first evening by catching the last floor show at the Tropicana nightclub, famous in the pre-Castro era. The show was as elaborate as ever, with dancers, singers, comedians, acrobats, and production numbers, but somehow it lacked the verve and spontaneity of other days. At a table in front of ours sat a dozen Soviet naval officers, chain-smoking, and chain-drinking vodka, their tunics half unbuttoned; they were quiet and orderly, but from the absence of conversation I sensed they were not having a very good time.

The next day was devoted to meetings with high government officials, including the president of Cuba, Osvaldo Dorticós Torrados. That was also the day for Fidel Castro's annual anti-U.S. speech — a fact we had not known until the eve of our departure from Washington. To keep out of sight while the whole country was listening to Castro, we attended a buffet supper at the home of the chargé d'affaires of the Swiss mission and watched the speech on television. The speech was quite virulent in tone (the CIA's role in the overthrow of the Allende government in Chile had just been revealed), but it was one of the shortest anti-American speeches Castro had ever delivered, and he read it carefully and calmly, without any of the gestures and bombast for which he had become famous.

When we met with Castro twenty-four hours later, he was apologetic — not for the speech but for the timing. "I hope it did not cause you any discomfort," he said, and explained that the speech had been scheduled before the time was fixed for our arrival. So he simply disregarded our presence in Havana and hoped we understood. We did not make an issue of what he had said on TV because we were more interested in what he would say to us.

On Sunday we toured Havana's docks and noted the weight of the Soviet Union's economic presence. The harbor was filled with Russian ships and even the fish crates had been made in the USSR. Then we visited the Valle de la Picadura, a major agricultural and livestock development center not far from Havana. The contrast between the shabby hotels and stores in urban Havana and the sleek and prosperous-looking agricultural center underlined for us the priorities of the Castro government. The buildings and the livestock and the facilities of the Valle de la Picadura looked like something that might have been put together by a gentleman farmer of Virginia, and even though it was a model farm and did not pretend to be an average Cuban agricultural establishment, it was very impressive. Ramon Castro, another brother of Fidel's, was in charge of agricultural development; he showed us around the farm and was our host for a sumptuous lunch: lobster, barbecued chicken, avocado salad, and fruits and vegetables and meats and delicacies of many kinds, served in what we might have thought to be a millionaire's country home.

On our way back to Havana, we visited a prison camp and talked to some political prisoners who were working outdoors. They looked well cared for and well fed. Some of them were quite articulate in English and perfectly willing to exchange ideas. I was struck by the length of their sentences: thirty years seemed to be normal, and many of them had already served about twelve years — that is, since the time of the Bay of Pigs. Some of them spoke of having been arrested when leaving their towns, on suspicion of planning to leave the country or to engage in counterrevolutionary activities. But none complained about injustice (though this may have been because their keepers were listening). They worked in the open air without any visible restraints, under conditions that, although undoubtedly hard, did not appear to be brutal.

That night we dined and talked with Fidel Castro for three and a half hours in his office at the Palace of the Revolution. He was smartly dressed in his military uniform, with gleaming paratroop boots, and he exuded confidence. We sat around a highly polished table that seemed rather long and formal for four people (Castro's vice prime minister for foreign relations, Carlos Rafael Rodriguez Rodriguez, joined us), and were served an excellent dinner by two white-jacketed and unobtrusive waiters.

After dinner, relaxing and smoking a cigar, with a brandy before him, Castro spoke easily and freely in English. He knew exactly what his policy was and where he stood in the world and seemed gratified to be there. But the CIA's activities in Chile were obviously of great concern to him, and he spoke of the need for the U.S. government to establish more control over the agency's clandestine operations; otherwise, he implied, the United States would face in other Latin American countries the same kind of problems it was having with Cuba. He did not mention the danger to him of assassination, or anything he knew about the attempts on his life, but in light of what was revealed later I can see that this must have been in his mind as well.

The purpose of our visit and talk was exploratory — to see what could be done to improve U.S.-Cuban relations. The limited antihijacking agreement already in effect, mutual respect for territorial waters, visits of relatives from the United States, and emigration from Cuba on a selected basis — all seemed to be working well, he thought. Castro said he wanted to better relations with the United States, and we discussed what could be done to reunite families and release some of the nine U.S. citizens then being held in Cuba. (A week after our return to the United States, Castro released four Americans who had been held on drug charges and stated it was a good-will gesture to Senator Pell and me.)

Castro distinguished between talks and negotiations. Negotiations, he said, could not begin until the United States lifted its trade embargo on Cuba. We pointed out that many people in the United States felt that the Soviet presence in Cuba was an equally important barrier to negotiations. Since neither the Soviets nor the embargo was likely to vanish, Castro made the point that *talks* on mutual problems could take place meanwhile. He indicated that the United States could signal its readiness for such talks by abstaining on a proposal to repeal the economic and diplomatic quarantine of Cuba that was due to come before the Organization of American States at a meeting in Quito that November. We reported this to the State Department upon our return and indeed the United States did observe a strict neutrality on that vote.

Castro also told us he looked forward to a common market in the Americas, which I, too, now feel is essential if we are to have real security and economic prosperity in the hemisphere. Such a market could help break the power of the OPEC oil trust by detaching the Latin American oil producers, Venezuela and Ecuador, from OPEC.

At a press conference in Washington after our return from Cuba, I declared that "the moment is propitious" for a better accommodation between the United States and Cuba. The major issues of security, human rights, exporting of revolution, and compensation for seized property still remained to be solved, I said, but "there are smaller steps which might be taken to sort of signal the thaw between the two countries." I suggested that we not insist on a Soviet withdrawal as a condition for the opening of talks, just as I felt Castro could not insist that the United States lift the trade embargo beforehand.

Our visit, and our report to the State Department and the Foreign Relations Committee, did create a better climate for rapprochement between the United States and Cuba, although the initiative was not picked up adequately and relations worsened again later. At the time, our trip received considerable publicity — not all of it favorable. The

New York Daily News later estimated that my visit to Cuba may have cost me two hundred fifty thousand votes in the election.

Meanwhile, Ramsey Clark was roaming the state campaigning hard against me, particularly for not demanding Nixon's resignation. In addition, Clark attacked me for accepting a $15,000 campaign contribution from Nelson Rockefeller at a time when Rockefeller's confirmation for vice president was before the Senate. (Clark, who regarded himself as a model of virtue, had announced that he would accept no more than $100 per family in campaign contributions — to which I later commented, "Beware the self-righteous man.") My opponent was also belaboring me for being a Republican, implying that all Republicans were as guilty as Nixon — notwithstanding my reputation for integrity.

I received reports on all this from my campaign aides when I returned from Cuba on Monday afternoon, September 30, and I realized my reelection was in danger. Up to then I had been busy in the Senate and had campaigned only sporadically, but that Monday I told my staff in Washington I simply had to go to New York to campaign; I was going to wash my hands of the Senate for a while and return to Washington only to vote on the most critical matters. I immediately arranged a street rally in front of the Time-Life building at Fiftieth Street and Sixth Avenue and ordered my campaign staff to recruit a band and post signs for the following Wednesday at noon.

So after Senator Pell and I had reported on Cuba to the Foreign Relations Committee and to the press, I finally got away from Washington on the seven o'clock plane Tuesday night. I was convinced if I had missed that plane and gone an hour later I would have lost the election right there. The first words I uttered when I took the microphone at the rally the next day were "I'm here." There were just five weeks to election day and it was nonstop all the way.

The differences at the time between the Democratic candidate and me were matters of character, style, competence, and record. Clark found it difficult to credit anyone else with good motives. He kept after me on the matter of campaign financing, claiming that because his contributions averaged $20 while mine averaged $500, the little people were for him. Rockefeller's contribution to my campaign, he said, was an example of the "old politics" in which legislators were swayed by moneyed interests. But it was nonsense to suggest that Rockefeller's contribution would affect my judgment on his confirmation, and the voters knew that. I pointed out that Nelson had contributed to all my campaigns since 1946 and that we had been friends and political allies for years; no one had any doubt I was going to vote to confirm him, campaign contribution or no. Nevertheless, the fear that Rockefeller might improperly use his great wealth delayed his confirmation until well after election day and kept the issue in the news, so Clark's attack hurt me for a while.

Late in the campaign, however, Clark overreached himself on the financial issue. In a face-to-face debate upstate, he attacked me for failing to support the position of Common Cause, the citizens' lobby, on public financing of elections. I happened to have with me just what I needed to refute that charge and when Clark had finished I produced it from my papers. It was a letter to me from John Gardner, the head of Common Cause, thanking me for "the considerable support you gave to the public finance issue" and commending me for my "fight on behalf of this important principle" of campaign financing. "As always," I said, after reading the letter aloud, "Mr. Clark has the record confused. . . . So much for Mr. Clark's authorities." One of my aides told me later that Clark visibly buckled, "like a fighter waiting for the end."

* * *

Ramsey Clark had a reputation in 1974 as an outspoken critic of the Vietnam War, but I was able to turn that issue to my advantage as well. In 1972 he had visited Hanoi and allowed himself to be used by North Vietnamese propaganda. In a famous broadcast over Hanoi Radio he said that North Vietnam "is pursuing a revolutionary cause of international significance. . . . Here is justice and equality." In the same broadcast he had criticized U.S. actions and described the devastation caused by U.S. air raids on the North Vietnamese capital. In my opinion Clark had shown poor judgment in making that statement while he was still in Hanoi, and I said so at the time. When I criticized him for that during the campaign he called me a "Nixon thug" who had tried to keep the American people from learning about what was happening in North Vietnam. A reporter then showed him a press clipping from 1972 in which I had described him as an "honorable and patriotic American" who had a right to say what he did but who would have been wiser to wait until he returned home to say it; Clark just shrugged that off.

But Clark's liberal, antiwar reputation just did not hold up — as I meticulously pointed out to the voters. As President Lyndon Johnson's attorney general, Clark had vigorously prosecuted Dr. Benjamin Spock and other war protesters. In 1968, in fact, he had proudly revealed statistics that showed that prosecutions of draft resisters under his administration of the Justice Department were at an all-time high. He had also helped coordinate the infiltration of groups of civil rights workers and black militants and antiwar protesters by agents of the FBI and military intelligence. And he had called the leaders of the peace movement "the Vietnam obstructionists . . . a bunch of eccentrics making propaganda."

It was only after he and Johnson had left office that Clark had suddenly spoken out against the war. A year after his prideful claim about Selective Service prosecutions he appeared before a Senate committee to declare that the punishments for those refusing induction were too severe. "War is bad enough," he told the committee, "without making criminals of those who refuse to serve." The draft laws, he said, caused young people to disrespect the law: "You have to have respect for law, but you can never have a respect for law if the law is not respectable." He proclaimed that he was opposed to the Vietnam War all along but had not spoken out or resigned from the Johnson administration because "the war was not my area of responsibility."

To my mind this was not the kind of person to be a senator. I spelled out in detail his record of inconsistency, and in a speech on October 20 I declared:

> Once Mr. Clark left the cabinet of Lyndon Johnson he abandoned his pursuit of the draft resisters. He abandoned his silence on the Vietnam War and he joined the ranks of the opposition that he had despised — with the zealousness only possible as a result of such a turnabout. . . . It is a far cry from the Ramsey Clark who considered it his job to allow black nationalists and other dissident groups to be infiltrated with FBI agents . . . to the Ramsey Clark who declares himself an exemplary civil libertarian . . . The question is not whether Mr. Clark was right to infiltrate, not whether he was right to prosecute, not whether he was right to do what he did in Hanoi. The question is whether or not we can believe in the constancy or stability of the views he proclaims today.

On all these issues Clark and I traded charges that related to our political styles. He claimed I was too willing to compromise. "The only way to lead is to lead," he said at one point. "You've got to fight for the things you believe in. Javits is not a fighter and I am." Clark even tried to belittle the ERISA bill because no one had opposed it on final passage: "How good a bill can it be when it passed unanimously?" he asked, ignoring the years of negotiation and compromise and trade-offs that were necessary to construct a monumental piece of legislation that all sides could support.

I tried to point out how unrealistic Clark's idealism was. "Over and over again," I said, Clark has "inveighed against compromise [and] preached the politics of self-righteousness." I predicted that if he were elected he would become one of that small group of senators whose bills never get out of committee and whose amendments are routinely voted down.

To answer Clark's charges that I had not taken a strong position on Nixon and Watergate, I produced with my media adviser, Julian Koenig, a TV spot emphasizing how I had fought the "imperial presidency." In that commercial I said:

> The danger of Nixon . . . was that as President he was the most powerful man on earth, more powerful than any shah, emperor, or dictator. . . . I fought in the Senate, not in words but in acts. I fought Nixon in my War Powers Act, the only act passed over a Nixon veto in this Congress. It means no more Vietnams. I fought Nixon with legislation for a special Watergate prosecutor. . . . And I led the fight for custody of the Nixon tapes. . . . The fight goes on — my National Institutions Act will mean no more Watergates. . . .

We used that hard-hitting commercial repeatedly in the closing weeks of the campaign and it put across my point that effective action is more important than sterile words.

What really turned the tide for me, however, was Ramsey Clark's "position paper" on the Middle East. He had proposed a Middle East development authority, like the Tennessee Valley Authority, to improve housing, health, irrigation, education, and so forth in all the nations of the region — Israel and the Arab states. The United Nations would administer the project, and the United States, the Soviet Union, the Arab oil-producing nations and the financial institutions would all contribute; the U.S. share would be $2 billion annually for ten years.

To neophytes in foreign affairs, such as Clark himself, this might have sounded like a good idea. But there were several things wrong with it — as I pointed out in my campaign speeches and statements. First of all, a majority of the United Nations, made up of Third-World countries, had already displayed a distinctly anti-Israel bias, and there was little hope that a development authority controlled by the United Nations would be fair to Israel. Second, the Clark scheme would bring the Soviet Union directly and officially into Middle East affairs, which certainly was not in accord with U.S. interests. Finally, the $2 billion a year that Clark wanted the United States to pour into an area already getting rich on oil money was completely unrealistic; there was no possibility whatever that Congress would approve a sum that was then larger than all our other foreign-aid commitments combined.

Buried within Clark's position paper, however, was an even more dangerous idea, which had received little attention until I picked it up and made a campaign issue of it. Although deploring the terror tactics of the Palestine Liberation Organization (PLO) and insisting that the United States must pledge "unequivocal" military aid to Israel, Clark's statement suggested the formation of a Palestinian state, "cojoined" to Jordan, in the West Bank and Gaza. It read: "The inclusion of Palestinian representatives in any peace discussion and indeed the eventual creation of a Palestinian state will be a solid guarantee of Israel's protection against terrorist attack. This is why Israeli leaders and most Israeli intellectuals endorse this approach."

I was very sensitive to the role of the Palestinians in the Middle East and to the nature of the PLO, which was (and is) dedicated to the liquidation of Israel and which has never, in word or deed, accepted UN Resolution 242, of 1967, the only foundation for peace in the Middle East. The preceding July I had visited Israel and had made a pilgrimage to the village of Maalot, which had been the scene of one of the most dreadful acts of the PLO. Terrorists had infiltrated into Israel, held children hostage in the Maalot school, and killed sixteen of them. It was a shocking event that had special significance for me, as some of the children had come to Maalot from Safed, where my mother was born.

Ramsey Clark claimed to be an ardent friend of Israel, but his unfamiliarity with the realities of the Middle East had led him to espouse a cause that threatened the very existence of Israel. I denounced his proposal — and that turned out to be the decisive issue of the campaign. It won to my side some of the people who might have voted against me because of Vietnam and Watergate.

On October 10 I blasted Clark's statement as "a gamble on the survival of the only free democratic state in the Middle East." Quoting his claim that Israelis favored a Palestinian state, I said:

> I don't know who qualifies as an "intellectual" by Mr. Clark's standards. But I know of no elected Israeli leader who would tolerate the creation of a Palestinian state ruled by terrorist organization leaders on the West Bank of the Jordan. Mr. Clark invalidates his own gesture of appeasement by stating that his suggestion for a new Arab state . . . is premised on a Palestinian "leadership" that is "as committed to Israel's continued existence as it is to the birth of a Palestinian state."

> Where on this earth will such a leadership of Palestinians who are committed to Israel's survival be found within the proximate future? Does he truly believe that the people of Israel should commit the lives of their children to the good will of people so embittered that they have sheltered and spawned the terrorists who

murdered children at Maalot, massacred innocents at Lud Airport and brought unceasing terror to the international airways? Not a chance, Mr. Clark.

The question became even more important a few days later, when the UN General Assembly voted to let the PLO take part in debates on the Middle East. I immediately condemned that action as a blow to the United Nations's credibility and as an unwarranted and dangerous precedent. The next day I again attacked Clark's stance. "There is much mischief in the advocacy of a West Bank state . . . because encouragement of its establishment not only encourages Arab extremists but also has the effect of impeding negotiations, hampering the chance of an agreement between Israel and each of its Arab neighbors."

Clark protested that I had distorted his position and he attempted to "clarify" it. He insisted that his Palestinian state would have no connection with the PLO and would not be independent but "cojoined in political union with Jordan and in economic relations with both Jordan and Israel." To which I retorted that he was "backtracking." Clark, I said, displays a "willingness to compromise Israel's security. . . . We can't afford a man who doesn't realize the implications of his own statements, . . . who knows so little about international relations that the significance of the presence or even serious consideration of a terrorist-dominated state on the West Bank and the Gaza Strip eludes his understanding."

A few days later, I found another chink in the armor of my opponent:

> Mr. Clark [I said] continues to maintain a most enigmatic silence over the shocking vote in the United Nations to invite the PLO terrorists to use the UN podium for propaganda purposes in support of its avowed goal of Israel's destruction. Even at this late hour I urge Mr. Clark to speak out in protest. His position on the Middle East is already too murky to permit equivocation on this life-and-death issue for Israel. If Mr. Clark still believes that the establishment of a Palestinian terrorist state on the West Bank is compatible with Israel's security he just doesn't have the judgment which is required of a United States senator from New York.

While Clark and I upbraided each other, the Conservative Party candidate, Barbara Keating, inveighed against both of us. Her main issues were high taxes and too much government spending — the classic conservative position — and neither Clark nor I tried to rebut her directly, even when all three of us appeared together in campaign debates. Because of President's Nixon's resignation, the Conservative Party had not been able to raise much money for the campaign, so we did not expect her to make a tremendous showing. I knew she would take some votes away from me, but there was little I could do about it because I had to keep after Clark.

On the morning of October 25 I picked up the *New York Times* and breathed a sigh of relief and satisfaction. In the lead editorial, the *Times* endorsed my reelection. The editorial suggested that I had erred on the side of caution on Watergate, and it stated that I was not a "flaming crusader." The *Times* applauded Clark's candor and sincerity, and said that the temptation to endorse him was strong. But, citing my experience and my record of "enlightened legislation," the editorial concluded that "on the basis of Senator Javits' proven ability to translate sound objectives into legislative reality, we believe the country will be better served by his reelection."

The *Times* had been one of the most vigorous, outspoken, and effective opponents of Nixon on Watergate, demanding time and again his prosecution and his resignation. Its endorsement was a decisive signal to the citizens of New York that my conduct was creditable and that I had maintained my liberal credentials in my third term.

As we expected, the 1974 elections registered a defeat for the Republican Party. We lost four seats in the Senate and forty-three in the House, as well as four governorships. But moderate or progressive Republicans like myself generally withstood the tide. I was reelected by the smallest plurality of my Senate career, three hundred sixty thousand votes, receiving 45 percent of the vote, with 38 percent for Clark and 16 percent for Keating. My trip to Cuba and the presence of a Conservative Party candidate in the race clearly cost me thousands of votes.

TWENTY-FOUR

Crisis in
New York City

New York City and its problems and needs have posed a dilemma for me many times. My conscience was often troubled by the thought that I might have been able to do more for the city — and get even more satisfaction myself — by becoming mayor than by serving as a U.S. senator. The temptation to seek the mayoralty of New York City has run like an underground stream through my career, surfacing in almost every mayoral election since my first try for the job in 1953, when Governor Tom Dewey promised me his support and then backed away.

Many people may wonder why anyone with a seat in the U.S. Senate would consider moving his workplace to New York's City Hall. The very words *Senate* and *City Hall* connote the difference in prestige and influence between the two posts. To a lot of people, a move to City Hall would have been a comedown for me, and in a protocol sense they are right: In many ways a senator is more "important," more "powerful" than a mayor.

But the mayor of New York City is not just "a mayor," because New York is not just "a city." It is a national city, a world city, and my great attachment to it transcends even the fact that it is the city of my birth and the city that is my home. In the far reaches of the world, people regard New York City as the symbol of the United States of America, and New York City represents the America of their dreams more than does any other city, state, or region of our country. The size and the variety and the vitality of New York City have always been sources of wonder for me. It is the country's and the world's leader in banking and commerce; it is the great port, the international center of art and music and dance, the mecca of tourism for visitors from everywhere; and it is a tremendous manufacturing center—even today. Seventy-five languages are spoken in New York, dozens of foreign-language newspapers are published and read in the city, and there are foreign-language television and radio programs. For me, despite its many problems, New York still has the luster and magic of a new town, with an adventure around every corner and behind every window, with human energy, ingenuity, and inventiveness coursing every street, changing every moment. It is still the most exciting city of modern civilization. And it is still a city that has a profound effect on what happens in other cities of the United States and on what happens even in distant lands that most New Yorkers have barely heard of.

Consequently, when New York City faced its grave financial crisis in 1975 I was determined that the city should not be forced to go into bankruptcy — even though the other New York senator at the time, Jim Buckley, seemed willing, for a while, to let that happen (and was defeated at the next election). I believed that if New York went into bankruptcy the city would be set back by decades and could no longer be the majestic national and world city it had become. I also felt that bankruptcy would imperil the entire financial situation of the country; bankruptcy would have a ripple effect on scores of other municipalities — and on many other states, too, as New York State would also be seriously involved. Such a course would also seriously damage the image of the United States in the eyes of the rest of the world.

Hence, I sought a leading role in the congressional struggle to have the U.S. government come to New York City's aid with temporary financial assistance to prevent it from going bankrupt and to give it time to correct some of the abuses and problems that had led to this sorry state of affairs. It was not an easy struggle because, as is well known, not all senators, and not all Americans, shared my views about our city. We had to fight prejudices based on false concepts (New York's problems are somehow different from the problems of other U.S. cities) and objections based on solid facts (New York City cannot become financially sound in the near future) in order to get the seasonal loan bill through the Senate in 1975 and to pass the loan guarantee bills in 1978. In those efforts I was able to pay back to the city that gave me birth, and which had done so much for me, some of the debt I felt I owed.

It is tempting to think that if I had become mayor of the city in the 1950s or the 1960s I might have been able to arrange things so that New York would not have faced the crisis it did. That may be a delusion. It is possible that I would have been buried under the same unmanageable weight of problems and traditions and methods and pressures and conflicting demands that trapped all the mayors of the city, even the good and honest and dedicated ones. (Ed Koch, the incumbent mayor, shows signs that he might be able to accomplish what others could not, but the real test will not come until the middle of 1982, when the federal loan guarantee expires.) The causes of the problem cannot be laid at the door of any one mayor or comptroller or city budget or finance director, and it is never certain whether any one leader or politician or elected official can ever do more than slightly speed up or slow down the inevitable march of history. I have the confidence to believe that I would have done well, but whether I could have reversed the trends, or redirected the steps of 8 million people to help themselves in an appreciable way, I cannot say.

Nevertheless, there are things I would have tried to do that have never been tried, even today, that I think might have made a difference. To understand these it is necessary to look at the causes of the cycle of events that brought New York City to the brink of bankruptcy in 1975.

There is no doubt that improvident, careless methods of accounting — budget gimmickry, it was called — and some challengeable selling of city securities by a few large banks pushed New York to the verge of default in 1975. But the causes of the city's economic and fiscal plight were much deeper and broader than that. The causes were rooted in the process of urbanization itself and the peculiar self-accelerating cycle of inward and outward migration that has affected every American city to some degree. They affected New York City more than most others because of New York City's political make-up and the attempt by successive New York municipal administrations, starting with La Guardia's, to provide services to the underprivileged that the underprivileged could not obtain for themselves. I was of course in favor of La Guardia's attempts to do this — in fact, as I have pointed out, that was one reason I found him attractive as a new kind of reformer; but the way in which it was done and the failure of the federal government and other state and governmental entities to contribute their share to this endeavor eventually put too great a burden on the city's finances.

New York has always been a mecca for people from the farms and small towns of America who come to the city to move up in the world and in their professions and to test themselves in the big time. They came when economic horizons were expanding, and even those among them who did not have special skills or talents or professional qualifications found work and did well. And if they did not do well they often returned to their hometowns or home states. But starting soon after the end of World War II, New York began to receive an influx of impoverished people who came to the city because there was no opportunity for them in their home areas. Many of them were Southern blacks, who came because of racial discrimination and economic stagnation in their home states. Others were Puerto Ricans, originally inspired to migrate by Congressman Vito Marcantonio, who wanted to create a new voting bloc in New York to build up his left-wing American Labor Party.

Southern blacks and Puerto Ricans alike came for jobs, for a better life, for better education for their children; and they found when they got here that even if they could not get a job New York's system of welfare and relief and subsidized housing and public health services were much better than at home. So they stayed, neighbors from home joined them, and New York started picking up the welfare tab for states that provided only minimal help for the poor.

In general, this happened spontaneously; the people gravitated naturally to where they could survive, like water flowing down a slope. In 1962, however, Southern segregationists deliberately encouraged the migration. At the time, teams of black and white "Freedom Riders" were traveling on buses and trains through the South in an attempt to integrate transportation. As a publicity stunt to counter that campaign, White Citizens Councils in Arkansas; Louisiana, and Mississippi chartered buses and handed out one-way tickets north to hundreds of impoverished blacks, many of whom were told that jobs and good housing awaited them. When these so-called reverse freedom riders arrived penniless and jobless in a score of Northern localities, including New York City, they immediately became an added burden on charity and welfare. (Some of them were sent to Cape Cod with the suggestion that President Kennedy open his summer home at Hyannis Port to take them in.)

Compared with the hundreds of thousands of poor blacks who migrated normally, the number of people involved in that cruel gambit was insignificant. But the racist organizers of the plan knew what they were doing. One of them said, "We expect to get a lot of people off the welfare rolls by sending them to other states where they can go on welfare there."

To carry this added burden of welfare and related services — and to pay for the wage gains of municipal employees — New York City had to raise taxes and go into debt. Raising taxes made it harder to attract new business or even to keep the businesses that were already in the city; as businesses left, the tax base declined, forcing further increases in taxes and accelerating the cycle. Simultaneously, the borrowing reached such proportions that it became unmanageable. Because it had established far-reaching social services for its residents during the La Guardia administration, the city found itself living beyond its means twenty years later. As early as 1953, when I made my first try for the mayoralty, I noted that New York City's per capita indebtedness already was the highest of any city in the country.

The wealth that was leaving New York in particular and the industrialized Northeast in general began accumulating in the South and Southwest of the United States — the Sunbelt. New industries established themselves in the Sunbelt to take advantage of lower labor costs, lower taxes, and the absence of unions, and those areas flourished, relatively free of the staggering costs of welfare and other services for the poor that New York and other Northeast cities had to carry without any significant federal help. It was interesting to remember that before World War II, when the shoe was on the other foot and we in the Northeast were relatively "rich" and the Sunbelt states were relatively "poor," federal programs and federal funds were administered in a way to reflect and alleviate that imbalance. But now that the shift had occurred, the Northeast was not getting a comparable break from the federal government.

Another key factor was the flight to the suburbs. The federal government had not built as much low- and middle-income housing in the cities as was really needed, despite our continuing efforts. But through the Veterans Administration and the Federal Housing Administration it had guaranteed low-cost mortgages for individual homeowners; coupled with new highways and parkways, many heavily financed by federal taxes, that had enabled the middle class to flee the cities for the suburbs. There are about 12 million people in the New York metropolitan area, but only about 8 million of them live in the city proper. The suburbanites are cut off from the city as citizens, in terms of political and moral support, and as taxpayers, in terms of financial support. Many of them, of course, work in the city, but even those who do not are linked to the city economically and are dependent upon it to some degree: New York serves them as a transportation center, as a market, and as a source of supply. But because the suburbs are politically distinct from the city, their residents are not accessible to the city as taxpayers and cannot be required to give it their fair share of support. Free of this burden, numerous communities right across the city line provide their residents with excellent public schools, sufficient law enforcement, and many municipal amenities for recreation and a better life that city residents just do not have.

Suburbanites who live within New York State do contribute to the city through the aid given by the state, but the state has never fully compensated New York City for the role it plays in the suburban economy. And those suburbanites who live in New Jersey or Connecticut are even further insulated from the needs of the metropolis — although they, too, benefit tremendously from their proximity to the greatest city in the world.

Other U.S. cities have faced and solved similar — if less severe — problems, yet New York City, for all the wealth and resources of its institutions and all the talent and ingenuity of its inhabitants, has not. And that is because the private sector, the business community of New York, has never been fully enlisted in the effort to make New York City a thriving and growing concern. In other cities that came alive after a period of decline — such as Boston, San Francisco, Pittsburgh, and Houston, to name just a few — private enterprise provided the capital and initiative and ability that were needed. Once fired with civic patriotism, the business people can get out and do the job that makes these cities what they are.

But that did not happen in New York. For one thing, the New York business community is too large and diverse to be easily mobilized for a local cause. Its leaders are so involved in national and international matters that the municipal problems of New York appear parochial in comparison. Civic boosterism seems redundant — if not downright corny — in the world's biggest city: It was only *after* the 1975 fiscal crisis that the "I Love New York" campaign began. So it is perhaps understandable that the business leaders of New York tended to remain aloof from the city's problems until the crisis of 1975.

The people of the city also bear some responsibility for the lack of business-government cooperation. The political and economic thinking of most New Yorkers is still dominated by the outmoded compulsion to oppose "the interests." In the old days, the interests were the industrial barons who controlled business and banking and railroads and built up enormous personal fortunes; opposing and limiting them made sense for the majority of the population. But the modern corporation, taxed, regulated, professionally managed — and owned by thousands of investors — is necessarily more sensitive to the needs of the community and it carries a vast potential for public good. To struggle against these "interests" in municipal affairs turns the world upside down, because private enterprise is precisely the element that can make a city function. While generally operating mass transit systems, government is really not properly equipped to do so, or to attract business and jobs to the city, or to adapt the city's physical shape and architecture to its changing historical needs. Only the private sector can do these things well.

Most citizens of New York do not fully understand this concept. There may be occasions for a clash between the people and the interests on the national and state levels, but the voters apply it to the municipal level too, even though the cooperation of the business community is precisely what is needed to save the city. Reflecting this popular mood, New York's mayors have never brought private enterprise into an effective working partnership with the city.

And that is where New York City went wrong. Fiorello La Guardia, that great civic patriot, began to clean up the city and make it more honest, but the people would have been suspicious of him if he had cooperated too closely with the business community in the interests of development. Besides, there seemed no need to do so at the time. New York City still had a lot of resources in La Guardia's day, a certain amount of fat that it could live on, so the city could afford financially to deliver services and root out corruption at the same time. The city was growing and no one predicted that one day its wealth would start draining away. With hindsight, it might be said that the slide began in La Guardia's time.

Neither Bill O'Dwyer nor Vincent Impellitteri, the next two mayors, had the vision to see what was needed — although the city debt was beginning to rise alarmingly in their administrations. And Bob Wagner, an intelligent and able mayor, kept the city in good order, but he broke no patterns either, and the slide continued.

John Lindsay, however, *was* an innovator. In his first term, he brought style and quality and a sense of intellect and history to the city; the attention he paid to music and the theater, and the manner in which he opened up the parks to the people, made New York a more interesting place to live in than it had been since the halcyon days before the First World War. He also displayed great courage in walking through the streets at a time of acute racial tension, and thereby kept tempers cool in New York when other cities were exploding. I was gratified that I had urged him to run in 1965 and had campaigned hard for his reelection in 1969, even though he did not have the Republican nomination that year and ran on the Liberal Party line.

But style is not a substitute for substance, and in Lindsay's second term people began to ask what was happening to the city's finances, to the labor contracts in the public services, and to the infrastructure and economy of the city. It was there that Lindsay's weaknesses showed. In the end it became apparent that Lindsay did not have the taste for hard slugging in collective bargaining with the municipal unions and that not enough private business had been attracted to the city.

That was particularly unfortunate, because with his style, education, and background John Lindsay could have become the long-needed bridge between the business community and City Hall — and a great deal of civic betterment might have crossed that bridge. The garment district of Seventh Avenue, for example, could have been turned into a sparkling showplace for the fashion industry if the cooperation and financing and intelligent planning of imaginative entrepreneurs had been enlisted in such a project. Or with the proper encouragement and planning and tax breaks, the young electronics industry could have been enticed to concentrate in New York, bringing many thousands of jobs; electronics was a natural industry for the city, because it requires skilled labor and does not need huge factories or bulk material. But that opportunity was lost. Intelligent plans for cooperative ownership for housing rehabilitation, as is being done now in some neighborhoods, could have saved many fine structures. With the proper kind of sophisticated cooperation between the public and private sectors — and with the private foundations, many of which are located in New York, also participating — the rapid deterioration of the city's schools, transit system, and housing could perhaps have been halted, and with that the seepage of business and jobs and wealth might have stopped as well. At least it would have been worth a try.

There were a few attempts, of which a relatively successful one was the rehabilitation of the Bedford-Stuyvesant black ghetto in Brooklyn. Senator Robert Kennedy initiated that idea and came to Mayor Lindsay and me to help get it started. We enlisted a number of business people and public-spirited citizens, including Andre Meyer, Bill Paley, Brooke Astor, Jock Whitney, Thomas Jones, Franklin Thomas — and of course the residents of the area. The project cleaned up decaying neighborhoods, attracted new business enterprise, and became a model for community development elsewhere.

Had I run for mayor and been elected, it would have come naturally to me to seek out business cooperation, for I have spent a great part of my career demonstrating that the private and public sectors can not only live together but can accomplish great things together. I do not know of a single major economic initiative I have taken in relevant legislation that has not involved the power of private enterprise. And nowhere could this partnership be more effective than in getting New York City to function as it should.

Several times I have tried to assemble such a partnership. In the spring of 1974 I called together a group of municipal and business leaders in an effort to create an industrial park on the site of the Penn Central railroad yards in the South Bronx; the project would have created thousands of jobs in that depressed and deteriorating area of the city and could have marked the first step in a significant urban renewal. Mayor Abe Beame, Senator James Buckley, Bronx Borough President Robert Abrams, George Champion, chairman of the New York City Economic Development Council, John Patterson, president of the South Bronx Economic Development Corporation, Congressman Herman Badillo, and New York City Economic Development Administrator Alfred Eisenpreis were among the officials who came to the first meeting in my New York office. The officials agreed in principle that the city would buy the land from Penn Central, and we lined up a number of businesses that were prepared to rent space from the city and open plants on the site. We worked quietly, without publicity, so that Penn Central would not raise the price of the land, and the news of the project did not leak out until we were almost ready to put it all together. But by then the severe recession of 1974 had hurt the city's finances. The fiscal crisis was almost upon us and the project that had promised so much for New York fell apart because the city could not raise the $10 million needed to buy the land.

The recession of 1974 strained the city's finances almost to the breaking point. Much of New York City's revenue comes from sales taxes and income taxes, and the business downturn reduced these revenues while simultaneously putting an even greater demand on city and state funds for welfare and other civic services. In March 1975 the major banks — some of which had been quietly selling New York City securities for some time — announced they would lend the city no more money. With its credit gone, the city faced the possibility that it might have to default on its obligations, and a cliff-hanging melodrama began: Week by week the city staved off default with stopgap measures, trying desperately to hang on to fiscal responsibility until the federal government could come to the rescue. And for nine months no one was sure Uncle Sam would show up in time — or at all.

Our effort to obtain Washington's assistance got a decidedly chilly reception. The general feeling in Congress and the Treasury Department and the White House was that the city had been living beyond its means for too long and that it was finally getting its comeuppance. When the crisis began, few people in Washington understood how close the city really was to bankruptcy or what bankruptcy would mean to the nation and to the world.

Part of the reluctance to help was based on sincere fiscal caution; unfortunately, another part of it reflected the prejudice and sometimes even hostility that many Americans felt toward New York City. I had been aware of these feelings for many years, for they were expressed repeatedly in Senate and House debates — particularly by Southern legislators during the civil rights struggles of the 1950s and 1960s. Every New Yorker has heard the comments about the noise and dirt and crowds of New York, the alleged general rudeness, the street-crime rate, the high prices. But these annoying criticisms — mostly by people who seldom visited the city and knew very little about it — were less important than the subtle ways in which anti–New York feelings were evidenced in the consciousness or the subconsciousness of federal legislators. The phobia against New York for a long time blocked the federal authorization and appropriations for the New York World's Fair of 1964 (which some members of Congress said was just a New York promotion project); it influenced the federal government to discriminate against the port of New York; and it denied New York its fair share of funds for education and for urban mass transportation.

New York was and remains a perfect symbol and target for attacks by rural demagogues. Moreover, New York contains within it several other symbols that are employed to conjure up all manner of evil: Wall Street, Madison Avenue, Park Avenue, Harlem, Greenwich Village. A federal official once told me that he rarely visited the city because it is "too big to cope with" and that he did all his considerable business with it by phone or letter. Senators and representatives from many regions of the country can make political hay at home by attacking New York.

I heard all the familiar arguments and more in the spring and summer of 1975 as I tried to persuade my colleagues in the Senate that New York had to be helped. I was told that New York had done it all to itself by corruption, inefficiency, and waste, that it was a den of iniquity anyhow, and that it ought to take its medicine, whatever the consequences. Then there was the easy excuse that if you do it for one city you have to do it for all cities — an argument that failed to recognize that New York was a national city and its fiscal collapse would pull down many other municipalities with it.

One of the arguments against federal aid for the city was that New Yorkers were not doing enough to help themselves. To counter that one we needed a new, highly visible group of public-spirited citizens who were willing to take up some of the tasks that the hard-pressed city government could not perform. In August 1975 I invited a group of business people, journalists, advertising people, religious leaders, labor leaders, and academics to a breakfast meeting at the Park Avenue offices of the Bristol-Meyers Corporation. The group was a reincarnation of the "good-government" forces that had long been active in mayoral politics.

Out of this effort came the Citizens Committee for New York City. Senator Buckley and I served as temporary cochairmen at first, but then I passed the ball to Osborn Elliott, now dean of the Graduate School of Journalism at Columbia University, who was just about to leave his post as chairman of the board and editor in chief of *Newsweek*. With a splendid board of directors under Elliott's gifted chairmanship, the Citizens Committee showed individual citizens how to help their city, and it revived the city's morale. The committee organized thousands of block associations, helped set up civilian street patrols, assisted neighborhood festivals, and promoted local cleanup and beautification projects — a particularly good one was sponsored by Molly Parnis Livingston, the fashion designer. When the New York Public Library laid off workers, the committee found volunteers to keep the libraries open. Most important of all, these activities of the committee and its volunteers proved to Congress that New Yorkers were interested in saving their city.

During the summer of 1975 the city and state were trying desperately to do the same thing. The city laid off workers, increased the transit fare, deferred capital spending, and took other economy steps. New York State set up the Municipal Assistance Corporation ("Big Mac") to sell long-term bonds, secured by earmarked municipal taxes, to help the city meet its short-term obligations. That plan was designed by Felix Rohatyn, the gifted financier who became chairman of Big Mac.

All these actions and our arguments on Capitol Hill convinced a few people in Washington that New York was serious about setting its financial house in order. In September the Senate's Banking, Housing, and Urban Affairs Committee began discussing a bill to provide federal guarantees for city bonds. Although I was not a member of the committee, I sat in on its hearings and discussions that fall and repeatedly made the case to my colleagues that every other state had at least one city, however small, that shared in some degree the problems that were crippling New York. If New York were allowed to go bankrupt, I said, many of those cities would eventually face the same threat.

The chairman of the Senate committee was Democrat William Proxmire of Wisconsin, a brilliant senator with a complex and fascinating personality who became a key factor in New York's survival in 1975 and three years later, when the city had to go back to Washington for further aid. Bill Proxmire is a true son of his region and heir to the Midwest progressive tradition of the La Follettes. His instincts are humanitarian and he has a great deal of common sense. But he is very conservative on fiscal matters, very suspicious of international commitments that can involve the United States in matters that are not its business — and he has a great penchant for discovering and ridiculing the foibles of the federal bureaucracy, to which he gives his Golden Fleece Awards. In his youth, Proxmire had once worked for a bank in New York City, so he understood finance and banking and balance sheets and accounting methods. He had a field day cross-examining the witnesses from New York who came before his committee seeking aid for the city. There *had* been some corruption and there *had* been some ridiculous and stupid bureaucratic blunders, and Bill Proxmire exposed them.

In 1975, Bill Proxmire realized how disastrous a New York bankruptcy would be, and after New York had tightened its belt, as he and others had been urging all summer, and after the city's finances had been placed under the control of the New York State Emergency Financial Control Board, Proxmire and his committee began writing a bill to provide federal guarantees for the New York City bonds that investors would not buy otherwise. In October, however, President Ford declared that he would veto any such legislation; New York, he felt, was not doing enough to help itself. Unfortunately, the famous *New York Daily News* headline on that story, FORD TO CITY: DROP DEAD, probably cost President Ford New York's electoral votes — and therefore the election — in 1976, although of course the President had not used those words.

All legislative work on the rescue proposal ceased momentarily after President Ford's veto threat. Later that month the city came to within two hours of defaulting and was saved only when the United Federation of Teachers agreed to invest some of its pension funds in New York bonds. (Other unions followed suit later.) That agreement enabled New York to keep afloat until December.

Then things began to fall into place, with President Ford and others. In my judgment, what finally prevailed over every other consideration was the belated recognition that a New York City bankruptcy would have a catastrophic effect on the capacity of other American cities to raise money in the financial markets and would adversely affect the economy of the whole world. Both Chancellor Helmut Schmidt of West Germany and President Valéry Giscard d'Estaing of France spoke to President Ford about it. The President asserted that his original hard line had convinced New York to come up with even more stringent financial controls (the New York State Legislature had raised the city's taxes and limited city spending), and he asked Congress to authorize "seasonal" loans to the city. These loans were to be granted to the city in the middle of its fiscal year so it could pay its salaries and meet other obligations; they had to be paid back the same year, when the city collected its taxes.

For three days that December the Senate debated the seasonal loan bill. It would cost the federal government nothing and the risk was minimal: Under the terms of the legislation these loans had to be paid back with interest before any other obligations. Yet the opponents of the bill, the traditional critics of New York, threatened a filibuster, and we had to invoke cloture in order to get the bill passed. (As it turned out, the U.S. government actually made a $30 million profit on the deal from the generous interest rates stipulated in the bill.) Proxmire argued for the bill on the floor of the Senate; I pointed out to my colleagues the "monumental contraction in city services" that had taken place since the crisis began. "Frankly," I said, "this is not the best bill ... from the point of view of preserving an enormous revenue source for the United States. But we are living in a pragmatic world. There is nothing much we can do about it. We are left breathing, period . . . We are not dead."

Finally, in a vote after midnight on December 5, the Senate passed the seasonal loan bill, by a vote of 57 to 30. The House had approved the measure a few days earlier. The bill granted the Treasury Department authority to lend New York City up to $2.3 billion at any one time, on a seasonal basis. It was a well-designed bill with strict compliance requirements — and it saved New York City.

Between the passage of that measure and its expiration in 1978, a remarkable turnaround took place in both the spirit and the finances of the city. The bicentennial celebration of 1976 and the Democratic Convention held in the city that year played a great part in improving New York's image, and the economies forced on the city began to take effect. But the long-range problems of the city were still not being solved.

To address the enduring problem of the city's economic development, I tried once more to get competing elements of the city to cooperate. It seemed to me that business and labor, in tandem, could do a lot of things to help bring the city out of the crisis. So in 1976, David Rockefeller, chairman of the Chase Manhattan Bank, Harry Van Arsdale, president of the New York City Central Labor Council, and I, with about a dozen more business and labor leaders, established the Business-Labor Working Group.

The group proved effective and influential — for a while. It took a stand in favor of Westway, the controversial highway project for Manhattan, as a means of boosting the city's economy; it agreed that welfare should be more of a federal responsibility; it agreed on tax abatements for new industries coming to the city; and it joined the city government in lobbying for city projects in Washington. It also succeeded in slowing down the flight of industry from the city: Labor-management "truth squads" talked to businessmen planning to move and showed them how they could solve their problems and remain in the city.

However, the Business-Labor Working Group eventually transformed itself into a predominantly business organization called the New York Partnership; the businessmen in it claim they can be more effective if labor is in an advisory capacity and free to act independently.

* * *

In 1978, the economies of the new city administration of Mayor Ed Koch were clearly moving the city toward fiscal responsibility. We still needed federal help — not emergency, seasonal loans but long-term guarantees that would enable the city to plan its recovery rationally. The administration of President Jimmy Carter, who had been elected with the help of New York voters in 1976, was favorable to the city, and New York now had another helpful senator, Daniel Patrick Moynihan, also elected in 1976.

But Senator Proxmire opposed long-term guarantees for the city. When the idea was broached he declared that the city no longer faced bankruptcy, that aid to the city would encourage too many other cities to ask for similar help, and that this would "weaken the incentive for fiscal discipline at the local level and erode the foundations of our federal system." So Senator Moynihan and I went to work on his committee. In his book *The Fleecing of America,* Senator Proxmire described what happened next. "Jack Javits and Pat Moynihan," he wrote, "did more to change the Senate Banking Committee from 'no' in January 1978 to 'yes' in June than any two senators I have ever seen operate on any issue in all my career."

Deep within himself, I feel, Bill Proxmire realized that the city had to be helped again. So although he personally opposed it, he did not prevent his committee from reporting out the necessary bill (drafted by Senator Richard Lugar, Indiana Republican). And when it came to debating the bill before the Senate, his fairness and objectivity, and his understanding of the facts and figures, helped the Senate come to an affirmative conclusion on the measure, notwithstanding Proxmire's opposition. Indeed this strange dichotomy on his part might well have been the reason the bill passed and was not doomed, as it could have been. In this case his opposition was nearly as valuable as his support of the 1975 bill.

In July 1978, after weeks of intense debate and negotiations and technical argument, Congress cleared a law authorizing the secretary of the treasury to guarantee New York City bonds for fifteen years, up to a total of $1.65 billion. Many limitations and requirements and controls were written into this legislation, and the seasonal help was abolished, but the crisis was over. We will face the next one in 1982, when the authority to issue loan guarantees runs out.

In June 1978, when the Banking Committee cleared the loan guarantee bill, I declared:

> New York has been vindicated and the work which has been done by myself and Senator Moynihan in sitting with the Banking Committee, cross-examining the witnesses, closely conferring and cooperating with the individual members of the committee has now paid off in a real understanding of New York's problems. . . . This represents the greatest victory of all, that Congress has accepted the responsibility . . . and that New York's actions in the last three years have won a certain confidence and support in the Congress, which now give it a chance to live.

TWENTY-FIVE

Our Troubled World

Political opponents often criticized me for spending too much time in the Senate on foreign policy and not enough on issues concerning my state. But I felt that only by giving both domestic and foreign policy their due could I attend conscientiously to the affairs of my state. Contemporary developments tie foreign policy so intimately to the fate of the U.S. economy and society that foreign and domestic policy become one and the same. Oil prices, worldwide inflation, the threat of nuclear destruction, international trade, and the aspirations of disadvantaged people in distant lands are not chips in some esoteric game that we play for fun: They affect the lives and the pocketbooks and the security of every American, every day, and they concern New Yorkers more than most because so much of our economy depends on commerce. Moreover, I regard foreign policy as critical because our successes and failures in it will determine whether we and our children live in freedom or survive in servitude — or perish in a nuclear holocaust.

The notion that we can ignore the rest of the world and expect it to follow our lead is a curious hangover from the immediate aftermath of World War II. We emerged from the war as the overwhelmingly dominant military, political, and economic power in the world, and some Americans look back upon that inherently unstable state of affairs with longing and nostalgia. They fail to recognize that it is our *relative* strength that has declined — as the other industrialized nations recovered from the war and as countries that were formerly powerless, such as China and the oil-producing Arab lands, acquired a measure of strength and influence.

The world has become much more complex and its nations and people are far more interdependent than we thought could be possible thirty-five or forty years ago. I have no regrets about the time and effort I expended learning about international problems and applying whatever skills I have to the attempts to solve them.

* * *

Almost everything that has happened in international affairs since the beginning of my congressional service has been colored by the ideological competition between our system and that of the Soviet Union. This competition grows out of two fundamental differences between our societies. The first of these is the relationship of the individual to the state: We hold that the state exists to serve the individual, while the Communists have it the other way around. We conceive of human rights as the right to travel freely, to be secure in person and property and communication, to have due process of law, to elect our representatives, and to choose our jobs, our place of residence, and so on. On the other hand, in the Communist world these rights are yielded to the state, which in return establishes the right to employment, health, education, and the constant care of the individual from the cradle to the grave. Therefore, when human rights are discussed between us, such as in the Helsinki Declaration of Human Rights of 1975, we and the Communists pass each other like ships in the night. They are talking about a totally different set of human rights and values than we are, and they accepted the Helsinki declaration only because in exchange for it they thought they got juridical acceptance of the division of Europe and our recognition of their control over East Germany and the East European satellite countries.

The second fundamental difference is the free world's capability to extend two powerful inducements to individual initiative: Credit and ownership, both of which are denied in the Communist system. Under the free-world system of credit the individual can give his labor today and receive back a piece of paper, in savings or life insurance or pension rights or social security or stocks and bonds, with reasonable confidence that it will be redeemed at a later date. The ownership opportunities in the Communist world are so limited that Rumania and Hungary, for example, regard it as a great concession to give individuals even a modicum of ownership of their own homes, something we regard as a basic right.

Our system, when clearly understood, has a great appeal to everyone, and therefore it is necessary for us to reach the people under Communism directly, notwithstanding their leaders' efforts to block that communication and to control the minds of their people so that whatever we say or do is received with suspicion and disbelief. We must struggle to break through and open up their society, through such means as the Voice of America and similar broadcasts, through tourism, through reciprocal press coverage and sports, through immigration and the cultural interchange that allows Soviet intellectuals, teachers, and students to see firsthand how democracy works.

While always trying to keep our door open to the Communists, to persuade them and show them what we are and how we do things, I have remained wary of their intentions and activities. The free world's security depends on the military power of the United States, and therefore, although it is regrettable that we have to spend so much on military preparedness, I did not compromise on this issue. On occasion I have voted against administration requests for greater sums to be spent on some esoteric weaponry, but this was because of my disagreement about whether we really needed a weapon or were merely pandering to the insatiable military appetite for ships, planes, tanks, and missiles. One of the best examples of this was my vote against the B-1 bomber, in which I agreed with President Carter that in the age of such advanced weapons as the Cruise missile this bomber was a throwback to another day and would become obsolete long before the multibillion-dollar program could get any planes ready for combat.

Simultaneously, I have tried at all times to improve our trade and cultural and sports relationships with the Communist world. When I returned from my first trip to the Soviet Union in 1962 I started a long campaign aimed at exchanging parliamentary delegations with the USSR. This was opposed by the House and Senate leaderships of both parties on the grounds that the Soviet Union did not have what we thought of as an independent parliament, and that therefore we should not receive them. But I worked at it and in my visit to Moscow in 1975 I got a promise from Soviet authorities that their delegation would include not only members of the Supreme Soviet but also ministers; eventually, in 1976, we did receive a Soviet delegation, which included their minister of foreign trade. These exchanges have continued since, interrupted only by the USSR's move into Afghanistan.

The differences between the two systems were clearly demonstrated after World War II when the Soviet Union reduced its Eastern European satellites to complete economic and military dependence on Moscow. The military control of the satellites by the USSR was evidenced in its worst form in the forceful suppression of the efforts to gain some element of freedom in Poland, East Germany, Hungary, and Czechoslovakia, and it created the aura of fear that haunts Eastern Europe. Only Polish workers have, for the moment, broken free of this suppression.

At the same time, we sought to strengthen our position by alliances with free and independent nations, accommodating as we did so all of the difficulties of fractious partners making unilateral decisions we do not like — such as France's withdrawal from NATO in 1966 and the more recent disagreements about how the Western alliance should respond to the Soviet Union's actions in Afghanistan.

Such disagreements are one price of freedom — a high price. The lack of harmony within the Atlantic alliance is the greatest single shortcoming of U.S. foreign policy. Europe — by which I mean free Europe — is the keystone of our security and the central arena in the overall East-West struggle; I say this notwithstanding my profound interest in Israel and the Middle East, my concern with the Vietnam War, and my dedication to the cause of economic development in Latin America and other Third World areas.

No problem facing the world is insoluble if Europe and the United States act together to solve it. Our highest objectives should be to harmonize policy with our European allies and to maintain the integrity of the European Economic Community, for only unity can provide Europe with the competence and strength and confidence to stand up as an independent entity against the combined weight of the Soviet Union and its satellites. Lacking such unity, if it appeared at some time that the Soviet Union was winning its competition with the United States, leaders of the weaker Western European countries might want to pick up and go with the eventual winner, and one by one, by a process of Finlandization, some nations of Western Europe could pass to Soviet control. No Western European country can stand alone, but together they can stand very effectively — a fact that would be too obvious to utter had not Charles De Gaulle ignored it.

Work on the Marshall Plan as a member of the Foreign Affairs Committee of the House of Representatives thrust me into the center of the effort for European unity. When I came to the Senate in 1957 I failed to get on the Foreign Relations Committee, so I quickly found another role in international affairs: At my request, Vice President Nixon, as president of the Senate, appointed me a delegate to the 1957 NATO Parliamentarians' Conference, which met in Paris that fall. The conference was not considered by the Senate to be of major importance at the time, and some of my colleagues regarded the Paris meeting as an unofficial holiday. But I made it clear I was willing to work at the job and so I was promptly chosen the *rapporteur* of the Economic Committee of that conference.

That post gave me a fruitful and fascinating opportunity to learn a great deal about European affairs — especially economic affairs. I later served this NATO organization as chairman of the Economic Committee, chairman of the Political Committee, and chairman of a special group known as the Committee of Nine, which reviewed NATO doctrine in the early 1970s; and through 1980 I remained an alternate member of the Standing Committee, the central operating body of the North Atlantic Assembly (which is what the NATO Parliamentarians' Conference is now called).

NATO work took me to Europe at least once every year and brought me into close contact with many emerging leaders. After that 1957 meeting I came home raving to my wife and my staff about a brilliant young French delegate to the Economic Committee; some day, I predicted, he would be president or prime minister of France. I got to know him well at ensuing meetings of the conference and I have visited and talked with Valéry Giscard d'Estaing from time to time since he became president of France. He has an iron will and a cool and rational mind that to me represents the spirit of France.

Although NATO is primarily a military alliance, our work in the NATO Parliamentarians' Conference was focused on the treaty's Article 2, which called for economic cooperation among the members. We aimed at strengthening the economic and monetary fabric of the NATO countries and encouraging their democratic institutions, so that peoples everywhere would be shown a true alternative to Communism. We were also interested in extending aid to the less-developed nations. In 1957, I introduced a resolution in the Parliamentarians' Conference calling for a special economic conference to coordinate such aid. That conference took place the following August in London, under my chairmanship, and decided that NATO itself should not get involved in this activity but that its members should cooperate in regional plans to aid development and establish collective guarantees to private investments in less-developed areas. The Western Europeans, who owed their own rapid recovery to the Marshall Plan, were very receptive to the idea of extending similar aid to the areas that needed it a decade later — an activity now carried out by the Development Assistance Group of the Organization for Economic Cooperation and Development (OECD).

We were doing fairly well in the NATO complex until the Vietnam War diverted the energies and the attention of the United States. The Soviet Union took advantage of our concentration on Vietnam and profited immensely from it — by developing and improving its military machine and by extending its influence in the Middle East, in the Mediterranean, and in other parts of the world. Facing the awesome military might of the Soviet Union, the leaders of Western Europe began to question the prudence and leadership of the United States, upon which they had based their security. President Charles De Gaulle of France withdrew his country from the NATO military command in 1966 and embarked on an independent foreign policy, and in 1970, West German Chancellor Willy Brandt opened his *Ostpolitik* dialogue with East Germany.

The long-range effects of this setback to Western unity are incalculable. For one thing, it led in the mid-1970s to Euro-Communism —

the threat that the Communist parties of Western Europe, who were professing to be nationalistic and free of Soviet domination, might come to power, particularly in France and Italy. In a long conversation with me in 1976, President Giscard expressed confidence that the people of France would not be taken in by the new Communist line, and he turned out to be right, for the Communist-Socialist alliance lost the parliamentary elections of 1978. Nevertheless, the lack of harmony within Western Europe keeps that threat alive.

President Giscard has also modified the Gaullist line and France now cooperates somewhat more with the other nations of Western Europe and with the United States. But the pure Gaullist ideal of a Western Europe led by France, not by the United States, still appeals to a great many of the French. In 1977 I discussed this view with its chief exponent, former premier Jacques Chirac, mayor of Paris and president of the Rassemblement Pour la République (RPR), the conservative Gaullist party. Chirac claimed that France needed to strengthen its armaments and acquire a real independent voice; he complained about what he saw as U.S. efforts to intervene in the construction of a united Europe, and he seemed to worry about a Western Europe dominated by Germany and the United States. I insisted that the United States had no desire to run Europe and I challenged him to discard what I called the old hat Gaullist theories. The United States, I reminded him, is the world's number-one producer, and the USSR is number two; France, I said, belongs with one or the other.

To that Chirac retorted with some asperity that a truly united Europe would be the second largest producer and maybe the first. The Gaullist line, he said, was a good one because it made France a strong and respected nation in the world. It was the softening of the Gaullist line, he said, that had hurt France the most.

A similar process has taken place in the Federal Republic of Germany, which followed U.S. policy toward the Soviet Union almost without question until Brandt broke loose with his *Ostpolitik;* that has now been revised under Chancellor Helmut Schmidt to become an independent West German policy pursued with a view toward establishing closer relations between West and East Germany. The Germans are bolder now — for example, they will accept nuclear missiles on their soil — but they are more critical of the United States on inflation, on trade, on the way we handle the Middle East, and recently on Afghanistan. Their criticism can be valuable — and at the same time may be troublesome, because in my view if the consensus on the unity of Europe ever broke completely apart, Germany might well revert to some form of neo-Nazism.

One reason it is so difficult to solve these problems is the economic weakness of Great Britain. By rights, the British should be playing a much greater leadership role in Europe, and that would help us too, because their outlook and their motives and objectives are generally closer to ours than other nations'. But the British people have been bled white by successive wars and their ambitions and energies and productivity have declined. They have passed from being an empire that administered a great part of the world and have become a nation whose main interests lie more in commerce than in political relations. Britain requires vast transfusions of capital to modernize its industrial plant, and it needs a major role in Europe to restore its sense of confidence and strength. The United States should accelerate that process because Britain is indispensable to the maintenance of world peace and stability.

In 1971 the North Atlantic Assembly decided to review NATO doctrine and it put me in charge of the exercise. I organized what was called the Committee of Nine, made up of leading statesmen from the principal NATO countries, including the former secretary general of NATO, Manlio Brosio of Italy, Walter Hallstein, former president of the EEC, and Canada's former prime minister Lester Pearson. I arranged for the committee to be financed through foundations and other voluntary contributions. Aided by major research organizations, including the Brookings Institution in Washington and the Institute for Strategic Studies in London, we undertook a two-year study of NATO's role in the world. In 1973 we produced a report that was considered the most authoritative analysis of NATO's strengths and weaknesses that had been made up to that time. In some respects the report was prescient: It recognized the possibilities of détente but also noted the accelerated development of strategic nuclear weapons by the Soviet Union.

The gravest threat in East-West relations is that the competition between the United States and the Soviet Union could break out into armed conflict and nuclear warfare. The growth of Soviet military strength increased our desire to limit the nuclear weaponry of the two great powers. The Strategic Arms Limitation Treaty of 1972 (SALT I) limited the deployment of both offensive intercontinental missiles and defensive antiballistic missile systems, but it was only the first step in this direction. As new and more sophisticated weapons systems were developed by both sides it became more imperative than ever to continue the process.

In 1978 some way had to be found to achieve and maintain equivalence of nuclear arms. The big question was what constituted equivalence. Since SALT I, the Soviet Union had expanded and improved that part of its nuclear arsenal which was not covered under SALT I, and had spent on defense three times as much of gross national product as we were spending. We had decided not to build the B-1 bomber or the neutron bomb. We were late in modernizing the Minuteman, our principal ICBM, and our production of the Trident nuclear missile was slow. In sum, we maintained the doctrine of "MAD" (Mutual Assured Destruction), which holds that since we and the Soviet Union both have sufficient nuclear power to wipe out the other, there is no need to build more, and that this mutual annihilation capability will itself prevent war. But by the late 1970s that had become a simplistic theory; the Soviets were proceeding on the assumption that they had to be equipped to *win* any war, even a nuclear exchange. Reliance on mutual deterrence became unrealistic when the Soviets, proceeding legally under the terms of SALT I, increased their nuclear *offensive* capability by placing multiple warheads (MIRVs) on their big missiles. MIRVs were our idea but we put them on smaller, more precisely targeted intercontinental ballistic missiles. When the Russians built missiles much bigger than our own and then placed MIRVs on those huge weapons, that gave them a formidable potential.

Visiting Moscow in the fall of 1978, I became convinced that the Soviet Union was seriously interested in SALT II, which was then being negotiated. At that time we were claiming that the Soviets were delaying the treaty, but they insisted that *we* were holding up agreement because of our worries about maintaining an adequate defense posture. In this case perhaps the Russians were more nearly right. I believe that the testimony we heard in the later Senate hearings indicated that the U.S. side recognized that the Soviet Union had gained such an enormous momentum in the development of nuclear and conventional armaments that there was a grave danger that it could establish superiority, and that when the impact of that became clear to the U.S. negotiators they slowed things down to examine the agreements more closely to make sure that by 1985, when SALT II was due to expire, we would not be in a weaker relative position than we were in 1978 and 1979.

The Soviets' desire for a genuine nuclear arms limitation agreement was based to a great extent on fear of the United States. The Russians knew that if the United States really became concerned about nuclear superiority and launched a massive buildup comparable to theirs, we would outdistance them — and since we are the only nation that has used nuclear weapons in war, they were afraid of a pre-emptive nuclear strike after we clearly had the upper hand.

It may seem unlikely to most Americans that we would strike first with a nuclear weapon — but that is what the Soviets inferred from the new nuclear targeting policy announced by President Carter in the summer of 1980. It is important for us to look at the question as the Soviets do. They have long memories; they lost 20 million people in World War II, and they remember that the Western powers sought to destroy their revolution by armed invasion after World War I. They note that we have never been invaded by a foreign power, an experience they endured as recently as World War II. We may think they are paranoid about our intentions, and we often say that we cannot trust them — but they feel they cannot quite trust us either.

In the summer and fall of 1979 I was closely involved in the Senate debate on the SALT II agreement, which would probably have been ratified had not the Soviet Union's invasion of Afghanistan late that year postponed the entire question. Underlying the testimony and argument about the details of the treaty was a concern about its psychological effects. Opponents of the treaty felt that it might give the Soviets so much confidence in their nuclear advantage that they would be emboldened to stir up more trouble for us around the world. The opponents also declared that the treaty would "tranquilize" us and make us complacent, thereby perpetuating our nuclear vulnerability. One expert who offered this tranquilizer theory was Paul Nitze, former deputy secretary of defense, who had helped negotiate the SALT I agreement but led the opposition to SALT II. In hearings before the Foreign Relations Committee, Nitze contended that the United States had fallen behind the Soviet Union in intercontinental nuclear weaponry and that the treaty would not allow us to catch up. Cross-examining him, I got him to admit that if he was right, it would be even more difficult for us to catch up without the restraints on Soviet arms development that were embodied in SALT II. Our failure, so far, to ratify SALT II has made the world a more dangerous place.

* * *

The competition between the superpowers, the United States and the USSR, has mainly taken place in struggles on the territory of the poorer nations of the world, such as the recent conflicts in Somalia and Ethiopia. I played a continuing role in the effort to help the less-developed countries attain a satisfactory standard of living without resorting to totalitarianism. My greatest contribution to this effort sprang from my interest in Latin America and my belief in the effectiveness of private enterprise. In the spring of 1961, concerned about the flight of capital from Latin America in the wake of Castro's takeover of Cuba, I suggested to the NATO Parliamentarians' Economic Committee, of which I was chairman, that private capital investment from the industrialized nations should supplement governmental aid to Latin America. The idea was applauded — no one could take issue with it — but it was easier said than done. Someone had to turn the idea into reality, so I set about it. My three years of work on this project resulted in the invention of an effective new vehicle for investment in economic development.

I started at home, with U.S. firms. George Moore, who was then president of the First National City Bank of New York, enthusiastically supported the idea, and at my request his bank put up some money to finance a preliminary study group. Standard Oil of New Jersey (now Exxon) provided financial support and the help of Emilio Collado, one of its directors. We also received help at the start from the Ford Foundation, and other corporations and foundations soon came aboard. To make the project bipartisan, and to tie it in with the Alliance for Progress, President Kennedy's government-to-government effort to aid Latin America, I enlisted Senator Hubert Humphrey, and he became one of the project's stalwart supporters.

In November 1962 the NATO Parliamentarians established a working party, under my chairmanship, to coordinate private and public development assistance for Latin America, and we fanned out to tap the resources and the ideas of bankers and businessmen throughout the industrialized free world. Senator Humphrey and I made speeches and proselytized businessmen and government officials and economists in the United States, and we recruited "apostles" to develop the idea in other countries. I approached Giovanni Agnelli, vice chairman of Fiat, who lent us the services of Aurelio Peccei, one of Fiat's economic advisers. Felipe Herrera of the Inter-American Development Bank assigned Julio Gonzalez del Solar to acquaint Latin American businessmen with what we were doing. Moore and Collado, who had excellent connections in Europe and Japan, enlisted a number of European and Japanese businessmen, including L. B. Wolters of Petrofina in Belgium, Kunio Miki of the Bank of Tokyo, and Marcus Wallenberg of Sweden, who at that time headed the Business and Industry Advisory Committee (BIAC) of the OECD.

We worked quickly, and by the following April the working party announced the formation of the Atlantic Community Development Group for Latin America (ADELA) and the appointment of three executive directors: Peccei for Europe, Gonzalez for Latin America, and Warren Wilhelm, loaned to us by Texaco, for the United States. Over the next nine months these three officials traveled extensively through the United States, Latin America, Canada, Europe, and Japan, speaking to hundreds of business executives, working out the details of how the new institution would function and lining up tentative investment commitments.

By this time the ultimate shape of the organization had emerged:

an international investment company in which large business enterprises from many countries have limited financial interests. The member firms have to be big enough to supply significant amounts of capital and technical assistance, but the investment company itself makes the investments — in projects that contribute to development and also can be expected to produce a profit. In order to make clear that the "colossus of the North," the United States, was not trying to use us to dominate the hemisphere, we stipulated that no one company could hold more than a $500,000 interest in the enterprise (a limit since increased to $1 million). Nevertheless, some Europeans worried at first that the United States would overwhelm its partners. One French business leader described the proposal as "hooking the small European carriages to the powerful United States locomotive which will pull us into the wild jungles of Latin America."

Despite French hesitation, most such fears were dispelled, and in January 1964, 102 public and private officials met in Paris and decided to proceed. A few months later the ADELA Investment Company was formally incorporated in Luxembourg with fifty-four corporate shareholders and a paid-up capital of $16 million. The Swedish banker Marcus Wallenberg was elected chairman of the board, and Ernst Keller, an international industrialist with long experience in Latin America, became managing director.

Wallenberg, a large, majestic, square-jawed Viking, looked like what he was — one of Europe's most powerful and important financiers — and he could be very imperious, as I found out during a formal conference at the Ritz Hotel on the Place Vendome in Paris. We were meeting in a magnificent room hung with tapestries. Several dozen businessmen, bankers, and government officials sat around a hollow square of tables covered with green baize; Wallenberg sat at the center of one side of the square, flanked by his retinue of the presidents of each of the national elements of the Business Advisory Committee of OECD. We discussed what sorts of directors we should appoint, how much capital we should have, what the limitation of each subscriber's capital should be, and similar details. Then came the question of the name: What would our company be called? Marcus Wallenberg leaned across his side of the conference table and thundered at me in a voice like Thor's: "Whatever name we choose, it will certainly not be called ADELA."

So I put on as stern an expression as I could and leaned toward him and declared, "Mr. Wallenberg, this company will be called, if I can help it, nothing *but* ADELA." With that mini-confrontation out of the way, we resolved the issue by calling it the ADELA Investment Company. Some months later I discovered that Adela is a popular woman's name in Latin America, which Wallenberg may have known.

Having developed the ADELA idea, put it through the NATO Parliamentarians, organized the commission, recruited the "apostles," and raised the money for the planning stages, I still faced the chore of recruiting directors. I think I made about a hundred long-distance and transatlantic phone calls to business executives in a dozen countries before I landed the first one who was willing to assume the responsibility of a totally new enterprise.

ADELA also needed to retain a law firm, and obviously it was not appropriate for it to engage mine. After considering the matter, I offered the business to Arthur Dean, who was then senior partner at Sullivan and Cromwell — John Foster Dulles's old firm. Dulles had died, but I am sure that Dean appreciated the irony: I had been a bone in the throat of that firm for years; now I was handing them an important and valuable client.

After those tasks were finished I had nothing further to do with ADELA officially. The company has distinguished itself by outreach: ascertaining the private enterprise needs of a country and then assembling the deals to help meet those needs. Most of the time ADELA puts up only a small amount of the funds for a new project, but it finds local entrepreneurs and other investors, negotiates for governmental approval and aid, lends management and technical services, gets the project launched, and monitors its operation. ADELA fills this crucial catalyst role by calling on the financial, managerial, and technical resources of its stockholders. The ADELA method encourages the development of small business and local economic entities, which are often neglected and by-passed by traditional investors who put their capital in mines, huge agricultural plantations, and heavy industry. Now capitalized at about $90 million, ADELA has handled $2 billion worth of business in Latin America, earning a modest profit and contributing significantly to the economic progress of this region so important to the security and economic well-being of the United States.

* * *

Unfortunately, despite all the effort and money expended in development aid in the past thirty years, we have not succeeded in significantly narrowing the gap between rich nations and poor. In a Senate speech in 1976, I stated the problem as it still existed three decades after World War II:

> We are an island of well-being in a sea of poverty on three continents and we cannot be heedless of the suffering or we will suffer for it. . . . We cannot exist safely and prosperously in a teeming world of poverty where the increasing political consciousness

among the world's poor raises the level of political tension and opens the way for explosive confrontations on economic and social issues. It is urgent that we take a global view of the world's economic problems because it is morally right and, vitally, because it is our only ultimate security in a turbulent world.

One roadblock to the solution of the North-South problem is the underdeveloped nations' resentment of the developed world. This is the legacy of colonialism, and although the United States bears little direct responsibility for that, we are often tarred with the same brush because we are rich and powerful. The resentments are so deep that the less-developed countries sometimes act against their own best economic interest in order to punish a former colonial power — or the industrialized world in general — for past sins. This recklessness may reflect despair: Fearing that they may never catch up to the industrialized nations, some of the underdeveloped lands seem to want to close the North-South gap by dragging down the developed countries — instead of by accepting the technological and capital assistance they need.

These resentments surfaced after the oil embargo of 1973–74 and the subsequent sharp increase in energy costs, which hit the less-developed countries (LDCs) very hard. An unhealthy new financial cycle was developing: Oil profits were being deposited in Western banks, which were lending ever-increasing amounts of money to the non-oil-producing LDCs — who of course used it to pay for oil. As the money went round and round, the LDCs sank deeper into debt. In May 1974, convinced that the world economic system was stacked against them, the LDCs came up with a plan to restructure it in their favor — the New International Economic Order.

The West balked at this, but by the following year we had to change our stand. An international energy conference in Paris could not even agree on an agenda because the LDCs and the Organization of Petroleum Exporting Countries (OPEC) refused to talk about energy except in the context of other international economic issues, and we had to agree that energy, finance, trade, and commodities, which were linked more closely than ever before, had to be discussed together. Secretary of State Henry Kissinger took the lead in framing a new, more cooperative U.S. policy, and Senator Gale McGee, Wyoming Democrat, and I argued for it in Congress.

In the spring of 1976, however, at a Nairobi meeting of the UN Commission on Trade and Development (UNCTAD), which I attended, the unrealistic demands of the LDCs frustrated our efforts to meet them halfway. At that, our hopes turned to a new and more promising forum for the North-South dialogue, which had been established late in 1975. This was the Conference on International Economic Co-operation (CIEC). After a series of preparatory meetings spanning eighteen months, the CIEC brought the ministers of thirty-five nations together in Paris in May 1977 for a major conference that was expected to reach solid agreements between the developed and underdeveloped worlds.

I attended the finale of the CIEC as one of three congressional advisers to Secretary of State Cyrus Vance. (The other two advisers were Senator Abraham Ribicoff and Representative Jonathan Bingham). We sat in on all the sessions, consulted frequently with Secretary Vance, and conferred with many other delegates.

To sum it up starkly, the conference was a disaster. The developing countries wanted their export earnings in commodities to be underwritten by the industrialized countries through a common fund and by means of an "index" system — under which the price of a commodity would fluctuate with the prices of a basket of manufactured goods. But the LDCs were not willing or able, in exchange for that, to guarantee steady supplies of raw materials. We objected that the index system would chain the world's economy to natural resource items that might eventually be replaced by technology, as metals have been replaced by some plastics. The industrialized countries offered general loan support where export earnings of the LDCs were deficient, but they would not agree to guarantee high commodity prices, and they insisted that without assurance of supply it would be impossible to get the developed countries to invest heavily in the LDCs.

The two sides also split on the issue of the LDCs' debt. The LDCs asked for automatic suspension of the debts of all developing countries; the Western countries were only willing to consider, on an individual basis, postponement of payments by countries truly unable to meet their debt service.

Finally, the conference foundered on the question of whether energy issues should be part of a continuing North-South dialogue. The OPEC nations said no: At this point they wanted to maintain their position as an oil cartel and negotiate as a unit, with the consuming countries acting as individuals or perhaps in some kind of users' association. OPEC did not want its freedom of pricing to be limited by any overall negotiations involving other commodities and development and aid. Our view was that it all had to go together; and on this disagreement the North-South dialogue through the CIEC, which had looked so promising, ended.

As a result of this experience, I came to the conclusion that we cannot assume that all developing countries deserve aid regardless of their economic policies. We can only help those that establish conditions congenial to capital investment and technological aid and that are willing to give some reciprocity: In exchange for development aid they must guarantee that their raw materials and their markets will be available to us, on fair terms, as ours must be to them. And they must allow the international financial institutions to monitor their performance. Of course there is a danger in such a selective policy: The Soviet Union would probably take the side of the other LDCs, regardless of what is good for their development, and this could lead to more "wars of national liberation." It is a risk we must take.

In an addendum to our report to Congress on the CIEC meeting, I emphasized that the failure to offer reciprocity was the main problem. The LDCs were asking us to triple our aid, I pointed out, but they "did not offer to respond with the production of more commodities, progress on human rights, or the reform of economic policies."

Tough choices have to be made on both sides, for the resentments of the poorer countries are often based on real grievances. Even in Latin America, despite ADELA, despite such enlightened if less than effective campaigns as the Good Neighbor Policy and the Alliance for Progress, distrust and jealousy and suspicion of the United States linger on. We still tend to take a patronizing attitude toward Latin America, and when we fail to score a resounding success with some project we say that the area is too difficult to deal with and we wash our hands of it. On their part, the Latin Americans sometimes expect more out of a partnership than they are entitled to. Also, it is a characteristic of their culture — which we should recognize and try to understand if we want to keep their friendship — that they insist stubbornly on the punctilio of their own protocol and that they are highly sensitive to anything they imagine might compromise their sovereignty and independence. But we must not forget that gunboat diplomacy was once the name of our game in Central America: The Latins remember, and that is why the 1978 debate over the ratification of the Panama Canal treaties was so important.

The Panama Canal debate was a gut issue on both sides, one of those rare subjects of conscience and strong feeling on which the normal processes of persuasion, manipulation, and trading have little effect in the Senate. There were two treaties involved: the Panama Canal Treaty itself, which regulates U.S. presence until Panama takes over the canal in the year 2000, and the Neutrality Treaty, which provides for the defense of the canal thereafter. The accords gave Panama an immediate voice in running the canal and a fair share of canal revenues, abolished the Canal Zone (which was in effect a U.S.

colony on Panama's territory), allowed the United States to continue to defend the canal and maintain armed forces in Panama until 2000, and provided for perpetual U.S. "go-to-the-head-of-the-line" privileges in times of war or emergency.

To my mind, the treaties were absolutely necessary to erase injustices and remove from the Western Hemisphere a vestige of colonialism — which has no place in the modern world. Panama was earning only about $2 million a year out of a total of $175 million in canal revenues, and Panamanians had not been permitted to become canal pilots. Resentment at this anachronistic state of affairs had been growing for years, not only in Panama itself but also in nearby countries. I had visited the area two years earlier and President Carlos Andrés Pérez of Venezuela and President Alfonso López Michelsen of Colombia had both told me that such treaties were needed as proof that the United States really intended to establish an equal and cooperative partnership with Latin America. "How can the United States, a leader of democracy in the world, take a colonial's stance?" the Venezuelan president wanted to know.

The opposition to the treaties was just as earnest and even more emotionally involved. Conservatives predicted that if the treaties were ratified the Panamanians would immediately seize the canal — ignoring the greater likelihood that they would try to seize it if the treaties did *not* go through. The opponents claimed that the United States "owned" the canal by virtue of having built and paid for it and that no change in its status was needed. "We stole it fair and square," said Senator Sam Hayakawa of California. "We should keep it." And he was only half joking.

The treaties aroused jingoistic passions even in people not normally regarded as conservatives, such as my old friend and ally from the House Foreign Affairs Committee days, John Davis Lodge. "We got tired of the Vietnam War," said Lodge, "we refused to help in Angola, and so now it is proposed that 217 million Americans should cave in and run away before the ominous threat of 1.5 million people in Panama." Lodge's comment explained why the issue had become emotional for so many Americans. Vietnam and Watergate had injured our country's pride, and for those who still thought a nation's greatness depended on raw power, Panama was a symbol of past glory and achievement that could not be given up. So, perhaps inevitably, the treaties were debated not on the basis of whether they represented a new, strong, and enlightened foreign policy, but on the basis of whether a weak and dispirited United States was going to abdicate responsibility and "give away" part of its own back yard.

There were also charges that we had been "coerced" into signing the treaties by Panamanian General Omar Torrijos Herrera, who was described as a latent Marxist, a dictator, and a narcotics smuggler. I had conferred with Torrijos for four hours on a trip to Panama and I saw him not as a typical leftist but as a Latin American *caudillo,* one of those authoritarian, personal rulers with whom the United States often has to deal. Such men are not democrats by any means, but they are patriotic — for they identify their own fate with that of their country.

Some opponents expressed legitimate worries about the future security of the canal. These were largely allayed by amendments permitting the United States to defend the canal against aggression, including aggression from within Panama. Moreover, the Joint Chiefs of Staff reminded the Senate that the canal, which is vulnerable to sabotage, could be defended more easily in a friendly environment than in the hostile "Yankee go home" mood that would certainly arise if we failed to ratify.

A reservation offered by Senator Dennis DeConcini, a freshman Democrat from Arizona, was accepted by the Senate — and it almost derailed the treaties. It gave the United States the right to reopen the canal by force if the operation of the waterway was blocked. Torrijos, who had to contend with extreme nationalists in Panama, declared with some heat that Panama would not accept "any reservation that dishonors the national dignity or is intended to impede the exercise of Panama's sovereignty." Thereupon we worked out another reservation which calmed down the critics in Panama and satisfied DeConcini; it declared that any U.S. action to keep the canal open "shall not have as its purpose or be interpreted as a right of intervention in the internal affairs of the Republic of Panama or interference with its political independence or sovereign integrity." With that hurdle cleared, the Senate ratified both treaties and Torrijos accepted the amendments.

On June 17, 1978, I and other members of the Foreign Relations Committee accompanied President Carter to Panama for the exchange of ratifications. Torrijos was wearing civilian clothes when he greeted us at the airport, but later he donned a glittering white military uniform to stand on a balcony beside President Carter and deliver a rousing speech to two hundred fifty thousand of his cheering people. The Panamanians turned the occasion into a fiesta, with bands and parades and dancing in the streets, for a new and promising era in the relations between North and South America had opened at the Panama Canal. I saw it as a major shift in U.S. policy, capping the efforts of four administrations and proving that a great power and a tiny country can deal with each other on a basis of equality.

TWENTY-SIX

The Explosive Middle East

Europe remains the key to U.S. security, but it is the Middle East, with its passions and violence — and oil — that has most frequently threatened that security and disrupted peace. Five times since World War II the Middle East tensions have erupted into open warfare, and even the periods of official peace are continually interrupted by fighting and bloodshed. We have been lucky in that the wars have not drawn the superpowers into direct conflict, but the danger always exists that the next time they might.

I was involved in many of the intricate, confusing, and frustrating attempts to work out an enduring peace settlement between Israel and her Arab neighbors. The key dispute for years was between the Arab demand that the Israelis withdraw from captured Arab territories *before* any negotiations took place and Israel's position that it would not give up its 1967 war gains until *after* new, secure boundaries had been set, through direct negotiations with the Arabs. Some of the Arab nations were refusing to recognize or negotiate with Israel under any circumstances. In April 1969, in this atmosphere of stalemate, Egypt repudiated the 1967 cease-fire, and the skirmishes along the Suez Canal and the Golan Heights escalated to a level of fighting that was just short of outright war — the "unofficial" war.

The following month I visited Israel and conferred with Prime Minister Golda Meir and her top ministers. At that time the United States was trying to arrange big-power talks to settle the Mideast question, but the Israelis — and especially Golda Meir — did not want other countries telling them what proposals to offer or accept. "We stood alone" in 1967, Mrs. Meir reminded me; she felt that Israel would only lose if the big powers arranged a settlement and that nothing but face-to-face talks with the Arabs could bring about peace.

During my visit, Pinchas Sapir, the secretary-general of Mrs. Meir's Labor Party, suggested that King Hussein of Jordan might be willing to sign a separate peace. Both Jordan and Egypt, Sapir believed, were under such pressure from extremist Arabs within their own countries that they would eventually be forced to take *some* action — either go to war or negotiate — in order to hold on to power, and he thought Hussein might move first. This idea was in line with my own thinking and I followed up on it later.

In January 1970, when I was in Israel again, my friends were worried. Secretary of State William Rogers had revealed a new "even-handed" peace plan that called for Israel to give up all the territory it had captured in 1967 in exchange for Arab assurances of a binding peace treaty. The Rogers plan would have left Israel with undefensible borders, and it seemed to encourage the Arabs to take an even harder line. The Israeli leaders also feared that Rogers was threatening to cut off U.S. support unless they endorsed his plan. Rogers had made clear that he was not suggesting any change in the U.S. policy of support for Israel, but this had been overlooked. This question of the extent of U.S. aid for Israel was to engage us all for years.

What Israel needed most were modern, supersonic jet fighter planes. Soon after the 1967 war, as part of a crash program to rearm the Arab states, the Soviet Union had begun sending MiG jet fighters to Egypt. Israel was in danger of becoming completely vulnerable to Egyptian air power unless it could get comparable aircraft, and the only planes that could match the new MiGs were the French Mirage and the U.S. Phantom F-4. As the French had cut off all arms sales to Israel after the 1967 war, and had even refused to deliver fifty Mirages that Israel had already paid for, Israel asked to buy Phantoms from us. But in the midst of the Vietnam War both the Johnson and Nixon administrations were skittish about further military commitments, and Congress had to remind them repeatedly of our responsibility to balance the Arabs' Soviet arms and thus deflect Arab efforts to eliminate Israel. Fortunately, Israel's popularity in the United States was flourishing during those years as a result of the 1967 victory, and Israel's friends could usually count on a substantial majority of Congress — and especially of the Senate — to respond when necessary.

In 1968 Congress wrote into a foreign-aid bill a provision directing the President to sell jets to Israel, and in the final days of his administration President Johnson announced the sale to Israel of fifty Phantoms. Those fifty aircraft, replacing the Mirages that Israel had expected to receive from France, were being delivered by early 1970; then France supplied some Mirages to Libya, Egypt's close ally, and the Soviets sent Russian MiG pilots and SAM missiles to Egypt. Israel needed more than those first fifty Phantoms, but the Nixon Administration refused to make a further specific commitment. So in May 1970 I took the lead in rallying seventy-three senators to sign a letter to Secretary of State Rogers urging that Israel be permitted to buy more Phantoms, and later in the year I worked with Senator Henry Jackson to pass legislation authorizing the administration to provide Israel with $500 million credits for buying arms. This clear message from Congress enabled President Nixon to promise Israel continued military and political support, and with those assurances — but still without any more Phantoms — Israel agreed in August to a cease-fire in the unofficial war.

But the following year we had to go through it all again. The State Department, which was anxious to get the Suez Canal reopened, thought it detected a new Egyptian willingness to negotiate, and the administration — despite the authority we had voted — continued to deny Israel the Phantoms. Nevertheless, the Soviet Union and Egypt insisted that Israel withdraw from captured territories before the canal could be opened and before further negotiations on boundaries took place. So in 1971 we got more than three-quarters of the Senate, seventy-eight members, to sponsor a resolution calling for the resumption of Phantom sales.

Senators Hugh Scott, Stuart Symington, Abe Ribicoff, and I were the principal sponsors of this resolution, and I pointed out in several debates that the planes were necessary not only to preserve the arms balance in the area but to help the negotiations that the State Department was working on. The Phantoms, I said, "will serve not only to sober the Arab and Soviet approach to resumed negotiations.... If Israel is assured of the military assistance it needs to maintain its deterrent strength, and feels secure against the Arab-Soviet threat, Israel is more likely to be in a position and a mood to negotiate with flexibility." But if Israel feels that its back is against the wall, if threats of withholding the planes are used to pressure Israel into making concessions, Israel will be "cautious" and "skeptical" at the negotiating table.

This prediction was borne out in November, when Israel refused to begin indirect talks with Egypt, which the United States had tried to arrange, unless it could buy more Phantoms. Later that month Senator Jackson and I led a move to force the administration to provide the planes, and this time we succeeded. In an amendment to the defense procurement bill, the Senate appropriated the $500 million in military credits to Israel we had authorized the previous year; half of that sum was earmarked for the purchase of Phantoms.

The amendment passed by the lopsided margin of 82 to 14, but the debate was more intense than the tally indicates. Our principal opponent was Senator William Fulbright, chairman of the Foreign Relations Committee, who took the State Department view that Israel was blocking peace; Fulbright believed that additional jets for Israel might contribute to a dangerous arms race and he wanted to leave the decision up to the administration. He also resented the overwhelming support in the Senate for Israel's cause. During a debate on a point of order against the amendment, Fulbright said that Israel

> is about the only country I can think of with sufficient influence to get funds earmarked. . . . There is no doubt it will get whatever it needs. . . . Per capita, no country in the world receives as much from this country as Israel. . . . If the Senate does not sustain this point of order we will say whenever we feel like it we will forget about authorizations and appropriating processes and if we have enough friends we will get enough money for our particular projects.

This brought to the surface an adversary situation that had developed in the Foreign Relations Committee between Chairman Fulbright and me. When I first joined the committee in 1969 Senator Fulbright was alarmed that my advocacy of Israel's cause would create a great deal of difficulty. As time went on he found that my usefulness to the committee on other issues counterbalanced what he considered my wrong-headed position on Israel. Eventually we worked well together on other matters, notwithstanding our profound differences on U.S. policy toward Israel.

Our amendment to the defense procurement bill all but required the administration to sell jets to Israel, and after a visit to Washington by Prime Minister Meir, the United States agreed to sell Israel forty-two Phantoms and ninety A-4 Skyhawks.

Shortly thereafter, in 1972, King Hussein of Jordan came to Washington and the administration agreed to sell jet planes to him as well. Hussein needed the planes to defend his government from the radical Palestinian guerrillas who were trying to topple him before he could sign a separate peace with Israel. He was serious about his quest for a Jordan-Israel peace, and while he was in Washington I learned his terms.

In July 1972 I was in Israel again and I relayed these views to the Israeli leaders. I made clear that I was not a middleman or negotiator, but I told them that with the U.S. government's consent I was reporting on what I thought might be done with Jordan. I felt strongly that Jordan rather than Egypt was the natural country to take the first Arab step toward peace with Israel — a point on which Henry Kissinger and I disagreed. Although the United States had no diplomatic relations with Egypt at the time, Kissinger was already in secret contact with Egyptian President Sadat, as he has revealed in his book *White House Years,* and not even the U.S. State Department knew that. Kissinger's goal of a phased Egyptian-Israeli withdrawal from the Suez Canal was of course later realized — but not until another major war, with much bloodshed and risk for the world, had taken place.

I outlined the views of Jordan as I believed them to be, first to Foreign Minister Abba Eban and then to Prime Minister Meir, her deputies, and several other Israeli ministers. I felt confident, I told them, that the king could deliver on any agreement he made with Israel, that the boundary question was negotiable as long as most of the population of the West Bank of the Jordan River was returned to Jordanian sovereignty, that the problems of a Mediterranean port for Jordan, a capital for the West Bank, and the care of the Moslem holy places in Jerusalem remained to be dealt with.

The Israelis were intrigued by these ideas, but Jerusalem was the main sticking point then — as it is today. They refused to consider any arrangement that would compromise Israeli sovereignty over Jerusalem.

I returned from that trip convinced that the Phantom sale and the support assistance we had also voted for Israel had given the Israelis a new confidence about their security and that they were moving in the direction of settling with Hussein rather than with Sadat, who seemed to have become a Soviet client.

But two weeks later the situation changed dramatically when President Sadat expelled the fifteen thousand Soviet military advisers in his country and took over the Soviet bases. This was not the good news that it appeared to be at first. The Soviets, who did not want to get into a military confrontation with the United States, had tried to restrain the Arabs from wild adventures against Israel, and yet they were unable to negotiate the pullback of Israeli forces that the Arabs wanted. Sadat was frustrated by the lack of a settlement, and he sent the advisers home to give himself freedom of action.

Over the next twelve months the tensions increased: Terrorists murdered Israeli athletes at the Olympic Village in Munich, and Israel made reprisal attacks on guerrilla bases in Syria and Lebanon. More jets were hijacked, more diplomats killed, and Egypt signed an agreement with the radical Qaddafi regime in Libya "unifying" the two countries.

Even more ominous was the emergence of the "oil weapon," the open threat by Arab oil producers to withhold supplies from countries aiding Israel. The possibility of such action had been discussed for years, but it had not been taken seriously because the oil producers clearly depended on oil revenues. By 1973, however, the members of the newly formed OPEC were in a much stronger position: They had nationalized and taken control of large portions of their oil industries and had raised oil prices enough so that they had a financial cushion that made the threat credible. By threatening to cut off our oil they wanted to blackmail us into ending support for Israel.

In August 1973 the chairman of the board of the Standard Oil Company of California echoed the Arab threat. He wrote to his company's stockholders and employees, citing the U.S. need for oil and appealing for "more positive support" for Arab efforts toward peace. In a public rebuttal, I pointed out that it was Arab intransigence that was blocking peace, and Arab oil money that was supporting terror. Israel, I declared, has "repeatedly offered to negotiate a settlement . . . without preconditions" and only Jordan among the Arab states "has expressed willingness to find a peaceful solution." And I went on:

> It is neither desirable nor necessary for our country to reverse its position of friendship with both Israel and the Arab states. . . . U.S. policy is not anti-Arab now, nor should it be in the future. But neither should U.S. policy be changed, in effect to be anti-Israel. . . . America has never permitted itself to be coerced. Yet [the chairman's] letter suggests we must give up a sound U.S. policy in response to the energy crisis, raising the issue of oil coercion. Such a change would be immoral and unnecessary. . . . The shah of Iran . . . pledged "never to withhold our oil as a political weapon." [That] principle should guide Iran's Arab neighbors as well as the American oil companies.

But it was already too late for such exhortations. At about the same time, the Saudis, who had declined to brandish the oil weapon in the past, promised Sadat that if war came they would indeed impose an oil embargo on Israel's friends. In a series of summit meetings among Arab leaders, even Hussein fell in line with his more militant brethren. Egypt, moreover, was beset by economic problems, and Sadat's generals were urging him to strike a blow quickly — not believing they would necessarily *win* a war but in hopes they could improve their position and break the diplomatic stalemate. On October 6, 1973, Yom Kippur, Egyptian and Syrian armies attacked Israeli forces at Suez and the Golan Heights; other Arab countries sent troops to help. Once more the Middle East was at war and Israel was fighting for its life.

The Yom Kippur attack caught Israel — and us — by surprise. The Israelis were confident that the arms they had been receiving and the buffer territory they held would enable them to defend themselves, and they did not believe that the Arabs would dare attack. In the first few days Israel suffered heavy casualties and lost so much equipment and supply that it had to appeal to the United States for an emergency airlift of materiel to keep fighting. After some delay, the United States responded, and by the time the United Nations and the big powers imposed a cease-fire, Israeli armies had crossed the Suez Canal, surrounded the city of Suez, and trapped twenty thousand Egyptian troops who had crossed earlier from the other direction.

Thereupon Secretary of State Henry Kissinger began his remarkable "shuttle diplomacy" and negotiated the first Sinai "disengagement" — so called because the Egyptians would not concede that they were signing a separate "peace" with Israel. Israeli troops pulled back about twenty miles from the Suez Canal and a UN force was placed between the opposing armies. A similar agreement disengaged Israeli and Syrian forces on the Golan Heights. Although the Israelis regarded the Yom Kippur war and its aftermath as something of a defeat (it cost Golda Meir her post as prime minister), the disengagement moved the Middle East closer to a permanent peace, for Arab nations had negotiated with Israel.

It took another year and a half of intermittent diplomatic shuttling to work out the second Sinai disengagement. Under this one the Israelis gave up the Sinai oil fields and two strategic mountain passes. Congress was directly involved in the second agreement because it included a provision that two hundred American civilian technicians would be stationed at early-warning listening posts between the two armies to monitor the truce. Both sides insisted on the American presence, but after Vietnam and the War Powers Resolution President Ford could not agree to send the volunteers without the concurrence of Congress. I argued strongly in favor of the authorizing resolution on the grounds that the two hundred unarmed Americans were essential to keep the truce and to encourage Israel and Egypt to take the next step toward peace. Opponents of the idea were worried that the assignment of Americans, even civilians, in such a volatile area could draw the United States into a conflict or at least commit us to a massive involvement.

To give Congress the confidence to approve that unusual and potentially risky operation, I introduced another resolution, requiring President Ford to reveal every relevant document and every promise the administration had made to induce Israel to accept the agreement. These included assurances of continued military supply, limitations on such supply to Arab nations, a pledge of an oil-purchase subsidy to make up for the oil Israel had been getting from the Sinai field, and promises to use the veto, if necessary, in support of Israel's position in the United Nations, where a majority of the General Assembly had by then lined up solidly against Israel.

The Israelis were not at all happy about publicizing all the agreements, but I was convinced that in the post-Vietnam, post-Watergate climate, secret agreements would be like a time bomb: If they leaked out later the entire structure of the peace arrangements might have been jeopardized and the popular and congressional support for Israel could have been seriously impaired. My resolution was passed, the facts were laid before Congress, and in October 1975 both the House and the Senate overwhelmingly voted to approve the dispatch of the technicians. With the help of those two hundred Americans, the truce held until Israel and Egypt signed their peace treaty in 1978.

The period between October 1973 and October 1975 was a momentous one for our nation and for me. Besides the Yom Kippur war and the Sinai disengagement agreements and the beginning of the world energy crisis, those years saw the Watergate affair climax with the resignation of President Nixon, the fall of Saigon to the North Vietnamese, and New York City teetering on the edge of bankruptcy; in the same two years the ERISA and the war powers bill were completed and enacted, I fought and won a reelection campaign, and I traveled to Cuba, China, Japan, Israel, Iran, London, Paris, Rome, Brussels, Bonn, and the Soviet Union.

Still another issue that concerned me deeply came to a head during that period. I had been speaking out for years about the persecution of Jews in the Soviet Union, many of whom wanted to emigrate to Israel and were not only prevented from doing so but were harassed and punished just for applying to leave. These activities of mine and my support of Israel had long since marked me as a troublemaker in the eyes of the Kremlin. In 1953 the official Soviet newspaper *Izvestia* had named me as one of the most prominent American Jews seeking to turn Israel into "an anti-Communist bastion of the United States in the Middle East." *Izvestia* had blasted me again in 1971 in an article titled "The Senator from Tel Aviv." That one described me as "odious," a "rabid Zionist" and "brother to the Israeli hawks" who, under the "camouflage" of a liberal, was "whipping up anti-Soviet hysteria" and "manipulating the White House [to] give unconditional support to Tel Aviv's aggressive policy."

The 1971 diatribe was published on the eve of a trip I was scheduled to make to the USSR, and it was apparently aimed at keeping me out of the Soviet Union at a time when nine Jews charged with "anti-Soviet activity" were about to go on trial in Leningrad. To make sure I understood, Tass, the Soviet news agency, called my office when the

Izvestia story came out and dictated it to one of my staff members over the phone. Realizing that I could accomplish nothing in the Soviet Union in such a poisoned atmosphere, I canceled my visit.

The following year, the Soviet Union's treatment of Jews became directly intertwined with U.S. government policy. The cruelties heaped on Jews seeking to leave the Soviet Union, the deprivation of jobs and living space, the public obloquy and even accusations of crime were so frequently employed as to have become an international scandal. Then, in the summer of 1972, after the Moscow summit meeting that started détente, the United States and the Soviet Union began negotiating a trade treaty, signed that fall, under which the United States granted most-favored-nation tariff status to the Soviet Union.

The Soviet need for trade, I thought, offered us an opportunity to help Jews and others in the USSR. On August 30, 1972, in a speech to an Emergency Rally for Soviet Jewry in New York's garment district, I declared that culture and commerce are directly related to freedom, and that "we should properly demand justice for Soviet Jewry as a condition for close economic relations with the USSR in trade and finance."

Ultimately, this concept was brought into law by the Jackson-Vanik amendment to the trade bill that Congress had to pass to implement the terms of the 1972 trade treaty. Senator Henry Jackson of Washington, who was a friend of Israel, a hard-liner on defense and on relations with the Soviets — and who was also a potential Democratic presidential candidate — took the lead on this issue, and I was closely involved in drafting the amendment to remove some of the needlessly provocative provisions originally proposed. In its essence, the amendment forbade the administration to grant trade credits or most-favored-nation tariff status to any country that imposed burdensome and unreasonable restrictions on its citizens' right to emigrate. Its purpose was to give Soviet Jews greater freedom to emigrate by making most-favored-nation treatment dependent upon the granting of this right.

The House passed the amendment and the bill in 1973, but the administration opposed the amendment out of fear that it might wreck the whole trade treaty; that stalled the bill in the Senate well into 1974. In an effort to get out of the impasse, Senators Jackson, Ribicoff, and I, as a team, began to negotiate with Secretary of State Kissinger, who had received some clarifications from the Soviet Union regarding its emigration policies. We were trying to reach an understanding about the conditions under which Jews could apply to leave the Soviet Union and how many could be expected to leave annually. It was contemplated that if this negotiation was successful, the Jackson-Vanik amendment would be altered so that it could function as a safeguard, protecting the rights of Jews to emigrate from the Soviet Union but still permitting the enhancement of trade between the United States and the Soviet Union — which the administration, and I, wanted to take place.

The negotiations continued for a considerable number of months and eventually an understanding was reached. It was spelled out in letters between Senator Jackson and Kissinger that a minimum of sixty thousand Jews would be able to leave the Soviet Union every year and that applicants for emigration permits would not be punished. Kissinger testified before the Senate Finance Committee that the agreement with the Soviets was not a formal government commitment. Nevertheless, on the basis of the understanding, we wrote into the bill a provision that the President could waive the Jackson-Vanik restrictions if he found that the policies of any country affected by them were leading substantially to free emigration. In the case of the Soviet Union, the waiver was to be automatic for eighteen months and then was to be reviewed. With that compromise, the Trade Act passed in December 1974.

The understanding broke down a few weeks later when the Soviet Union refused to enter into the 1972 commercial treaty on which the whole process was based. (The treaty was contingent on the granting of most-favored-nation status, and the Soviets chose to regard the Trade Act, containing the emigration compromise, as something less than that.) The Soviets claimed that they denounced the treaty because too much publicity had been given to the emigration compromise. There may have been some grains of truth in that charge, but it certainly did not justify the collapse of a negotiation that offered so much to both countries in improved relations and expanded mutual trade. In any case, the Soviet action put a new strain on relations between the two countries.

Later, the Soviets voluntarily opened the emigration gates in order to win us and Europe back to détente and SALT II. In 1979, the emigration of Soviet Jews reached an all-time high of fifty-one thousand. But then, just as precipitously, when SALT II ran into difficulty and the United States protested the Soviet intervention in Afghanistan, the barriers clanged shut again and only a trickle came out in 1980. Yet even when they cannot leave, it is the Jewish "refuseniks" themselves who believe most passionately that the Jackson-Vanik conditions should be continued, not relaxed.

This was all a clear illustration of how the USSR operates. Our steadfast policy regarding Jewish emigration from the Soviet Union is now a critical element of the struggle for world opinion that we are waging with the USSR. On the whole, the Soviet Union keeps the agreements it makes, but it is very technical about the construction of those agreements. And if agreements are not made, the Soviet Union does not hesitate to pursue a policy that is very harmful to us in order to make clear its displeasure. Notwithstanding all of its protestations about peace and human rights, the Kremlin can still be very inhuman when it is seeking to gain some purpose.

*　*　*

By about 1975 I began to notice a subtle shift in U.S. attitudes toward Israel and the Middle East. Israel's serious initial reverses in the Yom Kippur war and its need for U.S. material support had tempered the idea that the Israelis were supermen who could take on the Arabs forever and always prevail. Furthermore, under President Sadat, Egypt was no longer seen as a dangerous menace. Sadat's expulsion of the Soviet advisers, his recognition that his poverty-stricken country can only be developed with a tremendous infusion of Western capital, and his reasonableness in agreeing to the Sinai disengagements had transformed him into a friend of the United States — and his historic trip to Jerusalem, which later opened up the peace process, heightened that perception. Finally, the emergence of Arab oil as a major strategic factor in the world produced some support, in Western Europe and the Third World, for the Arab confrontationalist position on Israel. But the United States came out of all this with increased power and influence in the Middle East.

The Ford Administration reflected the changing attitude. When there was a hitch in negotiating the second Sinai disengagement in March 1975, Ford ordered a "reassessment" of U.S. Middle East policy, which in the context of the time seemed to mean a reassessment of U.S. support for Israel. The Senate, however, remained convinced of the importance of Israel to U.S. security; once more, seventy-five senators signed a letter to the White House in Israel's behalf, this one declaring that "a strong Israel constitutes a most reliable barrier to domination of the area by outside parties."

The administration's shift in policy led to sales of planes and missiles to Arab countries, and it was important to moderate the administration's prospective course. In 1976 I helped work out with President Ford and Secretary of State Kissinger a reduction by more than half in the number of Sidewinder and Maverick missiles being supplied to Saudi Arabia.

Two years after that I opposed a Carter Administration "package deal" that linked the sale of sophisticated military aircraft to Israel with the simultaneous sale of such planes to Saudi Arabia and Egypt. I was not against selling arms to the Arab countries: The Saudis were then considered to be a moderating influence in the Arab world and they needed the planes to defend their southern borders against Soviet mischief in South Yemen and the Horn of Africa; and Egypt, having cut its ties with the Soviet Union, clearly rated the provision of jet fighters. But I thought that joining the three different sets of considerations in one take-it-or-leave-it bill might signal Israel that the special relationship it had enjoyed with the United States in the past was dead. Fearing that it was gradually being surrounded by effectively armed and potentially hostile neighbors, Israel might be tempted to strike first, before those neighbors got too strong. So I led the fight against the entire package — which passed by a close vote.

By then I had already established what might be called new diplomatic relations of my own with the Arab leaders. My Washington friendships with Arab ambassadors led to invitations to visit their countries and confer with their heads of state and government. In the spring of 1976 I traveled to Egypt, Syria, and Jordan, and in July 1977 I went to Jordan and Egypt again and also to Saudi Arabia.

The period was one of intense diplomatic activity that climaxed with President Sadat's trip to Jerusalem in November 1977. The status of the West Bank and Jerusalem, the Israeli settlements policy, and the role of the PLO were the major points of dispute, and I discussed all of them with the Arab leaders I met and with Israeli leaders as well. Many officials and governments were involved in the search for peace at that time, and I cannot claim that I achieved any specific breakthrough. But I was in the thick of it all, and I served as an unofficial intermediary explaining the views of one side to the other. The cause of peace might also have been aided merely by the presence of an American senator of the Jewish faith, long identified as a staunch supporter of Israel, talking with Arab heads of state.

The first trip started in Egypt, which I had not visited in thirty years. I told President Sadat about the flight I had made from Cairo to Tel Aviv in 1946 and expressed the hope that I would some day be able to fly that route again (in a better plane) — to which he replied that future generations would have to decide that. Neither of us realized how fast things would move and that he would fly to Israel himself a year and a half later.

In 1976, President Sadat received me at his official residence in Giza, a suburb of Cairo and the site of the Great Pyramids. In 1977, we talked and had an elegant lunch at Sadat's modest but lovely palace located on a promontory thrusting into the Mediterranean near Alexandria, with exquisite architecture and outdoor walks and gardens — a beautiful, private, tranquil setting. And the city of Alexandria itself seemed much more prosperous and substantial than teeming, dusty Cairo. Sadat, very relaxed, smoking his pipe, was clad in a kind of fatigue uniform with a brown Russian-type blouse and well-fitting slacks. The U.S. ambassador to Egypt, Herman Eilts, and Egypt's ambassador to Washington, Ashraf Ghorbal, both of whom I knew well, were both with us, and we had about four hours of frank conversation and good food on that second visit.

President Sadat struck me as a clever man, an able statesman and negotiator, and a skillful and inspiring leader of his people. But he is not a detailed planner. He makes up his mind about what he wants to do and then goes around to get it confirmed by "consulting" others. I believe that what took him to Jerusalem later was not a considered, staffed-out plan but simply the instinct that the time was ripe for peace and that some dramatic gesture was needed. He was bold and confident enough to pick the trip to Jerusalem as a sure way to command world attention — and the attention of his Arab brethren, of which he received perhaps more than he wanted.

It concerned Sadat deeply that Egypt, as the principal Arab fighting force in the wars against Israel, had been bled white and that his country was still being beggared by the continuing need to prepare for war. I gathered that he thought the Arab world was exploiting him by letting Egypt bear the brunt of the wars that Arab irredentism and chauvinism insisted must be fought to drive the Israelis into the sea. He knew the situation prevented his country from making an economic comeback, and he saw peace as Egypt's only hope for the future.

Sadat's desire for peace stood out from the first meeting. The clearest evidence of it was the resettlement of two cities on the Nile, Ismailia and Port Said, which had been devastated in the 1973 war but had since been repopulated with six hundred thousand Egyptians. That seemed so significant to me that I later suggested publicly that the same might be done for the devastated city of Kuneitra, on the Golan Heights, which stands to this day as a monument to belligerence and enmity between Syria and Israel. If that city could be born again it would tell the Israelis that Syria was serious about peace.

By the time of my second visit, only four months before Sadat's breakthrough, he seemed even more confident. Almost all of the other Arab states, he told me, would support an Egyptian peace initiative. He was concerned only about whether Israel's new prime minister, Menachem Begin, was serious about making peace, and on this point I sought to assure him.

My one meeting with President Hafez al-Assad of Syria, on my

1976 trip, was more formal and constrained. At the Presidential Palace in Damascus, U.S. Ambassador to Syria Richard Murphy and I and an interpreter were conducted into a very spacious council chamber decorated with Arabic calligraphy. There was a row of what looked like desks at the head of the chamber and built-in upholstered seats all around the wall, leaving the center of the room quite open. President Assad sat at one of the desks at the head of the room, in the position of someone presiding over the occasion; he asked me to sit at a desk a few feet to his right, placed the interpreter at another desk to his left, and motioned Ambassador Murphy to the first seat along the wall.

Assad seemed to be running even more of a one-man show than Sadat. He is a shrewd and able trader, absolutely sure of himself, knowing exactly what he wants and willing to run great risks to attain it. I found him to be quick-witted and cool, and very agile in debate — quite a figure to contend with.

At the beginning, so that we could speak frankly, I made sure he had been told I was Jewish, which he had. He asserted that Syria did not mix religion and politics and he made a clear distinction between Judaism, which he recognized as one of the three revealed religions, and the policies of Israel, of which he was critical indeed. He said he doubted the Israelis' sincerity when they spoke of peace. Their plea for secure borders, he said, was only an "excuse for expansion"; they had claimed they needed the high ground of the Golan Heights to protect their settlements from Syrian artillery, but then, he said, they had built new settlements within rifle range of Syrian lines. In his view Israel merely wanted to take the land of others, and under no conceivable circumstances, he said, would Syria give up "one single meter of its territory" to Israel. This was his most earnest and constantly reiterated point.

I told him the case as I saw it, and said that we as statesmen had to go beyond the mistrust on both sides to seek peace. At one point I felt I had been lecturing him and I apologized and remarked that I was older than he was.

Assad insisted that only an overall peace settlement could work, and he criticized the moves for separate and step-by-step agreements that were then (1976) being explored with Egypt and Jordan. An overall agreement, he said, must include big-power guarantees — which he thought should satisfy Israel — plus the return of Arab territory and a state for the Palestinians. He was adamant on the PLO: When I suggested that if the PLO wanted to be treated like a government it should act responsibly — as Assad himself had acted in signing the Golan disengagement despite the views of some of his radical followers — the president acknowledged that but retorted that if we gave the PLO a state they would then act with the responsibility of a state.

I came away from this revealing discussion recognizing that Assad's Syria was a lot tougher than Sadat's Egypt, that Assad would fight for every square meter of land on the Golan Heights, and that it was highly unlikely that the rectification of Israel's borders could get very far with him. Nevertheless, I was convinced that this man could be treatied with.

My first visit to Saudi Arabia, in July 1977, was like entering a forbidden kingdom — the source of Islam and for so long a land closed to Jews. Foreign visitors to Saudi Arabia are received in Jidda, the busy seaport on the east coast. Jidda was swarming with people and vehicles and donkeys going every which way through a huge bazaar still under construction. I could detect no regularity of sidewalks or streets; it was all a bedlam of construction and noise and movement. One of the most notable sights in the city, however, was the quarters for the pilgrims on their way to Mecca. There must have been more than two thousand rooms in a series of three-story dormitories built right along the piers where the pilgrim ships dock. A million or two faithful from all over Islam move in and out of Saudi Arabia every year, and they have been doing so for centuries.

The new royal palace is far removed from this hullabaloo. There, I was shown into the presence of King Khalid, who was sitting in a large chair, dressed in traditional robes, with one leg elevated because of a circulatory ailment. On a divan on the other side of the room, deep in conversation with another gentleman and apparently paying no attention to my chat with the king, sat Prince Fahd, who is both crown prince and prime minister.

The king impressed me as modest and low-key; we talked about his health and his travels and Saudi Arabia's attempt to adapt to its enormous wealth. I proposed to the king my favorite theme: that this new wealth ought to be treated as a capital fund for investment in Saudi Arabia's own economic development, in the accelerated development of the poor countries, and in energy projects in both industrialized and developing countries. Then, when the oil gave out, Saudi Arabia would have extensive investments that would sustain it as a developed country. This should be done, I suggested, in cooperation with the industrialized countries of the world, from whence the wealth came in the first place.

The king said he appreciated my thoughtfulness. Aside from insisting that there could be no compromise with the integrity of the Moslem holy places in Jerusalem, the king said very little about Middle East problems. He was more interested in learning how the U.S. government operates, particularly our system of checks and balances and the "advise and consent" role of the Senate in foreign affairs. As something of an autocrat, he found it difficult to understand the limitations on our presidents' power.

After I left the king I spent about two hours with Prince Fahd. He was dressed in exactly the same kind of robes the king had worn: a brownish outer tunic and the traditional headdress of fine linen, embroidered with gold. We sat in comfortable red leather chairs at a desk in his office and Prince Fahd expressed even more strongly than the king the Saudi belief that Jerusalem had to be in Arab hands in order to ensure that the Moslem shrines were fully safeguarded. But he was practical in his thinking — I saw him as a man of affairs whose job it was to get business transacted — and I discussed with him also my hopes for effective Saudi participation in world economic development. This did not prevent him from speaking much more severely about Israel a year later, when I visited Saudi Arabia again with a group of my colleagues. At that time, Camp David had been successful and the Saudis were joining for a time the Arab confrontation front opposed to Sadat.

The high point of my 1977 journey to the Arab lands was a dinner to which Prince Saud al-Faisal, the Saudi foreign minister, invited me and Peter Lakeland, my foreign-policy aide, and U.S. Ambassador John C. West. The dinner was given at the home of the chief of royal protocol, who turned out, not surprisingly in Saudi Arabia, to be Prince Saud's uncle. Prince Saud, a Princeton graduate, was an engaging man who spoke perfect English. I had heard a little about him from Marian, who had met him at a party in New York and had enjoyed his company. I reminded him of that, privately, and he confirmed it with a smile, and that put us on a comfortable personal basis.

The ten Saudis present, all male, included some of Prince Saud's brothers and other public officials and businessmen. Almost all spoke good English, and in the informality of the setting we got into a rousing, somewhat heated discussion about the Arab-Israeli struggle. The Saudis maintained their view that Israel had to withdraw from the West Bank of the Jordan before peace could be arranged, and they ridiculed Prime Minister Begin's Biblical claim to Judea and Samaria. I argued that Israel's concern for security was justified after four wars in thirty years and that Israel needed new weapons simply to maintain parity with the Arabs. The table was pounded and voices rose, but cordiality survived and nobody got mad at anybody. The Saudis were as delighted as I was that we had all become passionate and stood our ground.

After dinner Prince Saud quietly — and with some delicacy — asked Ambassador West if a private talk with me would be in order. The ambassador of course said yes, and Prince Saud invited me into a study, where we talked very seriously for about forty minutes. The prince felt that his country was threatened on all sides, and the strategic map of Saudi Arabia demonstrated the claim. There were red arrows marking routes of invasion from almost every direction. I found it a revealing recital.

What was also interesting in Saudi Arabia was the absence of any discussion about an internal threat (which later surfaced in the attack on the Black Mosque in Mecca), although at least a quarter of the population of the country is made up of workers from other Arab nations and from Europe and Asia, whom the Saudis have to import because their own population is small and as yet mostly unskilled. Outside observers consider the presence of these non-Saudi elements — some of whom may already be under the influence of the PLO or other radical Arab groups — as another menace to the country. But to Prince Saud the main threats were from abroad — or at least that is how he explained it to me.

The Saudis obviously placed great stress on the fidelity of the United States to what they considered a security commitment to Saudi Arabia and on their determination to do their utmost to preserve friendship with the United States. For Saudi Arabia depended upon world economic and monetary stability for its own future, and all of that was intricately tied up in Saudi minds with the relationship to the United States.

The feeling of reliance on the United States that was revealed to me that evening made me realize that if the United States wielded its influence effectively, Saudi Arabia, with all the wealth it was acquiring, could be induced to become a constructive force for world economic development. Saudi unhappiness over the Camp David agreements altered the situation, but this attitude was again changed by the Iraq-Iran war, so watchfulness was needed.

* * *

Soon after he became President in 1977, Jimmy Carter began talking about a Palestinian homeland and offered to deal with the PLO if the PLO would accept UN Resolution 242 of 1967. These controversial statements revealed two things about the new U.S. President: his naiveté and inexperience in foreign affairs (in expecting more than the PLO would possibly deliver); and his sincere desire to bring about peace in the Middle East. President Carter's failure to understand the complexities of the Middle East situation, and his deep commitment to peace, which reflected his religious character, led him to take great political risks and stake his prestige on his ability to bring the opposing sides together. No President put more of his heart into the search for an Arab-Israeli peace, and I believe that Camp David and the subsequent Israel-Egypt treaty will emerge in the days ahead as one of the most significant achievements in the long effort to attain peace in the Middle East.

The advent of the new leadership in Washington was followed shortly by new leadership in Israel, and that, too, had a profound effect on succeeding events. The success of Menachem Begin's right-wing Likud party represented the victory of the old "revisionists," a militant, ideological faction of Zionism thought to have been eliminated by Ben-Gurion's mainstream policy. The revisionists and their military arm, the Irgun, of which Begin had been a member, refused to cooperate with the British authorities during World War II, and before that they had demanded a Jewish state on *both* banks of the Jordan River. The Ben-Gurion tradition held that Israel's existence is founded on law and history; Begin tends to base his claims on Biblical grounds — that the land was given to the Jewish people by God. Prime Minister Begin's policy on the West Bank settlements has caused me considerable anguish, and it has not improved Israel's status in the United States. However, just as Eisenhower, a general, made peace in Korea, and Nixon, a firm anti-Communist, opened the China door, Begin's credentials as a tough opponent of the Arabs enabled him to go where no moderate had dared to tread and to sign a peace treaty with Egypt.

In close correlation with the State Department, I played a number of roles in the complicated three-way negotiations that started with Sadat's 1977 trip to Jerusalem and culminated in the signing of the peace treaty at the White House in March 1979. At some stages I was directly involved, explaining the views of one party to another or giving advice about drafting compromise proposals. At other times I operated from the sidelines, privately or publicly urging whichever party was being intractable at the moment to take more reasonable positions. I tried to be objective, but some of my friends in the Jewish community were upset when I criticized one of Begin's negotiating propositions or his repeated use of the Biblical names Judea and Samaria for the West Bank provinces — names that were anathema to the Arab states because most of the people living in those areas today are Arabs.

Such an incident occurred in June 1978, during that difficult period between Sadat's Jerusalem trip and the Camp David summit. The U.S. government, in its role of mediator, had asked Israel whether it would be willing to commit itself to discuss "the permanent status" of the occupied territories after a five-year period of limited autonomy. The ambiguous Israeli response was that only "the future relations" of the parties would be discussed at that time, a subtle but important distinction which implied that Israel might want to retain sovereignty over the West Bank forever. I felt I had to do something to shake up the Israelis, so in a speech to the Senate I said that Israel's "disappointing" response was "the wrong signal, at the wrong time, and argues with the wrong party," and that the United States had been correct in expecting "a more positive reply."

My speech also criticized Sadat for not following up his original peace initiative with anything more than "public rhetoric," but it was my remarks about Israel that raised a small storm. The American Jewish Congress rebuked me for "climbing aboard the 'Let's put more pressure on Israel' bandwagon," and declared that "Senator Javits would have been better advised to offer his advice to the leaders of Jordan and Egypt." I received a batch of critical mail from constituents. But many thoughtful friends of Israel agreed with me, and in the long run my criticism helped bring the Israeli government around to a more realistic position, agreeing to open negotiations at the end of five years.

A few weeks later the shoe was on the other foot: The Egyptians announced their "new" peace plan, which was just as disappointing as the Israeli statement had been. It was, I declared publicly, "only a reiteration of the classic Arab position and as such it is even a retrogression from the situation at the time of President Sadat's . . . visit to Jerusalem." And I let Sadat know that I thought he had become hard-fisted when things seemed to be going his way.

Throughout, I tried to help and encourage President Carter in every way I could, urging him, in the weeks before Camp David, to make the best effort to bring the parties together. I told him that he should handle it personally, like a mediator in a labor dispute who locks the parties up until they get an agreement. Nobody could do that with Begin and Sadat except Carter, but he would have to give it time so that the parties could not go home to consult their cabinets and get lost in domestic politics. Carter was willing to do whatever was needed, but he had to be persuaded that his efforts would be fruitful.

That September, President Carter brought Begin and Sadat face to face at Camp David for the summit accords that electrified the world. But then the ball was fumbled. Carter, because of his inexperience, failed to insist that the two countries sign an agreement immediately, and both sides began to look back and wonder whether they had driven a hard enough bargain at Camp David. Begin thought he had unnecessarily offered too much in self-rule for the West Bank; Sadat saw that Israel's position with the United States had been impaired, and perhaps he dreamed of getting the United States to become *his* patron instead of the Israelis' patron. So they both dragged their heels.

At one point, at the request of the State Department, I carried to Israel a document comparing U.S., Israeli, and Egyptian drafts of a treaty, and I discussed them in detail with Begin and other Israeli officials. In December, when I was in Israel for Golda Meir's funeral, I spoke rather strongly to Prime Minister Begin, telling him that his support in the U.S. Congress was in danger of some erosion and that he should weigh the consequences of that against whatever risk he thought his country might be running if it signed a treaty. In January 1979 I urged President Carter to convene another summit, to invite Begin and Sadat to the White House and keep them there until they signed a treaty or broke off negotiations. After one White House meeting I told Carter, "Mr. President, you know if you keep at it, I think you can still pull this off."

Every delay caused new problems. The downfall of the shah of Iran frightened the Saudis, who, I thought, had been prepared to concur in substance with Egypt on the deal with Israel, and who were already supporting the Egyptian government with economic aid. With the shah overthrown, the Saudi royal family suddenly became more aware of its own vulnerability; it became wary of antagonizing other Arab states whose support it might need in a revolutionary situation, and this posed new problems in the negotiations. Remembering my conversation with Prince Saud in Jidda, I suggested to President Carter that the United States should give the Saudis some new assurances about their defense, and shortly thereafter Secretary of Defense Harold Brown flew to Saudi Arabia to do just that.

Nevertheless, by February 1979 I was very discouraged. It seemed that the opportunity had slipped through our fingers, that the great moments of Sadat's trip to Jerusalem, Begin's trip to Ismailia, and Carter bringing them both to Camp David, all had been wasted because no one had performed adequately. I felt that I too could have done more, perhaps by trying to rouse the Jewish community to the danger that the movement for peace could be derailed. I could have taken a plane and stormed about the United States saying, "Fellow Jews, here's your time. Demand peace, you can do it." But I was too involved with the details and the mechanics.

The turning point came early in March 1979. Begin was in Washington, and after a couple of days of fruitless talks President Carter, on Sunday, March 4, gave him a new U.S. proposal regarding the "linkage" of the West Bank issue to the peace treaty itself. Later that afternoon Carter called ten congressional leaders, including myself, to the White House. He gave us the impression that the situation still was grim and that Begin had not accepted or rejected the new proposals. The President asked for our support (it was after that meeting that I made the calls to Jewish leaders described in Chapter 15), and I told him that the new element needed was U.S. guarantees — of Israel's security, of financial and perhaps military support for Egypt, and of the security of the Saudi Arabian oil fields.

The next morning, at Blair House, Begin told a group of us that the proposals were so "interesting" he had cabled them to his cabinet, recommending they approve. Begin came to Capitol Hill later that day for meetings with House members and a group of seventy-five senators (and a private talk I arranged for him in my office with Senator Howard Baker, the minority leader). By that time the word had arrived that the Israeli cabinet had indeed approved the proposals. For the first time in months, the negotiations were back on track, and it was a happy scene as Begin walked through my office suite, shaking hands with the men and kissing the women. Two days later President Carter himself flew to the Middle East, where he hammered out the "final" compromise in meetings in Cairo and Jerusalem.

The news of his success brought tears to my eyes — but even that agreement was not quite final. At practically the last minute, when Sadat and Begin had already arrived in Washington to sign the treaties, with the documents prepared and everything agreed, Israeli Ambassador Ephraim Evron suddenly showed up in my office with a problem. The agreements provided for various kinds of U.S. economic support for Israel, but in the rush to get the treaties signed, the shape of the aid, whether it was to be loans or grants, had somehow not been determined. Israel was in a perilous financial condition, and the point was crucial. Since the implementation of the treaty was clearly in the U.S. interest, I told the ambassador that I would consider it my duty to get this straightened out; I immediately made calls to Senator Daniel Inouye, the Senate appropriations subcommittee chairman who would be involved in this matter, and to Senator Baker, and got their assurances that a substantial amount of the aid would be in grants. That removed the last hitch. On March 26, 1979, the historic treaty was signed.

The state dinner at the White House that night was for me the most memorable of all such occasions I had attended, because so many years of effort and anguish had preceded it. Marian could not join me

— she was teaching a class that night in New York — so I escorted Barbara Walters, who had interviewed both Begin and Sadat on her television program and knew them well. They liked and trusted her and together we went around to greet them and to share everyone's delight and happiness. At our table, we were seated next to a member of the Egyptian parliament, a veteran who had lost a leg in the 1973 war. On the other side of him sat an official of the Israeli foreign office, who had also fought in the war. Barbara and I watched as the two former enemies introduced themselves and then raised their glasses in a toast to peace — and to each other.

The treaty, of course, did not solve the problems of the Middle East; the status of Jerusalem and the role of the PLO and Israel's continuing settlements in the West Bank are still dangerous and difficult issues. But what I said at the time of the signing of the peace treaty still holds: that Egypt and Israel had made peace with the United States and now they were going to try to make peace with each other. They have not yet succeeded in settling all the issues between them, but at least they are still trying, and that is better than making war.

* * *

The violence and turmoil in the Middle East have been fueled for decades by a dangerous brew of dynastic and big-power rivalries, petroleum politics, and religious fanaticism. The same volatile concoction underlies the crisis in Iran. Fifty-two U.S. hostages were held in captivity for fourteen months, Iraq and Iran are at war — threatening an oil shortage that could make us long for the days of the "energy crisis" of the 1970s — and the future of the region is unfathomable. Perhaps it will all be solved and forgotten soon, but I doubt it.

My contact with events in Iran and U.S. policy toward Iran had been related to my membership in the Senate Foreign Relations Committee. But after the overthrow of the shah, a previously well-publicized incident caused me to be marked as an "enemy" of the Ayatollah Khomeini's regime, a feeling I did not reciprocate. Despite my outrage at the excesses of the Iranian revolution, particularly the taking of the hostages, I felt no enmity toward Iran or its people.

The earlier incident was Marian's employment by Ruder and Finn, a New York public-relations firm, to do publicity work for Iran Airlines. I had visited Iran in 1970 and 1975, and on the latter occasion Marian was with me. We had met the shah and his family. Together with other members of the Foreign Relations Committee, I had received the shah on some of his visits to Washington. Marian was impressed with his efforts to modernize his country, using the resources made available by the high price of oil.

Sometime in the fall of 1975, Marian told me that she wanted to help Iran in its modernization effort and that she was working out a public-relations program for Iran through Ruder and Finn. I did not ask for details, and if she gave me any at the time they went in one ear and out the other. I had been urging her for years to find work of her own and to devote herself to it (as indeed she had), hoping that if she did so she might be very busy too and stop protesting about the Senate being my "wife." It did not occur to me that anyone would challenge the propriety of her assignment.

Marian duly registered as an agent of a foreign government, as the law required (Iran Air was wholly owned by the Iranian government), and that brought the whole project out in the press as a public controversy. I had spent a lifetime building a reputation for integrity; I knew I could not possibly be influenced by my wife's connection with any foreign government, and it was inconceivable to me that anyone would make such a charge seriously. But I realized at once that our position was publicly untenable, that although everyone was jumping to the wrong conclusions their suspicions were reasonable considering the surface facts. So I asked Marian to resign from the account. She was deeply hurt, for she felt I was thwarting the career that I had encouraged initially, and she argued long and hard to save it; but I insisted and out of loyalty to me she agreed to step down. In her letter of resignation she cited "the unjustifiable criticism that has been leveled at my husband because of the appearance of possible conflict," and she added that "the American public is not yet ready to accept the separate roles of a husband and wife in professional affairs when one of them happens to be a public official."

Three years later the shah was overthrown. He had a tremendous drive to bring his country out of the Middle Ages, but he lost touch with his own people and he seemed to believe that his authority, his prestige in the world, his own influence, were identical with his country — that he, in fact, *was* Iran. And since the primary object of his rule by then seemed to his subjects to be not their welfare but the perpetuation of his own dynasty, the people rebelled, and as people do when they rebel in anger they become as cruel as the regime they topple.

I became concerned about these cruelties, particularly the summary executions; some of the victims of the firing squads were accused of atrocious crimes, but others, such as former prime minister Hoveida, whom I had met, were killed merely because they had served under the shah. And a Jewish businessman was executed just for the "crime" of being a "Zionist" and raising funds for Israel. In May 1979 I wrote and sponsored a Senate resolution deploring and protesting these actions.

The Senate leadership of both parties agreed to cosponsor it, the Foreign Relations Committee approved it unanimously, and on May 17 it passed the Senate without a negative vote or a murmur of dissent. I could have asked the majority and minority leaders to put their names at the top of the list, and my name in alphabetical order further down. But it had been my idea and I had been the author and I saw no reason not to handle it normally. We all considered it an honorable, restrained way to express our concern about events in a country with whose people we felt a bond of friendship, and we were very disappointed to find that the resolution was completely ignored by the press.

It was not, however, ignored by Iran. My seventy-fifth birthday was on May 18, 1979, and on Sunday, May 20, Marian and I were celebrating in New York at a big party with seventy-five friends. At about 2:30 in the afternoon, as we were having lunch, Ed Pinto, my press aide, phoned me from Washington with the news that Marian and I had been denounced as "criminals" by the regime in Teheran and had been summoned to appear before a revolutionary court. My "crime" was the Senate resolution and my position as "a leading Zionist"; Marian's was her work for Iran Air three years earlier. I did not want to mar the birthday festivities, so I said nothing to our guests and did not even mention it to Marian until they had gone. Then we called the New York City police and the State Department and were given police protection.

It was with some surprise that I learned from the morning papers some months later, in October 1979, that the President had decided to admit the shah to the United States for medical treatment. The Foreign Relations Committee had not been consulted on this decision, as it might have been, but the deed was done, and the remarkable aspect of our discussion of it that morning in the committee room was that none of us was alarmed. We decided it was no time to recriminate and that after the shah left we would try to find out why we had not been consulted. Little did we anticipate the crisis that soon overtook us.

The capture of the U.S. Embassy in Teheran and the seizure of sixty-three Americans by Iranian "students" demanding the return of the shah is a story too well known to be repeated here. With Senator Frank Church, chairman of the Foreign Relations Committee, and Senators Byrd and Baker, the majority and minority leaders, I was briefed daily on the situation by the State Department. My personal efforts were concentrated on making sure that the shah would leave when his treatment was completed and on trying to ensure that the constitutional rights of law-abiding Iranians in the United States would not be violated in retaliation.

I was also concerned, of course, with the action the United States could take to free the hostages, and I was disappointed in President Carter's announcement a few days later that he was only suspending all purchases of oil from Iran. I felt that the American people were so enraged by the seizure of the hostages that they would have endured almost any sacrifice, and that Carter could have used the opportunity to impose a real conservation policy, perhaps even gas rationing. This would have reduced our dependence on OPEC oil and might also have encouraged Western Europe and Japan to do more in our support; they might even have been able to boycott Iranian oil if our decreased use of OPEC oil had left more available to them from countries other than Iran. Such a boycott might have forced Iran to surrender the hostages within a matter of weeks. As it was, Iran continued to sell its oil and earn the foreign exchange it needed to import food and to survive.

We did not dream in those early days of the crisis that the hostages would languish in captivity for more than fourteen months. Our inability to get them out frustrated the nation. Once we missed the opportunity of moving in militarily in "hot pursuit," we were committed to go the peaceful route and sweat it out. We had the choice, but the President made the decision not to take direct military action and it was binding on the nation. From then on we were hostages ourselves to that fact. Only some attempt like the desert operation — which was a disaster but which I do not say was foolhardy — could have ended the crisis. Not even a blockade, in my opinion, would have been effective, for the Soviet Union could have broken it by sending food to Iran overland — thereby creating for itself a handy new satellite.

Whether or not the taking of the hostages was a punishment for our past errors of policy, as has been claimed, our inability to free them quickly was a sign of even greater failures: We had let our alliances fall into disarray, we had permitted our economy to become less competitive, we had allowed our defenses and our dollar to become weak. All these developments momentarily eroded the strength we needed to cope effectively with this outrage.

The prospect is not hopeful, and those who look for silver linings can only say that at least the crisis awakened us to our shortcomings and that perhaps we will now do something about them. Perhaps.

TWENTY-SEVEN

The Last Campaign

After an unbroken string of nine electoral victories I was defeated in my tenth run for public office. Nine out of ten is a good score in any league, but when the lone defeat comes at the end of a career, in a last campaign, and when one's record and achievements are well known, it hurts. As I write these lines I look forward to more years of service, but the United States Senate had become my life and it was hard to face the fact that while in full possession of all my powers I would not rise to be recognized in the U.S. Senate again.

The 1980 campaign was unusual in many respects: the large number of challengers, the presence on the ballot of three major candidates for the presidency and three for the Senate from New York, the nationwide Republican sweep, and the mistakes I made — mistakes that a political campaigner of my experience should have known how to avoid.

It was also an election of ironies. After twenty-four years in the Senate minority, having become the ranking minority member on the Foreign Relations Committee, I was dismissed in the year that my party became the majority in the Senate, when I would have become chairman of the committee — a lifelong dream. I was shown the promised land but was not permitted to enter it.

Furthermore, I was not sure for a long time that I wanted to seek another term, and after I decided that I did it turned out that my hesitation was at least partly responsible for my defeat.

To understand why I lost the election it is necessary to go back to why I ran. When I was elected to my fourth term, in 1974, I had not expected to even consider a fifth. Consequently, by the middle of 1979 I had performed only a minimum of the political fence-mending and fund-raising chores that I normally began in the year preceding an election year. But toward the end of 1978 I had started thinking about the 1980 campaign because it seemed likely then that Representative Jack Kemp of Buffalo would contest me in a primary for the Republican nomination if I did decide to run. I had engaged in two primary contests in the Liberal Party, but I had never experienced a Republican primary, and the outlook was unsettling.

Jack Kemp, a former star quarterback for the Buffalo Bills, was a popular and personable congressman who was making a career as a conservative, especially on tax issues. He was one of the authors of the Kemp-Roth bill, which proposed to cut income taxes 30 percent in three years, on the theory that a drastic tax cut would stimulate enough new initiative and enterprise to more than make up for the lost revenue. I felt it would be reckless in our highly inflationary economy to increase consumption without any assurance of increased productivity. So Jack Kemp and I had been on opposite sides of that issue, as well as on some labor issues and others.

Faced by the prospect of a conservative challenge, it was imperative that I try to discourage my potential opponent — just in case I decided to run. Late in 1978, at a dinner in Kemp's bailiwick of Buffalo, I declared that if I ran I would definitely be on the ballot; in short, I served notice that whether or not I was successful in a Republican primary I would run on election day, either on an independent line or on the ticket of the Liberal Party. The announcement had its intended impact. It made clear to conservative Republicans that they would have to reckon with me whether I won or lost the primary.

I was considered virtually unbeatable at that stage and everyone who coveted my job was waiting for me to make up my mind. There were few people, Democrats or Republicans, who relished the idea of taking me on. Early in 1979, for example, Queens Democratic leader Donald Manes was quoted in the press as saying: "Right now, everybody's a major candidate. I just want to see what happens when Javits announces whether he's running or not. Someone with twenty-four years in the Senate is not easy to knock off."

In May 1979 I passed two of those milestones that generate a lot of attention in the press and then are usually forgotten. As of May 4, I had served in the U.S. Senate longer than any of my predecessors from New York: twenty-two years, three months, and twenty-five days, eclipsing the record of Robert F. Wagner, Sr. My Senate colleagues voted a resolution of commendation, the mayor of New York City, Ed Koch, issued a proclamation of "public tribute," and the press was in constant attendance. Two weeks later, on May 18, I celebrated my seventy-fifth birthday, and the round of congratulations and interviews and articles was repeated.

That was a gratifying time, but it raised in everyone's mind the question I was not ready to answer. My intentions became a prime topic of public speculation, and for the next nine months I could not walk down a street, catch a cab, enter a restaurant, go to my club, attend a meeting, hold a press conference, pick up the telephone — without someone asking whether I was going to run again. At first I simply replied that I was not ready to decide, but as the questions multiplied I promised to announce my decision on or before Lincoln's Birthday, 1980. That seemed late enough to preserve my influence in the Senate if I decided to retire and early enough to mount a campaign if I decided to run again.

In October 1979, all but one of the Senate's Republicans signed a letter to me and to Barry Goldwater urging both of us to run again and promising to help us in any way they could. Barry and I were sitting next to each other in the Senate chamber soon afterward, and he asked me what I was going to do about it. "Well," I said, "I'll be thinking about it right along. I'll be going about my business just the same but it'll be on my mind. I don't think it will keep me awake nights. And there will come a stage, because I've set myself a deadline, when I'll just get down to it and decide. I'll gestate and come up with an answer."

Barry took quite a different tack: "Well, at first I'm not going to think about it at all. But what I'm going to do, as soon as I get a little time I'm going to get a sleeping bag, go up in the mountains, stretch out and think it over and make a decision." I guess that is the difference between Goldwater and Javits — or between Arizona and New York.

Soon after that I began to consult seriously with family and friends and colleagues. Marian did not really want me to run, but she was afraid that if I quit at my stage of life, having served in the Senate for so long, that I could atrophy and die, as other busy and committed men had died soon after retiring. And so she said that if I felt up to it I ought to do it.

But I had visions of all those concerts and plays and beautiful parties and dinners and wide-ranging conversations in my native New York, so many of which I had missed because the Senate sat late or I had another speech to make. In the later years it had been too tiring to make the round trip to New York just for a dinner party. And I thought that if I did retire I would teach at a university and practice law and earn some money, which would certainly keep me from dying of boredom. Although $60,000 a year as a senator and up to $25,000 more in honoraria is a lot of money, it did not seem like much compared to the quarter of a million dollars I was told I might earn as a lawyer every year without working half as hard as I did as a senator.

So life outside the Senate had many attractions for me, and I discounted Marian's reasons for my running.

Our children were divided. Joshua felt as Marian did, that carrying on in the Senate would be good for me, would keep up my interest in life. Joy, on the other hand, was enthusiastic about all the things I said I would do if I left the Senate. Carla was neutral, realizing that I would ultimately decide for myself.

John Trubin, my law partner, adviser, and campaign manager, and Jud Sommer, one of my principal political lieutenants, both thought it would be better for me not to run — unless I felt a very deep call of conscience to be a candidate again. They spoke as caring friends with a real solicitude for me — and against their own best interests: It certainly is nice to have a friend in the Senate, but they advised what they thought was best for me.

The barrage of questions kept up. I did not have a newspaper inquiry on any subject, a television appearance, or a radio request in which the reporter did not throw in the question of my candidacy, just for good measure. The reporters were hoping that I had made a decision and that they would get a lucky scoop. For the television programs I developed a stock response: "If I were going to commit hara-kiri, it wouldn't be on this show."

Many people refused to believe me, but I really was undecided. Although I had not intended to run for a fifth term, I was troubled by the overlapping crises in which our country found itself: the hostages in Iran, the Soviet takeover of Afghanistan, the threat to the oil supply of the Western world, the disarray among our allies, and our own economic woes. Added to these was what we were learning in the 1979 hearings on SALT II, that the Soviet Union's military strength had bounded ahead since 1969 — the year we decided to stand pat in strategic nuclear weaponry — and that the USSR might be close to attaining nuclear superiority. I felt we had to make the Soviet Union understand that we were determined to rearm, and that parity would again prevail, even if it took five years and much treasure.

These were compelling factors. As ranking minority member of the Foreign Relations Committee, I was at the peak of my influence while all of these critical international events were going on. My accumulated experience could undoubtedly be of great use to our country in a crisis like this. And on the domestic front, I considered myself the last major survivor of the progressive Republican tradition in New York. Nelson Rockefeller, Tom Dewey, and Irving Ives were gone, John Lindsay had joined the Democrats, and others were out of office. Younger New York Republicans — notably Ned Regan, New York

State comptroller, and Congressman Bill Green and State Senator Roy Goodman of Manhattan — were around and active, but I was the number-one progressive Republican in the country, anathema to the ultraconservatives in the Republican Party and to the leaders of New York's Conservative Party. If I retired, what I would be able to do thereafter would become problematic. I might have some influence and be able to help for a long time, but probably not in the way I could as a senator.

But then a question went through my mind: Is that just an ego trip? Am I really just afraid of losing my authority and power? Am I concerned I will not be happy as a civilian, just practicing law, perhaps in the international field, and teaching at a university — in the event I am not called on by a President for some foreign-policy mission in the way that Averell Harriman and John McCloy are even now still on call? I had no answer to that one.

And I was tired. I had worked very hard for all those years and felt entitled to some personal and private life. My physical condition was also something of a problem. I had developed a slackening in my abdominal muscles, which the doctors diagnosed as motor neuron disease and which made it somewhat difficult for me to walk; I was good for about ten blocks. I could climb stairs only if I rested at every floor, and I had stopped playing tennis. It was disconcerting to find myself impeded in this way.

Certainly I was still able to undertake a campaign and serve very effectively in the Senate. My own doctors, Jerome Posner and Arnold Drapkin, were divided on whether my condition would be aggravated by the tensions of a campaign and another term. They felt that on balance I would be taking less of a chance if I did not run, but if I really wanted to keep going they certainly would not stand in the way. The consulting specialists explained that the ailment tended to be slowly progressive, but they assured me that it in no way affected or would affect my brain; and I really thought that my mind had never functioned more clearly, more logically, more calmly and coolly than it did then, at the age of seventy-six.

Other considerations that crowded in on me related to the campaign itself, especially the threat of a primary challenge. As a progressive Republican, I was haunted by the fate that befell Clifford Case in New Jersey. Case was defeated in the 1978 Republican primary by an obscure conservative who thereupon lost the general election to Bill Bradley, a Democrat. The argument was made that Case was thus unceremoniously removed from politics because he was overconfident, did not keep his fences mended, was not adequately involved in the poli-

tics of his state, and did not campaign hard enough in the primary —
and that he was much more interested in foreign policy (he preceded
me as the ranking minority member of the Foreign Relations Committee). I could not blame his defeat entirely on his local problems or
on mistakes he might have made, for I admired him greatly. I had to
recognize the conservatism of many Republicans who vote in primaries
and who seemed more eager in New Jersey to defeat Clifford Case than
to keep the Senate seat Republican.

The 1979 polls showed me easily beating any potential rival for
the nomination and winning the general election handily. But I realized that in a Republican primary the plebiscite would be on me, even
if my opponent or opponents were unknown. Jack Kemp graciously
announced early in 1979 that he would not run if I did, but two other
Republican rivals had surfaced: Bruce Caputo, a former congressman
from Westchester, who had been a candidate for lieutenant governor
in 1978, and Alfonse D'Amato, who was supervisor of the town of
Hempstead on Long Island. D'Amato was not well known at the time,
but it had not taken a major personality to upset Case in New Jersey,
and I realized even then that it would not take one to give me the same
kind of trouble. Any challenger who could bring out the conservatives
in the Republican Party of New York was a threat.

On Wednesday night, February 6, 1980, I was sure I was not going to run. I had attended a few receptions around Washington and
had come back to my Capitol office at about eight. I had mail to sign,
memoranda from my staff to look over, and material to read to keep
me up to speed on some of the policy issues in which I was involved.
I got through at about quarter of ten. I had not eaten dinner, the
Capitol was practically empty, and as I put out the light in my office
and tucked under my arm envelopes with some remaining papers I
still might wish to look at, I suddenly said to myself, "If you run for
reelection, this is what you are going to do for the next six years. Is
this the best you can do with your life?" And the answer at that moment was no.

Nonetheless, so great is the discipline of habit that in the next few
days, before coming to a firm conclusion, I kept talking with a number
of my close friends to see whether they would join my campaign committee if I did run. And, since I had not yet made up my mind, I postponed the announcement. It would not be made in the week of Lincoln's Birthday after all.

On February 11 I went to Massachusetts General Hospital in Boston for an all-day review of my physical condition. The check-up indicated no reason why I should not be a candidate, but when I came

back to New York after a trip to Lake Placid for the opening ceremony of the Winter Olympics, I still felt I should not run.

On Thursday morning, the fourteenth of February, Senator Ted Stevens of Alaska, the minority whip, and I had breakfast with Secretary of State Cyrus Vance to get a briefing on the Iran hostage situation. What we learned from Vance intensified my feeling that I should step aside: The secretary reported a real possibility that the hostages in Iran would be released by arrangement with a United Nations commission appointed to consider Iran's grievances. It seemed to me that the release of the hostages might lead to a resolution of the Afghanistan situation and might revive the SALT II treaty. Such a dramatic solution to the crises would provide a suitable moment to announce my retirement. I think I was grasping for someone or some event to tell me that it was now all right to step down.

With Steve Matthews, my press aide, and Joe Fristachi, who ran my New York office, I tentatively scheduled my announcement press conference for Monday, February 18. Early on Friday morning, the fifteenth, I left for St. Petersburg, Florida, where I was due to give a lecture Saturday night. On the plane, I wrote for the Monday press conference a statement that I would not run. But then I thought about it some more. If the release of the hostages was to provide the proper moment for retirement from the Senate, then it seemed prudent to wait to see if it would really happen before I made the announcement. So when I got off the plane at Tampa, I telephoned my office and postponed the press conference for a week, until February 25.

The successive postponements triggered even more speculation. All the "experts" had theories about what the delay meant, and just as many of them reported I would run as reported I would not. It amused me to see these serious predictions and stories from "sources," because I did not yet know the outcome myself. Barbara Walters predicted I would not run, and because of her professional reputation and her known friendship with Marian and me, she was widely believed. But Barbara, too, was guessing, although it was a good guess at the time.

When I got on the plane back to Washington on Sunday afternoon, the newspapers and television were reporting that the United Nations's arrangements to free the hostages in Iran had slowed down and that we were faced once more with bewildering uncertainties and riddles about what was happening in that chaotic country. State Department briefings on Monday confirmed that the effort to bring back our people was not going smoothly, and I began to wonder whether the United States was doing all it could. From that question it was only a small step for my conscience to ask whether I had any business leaving my post of duty while the troubles of the United States proliferated.

On Tuesday night, the nineteenth, I flew to the Mayo Clinic, at Rochester, Minnesota, for another opinion on my ailment. The Mayo Clinic was a marvel of organization and professional efficiency, and all the doctors were first-rate. Their findings and diagnoses repeated what I had already been told. They agreed that there was nothing I could do about the condition except to exercise to strengthen muscles that were not affected, to supplement my energy with vitamins, and to avoid getting tired — no panting, as the doctors put it.

I realized now that it was entirely up to me to decide whether I could "hack it" in a campaign and in further service in the Senate. No doctor was going to be able to give an answer clear enough, one way or the other, to make the decision for me — as perhaps I had hoped one would. So, leaning now toward becoming a candidate, I called a final meeting on Saturday, February 23, with John Trubin, Dick Clurman, Joe Fristachi, and Steve Matthews. After two hours we arrived at a familiar equation: that if I wanted to be kind to myself as a person, I should not run, and that the only reason for running would be some inner call of duty that I could not resist, coupled with the confidence that I could get through a campaign and still have enough health and energy left to serve effectively if I were reelected.

And then began my weekend agony: The press conference was scheduled for Monday, the twenty-fifth, and I could not postpone it again. But no matter how I tried to figure out what I ought to do, it came out exactly even on each side. On Saturday night I sat down with a ruled yellow pad and ran a line down the middle and wrote the pros on one side and the cons on the other — it still balanced out. Even the question of whether I *could* do it physically was a stand-off, with my family doctor recommending that I step down and with the neurologists saying I could do it if I wished to, that no one knew when, if ever, the "indolent" progress of my disease would disable me — and that even then it would not affect my mind. As one doctor had said, rather bluntly, "You can think even in a wheelchair, and do your job as a senator from that, should things ever get that bad."

None of my children were in town that Saturday night, and Marian had gone to California to spend two weeks in Santa Monica writing an article on the Pritikin Institute of Diet and Exercise for a magazine. She had postponed the trip, hoping that I would announce my decision on the fourteenth and then on the eighteenth, but when it got to be the twenty-fifth, she could not wait any longer without defaulting on her deadline, which I certainly did not wish her to do.

That Sunday, February twenty-fourth, I was still undecided. I had written my statement on a small Senate pad in longhand; I carried it about with me and had revised it several times. Essentially it said that the decision was close and agonizing, but considering that I would still be in the Senate for nearly another year and that even thereafter I would hope to be active, on balance I thought I had better not run.

I lunched at the Harmonie Club with Dick and Shirley Clurman and their son, Michael, and other friends. It was purely a social occasion, but afterward I took Dick aside and showed him the statement, not because I had made up my mind — I had not — but to get his reaction. He had no quarrel with the decision but he thought the statement was terrible. "It's a deathbed statement," he said. "You can't go out as if now your life is over." He thought I should be more enthusiastic about the decision and write a statement to reflect the enthusiasm. And of course, he was right; the prospect of not running again did make me feel terrible. A new decision began to come together at that point, but I was still not sure of it.

I slept very little that Sunday night as I examined all the considerations again. On the side of running were the acute national and world crises and the pattern of my life that was based upon my role as a U.S. senator. I also considered my life in Washington and the satisfactions of participating in the great affairs of mankind. I felt that I had benefitted millions of Americans through my legislation on domestic matters and that I had aided my country by helping to shape foreign policy on some of the greatest events of our time. It was all very heady, very difficult to give up. And against that, in addition to my physical condition, I had to balance the lure of life in New York.

On Monday I got up at 5:30 A.M., still unsure which way it would go. I tried to call my son Joshua, a lawyer in Los Angeles, to see if he had any helpful last-minute thoughts — but as luck would have it, like an episode in a play, he was away for the weekend. The phone did not answer. And so I simply had to make this decision alone.

In the final analysis what took over my thinking was the call of duty and conscience — and the call of what I knew how to do best, which was to be a United States senator. There was no argument to stand up against that. By the time I had done my morning exercises and washed up and prepared to go out, I had pretty much decided that that was my fate, and that I had no way out, and that I had to express my willingness to serve the people again — and let the voters make the final decision.

None of the friends or staff members with whom I had conferred knew my decision. I had revised the statement from a no to a yes, and it was still tucked in my pocket on the sheets of a Senate pad, with all the insertions and erasures just as I made them. I met for breakfast at the Waldorf-Astoria Hotel with the same four men I had seen on Saturday. Without disclosing what I was going to do, I asked some further questions on the political situation. Clurman and Trubin were puzzled to find us going over ground we had covered before. I then attempted to reach Marian but she was reported to be running on the beach and unavailable.

Arriving at my office about ten, I looked over my statement again. At about eleven o'clock, exactly one hour before my press conference was to begin, I called in Joe Fristachi and Steve Matthews, took the statement out of my pocket, laid it before me, slapped my palm down on it, and said, "Gentlemen, this is it, I'm announcing for reelection." They actually cheered, they were so elated; they had certainly favored my running — though they had not tried to sway me.

I tried to call Joy and Carla, again without success. So I put the statement in my pocket and with my two assistants walked over to the Biltmore Hotel. There I immediately saw Trubin and Clurman and called them into a side room that was being prepared for a luncheon. While the waiters tried to shoo us out, I told my friends that I had decided to run. They were quite surprised and very enthusiastic: I think they would have been enthusiastic about any firm decision, as they both knew how much it had taken out of me — and them — to make it.

I then walked down the corridor to the Music Room of the Biltmore, said hello to a dozen of my friends (we had invited lots of Javits partisans as well as the media), and stepped up behind a thicket of microphones on the podium. I took the announcement out of my pocket, said that no one knew what I was going to say, but that I was ready and here goes. I spoke for about ten minutes, outlining all the considerations I had been struggling with for months, and maintaining the suspense until the last line. And then I got to it. I have committed myself to make a decision now, I said, "and pursuant to that commitment, I declare that I am a candidate. . . ." My friends in the audience did not let me finish, and I had to repeat the whole sentence after the tumult died down, ". . . for reelection to the U.S. Senate in 1980." I am told that my manner and voice shifted visibly upward at that moment, and I can believe it. For there I was, following my mission, offering myself to the public once more.

*　*　*

My prospects looked good at the time of my announcement and the decision was the right one, but my well-publicized delay in making it introduced a note of ambivalence that permeated my entire campaign and gave the eventual winner his chance. The whole exercise leading up to my announcement turned out to be a major strategic mistake. I thought the people would not expect me to leap at another election at my age, having served as long as I had — but they did. Just as there is no upper age limit for election to the Senate, so there is little concession given to age or length of service. Every campaign is a first campaign and you have to go out to win it from the starting line, which is quite properly early in the year before the election. With hindsight I realize that at the end of 1978 I should have said that of course I expected to stand for reelection — and then I could have deferred a formal declaration until even later in 1980.

Three strong candidates had emerged in the Democratic Party, but polls indicated I would run ahead of anybody — if I got the Republican nomination. And that, of course, turned out to be the rub. Leading the conservative contenders for the nomination — but still almost invisible to the general public throughout the state — was Alfonse D'Amato of Hempstead. D'Amato had the backing of the Nassau County Republican chairman, Joseph Margiotta, who ran a tough and powerful political machine very much like the old Tammany Hall. Margiotta said later that if I had declared my candidacy in 1979 he would have backed me in the interests of party unity — in which case there might have been no primary. When the Republican Party's state committee met in June to select a senatorial candidate, I received 65 percent of the vote and the official party "designation." But D'Amato — with the support of Margiotta and other leaders Margiotta rallied, mainly on Long Island — got 35 percent, which entitled him to fight it out with me for the nomination in a September primary election — the only Republican primary challenge I ever faced.

I was also handicapped by the passing of Nelson Rockefeller. Had he been on the scene I believe I might have made a decision sooner. Even if I had still delayed, Rockefeller might have helped to obtain the nomination for me, without the primary. Nelson had a genius for dealing with county chairmen. He cajoled them; he dazzled them with his personality and the luster of his family name. Although he had chosen to withdraw completely from politics, I am sure he would have done this for me had I appealed to him at the right time and had he been around to do it.

D'Amato, an ultraconservative, had plenty of substantive issues to argue about with me, but he chose to focus his primary campaign on my age and health. The three television commercials he introduced early in August were described by a *New York Times* reporter as "among the roughest that New York politicians could remember." One of them, referring to me, said, "And now, at age seventy-six and in fail-ing health, he wants six more years." A few weeks later D'Amato him-self was quoted in the press as saying about me: "You take a look at the guy and you tell me if he'll last six more years."

These commercials and comments were ruthless and cruel and I called them crude and vulgar and "below the belt." But that did not get through to the voters, because I had named my ailment myself when I announced my candidacy, and medical analyses in the press thereafter made matters worse. Doctors had to declare that some types of motor neuron disease were fatal, such as the disease that killed ball-player Lou Gehrig; I did not have that kind, but it was a nice distinc-tion that was very hard to explain. So I had started on the wrong foot, and D'Amato took advantage of that.

Then, instead of zeroing in on D'Amato and his connection with Margiotta's political machine, I responded to his charges and explained again why I was running. In one of my commercials I said,

> I run for reelection because I must. Our country is in trouble at home and abroad. The decisions of the next few years are crucial to America's future. You've honored me with seniority and prestige in the Senate. I'm in a position to make a difference. I know my age, all the spirit of seventy-six. I know my health; I would not run if I could not serve. I owe my country everything. I have no choice but to run.

I had other TV commercials too, of course, including endorsements from former President Gerald Ford and from George Bush and Senators Howard Baker and Barry Goldwater and other Republican senators, but every time I mentioned my health and age it apparently reminded the voters of my opponent's attack, which he ruthlessly pressed with large expenditures on TV. Indeed, the public came to believe that age had induced in me an illness that made it unlikely that I could serve out my term, and that attitude persisted.

Furthermore, I had not organized my staff sufficiently to respond to unexpected developments. As in every campaign, we heard rumors that, if true, could have devastated my opponent. But we could not use them without verification, and our investigatory work fell short. In retrospect, I feel that when I did attack my opponent I picked the wrong target. In a debate at the *New York Daily News,* for example, I criticized the "crudeness and vulgarity" of his campaign and called him "temperamentally unfit" to be a senator. But the voters appar-ently cared little about campaign tactics or that D'Amato was sullying the dignity of the office of senator.

In the final week of the primary campaign it was revealed that my opponent had a role in a scheme requiring county employees in Nassau County to "kick back" one percent of their salaries to the Republican organization. For some reason, I did not go after him adequately on that. I said I regretted that this scandal had suddenly come up — because in my mind it diverted the primary debate from a discussion of the major issues. But I should have been out on the streets yelling about it at the top of my lungs. If an opportunity like that had arisen in any of my earlier campaigns I would have bought $500,000 worth of television time in three days to blast my opponent for such an unsavory practice — the existence of which D'Amato ultimately had to admit.

Although I had always worried about a Republican primary, I did not deploy my resources effectively enough to beat back the challenge. My finance committee raised a million dollars, but a good deal of that went into an enormous telephone campaign to urge thousands of registered Republicans to vote for me in the primary. I thought that this rifle-shot approach to individuals would produce the greatest dividends in a primary, where 20 percent of the enrolled voters represents a pretty good turnout.

We spent $200,000 on the phone banks and put a lot of people to work on it for a long time, statewide. I had used phone banks in the past, but never anything approaching the magnitude of this one — which turned out to be not nearly as effective as we had anticipated. If we had spent that money on TV we could have bought 25 percent more air time, and that is a lot.

D'Amato put almost all of his campaign funds into TV and made a greater impact. Whether that was because his television campaign was so rough and abrasive or because television is just a more effective medium than the targeted approach of the telephone is a question I cannot yet answer. But it does seem that a telephone message goes in one ear and out the other and is quickly forgotten; television is repeated and continuous and it gradually bears in upon the listener.

By the end of the primary campaign I had been endorsed by almost all the trade unions, by the *Times,* the *Post,* the *Daily News,* the *Buffalo Courier-Express,* and the *Watertown Daily Times,* and by many radio and television stations in the state. Former President Gerald Ford appeared in New York on several occasions to endorse me and speak in my behalf, and in the closing days nine Republican senators (Boschwitz, Chaffee, Cohen, Danforth, Heinz, Kassebaum, Simpson, Stafford, and Stevens) campaigned for me around the state. D'Amato had been endorsed by all the ultraconservative organizations, including the National Rifle Association, which had praised his stand against handgun-control laws. The gun lobby even quoted him as opposed to the ban on the

"Saturday-night special." From the point of view of people in the cities concerned about street crime, that position alone should have been enough to defeat him.

Meanwhile, the Democrats were engaged in a bitter primary battle of their own. The leading candidates were Bess Myerson, a former Miss America and New York City Consumer Affairs Commissioner; Representative Elizabeth Holtzman of Brooklyn; and former mayor of New York John Lindsay. Governor Hugh Carey, a Democrat, was supporting Myerson, and late in August he tried to help her by declaring that the Senate seat was a "Jewish seat." In fact, only one of my predecessors, Herbert Lehman, had been Jewish; and there were two Jews in the Democratic contest anyway, Myerson and Holtzman. But Carey's statement had set everyone on edge and may have caused enough resentment to affect the outcome in November.

On primary day, September 9, Margiotta's political machine pulled out an unusually heavy Republican vote in the Long Island suburbs — and nearly three-quarters of it went to D'Amato. Elsewhere, however, the turnout was light, and that hurt me. Committed conservatives in the party sensed they had a chance to get rid of me at last, and they seem to have voted in large numbers. Many moderate Republicans who favored me but were impressed with the health argument apparently just stayed home. I captured Manhattan and Westchester and most of the counties upstate, but D'Amato took the rest of New York City and its suburbs and received 56 percent of the vote statewide. Representative Holtzman won the Democratic nomination with a substantial plurality of 41 percent.

I put a brave face on it as I stepped before the television cameras that night. I promised that I would continue the campaign as the Liberal Party candidate, and I declared: "I've lived a full and interesting life, but there's one thing I haven't had, and that is a defeat at the polls. It's very healthy." Healthy or not, I had been handed what the *New York Times* called a "stunning defeat," and I was as stunned as anyone.

Immediately after the primary we mounted a last-minute petition drive for an independent ballot line, which I needed because the party allegiances were so mixed up. As the Liberal Party candidate for senator, I was on the same ticket with presidential candidate John Anderson — but I was supporting Ronald Reagan for the presidency and most of my trade union supporters were backing Jimmy Carter. Since Anderson could take enough votes from Carter to swing the state to Reagan, union leaders were reluctant to urge their members to go to the Liberal line to vote for me. If I had an independent line, unionists could vote for me without being tempted to vote for Anderson.

We needed to gather twenty thousand signatures of registered voters who had not voted in the primary, and we had to get at least one hundred from at least twenty congressional districts. Such a drive normally takes six weeks and we had less than one. Despite the help of about a thousand volunteers from the New York State United Teachers, we did not make it; we had enough signatures but no time left to check and process them. So I had to run on the Liberal line alone and hope the unions stayed with me.

Then there was the problem of money. The Republican Senatorial Campaign Committee had previously decided to allocate $770,000 to my general election campaign, but after the primary they were obliged to back the official Republican candidate, and they could give nothing to me. I needed at least a million dollars, the same amount I had raised and spent for the primary, but I doubted I could raise more than about $400,000 — and my chances of winning on the Liberal Party line alone did not justify borrowing a large sum that would hang over my head as a debt if I lost.

So again the campaign marked time for several weeks while I tried to find out whether I could raise enough money to continue. After extensive canvassing of my friends and supporters, I found that I would be able to get some support but not as much as I had received in the primary — not what I really needed or had hoped for — and therefore I had to decide whether it was worthwhile to continue nevertheless. I decided to keep going, but this hesitation, like my ambivalence about running in the first place, encouraged speculation that I would withdraw. As late as October 14, three weeks before the election, I found it necessary to issue a press release to state that "I am in the race to stay."

I thought that I had to deal with *both* my opponents and capture the middle ground between them. "I do not believe," I said, "the people of this state are willing to accept doctrinaire naiveté on the left, as in Miss Holtzman's attitude toward defense and energy, any more than they are interested in rigid extremism on the right, as in Mr. D'Amato's general outlook and philosophy."

As to my opponents, D'Amato called off his attack on my age and health, and Holtzman, to her credit, never joined it.

The most important issue separating Holtzman and me was defense. In Congress she had voted against almost every defense appropriation and authorization, except when they were inextricably tied up with civilian expenditures. Bess Myerson had brought this up in the Democratic primary, D'Amato of course zeroed in on it too, and I felt I had to point it out as well, because Holtzman's attitude toward defense was dangerously naive. With that, and D'Amato's claims that the middle class was being exploited by taxes and regulation, Holtzman's lead suddenly melted away like snow in the summer, very much as my commanding lead had dissolved in the primary.

Consequently I began to get a great deal of pressure to withdraw from the race in order to prevent D'Amato's victory. Many people thought I had no chance to be elected — I was consistently third in all the polls, though still within reach — and the general view among liberals was that I would take enough votes away from Holtzman to allow D'Amato to get in — just as Charles Goodell had split the liberal vote in 1970 and permitted Jim Buckley to be elected with 39 percent of the vote.

On October 30 the *New York Times* stated that it still considered me the best candidate of the three, but that "with this last hurrah" Javits "may lose even more than the seat he has held with distinction for twenty-four years. He may also weaken the progressive causes to which he devoted his political life. . . . If he shares the judgment that he cannot win, Senator Javits should complete a brilliant career with a selfless, principled withdrawal."

The next day, however, the *New York Post* declared that the *Times* editorial was as "barren of logic as it is devoid of principle." My public life, the *Post* said, "cannot — and should not — be terminated by the crocodile-team of *Times* editorial writers morosely pondering the arithmetic of opinion polls and cravenly trumpeting retreat."

I gave the suggestions that I withdraw the careful consideration they deserved — and I found two serious flaws in them. First of all, when I decided to run I had given the people the option of deciding my future; for me, there could be no other way in which I would be dismissed. I felt I could not retire just because I was running third in the polls. The final preelection polls all showed me behind, but none of them indicated that I was out of the running altogether. In addition, there was no assurance that, if I withdrew, my supporters would all vote for Holtzman. There were certainly many moderate but loyal Republicans upstate willing to go to the Liberal line to vote for me but who would never have voted for a Democrat from Brooklyn.

It had been suggested in the press that before announcing her own candidacy Holtzman should have come to me, another liberal, to find out if I was going to retire. I do not go along with that idea. She was not obliged to ask me — and by the same token, I had no obligation to withdraw in her favor when she found herself in trouble as the election approached.

As the campaign neared its end, I began to have problems with my trade union support. The state AFL-CIO had supported me in the primary, which was extremely unusual, but my loss of the primary and my failure to get an independent line on the ballot cost me the backing of a number of public-employees' unions, notably District 37 State & Municipal Workers, headed by Victor Gotbaum. Indeed, Gotbaum tried to persuade the New York State AFL-CIO to withdraw its endorsement of me on the grounds that votes for the Liberal Party would hurt President Carter. But Ray Corbett, president of the New York State AFL-CIO, Harry Van Arsdale, president of the New York City Central Labor Council, representing employees of the private sector, and Al Shanker, president of the United Federation of Teachers, stood fast. As late as October 23, thirteen prominent New York State labor leaders joined in a statement rejecting the suggestion that I withdraw and urging me to continue to "campaign strongly" because New York needed my "unquestioned power and influence in the Senate." Among the labor leaders signing that statement were Corbett, Van Arsdale, Shanker, and Tom Hobart, president of the New York State United Teachers.

But a week later, with the polls showing no improvement in my position, the Teachers Union got worried. Shanker came to see me about ten days before the election to discuss the problem, and a few days later Hobart informed me that the Teachers Union, also a public-employees' union, had to withdraw its support; its members, he said, were straining at the leash to vote for Holtzman to prevent a D'Amato victory and to be sure that Carter got every vote that he could in New York.

And so, although I still retained the official endorsement of the New York State AFL-CIO and of the New York City Central Labor Council, I lost an important element of union help at the eleventh hour. It was most distressing and discouraging, but I continued in the race, my spirits considerably uplifted by the fact that I had the endorsement of most of the major newspapers in the state, including the *Rochester Times-Union,* the *Rochester Democratic Chronicle,* the *Buffalo Evening News,* and the *Syracuse Post-Standard,* plus all the papers that had backed me in the primary except the *Times.*

In the final week of the campaign, after the Carter-Reagan debate, the U.S. electorate shifted massively from Carter to Reagan. It was a glacial shift that took a few days to manifest itself, but by election day it reached its crest. The Republican Party and the country were swept by a conservative tide.

Alfonse D'Amato was clearly a part of that tide, and in the final analysis that was what brought him his narrow victory. Governor

Reagan carried the state with 2,894,000 votes, a plurality of 166,000 over President Carter, while D'Amato won with only 2,699,000 votes, 45.1 percent of the total, a margin of 81,000 over Holtzman, who received 43.7 percent.

Not surprisingly, some of the people who had urged me to withdraw blamed me for Holtzman's defeat, and the closeness of the vote between D'Amato and Holtzman does give colorable support to their claim. A careful analysis of the vote conducted by my staff indicated that in the Reagan landslide — a situation which Miss Holtzman's friends never' contemplated — D'Amato would have still been elected (by about sixty-seven thousand votes instead of eighty-one thousand) if I had withdrawn from the race.

My final vote tally of only 11 percent (half of what was predicted by the final preelection polls) was a disappointment, of course, but liberal and progressive senators and representatives all across the country were turned out of office that day. My ballgame was lost in the primary. I would have lost more had I stepped away from what I felt was my responsibility, had I decided not to seek a fifth Senate term. The voters of New York dismissed me, but they had also made me what I am in politics; they had given me an unparalleled opportunity to serve, and I am satisfied.

*　*　*

On the Sunday afternoon before the election I took the violinist Isaac Stern and his wife, Vera, and my family to the Lower East Side. It was a campaign ritual: In every statewide election I had made the pilgrimage to Stanton and Orchard streets to renew old ties, refresh my recollection of old sites, and revive my feelings for the place and the people of my origins. This time the moment was especially poignant, for the polls were erasing the dreams of electoral miracles. I felt that my career as a senator was about to end.

First we went to Delancey Street for lunch at Ratner's, which has been a dairy restaurant since the beginning of time, it seems, though I do not know whether the original Ratner family is still in charge. The barley soup and the matzoh-ball soup and the cheese blintzes were as good as ever, and as I sat with the Sterns and my family in the midst of the Sunday throng, many patrons came to our table to shake hands or have a word with me and I began to shed the tensions of the campaign.

After lunch we rode the two blocks to Orchard Street, which is still a major shopping area. The pushcarts of my youth are gone now, their place taken by sidewalk stands displaying the wares of dozens of small shops. People from all over New York and neighboring states come to Orchard Street on Sunday to shop for bargains in everything from suits and dresses to handbags, notions, toys, and groceries. As we walked up the middle of the narrow street, closed to vehicles, at least every other person stopped to shake my hand. My campaign workers gave out handbills and I took great pleasure in introducing Isaac Stern to as many people as I could.

At the corner of Stanton and Orchard I pointed out to Isaac and Vera the building where I had been born, which was now boarded up, and I described the scene as it had been so many years before: the swarming tenements, the street full of pushcarts and the shouts of the hawkers — including me. I felt detached from the campaign just ending and from the unhappy arithmetic of the polls. I felt warmly received, completely at one with the world in which I was moving and as if it had always been this way. I remembered my boyhood on these streets, and my father toiling in the hallways of the tenements, and the hard struggle of our neighbors' lives — and I thought of where I had gone and what I had done. And as I shook hands with so many people there on the street corner where it all began for me, I realized that they knew what I was and that they knew what I had accomplished for them and for all of us, and I saw that one defeat meant little on the long road I have traveled.

Index

Index

Abel, I. W., 381
Abourezk, James, 252
Abrams, Robert, 441
Abs, Herman, 287
Academy of Arts and Sciences, 95
Acheson, Dean, 179
Actors' Equity, 309, 311
Adams, Sherman, 219, 220
Adams Chronicles, The, 319
ADELA Investment Company, 458–59. *See also* Atlantic Community Development Group for Latin America
Adenauer, Konrad, 188
Adler, Jacob, 305
Admiration Clothes, 11
AFL-CIO, 388; New York State, 505–6
Agnelli, Giovanni, 457
Agnew, Spiro, 360, 370, 415, 418
Agriculture, Department of, 108
Aiken, George D., 299, 334, 388
Albert, Carl, 418
Allen, James, 252, 375–76
Allende, Salvador, 424
Alliance for Progress, 457, 462
Amalgamated Clothing Workers' Union, 389
American Academy of Dramatic Arts, 313
American Council for the Arts, 318
American Federation of Musicians, 312
American Guild of Musical Artists, 312
American Israel Public Affairs Committee (AIPAC), 167, 279–80
American Jewish Committee, 83, 213, 279

American Jewish Congress, 279, 281, 483
American Labor Party (ALP), 86, 87, 95, 99, 111, 437; Communist influence in, 215–16; and accusations against JKJ, 225, 226, 233, 234, 235, 237
American Legion, 165
American Medical Association (AMA), 146, 147, 293, 300
American Motors, 353
American Oil Company, 83
Americans for Democratic Action, 153
American Veterans Committee (AVC), 102–3, 142
Anderson, Clinton P., 334; national health-care proposal of, 295–99, 365
Anderson, John, 503
Anglo-American Committee of Inquiry on Palestine, 83, 108
Arab League, 178, 282
Arden, Eve, 59
Arnold, Henry "Hap," 66
Art in America magazine, 309
Arts Endowment, 316–17, 318, 319
Assad, Hafez al-, 477–79
Associated Press, 108
Association of Committees for Inter-American Placement (ACIP), 57–58, 62, 363
Atlantic Community Development Group for Latin America (ADELA), 457–59, 462
Atomic Energy Commission, 317
Aurelio, Richard, 395
Austin, Warren, 167, 177

Badillo, Herman, 441
Baker, Howard, 269–70, 485, 488, 501
Baker, Walter C., 58–59
Balfour Declaration (1917), 83
Baltimore Sun, 228
Bank of Tokyo, 457
Bar Association of New York, 40
Baron, Murray, 234, 235, 237
Beame, Abe, 374, 441
Beard, Charles, 21
Beard, Mary, 21
Begin, Menachem, 289, 477, 480, 482, 483–85
Belkin, Samuel, 98
Bellamy, Ralph, 311
Ben-Gurion, David, 178, 180, 272, 276, 288, 482; JKJ's meeting with, 273–74, 275
Ben-Gurion, Mrs. David, 288–89
Bennington College, 57
Bentsen, Lloyd, 384
Benzell, Mimi, 311
Berkman, Alexander, 14
Berle, Adolph A., Jr., 190
Bevin, Ernest, 179
Bickel, Alexander, 408
Bill of Rights Procedures Act, 417
Bingham, Jonathan, 461
Binghamton (New York) *Sun-Bulletin,* 200
Birk, Louis, 97
Black, Algernon, 14
Black, Eugene, 287
Blaustein, Jacob, 83
Bloom, Sol, 201
Blue Cross/Blue Shield, 147, 301
Blumenthal, Al, 374
B'nai B'rith, 279
Bolton, Frances, 143
Bonnet, Henri, 125
Bonnet, Madame, 125
Borris, Clara, 118–19
Borris, Marian. *See* Javits, Marian Borris
Bradley, Bill, 494
Bradley, Omar, 186
Brancusi, Constantin, *Bird in Space,* 308
Brandt, Willy, 188, 452, 453
Bransten, Louise, 81–82, 221–22, 230, 232–33, 237

Braque, Georges, 308
Brewster, Kingman, 58
Brezhnev Doctrine, 164
Bridgeport, Connecticut, *Sunday Herald,* 80, 84
Bridges, Harry, 82
Brisbane, Arthur, 22
Bristol-Meyers Corporation, 443
British Arts Council, 306
Bronx County Bar Association, 152
Brooke, Edward, 263, 401
Brookings Institution, 454
Brooklyn *Jewish Examiner,* 218–19
Brooks, Ned, 237
Brosio, Manlio, 454
Brown, Harold, 484
Brownell, Herbert, 221, 224, 226, 327
Brown University, 316
Brown v. *The Board of Education of Topeka, Kansas,* 321
Bryan, Frederick VanPelt, 208
Buckle, Henry Thomas, 28, 154, 162; *History of Civilization in England,* 21–22
Buckley, James, 358, 359, 360, 415, 441, 505; his call for Nixon resignation, 418–19; and threatened bankruptcy of New York City, 435; and Citizens Committee for New York City, 443
Buffalo Courier-Express, 223, 502
Buffalo Evening News, 506
Bundy, McGeorge, 406
Bureau of the Budget, 310, 313
Bureau of Public Relations, Inc., 78–79, 81, 89
Burnett, Daniel F., 23
Bush, George, 501
Business-Labor Working Group, 446
Butler, Nicholas Murray, 97
Byrd, Harry F., Sr., 308–9
Byrd, Robert C., 270, 391, 488

Camp David agreements, 481, 482, 483–84
Caputo, Bruce, 495
Carey, Hugh, 503
Carlyle, Thomas, 21
Carnegie Endowment for International Peace, 287

Carter, Jimmy, 289, 447, 464, 503, 506; and Carter Doctrine, 274; and national health care, 302; his attempt to rescue hostages. in Iran, 413–14, 489; and B-1 bomber, 450; nuclear targeting policy of, 455–56; Middle East policy of, 475–76, 481–82; and Camp David agreements, 483–84; and Israel-Egypt agreement, 484–86
Carter, Tim Lee, 303
Casals, Pablo, 310
Case, Clifford, 258, 299, 325, 339–40, 388, 494–95
Castro, Fidel, 423, 424, 425–26, 456
Castro, Ramon, 425
Castro, Raul, 423
Celler, Emanuel "Manny," 167, 174, 280, 306
Century Club (New York), 56
Champion, George, 441
Chase Manhattan Bank, 446
Chase National Bank, 41, 44, 53
Chelf, Frank, 169, 172–73, 175
Chemical Warfare Service (CWS), JKJ's work for, 58–60, 61–64, 65–66, 72, 76, 80, 84
Chicago, University of, 57
Chicago Lyric Opera Company, 312
Chicago Tribune, 238
Chiperfield, Robert B., 181–82
Chirac, Jacques, 453
Christian Front, 99
Church, Frank, 401, 403, 488
CIA (Central Intelligence Agency), 424, 425
Citizens' Committee for (Jack) Javits, 97, 103
Citizens Committee for New York City, 443–44
Citizens for Javits, 241
Citizens' Non-Partisan Committee (CNPC), 192, 194, 196, 197
Citizens' Union, 191
Civil Rights Act: (1960), 341–42; (1964), 266, 342, 343–46, 351
Civil Rights Commission, U.S., 341
Clark, Joseph S., 309, 312, 313
Clark, Ramsey, 416; his 1974 campaign against JKJ, 427–33
Clay, Lucius D., 185

Cloisters, 95
Clurman, Michael, 498
Clurman, Richard, 238, 420, 497, 498, 499
Clurman, Shirley, 420, 498
Cohn, Roy, 152, 218
Cole, Albert, 150–51
Collado, Emilio, 457
Columbia Law School, 103, 142
Columbia-Presbyterian Medical Center, 95
Columbia University, 22, 94, 95, 97, 98, 108; Eisenhower's presidency of, 220; Graduate School of Journalism at, 443
Comédie Française (France), 309
Commager, Henry Steele, 406
Commission of Fine Arts, 307
Committee for European Economic Cooperation, 182
Common Cause, 270, 428
Communist Party, 81, 82, 86, 87, 99; and Mundt-Nixon bill, 112, 151; and McCarthyism, 152; attempt to connect JKJ with, 213–38 passim
Community Mental Health Centers, 304
Conference on International Economic Cooperation (CIEC), 461, 462
Congressional Budget and Impoundment Control Act, 417
Congressional Quarterly Almanac, 390–91
Congressional Record, 133, 269
Conine, Ernest, 403
Connolly, Eugene P., 99–100, 103, 111, 216
Coolidge, Calvin, 45
Cooper, John Sherman, 299–300, 388, 401, 403, 408
Corbett, Ray, 506
Costello, Frank, 190
Council for the Encouragement of Music and the Arts (CEMA), 306
Cox, Archibald, 413, 418
Crews, John, 192, 201, 202, 224
Crone, Leonard, 24
Crown Zellerbach Corporation, 58, 81
Crum, Bartley C., 81, 82–83, 89, 108

Cummings, Frank, 380, 402
Curran, Tom, 96, 190–91, 204; and JKJ's New York City mayoral campaign, 192–99 *passim*
Curtis, Carl, 383, 384
Cusick, Peter, 56, 97, 195

Daily Worker, The, 81, 221, 231
D'Amato, Alfonse, 495; his 1980 campaign for Senate, 500–507
Danenberg, Leigh, 80
Darrow, Clarence, 82
Daughters of the American Revolution, 165
Davenport, Russell, 153
Davis, John W., 45
Davis, Murray, 237
Dean, Arthur, 459
Debs, Eugene, 14
DeConcini, Dennis, 464
De Gaulle, Charles, 286, 451, 452
Del Vecchio, Frank, 209
De Mille, Agnes, 305
Democratic Convention: (1924), 45; (1956), 222–23
Democratic Party, 11, 45, 95, 198, 201, 500
DeSapio, Carmine, 201
Dewey, Thomas E., 109, 111, 112, 113, 207, 493; and rent increases, 151, 193; JKJ's differences with, 192–93, 255; and JKJ's New York City mayoral campaign, 194, 196, 198–200, 371, 434; retirement of, 200, 202; and JKJ's campaign for attorney general of New York State, 202–3, 208, 209; urged to run for Senate, 219, 220; and JKJ's run for Senate, 222, 223, 224, 236–37, 238
Dirksen, Everett M., 184, 259, 263, 266; and civil rights, 338, 341, 344–46, 347; and cloture, 340
Dodd, Bella, 99, 231; accusations against JKJ, 213–14, 215–16, 221–22, 233–34, 235, 237
Donegan, Horace W. B., 148
Donovan, James B., 366
Dorn, William Jennings Bryan, 175
Douglas, Helen Gahagan, 161, 163–64

Douglas, Paul, 258, 261–62, 307; and civil rights, 325–29, 332, 333, 337, 338, 340, 341, 344
Drapkin, Arnold, 494
Dubinsky, David, 86, 88
Dulles, John Foster, 42–43, 44, 84, 239, 246, 249; and Sullivan and Cromwell, 42, 459; and Israel, 179–81, 202, 275; and Suez crisis, 247, 248
Dunham, Katherine, 311

Eagleton, Thomas F., and war powers issue, 403–13 *passim,* 416
Eastland, James O., 325, 326, 327, 330; and accusations against JKJ, 213–14, 221, 222, 223, 224, 229–35 *passim*
Eaton, Charles A., 159, 169, 177, 181–82
Eban, Abba, 469
Economic Cooperation Act (1948), 182
Ehrlich, Philip S., 81, 82, 83, 84, 216; and accusations against JKJ, 223, 230, 232, 233
Eilts, Herman, 477
Eisenhower, Dwight D., 68, 153, 191, 195, 217, 239; Views of, on Israel, 180, 181; and JKJ's run for Senate, 220, 246; and 1956 Republican National Convention, 223; and civil rights, 243, 323, 325, 327, 328, 336–37; his heart attack, 244; and Suez crisis, 246, 247, 248, 279; reelection of, 250–51; his friendship with JKJ, 255; and Soviet-Israeli arms deal, 272; and Ben-Gurion, 273; and Eisenhower Doctrine, 274–75;, 277; Middle East policy of, 276–77; opposition of, to Forand health plan, 293, 294; cities carried by, in 1956, 355; anti-union legislation of, 388
Eisenpreis, Alfred, 441
Elliott, Lowell A., 62
Elliott, Osborn, 443
Emergency Committee to Save Public Housing, 148
Emergency Financial Control Board (New York), 444–45

Emergency Ralley for Soviet Jewry, 473

Employment Retirement Income Security Act (ERISA), 378, 387, 422, 429; provisions of, 379–80; events leading to passage of, 380–85; passage of, 385; benefits of, 385–86

English, Paul X., 62–63

Equal Employment Opportunity Commission (EEOC), 343, 345, 346

Equal Rights Amendment (ERA), 110

ERISA. See Employment Retirement Income Security Act

Ervin, Sam, 260–61, 325, 328, 329, 330, 333

Espionage Act (1917), 19

European Economic Community (EEC), 184, 451, 454

European Recovery Program. See Marshall Plan

Evans, Rowland, 336

Evron, Ephraim, 485

Ewing, Oscar R., 146

Ewing Plan, 146, 147, 293

Exodus, 171

Eytan, Walter, 278

Fahd, Prince, 479, 480

Fair Employment Practices Committee (FEPC), 336

Farah Company, 389

Faubus, Orval, 336–37

Faw, Duane, 103, 142

FBI (Federal Bureau of Investigation), 221, 232, 429

Federal Housing Administration, 438

Feinstein, Herman, 11

Fiat, 457

Field, Frederick Vanderbilt, 80–81, 221, 231

Fight for Freedom Committee, 56, 97

Finkelstein, Louis, 98

First National City Bank of New York, 457

Fisher, Max, 282, 353–54

Fleming, Arthur, 300

Flynn, Daniel, 95, 99, 103, 111

Foley, Raymond, 148

Forand, Aime J., 293, 294, 295

Ford, George B., 98–99, 155

Ford, Gerald, 267, 374, 413, 445, 501, 503; and ERISA, 385, 422; and unemployment compensation, 387; confirmation of, as vice president, 418; and Middle East policy, 471, 475

Ford Foundation, 406, 457

Fortune magazine, 153

Freyberg, Morris, 101

Fristachi, Joe, 496, 497, 499

Frost, Robert, 309

Fulbright, William, 330, 393, 397, 467–68; and war powers issue, 408, 409, 410

Fulton, James, 117, 118, 120, 121, 158–59; and displaced persons, 169–70; 175; and accusations against JKJ, 229

Fusion Party, 85, 86, 189, 192, 193

Gardner, John, 428

Garment, Len, 318

Gavin, Leon H., 132–33, 135, 137

Gehrig, Lou, 501

General Electric Company, 58, 77, 78–79, 85, 89

General Investment Corporation, 53–54, 55, 59, 61

General Motors, 78

Ghorbal, Ashraf, 477

Gibbon, Edward, Decline and Fall of the Roman Empire, 21

Gifford, James P., 103

Gifford-Wood Company, 381

Giscard d'Estaing, Valéry, 445, 452, 453

Goldberg, Arthur, 281, 286, 310–11

Goldman, Emma, 14

Goldman, Manuel, 201

Goldsmith, Arthur, 195

Goldstein, Jonah, JKJ's work in mayoral campaign of, 85, 86–90, 92, 115, 189

Goldstein, Nathaniel, 200, 204

Goldwater, Barry, 266, 295, 300, 355, 357, 360; nomination of, for President, 347, 350–51; Conscience of a Conservative, 348; ultraconservative movement led by, 348–53,

Goldwater, Barry (cont.)
  357–58, 359; antiunion bill of,
  388; and war powers issue, 406–7,
  408, 413, 414; and Nixon resig-
  nation, 421; urged to run again
  for Senate, 492; and JKJ's 1980
  campaign for Senate, 501
Gonzalez del Solar, Julio, 457
Goodell, Charles, 360, 415, 505
Goodman, Roy, 494
Good Neighbor Policy, 462
Gordon, Mike, 384–85
Gossett, Ed, 148, 174
Gotbaum, Victor, 506
Great Depression, 20, 39, 53, 116
Green, Bill, 494
Green, Theodore Francis, 340
Gregerson, Halfdan, 57, 58, 363
Griffin, Robert P., 389
Groat, Bill, 234
Gross, H. R., 317
Gruening, Ernest, 284
Gwinn, Ralph W., 184

Hadassah, 279
Hager, Helen, 256
Haldeman, H. R., 418
Hall, Gladys, 237
Hall, Len, 215, 224, 237
Halleck, Charles, 141
Halley, Rudolph, 192, 194, 196, 197,
  198, 200
Hallstein, Walter, 454
Hammarskjöld, Dag, 276
Hanks, Nancy, 318
Harriman, Averell, 201, 207–10, 243,
  363, 364, 494
Hart, Philip, 262
Hartley, Fred A., 137–38
Harvard University, 57
Hatch, Orrin G., 390, 391
Hatfield, Mark O., 263, 401
Hatters' Union, 86
Hayakawa, Sam, 463
Hayes, Helen, 311
Hays, Mortimer, 53–54
Hays, Podell and Shulman, 53
Hayworth, Rita, 82
Health, Education and Welfare, De-
  partment of, 302, 310, 317
Health Insurance for the Aged Act,
  294

Hearst, William Randolph, 82
Hebrew University, 157
Heck, Oswald, 224
Heckscher, August, 313
Helsinki Declaration of Human
  Rights (1975), 449
Hennings, Thomas C., 325, 329
Herrera, Felipe, 457
Hershey, Lewis B., 363
Herter, Christian, 169, 195, 212, 244,
  281
Hertzberg, Arthur, 281
Hickok Manufacturing Company,
  382
Hill, Billy, 200–201, 224
Hill, Lister, 311
Hill, Robert C., 283
Hillquit, Morris, 13, 14
Hiss, Alger, 84
Hitler, Adolf, 55, 56, 57, 83, 108,
  271; and chemical warfare, 66;
  refugees from, 169
Hobart, Tom, 506
Holifield, Chet, 133, 161, 163
Holland, Spessard, 332, 338
Holtzman, Elizabeth, 503, 504–5,
  506, 507
Hoover, Herbert, 45
Hostages, American, in Iran, 486,
  488–89, 496
House Banking and Currency Com-
  mittee, 143
House Education and Labor Com-
  mittee, 137, 139
House Foreign Affairs Committee,
  136, 140, 143, 155, 158, 229; and
  food-relief bill, 159–63; successor
  to, 164; subcommittee of, on European refugees, 169–70; and
  European Recovery Program, 181;
  Subcommittee on Foreign Economic Policy of, 183; and U.S.
  occupation of Germany, 185; and
  aid to Israel, 280; Zablocki's chairmanship of, 405–6; and war powers issue, 409; and European unity,
  451
House International Relations Committee, 164
House Judiciary Committee, 169,
  172, 174; and Watergate, 418, 420,
  421

House Un-American Activities Committee, 151–52, 217, 232
House Ways and Means Committee, 294, 295, 300
Housing Act (1949), 145, 147, 148, 149
Housing and Home Finance Agency, 148
Hoveida, Amir Abbas, 487
Hughes, Harold, 303, 304
Hughes, Thomas L., 287
Humanities ·Endowment, 316–17, 318–19
Humphrey, Hubert, 258, 457; his support for the arts, 307, 309, 312–13; and civil rights, 325–26, 329, 333, 344
Hurok, Sol, 311
Hussein, King, 288, 465–66, 468, 469, 470

Immigration Act (1924), 109
Impellitteri, Vincent, 148, 189–90, 191, 440
Independent Veterans' Committee, 103
Information Agency, U.S. (USIA), 263–64
Institute of Museum Services, 319
Institute for Strategic Studies, 454
Inter-American Development Bank, 457
International Association of Machinists, 392
International Ladies' Garment Workers' Union (ILGWU), 86, 111
International Match Corporation, 40, 41
International Refugee Organization (IRO), 165, 169–70
International Trade Organization (ITO), 119, 169
Investors Fairplay League, 85
Iran, shah of, 486, 487, 488
Issues and Answers, 349
Ives, Irving, 166, 181, 275, 314, 337, 493; his campaign for governor of New York, 202–10 passim
Ives-Quinn bill, 202
Ivy Republican Club, 46
Izvestia, 179, 472–73

Jackson, Henry, 289, 467, 473–74
Jackson, Percival, 59
Jackson-Vanik Trade Act amendment, 279, 473–74
Javits, Benjamin (brother), 2, 5, 6, 12, 18, 85; abandoning of orthodoxy by, 8–10, 13; his influence on JKJ, 12–15, 16, 19–20; his job as debt collector, 20, 21, 24; law practice of, 23, 25, 40, 48; disagreements between JKJ and, 25–26, 52–53, 55–56; marriage of, 26; JKJ's letters from Europe to, 27–38; and Kreuger case, 41–42; financial relationship between JKJ and, 50–51, 52, 129; his faith in corporate business system, 52–53, 77; and World War II, 55–56; and election of 1940, 57; closeness between JKJ and, 64; and JKJ's first congressional campaign, 97, 103; and Marian Javits, 116, 117; and accusations against his brother, 215; and JKJ's campaign for Senate, 241; death of, 416
Javits, Carla (daughter), 129–30, 211, 214, 318, 493; birth of, 124, 128
Javits, Ida Littman (mother), 4–5, 7–8, 11–12, 16, 25; characterized, 9, 17, 19; her move to Brooklyn, 14–15; death of her husband, 15; remarriage of, 26; and Marian Javits, 116
Javits, Jacob K.
  PERSONAL DATA: birth and early years, 1–15; public-speaking talent of, 6, 18, 175; influence of brother Benjamin on, 12–15, 16, 19–20; first political awareness of, 13; death of his father, 15, 18; education of, 16–26 passim; early political activities of, 18–19; early jobs of, 21, 23–25; disagreements between brother Benjamin and, 25–26, 52–53, 55–56; admitted to the bar, 26, 27; his letters to Benjamin from Europe, 27–38; law practice of, 38–39, 48–49, 123; and Kreuger case, 39–44, 45, 46; and Tammany corruption, 45–

Javits, Jacob K. (cont.)
46; and La Guardia, 46; and Standard Gas & Electric Company case, 46–48; marriage of, to Marjorie Ringling, 49–51; financial relationship between Ben and, 50–51, 52, 129; his divorce from Marjorie Ringling, 51; and General Investment Corporation case, 53–54, 55, 59, 61; his role in World War II, 55–76 *passim;* and election of 1940, 57; and Chemical Warfare Service (CWS), 58–60, 61–64, 65–66, 72, 76; and Hollace Shaw, 59–61, 63, 65, 69, 70–71, 81; health of, 63–64, 494, 495, 497, 501; and army's Command and General Staff College, 64–65; his wartime tour of Europe and North Africa, 66–69; his wartime tour of Pacific, 72–74, 75; his work for General Electric Company, 77–79; and United Nations founding conference, 80, 83–84, 221, 232; and Jonah Goldstein's campaign for mayor of New York, 85–90; and Marian Borris, 88–89, 113; marriage of, to Marian Borris, 114–31; births of his children, 121, 122, 124; in New York politics, 189–212; his refusal of New York city council presidency, 190–91; accusations against, 213–38; *Order of Battle,* 348; *Who Makes War,* 402; agony of his decision to run for 1980 reelection, 491–99
CAMPAIGNS: first congressional (1946), 91–111 *passim;* second congressional (1948), 111–13; for attorney general of New York State, 128, 200–212; for mayor of New York City, 191–200; for Senate (1956), 239–51 *passim;* for Senate (1962), 365–67; for Senate (1968), 357–58, 359–60; for Senate (1974), 415–16, 422, 427–33; for Senate (1980), 490–91, 499–508

CONGRESSMAN IN DOMESTIC AFFAIRS, 132–37; on labor-management relations, 137–40; on housing, 140–45, 147–49; on rent control, 145–46, 149–51; on national health care, 146–47; on civil liberties and subversion, 151–53
CONGRESSMAN IN FOREIGN AFFAIRS, 154–56; and Jewish homeland in Palestine, 156–57, 165, 166–69, 175, 176–78; 182; and food-relief bill for Greece and Turkey, 159–64; and displaced persons, 164–66, 169–75; and United States and Israel, 178–81; and Marshall Plan, 181–84; and West Germany, 184–88
SENATOR IN DOMESTIC AFFAIRS, 252–56, 264–68; and civil rights, 256, 259–62, 268–69, 320–46; and Senate Rule XXII (cloture issue), 256–59, 264, 269–70, 322, 324, 340, 346, 375–76; and Wednesday Club, 262–63; and Lyndon Johnson, 263–64; on national health care, 291–304; on venereal disease, 302–3; on marijuana, 303–4; on alcoholism, 304; and the arts, 305–19; and division within Republican Party, 347–53, 355; vice-presidential foray of, 353–57; and New York Conservative Party, 357–58, 359–60; and Richard Nixon, 358–59; and 1976 Republican National Convention, 360–61; and Nelson Rockefeller, 362–77; his refusal to run for mayor of New York City, 371–72; labor legislation shaped by, 378–92; and presidential war powers, 402–14; and Watergate, 416–17, 433; and problem of Nixon resignation, 417–22, 427; and threatened bankruptcy of New York City, 434–47
SENATOR IN FOREIGN AFFAIRS, 448; and United States and Israel, 271–90; and Vietnam War, 393–401, 403; his trip to

Cuba, 422–27; and US-USSR competition, 449–51; and work for NATO, 451–52, 454, 456, 457; and SALT I, 454–55; and SALT II, 455–56; and ADEIA, 457–59; and LDCs, 460–62; and Panama Canal debate, 462–64; and Middle East, 465–72, 475–86; and persecution of Jews in Soviet Union, 472–75; and crisis in Iran, 486–89

Javits, Joan (niece), 118
Javits, Joshua (son), 124, 129–30, 359, 493, 498; birth of, 122
Javits, Joy Deborah (daughter), 122, 124, 129–30, 399, 493; birth of, 121
Javits, Lily (sister-in-law), 26, 27, 50, 116; and JKJ's letters from Europe, 29, 32–33, 35
Javits, Marian Borris (second wife), 88–89, 113; marriage of, to JKJ, 114–31; births of her children, 121, 122, 124; on accusations against her husband, 214–15; and JKJ's campaign for Senate, 241; and the arts, 305, 306, 307, 313, 317; and Vietnam War, 399–400; and Watergate, 420; and Iran Airlines, 486–87; 488; and JKJ's decision to run for reelection in 1980, 492–93, 497
Javits, Marjorie Ringling (first wife), 49–51, 305
Javits, Moore and Trubin, 212
Javits, Morris (father), 2–5, 8–9, 11; death of, 15, 18
Javits & Javits, 25, 38, 58, 66, 85, 123; and Kreuger case, 39–44; and Standard Gas & Electric Company case, 46–48; and General Investment Corporation case, 53–54, 61; and JKJ's campaign for attorney general of New York State, 204
Jefferson, Thomas, 402
Jenner, William, 231, 235, 236, 237, 238
Jenner-Butler bill, 264
Jewish Agency, 282
Jewish Agency for Palestine, 157
Jewish Memorial Hospital, 121

Jewish Theological Seminary, 95, 98
John F. Kennedy Center for the Performing Arts, 308
Johns, Jasper, 313
Johnson, Joseph E., 287
Johnson, Lyndon B., 263–64, 266, 281, 295, 314; and Senate Rule XXII, 258–59; Middle East policy of, 285; and national health care, 297, 300; and humanities foundation, 316, 317; and civil rights, 323–25, 328, 329, 331, 335–46 passim; and 1964 presidential election, 351, 352, 353; Vietnam policy of, attacked by Romney, 356; and 1968 New Hampshire primary, 369; his withdrawal from presidential contest, 370; and pension regulations, 380; and Vietnam War, 394, 397, 398, 402; and Ramsey Clark, 428–29; and sale of jets to Israel, 466
Joint Committee on Internal Revenue Taxation, 384
Joint Economic Committee, 265, 377
Joint (Senate-House) Committee on National and International Movements, 152, 153
Jordahl, Anders, 43–44
J. P. Stevens Company, 389
Judd, Walter, 229–30, 280–81
Juilliard School of Music, 95
Justice Department, 223, 226, 323, 326, 342; and Vietnam War, 400; and Watergate, 413; Ramsey Clark's administration of, 428

Kaiser-Permanente plan, 147
Katz, Michael, 19, 292
Kaufman, Bob, 206
Keating, Barbara, 415–16, 432-33
Keating, Kenneth B., 299–300, 314, 337–38, 341, 416
Keeney, Barnaby C., 316
Kefauver committee, 190, 192
Keller, Ernst, 458
Kelley, Sheila, 206, 208, 240–41
Kemp, Jack, 490–91, 495
Kemp-Roth bill, 491
Kempton, Murray, 366
Kenen, Isaiah "Si," 167, 279–80

Kenna, Frank, 190–91, 192, 194, 198, 199
Kennedy, Edward, 287, 301, 302
Kennedy, John F., 84, 103, 139, 147, 266, 437; on housing, 142, 143; and 1956 Democratic Convention, 222–23; national health-insurance proposal of, 293–300; his support for arts establishment, 309–10, 312, 313; assassination of, 313–14; and civil rights, 334, 342, 343; troops sent by, to University of Mississippi, 350; cities carried by, in 1960, 355; and Catholic issue, 355; labor legislation introduced by, 388; and Vietnam War, 402; his Alliance for Progress, 457
Kennedy, Robert F., 342, 345, 360, 369, 399, 441; assassination of, 415
Kenney, George, 73
Kent State University, 400
Kerr, Robert, 300
Kerr-Mills Act, 299, 300
Kessler, David, 305
Khalid, King, 479–80
Khan, Aly, 82
Khomeini, Ayatollah, 486
Kidder, Peabody, 53
King, Martin Luther, Jr., 342; assassination of, 370
Kissinger, Henry, 95, 256, 267–68, 422, 460; and US-Israel relations, 282; and Middle East peace, 468–69, 471, 475; *White House Years*, 469; and persecution of Jews in Soviet Union, 473–74
Klein, Arthur, 177
Knowland, William, 327, 328, 336
Koch, Ed, 435–36, 446, 491
Koenig, Julian, 430
Koenig, Sam, 92, 234
Korean War, 153, 186, 244
Kramer, Morris, 101
Kreuger, Ivar, 39, 40–44, 45
Kreuger and Toll, 41, 42–44, 46
Krupp, Alfred, 187
Kuchel, Thomas, 300, 329, 344
Ky, Nguyen Cao, 395, 397

Labor, Department of, 143, 382
Labor-relations laws, failure to reform, 388, 389–92

La Follette, Robert, 349
La Guardia, Fiorello, 46, 57, 59, 189, 198, 436; and 1945 New York mayoral campaign, 85, 86, 87, 89; and JKJ's New York City mayoral campaign, 192; progressive Republicanism of, 349; his cleanup of New York City, 439–40
La Guardia, Marie, 192
Lakeland, Peter, 278–79, 402, 408, 411, 480
Landrum, Phil M., 389
Landrum-Griffin Act (1959), 388, 389
Larson, Arthur, 263
Latin American Institute (Washington), 62
Lawley, Ray, 201
Lawrence, Gertrude, 123
Lawrence, Jock, 195
Lax and Burgheimer, 24
League of Nations, 83, 156, 177
Lee, Higginson and Company, 41 42
Lefkowitz, Louis, 364, 372
Lehman, Herbert, 198, 218–19, 220, 222, 239, 503; retirement of, 223; and the arts, 306
Leinsdorf, Erich, 311
Lepler, Samuel, 94, 95, 234
Less-developed countries (LDCs), 460–62
Liberal Party, 86, 87, 88, 416; and JKJ's 1946 congressional campaign, 95, 96, 99–100, 101–3, 216; and JKJ's 1948 congressional campaign, 111; and JKJ's New York City mayoral campaign, 192, 193, 194, 195–96, 197
Library of Congress, 317
Liebman, Joshua Loth, 119
Life magazine, 234
Lincoln, Abraham, 348, 352
Lincoln Center Opera House (New York), 312
Lincoln Center for the Performing Arts (New York), 313
Lindsay, John, 310, 311, 365, 369, 493, 503; and New York City mayoralty, 373, 440
Lodge, Henry Cabot, Jr., 153, 276, 295, 395
Lodge, John Davis, 158–59, 195, 463

Loeb, John, Sr., 212, 241
Loevin, Sidney, 101
London, Meyer, 13
Long, Russell, 262, 332, 382–84, 386, 387
Long Island Press, 228
Los Angeles Times, 403
Luce, Clare Boothe, 123
Luce, Henry R., 123, 153, 241
Lundy, James, 364

MacArthur, Douglas, 72, 73
McCarran, Pat, 174, 175, 223
McCarran Internal Security Act, 152, 218
McCarthy, Eugene, 369
McCarthy, Joseph, 103, 142, 152, 215, 218, 236; censuring of, 255
McClellan, John, 304
McCloy, John J., 186, 494
McCook, Philip J., 53–54
McCrary, Tex, 220, 226, 236, 255
McGee, Gale, 460
McGovern, George, 401
McGovern, R. Raymond, 209, 224, 238
Mack, Julian, 43
McNamara, Pat, 328
Macomber, William B., Jr., 287–88
"MAD" (Mutual Assured Destruction), 455
Magnes, Judah, 157
Mahoney, J. Daniel, 357
Malkin, Herbert, 195
Mandel, Benjamin, 232
Manes, Donald, 491
Manhattanville College, 95
Mansfield, Mike, 161, 289, 314, 344, 346, 375
Manuilski, Dimitri, 223
Marcantonio, Vito, 145, 437
Marchi, John, 373, 374
Margiotta, Joseph, 500, 501, 503
Marley, Harry, 201
Marshall, George C., 167, 177, 182, 236
Marshall Plan (European Recovery Program), 93, 169, 179, 181–84, 451, 452
Martin, Joseph W., Jr., 136–37
Marx, Karl, 22; *Das Kapital,* 21
Massachusetts General Hospital, 495

Mathias, Charles, 375, 407, 417
Matthews, Steve, 496, 497, 499
Maudling, Reginald, 287
Mayo Clinic, 497
Medicare, 297, 299, 300–301, 305, 316
Meet the Press, 236, 237–38
Meir, Golda, 176–77, 276, 277, 278–79, 288; her meeting with Senate, 289; JKJ's meetings with, in Israel, 465, 469; and sale of jets to Israel, 468; and Yom Kippur war, 471; funeral of, 484
Melody, Jim, 6–7, 11
Meredith, James, 350
Metropolitan Opera (New York), 310, 311
Metzenbaum, Howard, 252
Michelsen, Alfonso López, 463
Middle East Commission, 287
Miki, Kunio, 457
Millbank Tweed & Hope, 54
Miller, William E., 350
Mills, Wilbur, 294, 300
MIRVs, 455
Mississippi, University of, 350
Mitchell, Clarence, 322–23
Mitchell, John, 418
Mittleman, Mr. (JKJ's teacher), 17, 66
Mondale, Walter, 375
Moore, George, 457
Moore, James, 211–12, 230
Morgenthau, Robert, 366
Morgenthau plan, 185, 186
Morhouse, L. Judson, 224, 225, 226–27, 230
Morris, Newbold, 85–86, 87, 89, 104, 241
Morris, Richard B., 406
Morris, Robert, 214, 222, 235, 238; his questioning of JKJ in Senate committee hearing, 230–34
Morse, Wayne, 104, 283, 334, 392
Moynihan, Daniel Patrick, 447
Mudge, Stern, Williams & Tucker, 54
Mundt, Karl E., 162–63, 328
Mundt-Nixon bill, 112, 151, 162, 217, 244
Municipal Assistance Corporation (New York), 444

Murphy, Richard, 478
Museum of Modern Art (New York), 308
Muskie, Edmund S., 417
Mussolini, Benito, 33
Mutual Security Act (1953), 181, 283
Mutual Security Agency, 201
Mutual Security Assistance bill, 280–81
Myerson, Bess, 503, 504
Myrdal, Gunnar, 287

Nasser, Gamal Abdel, 247, 273–74, 276–77, 283–84, 285; and Six-Day War, 286
National Association for the Advancement of Colored People (NAACP), 148, 322
National Civil Liberties Clearing House, 152
National Commission on Marijuana and Drug Abuse, 303–4
National Committee on Health Care of the Aging, 300
National Council on the Arts, 312, 315
National Council of Jewish Women, 279
National Endowment for the Arts, 140
National Foundation on the Arts and Humanities, 305, 306, 316–19
National Foundation on the Arts and Humanities Act, 317–18
National Health Insurance for Mothers and Children Act, 301–2
National Heart Act (1948), 146
National Heart Institute, 146
National Institute on Alcohol Abuse and Alcoholism, 304
National Institutes of Health, 311
National Labor Relations Act (1935), 389
National Labor Relations Board (NLRB), 388, 389–90
National Liberation Front (NLF), 399
National Music Council, 307
National Paper Trade Association, 70

National Public Housing Conference, 144
National Recovery Act, 51
National Republican Club, 153
National Rifle Association, 502
National Security Act (1947), 402–3
National Veterans' Housing Conference, 142–43
National Women's Party, 110
NATO (North Atlantic Treaty Organization), 164, 184, 266, 285, 351, 407; France's withdrawal from, 450, 452; JKJ's work on committees of, 451–52 454, 456, 457; Committee of Nine of, 454; and ADELA, 459
Nelson, Gaylord, 384, 386–87
Neuberger, Richard, 264
Neutrality Treaty, 462–64
Newsday, 238, 420
Newsweek, 443
Newton, Audrey Swift, 97
New York City, threatened bankruptcy of, 434–47
New York City Central Labor Council, 446, 506
New York Conservative Party, 357–58, 359–60, 415, 432–33
New York Daily Mirror, 196, 228
New York Daily News, 194, 196, 216, 427, 445; and JKJ's 1980 campaign for reelection, 501, 502
New York Evening Journal, 22
New York Herald Tribune, 30, 197, 336, 363, 395; JKJ's campaign letters to, 92–94, 97, 100, 104, 140, 154; on JKJ's campaign for Senate, 241, 242
New York for Javits, 196
New York Partnership, 446
New York Post, 194, 196, 209, 228, 366, 372; and JKJ's 1980 campaign for reelection, 502, 505
New York State United Teachers, 504, 506
New York State Teachers Union, 99, 233
New York Times, 43, 135, 194, 197, 254, 269; on JKJ's campaign for attorney general of New York State, 208, 209; and JKJ's alleged Communist affiliations, 227–28,

234, 235; on JKJ's campaign for Senate, 241–42; on Social Security amendment, 299; on civil rights, 325; *Magazine*, JKJ's article in, 352–53; on Romney's brainwashing statement, 356; and Rockefeller announcement of his candidacy for President, 370; and Nixon resignation, 420; its endorsement of JKJ's reelections, 433, 502; on D'Amato campaign for Senate, 500; on JKJ's 1980 campaign, 502, 503, 505
New York University Law School, 22, 23
New York World-Telegram, 237, 249
Nguyen Cao Ky, 395, 397
Nields, John P., 47–48
Niles, David K., 63, 66, 89, 119
Nimitz, Chester, 72–73
Nitze, Paul, 456
Nixon, Richard, 164, 212, 223, 235, 243–44, 318; and Senate Rule XXII, 257; and Golda Meir, 289; and health insurance plan, 294–98, 301; and alcoholism legislation, 304; in eclipse, 353, 358, 359; nomination of, for President, 357; JKJ's relationship with, 358–59; and Rockefeller presidential campaign, 364–65; and 1968 presidential campaign, 369, 370, 371; on JKJ's run for mayor of New York City, 371; and Vietnam War, 400, 401, 402, 409; and War Powers Resolution, 402, 408, 410, 413, 414, 416, 430; and Watergate, 409, 413, 417–22, 433; and NATO Parliamentarians' Conference, 451; and support for Israel, 466–67
Norris, George, 57, 200, 349
Norris–La Guardia Committee, 57

O'Doherty, Keiran, 357, 358
O'Dwyer, Paul, 107, 111, 112, 113, 360
O'Dwyer, William, 85, 86, 87, 89, 107, 144; resignation of, as New York City mayor, 189; and organized crime, 190; rise of city debt during administration of, 440

Office of Price Administration (OPA), 100–101, 110, 133–34, 184
O'Mahoney, Joseph C., 328
OPEC (Organization of Petroleum Exporting Countries), 426, 460, 461, 470, 489
Operation Overlord, 70
Organization of American States, 426
Organization for Economic Cooperation and Development (OECD), 452, 457, 458
Ostpolitik, 452, 453

Palestine Liberation Organization (PLO), 431–32, 476, 478–79, 481
Paley, William, 241
Palmer, Archibald, 38
Panama Canal debate, 462–64
Panama Canal Treaty, 462–64
Pastore, John, 262
Patterson, John, 441
Patterson, Robert P., 162
Peace Corps, 103
Pearl Harbor day, 59, 60
Pearson, Drew, 135, 165
Pearson, James, 263
Pearson, Lester, 287, 454
Peccei, Aurelio, 457
Pell, Claiborne, 311, 313, 314–15, 427; and humanities foundation, 316, 319; and U.S. policy toward Cuba, 422; his visit to Cuba, 422–26
Pension Benefit Guarantee Corporation, 380
Pension Commission, U.S., proposed, 380
Pension Reform Act. *See* Employment Retirement Income Security Act
Percy, Charles, 263
Pérez, Carlos Andrés, 463
Petrofina, 457
Pette, Nicholas, 88
Pfeifer, Joseph, 169
Phillips, Cabell, 325
Picasso, Pablo, 308
Pinto, Ed, 488
Pius XII, Pope, 35–36, 155
Plessy v. *Ferguson*, 321

PM, 171
Portal-to-Portal Act, 132–33, 137
Porter, William, 61, 62, 64, 79
Posner, Jerome, 494
Powell v. *Texas,* 304
Pratt, Robert, 381–82
Price Control Act, 100
Pritikin Institute of Diet and Exercise, 497
Progressive Party, 112
Proskauer, Joseph, 83
Prouty, Winston L., 340
Proxmire, William, 444–45; *The Fleecing of America,* 447
Pryor, Sam, 136

Qaddafi, Muammar al-, 469
Queen Mary, 117, 158

Randolph, A. Philip, 343
Rankin, John, 160, 175
Rassemblement Pour la République (RPR), 453
Ratner's, 507
Rauschenberg, Robert, 313
Reagan, Ronald, 503, 506, 507
Reconstruction Finance Corporation, 83
Regan, Ned, 493–94
Reid, Ogden R., 394–95
Rein, Norman, 99, 103
Republican Advance, 153, 190
Republican National Committee, 350, 352
Republican National Convention: (1956), 222–23; (1964), 347, 350–51, 360; (1976), 360–61
Republican Party, 11, 85, 86, 87; JKJ's enrollment in, 44, 45–46; and JKJ's 1946 campaign for congressional seat, 91–111 *passim,* 216; its control of both houses of Congress, 134, 135; and JKJ's New York City mayoral campaign, 192, 193, 194, 195, 196, 197; divisions within, 347–53, 355, 357–61
Republicans for Progress, 352
Rhodes, John, 421
Ribicoff, Abraham, 268–69, 289, 461, 467, 473; and unemployment compensation, 386–87

Rich, Robert F., 174–75
Richards, James P., 229
Richardson, Elliot L., 418
Riegelman, Harold, 199, 200
Ringling, Alfred, 49
Ringling, John, 49, 50, 51
Ringling, Marjorie. *See* Javits, Marjorie Ringling
Ringling Brothers, Barnum and Bailey Circus, 50
Ripon Society, 153
Rochester Democratic Chronicle, 506
Rochester Times-Union, 506
Rockefeller, David, 192, 446
Rockefeller, Happy, 367
Rockefeller, Nelson A., 84, 153, 212, 264, 353, 493; and Inter-American Affairs, 58, 362, 363; and JKJ's campaign for Senate, 241; arts council established by, 309; re-election of, as governor, 312; and 1964 Republican National Convention, 350, 351; and Romney-Javits ticket for President, 354; JKJ's support for, 357, 359; progressive Republicanism of, 357–58; and New York Conservative Party, 360; JKJ's relationship with, 362–77; vice presidency of, 374–76; death of, 377, 500; his campaign contribution to JKJ, 427–28
Rockefeller Brothers Fund, 318
Rodgers, Richard, 311
Rodriguez, Carlos Rafael Rodriguez, 425
Roffman, Dick, 97
Rogers, Paul G., 303
Rogers, William P., 406, 466, 467
Rohatyn, Felix, 444
Roll, Sir Eric, 287
Roman, Sam, 146, 195, 212, 224
Romney, George, 369; his attempt to obtain nomination for President, 353–57, 359, 367–68
Roosevelt, Eleanor, 16
Roosevelt, Franklin D., 45–46, 63, 86, 201; JKJ's support for, 56–57, 239; death of, 80; and civil rights, 243, 321; and the arts, 307; New Deal of, 349

Roosevelt, Franklin D., Jr., 128, 142, 239, 240; his nomination for attorney general of New York State, 201–11 passim
Root, Oren, 241
Roper, Elmo, 97, 104
Rose, Alex, 86, 88, 96, 374; and accusations against JKJ, 225, 233, 234, 235
Rosenbaum, David, 269
Rosenthal, Hal, 287
Royal Ballet (Great Britain), 309
Rubinstein, Artur, 88
Ruckelshaus, William D., 418
Ruder and Finn, 486–87
Rusk, Dean, 285
Russell, Richard B., 256, 258, 259–60, 291; and civil rights, 259, 260, 261, 323–46 passim

Sacco-Vanzetti case, 30–31
Sadat, Anwar, 469, 470, 475, 479, 482–83; JKJ's meetings with, in Egypt, 476–77; and Camp David agreements, 483–84; and Egypt-Israel agreement, 484–85
SALT I, 454–55
SALT II, 455–56, 474, 493, 496
Sapir, Pinchas, 465
"Saturday Night Massacre," 413, 418
Saud al-Faisal, Prince, 480–81, 484
Scheuer, James H., 301
Schmidt, Helmut, 188, 445, 453
Schwartz, Arthur, 87–88, 89, 234, 241; and JKJ's first congressional campaign, 92, 94, 95
Scott, Hugh, 289, 421, 467
Scranton, William, 350–51
Seabury, Samuel, 45
SEATO (Southeast Asia Treaty Organization), 393, 406
Securities and Exchange Commission, 54, 380
Select Committee on Foreign Aid, 169
Selective Service System, 363
Senate Appropriations Committee, 134, 259, 260
Senate Armed Services Committee, 259, 404

Senate Banking, Housing, and Urban Affairs Committee, 444–45, 447
Senate Banking and Currency Committee, 206, 265
Senate Committee on Government Affairs, 304
Senate Finance Committee, 295, 309, 382–84, 474; and unemployment compensation, 386–87
Senate Foreign Relations Committee, 161, 260, 265, 266, 292, 495; Western Hemisphere Subcommittee of, 377; Fulbright's chairmanship of, 393, 467–68; and Cambodian incursion, 402; and war powers issue, 406, 408; and U.S. policy toward Cuba, 426, 427; and nuclear weaponry, 456; and crisis in Iran, 486, 488; JKJ as ranking minority member on, 490, 493
Senate Judiciary Committee, 174, 265, 408; Internal Security Subcommittee of, 213–14, 215, 221–22, 223, 224, 231, 236; and civil rights, 325–27, 329, 338, 341, 343; and war powers issue, 408–9
Senate Labor and Human Resources Committee, (Senate Labor and Public Welfare Committee), 265, 266, 292, 301, 310, 311, 378, 389; and Frank Cummings, 380; Harrison Williams's chairmanship of, 380–81; and events leading to passage of ERISA, 382, 383; and John Kennedy's labor legislation, 388
Senate Special Committee on Aging, 300
Senate Special Committee on Interstate Crime, 190
Shafer, Raymond P., 303
Shanker, Al, 506
Shapiro, Morris, 96, 99
Sharett, Moshe, 176, 177
Shaw, Anne, 61
Shaw, Hollace, 305; JKJ's relationship with, 59–61, 63, 65, 69, 70–71, 81
Shaw, Jim, 61, 74
Shaw, Maxine, 103

Shaw, Robert, 61, 103
Simon, Caroline K., 241
Six-Day War (1967), 281, 286–87
Smith, Al, 45
Smith, Margaret Chase, 299, 340, 388
Smith College, 57
Smithsonian Institution, 307, 317
Socialism, Socialist Party, 14, 18–19, 44, 52, 53
Social Security system, 294, 295, 296, 299, 301; Old Age and Survivors' Insurance (OASI) of, 293, 299; and private pension plans, 378; and ERISA, 385, 386
Sommer, Frank Henry, 22
Sommer, Jud, 493
Sourwine, Jay, 223–24, 226, 227, 235
Spielberg, Arthur, 104, 113
Spitalny, Phil, 63
Spock, Benjamin, 428
Spong, William, 407, 408
Sprague, J. Russell, 201, 202, 224
Standard Gas & Electric Company, 46–48
Standard Oil Company of California, 470
Standard Oil of New Jersey (now Exxon), 457
Stark, Abe, 242
Stassen, Harold, 104, 355
State Department, 152, 167, 168, 177, 179, 469; and Arab League's boycott of Israel, 282–83; and the arts, 307, 317; and U.S. policy toward Cuba, 422–23, 426; and jets for Israel, 467, 468; and American hostages in Iran, 496
Steel, Johannes, 95, 96, 99
Stennis, John C., 329, 331, 404–5, 407, 408
Stern, Isaac, 507–8
Stern, Vera, 507–8
Stevens, Rise, 311
Stevens, Roger, 318
Stevens, Ted, 496
Stevenson, Adlai, 239, 244, 246, 250
Stone, I. F., 225
Storch, Shirley, 97
Straight, Michael, 318
Strasberg, Lee, 123
Strategic Arms Limitation Treaty. See SALT I; SALT II

Stratton, William G., 165–66, 172
Stravinsky, Igor, 310
Studebaker automobile company, 379
Subversive Activities Control Board, 152
Sullivan and Cromwell, 42, 54, 459
Supreme Court, U.S., 261, 264, 304, 327; civil rights decisions of, 321, 323, 337
Symington, Stuart, 285, 286, 467
Syracuse Post-Standard, 506
Szold & Brandwen, 53

Taber, John, 133–34, 135, 184
Taft, Robert A., 109–10, 144, 153
Taft-Ellender-Wagner bill, 141, 142, 143
Taft-Hartley Act, 111, 137–40, 202, 388, 389
Talmadge, Herman, 258, 336
Tammany Hall, 11, 45, 85–86, 95, 100; corruption in, 45, 46, 190, 191, 320; and JKJ's New York City mayoral campaign, 194, 195
Teamsters Union, 388; Central States Pension Fund of, 382
Texaco, 457
Thant, U, 284, 285
Thomashefsky, Boris, 305
Thompson, Frank, 310, 311, 315
Thurmond, Jean, 336
Thurmond, Strom, 314, 315, 317, 336
Time magazine, 354–55, 420
Tonkin Gulf Resolution, 393–94, 397, 406–7
Torrados, Osvaldo Dorticós, 424
Torrens, James, 95, 99, 100
Torrijos Herrera, Omar, 464
Trade Act (1974), 474
Treasury Department, 310, 446; Section of Painting and Sculpture in, 307
Trubin, John, 204, 211–12, 240, 250; and JKJ's decision to run for 1980 reelection, 493, 497, 498
Truman, Harry, 80, 100, 107, 137, 189, 201; his defeat of Dewey, 113; his veto of Taft-Hartley bill, 138–39; on housing, 143, 145, 147, 148; on national health program, 146; and McCarran Internal Security

Act, 152; and aid to Greece and Turkey, 156, 159; and Truman Doctrine, 159, 161, 164, 274; and Palestine partition plan, 168, 177; and displaced persons bill, 174; and U.S. recognition of Israel, 178; and Marshall Plan, 182; and German rearmament, 186–87; and civil rights, 243, 321
Twyman, Robert J., 167

Unemployment compensation, 386–87
Union Theological Seminary, 95, 98
United Auto Workers, 381
United Federation of Teachers, 445, 506
United Mine Workers (UMW), 137
United Nations (UN), 75–76, 102, 104, 110, 166–67; founding conference of, 84, 221, 232; and Palestine partition plan, 119, 168, 176–78; and Greek-Turkish aid bill, 161–62, 163, 164; attempts of, to establish peace in Israel, 181; and Suez crisis, 248; Relief and Works Agency (UNRWA), 273, 280; Emergency Force (UNEF), 275, 276, 277, 283, 284–85; Goldberg's ambassadorship to, 281; Resolution 242, 286, 287; and Vietnam War, 393, 394; and Palestine Liberation Organization, 431, 432; Commission on Trade and Development (UNCTAD), 460; and American hostages in Iran, 496
United Press, 108, 135
United States Arts Foundation, proposed, 307
United Steelworkers of America, 381
Untermeyer, Samuel, 42, 43, 46
U.S.-Japan Friendship Commission, 75
U.S. News and World Report, 354

Van Arsdale, Harry, 446, 506
Vance, Cyrus, 461, 496
Vandenberg, Arthur, 161, 163, 182
Van Dusen, Henry P., 98
Veterans Administration, 51, 438

Veterans' Housing Act, 142
Vietnam War, 126, 356–57, 416; student demonstrations against, 370, 399–400, 401; JKJ's early views on, 393–98; JKJ's later views on, 398–401; escalation of, 409
Voice of America, 449
Vorys, John M., 182, 183

Wagner, Robert F., Jr., 142, 148, 196, 200, 227; his campaign for Senate, 238, 239–50 passim; waning of his popularity, 372; and New York City mayoralty, 373, 374
Wagner, Robert F., Sr., 239–40, 491
Waitt, Alden, 65, 70, 76; his wartime tour of Europe and North Africa, 66–68; his wartime tour of Pacific, 72, 75
Walker, Jimmy, 45
Wallace, Henry A., 112
Wallenberg, Marcus, 457, 458–59
Walter Reed Hospital, 63–64, 288
Walters, Barbara, 486, 496
Warburg, Paul, 241
Warhol, Andy, 313
War Powers Resolution (1973), 256, 263, 394, 409, 417; genesis of, 402; Nixon's veto of, 402, 410, 413, 416, 430; John Stennis's contribution to, 404, 407; enactment of, 409–13; invoking of, 413–14; critics of, 414
War Production Board, 58
Warren, Lucian, 223
Washington Post, 158, 228–29
Watergate, 260, 261, 409; effect on Republican credibility of, 416; unfolding of, 416–17; and problem of Nixon resignation, 417–22, 427
Watertown Daily Times, 502
Watson, Thomas J., 241
Wednesday Club, 262–63
Weicker, Lowell, 263
Weizmann, Chaim, 177
West, John C., 480, 481
Westmoreland, William C., 395, 396
White, Sir Eric Wyndham, 287
White, Theodore: The Making of the President 1964, 351; The Making of the President 1968, 356

White Citizens Councils, 437
Whitney, John Hay "Jock," 94, 153, 212, 363, 372
Wicker, Tom, 299
Wilhelm, Warren, 457
Wilkins, Roy, 148, 343
Williams, Harrison "Pete," 387, 391; and ERISA fight, 380–81, 382, 383, 384
Willkie, Edith, 104, 196, 241
Willkie, Philip, 110–11
Willkie, Wendell, 56–57, 104, 110, 153
Wilson, Charles "Electric Charlie," 58, 77, 78–79, 84–85
Wilson, Charles "Engine Charlie," 78, 205–6
Wilson, Harold, 170, 398
Wilson, Malcolm, 364
Wolters, L. B., 457
Woodcock, Leonard, 381

Woodring, Harry, 55
Woods, Tighe, 149–50
Woodworth; Larry, 384–85
WQXR, 110

Yale University, 57, 58; Law School, 408
Yates, Sidney, 289
Yeshiva University, 95, 98
Yom Kippur war, 470–71, 472, 475
Young New York for Javits, 194
Young Republican Clubs, 189, 193

Zablocki, Clement, 405–6, 409, 410, 411
Zellerbach, David, 58, 63, 65, 83
Zellerbach, Doris, 81
Zellerbach, Harold, 58, 63, 81, 83, 89
Zionist Organization of America, 279